Sam Houston

Nov 2015

Sam Houston, ca. 1858

Courtesy National Portrait Gallery, Smithsonian Institution

SAM HOUSTON

James L. Haley

UNIVERSITY OF OKLAHOMA PRESS • NORMAN

Also by James L. Haley

Nonfiction

Texas: From Spindletop to World War II
(New York, 1993)
Most Excellent Sir: Letters Received by Sam Houston, President of the Republic of Texas, at Columbia, 1836–1837 (Austin, 1987)
Texas: An Album of History (Garden City, N.Y., 1985)
Apaches: A History and Culture Portrait (Garden City, N.Y., 1981)
The Buffalo War: A History of the Red River Indian Uprising of 1874 (Garden City, N.Y., 1976)

Fiction

Final Refuge (New York, 1994)
The Lions of Tsavo (New York, 1989)
The Kings of San Carlos (Garden City, N.Y., 1987)

Library of Congress Cataloging-in-Publication Data

Haley, James L.
    Sam Houston/by James L. Haley
        p.   cm.
    Includes bibliographical references and index.
    ISBN 978-0-8061-3644-8 (paper)
        1. Houston, Sam, 1793–1863
    2. Governors—Texas—Biography   3. Legislators—United States—Biography.
    4. United States. Congress. Senate—Biography   5. Texas—History—To 1846
    I. Title

    F390.H84 H34 2001
    976.4'04'092—dc21
    [B]

                                                                2001045108

The paper in this book meets the guidelines for permanence and durability of the Committee on Production Guidelines for Book Longevity of the Council on Library Resources, Inc. ∞

Copyright © 2002 by the University of Oklahoma Press, Norman, Publishing Division of the University. Manufactured in the U.S.A. First printing of the paperback edition, 2004.

5 6 7 8 9 10

Dedication

Americans who care much about the arts, and there are not that many of us unfortunately, have slipped into a complacency that assumes the days of patronage are gone. After all, we have the National Endowment for the Arts, various corporate sponsorships, and several private foundations involved in all the many disciplines. But connections, we often forget, usually come with strings. Nor can one depend, in today's publishing environment, on the forces of the marketplace to select the meritorious from the merely commercial. For many of us, we who feel our artistic and social responsibilities but may not feel quite right about supporting ourselves from the public treasury, for us the days of patronage—of Papa Haydn slipping in the back door of the palace to collect his paycheck—are still very much around. And writing is surely the least visible of the arts: no gala concert for the pension fund, no professional consultants to stage media blitzes, no slowly filling billboard thermometer by the freeway with a post-office box number to which to send your tax-deductible contribution. This latter, of course, is the crux of the issue: arts institutions are tax-exempt, artists are not. Yet without the artists, there would be no institutions.

Few of those who today read the poetry of Edwin Arlington Robinson stop to speculate whether he would have made a career at all if Theodore Roosevelt had not admired—and promoted—his work. And bitter, bitter gall it was for Samuel Clemens, when on the edge of bankruptcy, to turn to Standard Oil's Henry H. Rogers, one of the Gilded Age barons whom he lampooned so mercilessly. But Mark Twain accepted his help.

This biography of Sam Houston was difficult, time consuming, and expensive to research and prepare. Within the straitened abilities of academic publishing, the University of Oklahoma Press has been both generous in its advance and patient in turning over the months on its calendar. Nevertheless, there was a deep abyss between my ambitions for the book and the reality of paying the bills for the fifteen years it took to accomplish. Nor would it be accomplished yet but for the repeated intercession of just such an angel of the public conscience, a patron, whose purse supported my research almost from the start. As Mark Twain wrote of Henry Rogers: "He did these saving things at no cost to my self-love, no hurt to my pride; indeed, he did them with so delicate an art that I almost seemed to have done them myself. By no sign, no hint, no word did he ever betray any consciousness that I was under obligations to him. I have never been so great as that and I have not known another who was." To Sam Houston's literary patron, this work is respectfully and affectionately dedicated:

Joel Rudd

If Houston had brought about the annexation of Canada to the
United States, instead of Texas, there would be statues and monuments
to him all over the North, and he would long ago have been
ranked with Washington as one of America's immortals.

—Samuel G. Heiskell
Andrew Jackson and Early Tennessee History

The failure of the Sam Houston legend to outstrip the facts
concerning him resulted from the sheer difficulty
of elaborating upon the startling truth.

—William Ransom Hogan
The Texas Republic

The great man of the age is the one who can put into words
the will of his age, tell his age what its will is, and accomplish it.
What he does is the heart and essence of his age; he actualizes his age.

—G. W. F. Hegel
The Philosophy of Right

I stand the last almost of a race.

—Sam Houston

Contents

Illustrations

Preface

I was well into research for this biography of Sam Houston when I chanced across the previously quoted passage from Hegel. I was surprised to see it, for Hegel's "Great Man" school of history has been defunct for so long that those who remember it at all recall it as a curiosity from a simpler time when the study of history was less sophisticated than it is today. While I am not interested in reopening the "Great Man" academy, some historians today are rethinking the degree to which individuals can have a significant impact on their times. More to the point, there are aspects of Hegel's philosophy that bear peculiarly on the story of Sam Houston. Perhaps it is no accident that they were virtually contemporaries. To Hegel, life was about the subjection of will and passion to reason; Sam Houston lived that. To Hegel, the individual was actualized through participation in the state; Sam Houston lived that too. And to Hegel, America represented a land of future promise, where some ultimate destiny of universal freedom would reveal itself. He forecast this dimly, thinking that it might take place in a war between North America and South America; how narrowly he missed predicting that the war for freedom would take place between the North and South of the United States. The difference between Hegel's thinking and Houston's life was that Houston, having harnessed his passions and while participating in the state, labored mightily for reason to triumph over the horror of that war Hegel seemed anxious to glorify.

Certainly, at no time in American history were the circumstances better arranged for a powerful personality to leave an imprint. The middle third of the nineteenth century was a curious period, as the growing pains of western expansion and deepening sectional hostility over slavery produced a time of political stagnation, an era in which Congress held prominence over the presidency. No charismatic or preeminent chief executive was sworn in from Andrew Jackson in 1832 until the inauguration of Abraham Lincoln in 1861. A few able leaders emerged in Congress such as Daniel Webster and Henry Clay, but none of them of a stature to symbolize the American spirit.

One figure only stands like a colossus astride the middle decades of the 1800s: Sam Houston. As a protégé of Jackson, he became a congressman from and then the governor of Tennessee before emigrating to Texas in 1832. As commanding general of the Texan revolutionary army, he fought one of the pivotal battles in history, and he later served two terms as president of the Republic of Texas. After Texas' annexation to the United States, he returned to Washington for thirteen years as senator. In 1859 Houston was elected governor of Texas on a pro-Union platform, for which stance he was removed from office by the secessionists who marched Texas into the Civil War. He lived two years in retirement, disgraced in Confederate eyes, and died in 1863.

He was a creation of enormous contradictions. The Sam Houston who loved classical literature and could recite lengthy segments of Homer, whose usable vocabulary exceeded that of any of his contemporaries, hated school so much that he deserted the classroom after less than a year of formal education. The Houston whose restless energy spurred him through sleepless nights of work and study was so bored by regular jobs that at sixteen he fled his family to live with Cherokee Indians. The young man who lived as the adopted son of a Cherokee chief, receiving the native name Raven after a totem of good fortune (but also, according to one who knew him during his Cherokee years, a totem of wandering), later received near-fatal wounds fighting other Indians—Creeks—while serving under Andrew Jackson. And the Houston who, as Senator, sought protection for American settlers on the frontier, also thundered against the government's brutal treachery toward Native Americans.

The Sam Houston who disliked the institution of slavery, and who was known to buy slaves out from under cruel "drivers" whom he loathed, saw to it that his own slaves learned to read and write, eat with flatware, and save the money they earned from outside employment. When he freed his own slaves in 1862, they wept and vowed to stay with the family.[1] Yet this same Houston insisted upon the constitutional right of Southern states to allow slavery if they chose, and in 1855 he delivered a scorching speech to abolitionists in their high stronghold, Boston, indicting their hypocrisy with the charge that the only reason they no longer owned slaves themselves was that, with a flood of cheap immigrant labor to exploit, it did not profit them to do so.

And the battle-scarred soldier, whose boyhood wounds never healed and who rallied his army at San Jacinto with the cry "Remember the Alamo!" campaigned to the last of his strength to prevent the Civil War and keep the Union together. Indeed, the prescient statesman who predicted the exact sequence of events leading to the Civil War, six years before the fact, and that a victorious North would "reap a harvest of . . . assassination," eleven years before the fact, was also the wagging stump-speaker who could heap breathtaking invective upon his opponents. He delighted audiences with his famous story-telling, like the time he retained a man as state geologist, he said, for discovering "six distinct strata of filth" on the neck of a rival.

A world-class roué with prodigious appetites for liquor and sex, although there is more evidence for the former than the latter, it was rumored that only the specters of previous scandals—a divorce, a liaison with an Indian woman, and a second marriage to a woman less than half his age—cost Houston a presidential nomination when, according to the most astute observers, he would have trounced Lincoln and possibly headed off the Civil War: a fascinating proposition. Yet Houston the rake astounded his closest friends by reforming in middle age, after his marriage to Margaret Lea produced a blissful home life and a coachful of rowdy children. He gained piety without losing his mirth, converting to the Baptist faith in his late fifties with the hope that, if *his* many sins had truly been washed away, the Lord would find a way to help the fish survive in such polluted water. Acknowledging that his "pocketbook had been baptized, too," he underwrote half the minister's salary. Nevertheless, Houston maintained a studied contempt for what he called "political preachers" and blocked their attempts to write religion into law—one of many timely lessons for our own era.

To historians who seek to interpret the meaning of America's experience, Houston has proved an irresistible subject. Sue Flanagan, author of the unique *Sam Houston's Texas,* described his effect on her increasing interest, which "grew from a weekend fever to a full-time disease" whose only cure was the completion of her photo-travelogue of his Texas career.[2] Since Houston's death, no fewer than sixty biographies have appeared. Why yet another?

First, most of the early works about him are discountable for their partisanship. Houston himself took a kind of dark delight in knowing that his personality was so strong that the political questions of his day were often argued not on their own merits but upon his position on the issue: Houston, people asked, or anti-Houston? The two authorized biographies, Charles Lester's *Sam Houston and His Republic* (1846; a revised edition was released in 1855 bearing the title *The Life of Sam Houston (The Only Authentic Memoir of Him Ever Published)* and William Carey Crane's *Life and Select Literary Remains* (1884), offer voluminous facts but are virtually uncritical. The exposés by his enemies, in book and pamphlet and article, are sometimes stunning for the sheer relentlessness of their vituperation. For fifty years after his death, most biographers were either hell-bent to expose him as a fraud and charlatan or equally intent upon his exoneration. By World War I, more objective historians began to discern Houston as a figure of great, but obscured, importance. "Injustice has been done to Sam Houston," wrote Samuel Heiskell on the very first page of his monumental *Andrew Jackson and Early Tennessee History.* "If Houston had brought about the annexation of Canada to the United States, [instead] of Texas, there would be statues and monuments to him all over the North, and he would long ago have been ranked with Washington as one of America's immortals."[3]

Second, of all the biographies now on the shelf, many writers were sensible of Houston's position in the history of the times, and they developed an awe of him that they tried to name at least in the subtitles of their books: "Titan," "Colossus," "Giant." Of those works, only three, to my mind, have maintained their currency to the present day: Marquis James's *The Raven,* which appeared in 1929 and won the Pulitzer Prize for biography the following year; Llerena Friend's *Sam Houston: The Great Designer,* published in 1954; and M. K. Wisehart's *American Giant,* released in 1962. But they are now insufficient for a complete portrait of his life.

The Raven, while notable for its oral sources that could not now be duplicated (but also cannot now be corroborated), is largely outdated by the mass of research accomplished since its appearance. Moreover, the book, produced at the height of the so-called Golden Age of biography, was written at a time when the most influential practitioners of the art, like Lytton Strachey and Virginia Woolf, were advocating the acceptability of fictionalizing certain elements of the story if that helped arrive at a more complete understanding of the subject than the known facts alone could sustain. James, it is now believed, adopted this doctrine freely. I have never accepted that view of the biographical art, but *The Raven* remains the most famous and frequently cited of the Houston biographies; my own labor in primary resources has increased my respect for it as the most densely researched volume ever written about the man. Such has been its influence on later biographers that at times they assume that all examination of Sam Houston began with it. Gregg Cantrell, in a perceptive tandem review of the 1993 Houston bicentennial biographies, wrote, "No professional writer attempted a full-length Houston biography until . . . *The Raven*." However, one of the inevitably and traditionally related Houston scenes that Cantrell dated to *The Raven*, and whose validity he subsequently questioned, namely Houston's last words, "Texas, Texas . . . Margaret," stems not from *The Raven* but from Alfred M. Williams's *Sam Houston and the War of Independence in Texas* (1893).[4] It was related to Williams by Houston's second daughter, Maggie, who was at the bedside. Oddly, then, some of the sources of "new" Houston material upon which I have drawn are not recent archival discoveries but biographies older than *The Raven*, books of which Marquis James made only incomplete use and that have remained largely unexamined since their own time.

Friend's superb book was by design a political analysis of Houston's Texas career. There was, somewhat to Friend's own apparent regret, little information on Houston's formative years—she had him grown up and out of Tennessee in fewer than thirty pages—and there was little focus on what made the man tick. Some of that was provided by Wisehart; in my decade and a half of learning to gauge the general's moods and what he might be really up to, I have come to enjoy *American Giant* as the most intuitive of the existing biographies.

However, and third, much new material has come to light in recent years, and these sources have been only lightly glossed over—or else missed completely—by the latest generation of Houston biographies. One of the primary sources used for this volume, the Andrew Jackson Houston Collection of over four thousand largely unique Houston papers, remained in the family's possession until 1973. Although there is evidence to suggest that Marquis James used a portion of them when they were still in A. J. Houston's custody, and Marshall De Bruhl surveyed many of the papers during research for *Sword of San Jacinto*, these documents remain underutilized. Their import has been enormous, but they are not the only new materials to surface since the last time Sam Houston's story was told. The staff of the Texas State Library in Austin, custodians of the A. J. Houston Collection, were jarred to learn in mid-1987 that A. J. Houston's daughters had separately donated hundreds of other Sam Houston papers to the Catholic Archives of Texas, located, of all places, barely four blocks away. (The first time I visited the Diocese Chancery to view this collection, late in 1996, I was stunned by its richness. I asked the archivist whether any of Houston's half-dozen or so 1993 bicentennial biographers had come down to use the papers, and she said no, but "We have been waiting for years for someone to come.") The massive daybook of Houston's second term as president of Texas was donated by Houston descendents to the Sam Houston Regional Library in Liberty, Texas, as recently as December of 1986. The Sam Houston Memorial Museum in Huntsville, Texas, only recently acquired the Franklin Williams Collection of Sam and Margaret Houston's private correspondence, and one descendent, Madge Thornall Roberts, is now collating and publishing a further four volumes of these family letters. Thus, it seemed clear to me that there were new sheaves to bring in, and this belief was not altered by the spate of Houston biographies that appeared for the bicentennial of his birth in March of 1993. Those books, while giving mostly acceptable chronology, did little to extend the tunnels in the mine of source materials.

(Even utilizing the new resources, I cannot claim that this book is definitive. One collection of papers was inaccessible because the library was closed for renovation; another had just received a gift of Houston papers, which were not yet available for research. I have since learned that many of these papers are printed in the eight volumes of *The Writings of Sam Houston,* but that several are not. In any event, *no* single-volume biography of Sam Houston could even approach telling his story completely, anyway. A definitive Houston biography would require a minimum of three volumes.)

But, fourth, and the main reason for this book—what compelled me to write about Houston even as sixty others have been compelled to write about Houston—is that he has survived scholarly scrutiny with his mysteries intact. During my research, I was chatting with the curator of one of the primary repositories of Sam Houston materials. We were talking about the general's relationship with Margaret when he asked me if I did not think it remarkable how Houston always seemed to turn to her for approval. Houston was always distant from his own mother and seemed to need from Margaret reassurance and maternal comfort. Not ten minutes later, I was discussing the same subject, separately, with the director of the same institution, who asked me if I did not think it remarkable how Houston always seemed to treat Margaret like a child to be alternately guided and humored. In a strange way, this inconsistency of perceptions did not surprise me in the least, for there is something so compelling about Sam Houston's life story that it causes even the most objective and scholarly people to personalize their interpretations.

During his own lifetime, Houston's reputation survived both the silly "exposés" penned by his enemies and some equally silly refutations from his own pen. His more tantalizing personal enigmas survived the vestal flamekeeping of the 1920s and 1930s, when history—and especially Texas history—was largely the province of well-bred, hero-worshipping spinsters who, though they might whisper their suspicions within the hush of an archive, would never publish them. His luster survived the opposite extreme—the 1960s and 1970s, the golden age of liberal revisionism. Those were the days when Shakespeare was performed in the nude and the surest route to tenure in the history department was to tout a dissertation suggesting that somebody big probably died of syphilis. And I have no doubt that he will survive the hatchet attacks of the "New History" and the politically correct, the postmodernists and the deconstructionists, all those who drag to the bar persons of historical import for failing to perceive their world through the enlightened sensitivity (if such it really is) of our newly opened twenty-first century eyes. (The New Historians would be surprised at how much Sam Houston himself had in common with them. "Bear in mind," he once wrote a correspondent, "that all Histories from the Rock of Plymouth, and Jamestown to the present time, have been made by white men, and a man who tells his own story, is *always right* until the *adversary's tale is told*.")[5]

But, certainly, these writers have asked mighty questions: Was Houston indeed the friend of the Indian, as he postured, or did he cynically use them to create a certain image of himself for public appreciation? Was he indeed the hero of San Jacinto, or as some have claimed, a tepid chronic retreater who fought only in the face of certain mutiny if he did not engage the enemy? In his two terms as president of the Republic of Texas, was he indeed the iron prow of the ship of state, hazarding even his personal credit to shore up that of his country, or was he a befuddled drunk, spouting grandiloquence like a periodic geyser when he sobered up enough to say anything at all? Was he indeed the architect of Texas's annexation to the United States, thereby throwing open the gates to the Pacific, or did he follow the lead of Anson Jones and others and then claim the credit for himself? Was he, as the still-bitter descendents of his rivals maintain, merely more adept at manipulating the press? Most tantalizing of all, as the Civil War neared and Houston removed himself from presidential contention, could he have beaten Lincoln? If he had beaten Lincoln, could he have headed off the war?

Perhaps at last enough time has passed—nearly 140 years since he died— that enough of the partisanship has faded, enough new sources have come to light, and enough technology has been injected into the stale ether of historiographical methodology for General Houston to finally yield up his secrets. Pale thought. How naïve to plot that something as narcissistically high tech as a computer cross-reference of his many correspondents could help uncover the political intrigues of a man who learned from Indians how to cover his tracks. Will he be chuckling at me from his grave? I think not, because to me, the great mystery of Sam Houston is not political, but human. I am certain that some readers would prefer a more political treatment of Houston's life—as indeed I was rather energetically informed in one preliminary manuscript evaluation. That, however, is not the book I chose to write, and I am content that *The Great Designer* should remain the most detailed political study. My book, much of which concerns politics, is yet a political study only as it reflects the heart of the man: My search for the Raven is a personal one. How did he do it? How could such a man—a rake, a confessed alcoholic who lost out of his life whole years ridden by fits of the most abject depression—rise above the turbulence of his soul to stake out a career that Caesars might have envied? If we can discover that, then Houston will teach us much of how the human spirit can triumph over the demons that lie in wait.

• • •

In the book *Apaches: A History and Culture Portrait,* I included a preface that generated some amount of comment because it not only introduced my principal thesis—that a discovery of Apache Indian culture had a major impact on the study of the history—but also included remarks on the politicized atmosphere in which the writing of Native Americana is done today. A preface, I thought, should be a cleansing thing, a personal confession by the author to his reader. I wanted to unshoulder my doubts and prejudices of the subject area at once, in a lump, in the preface, so the body of the work would not be burdened with them. The periodical *Choice* reviewed the preface as a "masterpiece"; others were rather less charitable and considerably more annoyed. It was only seven years later that I was shown the great Walter Prescott Webb's essay, "An Honest Preface," in which he struck closer to the mark: "In a Preface the author is supposed to take the reader into his confidence, let him in on a deep and mysterious secret, and tell him the truth. What the author really does is to introduce himself with an air of assumed modesty, try to forestall and fend off the critics, and persuade the reader to go on with the job and buy the book."[6]

So to be honest, in Webb's sense of honesty, this is a long book, and imperfect. One preliminary manuscript evaluation found my treatment of Houston's life "uneven," a charge to which I plead at least a little guilty, largely because so much of the material herein is presented in print for the very first time. By way of analogy, I would suggest that in the 1980s the Reagan administration found it manifestly impossible to cut taxes, strengthen the military, and balance the budget. Just so, in preparing this volume, I found it manifestly impossible to present so much new material, still recite the complete Sam Houston canon, and stay under my contractual length of a quarter-million words. Something had to give. I chose to give precedence to the new insights into his life and to emphasize those aspects of his career that Houston himself held most important—hence the greater than usual detail on his dealings with Native Americans. This came at the cost of perhaps having to short shrift other aspects of his career already in the books—his land dealings with James Prentiss, for instance, or his quarrel with the Texas Navy, or details of the political maneuvers leading toward annexation.

I regret this, but even after making such excisions (and even after caving in to eleventh-hour jawboning from the publisher to cut additional length from the finished manuscript), the book is still rather long. I did not start off to write a long book, and I myself seldom work up the courage (by which I mean trust in the author) to risk investing the time to read a long book. But biography is not a science, it is an art, even as storytelling is an art, and the biographer-as-storyteller must command the reins of a galloping team of factors: what style; what progression; what pace; what blend of story, thesis, and subtext will eventually arrive at a true revelation of the subject? What audience does one write to, the most astute or the general reader who perhaps needs to have points clarified more directly? General Houston did not reveal himself to me quickly, and his story is one that cannot be quickly told. But it is a majestic story and one whose appeal, happily for me, lies now where it always has, with Houston himself, and does not depend upon the skill or lack of skill on the part of those who write about him.

I would close with a few words about the construction of this volume. There is a famous story about that wonderful writer Mari Sandoz, who, having completed a great deal of work on her biography of Crazy Horse, was struggling to present the information in the most effective way. Eventually, it is said, she threw the manuscript on the floor and began physically rearranging chapters to see if that would help. I doubt that I know a single author of serious nonfiction who has not at one time or another been reduced to that seemingly crude practice.

This new presentation of Sam Houston's life story, a life itself long and eventful but then jumbled and complicated by the heavy shelf of existing biographies with their often irreconcilable theories, presented a task of gruesome complexity. Scaling the continental divide of my notes, the watershed proved to be this: I might on the one hand give the narrative flow of his life secondary status and concentrate instead on addressing the large scholarly issues previously listed. Such a book would necessarily take on the function, if not the form, of a series of essays, analyzing the well-known facts and reinterpreting them in light of new source materials. Or I might on the other hand simply unwrap the story in its slower chronology and trust that the legion of Houston-watchers will know when I am departing from an established orthodoxy or when I am presenting events in a light different from that previously cast. For the most part, although there are exceptions to prove the rule, I have taken the latter option because I wanted to write a biography of the flesh-and-blood man, not publish some declaration of theses to nail to the door of the history department. Sam Houston's story deserves a wider audience than a series of lectures would find.

I have also elected to present original materials, where quoted, in their expressive, rustic illiteracy, when that could be done without undue confusion. While I was editing a portion of the Texas State Archives' A. J. Houston papers for reproduction and publication, I was struck by how leaving such illiterate foibles intact went far to preserve the life under discussion in the color of its times.[7] Besides, nothing, it seems to me, so impedes the flow of historical narrative as a compulsively correct use of "[*sic*]," the use of which also begs the proposition that the editors, if not the author, know how to spell and use correct grammar.

There is one final aspect of writing a Houston biography that demands mention: the interest of local folks—Texans and especially East Texans. The only possible comparison is with an unrelated genre. Among mystery writers, there is an unwritten rule—or it may even be written somewhere—that you simply do not give a lecture about Sherlock Holmes unless you have mastered the entire canon and all its permutations. If you try to fake it, "they" will get you. "They," of course, are the panoplied host of Holmesian fanatics, many of whom hold steady jobs and are otherwise satisfactorily integrated into adult society, but who become bug-snatching Renfields at the mere mention of their hero and his career. Speak or write about Holmes and get something wrong, and "they" will skin you alive.

That is not unlike writing about Sam Houston in Texas. I once watched a well-known and favorably reputed historian whose field of specialty was not Sam Houston, but whose field Houston touched upon, give an invited lecture at the Sam Houston Memorial Museum in Huntsville, before what he might have assumed to be a friendly audience of buffs, mavens, hobbyists, and locals. After the lecture he took questions, and it was obvious from the second one that the poor man was in over his head. He went down like a pudu in a school of piranhas. Anyone who writes about Sam Houston had damned well better know it all, or when the locals get hold of him, he will find himself trapped in a scene from *Night of the Living Dead.* It is a lesser-known aspect of Texans' devotion to their history that, though many locals may be mere peasants and housewives, they probably know more about their past than the tenured poobah who jets in from Harvard or Berkeley to illuminate the New History for them.

If this book earns the approval of the locals, anything else will be window dressing.

Acknowledgments

In the fifteen years I have worked on this volume, during which time my favorite photograph of General Houston has sat, smirking down at me from atop my computer, daring me to find him out, I have accumulated many debts to historians, archivists, curators, buffs, mavens, and just plain folks. No mere acknowledgment of assistance can convey how much this book gained from them, nor the fact that aid from all was given fulsomely and without fail.

Those in Austin are: Kinga Perzynska and Susan Eason at the Catholic Archives of Texas in the Chancery of the Austin Diocese; Michael Moore at the Texas Land Office; Carl McQueary at the Republic of Texas Museum; Jane Karotkin at the Friends of the Governor's Mansion; Jean Carefoot, Donaly Brice, John Anderson, Bill Simmons, Sergio Velasco, and others at the Texas State Library and Archives; and the staffs of the Austin History Center of the Austin Public Library and the Center for American History at the University of Texas.

In Huntsville, they are: Patrick Nolan, Mac Woodward, and Dick Rice at the Sam Houston Memorial Museum; Paul Culp at the Thomason Room (Special Collections) of the Newton Gresham Library at Sam Houston State University; County Clerk James Patton; Education Minister Carroll Williams of the First Baptist Church; and a special thanks to Brownie Moore for her helpful exhortations.

Others elsewhere include: Wayne C. Moore, Archivist at the Tennessee State Library and Archives in Nashville; J. C. Martin, Lisa Struthers, and Brian Butcher at the San Jacinto Museum of History in La Porte; Robert L. Schaadt, Darlene Mott, and Venus Booker at the Sam Houston Regional Library and Research Center in Liberty, Texas; Rev. Paul Sevar at the Texas Baptist Historical Center-Museum in Independence; Linda Nicklas at the Steen Library of Stephen F. Austin University in Nacogdoches; Amy Johns Tartaglia at the Fort Bend Museum in Richmond, Texas; and Martha Utterback at the Daughters of the Republic of Texas Museum and Research Library at the Alamo in San Antonio.

And in miscellany, but by no means of lesser value, for various hints offered, aid rendered, and interest extended, I am indebted to Mickey Lanford, Jack Jackson, Dorman Winfrey, and Ron Tyler of Austin; Kathryn J. Farley, Nancy Burch, and the Hon. William P. Hobby Jr. of Houston; Dr. Randolph B. "Mike" Campbell of Denton; and Vernadine and Don Richardson of Lufkin. I extend homage to Madge Thornall Roberts of San Antonio, whose years of labor to collate and publish Sam and Margaret Houston's private correspondence have added a dimension to their history previously untapped, and to her editor, Charlotte Wright, who very kindly made galleys of Madge's latest work available to me so I would not have to wait on the book. In addition to the patron to whom this volume is dedicated, my research has over time been supported by grants or loans (at least they will be loans if I ever manage to repay them) from

Michael Alexander, Jane Karotkin, and Bill Young of Austin; Greg Bowden of Corpus Christi; and Kelley Beck and Dana Howells of Los Angeles.

For editorial oversight and guidance at the University of Oklahoma Press through a long process, I am indebted to Chuck Rankin, Alice Stanton, Jean Hurtado, and Susan Garrett—and many thanks to Kevin Brock of Fayetteville, Arkansas, for an insightful and rigorous copyedit. Finally, a word about John N. Drayton, director of the University of Oklahoma Press. I knew going in that he was one of the most respected figures in scholarly publishing. I did not know—and bless his heart, neither did he—how long his patience and determination would be challenged. Every time I thought I had Sam Houston nailed down, a new cache of papers would surface that had to be assayed and mined, and then I would run out of money and have to go write a novel to pay bills. (I was young; I was stupid; I thought one could pay bills by writing novels.) Years rolled by. When Sharlot Hall, the indefatigable historian of Arizona, found herself similarly bogged down in trying to write her state's history, her publisher eventually let her out of the contract, but with the cruel stipulation that she never write an Arizona history. It broke her heart. John Drayton had every right to call in his Sam Houston contract in similar fashion, but he did not. I will never forget that.

Sam Houston

1

THE RUNAWAY GROCERY BOY

The fledgling United States secured its independence with victory in battle at Yorktown, Virginia, in October of 1781. In the Treaty of Paris two years later, Great Britain was not only compelled to accept defeat but the American negotiators, Benjamin Franklin and John Jay, also played skillfully on the rivalry between England and France. Their former enemy proved so anxious to keep America out of the French orbit that, in the end, Franklin and Jay euchred Britain out of her land claims as far west as the Mississippi River. It was a loss said to have cost England's brittle king, George III, his last grip on reality.

But America was not a country, it was a "league of friendship" among thirteen independent and jealous states, "bound" together by the largely nonbinding Articles of Confederation, which had been drafted during the second year of the Revolution. This form of national government, with multiple currencies and domestic tariffs and tax contributions paid to the central authority whenever the states felt generous, proved intolerable. In 1786, delegates gathered in Annapolis and proposed that a convention be held the following year in Philadelphia to draft a revised instrument of government.

That convention opened on May 25, 1787, in Philadelphia's Independence Hall, and during sixteen sweltering weeks in that hothouse of summer sweat and contesting intellect, thirty-nine delegates forged the greatest political compact ever conceived, the Constitution of the United States, which was signed on September 17. Upon ratification by nine of the thirteen states, the Constitution was to become binding on those states who consented to it, and most did so quickly. But of the four leading states, Virginia, Massachusetts, New York, and Pennsylvania, only the fourth moved with speed. Massachusetts refused to sign on until it was agreed that a Bill of Rights would soon be submitted as amendments. In New York, Alexander Hamilton had to threaten to split New York City off from the rest of the state before that legislature complied. But the hardest fight was in Virginia, where James Monroe and Patrick Henry fought against it. James Madison and John Marshall undertook a parliamentary brawl to save it, and in the end they prevailed by a vote of 89 to 79.

In a way it was appropriate that the toughest test came in Virginia because, of the original thirteen states, it stood just a forehead taller than the others. Massachusetts had produced the blunt but brilliant John Adams, and New York produced the lawyering Jay and the calculating Hamilton. Pennsylvania, founded by Quakers, contributed the deeply loved Franklin. But of founding stock, Virginia stood preeminent. Washington, Jefferson, Madison, and Marshall alone defeated all comers to that claim. But just as the United States now was a union of diversity, so too was Virginia. There was not one Virginia—there were two.

There was the Virginia of the tidewater, of Jamestown and the other early settlements. Predominantly English, many residents had been in the New World for generations before revolution was ever thought of. They now regarded themselves as America's aristocracy, and their world, and their snobbery, extended inland to the eastern flank of the Appalachians. Their only interest in Virginia west of the mountains was as land speculators. People living in that wilderness they regarded as mostly ruffians—guaranteed their rights under the Constitution now, and that was well enough, but a breed apart and set a little down. To well-bred Virginians of the tidewater, intermarriage, for instance, with the mountain people was unthinkable.

This was unfair, for many of the western Virginians were every bit as well educated and cultured as those of the tidewater—a few, like Jefferson, moreso. But the realities of living in the western lands were different. There, a livelihood still had to be wrested from the wilderness; the conditions were raw, and the opportunities to rise by one's own merit were fresher. It should be no surprise, then, that the difference between eastern and western Virginia also defined the first meaningful divergence in American political philosophy, the split between Federalists and Jeffersonian Democrats. It was no accident that Washington's beloved Mount Vernon overlooked the sloughing tides of the Potomac, while Jefferson's equally beloved Monticello sat atop its Little Mountain near the Blue Ridge like a gracious Greek eyrie.

One part of the tidewater's ledger against the west was true enough. The Virginians of the mountains, and of the broad valley of the Shenandoah River just beyond, were a different breed. That region was not settled primarily by Virginians who went west over the mountains. It was settled rather by Scots-Irish immigrants who came down the Great Philadelphia Wagon Road from the population centers of the Northeast. Many were of families who had been familiar with each other for generations: the clans Davidson, McCormick, Paxton, McCorkle, Houston, Stuart, and others. They had come southwest, up the Shenandoah Valley all the way to its headwaters and beyond, before settling in the environs of Rockbridge County and the town of Lexington.

At the time Virginia acquiesced to the Constitution, if there was a first among equals of these very democratic families, it was the Houstons, and more particularly the family of Capt. Samuel Houston of Timber Ridge plantation in Rockbridge County, seven miles east of Lexington. During the Revolution he had served as captain and paymaster of Morgan's Rifle Brigade, the closest thing to an elite unit in the Continental army. He gained enough of a reputation to return home and in 1783 marry Elizabeth Paxton, daughter of the richest man in the region. When he inherited his father Robert Houston's Timber Ridge, with its fine, two-story porticoed mansion, Captain Houston seemed justified in thinking himself a fitting scion of his family.

· · ·

Reckoning of the modern genealogy usually begins with Sir John Houston, builder of the family's baronial estate near Johnstone, Scotland, in the late 1600s, but the ancestry stretches much further back to one Sir Hugh of Padivan, a Norman knight and retainer of William the Conqueror. For later service in racing through the thick of battle to save the life of Malcolm, king of Scotland, Sir Hugh received an addition to his coat of arms: two swift greyhounds supporting the motto "IN TEMPORE" over his older Norman escutcheon of three ravens. He also received an estate in Renfrew, and the settlement that grew up around it became known as Hughstown, the common source of variant family spellings of Houstoun, Houston, and Huston.[1]

Sam Houston's great-grandfather John Houston, son of the above John Houston who built the castle, after a lengthy sojourn in Ireland immigrated to America in 1735, accompanied by his aged mother, his wife Margaret Mary (née Cunningham), and six of their seven children.[2] They prospered many years in Pennsylvania, but eventually the prevalence of Germans, with their Lutheranism, and the call of greater opportunities to be had in the Virginia Appalachians led him to join the train of Scots-Irish Presbyterians that creaked and rumbled up the Great Philadelphia Wagon Road into the Shenandoah Valley. He purchased the land east of Lexington, and as he slowly added slaves and acres to his Timber Ridge plantation, his means and social prominence led to the people calling him "squire." The title was unofficial, but he took his *noblesse oblige* seriously, building a stone church for his neighbors to worship in and serving them as soldier and judge. In 1754 the squire, then about sixty-five years old, was killed, according to family tradition, by a limb falling from a burning tree. Ownership of Timber Ridge passed to his son Robert, who continued its skillful management until in good time he bequeathed it to his son Capt. Samuel Houston, formerly of Morgan's Rifle Brigade.

Like his father, Samuel Houston was a second son, and like his father he had married well. Elizabeth Paxton bore him four sons—Paxton, Robert, James, and John—before her fifth confinement produced yet another boy, this one selected to bear his father's name: Sam Houston was born on March 2, 1793. In the following years four more children appeared: a sixth son, William, and finally three daughters, Isabella, Mary, and Eliza Ann. But unlike his father, Samuel Houston was not a skillful manager. In the years after the Revolution, Captain Houston served as inspector of the frontier militias, a post that he enjoyed and at which he excelled, for he relished the ruggedness of military life. It came at a cost, however, for militia officers were expected to pay their own expenses. Although the job required long absences from home, Houston managed to keep up a commitment to improving his community, including a lively interest in education. As early as May of 1776, he and Capt. Hamilton Stuart donated several acres of land in the village of Timber Ridge for the establishment of an academy, upon which land his neighbors underwrote the erection of a lofted hewn-log structure twenty-four by twenty-eight feet. The academy, rather daringly named Liberty Hall, prospered and later relocated. In 1798 the corresponding clerk of the Board of Directors, still Captain Houston, wrote former president George Washington seeking his sanction to rename the institution in his honor. Washington agreed.[3] Over time, however, Captain Houston's militia expenses, time spent tending to what he perceived as his civic responsibilities, and most of all his long absences from and inattention to Timber Ridge left the plantation hopelessly in debt.

Financial ruin in the era of the open frontier was commonly handled in a fashion no longer available: sell out, patent raw land in a new place, and begin again. Although he was now sixty-two years old, Captain Houston resolved to do exactly this. Some of his relations had already established themselves in the hills of east-central Tennessee and were doing well. Arranging to sell what was left of three generations of effort for a thousand pounds, he bought land near his kin around the settlement of Maryville, fifteen miles south of Knoxville, and spent $174 on a large wagon and a five-horse hitch to make the move. Then in the spring of 1807, while fulfilling his duties as militia inspector, Captain Houston died unexpectedly at Dennis Callaghan's tavern on the New Road to Kentucky. He was buried in a cemetery near the High Bridge—a scenic natural feature now known as Natural Bridge—fifteen miles southwest of Timber Ridge and one mile from Forest Tavern, a substantial operation run by his cousin Matthew Houston.

The following November, his widow and their favorite son, John, who inherited the captain's sword and a share double that of the other children, appeared in court to probate the estate—five slaves, all women and children, and an assortment of personal property appraised at $3,659.84. After the creditors had lined up for payment, she was left with enough, and Elizabeth Paxton Houston, aged fifty-two, with feelings unknown, loaded up all she thought necessary in two wagons and struck southwest up the valley.

•   •   •

Through his educational interests, Captain Houston had accumulated a library that was, by frontier standards, luxurious. His first four boys, occupied with schooling and work, seem to have taken little notice. It was his fifth son and namesake, Sam, thirteen at the time of his father's death, who could lose himself in the shelves of books even to the detriment of his formal education. He was, in fact, more truant than in attendance, finding he could work up little interest for mathematics when he had Pope's translation of the *Iliad* waiting for him at home. He was better about church, attending services with the family in the stone edifice built by his great-grandfather, Squire John, but from his often-incorrigible behavior, no one took him for an aspirant to the cloth. Young Sam was big for his age. Traditional history in Rockbridge County has it that shortly before the move to Tennessee, curious about his height, he flattened himself against the frame of his cellar door, leveled a pistol over his head, and fired. Judged by the bullet hole, if his aim was steady, he stood five feet, eleven inches—an estimate that corresponds with Houston's own reckoning that around this time he stood "nearly six feet tall." In the years after Elizabeth Paxton Houston moved her brood to Tennessee, her Virginia home was razed and the foundation partly incorporated into Church Hill, the family seat of Washington College trustee Horatio Thompson. The newer dwelling cannibalized the Houston house for its locks and hinges, a mantel, and the cellar door with the bullet hole in the frame.[4]

The road southwest followed the James River valley. The family would have passed the High Bridge and probably spent the night a mile farther on at Forest Tavern. Matthew Houston had built the place three years before Sam was born, and it was one of the boy's favorite romping places. This may well have been the uncle who, as Elizabeth Houston's two wagons rumbled away to a new life, shook his head about the boy's future. "I have no hope for Sam," he sighed. "He is so wild."[5]

In 1807 the United States of America was thirty-one years old; the state of Tennessee was eleven. Thomas Jefferson was ending his second term as president, and the frontier had hardly moved west of the Appalachian Mountains. When the widow Houston packed her necessities and immigrated to Tennessee, she showed uncommon courage and determination, traits that, from all accounts, matched her large build and forceful personality. In the Appalachian foothills of east-central Tennessee, she reached Maryville and then continued up Baker's Creek into the higher and more rugged hills until she reached her relations and her 419-acre farm. There she started anew. She cleared land, built a house, and planted crops. All the children shouldered their share of the labor; a better manager than her husband, she soon acquired an interest in a Maryville mercantile.

Within a few years of the move, the eldest son, Paxton, and the eldest daughter, Isabella, died, and her second son, Robert, also died without issue. Elizabeth Paxton Houston then came to depend upon her next two sons, James and John, to operate the farm, help run the store in Maryville, and help raise the other children properly. Sam was a different case. He was good looking, made friends easily, and never wanted for companions when he roughhoused through the woods. Like his father, however, he was a combination of ambition and indolence, a mix of big dreams and, apparently, an averseness to work. For his education, Sam was enrolled in the Porter Academy, with some hope that he would have greater success as a pupil than he had in Virginia. Certainly the young dreamer had shown a passion for his father's books. The Houston library had come to Tennessee with the family, and in those volumes Sam could abandon the dreary reality of pulling stumps and hoeing corn. Reliving the epics of Homer and Virgil, he compared these legends with actual events as recorded in Rollins's *Ancient History*. His fascination with Morse's two-volume *Geography* manifested itself throughout his life with references and allusions that left his many correspondents scratching their heads. But although the young Houston could secret himself away for hours enraptured by the classics, in a classroom he remained, from all indications, terrible. "Often I had determined to whip Sam Houston," recalled Maryville schoolmaster Dr. Isaac Anderson of that era when teachers ruled with the rod, "but he would come up with such a pretty dish of excuses that I could not do it."[6] He had wit quick enough to escape a beating, but a lifetime later, in a letter to his own son, Sam Houston admitted that he was able to endure formal education for less than a year altogether. About the only thing that interested him in school was the sound and use of language, and even when playing hooky he would draw within earshot to absorb the spelling lessons. Otherwise, he could not be bothered with classes.

It probably did not help that two of Porter Academy's trustees were his brothers James and John, whom he derisively referred to as the "Holy Apostles"—an attitude that also summed up the surface, but not the depth, of his attitude toward religion. In this truant youth the current of spirituality ran deep but muddy. His mother was a strict Presbyterian, and although young Sam sensed the reality of the Almighty, he found in the dour frontier sermons on hellfire and damnation more to terrorize than to uplift him—a confusion that lasted through most of his life. What he did find appealing was the free and unsophisticated spiritual expression of the Native Americans. The Houston farm lay almost at the boundary of the Cherokee Nation, and with easy access and trade across the border, Sam Houston found plenty of opportunities to gratify his curiosity about this most advanced of the so-called Five Civilized Tribes.

The "Holy Apostles" could not have cared less about the Cherokees, and when repeated attempts to get Sam to take an interest in the farm came to naught, they and their mother decided to put him to work in the Maryville store. However, except for his chums and the Cherokees who came in to trade, this was a labor he found even less bearable. The youth withstood his family's hounding for three years, then one day he did not come in to work. Sam Houston, age sixteen, a dreaming, frustrated grocery boy, ran away from home. Ever afterward he corresponded warmly with his cousins; kept informed of the welfare of his only younger brother, William; and retained an affectionate solicitude for his sisters. But of his immediate family whom he found guilty of ill using him, he was—except for one brief interlude in 1815—free. He did once write a touching tribute to his mother, in his autobiography, characterizing her as "an extraordinary woman . . . distinguished by a full, rather tall, and matronly form, a fine carriage, and an impressive and dignified countenance. She was gifted with intellectual and moral qualities, which elevated her, in a still more striking manner, above most of her sex. Her life shone with purity and benevolence, and . . . her name was called with gratitude by the poor and the suffering." Houston's autobiography, though, was published to enhance his presidential prospects in a day when family loyalty was a paramount virtue.[7] The fact was that in after years he hardly spoke the names of his mother or older brothers.

• • •

What would Sam Houston's life have been had he not bucked the family traces, had he knuckled under to his mother and brothers and spent himself guiding a plow and shelving dry goods—if, in sum, he had been satisfied reading Homer's *Odyssey* instead of setting off to create his own? The only thing known is that he was not content there. Perhaps after leafing through his father's classics one last time— Greece and Rome and the Renaissance—Sam Houston disappeared into the woods.

His family's loss, certainly, was history's gain. But how very odd that at that small spot on the vast continent the heritage of western civilization, leather-bound in the Houston library, lay separated only by a hewn threshold from the dark forest of possibility. And how luminously eerie that it was Sam Houston and not another who crossed it. Doubtless the frontier presented the same stark choice to other restless youths, but they were boys who did knuckle under to their families and became clerks and plowmen. Perhaps their libraries—if they had libraries—did not fire their imaginations; perhaps they could not grasp the scope of what could be accomplished on the boundless, sparsely cast stage of North America. Maybe others took the challenge only to be felled by disease, or Indians, or melancholy, or drink; certainly in subsequent years Sam Houston only narrowly escaped death at the hand of each. Most frontier youths chose to grasp what comforts the age could afford them—a hearth, a family, a job. Most people do live for lesser things than greatness, but that is nature's way: a million seeds are shed that one may root.

When he left, Sam headed southwest, skirting the flank of the Appalachians, until he came to an Indian settlement clustered on an island in the Hiwassee River above its confluence with the Tennessee. The town had been the birthplace in 1770 or 1771 of the great Cherokee leader The Ridge and was now guided by Oolooteka ("He Puts away the Drum"), known to the whites as John Jolly. The name of the village, and river, came from *Ayuhwa-si*, the Cherokee word for "meadow." Moravian missionaries visiting the place a few years earlier had found about three hundred people living there, mostly Cherokees but also a few whites who, like young Houston, had bucked against an American society that placed a great premium on conformity.[8] The Moravians believed the population was in decline owing to its location, which they described as low, damp, and unhealthy. When Houston arrived there, though, he must have thought he had found a new utopia. The Hiwassee was "a cold, clear torrent that brawled from a cleft in the Great Smoky Mountains. . . . Along the edge of the village spread fields of corn, beans, pumpkins, sweet potatoes, and tobacco, while beyond rippled a prairie of waving grass. The grass sheltered countless strawberry plants, and when the berries were ripe, the ground seemed carpeted in crimson. The plain was bordered by forests of oak, maple, pine, sourwood, and hickory trees. Peach and wild apples abounded, along with several kinds of plums, and at either end of the straggling settlement the forest walls closed down against the river, vine-draped and flowery."[9]

The strapping, precocious youth became a favorite of Oolooteka, who adopted him, and Houston became known in Hiwassee by a Cherokee name, the Raven, in that tribe's cosmology a great symbol for good luck—but also, according to one contemporary source, a symbol of wandering. It is unknown whether the chief bestowed it on Houston or whether the headstrong boy, aware of the ravens on his existing family crest and now aware of the bird's role in Cherokee mythology, appropriated it to himself. But along with the Cherokee name he adopted their dress and ways and, remarkably for a lad who had been a dullard in school, became fluent in their language. Oolooteka's interest in him was natural, for the young Raven had done what the chief himself had done: walked out of a strife-filled existence to go do better for himself. The Cherokee Indians lived up to their billing as "civilized" by splitting into acrimonious factions over what their response to increasing Anglo presence should be. Oolooteka was a maverick, moving to his island in the river to get away from the rest of his people and their clamoring, and earning his new name, John Jolly, by his geniality toward the whites. Doubtless he understood the Raven better than anyone in Sam's own home.

He had left his family but took no trouble to hide himself. When after several weeks his mother sent the "Holy Apostles" out to find him, they did so easily and remonstrated with him to come home. He informed them rather haughtily that he preferred measuring deer tracks to tape, and that he had endured quite enough of their tyranny. The brothers could see for themselves that Sam had acquired a new set of Cherokee friends, including young women in greater familiarity than Presbyterian propriety would approve, and they left him there—as he was afterward fond of saying—to make love and read Homer's *Iliad*. (Importantly, however, this was an era when the phrase "make love" usually meant innocent courting, not having sex. Others familiar with the Cherokee Nation recalled that if Houston had been ruining the girls' virtue, their families would have let him know straightaway that he was wearing out his welcome.)

Young Houston based himself with the Hiwassee Cherokees for the next three years, but he was not anchored there. He returned home every several months to visit with and wheedle money from his mother. He was generous in returning to his Cherokees with gifts bought, mostly on credit, from stores such as Sheffy's in Kingston, a settlement some thirty miles west of Maryville at the confluence of the Big and Little Tennessee Rivers. There were also stories that Houston had acquired too great a fondness for liquor, which helped put him in such debt that he must either default and become known as a youth of no character or find some manner of employment. In 1811 a thirteen-year-old lad named Willoughby Williams discovered Houston clerking at Sheffy's. "The Indian trade being much valued, his services were highly appreciated from the fact that he spoke with fluency the Cherokee language. He was especially kind to me, and much of my time was spent in his company."[10]

Nor was this Houston's only occupation, for at some time during 1812 he returned to Maryville and announced his intention to open, of all things, a school, which would have come as rather a shock to Porter Academy's Dr. Isaac Anderson. Houston established the venture a few miles north of Maryville and, to the surprise of onlookers, made a success of it. Despite his modest qualifications, Houston hiked the tuition to eight dollars per term, payable one-third in cash, one-third in cotton cloth, and one-third in corn at three bushels per dollar. In his mature years, Houston recalled of his schoolmastering that at lunch, "which I and my pupils ate together out of our baskets, I would go into the woods and cut me a 'sour wood' stick, trim it carefully in circular spirals and thrust one-half of it into the fire, which would turn it blue, leaving the other half white. With this emblem of . . . authority in my hand, dressed in a hunting-shirt of flowered calico, a long queue down my back . . . I experienced a higher feeling of dignity and self-satisfaction than from any office or honor which I have since held."[11] While Houston may have been indulging in a bit of hyperbole from the fondness of the memory, the vignette provides a useful additional tidbit: at the age of nineteen, his life-long affinity for the whittling knife was already begun. And apparently, Houston also had less genteel ways of keeping rowdier students in line. In later years a set of leaden knuckles with Houston's name inscribed in them was discovered wedged above the schoolroom's doorcasing.[12]

In March 1813, finding himself again in debt, Houston spoke of his difficulties to Charles Norwood, a friend only a couple of weeks younger than himself, to ask for a loan. Norwood had grown up on a farm three miles removed from the Houstons, and in their adolescence he had been a partner in mischief. Norwood pointed out that the U.S. Army was in Maryville recruiting and paid a cash bounty for signing up.[13] This Houston did, although the silver dollar taken symbolically from the drumhead as a token of enlistment would not have covered much debt. Indeed, Norwood may have fancied too great a role for himself in setting Sam Houston on a military career, for Willoughby Williams was emphatic in his memory that Houston's enlistment took place not in Maryville but in Kingston: "Robert H. McEwen, of Nashville, cousin of General Houston, and myself, were standing together on the street and saw Houston take his dollar from the drum and enlist as a private. . . . [H]e was taken immediately to the barracks, dressed as a soldier, and appointed the same day as a sergeant."[14]

Why did Sam Houston join the army? Although he taught school near Maryville during the term, the fact that he continued to clerk at Sheffy's store in Kingston when school was not in session was evidence enough that he was desperate for money, since he hated clerking with a passion. From this shuttling drudgery, that silver dollar on the drum provided merciful release; the pay was not generous, but it got him out of town and into a life with possibilities.

Willoughby Williams in his dotage remembered one detail with accuracy: Houston's service record shows him entering the army with the rank of sergeant. Some of young Houston's friends, familiar with his father's career, upbraided him for joining as a ranker when, in their view, he should have applied for a commission. Houston scolded them with a curiously Elizabethan retort: "Go to, with your stuff; I would much sooner honor the ranks, than disgrace an appointment. You don't know me now, but you shall hear of me." Half an eventful lifetime later, Sam Houston wrote that this was his first speech, a comment made in that authorized memoir composed to enhance his profile as presidential timber. That purpose doubtless accounts for much of the book's excessive theatricality, in which one can almost hear the nuggets of fact being hammered into frontierish legend. A case in point immediately follows that first speech. It was a fact that Houston had joined the army, but there was still one hurdle to clear. The age of legal enlistment as an adult was twenty-one. Houston had just turned twenty, and he needed his mother's consent. She gave it, but Houston's rendering of that fact in his autobiography bridges the gap between history and melodrama. "There, my son," he has her saying, "take this musket and never disgrace it; for remember, I had rather all my sons should fill one honorable grave, than that one of them should turn his back to save his life. Go, and remember, too, that while the door of my cottage is always open to brave men, it is eternally shut against cowards." So saying, she slipped onto his finger a simple gold band, so thin that it was almost wire, just stout enough to have the word "Honor" engraved along the inner curve. That much again is true, for he wore this ring until his widow removed it at the moment of his death. How inevitable that the complexity of separating Houston fact from Houston legend begins with Houston himself, for that was his intention.[15]

Still, the military was an obvious career choice for Sam Houston, and not only because his father had been an officer in the Revolutionary War. At age seventeen, young Sam had been fined five dollars "for committing a contempt to this Court . . . in disorderly, riotously, wantonly, with an assembly of militia annoying the court with the noise of a Drum . . . and with force and arms disturbing the Good order of said Court and abusing their Sheriff and demeaning themselves against the peace and dignity of the State." Houston, however, was not the ringleader in that episode; his friend John B. Cusack was fined ten dollars.[16] Sam Houston once wrote that one of his strongest early impressions was the pride he felt in his father's career, and once he was himself done with beating a drum outside the Blount County Courthouse and enlisted in the real army, he seemed to have no difficulty jettisoning the nature-will-provide indolence of his Cherokee idyll. In fact, he showed aptitude for the drill and a natural instinct for leadership that cannot be taught. His physical attributes helped; he was powerfully built, and at six feet, two inches tall, he towered over most men of the day. He had a deep, commanding voice and a striking appearance centered about a cleft chin and eyes of a transfixing and brilliant blue. He could, as they say, fill a room.

The War of 1812 was then being waged in grim earnest, and reprising an old stratagem, the British sought to enlist Native American allies to defeat her former colonies. The Cherokees, however, had repeatedly been loyal to the American government—once in spurning the Shawnee chief Tecumseh by refusing to join his projected native alliance and now in refusing the British enticements. The British had more luck with the Creek Indians, who lately had massacred a large number of white refugees near Fort Mims, Alabama. The officer sent to punish them, Gen. Andrew Jackson, commanded a disparate force of army regulars, Cherokee allies, and some friendly Creeks in addition to militia units from Georgia and his own state of Tennessee. Operating from Fort Strother on the Coosa River in Alabama, he had enjoyed only mixed success. Repeatedly frustrated by his undisciplined and undependable militia volunteers, faced with daily mutiny and near mutiny, Jackson held his force together by the ferocity of his character and in one instance by lit matches held over cannon aimed at his own men. Jackson requested an infusion of infantry regulars to provide the others an example of proper military operation.[17]

Thomas Hart Benton. At the time Sam Houston's regiment was merged into the Thirty-ninth Infantry, its lieutenant colonel was Thomas Hart Benton, who was so impressed by Houston's soldierly qualities that he brought him to the attention of Andrew Jackson. By the time Houston entered Congress, Benton represented Missouri in the Senate, where in a thirty-year career he was a consistent advocate of western expansion.

Courtesy Library of Congress

Not long after Sam Houston's enlistment, his Seventh Infantry was merged into the Thirty-ninth Regiment, where Houston's capabilities were noticed by the lieutenant colonel, Thomas Hart Benton (who went on to play his own role in America's westward expansion). As the officer to whom Houston first reported, Benton "marked in him soldierly and gentlemanly qualities . . . frank, generous, brave, ready to do . . . and always prompt to answer the call." At the end of July 1813, Houston was promoted to ensign, and then on the last day of the year he became a third lieutenant, all less than a year from his underage enlistment.[18] The Thirty-ninth got the call to march to Jackson's aid and reached him at Fort Strother on February 13, 1814. It was Houston's first sight of the raptor-eyed Jackson, with his wild shock of hair and his deeply fascinating mixture of culture, violence, chivalry, and blood-curdling temper.

After a setback at a place called the Holy Ground, about one thousand hostile Creek Indians—frequently called Red Sticks for the emblem that signified a decision in council for war—retreated down the Coosa River to where it joined the Tallapoosa in east-central Alabama. Led by a mixed-race chief named Weatherford (sometimes rendered Weathersford), the hostiles fortified themselves into a tight, eighty-acre loop of the Tallapoosa known as Tohopeka, or the Horseshoe Bend. Surrounded by water on three sides—the shore lined with banked canoes in which to escape, if need be—the warriors constructed log breastworks across the narrow neck on the landward side and awaited the next contest with Jackson and his patch-quilt army.

Jackson arrived in the vicinity on March 26 with about three thousand infantry, militia, allied Cherokees, and friendly Creeks, and he saw straightaway that routing the Red Sticks would be no easy task. "Nature furnishes few situations so eligible for defense," he wrote in his battle report, "and barbarians have never rendered one more secure by art. Across the neck of the bend which leads into it from the north, [the Creeks] had erected a breastwork of the greatest compactness and strength from five to eight feet high and prepared with double portholes very artfully arranged. . . . An army could not approach it without being exposed to a double and cross fire from the enemy, who lay in perfect security behind it." High praise for the effort of mere "barbarians."[19]

The following afternoon, having given the hostile Creeks a chance to clear their dependents from the field, Jackson determined to attack the Red Sticks on all sides. His strategy for the day was straightforward enough: he had his Cherokees slink into the river and swim back with as many of Weatherford's canoes as they could pull away. They and some of the regulars surrounded the curve of the Horseshoe Bend along the opposite bank to fire into the Creek rear and prevent their escape while he sought to reduce their fortifications with artillery. He also retained the militia with him to keep the Creeks' heads down during the bombardment. Once he believed the defenses were softened, Jackson ordered an assault, and the Thirty-ninth Infantry led the way. The breastworks had been battered by Jackson's guns, but the fire from behind them was murderous. Maj. Lemuel Montgomery, one of Jackson's favorite officers and the man for whom Alabama's future capital was named, was the first man over the top and was killed instantly. Third lieutenant and platoon leader Houston was over immediately after him, waving with his sword for his men to follow. They did so, becoming engaged in fighting that was desperate and hand-to-hand. Suddenly there was the zip of an arrow, and Houston felt a sticking agony low in his right groin as two other officers of his regiment were killed nearby—falling near his side was Maryville friend William Wallace, two of whose brothers later married his younger sister, Mary.[20] Though he was hobbled, the young lieutenant continued to fight powerfully until the Red Sticks abandoned the breastwork and retreated to a fortified redoubt in a rocky ravine. Houston pulled a fellow lieutenant aside for help in extracting the arrow. The officer tried, but when it would not budge, Houston raised his sword and threatened him with a bellow. The arrow was barbed, and when it withdrew it did so with tissue and such a torrent of blood that Houston was forced to leave the barricade and find a surgeon to stop the flow.

As he was recovering, General Jackson happened by and ordered Houston out of the fight for the remainder of the day. The battle was going their way, and the Creeks were now holed up in their log-roofed redoubt in the ravine. After attempting to weaken this position also with artillery, Jackson called for volunteers to storm it. For his memoir, Houston related that had it not been for that reckless boast to his family, he would have sat as still as his fellows. But, having sworn that they should hear of him, he took a musket and called on those of his platoon who dared so to follow him. Making his way painfully down the side of the ravine, Houston advanced until he was stopped fifteen feet from the redoubt by two musket balls that hit his right arm and shoulder simultaneously. He called on his men to charge, but no one responded, and when he turned Houston was horrified to discover he was alone. His right arm useless and with darkness having fallen, he made his way back to the top of the ravine and collapsed.

Ultimately, the redoubt was taken not by storm but by setting it afire, and the battle was a crushing defeat for Weatherford's Creeks, losing perhaps 800 killed. Jackson lost only 49 dead (26 white, 18 Cherokee allies, and 5 friendly Creeks) and 157 wounded, some of whom, including Lieutenant Houston, were likely also to die. By firelight a surgeon dressed his mangled groin as best he could and removed the ball from his upper right arm. A second doctor told the first to save the trouble; this man, he said, had lost so much blood he could not last until morning. So Sam Houston was laid aside, on the ground, as the surgeons labored over those they had a chance of saving. He lay there all night, cold and in pain, refusing to die. With the surgeon's prediction confounded by morning, Houston was placed on a litter and dragged sixty agonizing miles to Fort Williams, where, it was assumed, he could finally die in some better comfort.

With the Creek threat having been crushed, the Tennessee militia was mustered out. They placed the still-breathing lieutenant on another litter, between two horses, and headed for home. With the ball still in his shoulder and with onsetting septicemia, the torture of being dragged home was relieved only by whiskey and occasional blackouts.

The traditional history, which has Houston arriving home unexpected and so emaciated his mother did not at first recognize him, is a product of his later political mythmaking. In fact, at the latter stage of his long and painful journey home, his boyhood friend Willoughby Williams and cousin Robert McEwen met Houston "some distance from Kingston on a litter supported by two horses. He was greatly emaciated, suffering at the same time from wounds and the measles. We took him to the house of his relative, Squire John McEwen . . . where he remained for some time, and from thence he went to the house of his mother in Blount County." It is unthinkable that the McEwens would not have informed Elizabeth Paxton Houston of her son's condition and imminent return. She may well have been jarred by her son's wasted appearance, but his arrival would not have been unexpected.[21]

But at least he was home, and whatever his previous differences with his family, home was a comfort—and, as he once boasted, he returned home a hero. Even the army finally decided to quit waiting for him to die, and after a rest he was ordered to Washington for expert medical treatment. When he arrived there he stared at the ruins of the Capitol and the White House, burned by the British the previous summer, and had no inkling that it was not the last capital he would see in ashes. The doctors there were of no help, and as he made his way home he stopped to visit relatives in Virginia. March of 1815 found him back in Maryville, his wounds still unhealed, when he heard of Jackson's glittering victory at the battle of New Orleans, after which he learned that the war had ended. Peace surely meant a reduction in the size of the army, with young officers—especially officers of volunteers like himself—to be mustered out to look after themselves. On the first of March, he wrote to Secretary of War James Monroe applying for a commission in the regular army; he then also wrote to John Rhea, East Tennessee's elderly six-term congressman, requesting him to use his influence to see that it came through. The latter is a curious missive, being Houston's first documented attempt to get a string pulled in his behalf—his student work in the art of patronage. As such, it contains none of the subtlety and smoothness of his later maneuvering style and, in fact, displays a kind of testy self-consciousness at having to ask a favor of anyone: "I have fought and bled for my country in consequence of which I am in some measure rendered unfit for other business. You are not a stranger to the manner in which I enter'd the army at a time I had not friends to patronize me & by my own merits or good fortune have been promoted & I think it consistent with a virtuous government to reward bravery & merit both of which I claim. You will be so good as to use your influence to have me continued in the army. I would not have intruded on you had you not assured me when I saw you last that you would be happy to serve me if it was in your power." It was only after signing the letter that it occurred to Lieutenant Houston that being unfit for other business might also disqualify him from a further military career. "P.S.," he added hastily, "My wound is nearly healed and my health is entirely recovered."[22] It was a youthful gaffe he would not repeat, but it was hardly the last time he leaned on his war wounds to get some consideration.

Rhea complied with a pleasant endorsement of "this fine young man" to Monroe.[23] By the end of April, Houston must have heard no news, for at that time he wrote a family friend lamenting how his situation would likely prolong his undesired bachelorhood: "I suppose it will be impracticable for a disbanded officer to marry for the[y] will be regarded as cloathes, out of fashion . . . but I will not despond, before I am disappointed, and I suppose that will be some time for I will not court any of the Dear Girles before I make a fortune and if I come no better speed than I have done heretofore it will take some time." As far as making that fortune was concerned, Houston supposed if he were forced into civilian life he would have to "pursue some course for a livelihood which will not be laborious as my wounds are not near well." (So much for his "entirely recovered health.") This letter piques the interest in one other way—its closing, which contains a chilly premonition of the intrigues that soon would begin swirling about him: "Please present my warmest respects to your mother, and all whom you believe are my friends."[24]

Young Houston should have been just a little more patient; five days before confessing his anxieties, his commission as a second lieutenant in the Thirty-ninth Infantry Regiment was finally issued, dated April 20, 1815, but with the rank to date from the preceding May 20.[25] Even better news, an army surgeon in Knoxville concluded that Houston might finally mend if the ball in his shoulder could be removed. To get the best treatment, he was transferred from the Thirty-ninth Infantry to the First, stationed in New Orleans. He departed Tennessee with several volumes of his father's library to keep him company during the next stage of his recovery. In New Orleans, the ball was finally removed in a grisly procedure during which he nearly bled to death, but still the wounds would not heal, and in the spring of 1816 he was ordered to New York for still more treatment. This journey afforded Houston his first look at the vibrant city that in future provided some of his warmest support.

Throughout his long recovery from Tohopeka, first being dragged by litter and then riding painfully from doctor to doctor, Lieutenant Houston drew pay from each post in which he found himself. During the summer of 1818, his head having finally cleared, he realized that he had possibly drawn pay for the same months from two different posts. He could not be certain that he had, but Houston reported himself to the paymaster all the same. "If I did I have commited myself," he wrote, "but hope you will not take advantage of me but let me know the amount of the error & I will on the shortest notice transmit it to you."[26] The letter began a reputation for transparent fiduciary honesty that held fast against repeated efforts over the years by political enemies to catch him in some fraud. It was a reputation maintained largely because of his fanatical record keeping—a mania that would prove its value presently.

2

THE INDIAN AGENT

If Sam Houston had died of his 1814 wounds, as by all medical probability he should have died, he would have been remembered only in local history as a gallant young idiot, a footnote on the page of Horseshoe Bend. But with Houston having survived the neglect of army doctors, his ticket to prominence was endorsed by the kindly notice of Andrew Jackson himself. The traditional history is that Jackson marked Houston for advancement because of his bravery at Tohopeka, but there is more to the story. After the battle, Jackson wept like a child over Lemuel Montgomery's body, lamenting, "I have lost the flower of my army." He made out two reports of the battle, one to regular-army brass on March 28 and a more complete version to Tennessee governor Willie Blount three days later; in neither account does Sam Houston's name appear.[1] The general certainly did note and remember Houston's bravery under hellish fire and doubtless smiled at his refusal to expire on cue for the army doctors who gave up on him. He also admired the qualities that made Houston a good officer: honesty, leadership, and attention to duty. But what cemented their relationship was the young man's response to a later situation in which loyalty to his country was placed opposite his personal concept of honor—a corner from which no officer, and certainly no Southerner, could escape with ease.

Just as Oolooteka had seen in Houston a mirror of his own free spiritedness and desire to be let alone to live amiably with people, just so Andrew Jackson saw things in this maimed lieutenant to draw his sympathy. Like Houston, he had had a tempestuous youth and the advantage of being mentored by solicitous elders. Still childless at age forty-six, it is possible Jackson saw in Houston the distant image of his own apprentice years of brief tenures and abrupt resignations. And in seeing himself, perhaps he saw the son he never had, a willing lad on whom he could settle not just his experience but also his affection. Jackson always collected

Andrew Jackson. From the days of his army service, Houston respected and admired Andrew Jackson. He acted, however, more as a protégé of Tennessee governor Joseph McMinn and was drawn closer to Jackson's orbit after McMinn's death. Houston was attracted to Jackson's ideal of "mass democracy" but found the Old Chief's behavior occasionally inconsistent with his rhetoric as he attempted to pick office holders from among party loyalists. Still, Jackson's frequent recruitment of young protégés was a model Houston followed his entire adult life.

Courtesy National Archives

about him wards and protégés to help through life, a trait that Houston in his own maturity actualized more than once (until his own belated fatherhood).

Nor was Houston always an easy apprentice. Asking of Jackson first one job but then suddenly desiring another, Houston seemed to be engaged in some youthful inner struggle to find himself, as though he was aware of his inexperience and struggling to make the most of the opportunities put in his hands. Jackson bore Houston's changes of heart patiently and paternally, endorsing his shifting requests and smoothing the way for him. With the lieutenant's shoulder and groin still healing, orders came on New Year's Day, 1817, assigning him to the adjutant general of the Southern Division in Nashville, whose commander was Jackson, now a major general in the regular army. Before reporting for duty, he had several weeks' furlough to visit relatives in Maryville, where he temporarily forgot his pledge not to court any of the "Dear Girles" before raising a fortune. The young woman is now known only as Miss M—— and was characterized by a Houston intimate as the "Princess of E. T.," meaning East Tennessee. It was not a simple matter, for the woman was torn between him and another suitor, and by the time Houston arrived for duty in Nashville, he was neither free nor spoken for.

On March 5, 1817, he was promoted to first lieutenant, his rank to count as such from the previous May 1. His clerical duties in the adjutant general's office were light, designed to keep him busy while giving his draining wounds a chance to heal, and Houston used the respite to mix in society. During this period he added to his résumé other requirements of genteel adulthood; he submitted to the mysteries of Masonry; initiated into Cumberland Lodge No. 8, AF & AM, on April 19, 1817; passed on June 20; and raised on July 22.[2] Feeling out of his depth in his entanglement with the "Princess of E.T.," he requested a buddy from his romping days, Jesse Beene of Knoxville, to speak to her. Hoping for release, the reply he got, addressed to "My Dear Friend Sam," made things even harder: "You know that J. Beene is your friend & if I were to advise you it would be to speedily marry M—— by moonshine or any other way most handy." It seemed that Miss M—— had thrown Houston's rival "sky high and . . . She is . . . ready to leave mother home friends and every thing dear to her . . . and go with you to earth's remotest bounds."[3] That was not what Houston wanted to hear, but soon he was summoned to Jackson and presented with a challenge that caused him to disengage himself from Miss M—— without further ceremony.

Two years earlier, the government had concluded a treaty with several Cherokee chiefs by which the Indians ceded their Tennessee lands to the United States in exchange for new territory and liberal subsistence west of the Mississippi River. The signatories were underling chiefs who had no authority to speak for all the Cherokees resident on that land—one of whom was Sam Houston's adopted father He Puts away the Drum, Oolooteka. Houston recognized in a heartbeat the irony and injustice that John Jolly, who had removed to his island in the Hiwassee to get away from fractious and quarreling would-be leaders and live congenially with his white neighbors, now was to be evicted and forced to a strange and distant country. Worse than that, Cherokee tradition looked favorably on the East, place of the sunrise, but the West, where night consumed the sun, was considered the home of Black Evil. John Jolly did not want to go. Still worse, Oolooteka's older brother, Tahlontusky, who had earlier led a splinter group of Cherokees of their own volition to the Indian Territory, had returned with a sour report of the land's quality, of the government's fidelity to its promises, and of their neighbors there, Osage Indians who were always looking for an excuse to fight—which was understandable because the government had moved the Cherokees onto land the Osages considered their own. And now Tahlontusky was back in Tennessee en route to Washington to petition President Monroe to recognize the complete independence of his band from the rest of the Cherokees.

The western Cherokees had been at something of a disadvantage against the Osages, for after generations of peaceful accommodation to the whites, they had all but forgotten the arts of war. In the spring of 1818, though, as it became clear that the United States meant to enforce the rump treaty made by the pretender chiefs, the Hiwassee River bands were so angry they were remembering hard how to fight. With Indian affairs being administered by the War Department, the Cherokee agent was Col. Return J. Meigs, a capable officer and one not unsympathetic to John Jolly's Indians. To Jackson he suggested that what was needed was a subagent appointed to the Hiwassee Cherokees, a man whom the people would trust implicitly but who could be counted on to carry out government policy. Meigs asked for Lt. Sam Houston.[4] Jackson's star had continued ascendant after his victory at New Orleans, and just now he was preoccupied with growing trouble in Spanish Florida. He could not give the Cherokees his attention and needed Houston to handle the situation.

The bandaged lieutenant was deeply conflicted. He was an officer of the United States Army sworn loyal to a government that, he realized, was dealing treacherously with innocent people with whom he was intimately connected. Houston might resign his commission, but then the duty could fall to another who would treat his Hiwassee Cherokees less gently. What might have proved to be an insuperable conflict of conscience Houston navigated by concentrating on the existing realities of the situation. When one cannot do what is completely right, he reasoned, sometimes one has to do the best that is possible under circumstances one is powerless to change. It was a principle he first implemented here in accepting the assignment as subagent to his adopted people, and it did not change in later years when he adhered to it during the sectional schism over slavery. He told Jackson he would do it, and through Tennessee's governor Joseph McMinn, his appointment was arranged in Washington. When it came through on October 21, 1817, Houston received the news from Jackson's own hand. On the spot he wrote out his acceptance, indicating his determination to make a success of the job in signing his acknowledgment, "Sam Houston, Sub-Agt."[5]

Colonel Meigs was aware of Lieutenant Houston's ambivalence to the duty and wrote him four tightly scripted pages of instructions, assuring him that those Cherokees who agreed to leave for the West "will have in every sense the most liberal patronage, countenance & support of the Government—the emigrants are not going from home on the contrary they are going home in the best sense of the word."[6] It was clear from Meigs's orders, however, that Houston had finally crossed the political threshold. He was now an instrument of national policy, and Meigs emphasized that in making his decisions, whatever his personal sympathies, Houston was to be guided by the object of facilitating the Cherokee removal.

The situation seemed clear enough for Houston to administer, but he quickly discovered that Colonel Meigs was less familiar than he should have been with the workings of the Hiwassee subagency itself. When he arrived on station, what he found was an apparatus as entrenched as it was corrupt and politically well connected. If Houston was to act honorably by his adopted people, he would have to take on a hostile power structure, exposing the seedling of his career to a hailstorm from the very start. It gave him pause, but he did it. Dogged by ill health during the first several weeks of his residence, Houston told all in a long letter, not to Meigs but to Jackson: "When I arrived here Mr. Smith act'g assist. agent, had been absent from the Agency, twenty-two days. . . . I called on his *agent* (a Brother-in-law of his) for funds, agreeably to the instructions of Col. Meigs. When I called, out of 2000$ only 884$ could be produced, and the notes not current." This, however, was not the real source of alarm that prompted him to seek Jackson's protection. Houston had heard "from good authority, that Mr. Smith A.A.A. has a store at the garrison, and also keeps spirits, & (from Good authority I have learned), sells them. . . . You know General Jackson? how difficult it is to keep Indians sober? and also how impossible it is to transact business with them when intoxicated?" The twenty-four-year-old lieutenant of infantry had therefore shut down Smith's establishment and removed the agency from the army garrison onto Cherokee Nation soil, where he could interdict the liquor. "Mr. Smith is much exasperated," he continued, "and I expect, will remonstrate against it, to the dept. of war."[7]

On further reflection of the political repercussions, Houston soon after decided to make a preemptive strike and wrote a second account of his side of the affair directly to Secretary of War George Graham amplifying his reasons for the move. He pointed out, first, that the garrison was located outside the boundaries of the Cherokee Nation, and "Indians have an aversion to transacting business among whites," and second, "I could not prohibit sale of spirits to them, and it is an established maxim with Indians to get intoxicated when they can get liquor." Sensing the need to haul up some authority behind him, he added that his decision "has also been sanctioned by His Excellency Jos. McMinn, as being the only fit one at this *crisis* of emigration." Finally, he pointed out that moving the depot into the Nation also had a salutary effect on the Cherokees' willingness to emigrate: Part of the bargain was that Indians who agreed to leave would be given new muskets, and Houston was able to report that "Eighty-three Guns &c have been issued, since the issues commenced, and one fourth of the number have been issued to Indians who were attracted to this place by curiosity & business, and had no intention of emigrating to Arkansaw, until they came here, and caught the contagion. . . . I am not able to state the precise number . . . as [it] is daily increasing, tho' I believe, I may with safety, say, near Five hundred, in toto."[8] During these cold days Houston found himself embattled on another front. Having discovered slave smugglers from Florida attempting to slip blacks through the Cherokee Nation into the United States, he did not wait for instructions to break up the ring, but did so on his own initiative.

With the Hiwassee subagency more or less under his control, Houston met with Oolooteka and his chiefs, not as adopted son but as representative of the United States. He freely admitted that the situation was unfair, but the government had Cherokee names on a treaty that ceded the eastern lands and agreed to removal to the West. It was true, he argued, that they might resist by force of arms, but what chance had they against the might of the U.S. Army? With allies they might make a fight of it, but none were at hand. The stick he matched with a carrot, adding his solemn opinion that the government had made its pledges in good faith, and if they agreed to the removal they would be generously provided for. Sadly but peaceably, John Jolly agreed to leave his homeland. He did, however, wish for words of his own to be taken to the far-away secretary of war emphasizing his desire that his people be understood as peaceable and cooperative. "You must not think that by removing we will return to the savage life. You have taught us to be Herdsmen and cultivators. . . . Numbers of our young people can read and write, they can read what we call the Preachers Book." Sam Houston may well have helped his adoptive father place his people in the most favorable light.[9]

Although he was under Meigs's authority and corresponding with Jackson, the man most helpful to the embattled subagent was Governor McMinn, who took a liking to the earnest young officer and gave him close guidance. There was a third circumstance at the Hiwassee Agency during those first weeks that required Houston to crawl out on a limb. It was midwinter, and many of the Cherokee families slated for removal were ill equipped to face the journey. From Governor McMinn's advice, he was persuaded to "issue some blankets to women, who can produce vouchers to satisfy me that they are really the only heads of families. In this transaction, I am aware that the *responsibility* rests on *my own shoulders*. I would not have been induced to act thus, but some are in a destitute situation, and a few blankets will answer the present emergency." Trying to put the best spin possible on the irregular disbursement, one he knew Jackson would approve, he added, "It will, at this season be a stimulus to emigration."[10] Taken as a whole, the opening months of Houston's tenure as subagent to his Cherokees was a seminally instructive time. He learned that there are circumstances in which initiative must be taken, but that in so doing enmities can be incurred that might prove lethal to a fledgling career. His correspondence reflected an awareness of this liability, but it was not until the next year that he suffered the consequences.

To persuade the Tennessee Cherokees of the good faith of the United States, a delegation of chiefs—including John Jolly's elderly brother Tahlontusky, whom McMinn assured the new secretary of war, John C. Calhoun, was "considered in the light of a king among his people"—was assembled to trek to Washington to meet the president. Houston reported on December 21 that all of them had arrived but one, Ta-ka-to-kah, and the other chiefs had set a meeting for the twenty-fifth to elect a replacement. Governor McMinn, who was going to Washington separately, assigned the duty of escorting the chiefs to Lieutenant Houston. While he endorsed Houston in the highest terms to Calhoun, McMinn felt himself responsible that the affair should come off well. In charging Houston with this important mission, the governor was aware that this was the most serious responsibility the young officer had yet undertaken, and McMinn was anxious that nothing should go wrong. His instructions of January 2, 1818, were trusting but meticulous, revealing his transparent honesty and good will. "Dear Samuel—In the event of our not meeting on this side of Knoxville you will please take the Chiefs to Mr. Rheas, and say to him I will [illegible] on his keeping them upon the very lowest Terms so as to indemnify himself. The horses must be taken to [illegible] unless Rhea will keep them at 25 Cents per day."

Winter travel in the Appalachians could be brutal. McMinn preceded Houston and the chiefs to Washington, and on January 16 wrote Houston that he was supplying him with an additional $650 credit to cover any contingencies in seeing to the chiefs' well being. "Dear Samuel—You will proceed to Washington . . . by the nearest and best route," but without trying to move the chiefs more than twenty-five miles per day; he should make certain that the inns they stopped at could accommodate the entire party comfortably, "particularly as you approach the City when fuel becomes an object," and he should see to it that the chiefs ate good breakfasts before starting off in the mornings. Further, with an eye toward the venerated Tahlontusky,

> You will favor as much as practicable the ill health of the old chiefs, by slow and regular movements. . . .
>
> You will use proper economy in the disbursement of your funds—this can be done with one hand while with the other you can administer liberally to the wants and comforts of those committed to your care.
>
> I have a singular dislike to the intemperate use of Spirits amongst men on business, particularly in the elevated character in which you and the Delegation

stand. You are going to see the chief of one of the greatest nations on the
Globe. . . . I have your honor and the interest of the delegation very much
at heart, and no mortification could wound my feeling, with equal depth to
that of hearing of a single case of intemperance (much less drunkenness)
charged to any one of the company.

There is something in the tone of McMinn's instructions here that gives the
impression that his admonition to sobriety may have been directed as much at
Lieutenant Houston as to the Cherokees in his charge, and it is certain that the
turbulent young officer was gaining a hard reputation with the bottle. Still, some
alcohol was seen as necessary to the chiefs' comfort in bitter winter travel, and
McMinn recommended that Houston acquire "one great bottle" from which to
administer whiskey to the chiefs responsibly. Once in Washington, "having made
the necessary preparations for appearing at Court, you will report yourself to the
Secretary of War, who will give you the necessary information relative to the most
suitable place for your lodgings, and at what period the chiefs can have an interview. You will also render him an accurate account of your expenses and of the
money you will have on hand, and await his pleasure."[11]

The Cherokee delegation arrived in Washington, D.C., on February 5, 1818,
and the chiefs were received with faultless courtesy by War Secretary Calhoun.
Lieutenant Houston attended, clothed in native fashion—the argument can cut
either way whether it was to make a show of himself or out of respect for his
charges. Calhoun cordially invited the Cherokees to exit to the adjoining room,
where the Great Father himself, President Monroe, awaited them. When he asked
Houston to stay behind a moment, the young lieutenant had no idea he was in for
the verbal hiding of his life. How dare he, Calhoun demanded, an officer in the
United States Army, appear at an official function in such a costume? Houston's
protest that, while he was indeed an officer, he was also these Indians' agent, and
he had adopted their dress out of respect for them, got him nowhere, and Calhoun
dismissed him with an angry warning never to repeat such a stunt. Houston withstood the barrage, but his hatred for Calhoun never, ever abated.

There is a story that Houston had "frequently" been seen in Washington
wearing a loincloth and blanket, and if his appearance before Calhoun came after
unheeded warnings about his attire, it would make the secretary's outburst more
understandable.[12] But worse followed. Some days later he was summoned back
into the secretary of war's presence and informed that charges had been preferred
against him for complicity in slave running. It seemed that the smugglers whose
traffic he shut down had friends in Congress. This time Houston was prepared. He
had known instinctively from the first days of his agency—and had warned Jackson—that he was making enemies who would strike at him one day, and he carried
in his head a minute command of every aspect of his tenure. Houston's self-defense
before Calhoun was so forceful and nimble that the secretary backed down, and
President Monroe himself consented to an investigation, which quickly proved
Houston's innocence. The real slavers had used their congressional connections
to try to tar Houston with their own brush but failed completely.

John C. Calhoun. While Calhoun and Houston were inimical virtually from the moment they met, Jackson did not recognize the South
Carolinian's true colors until the twin issues of nullification and Peggy
Eaton aroused his hostility. Calhoun became the first vice president of
the United States to resign, after which he devoted himself to the
slaveocracy.

Courtesy National Archives

Lieutenant Houston was still hot about the incident when he made a lengthy
report of it to Andrew Jackson later in the year. He was armed with letters from
the principals concerned, which he labeled like exhibits in evidence, "I told [Cal-
houn] if he wished it, that I would submit the letters of Morgan with a statement
of facts to him, he said it might be proper. I then gave him copies of A, B, C & D.
Some days after I call'd on him and spoke of the Documents, and asked if he was
satisfied; he said perfectly, and that he had submitted them to the President, and my
conduct was approbated, as very proper, and the views of Morgan, as declared in
letter B unlawful & improper."

Houston had been exonerated by Monroe himself. What left him so angry about the whole affair was that this finding of fact had to stand as its own reward. "I then observed to the Secy. that a written expression of his approbation would be grateful to me, but he said it was not necessary, as the charges were not in writing."[13] In his few months as Cherokee subagent, Houston had learned to defend himself by keeping records so meticulous as to leave him invulnerable; now he found that he could still be slandered at the very pinnacle of government and had to be satisfied with an oral tut-tut that written exoneration was unnecessary. He never received an apology for the calumny from anyone, which was another offense he marked down against Calhoun. Deciding that he had no future in the army, Houston set pen to paper:

> Washington City
> March 1st 1818
>
> Sir
> You will please accept this as my resignation to take effect from this date.
>
> > I have the honor to be
> > Your Most Obt Servt
> > /s/ Sam Houston
> > 1st Lieut 1st Infy
>
> Genl D. Parker
> A & Ins Genl.
> W. City

Having learned the value of keeping possession of all his papers, he penned a postscript: "I will thank you to give me my commission, which I am entitled to by my last promotion." General orders were issued the same day: "The resignation of 1st Lieut. Samuel Houston of the 1st Infantry is accepted to take effect 1st of March 1818. By order / D. Parker Adj Genl." The army was not sorry to be rid of an officer who dressed in Indian costumes.[14]

This brief, truculent exchange closed the era of Houston's developmental years. Half a lifetime later, during one of his grueling political campaigns across the vastness of Texas, he counseled his slave boy, Jeff Hamilton, to always notice the landmarks of the country through which he traveled. Then, if he ever came that way again, his memory would carry him safely through.[15] As galling as were the circumstances under which Lieutenant Houston resigned, his five-year military career and six brief months as Indian agent had been a journey whose landmarks he himself memorized to the smallest detail. Today its landscape shocks the viewer, not for its topography but because it foreshadowed in small the Texas experience to come.

From the doleful misadventures of the Tennessee militia, clad in their homespun, shouldering their unmatched weapons, and following their penchant to slip back home whenever they got bored, measured against the ruthless precision of Jackson's infantry, it was stamped on Houston's mind like a die-cut that military discipline was essential to the success of a campaign. Volunteers, whatever their initial zeal, could not be relied upon in a critical venture. Marquis James in *The Raven* drew a connection between Houston's love of fine clothes and the superior visage he cut in the spanking bright uniform of the regular army.[16] Truly, Sam Houston always harbored a weakness for striking apparel, but what he committed to memory was not pantaloons. Instead, he marked the deadly, daily struggle Jackson had holding his militia together, and then with discipline instilled, the crushing, lopsided victories the general pasted on Weatherford's Creeks at Tohopeka (800 hostile dead against 49 of his own) and on the British at New Orleans (2,100 casualties against 21).

Leading his platoon to the last Creek redoubt at Horseshoe Bend, Houston was nearly blown to shreds. As his men dove for cover, he had to crawl to safety on his own strength. One might lead men but must not advance too far ahead of them nor call upon them for valor equal to one's own. His shabby treatment by military doctors, given up for dead by everyone but himself, steeled Houston for his painful recovery after San Jacinto over twenty years later. The ease with which Indian treaties were discarded, even by a man he loved as much as Jackson, presaged the fate of his Texas Cherokees by a quarter-century. Then, to be set up and framed by ruffians to take the rap for crimes of their own, not to mention being humiliated by Calhoun and other political dandies, taught him how some men can rise to great power and still be mean, shallow, and worst of all, unperceptive. Later in Texas, Mirabeau Lamar and David Burnet could pull nothing he had not seen before. Taken in sum, this largely unhappy segment of his life provides a crucial insight into understanding the later man: he was not one who had to relearn lessons—ever. In later years, Ashbel Smith referred to Houston's memory as "awful," no small compliment in the nineteenth century, when that word conveyed the opposite meaning than it does today.[17] And beyond that, these bitter lessons were not just remembered, but they became part of his instinct, the way a bear once wounded avoids entering a dangerous place long after the memory of the encounter itself has faded.

But if Calhoun and his crowd were the men who hardened Houston, the men who made him wily and taught him to keep his own counsel, there was another, gentler side to Houston's early development, influences exercised by several men, some of whom have been all but forgotten by his biographers. Jackson tutored him, yes, but before Jackson there was Oolooteka, who took in the fatherless youth. Houston had found refuge from an impossible situation by removing himself from the scene of never-ending conflict. John Jolly had already done that, and it was a shared experience they exchanged repeatedly like a cherished heirloom: Oolooteka had fled to his Hiwassee island to escape the endless backbiting of other chiefs; Houston escaped family tyranny in his youth by seeking sanctuary among the Indians. The Cherokees removed to Arkansas in 1818, and they sheltered Houston again in 1832. Oolooteka demonstrated repeatedly that fatalism and acceptance in the face of adversity could preserve the core of one's soul to find happiness another day.

And after Jackson there was John Rhea, the congressman from Houston's East Tennessee district. An elderly bachelor who had fought in the American Revolution, kindly and deeply religious, rich and cultured, he was a man of contradictions startlingly similar to those Houston displayed throughout his own life. Rhea was a Jackson intimate, a western rustic who may have had a hand in encouraging Jackson to invade Florida. But he was also a man of letters who was a founding trustee of no fewer than three universities. He was a Southerner opposed to slavery and did not hesitate to speak his mind about it.[18]

Then there was Joseph McMinn, three-time governor of Tennessee first elected in 1814, an early advocate of penal reform—a sensitivity that was a hallmark of Houston's own brief gubernatorial tenure more than forty years later. McMinn's "Dear Samuel" letters guiding the lieutenant through the Cherokee chiefs' trek to Washington are the very models of those written by a kindly mentor to an appreciated young talent. McMinn pushed hard for internal improvements in his state, a recurrent theme in Houston's own career. But more importantly, when after six years as governor McMinn became the Cherokee agent (a year before his death at age sixty-six), he favored Jackson's removal policy but was so vigorous in defending Cherokee territory against unlawful encroachment that he burned out white squatters on Indian land, which nearly sparked a rebellion against federal authority.[19] The lifelong complexity of Houston's policy toward Indians, favoring their pacification while insisting that they control themselves or else be controlled, has embroiled scholars ever since. Some have claimed that Houston's professed sympathy for Native Americans was a politically motivated sham, that his was really only the mind of Jackson wrapped in a Cherokee turban. However, from Houston's very first days as Hiwassee subagent, he sought and accepted the tutelage of McMinn, even to the point—as in the case of the winter blanket issue—of defending his conduct to Jackson by invoking the "it will be good for removal" excuse to justify his course.

If Houston had been colluding with Jackson on how to trick and cheat the Cherokees, there would have been no need for any of that debacle in Washington during their treaty visit. On the contrary, Houston was doing everything he could, given the distasteful situation, to look after their interests, as evidenced by the Cherokees themselves. These were not stupid people; they were well established as first in rank among the "Civilized Tribes," and their statecraft, as integrated into their native customs, showed considerable sophistication. They had already been disappointed repeatedly by putting their trust in the American government, but they did not hold Houston responsible for its shortcomings; indeed, they welcomed him back as a refugee among them eleven years later. And McMinn's policy of using thrift elsewhere in order to subsist the natives more liberally was a theme that Houston not only continued but also amplified in Texas. From all these things, and McMinn's own complex thinking about the vexsome natives and the paternal tone of his letters to Houston during the Washington meeting, it seems apparent that Sam Houston took his Indian cue, not from Jackson, but from Joseph McMinn.

· · ·

Although Houston, while in Washington with the Cherokee delegation, took fire from Calhoun and then the cabal of well-connected slave runners, his earlier vigilant solicitude for the Cherokees' welfare had the desired effect back in the deep woods of southeastern Tennessee. Barely a month after the emergency issue of blankets, McMinn wrote him, "Mr. Rockhold called on me yesterday evening direct from the Garrison . . . and observed that he had never seen a more sudden change on the minds of so many people, he observed that even those who used to be the most inv[et]erate enemies [of the removal policy] had become entirely the reverse."[20]

Once Houston was out of the army, he retained his post as subagent to the Hiwassee Cherokees, and McMinn was still his boss. He instructed Houston on April 22 to tour the Indian towns—Sleeping Rabbit's village, the Widow Wolf's and the Ridge's village, among others—to explain the terms of the westward removal. By the first of May, Houston was at Wills Town, where he received word from a very pleased McMinn that he had been able to procure one thousand bushels of corn on favorable terms to aid in the removal. "I must suppose that you will consider that I am one of the sons of fortune. . . . I wish you to say to the Chiefs in Council that I will send in all 1500 bushels of corn, and what flour I can procure." McMinn was also certain that the Cherokees would be pleased that he had secured the appointment of Dick Taylor as their agent, "a man of . . . high reputation, and who is one of their own blood."[21]

Clad in a new issue of government blankets and carrying a new issue of government muskets, John Jolly and his people boarded a succession of flatboats on the Tennessee River and floated downstream for Arkansas Territory. In sum, the removal of the Hiwassee Cherokees under the terms of the 1818 treaty, while the result of a morally impeachable policy, was carried out with liberal subsistence and reasonably adequate transportation. It exhibited none of the horror of the later "Trail of Tears" during the forced removal, although once they arrived in Arkansas, the Cherokees discovered they had been assigned territory that both the Quapaw and Osage Indians regarded as their hunting ground. The latter tribe's brutality toward the newcomers, who had "all but forgotten how to fight," caused the Cherokees' later removal yet again across the Arkansas border into the Grand and Verdigris River country of the Indian Territory.[22]

Andrew Jackson was one who looked at the big questions and judged others by their results: Sam Houston had accomplished his task. He had done the government's dirty work to people he loved and done it in a fashion that allowed them to understand and accept what was happening and not blame him for it. For his thanks he had been bawled out and insulted, and though McMinn assured him he had done well, there was still something unseemly about it all, exemplified as McMinn wrote to Calhoun later in the year his congratulations on the removal, "corrupt as it may appear" to have "purchased" the cooperation of the chiefs. Having no intention of being blamed for the sins of federal Indian affairs, Houston finally quit the Indian agency business. He went to see McMinn on June 13 for reassurance, and as Houston waited the governor wrote a letter of recommendation: "Sir, I have learned this evening of your in[ten]tion to leave Town tomorrow morning. . . . justice requires me to state that you have in every instance which has come under my view acted with Integrity and firmness, as Sub agent for the Cherokee Nation."

Houston, not yet entirely sure where he stood with the great Jackson, made certain to send him this testimonial. But not wanting to lose track of McMinn's vindication, he penned a note on the letter's outer fold: "Genl Jackson, Please return this when convenient."[23]

3

THE POLITICAL PROTÉGÉ

Sam Houston did not leave Gov. Joseph McMinn's service without a plan: he had resolved to study the law. Moving to Nashville, he approached Judge James Trimble, originally from Rockbridge County, Virginia, whose family had been friends of the Houstons for three generations. In this era before the proliferation of law schools, the law was learned by apprenticeship, and Trimble agreed to take on Houston, outlining the usual course of reading—including *Blackstone's Commentaries* and *Coke on Littleton*. The young veteran's powers of memory, which had already found not challenge but solace in committing the *Iliad* to permanent recall, astonished his mentor. Before the end of the year, Trimble sponsored Houston at the Tennessee bar; he passed and was admitted, having read in less than six months law that would have occupied a less-determined mind for a year and a half.

Even that course of study, which Houston himself termed "severe," left him time for a social life. Most notably, he fell in with one Noah Ludlow, the creative spirit behind the Dramatic Club of Nashville. Many of the city's leading citizens such as Andrew Jackson were at least honorary members; others such as John Eaton actively took part. When not memorizing law, Houston took to memorizing lines, and trod the boards in such roles as a hotel porter with a weakness for liquor in *We Fly by Night*—a character perhaps not too difficult for him to commune with, although that role almost did not come off. Required to wear a red wig and, playing a drunk, a red nose, he nearly heeded his own deep aversion to ridicule, but Ludlow, with some help from Eaton, persuaded Houston to perform. Once he got on stage, he loved it. He also played a villain in John Home's *Douglas* and, maybe his most challenging role, a conflicted officer required to execute his own son in Mercier's *Le Deserteur*. Ludlow was more impressed with Houston's size than his stage presence in serious drama, but in comedic roles allowed that he "never met a man who had a keener sense of the ridiculous." The Nashville Dramatic Club dimmed its lights when Ludlow moved to New Orleans; otherwise, Sam Houston might have had a vastly different life.[1]

He opened a law office in the town of Lebanon, strategically located about thirty miles east of Nashville and about the same distance north of the state capital, then at Murfreesboro. In this endeavor Houston was once again the beneficiary of a mentor's kindly notice, this time Lebanon merchant Isaac Golladay. With no discernable motivation other than goodness of heart, Golladay clothed Houston, on credit, at his store; rented him an office at a dollar a month; and recommended his services to the town's best people. Golladay also served Lebanon as postmaster, and in this era when postage was expensive and paid by the recipient, he nevertheless gave Houston his letters, forgiving the twenty-five-cent charge apiece. And therein may lie the tale—the office of postmaster being a patronage position, it is not beyond possibility that Golladay was buttonholed by Jackson, or John Rhea, or McMinn, or by a combination of forces, with a nod toward young Houston and a whisper to look after him. If indeed that happened, their confidence was truly kept, for Houston never caught scent of it. Throughout his life he held Golladay in his personal pantheon of men who had selflessly helped him, which for all that can be proved, must stand as the truth.

Thus Houston, who began a career under the mentorship of John Jolly, Jackson, Rhea, McMinn, now added the names of James Trimble and Isaac Golladay to the roster of men he remembered with gratitude. It is scarcely any wonder that, later in his life, observers were struck at how readily Sam Houston took promising young men under his protection and tried to advance them. Under Golladay's sponsorship he took a shine to the practice of law and began making money in a profession that gave exercise to both his calculating mind and his growing gift for oratory. "As for myself," he wrote in a chatty letter to Governor McMinn at the end of April 1819, "I am moving on the business of the Law and do better than I had hoped at the start. I am not idle nor lazy, and you may remark a change in this." Houston's joking of his purported laziness had its roots in the two men's different backgrounds: McMinn was an East Tennessee farmer who reaped bountiful crops and sometimes rhapsodized to Houston of his love of tilling the soil, a labor Houston shunned. The young Lebanon counselor was ambitious too, having determined to seek a state office—solicitor general of the Nashville District, the equivalent in modern parlance of a prosecuting district attorney—that might have seemed presumptuous for a lawyer of less than one year's experience. But Houston had also become less bashful about asking favors; in the same letter he told McMinn that in his contemplated campaign: "I am resolved in combining all the might that I can by popularity muster. Governor you can help me up the rugged hill of life."[2]

At the time Houston was angling for McMinn's aid in winning the solicitor generalship, Jackson, interestingly, was urging Secretary of War John C. Calhoun to take the young veteran back into the Indian service. Knowing of the rift between the irascible secretary of war and the headstrong former subagent, Jackson assured Calhoun at the end of September 1819 that if Houston were made agent to all the Cherokees, "he can draw to the Arkansas in a few years the whole strength of the

Cherokee Nation. . . . I have no hesitation in saying that Col. Sam Houston is better qualified for this station than any man of his age I am acquainted with; he is honourable, honest and brave . . . and well calculated to wield the Indians beneficially for their own happiness, and the interests of the U States."[3]

Houston's success with the Hiwassee Cherokees had certainly made a believer out of Jackson, but Houston seems still to have been more McMinn's protégé than his, for only a couple of weeks later he was indeed elected Nashville's solicitor general. McMinn took hearty satisfaction in signing the proclamation of Houston's assumption of office. It was time to leave Lebanon, a town that had shown the young man much favor. He gave "a kind of farewell address" on the courthouse steps. "Gentlemen," he said, "The time has come when I must bid you farewell. Although duty calls me away, yet I must confess that it is with feelings of sincere regret that I leave you. I shall ever remember with emotions of gratitude the kindness which I have received at your hands. I came among you poor and a stranger, and you extended the hand of welcome, and received me kindly. I was naked, and ye clothed me; I was hungry, and ye fed me." It was a tribute delivered with such class and sincerity that many in the audience left in tears.[4] He departed for Nashville, which was becoming the gravitational point for men of ability from the surrounding communities. Houston lost no time making connections there, even taking an active role in the Tennessee Antiquarian Society, the state's first association of learned men—not bad for one with less than a year of formal education. Carrying a social profile brought with it the need for money, and while solicitor general was a fine-sounding title, it did not pay well. As was not unusual for him, Houston abruptly resigned the office he had sought "with all the popularity he could muster" before the end of his two-year term and went into private legal practice. He moved into an office on Market Street and took out an advertisement the day after Christmas, 1821, assuring prospective clients that if they called during his hours they would find him "where he ought to be."[5]

But like his father, the one-time inspector of militia, Houston found comfort in the hale company of officers and fraternized with them often at the Nashville Inn. McMinn had already appointed him to the largely honorary post of adjutant general, and his fellow officers began to speak of Houston as their future leader. Near the end of October, McMinn, far from annoyed that Houston had abandoned the office to which he had helped him get elected, forwarded a hint from Houston's friend Maj. John D. Bowan that the major would be willing to serve as Houston's aide "in event of your being elected of which there is no doubt."[6] In 1821 the field officers of the Tennessee Militia's southern command did indeed elect Houston to the rank of major general. It was a post that brought him into regular correspondence with Secretary of War Calhoun, and his transactions with him on state militia business were formal and respectful. But there was one matter remaining from their previous intercourse that Calhoun maliciously protracted.

Houston's official ties to the Hiwassee Cherokees had come to an end except for one item that the new major general of militia could not shake loose. Shortly after the election, a hostile auditor declared the accounts of his tenure as subagent to be short by $67.52. If there was any single point on which Houston's career had been above reproach, it was his management of money, from reporting himself for a double draw of pay he was not even sure he had committed to alerting Jackson of the shortfall at the Hiwassee agency as soon as Houston arrived there. He must have refused to pay the alleged shortage, for the next paper to issue on the subject were instructions to Henry Crabb, U.S. attorney for Tennessee, to sue Houston for the amount. The matter dragged on for months, just the kind of bee in his hat that could drive Houston into a frenzy. Not until the following April did a Treasury Department auditor weigh in with a comment that Houston's expense claim of $237.61 was still payable, and until the shortage was clarified, the $67.52 could be withheld from that amount. Two days later the U.S. attorney was sent instructions to dismiss the suit.[7] When Houston received a voucher for his expenses, it was still short; his transportation charge had been disallowed, and apparently he was docked the costs of the lawsuit against him.

General Houston—for his post as adjutant general accorded him that address— thought he began to smell Calhoun behind it and let loose on him in a letter in early June: He had submitted his accounts for auditing on three different occasions, he wrote, and each time they had been "treated with contempt" before the suit was brought. "I am at a loss to account for this. . . . If a suit had been instituted against me, on improper grounds, when the United States owed me a ballance . . . ought I to be charged costs? Perhaps this is a rule established at the City, but it won't meet our Backwoods notions of Justice." He concluded that he wanted to hear nothing further from the federal attorney involved, whom he believed inimical to him, and rather highly suggested a replacement he believed would be more impartial.[8]

Halfway through 1822 the War Department finally sent him a draft for $170.09, the difference between his approved expense claim and the $67.52 that was still in dispute. However, it was not payable at any of the principal cities in the United States, as Houston had requested, but on the Bank of Nashville, where Houston would have had to cash it for notes or silver at twenty-seven cents on the dollar. This latest obstacle was more than Houston could bear. "I can see no reason for the course of conduct pursued by you," he exploded at Calhoun, "unless it be that I am the same man against whom you conceived so strong a prejudice in 1818, when I was assist. Indian Agent. . . . Sir I could have forgotten the unprovoked injuries inflicted upon me, if you were not disposed to continue them. But your reiteration shall not be unregarded. I will remember your personal bad treatment . . . as a man. As a citizen of Tennessee I will mark your Treaty of 1819 with the Cherokees . . . replete with mischief to our state." Not brooking the cheap check, he returned the draft for appropriate processing and eventually received pay—except for his transportation, for which he was not reimbursed—in a form he accepted.[9]

Late in 1822 Sam Houston, private attorney and militia general, suffered a bad case of influenza, but by February of 1823 he had come out of it and announced his candidacy for Congress. The decennial census of 1820 had increased Tennessee's representation in the House from six seats to nine, and it was in the Ninth District, which included Nashville, that Houston stood for election. Jackson and McMinn saw to it that he ran unopposed. This provided him the opportunity to reflect on his first five years in politics. "Permit me to assure you, Governor," he wrote McMinn, "that . . . I can never be unmindful that in the commencement of my career you were not an inefficient friend." Still, his impending elevation to the federal house was "*not* by the consent of all parties, or persons. . . . They smile at me, and seem kind, but like the rose, there is a thorn under it."[10]

One of the thorns thus alluded to was a falling out between Houston and another McMinn protégé, Daniel Graham. Some six weeks after the above letter, Houston wrote McMinn a protest so hurried that he forgot to punctuate it: "You wou'd dislike that any difference shou'd take place between your 'political sons' and no one would deprecate the event more than myself. . . . But I apprehend a coolness on the part of Major G——m I am not satisfied of the fact, and will make every allowance until I ascertain the truth I never quit a friend until I see a disinclination on his part to be friendly with me I dearly love my friends because they have been everything to me I part with them as a Miser does his treasure with anguish and regret."[11] One might perceive different shadows behind this outburst—a certain faint damning of his family, that they meant so little to him that his friends had become everything, and perhaps a certain young terror that his destiny, having drawn its first blood at Horseshoe Bend, was about to carve it first pound of flesh from his psyche as well. It should not therefore be much of a surprise that Houston closed his letter to McMinn, "Unalterably thy friend," the first showing of an idiosyncrasy that pervades a long life of prolific correspondence. In an age when official or business letters commonly closed, "Your obedient servant," Houston habitually closed letters to those he trusted with such poetically tied bows as "Ever thine truly," or "Truly thy friend." Considering his family background and what his career cost him in friendships, it was no idle affectation.

In the case of resigning the friendship of Daniel Graham, what Houston probably did not realize was that Graham had desired to run for the Ninth District seat himself, but McMinn pulled Graham aside and dissuaded him, smoothing the path for his favorite.[12] It was one of the last services McMinn performed for Houston; the former governor took up a new post as Cherokee agent, but he died soon afterward and was buried at the Cherokee Agency. Houston was elected to the Eighteenth Congress on September 13, 1823, and set out for Washington almost immediately, probably stopping to visit with relatives in Rockbridge County, Virginia, and gloat—if the story of what he told his Uncle Matthew was true—over his returning as a congressman. In addition, there was one other pilgrimage he wanted to make, and he got Andrew Jackson to write him a letter of introduction.

Thomas Jefferson, third president of the United States and author of the Declaration of Independence, became in his old age an icon accorded unequalled reverence. Whenever he received admirers at his hilltop villa, he liked to make them wait in the entrance hall, giving them a chance to admire the "museum" he had crowded onto its high walls—paintings acquired during his tenure as American minister to France; maps and specimens from the Lewis and Clark expedition, whose journey he had commissioned to explore the Louisiana Territory he had purchased; gadgets such as the seven-day calendar clock he had himself devised. No one anticipating an audience could pace the great hall of the gracious yet egalitarian house that Jefferson had himself designed without being cowed by the sheer brilliance of the man.

Autumn of 1823 found the eighty-year-old Sage of Monticello's entrance hall stalked by a tall Tennesseean of thirty, stiff from war wounds in his shoulder and groin that would not heal, his perceptive gaze absorbing the treasures—and the meaning—of Jefferson's "museum." Perhaps he felt nervously in his coat for Jackson's letter:

> Hermitage October 4th 1823
> Dear Sir,
> This letter will be handed you by Genl Saml Houston, a representative to Congress from this State, and a particular friend of mine to whom I beg leave to introduce to you. . . . He has attained his present standing without the extrensic advantages of fortune & education, and has sustained in his various promotions from the common soldier to the Major General the character of the high minded & honorable man—as such I present him to you. . . .
> With a sincere wish that good health and happy days are still yours, I remain your friend and very obliged servant.
> Andrew Jackson[13]

What the past imparted to the future in this meeting was never set to paper, but Sam Houston was ever moved when he approached close to something that touched the roots of American democracy, and if any man in America could command his homage, it was the author of the Declaration of Independence and spiritual precursor of Andrew Jackson. Houston ranked Jackson only slightly behind Jefferson in greatness, and he was soon elated to learn that Old Hickory would be in Washington with him. Jackson's popularity reached greater heights than ever once he precipitated the cession of Florida, and six weeks after Houston was elected to Congress, the Tennessee legislature sent Jackson to the U.S. Senate. The two were able to spend time together, and Houston found himself studying even his mentor's manners. "He makes as fine a bow," he wrote, "as any man I have seen at Court." At one point in 1823, Houston and Jackson paid a joint visit to Washington College, for whose early welfare Capt. Samuel Houston had been so solicitous.[14]

Arriving in Washington, Houston was delighted to renew his acquaintance with E. G. M. Butler, who in his youth had been Andrew Jackson's ward before going to West Point in 1816. Houston was on a mission to cut the right figure in the House, and according to Butler, "He made me accompany him to every hat store in Washington in search of a hat with 'a very narrow rim.'" Thus outfitted, Sam Houston felt himself ready to take on the world. His six foot, two inch frame bore such presence that he was commonly credited with standing as much as four inches taller. He was powerfully built and muscled, with enormous hands and thick strong fingers, his impressive frame solidly planted on feet so large that the measure around the instep was greater than their length.[15] With his narrow-rim

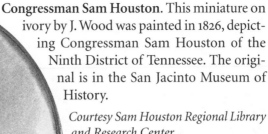

Congressman Sam Houston. This miniature on ivory by J. Wood was painted in 1826, depicting Congressman Sam Houston of the Ninth District of Tennessee. The original is in the San Jacinto Museum of History.

Courtesy Sam Houston Regional Library and Research Center

hat compressing ample chestnut-brown hair, Houston took in the Capitol and House chamber with his piercing blue eyes. Butler and Houston inspected the room together, when Houston, "having selected his seat, as he imagined, he turned to me, and remarked, 'Now, Butler, I am a Member of Congress, and I will show Mr. Calhoun that I have not forgotten his insult to me when a poor lieutenant.'"[16]

Indeed, one of the first items to which Houston turned his attention was the recovery of certain expenses never reimbursed for his Cherokee duty. This meant taking up the cudgels against Calhoun, the long-time secretary of war who was now the closest thing a man of Houston's age and experience could have to an archenemy. Houston's expenditures were long since repaid, but his cost of transportation had been disallowed, he felt unfairly. "I found my own transportation," he now complained to Calhoun in a large and emphatic hand, "my own horse, my own equipage—the duty was extraordinary. . . . I really do consider that there is no item in my acct for which I am more entitled to pay than I am for transportation."[17] Not just a new member of Congress but a new member of the Military Affairs Committee that oversaw Calhoun's War Department (and budget), Houston won his point—and eventually Calhoun's endorsement to a reimbursement of thirty dollars: "Gen Houston not being bound to furnish a horse to perform the journey, the charge for the use of the horse is allowed. J.C.C."[18] The thirty dollars was not the point; wringing vindication from Calhoun was the point, and Houston could only have savored this early victory. Of course, his position was not hurt by the fact that Andrew Jackson had become chairman of the Senate Military Affairs Committee.

Houston remained contemptuous of Calhoun, but to his colleagues in the Congress he developed a more favorable deference; at the time he took his seat he

U.S. Capitol. After desultory progress under several architects, the push to finish the federal capitol began in 1818 under Charles Bulfinch, but it was still under construction during Houston's tenure in the House of Representatives. This phase was completed in 1830.

Courtesy Library of Congress

found himself in a den ruled by lions of genuine ability: the dean of the House was John Randolph of Virginia, who first took his seat when Sam Houston was six years old; the Speaker was Henry Clay of Kentucky, a dangerous enemy of Jackson's but a brilliant debater and adroit dealmaker who had engineered the Missouri Compromise in 1820; and Daniel Webster of Boston was a legal wizard who had won seminal victories before the U.S. Supreme Court and was in no way inferior to Clay as an orator. These great men were soon to leave the House for the Senate—Clay and Randolph in 1825 and Webster in 1827—but Houston's exposure to titans in action gave him a high frame of reference for honing his own skills in debate and political maneuver. At last in a venue of men worth his time, Sam Houston packed his considerable ego away and settled down to learn and work. On January 22, 1824, he made his first important speech in the House, a peculiarly appropriate one for a devotee of Homer, supporting American recognition of Greek independence. His remarks were expansive enough to reason his argument, though without the confident verbosity of his later years. They were carefully crafted, his supporting arguments lined up, 1-2-3, like a student's exercise in rhetoric. The stamp of his later style is there without question, first in his self-deprecation at "trespassing upon the patience of the House . . . to give his feeble aid on the subject" and not least in his preference to eschew declamation in favor of pointed, leading questions. He even managed to work in a little something from his Morse's *Geography*:

> What sentiment has the President expressed upon this subject? Does he say that we should not interest ourselves for the Greeks? Does he not, rather, express the deepest solicitude concerning their affairs? . . .
>
> And can it be supposed that the passage of this resolution will bare another Turkish scimetar against the Greeks? No. . . . If they have determined to crush the Greeks, will they not do it in defiance of us? Has [the Turk] ever paid any regard to us? Has he ever rendered us any service as a nation? Does our flag protect our property upon the Bosphorus? Has not our commerce rather been protected by the Greeks? . . .
>
> Let us, then, as far as we can, consistently with our relations with foreign nations, hail [the Greeks] as brethren and cheer them in their struggle.[19]

Other passages in the four-page speech score further points and anticipate and answer arguments against the resolution. As a first effort, it was well formed and tidy, but his support was moral only, for he voted against a measure in the following session to appropriate a $50,000 contribution to the cause. It was worthy, he admitted, but ought to be a matter of private charity. He also voted stingy at home, opposing a $26,000 appropriation for improvements to the White House. As he was lodging with a Mrs. Wilson, perhaps the accommodations at her boarding house were sufficiently Spartan that he saw no need for a two-story portico on the south front of the president's mansion.

Sam Houston got his congressional schooling in weighty issues whose constitutionality was not yet decided. He voted against Randolph and with Webster and Clay for federal funding of interstate improvements. There were acrimonious, section-based tariff debates, and he saw first-hand how readily the Southern states, especially South Carolina, were willing to haul up their big gun, the threat of nullification—the still untested doctrine that the rights of a sovereign state trumped any federal statute—to get their way. And this heady work was relieved by heady diversions, as the House fêted America's great revolutionary friend, the Marquis de Lafayette. Houston had ample opportunity to socialize with the great nobleman in Washington, as Lafayette lodged at O'Neill's Tavern with the Jacksons and Eatons, and he saw him again the following year at the Hermitage. He listened raptly as the celebrated patriot expounded on two themes that particularly haunted Houston for the rest of his career. The first was the absolute necessity, whatever the internal conflicts, that the American Union remain indissoluble. America was, said Lafayette the following year, "an union, sir, so essential, not only to the fate of each member of the confederacy, but also to the general fate of mankind, that the least breach of it would be hailed with barbarian joy, by . . . European aristocracy and despotism." His second theme was the inexorable progress of natural law that must eventually culminate in the emancipation of the slaves. As cheap foreign labor became more economical to employ than slaves, beginning in the North but progressing eventually to the South, the nightmare precipitated by waves of unemployed and economically irrelevant blacks caused him to express "the gravest apprehension for the future of the Gulf states."[20] Thirty years later, when Sam Houston scolded an audience of Boston abolitionists on the hypocrisy of freeing their slaves only after acquiring cheap foreign labor, he was elaborating on ideas articulated by, if not first heard from, Lafayette. Their conversations also had a lighter side, for at some point Lafayette claimed that if some now-forgotten condition did not occur, he could, in his heavy accent, "no die 'appie." Houston was enchanted, and he mimicked the phrase for the rest of his life.

Overall, Houston's first session in Congress not only cleared his head and enlarged his sense of himself but also taught him the necessity of tending to the daily grind. With the congressional seat came the inevitable parade of office seekers, and Houston acquired admirable slickness in endorsing an applicant for a patronage position, but without promising anything. When a Tennessee colleague recommended a mutual friend to a Cherokee agency post, Houston replied: "Your mention of my friend Genl Martin's name as an applicant for the agency is all sufficient to present him with all the advantages that a *recommendation* of 500 cou'd have done. But his name is about the fifteenth that has been sent in. The Secy of War has not yet determined whether the appointment will be made from the state of Tennessee or Georgia."[21] Whatever John Martin's chances were of winning the Cherokee agency, at least there was a new secretary of war for Houston to transact with. John C. Calhoun, who in that post had nettled Houston since 1817, had become vice president as a result of the election of 1824, a contest in which lay a mighty tale. If Houston's conversations with Lafayette played a part in framing the political issues that dogged him throughout his career, the presidential contest of 1824 was the anvil on which Houston's political personality was hammered into shape.

Senator Jackson, war hero and populist, was wildly cheered by the swelling frontier population even as the well-mannered political establishment regarded him with fear and contempt. Jackson was swept into the presidential nomination by an irresistible popular tide, and on the fractionated ballot of 1824, Jackson received the plurality of electoral votes with ninety-nine; John Quincy Adams of Massachusetts, eighty-four; the independent William Crawford of Virginia, forty-one; and Speaker of the House Henry Clay of Kentucky, who could not abide Jackson, thirty-seven. Crawford soon after was felled by a stroke, and with no candidate having a majority, the issue was thrown into the House of Representatives. Houston watched horrified as Clay, ignoring the instructions of the Kentucky legislature, threw his support to Adams, who had received not a single elector in Kentucky. Adams became president, and Clay, to the cries of "Corrupt bargain!" took the post of secretary of state in his administration. To the end of his days, Sam Houston squinted with suspicion at any venue, whether cabal, meeting, caucus, political party, or especially convention, that presumed to lift the elective power out of the hands of the people themselves. Any such convocation, in his view, had a heavy burden to prove that it was furthering, not frustrating, the popular will. And ultimately, it was party management, and his lifelong distaste for it, that played the largest role in preventing him from assuming the nation's highest office. Even at the time of Adams's ascendancy, he felt so strongly about the people's absolute sovereignty that he had a circular printed and distributed among his Tennessee constituents, in which he grieved that there seemed to be:

> a manifest defect in the Constitution in relation to the election of President. . . . One candidate had a decided preference in eleven out of twenty-four States by the people; yet, when the power passed from their hands and devolved on the House of Representatives, the voice of the people was not, in many instances, regarded. . . .
>
> The individual [Jackson] who was manifestly the choice of the majority of the people was not elevated to that distinguished situation for which his qualifications so pre-eminently fitted him. . . . This is a subject of serious consideration for the citizens of the United States, and it will be for them to say, on some subsequent occasion, whether their voice shall be heard and their rights respected, or whether they will tamely yield those inestimable rights to the unhallowed dictation of politicians, who may choose to barter them for their own individual aggrandizement.[22]

Politically shaken by the time the Eighteenth Congress adjourned, Sam Houston turned his attention to other matters. Having once vowed not to court any of the "dear Girles" before he had made a situation for himself, young Houston seems to have considered that goal now achieved, for in early 1825 he was sufficiently involved with a woman to be expecting marriage. "I regret to hear that you have been unsuccessful in love affairs," he wrote his Tennessee friend A. M. Hughes, "but have taken the best course possible to be extricated, by taking a new chase! For my single self I do not know yet the sweets of matrimony, but in March or April, next I will; unless something should take place not to be expected, or wished for! To have been married on my way [to Washington] would not have answered a good purpose. My errand here is to attend to the business of my constituents, and not to spend 'honey moons.' *Every thing in due season!*"[23]

However, Houston's season of matrimony was not yet arrived. Unlike the Miss M—— that Jesse Beene once urged on him, this Miss M—— has an identification that can at least tentatively attach to her. Probably she was Mariah Campbell, sister and hostess of a bachelor congressman from South Carolina, an identity that would fit her apparent residence of Lancaster, South Carolina, from where Houston wrote his cousin John: "The political ferment at home is very great. My summer must needs be very active, and . . . I felt bound in honor to let Miss M—— know all . . . and she concluded to defer matters until fall."[24]

By the time autumn arrived, the romance had cooled with the weather. At whose behest the engagement—if that—was broken off is not known. However, the relationship was indicative of another emerging Houston life pattern. Apparently, he had the opportunity to marry this woman early in 1825, but he put it off owing to the press of business in Washington. They then seem to have made nuptial plans for the summer, which Houston again postponed on account of the "political ferment at home." Neither now nor later in life did Sam Houston allow his desire for a domestic life precedence over the political call—a fact to which Margaret Lea, his future wife, would in later years have to resign herself.

Houston had, however, been persistent in attending the fairer sex. In Virginia, he had paid some court to a Miss Sophia Reid, the granddaughter of a Tennessee friend, which came to naught. But he did seem chastened by his earlier Miss M——experience, writing that winter to his friend from army days, William Worth: "I am making myself less frequent in the Lady World than I have been. I must keep up my Dignity, or rather I must attend more to politics and less to love."[25] Afterward, though, came another in the succession of his Misses M——s: he began calling on Mary Parke Custis, heiress of Arlington mansion and descendant by marriage of George Washington. Houston was not unreasonable in thinking he had the inside track; apparently they had the friendship of Lafayette in common, for G. W. Parke Custis was disseminating the Frenchman's views on emancipation. In addition, they had his father's war service to chat about and the land scrip with which the first president had endowed Capt. Samuel Houston's academy. But in this instance, the ambitious suitor reached too high, and Miss Custis had to tell him that he lost out to a bashful cadet named Robert E. Lee. This misfire he took less well than his others, questioning "the good taste and discernment of Mary Custis who preferred to tie herself by long engagement to that shy underclassman at West Point when she might have been Houston's bride and the belle of Washington society."[26] And with this setback another lifetime trait asserted itself: his habit, on occasions of moment, of referring to himself in the third person, a style adopted from the Cherokees.

• • •

Until the right lady came along, he could make do with politics. Jackson was sensible of the role he had played in Houston's rise, and he was proud of his protégé, but his mentoring was not altruistic. He expected service and loyalty in return, as he did from all his able minions, and never hesitated to scratch out notes to Houston expressing his needs. The young congressman performed admirably, even becoming on occasion a kind of lightning rod to draw the wrath of Jackson's enemies upon himself. During 1825 this ran him afoul of a General Gibbs. The nature of their dispute is now indistinct, but a committee of gentlemen was formed to investigate their differences and affidavits were sworn: A. R. Mathis swore that Gibbs had given a speech in which he said John Eaton was an enemy of Jackson; T. Scruggs swore that he did not remember the details of the speech; William D. Phillips swore that Gibbs's speech was violent and abusive; J. F. Williams swore that Gibbs said his enemies were spreading rumors to wreck the election; and Benjamin Williams swore that Gibbs had charged Eaton with saying that Jackson was a tyrant. Houston apparently needed to know why Eaton would say such a thing. Had they been old women over their tea, the subject would have been considered gossip, but being Southern gentlemen, honor was at stake, and vast time and energy was expended to see who would fight and who should get killed. It was, in its patented antebellum way, rather pathetic.[27]

Ultimately, a committee of Masonic gentlemen, for the principals were all Masons, was formed to investigate the whole silly tempest, but they took no action, and by spring 1826 things escalated to Houston accepting a challenge. It does seem that Felix Grundy had an opportunity to ameliorate the quarrel but replied, "Never mind, let them go on, if they all get killed it will only make more room for the balance of us." Houston blamed Grundy for the impending duel and attacked him and his retainers in a paper to be published in case of his death as a group "timid as hares, ferocious as wolves, and servile as spaniels . . . , they must be hissed at, and backed. . . . My firm and undeviating attachment to Genl Jackson has caused me all the enemies I have, and I glory in the firmness of my attachment." If he should perish, "I will die proud in the assurance that I deserve, and possess his perfect confidence." Sam Houston was bound by a standing admonition from Jackson not to duel, and in this particular case the general intervened with a suggestion that Houston cool down, assuring him that he remained on friendly terms with both Eaton and Houston, which may or may not be why Houston and Gibbs never fought. Eventually, the Grand Lodge of Tennessee absolved all parties from blame.[28]

Houston's loyalty to Jackson, not to mention the creditable job he did in the Eighteenth Congress, got him easily reelected for a second term, but the following year the testy young congressman was not so lucky in evading a fight with one Gen. William A. White, a leading lawyer in Gallatin, Tennessee. The duel they fought, as Houston later explained, arose out of his attending to the wishes of his constituents. "The Postmaster at Nashville resigned, and about 650 persons had recommended as his successor a young man who had been long an assistant in the office and every way qualified to do its duties. This recommendation was supported by . . . ten out of eleven of your Members of Congress. These recommendations were disregarded, and a man appointed with but very few recommendations in his favor, but he was a partisan of those in power." Houston protested the appointment in the strongest terms to the Adams administration, and someone saw to it that his comments reached the successful applicant.

The administration's choice for postmaster, a man named Erwin, was also the brother of the son-in-law of Henry Clay, Adams's "corrupt bargain" secretary of state. Erwin demanded that Houston retract his statements, but the congressman refused, which in the South constituted an affront to Erwin's honor. Houston was so popular in Nashville that the Adams people could not find a second to deliver Erwin's challenge. They approached General White, but he declined, "not feeling any hostility towards Houston." Erwin's partisans therefore employed the services of a professional duelist from Missouri with the likely name of John T. Smith. The latter delivered the challenge to Houston's second, one Colonel McGregor, who refused to receive it on the grounds that Smith was not a citizen of Tennessee. Smith then sought out Houston himself at the Nashville Inn, and in the company of General White as his witness, presented the note himself. Again Houston refused it, but after some needling from White offered to entertain a challenge from the general instead. White said he was prepared.

"The saddle is on the other horse, General," snorted Houston, "and that is enough to be understood between gentlemen."

"If I call on you there will be no shuffling, I suppose," White answered.

"Try me, sir."[29]

Then, nothing. Erwin did not pursue the matter, and the Missourian decamped as suddenly as he had appeared. After several days White sent Houston a challenge, explaining that he was bound in honor to fight him even though he and Houston had no personal quarrel. Houston accepted the challenge, acknowledging that he had no personal quarrel with White. Such was the nature of Southern chivalry.

Sam Houston, who had gained honor on the field of battle, had never yet battled on the field of honor. He chose pistols at fifteen feet—a courtly gesture to White's known poor marksmanship—and practiced in the meadows about the Hermitage, following Jackson's advice to bite a bullet to steady his aim. The duel took place on September 23, 1826, in Simpson County, Kentucky, just across the state line. Houston returned unharmed; White was dangerously wounded through the groin, but he lived. The two men made up as White lay on the ground, believing himself dying.

Only two months after the duel with White, the ever-touchy Jackson pressed Houston to learn from a couple of their mutual acquaintances what Navy Secretary Samuel Southard had said about him at a certain dinner, and Houston's handling of the affair showed him gaining in a new political skill: having fought one duel and nearly a second, he now took it upon himself to start calming down the Old Chief before matters got out of hand. In this instance, Southard criticized Jackson's defense of New Orleans. Jackson heard about it, wrote out a blistering note to Southard demanding an explanation, and sent it, unsealed, to Houston to read and deliver. Houston took it upon himself to make sufficient inquiry to learn that the account Jackson had heard was exaggerated. "Your friends," he wrote Jackson after stowing the angry note, "are of the opinion that the better course, is for you to make no application yourself, but to permit it to come through some other channel. . . . It is now a desirable matter with all your friends, to keep you out of collision" lest Jackson damage his presidential prospects. "If you write directly thro' me to Mr. Southard, I pray you, let it be in the mildest, calmest tone of expression—The very fact of his conduct, and statement, will most effectually damn him."

Pushing all the right Southern buttons—that he would never allow Jackson's personal honor to be compromised for political advantage—Houston went on to offer himself as the "other channel" for handling the matter. That the young congressman was successful in defusing a potentially nasty dust-up between Jackson and a powerful political clique caused other Jackson protégés to begin deferring to Houston as the first among equals.[30]

Houston's addition of subtlety to his repertoire was an important achievement, now that he had decided to run for governor of Tennessee, but it did not mean that he had lost popularity by resorting to pistols—as Jackson himself was happy to point out: "I have received several letters from the western district since you left Nashville, the *current has changed* there, and you will (unless a mighty change) receive an overwhelming majority. The result of your political quarrel . . . has put down the faction, and unanimity and harmony will pervade our whole state."[31] The state, perhaps, but not within Old Hickory's own camp, as just the slightest discomfort now developed between Jackson and Houston. Tennessee's governor for three terms had been the calculating and decidedly unsentimental William Carroll, who was barred by the state constitution from a fourth consecutive term. As the deal was apparently worked out and presented to Houston, he would become governor for one term, his place in Congress to be taken by James Knox Polk, another Jackson protégé. Houston would then relinquish the gubernatorial chair back to Carroll, who would support Houston for the Senate. Of the whole group, Houston was the only one who believed that they were behaving not much better than the scoundrels of the "corrupt bargain" of 1824. Election was the province of the people, not some cabal, even if it was headed by Jackson. Houston ran for governor without signing on to the deal, but Carroll, apparently believing that Houston was merely posturing for public exposure, supported him anyway.

In seeking the highest office in Tennessee, Houston faced two men who had each held it before: Willie Blount and Newton Cannon, the latter more formidable than the former. In June of 1827, a grand jury in Simpson County, Kentucky, indicted Houston in the duel with General White, and the Kentucky governor sent a requisition for Houston's arrest to his Tennessee counterpart. The authorities ignored it, and the matter died for want of cooperation. The roots of the indictment were political, and knowing he had not been hurt politically by the duel, Houston made this an issue. Shortly before the election, a dinner was given in his honor at Tellico, during which he summarized the circumstances of his fight with White, reiterated his opposition to dueling in principle, and expressed his relief that White was not permanently disabled. "But here the matter, it seems, was not to rest," he declared. "Houston, shall not be Governor, is the decree of those in power and their minions. *A witness is sent from Tennessee to Kentucky*, an indictment is there framed and a grand jury procured to find a true bill, and I am proclaimed a felon. Yes! *A felon*!. . . . If my fellow citizens think me in the light of a horse-thief, a felon, they ought not to vote for me; but if they view me as acting involuntarily, from a necessity imposed by others, I hope they will vote for me, and should I be favored with a majority, I will be Governor of Tennessee."[32]

In Houston's 1827 campaign, one sees the first manifestation of the mature man. His rise during the previous ten years was meteoric, from an infantry lieutenant resigning under the disgust of the secretary of war to a strong gubernatorial candidate. It was a rise accomplished without support from his family; Nashville was some one hundred fifty miles west of the rolling foothills of Maryville, and his contact with his mother and siblings seems to have been minimal. It was, in the context of the times, a speed of advancement reserved for protégés of Andrew Jackson.

But of equal importance was the force of Houston's own personality. Roughly shaped by the hardships of war, pain, and intrigue, he now gained polish and subtlety from contact with society. He was good looking and knew it, witty and playful with his friends. He understood the psychological complexities of Jacksonian rusticism and what was required of him. His becoming a Mason, for instance, netted him the political connections such membership entailed. At the same time, he knew the public must never lose its perception of him as a man who answered only to his own conscience; he made no apology when he was suspended from the Masons for dueling. While he utilized the debating skills honed in Congress, he learned to pack Homer away and speak to the people in homespun language they could understand. And to this studied Jacksonian identity he added turns of his own invention. First, to the plainspoken severity expected of him he added, possibly as a holdover from his amateur thespian days, a talent for irony and sarcasm that could carry the day in a debate where reason and even invective would fall equally short. Second, he proved himself a more adroit navigator than his contemporaries. Tennessee politics at this time was full bodied and bare knuckled, even among the Jacksonian Democrats, and Houston's two principal mentors had squared off in opposing factions: Jackson began his career as a supporter of William Blount and McMinn as a partisan of John Sevier.[33] For Houston to emerge so prominently and still keep the affections of both men was no small accomplishment.

On election day, August 2, Houston left nothing to chance, appearing at all the polling places in Nashville dressed fabulously from his richly embroidered silk socks and polished-buckle pumps to his black beaver hat. A ruffled shirt billowed from beneath a trim black satin waistcoat, and instead of an overcoat he sported a splendid Indian hunting shirt held in place with a red beaded sash. "He was the observed of all the observers," according to one of the latter.[34] Houston's sudden appearance astride a handsome gray had the desired affect on the voters, and he was elected with a majority of 12,000 votes out of fewer than 75,000 cast—a very solid win.

The inauguration took place on October 1, 1827, at Nashville's First Baptist Church. Houston's speech was brief and decorous, mentioning with deference both federal and state prerogatives but taking up no contentious issues. He pronounced himself proud to have come to reside in Tennessee, although his rise had occurred without the usually necessary social advantages. "However wayward and devious my course may have been in youth," he was relieved to say, "her citizens have magnanimously upheld me" in his succession of offices.[35] The speech made no mention of that omnipresent benefactor behind him, without whose approval those magnanimous citizens would never have noticed him: on inauguration day of 1827, Gov. Sam Houston was thirty-four years old; Andrew Jackson, a dyspeptic fifty-nine. There was little doubt that Old Hickory would be elected president the next year. If he lived through two terms—and although he was often sick he was counted far too tough to die—he would need a successor, and most eyes roamed no farther than the tall, handsome young chief executive of Tennessee. But Houston's coronet as heir still lacked one jewel, even as his life, for all the parties and banter, concealed one void he yearned to fill: he needed a wife.

4

SPLICED TO A RIB

As Governor Houston undertook his administration, he followed through on programs such as reforming and regulating the state banks that were begun by his predecessor. If this gave the watchful Carroll any feeling of ease that Houston would be a one-term caretaker, however, he was disabused of that notion when Houston went off on an internal improvements streak. The new governor's popularity only increased as he advocated navigational engineering on the Tennessee River, including a canal to get around Muscle Shoals so that East Tennesseeans could get their wares to markets throughout the South. As one of his biographers noted, Sam Houston "anticipated the Tennessee Valley Authority by almost a century."[1] In the same vein, he won an appropriation to build a hospital in Memphis for the relief of travelers who fell ill on the Mississippi riverboats, since they often landed in Memphis for treatment. His understanding of the common benefits of internal improvements implied common responsibility as well, and he memorialized the governors of other states bordering the Mississippi and Ohio Rivers for contributions to the hospital.[2]

He also undertook a unique land policy. In some sections of the state, immigrants had been living on public domain, on parcels the state had begun to sell them on the principle of trying to get the highest price possible. This made financial sense, Houston admitted to the legislature, and those who had bought under these terms were obligated to pay, yet "the contract in some of its leading features, bears the stamp of . . . duress. The occupants of that country were with very few exceptions poor, and destitute of visible effects of any kind; they had migrated from the older states because they were poor." Some of these homesteaders could now not meet the payments, and Houston asked the legislature to find some way to adjust their notes to allow them to stay on their land. Proceeds from the sale of unsettled public domain, he recommended, should be allocated to internal improvements and general education.[3]

Amid the governor's new responsibilities, he was daily reminded of older associations and loyalties. His gubernatorial proclamations were attested by Daniel
Graham, secretary of state, so it seems evident that he made up with the other
"political son" of the late Governor McMinn, Graham having been piqued at one
time for being passed over for the Ninth District congressional seat that went to
Houston. The governor was still busy on Jackson's behalf as well, whether in forwarding a letter from Carter Beverly to the senator explaining why he was not
responsible for a letter critical of Jackson that had been attributed to him or in
forwarding a lock of the Old Chief's hair to a Mrs. Morse in New Orleans.[4] But he
did not lack for enemies. Gen. William White of Kentucky had recovered sufficiently from the groin wound received in his duel with Houston to contribute to
a newspaper shortly after the election that Houston soon would be "stripped of his
little brief authority, and neither the name or influence of a great man, nor the
misdirected sympathies of a deluded people, will screen him from . . . punishment."[5] And he was making one particular enemy at home: the more popular
Houston became, the more certain Billy Carroll grew that if he wanted the gubernatorial chair back, he would have to fight for it.

The tranquil atmosphere of the Hermitage was not disturbed by this. There
was some consensus among Old Hickory's retainers that whoever lost out in the
next governor's race would have the next open Senate seat, although Jackson
wanted that chair for Felix Grundy. But now was a time to appear the happy family.
Houston helped to host Jackson in a grand dinner at the Nashville Inn on Christmas
Eve of 1827, and three days later most of the political royalty of Tennessee boarded
the riverboat *Pocahontas* for a slow progress to New Orleans. Partly it was to com-
memorate Jackson's victory in the battle that sealed the War of 1812; it also served
to give that section of the country a good look at their almost-certain next president. Rachel Jackson spent most of her time in her cabin, but when she emerged
she was smiling and gracious, pretending not to be hurt by politically motivated
smears against her from Henry Clay's camp. The Old Chief was irascible as ever,
threatening to shoot at small boats that approached too near the *Pocahontas*. Even
New York's Tammany Hall deputized James A. Hamilton to make the cruise to represent Martin Van Buren's wing of the party. The trip was almost a Roman triumph.
After a ceremony at the battleground, the city of New Orleans fêted Jackson on January 9, 1828. Houston had not been there since an army surgeon nearly killed him
in removing the second Tohopeka musket ball from his shoulder, and he desired
to reacquaint himself with the city's charms. He had made friends with Hamilton—
one of the first of many Tammany connections—and as one evening of oratory in
tribute to Jackson extended beyond endurance, the two cut out for some bachelor
mischief, crashing a quadroon ball being held in the same hotel.[6]

During most of 1828, the laborers in Jackson's political workshop managed to
table their own differences and cooperate in getting Old Hickory elected. Much of
their correspondence remained of the Southern gentlemen's who-said-what-about-
whom variety, and Governor Houston served as the clearinghouse of what they
called their "Literary Bureau." The result of their efforts almost always vindicated

Jackson, and letters were published to good effect in countering appallingly personal attacks on him and his wife. Their greatest asset, of course, was Old Hickory's juggernaut of popularity; the omens were good. Houston as Literary Bureau received one letter, for instance, from a contact in Illinois asserting that sentiment for Jackson was stronger than one could gather just by reading the press, even in those sectors where he was not expected to do well. "Newspapers say anything for money, and ... government patronage pays for the ink and paper and leaves a little to liquor." The people, he was sure, were really for Jackson.[7] Old Hickory won the election going away.

. . .

While Governor Houston was yet unmarried and had disowned most of his immediate family, that space in his heart was taken up by his favorite cousin, Washington resident John H. Houston, known to the family as Jack; his wife Gertrude; and their daughter Mary, for whom Sam Houston had stood as godfather. And in the autumn of 1828 he had new cause to revel in their regard. "I am rejoiced," he wrote to Jack, "that my dear Cousin Gertrude has presented you with a lovely boy, and I will suppose ... that the Boy was called 'Sam' for me. Tell my dear Cousin that I trust in God that by the 4th of March next that I will be in the City and stand sponsor for the *lad*, and then I will see my dear little Mary, and I will be as happy for a while at least as tho' I had been more *provident in my youth*." He adjured his cousin to teach the little girl to pray for him, for "I need the prayers of all pure beings." To Gertrude, he enclosed flowers picked from Jackson's gardens and the best wishes of the Old Chief.

These were fine days at the Hermitage, the interval between the election and the inauguration being intended for a combination of preparing an administration and celebrating. Having been in public life for some years now himself, Houston presented a little gift of his own to the president-elect: his promise not to pester him with recommendations for patronage jobs. Amid all the festivities, marriage was much on Houston's mind, and his appraising eye cast actively about. With him at Jackson's estate was James Knox Polk, two years younger than Houston and newly wedded to Sarah Childress, who drew the crown prince's admiration: "Mrs. Polk is not only a fine young lady," Houston wrote to cousin Jack, "but she has the '*Quills*' to the amount of many thousands—say $40,000.00. ... I am not married yet but it may be the case in a few weeks, and should it—*you* shall *hear* of it, before the news papers can reach you."[8]

The young lady who had so claimed his notice was Eliza Allen of the town of Gallatin, the seat of Sumner County, immediately northeast of Nashville. She was eighteen and beautiful, her family powerful, well connected, and ambitious to be even better connected. Houston had served in Congress with her uncle, Robert Allen—at least one invitation survives from 1828, inviting Houston to spend the Fourth of July with the Allen family.[9] Through Robert, he became acquainted with his younger brother, John Allen, the owner of thirty-nine slaves who worked his Allenwood estate along a bend of the Cumberland River south of Gallatin, home to many of Tennessee's finest families. The month after the July visit, Houston sought out John Allen and told him he wanted to marry Eliza. Father and uncle agreed, and as far as Houston knew, so did Eliza, for she accepted his proposal. Three weeks after Houston's letter to Jack, she turned nineteen; he was thirty-five. Society mavens clucked over the age difference, but it seemed not to matter to the Allens.

Jackson had been after Houston for years to marry and was jubilant that his political heir was finally going to settle down, but the Old Chief first had to endure an enormous loss: three days before Christmas, his beloved wife died. Houston had adored his genial and much-wronged "Aunt Rachel," as he referred to her both personally and in his letters. He helped carry her to her grave on Christmas Eve and did what he could to comfort the shattered Jackson. Just as Houston's engagement when a freshman in Congress fell victim to his career, so now politics again intruded as a major and unpleasant distraction during the weeks leading up to his marriage to Eliza Allen. The wedding was set for January 22, 1829, but Jackson was broken over losing Rachel; many of Tennessee's political worthies were already in Washington preparing for the new president's arrival, and no sooner was Old Hickory safely elected than his underlings began snapping at each other for position. With Carroll and Houston on a collision course over the governorship, the Old Chief tried to broker some settlement but instead became trapped between them. Jackson thought it best to begin the tedious journey to Washington and, leaving his blessing over the governor's upcoming nuptials, boarded a riverboat on January 18. Houston accompanied him to the dock. Carroll's popularity was declining, and the word was that Jackson was looking to Houston to keep Tennessee in political line as he assumed national leadership. Not to make too fine a point of it, Carroll that day announced his candidacy to reclaim the governorship.

Whether or not politics was the cause cannot be known, but apparently Houston and Eliza Allen had a quarrel in early December. "I have as usual had 'a small blow up,'" he wrote his congressman-friend John Marable on December 8, six days after Eliza's birthday. "What the devil is the matter with the gals I cant say but there has been hell to pay and no pitch hot!" He was endeavoring to patch things up and still hoped for the best. "May God bless you, and it may be that I will splice myself with a rib. Thine ever, Sam Houston."[10] Unlike 1825, politics would not derail these nuptials, for Sam Houston was well and truly smitten. He imparted some of his feelings to a friend from his youth, Frank Chambers. "Sam Houston and I were in our teens together," recalled Chambers. "He and I were children of nature, and full of enthusiasm. I married a rich woman and sunk into the oblivion of wealth . . . he was among the Indians for some time and I lost sight of him." Houston and Chambers reconnected when the former emerged in prominence, and as the date for the wedding neared, "I had a half notion that he was crazy. . . . I could see that it was the one love of his life. He was one of those rare men who are in earnest. He was so sincere that he was not conscious of how sincere he was . . . . But he had a doubt that made him miserable."[11]

Houston was doubtless made even more miserable if, as he claimed years later, a raven fell into the road before him as he rode toward Allenwood for the wedding—

a terrible omen. But there was no turning back now, and the marriage was conducted on January 22, 1829, by the Presbyterian Dr. William Hume, a fellow member
of the Antiquarian Society. The midwinter weather was worsening, and the newlyweds retired to a room in the Allens' house. The couple departed the next day for
Nashville, but a few miles short of there, the intensifying snowstorm prompted them
to stop for the night at Locust Grove, the comfortable seat of their mutual family
friends Robert and Martha Martin. In the morning Eliza came late down the stairs;
her husband had already been up for a while and was at that moment embroiled
in a snowball fight on the front lawn with the Martins' two daughters. In her
unpublished memoir, Martha Martin recalled looking out the window at the fracas
and then getting Eliza's attention: "I said to her: it seems as if General Houston is
getting the worst of the snowballing; you had better go out and help him. Looking
seriously at me, Mrs. Houston said: 'I wish they would kill him.' I looked astonished
to hear such a remark from a bride of not yet forty-eight hours, when she repeated
in the same voice, 'yes, I wish from the bottom of my heart that they would kill him.'"[12]

Whatever toxin it was that poisoned the Houstons' marriage had already set in.
Mrs. Martin, one of the best known and most gracious hostesses of the Nashville
environs, was flabbergasted but remained discreet. She said nothing to Houston.
The couple proceeded on to Nashville, houseguesting for a few days with Houston's
cousin Robert McEwen and his wife before settling into the Nashville Inn.[13] Eliza,
no longer among her own people, said little; to Mrs. McEwen the couple seemed
secluded and affectionate, as one would expect of newlyweds. At the Nashville Inn,
however, the Martins called on the couple several times and saw them, though
never together.

Of Eliza Allen as first lady of Tennessee, there are precious few glimpses, and
what survives is not particularly flattering: "One evening when cousin Eliza was
worn out by fashionable dining and throngs of company . . . a fashionable gossip
entered . . . and she exclaimed involuntarily: 'Oh, yonder comes that horrible Mrs.
S—— to bore me to death. I wish she would stay at home or torment somebody
else.' Yet she sprang up, adjusted her beautiful toilet, put on her sweetest smiles, and
met 'the horrible Mrs. S——' with a kiss and protestations of joy at her coming. . . .
That night General Houston rebuked her sharply for such insincerity, which
caused my beautiful cousin to weep all night."[14]

As Houston went about his gubernatorial duties, at least one of his old friends,
Frank Chambers, perceived that all was not well. "During the next week or two
Governor Houston looked years older. I saw that the beautiful young wife would
be but dead sea fruit to him. . . . I saw that his heart was broken."

Even in the midst of personal crisis, politics made their demands, and Houston
and Carroll were scheduled to debate at Cockrell's Spring, ten miles distant from
Nashville; perhaps Houston told Eliza he might spend the night out of town. An
enormous throng was gathering to hear the two great figures go at each other, and
Houston used the good offices of his friend in youth, Willoughby Williams, who
now served Nashville as sheriff, to work the crowd and let him know what they
were saying. As Williams rode with Houston back toward Nashville, he told him

the evening, as far as the audience was concerned, went well for him. Within sight of the city they separated; Williams returned to Cockrell's Spring and Houston continued to the Nashville Inn. Eliza was gone.[15]

What in heaven's name was going on here? The circumstances and particulars of the separation have been both bait and bane of Houston watchers then and ever since. Houston himself, as riveted into an almost ironclad traditional history, never spoke of it—save two or three possible exceptions. Indeed, every new Houston biography that appears seems most avidly searched, not for insights on the Texas Revolution, nor annexation, nor the Civil War, nor Houston's prospects for the presidency but rather is scrutinized for new tidbits about Eliza and the failed marriage. What, indeed, was going on here?

Piecing together all available sources, the most likely reconstruction of events is this: After the ceremony at Allenwood the newlyweds spent the night there. Once secluded, as Houston related to his Washington pastor many years later, he could see that Eliza was pale and nervous beyond the mere strains of the ceremony. He told her he had sensed her discomfort for some time and inquired after her difficulty. To his horror, she disclosed that she was and had been in love with someone else. Houston may or may not have accused her of being unfaithful, but he did sleep on a couch. The identity of her beloved is not certain, though he was probably a consumptive young lawyer named Will Tyree, whom Eliza jilted at the insistence of her family. When the crestfallen Houston asked how she could marry him despite her feelings, she admitted that it was to advance her family's position. Houston, according to one family tradition, stalked to a writing desk and slashed out a resignation from the governorship, gave it to her, and said, "There, madam, is your position!" Of course, Houston did not actually resign until April 16, but it is just the sort of dramatic gesture he would have made and was probably the reason the pastor who ministered to Houston later in life related that he resigned immediately after the wedding.[16]

Leaving her parents none the wiser, the unhappy pair headed for Nashville, being forced by weather to stop at Locust Grove. During that night, apparently, some attempt was made to make the best of their situation and reconcile, and some intimacies may have been exchanged. They then began their unhappy coexistence at the Nashville Inn, both increasing in misery. If Houston had indeed accused her of being unfaithful, Eliza was trapped, for if she fled it could be interpreted as an admission of guilt—a very real consideration in the antebellum South.[17] Therefore, Eliza referred Houston to her family physician, Dr. John Shelby, whom Houston knew well and who had been her doctor since she was a girl. As one biographer has suggested, he could add little as a character witness for Eliza, but he might be able to persuade Houston of her physical chastity. Houston pronounced himself satisfied after the interview, but matters between them did not improve. Indeed, this was the point at which Eliza could assert herself, for her actions could not now be questioned. She wanted out.

During the enormous emotional throes of the impending separation, Houston penned a letter to Eliza's father that was desolate in its desire to erase all trace of the commotion, reunite with Eliza, and begin again as though nothing had happened:

> Mr. Allen The most unpleasant & unhappy circumstance has just taken place in the family, & one that was entirely unnecessary at this time. Whatever had been my feelings or opinions in relation to Eliza at one time, I have been satisfied & it is now unfit that anything should be adverted to. Eliza will do me the justice to say that she believes I was really unhappy That I was *satisfied & believed her virtuous*, I had assured her on last night & this morning. . . . That I have & do love Eliza none can doubt,—that she is the only earthly object dear to me God will bear witness. . . .
>
> She was cold to me, & I thought did not love me. She owns that such was one cause of my unhappiness. You can judge how unhappy I was to think I was united to a woman that did not love me. . . . You may rest assured that nothing on my part shall be wanting to restore [harmony]. Let me know what is to be done.[18]

A little conjecture, if I may. Consider the position and options of a young woman like Eliza: beautiful, vivacious, accomplished—the kind of woman to whom Houston was attracted all his life. Place such a girl in a wealthy and ambitious family like the Allens. Suppose the men in such a girl's family desired her to marry, against her heart's wish, an eligible, powerful older man. Given the time and place—the antebellum South—and the position of women in it, how, if she had set her mind to it, could she have opposed them? What weapons, beyond her own will, could she have brought to bear?

Consider how, in the antebellum South, the source of a man's strength and pride, indeed the definition of his very manhood, was irretrievably entwined in his notion of honor. As the daughter of Colonel Allen, Eliza could do precious little, unless she found some way of turning the men's idea of honor against them. Suppose, for a moment, that she decided to enter the marriage with every intention of spurning her groom—to marry sweetly, already planning to return in disheveled horror. Her family would be forced—for its own sake, not hers—to take her back and incite public sympathy for their abused child. The galled husband, forbidden by the code of gentlemen to gainsay the complaint of an aggrieved bride, would be compelled to silence, imprisoned in his own silly chivalry. He might even (not to make too fine a point of it) be driven to drink, if not by the split itself then surely by the walleyed injustice of being both ruined and muzzled in the same brilliant, betraying stroke. From Eliza's standpoint, however, it would be a coup with the mark of genius.

Suppose, alternatively, that Eliza did not plan her escape with such forethought, but having obediently married and finding herself wretchedly unhappy, she merely rode the circumstances to the same result. If she had gone home in misery to face her father's and uncle's punishment, any course of action to save the Allen family from disgrace would have dictated exactly the same sequence of events: defend Eliza and rake scorn upon the silenced Houston. Two different grounds for her actions subsequently gained currency in both families: one that she was grieving for the former beau, and the other that she was demoralized by the sight of Houston's war wounds. In either case, for her to have merely allowed the situation to carry her to escape would be by far the more charitable scenario. It would also be the more plausible, if only she, like Houston, had kept her mouth shut. But she did not, and the Allens and their retainers were never shy about publishing exonerations of her. Apparently, she later told her troubles to a relation who wrote over the initials "M.B.H." in the *New Orleans Picayune* in 1871, publicizing Eliza's sentiment that Houston "was a maniac on the subject of female virtue, and did not believe a pure woman lived. He upbraided her the first night he married, and every day afterward as long as he lived with her, acting now the fond husband and in ten minutes a furious maniac, the victim of ungovernable jealousy."[19]

Eliza did maintain her own kind of consistency, telling a second and more complete version in a document that has become somewhat better known. If it is credible, her account survived, several hands removed. She offered it, under oath of confidence, to her lifelong friend Balie Peyton, a prominent citizen and cagey stump speaker who in his time represented Andrew Jackson's district in Congress and served as minister to Chile. Peyton recounted it on his deathbed to his daughter Emily, who wrote it down and tucked it away with many other family papers, which were left to a niece in whose attic it surfaced in 1960. Eliza Allen Houston's own account of the rift takes one's breath away:

> I left General Houston because I found he was a demented man. I believe him to be crazy! He is insanely jealous and suspicious. He required of me not to speak to anyone, and to lock myself in my room if he was absent even for a few moments, and this when we were guests in my own aunt's house! On one occasion he went away early to attend to affairs in the city of Nashville, . . . and after he was gone, I found he had locked the door and carried off the key, leaving me a prisoner until late at night, without food, debarred from the society of my relatives, and a prey to chagrin, mortification and hunger. He gave additional evidence of an unsound mind by his belief in ghosts—he was timid and averse to being alone at night on account of these imaginary and supernatural influences. . . . I should never have consented to marry him had I not been attracted by his brilliant conversation and his handsome and commanding presence. I parted from General Houston because he evinced no confidence in my integrity and had no respect for my intelligence, or trust in my discretion. I could tell you many incidents to prove this, but I would not say, or do, anything to injure him.[20]

There are, of course, preliminary obstacles to accepting this account. First, Balie Peyton was Eliza's dear and courtly friend, reason enough for him to place her in the best possible light after half a century of whispers and innuendo. Did he weave the story of whole cloth in order to polish her tarnished reputation? If that had been his intention, he probably would have had it published, not merely related it to his daughter. Second, Peyton did recall these events in 1878, some forty-nine

Balie Peyton. Eliza Allen Houston made certain that all images of herself were destroyed before she died, but a daguerreotype of her courtly friend and later champion Balie Peyton survives. After a stint in Congress, he later served as minister to Chile.

Courtesy Library of Congress

years after they occurred, a long time for memory to alter or embellish. Third, Emily Peyton's own motive was not unimpeachable: as a girl she had known Eliza Houston in her later life as Eliza Douglass, a woman she admired. She inquired the divorce story of her father after reading speculation in a Nashville newspaper and getting angry. And in putting pen to paper she avowed that it was "my privilege, my duty to *prove* Eliza not guilty of coldness, and blameless in the episode."[21]

If these doubts are assuaged, and if what survives is an accurate reflection of what Eliza Houston told Balie Peyton in hushed confidence in the wake of her separation, then it is hardly the account of a trembling waif gone home in fear of her ambitious father's punishment. In the first place, in none of Houston's other serious relationships with women, with the Misses M———s of East Tennessee and South Carolina, with Diana Rogers, with Anna Raguet, or with Margaret Lea—is there the slightest hint of such insane jealousy, nor was there, apparently, during his courtship with Eliza. Is it reasonable to expect such a bizarre change of behavior literally overnight, which then never recurred in a life of seventy years?

Another problem is charging Houston with a fear of ghosts. If for whatever reason Eliza spurned her groom from the marriage bed, one can easily imagine Houston feigning fear of the dark and of ghosts while playfully trying to cajole his way into her arms. Nothing, in fact, would be more within Houston's character than such whining banter. It would be a very low blow indeed for Eliza to have cited this clever whimpering as evidence of madness. In all the rest of Houston's life, the only other mention of superstition was his notice of omens, and they were all self-proclaimed, after the fact, without witnesses, and entirely concerned with the circling or fall from flight of ravens or eagles—and all were at least partly con-trived by himself to enhance his political image as a "Man of the Woods." There are no other references in his life to ghosts, save two, both of which occurred during the Civil War: once when he played a practical joke on two of his little slave girls whom he caught stealing from the kitchen, and another time when he got a kick out of "spooking" Jeff Hamilton on a wistful visit to the battlefield at San Jacinto. In both cases, the issue was not his fear of ghosts, but theirs.[22]

Finally, during the whole itinerary of their brief marriage—from her father's house, to the Martins' at Locust Grove, to the McEwens,' to the Nashville Inn—where is the record of a sojourn with an Allen aunt? If such a visit occurred, it is possible that Houston would have been given the key to the bedroom in deference to their newly wedded privacy. But if he had locked her in the bedroom, is it believable that Eliza, in her own aunt's house, would have sat there all day with-out pounding on the door for release? Not likely from a girl who had already told Martha Martin she wished he was dead. Is it believable that the aunt would not have knocked on the door at some time during the day and inquired after Eliza's health? Is it believable that the Allen family, after the separation, would have kept such an outrage quiet when they were scrambling to make Houston take the rap for the failed marriage on every other front? Later, Robert and Martha Martin both saw Eliza and Houston on subsequent visits to Nashville; they just did not see the two together as a couple. Eliza was under no house arrest, at least not at that time. And then there was the account that Eliza's cousin gave to Rufus Burleson about her encounter with "that horrible Mrs. S———, . . . when cousin Eliza was worn out by fashionable dining and throngs of company." That would have been quite a trick for a woman held prisoner in her room.

Nothing about Eliza's story rings true. Further, one keeps coming back to that morning at Locust Grove. Governor Houston, tossing snowballs on the front lawn, was not acting like a man whose life and career had just been blasted. It was Eliza who came downstairs in a hateful frame of mind. Even if all of Eliza's accusations in the Balie Peyton account were true, they could not possibly have transpired by the second day of the marriage, when Eliza looked squarely at Martha Martin and said, "I wish with all my heart they would kill him."

Had Eliza determined at that early time to free herself? It is speculation to be sure, but it is a pole from which no compass points askew—especially in view of the fact that the Allen family's behavior immediately after the separation was also very curious. They could hardly call Houston to the field of honor after his pathetic "What is to be done?" letter showed so clearly that he desired a reconciliation. It was equally clear from the letter, and from all her conduct, that Eliza did not desire it. Thus, while the Allens were willing to let Houston take the fall and even formed a committee of gentlemen to make sufficient inquiries to clear her name, they seemed not to be pleased with her conduct.

At least that was the perception of the most interested onlookers, including Nashville resident Emily Drennen, who thought the Allens were behaving very strangely: "There is a thouseand diferent tails afloat. He had resined, and poor fellow is miserable enough. . . . He is very sick and has been ever since. . . . And what is more astonishing none of her connection has been near. If he was in fault I should think some of them would resent it. He never has said any thing to any one not even his brother about her. . . . He says time will show who is to blame. The reason he does not tell. I expect you are tyered of this but I feel so interested."[23]

•   •   •

And people have been interested ever since. What then is one to make of this terrible personal episode? The issue of the separation, whether gleaned from Houston's "What is to be done?" letter, from the demeanor of the Allen family, or from Emily Peyton's manuscript, was Eliza's abandonment of her husband. What evidence survives of her temperament? Eliza herself, curiously enough, saw to it that little physical evidence survived her—not a letter, not a photograph, not even a tombstone. She desired oblivion. The warmest testimonial that her champion, Emily Peyton, could recall from her childhood was that "it was true that she did not belong to that class of persons who 'wear their hearts on their sleeves' . . . but she was capable of lasting affection to those she esteemed." Balie Peyton recalled from the mist of his platonic warmth for her, "no one could presume to take a liberty with Eliza Allen."[24] One wonders if it is significant that at no point in Eliza's defense of herself did she say she loved Sam Houston. "She would not injure him." "She would never have consented to marry him if she had not been attracted." The word "love" is conspicuous only by its absence.

It is clear from all the evidence that it was Eliza who walked out on Houston, not the other way around. But why did she do it? Many a woman in her time and place endured loveless marriages to men much older and less attractive than Houston for the sake of security and family advantage. Was it merely spunk or the determination to live only with a man she passionately loved? In answer, there is a longstanding Allen family tradition that Eliza was revolted by the oozing wound in Houston's groin—the "running sore," she reputedly called it late in life to her son-in-law, Dr. William Haggard.[25] Marquis James mentioned that possibility in *The Raven*, but it was only in 1962 that Louise Davis, who first published Balie Peyton's account, interviewed a number of Allen descendents and was surprised to discover that Eliza had spoken of Houston's sore to not one relative but two; as the family branches diverged, each preserved her confidence in such secrecy that eventually neither one was aware that the other knew. This seems to indicate, first, that Houston's wound had indeed played some role in her decision to leave him; second, for a woman who made her confidantes swear to secrecy, Eliza talked an awful lot; and third, if what she told Balie Peyton was the truth, it was not the whole truth. It would also explain, in addition to Houston's inability by social convention to defend himself, that his silence was doubly ensured by the nature of the problem. It is doubtful whether his pride could have withstood having it known to the whole world that he had been spurned because his war wounds had left him sexually disgusting.

Houston, certainly, was desperate to repair the marriage, and his frame of mind was truly expressed in his letter to John Allen. Its honesty is underwritten by various circumstances. He wrote it *ante litem motam*, at a moment of personal extremity when artifice would have been the last thing on his mind. Second, he wrote it to his father-in-law, a gentleman whose bruised honor Houston would not have dared provoke further with any sham that might be uncovered; Houston would not have dared to say, "Eliza will do me the justice," or even give a distorted version of the facts, when Eliza could contradict him in a second to her insulted menfolk. Lastly, the letter came to light not at Houston's instance but at that of the "committee" later formed to vindicate the bride's honor; Houston never intended any eyes but John Allen's to see the paper. It is clear from the letter that, whatever Houston did, he was provoked. Apparently, Eliza could not deny that she had been "cold" to him, and whether that chill was occasioned by her pining for her previous suitor or whether she was demoralized at the thought of making love to a man who had blood and pus oozing from a supporating hole in his groin, she would not have anything, intimately, to do with him. Almost certainly, both circumstances contributed to her determination to escape.

Emily Drennen's breathless gossip mirrored in small the avid feelings of the public. When Houston returned from the debate at Cockrell's Spring and found Eliza gone, rumor and talk raced across the city as fast as the governor could cloak himself in seclusion in his quarters at the Nashville Inn. His enemies, doubtless spurred on by partisans of Billy Carroll, hoisted placards accusing Houston of the grossest defamations of a pure young lady. He was even hanged in effigy, first in Nashville and then elsewhere as the news traveled. From his confinement, attended only by his closest friends, Houston sent for Reverend Hume, who had married the couple, and the distraught governor, who was not a member of a church, asked to be baptized. Hume took the matter up with the Reverend Obadiah Jennings, pastor of the First Presbyterian Church in Nashville, and together they declined, "on good grounds, as we think." More to the point was the fact that Obadiah Jennings was the father-in-law of Balie Peyton's law partner, Henry Wise. The Allens and their partisans were nothing if not tightly interconnected, and as Jennings himself admitted, "the respectable connections of the lady . . . were much offended."[26]

Abandoned by his wife and now forsaken by the church, Houston was beside himself. Sheriff Willoughby Williams had been out of town since the debate at Cockrell's Spring, and finding the city in commotion when he returned, called on Houston at the Nashville Inn. He got as far as the front desk before hotel clerk Daniel Carter asked if he had heard the news.

"What news?" Williams asked.

"General Houston and his wife have separated and she has gone home to her father."

Williams bounded up the stairs and was admitted to Houston's rooms, where he found him, "deeply mortified," in the company of Dr. John Shelby. As later related by Houston, Williams was bewildered by the onslaught of people demanding to know what had happened. "What can I say to them, Governor?"

"There is nothing to say, Billy."

"But you've got to say something, Governor. You owe it to yourself and your friends."

"This is a painful but a private matter, Billy. I do not recognize the right of the people to interfere. I shall treat the public as though it had never happened."

Williams protested that this was a disastrous course, but Houston ended the discussion by laying a hand on Williams's shoulder. "Whatever may be said by the lady or her friends, it is no part of the conduct of a gallant and generous man to take up arms against a woman. If my character cannot stand the shock, let me lose it."[27] This record of the conversation was part of Houston's memoir, composed much later with a view toward political visibility, and many of its key scenes are staged just a bit too theatrically to merit heavy historical reliance. What is interesting here, however, and what vouchsafes the sentiment if not the pose, is Houston's use of the very words—"take up arms against a woman"—that Andrew Jackson had uttered in defense of Peggy Eaton and in condemning Duff Green for attacking the wife of John Quincy Adams. Houston knew the words well, and it is virtually the only phrase he would have used.

Willoughby Williams was not the only man who rallied to Houston's side. Another who called at the Nashville Inn was John Overton, chief justice of the Tennessee Supreme Court. Asking no questions, he came merely to demonstrate his friendship and to see if there was anything he could do. Houston never forgot that.

Pulling himself together, the governor determined to make a final attempt to salvage his marriage. On the evening of April 15, he rode to Allenwood and pleaded to see Eliza, who consented with the condition that one of her aunts be present. On his knees he begged forgiveness and wept, but now that she was free of him she had no intention of going back. Returning from this disastrous interview, Houston, if the story is to be believed, sought out his friend Chambers:

> About 1 o'clock in the morning I was waiting and smoking as he staggered into the room. His face was rigid. His eyes had a strange stare. He looked like some magnificent ruin. . . .
>
> He sat upright in his chair finally, and running his fingers through his hair, said: "It was so infamous, so cruel, so vile. . . . Cursed be the human fiends

who force a woman to live with a man whom she does not love. Just think
of it, the unending torture . . . she has never loved me, her parents forced her
to marry me. She loved another from the first.

Houston, according to Chambers, concluded that it was better for one person to
live in misery than two, and he had decided to take Eliza back to her father's house.
That is dubious; it is far more likely that she either left on her own or sent for her
father to come fetch her without giving Houston an opportunity to use his formidable powers of persuasion. However, Houston did not, nor did he ever, blame
Eliza for not loving him—a stance consistent with his later oft-repeated defenses
of her character. He did blame the Allens bitterly for forcing her into the marriage.
Nevertheless, it was a disgrace he could not live down; he considered himself a
ruined man and told Chambers he would resign the governorship the following
day and remove to Arkansas Territory to reside again with the Cherokees. Houston,
in tears, required that his confidence be kept until he was dead, after which Chambers was to "do what good you can to transmute this evil; that you will let the
world know why I surrendered my wife."[28]

While Emily Drennen may thus have been correct in her assumption that
Houston had supplied details of the calamity to at least one of his friends, he was
stoically silent to others, and that silence became legendary, although by the end
of his life it was more legendary than actual. Drennen was correct on other points
as well. Houston had been ill, had remained in seclusion, did intend leaving Tennessee forever, and, most terrible of all, he had resigned his office.

The letter, dated April 16, 1829, was addressed to the presiding officer of the
state senate, Gen. William Hall. "That veneration for public opinion by which I
have measured every act of my official life," Houston wrote, "has taught me to hold
no delegated power which would not daily be renewed by my constituents. . . .
Delicately circumstanced as I am, & by my own misfortunes more than by the
fault or contrivance of anyone, it is certainly due myself & more respectful to the
world, that I should retire from a position which, in the public judgment, I might
seem to occupy by questionable authority."[29] Calling to see Houston the day he
resigned was Tennessee's first-term congressman and fellow Jackson protégé,
David Crockett, who asked what the former governor intended to do now. As an
infantry lieutenant and Indian agent, Houston had exiled his Hiwassee Cherokees
west to the Arkansas Territory; now, he replied, he intended to share their exile
with them.[30]

Once the lion had fallen, it took little time for the jackals to begin trotting in
from the hills to feed on his carcass. Henry Wise, Obadiah Jennings's son-in-law
and Balie Peyton's law partner, memorialized the Houstons' courtship and marriage
in a melodramatic summary that was as cruel as it was outrageous: "Houston,
then advanced in life, spent in dissipation . . . sought to strengthen himself and
insure his election. . . . Her family was sought by Samuel Houston from which to
select a victim, not of his love, but of his selfish electioneering for influence to save
him in office." Eliza Allen, he continued, was in love with another man, but "the

eye of the ogre fell upon her. . . . the family were flattered by the governor, and she was torn from her youth and her pure, natural, maiden love, to become the victim of his jealousy, and his heartless, selfish ambition!"[31]

"*Sic transit gloria mundi*," clucked the good Reverend Hume. "Oh, what a fall for a major general, a member of congress and a Governor. . . . I am sorry for him, and more sorry for the young lady he has left." And there was the beginning of the Eliza legend that Houston was too exhausted to contest: that he had left her, not the other way around.[32] He borrowed traveling money, and on April 23, accompanied by his friends Dr. Shelby and Willoughby Williams and with a traveling companion, an Irishman named H. Haralson, Houston went down to the wharf on the Cumberland River and boarded the river packet *Red Rover* bound for Cairo, Memphis, Helena, the White River, and ultimately Little Rock in Arkansas Territory.

5

THE MOST UNHAPPY MAN NOW LIVING

Speculation that Houston's rupture with Eliza was a deliberate plot of his to mask his projected conquest of Texas—or even worse, that the whole thing was Andrew Jackson's idea—date from barely a month after the separation. That there was collusion between Jackson and Houston for the Americanization of Texas seems all but certain, but it does not date from this early time. In the first place, Jackson had spent years grooming Houston to be his heir, not his errand boy. In the second place, Texas might well be had by less fantastical measures, and although Jackson never hesitated to shoot, he invariably tried diplomacy first, however crudely, and in the case of approaching Mexico to purchase Texas, it was rather crudely. Finally, such a usage of a young woman was unthinkable to a man of his stamp. Probably the sheer unbelievability of the idea has been the source of much of its currency, but in all of Jackson's life—and there is much to blame him for—his chivalry toward women was constant. From his shared humiliation with Rachel, to his rebuke of Duff Green for defending Rachel by attacking Mrs. Adams, to his repeated defense of Peggy Eaton in that sad affair, it is plain that the calculated ruin of Eliza Allen would never have occurred to Andrew Jackson.

The idea that Houston of his own volition spurned Eliza as his ticket to Texas is equally improbable. The origin of this story was Rachel Jackson's nephew, Daniel S. Donelson, who was point man in Jackson's effort to purchase Texas and not a friend of Houston anyway. Whatever Donelson may actually have heard, it was, to him, worth such an embellishment—that Houston never intended to keep Eliza—to alert Jackson to the danger of having Houston loose in the Southwest. However, every reasonable consideration is against it. Houston's bearing toward women was every bit as courtly as Jackson's, but putting that aside, to be governor of Tennessee with Old Hickory in the White House was as close to being the Prince of Wales as American blood could approach. Houston was the all-but-anointed heir of the most popular president since Washington himself. Texas, however, was a swamp of intrigue into which American filibusters had wandered and died for thirty years. No man as smart as Houston would have thrown away such bright prospects for something so dark and dubious. Then too, if Houston had meant to go to Texas, he would have gone to Texas. But he did not. The three years after resigning as governor he spent in and out of the thick woods of the Verdigris River bottoms, where there is no evidence of his beating the drum to recruit Cherokee filibusters to invade Texas. And it is certain that if it were Houston who had abandoned Eliza and not the other way around, then both the Allen family that was laboring to restore her reputation and Eliza herself, who had been capable of uttering a death wish against him on the second day of their marriage, would have made sure that the whole world knew of it.

The only conclusion to write to the whole business with Eliza Allen of Gallatin is to recognize it as a humiliation and debacle of dizzying proportions, a catastrophe from which a lesser man might never have recovered. Many years later Houston told a Baptist minister and family friend that as the *Red Rover* descended the Cumberland River on its way to the Tennessee, the

> brothers of Mrs. Houston, riding direct across the country, overtook us at Clarksville, Tenn. They came aboard, greatly excited and heavily armed, and said: "Governor Houston, the manner in which you have left Nashville has filled the city with . . . rumors, among others, that you are goaded to madness and exile by detecting our sister in crime. We demand that you give a written denial of this, or go back and prove it." I replied, "I will neither go back nor write a retraction, but in the presence of the captain and these well-known gentlemen, I request you to go back and publish in the Nashville papers that if any wretch ever dares to utter a word against the purity of Mrs. Houston I will come back and write the libel in his heart's blood."

That evening, he said, he considered throwing himself from the upper deck of the boat. "But at that awful moment an eagle swooped down near my head, and soaring aloft with wildest screams, was lost in the rays of the setting sun. I knew that a great duty and glorious destiny awaited me in the West."[1] Sam Houston never lost his faith in native augury, but the sweep of this particular eagle may have been embellished. However, that he was considering suicide seems possible, for previous to docking in Clarksville he wrote out and sealed a testament, which he left the boat long enough to deposit with his friend Thomas Howser, with the mysterious instruction that it was to be opened "only when you think my honor requires it." Just in case his verbal testament to Chambers never became public, Houston wanted insurance that his side of the debacle would not die with him.[2]

The *Red Rover* descended the Tennessee to the Ohio, and Houston and H. Haralson disembarked at Cairo, Illinois, on the Mississippi opposite the mouth of the Ohio. There they bought a flatboat and hired the boatman to take them downriver. They stopped in Memphis to replenish supplies—liquor most notably—and then proceeded to Helena, Arkansas. There is a traditional story that at some point on this journey, after a spell of drinking, Haralson ventured to ask Houston why he and Eliza had separated, and Houston told him the same thing he told Chambers: she did not love him. But of what passes between two drunks on a flatboat in the middle of a river, none can be certain. There was another story that at Helena, Houston made the acquaintance of Louisiana slave trader and legendary knife fighter Jim Bowie. This story, however, has its origins in *The Raven* and is almost surely false; Houston and Bowie did not meet for another three and a half years.[3]

Houston and Haralson sold their flatboat at the mouth of the Arkansas and arrived in Little Rock on May 8. There Houston chanced to meet up with Charles F. M. Noland, a figure now obscure, though apparently they had been bosom friends in days past. Houston also knew Noland's father; they were Virginians, so the association may have extended back that far. Noland soon sat down and wrote his father an account of their meeting, and he was clear in his estimation of who was at fault: "Merciful God! is it possible that society is to be deprived of one of its greatest ornaments, and the United States of one of her most valiant sons, through the dishonor and baseness of a woman? . . . He wishes to go to the Rocky Mountains, to visit that tract of country between the mouth of the Oregon and California Bay."

Noland had every reason to view Houston with alarm, for the drunken spectacle that he exhibited showed every evidence of his having been brought to the lowest point of his life. One night he and Haralson, with some hail-fellow-well-met named Linton, disappeared into the woods for a bacchanal. Linton was another Latin-spouting border figure, so Houston may not have been the only one classically educated enough to know about Maenads and the drunken orgies associated with the worship of Bacchus. But somewhere in the woods the three men built a fire and danced around it, drinking and sacrificing articles of their clothing to the flames until little was left to the imagination. What Linton did not know was that Haralson and Houston had extra clothing, and after the revelry those two crept back to Little Rock, leaving Linton passed out and naked next to the fire.[4]

Houston's contemplation of life as a mountain man was a motif that surfaced a few more times in the coming months—Matthew Maury reported a similar verbal speculation two years later—but really it only indicates the blankness with which Houston viewed his future as he cast about for a calling. All his options were open.[5] His words to Noland did not fall on other idle ears, however, as Houston's companionable drunk, Haralson, sent a report of it to Jackson's new secretary of war, John Eaton. This gave rise to rumors that Houston was planning to establish an Indian empire somewhere in the West, which he probably was not, and to later speculation that Haralson had ingratiated himself into Houston's favor merely as a spy for the administration, which indeed he may have been.[6]

Immediately after the bacchanal, Houston and Haralson resumed their journey upstream on board a smaller, shallow-draught boat called the *Facility*, crossing the line into the Cherokee Nation in what is now Oklahoma late in June 1829 and reaching the army's farthest, and by repute wildest, outpost of Cantonment Gibson near the confluence of the Arkansas and Verdigris Rivers. On a moonlit evening,

Houston stepped off the boat at a clearing at Webber's Falls and into the arms of John Jolly: "The old chief threw his arms around him and embraced him with great affection. 'My son,' said he, 'eleven winters have passed since we met. . . . I have heard that a dark cloud had fallen on the white path you were walking, and when it fell in your way you turned your thought to my wigwam. I am glad of it—it was done by the Great Spirit. . . . We are in trouble and the Great Spirit has sent you to give us council, and take trouble away from us. I know you will be our friend . . . and you will tell our sorrows to the great father, General Jackson. My wigwam is yours—my home is yours—my people are yours—rest with us." The noble-savage romance depicted in Houston's *Authentic Memoir* is a bit overstated. The clearing may have been moonlit, but the path to John Jolly's "wigwam" was lit by torches borne by the chief's slaves, and that "wigwam" was described by other visitors as "almost a palace."[7]

No sooner was Houston safe in John Jolly's arms, hearing him soothe, "Rest with us," than his enemies in Washington began urging Jackson away from him. The paddlewheel of the *Red Rover* had roiled a muck of White House intrigue about Houston and his intentions. In fact, Daniel Donelson wrote his alarm-bell letter that Houston's divorce was a sham to filibuster Texas on May 22—the very time, perhaps to the day, that Houston reached Webber's Falls. There can be no doubt that Sam Houston loved his two foster fathers equally, but as his red father embraced him, his white father began to distance himself as Houston watched in helpless exile.

What probably happened was this. Andrew Jackson was not a man to whom one reacted with equanimity. One either loved him or hated him. But the devotion he inspired among those who served him was a fidelity prone to intrigues among those intimates whose only shared loyalty was to Jackson.[8] Often they could not otherwise abide each other, and if one of them thought another was about some business that would embarrass the Old Chief, he did not hesitate to bear tales. Such a one was Daniel Donelson. In March of 1829, before the newly wedded Houstons separated, the governor, according to Donelson, asserted to him that William Wharton, a former Tennessee lawyer and now well-connected Texas colonist, was Houston's agent to sabotage Mexican control in Texas, after which he would send for Houston at the proper time. (This would probably have been quite a surprise to John Wharton, who was writing to Houston that he really should come out to Texas for a visit sometime.) Unknown to Donelson, of course, the Houstons' marriage was already on the rocks, and if the despondent governor said anything to him, it was probably more in the vein of trying to conjecture some future for himself. If Houston used Wharton's name to Donelson, it may have been in the context that he (Houston) could turn Wharton into his agent if he wished.[9] But as the Houstons separated only a short time later, and Wharton returned to Texas at just the same time, Donelson took it upon himself to conclude that the marriage had been a sham and the separation a ruse to spring Houston into the Southwest. William Wharton himself was certainly not acting as if Houston's flight to the West was part of a plan. After Houston's riverboat chum and Eaton's probable spy, H. Haralson, made it back to Tennessee, he wrote the ex-governor-in-extremis that his friends were worried about him. "John A. Wharton is your steady friend . . . I am not so sure about Collinsworth—Wm. Wharton is cold and says but little," but that may have had more to do with Wharton's dislike of Haralson.[10] Nevertheless, Donelson wrote accounts of the Houston scandal and sent them to his brother, Andrew Jackson Donelson, in Washington. A. J. Donelson was the president's private secretary, and the Old Chief was told all. "My God," said Jackson when he heard of the separation, "is the man mad?"

Another such loyalist among Jackson's "kitchen cabinet" was Duff Green, editor of the *United States Telegraph*. He was an in-law of John C. Calhoun—grounds enough for Houston's enmity—and also a friend of a man named Hamtramack, whom Houston would soon cause to be dismissed from his post as an agent to the Osages. Jackson knew from their previous dealings that Duff Green could be a scoundrel, but even as Henry VIII listened to Cromwell when there was evidence (of whatever manufacture) in his hands, Jackson heard Green out when he arrived with a document incriminating Houston.[11]

During his despair over Eliza, Houston had asserted to one of his good friends, Tennessee representative John Marable, that he intended to repair westward and "conquer Mexico or Texas, and be worth two millions in two years." Marable had betrayed the confidence, perhaps innocently, in a letter to Green, which Jackson now squinted over. The president defended Houston, believing that whatever he had said to Marable he intended only as some embellished assertion that he would make something of himself yet, that he had shaken his fist over his shoulder even as he skulked away from civilization. But the seed of discord had been planted, and Jackson could take no chances. From his perspective, he could not afford to let Houston, sane or mad, roll about his decks like a loose cannon at a time when he was attempting to soothe relations with Mexico and acquire Texas by purchase. If Mexico suspected for a minute that Jackson had unleashed Houston as a filibuster, the scheme would be wrecked. Jackson had powerful enemies in Congress who opposed any idea of Texas entering the federal union, which would dilute their power in Congress and give ascendancy to the slaveholding South. It would take but little for them to believe that Jackson and Houston were acting in collusion. They knew Jackson wanted Texas, they knew Houston already had financial interests in Texas and was headed west, and they knew Houston was Jackson's man.

But, was he?

Describing himself as "doubtless, the most unhappy man now living," Houston wrote Jackson from Little Rock. Of his "domestic misfortune . . . I say nothing." Rather, what preyed on his mind was word that Jackson had been told of Houston's supposed scheming for Texas. "I do not distinctly understand the extent of the information, or its character, but I Suppose it was intended to complete my ruin." That was a good guess, for someone who had no specifics at hand. From this distance there was no way he could offset the combined assault of Duff Green, the Donelsons, and perhaps occasionally Eaton—to say nothing of William Carroll—on the vulnerable Jackson. But still, "I can not brook the idea of your supposing me capable, of an act that would . . . blot the escutcheon of human nature!" In an impassioned torrent, Houston referred Jackson to his valor in battle and his public career up to the point of his downfall. "To what would they all amount" if he compromised the honor and safety of his country? "Nothing!" Houston reaffirmed his personal affection for Jackson and offered to serve him in some private capacity, but apart from that he would live among the Indians and allow nature's gifts to satisfy nature's wants.[12]

Sam Houston had returned to the Cherokees, but it would go too far to suggest that he was completely cut off from the land of the living. After reaching the safety of Cantonment Gibson and the hearth of John Jolly, Houston pulled himself together enough to write a series of letters to many of his friends on May 29. Only two weeks after describing himself to Jackson as the "most unhappy" man now living, Houston assured his friends that he was happy and contented, and their replies drifted out to him all summer, renewing their affection. First in line was Daniel Graham, his secretary of state in Tennessee, whose friendship he had once resigned over possession of the Ninth Congressional District seat. Graham's letter was discreet, newsy, and kind, not touching upon his troubles.

Others felt the need to eulogize or to offer help. "As I never was a friend in sunshine alone," wrote J. P. Clarke, "neither can I now be the deserter of Friendship in adversity. . . . when the reality of your absence pressed on me still it would seem a disturbed dream—a thing of air—and yet, at times, I can hardly trust the evidence of my senses upon the subject of your absence. . . . Your friends here beg me to say—that you are not forgotten by them." And those friends, he added, most particularly regretted that Houston's disappearance left the gubernatorial field to Carroll, who "now walks over the Turf—and must & will be the 'big man of Tennessee.'" (Carroll, for his part, wasted no time in letting Jackson know what a mistake he had made in ever placing his confidence in Houston. The President was still reeling from news of Houston's downfall when Carroll assured him that, after all, Houston was "always . . . a man of weak and unsettled mind, without resources, and incapable of manfully meeting a reverse of fortune. . . . and charity requires us to place it to the account of insanity." Carroll was elected governor by default.)[13]

Gen. Richard Dunlap was more practical in his words for the exile: "I see that Maj. McClellan the Osage agent is dead—I will write today to the President to give you this place & altho it is below you . . . you ought not to think of living entirely, a life of an inactive man." As it turned out, the Osages already had a new agent who was about to collide with Houston, but even the crusty Dunlap could not forbear philosophizing. "Houston what a mighty fall was yours; and one of *your own choice*—It was a *deep* wound to your friends—your misfortune gave you strength with the people, but I can well appreciate that honorable delicacy which forbids you" to return to a situation "which must have drawn blood from every feeling in your heart." Unlike Dunlap, one General Howard preferred to reinforce Houston's announced sense of recovery: "This day I rec'd your letter of the 29th May, and am so much gratified at receiving it. . . . Nothing could have given me so much satisfaction than the fact, that you disclose, that 'Houston is himself again' and that he has been able to withstand the boldest shock which misfortune could give." Family friend Richard S. Williams of Natchez was equally upbeat: "Although a Cherokee," he chided, "you are Sam Houston—*you are Williams friend* and visit me you must." After conveying family news he encouraged him, "Think no more of your misfortunes! They have been great it is true, but all you have to do is take care of your noble self, and be happy."[14]

Until happiness, there was activity. In fact, he was allowed little time to recover from his journey before natives from most of the tribes in the area sought him out to help settle difficulties, because they knew he was close to the Great White Father. An appeal to Houston was seen as a shortcut to Jackson, and first in line, of all people, were the Osages. The most influential white man among them, Maj. Auguste Pierre Chouteau, trader and former agent, sent an emissary to fetch Houston to visit him in his sprawling estate on the Six Bull River some one hundred miles to the northwest. The traditionally clad Osage emissary raised a small alarm when he arrived during a garden party at John Jolly's "wigwam," and to everyone's surprise Houston and Haralson departed with him at once. In his demeanor toward Indians, Chouteau was Houston's kindred spirit; his generosity and fairness to them generated a loyalty that the Osages never accorded another white man. Houston knew the feeling. In another of his secretive reports to Eaton, Haralson wrote that the Osages were grievously dissatisfied with their new agent, Maj. John Hamtramack, and upon his and Houston's arriving at Chouteau's mansion, they were met "by a parcel of the Osage Indians . . . [who] insisted that Genl Houston . . . and myself go with them to the agency. We told them we would go and see what passed between them and their agent."[15] Chouteau explained that all the Osages wanted was impartial witnesses at their issue, and a line of Indians complained of frauds that Hamtramack was perpetrating. The Osages had no particular reason to trust Houston, or any other Cherokees, but they trusted Chouteau and were pleased that Houston witnessed and endorsed their petition, although Houston quite honestly disavowed any particular knowledge of the charges. Then the Creek Indians, seeing that Houston had gained influence among the Osages, with whom they had never been friendly, began asking him to mediate their disputes with that tribe. And then the Choctaws asked if he would write a letter to Secretary of War Eaton outlining their needs as well.

Houston, upon finding himself useful, began to find himself. John Jolly quickly perceived what an asset he had procured, and he had his own plans for his returned prodigal son. The peaceable Oolooteka had a Cherokee war faction he desired to face down and asked Houston to represent him at a council on Maynard Bayou. It seemed that a group of Cherokees traveling in Texas had been attacked by a war party of Tawakoni Indians and now some of the young men wanted to stage a revenge raid. "I attended the Dance and Talk," Houston reported to Col. Matthew Arbuckle at Cantonment Gibson, "and had the mortification to witness (in despite of all my efforts) the raising of the Tomahawk of war." He was successful, however, in discouraging a number of Creeks who were tempted to join in. Overall, Sam Houston was acting like anything but a man who intended to conquer Texas at the head of a thundering horde of savages.[16]

Houston traveled hundreds of miles among the various Indian Territory tribes during the summer of 1829; back with John Jolly, his thoughts turned to his other adopted family, that of his cousin John H. Houston in Washington. "My friend Dr. Baylor will hand you this letter," he wrote from Cantonment Gibson on June 24. "He is worthy of your friendship, and that is all that I could say of any man. He will kiss my dear God Daughter, and will tell you all about me. The world may care nothing for me, but . . . you and My Dear Cousin Gertrude, and my Daughter will always love me." Settled among the Indians, their speech patterns had already become his own. "Write to me," he concluded to Jack, "[your] letters will reach my Wigwam, and they will bring me happiness."[17] The Dr. Baylor whom Houston recommended to his cousin has fallen from history, but Houston entrusted other letters to Haralson, who returned to Tennessee at the same time; Baylor and Haralson may have journeyed together. Houston and Haralson had covered many miles together, and the partially restored exile could recommend him safely as a traveling companion. The two are not known to have met again.

The Raven's Indian mediations came to a sudden halt in the middle of August, when he fell gravely ill from fever and chills—probably malaria—that lasted, some days better and some worse, for over a month. On his better days, he had a chance to read over the many letters from the States. Their chatty news and invitations to come back and sojourn indicate that it had not sunk in with many of Houston's friends that he was gone for good. Haralson knew better, and of those who had an idea that Houston's removal was permanent, it was Haralson who remonstrated hardest to get him home. In an eight-page letter he played the family card: Houston's younger brother William was very ill, and of Houston's sister Eliza, who had always had a precariously balanced mind, Haralson wrote that the "Doct thinks that if the [letter you addressed] to Eliza is sent it will cause her to derange. She I am told is in a delicate state of health." Jack Houston, with Gertrude and little Eliza, received the exile's missive about how a letter from them would bring happiness to his wigwam; their reply through Haralson must have driven Houston near mad with nostalgia: "Your little god Daughter requested me to say to you that when I returned she would write you a long letter and to keep in fine spirits, and that she lived in hopes yet to *imbrace* her Uncle Sam. She [has] a smile more precious than gold."[18]

But he could not return—not yet. Sometime during his crisscrossing the traces in Indian Territory on his missions to keep peace among the native nations, he managed to find time to set up his own household, which he christened Wigwam Neosho, establishing there a trading post in the thick bottom forest midway between the Grand and Verdigris Rivers some three miles above their almost joint confluence with the Arkansas River. (Apart from this general description, the site of Houston's trading post has been lost. The log structure apparently burned during or just after the Civil War, and over the years since then no fewer than eight different locations have been touted as the true site of Wigwam Neosho. By far the best claimant is known as the "Boling Place," where excavations later revealed smoothed foundation stones and piles of ironware, broken crockery, and other detritus that one would expect to find at the site of a trading post.) It was a well-chosen location;

Cantonment Gibson lay three miles to the southeast, a branch of Chouteau's out-post at Three Forks was three miles to the northwest.[19] Sam Houston was no more fond of playing storekeeper than he had been in Maryville, but he had a more compelling reason for building Wigwam Neosho: he had taken a wife.

Her name was Diana Rogers Gentry. She was tall, handsome, and in her mid-thirties, the widow of a white blacksmith killed in a clash with Osages and the half-sister of Houston's friend and John Jolly's probable successor, John Rogers. Even as Houston romanticized his hewn-log trading post as "Wigwam" Neosho, likewise have subsequent writers made Diana Rogers sound more exotic by trying to find native roots in her name. Some have opted to call her Tiana; one of her purported headstones reads TALIHINA. Surviving documents, however, bear the name Diana, although like John Jolly and Houston himself, she probably had her choice of names depending on what society she moved in. The degree of formality of the couple's relationship is also debatable. Anglos who intermarried into the tribe were required to have a ceremony conducted by Cherokee civil authority. But that may have been moot in Houston's case because he by then either was or would shortly be granted Cherokee citizenship, and Diana Rogers was not a full-blood. The natives regarded such relationships with more flexibility than Tennessee's high society—in fact, Houston's friend Chouteau often provided feminine company to visitors as a gesture of hospitality. But there is no doubt that Houston was deeply attached to Diana Rogers.

Whether he suffered malaria or delirium tremens, he found comfort in her care. He was generally losing his battle with alcohol, and on occasion he would get so drunk at Cantonment Gibson that Diana would go into the post and bring him home slung across his horse. One visitor who saw him at his low ebb was Arkansas judge Williamson Oldham, who had been acquainted with him in Tennessee. When-ever he saw Houston in Cantonment Gibson, the fallen governor was habitually in Cherokee dress and refused to even speak English with anyone.[20]

· · ·

Six weeks after he wrote to Jackson describing himself as the most unhappy man alive, Houston might have expected to hear some word of comfort from Old Hickory about his personal extremity. This he did, in a letter dated June 21, 1829, wherein Jackson expressed his shock at the change. When last they saw one another, on January 18, Jackson's grief at parting was "as much as I could well bear," but, "I then viewed you as on the brink of happiness, and rejoiced. About to be united in marriage to a beautiful young lady . . .—you the Governor of the State, and holding the affections of the people. . . . What reverse of fortune! How unstable are all human affairs!" If, as it is sometimes alleged, Jackson and Houston conspired in the ruin of Eliza Allen to spring Houston to Texas, the intimate correspondence between the two confederates is a field barren of evidence. Elsewhere in the letter, Jackson clarified exactly what it was he had heard against Houston. "It has been communicated to me that you had the *illegal enterprise* in view of conquering Texas; that you had declared that you would, in less than two years, be *emperor* of that country by conquest. I must really have thought you deranged to have believed you had so wild a scheme in contemplation, and particularly when it was communicated that the physical force to be employed was the Cherokee Indians. Indeed, my dear Sir, I cannot believe you have any such chimerical visionary scheme in view. Your pledge of honor to the contrary is a sufficient guarantee that you will never engage in any enterprise injurious to your country that would tarnish your fame."[21] From Jackson's tut-tut that Houston's word of honor was good against the rumors, it is unclear whether Jackson was acknowledging Houston's anguished letter as sufficient proof or if he was hinting that a further disclaimer would be welcome. Marquis James assumed the latter while admitting that he found no additional correspondence on the subject.[22] If he was right, then Houston must have stopped to consider Jackson's implied mistrust. If Jackson truly did not believe the story, he would not have required Houston's further word of honor in surety against it. And Jackson's subsequent acts betray a frame of mind that he might well have believed at least part of the allegation. To his own notebook he committed, "As a precautionary measure I directed the Secretary of War to write and enclose Mr. Pope, Govr of Arkansas the extract [of Green's story] and instruct him if such illegal project should be discovered to exist to adopt prompt measures to put it down and give the government the earliest intelligence of such illegal enterprise with the names of all concerned therein."[23]

Jackson also, apparently, had Houston's mail opened. James asserted this without evidence in *The Raven*, but certainly Houston was aware during the early months of his exile that his mail had been opened by somebody.[24] At the end of the year, in writing Tennessee ally John Overton of his travel plans, he cautioned, "If you do me the favor to write, be pleased to enclose it to Judge White's care! If this were not done the curious would open my letter as they have done this summer before they reach me."[25] Could Houston have known that "the curious" were the spying minions of the eagle-eyed Jackson? That is doubtful. But all evidence of this period strengthens a view that if Jackson and Houston conspired about Texas, they were not doing it yet. It is clear that Jackson did not send Houston west, but once he was there, it is entirely possible that the cogwheels began cranking in Jackson's calculating mind. Less than two weeks before writing to Houston, the president wrote to Judge Overton, "I have long since been aware of the importance of Texas to the United States, and of the real necessity of extending our boundary west of the Sabine. . . . I shall keep my eye on this object & the first propitious moment make the attempt to regain the Territory as far south & west as the great Desert." Sam Houston and Texas were certainly in Jackson's mind at the same time, but if that set his mind working, his exiled prince had no inkling. On the contrary, if Houston sensed his loss of stature with Jackson, it could only have intensified the early agony of his exile.[26]

Houston's Cherokees, however, were doing more to make him feel at home. In reward for past service and in expectation of more service to come, and perhaps also in some fear that he might undertake that expedition to the far Columbia River country he mentioned from time to time, his adopted people granted him an extraordinary mark of favor on October 21, 1829: "In consideration of his former acquaintance with and services rendered to the Indians, and his present disposition to improve their condition and benefit their scircumstances . . . , we do as a committee appointed by principal chief John Jolly, Solemnly, firmly [illegible] Grant to him forever all the rights, privileges and immunities of a Citizen of the Cherokee Nation." John Jolly made the requisite "x" between the words "his mark," as did Walter Webber and Aaron Price, president and vice president of the committee.[27] The Cherokee chiefs, it turned out, had a specific service in mind. A delegation was forming up to go to Washington to negotiate a variety of issues—land surveys, ration contracts, further conflict with the Osages, and the anticipated arrival of more Cherokees from the East—and the best way to utilize the Raven's influence with Jackson was to send him, and send him as a citizen of the nation.

The final days of 1829 found Sam Houston on the deck of the riverboat *Amazon* on his way to Washington, watching the dark forest bank of Tennessee slip by. It kindled feelings both melancholy and reflective, and he penned a letter to Judge Overton, who had visited him at the Nashville Inn immediately after Eliza left him. "In prosperity you regarded me well, and generously," he wrote, "but when the *darkest*, direst hour of human misery was passing by, you called upon me to *sustain* me by . . . philosophy, and friendship. The hour of anguish has passed by, and my soul feels . . . gratitude to the man who dared to lend the moral aid of his presence." Houston went on to warn Overton that there would be much unfounded speculation on the nature of his trip but assured him he was not going to solicit any favors from Jackson. "It is probable that I may return thro' Tennessee, and if I should, I hope to see you, and your family, in health and happiness," at which time he would discuss the nature of his Washington business.[28] As soon as he reached Fredericktown, Maryland, Houston dashed a note off to cousin Jack, and they had their reunion the next evening over dinner at Brown's Indian Queen Hotel, where Houston placed himself in residence.

He reunited with Jackson at a reception for the diplomatic corps; Houston, as the at least unofficial Cherokee ambassador and citizen of their nation, wore traditional dress. The reaction was vastly different from what he received from Calhoun in 1818: Jackson embraced him like a son restored. As Old Hickory's other protégés kept the Old Chief suspicious of Houston's activities, official contact between the two fell off, but they genuinely cared for each other. Jackson sent a private letter, suggesting that Houston might do well to locate permanently in Arkansas. Houston rejected this because "in that Territory there is no field for distinction—it is fraught with *factions*; and if my object were to obtain wealth, it must be done by fraud, and peculation upon the Government, and many perjuries would be necessary!" He noted instead that many of his old Tennessee friends were settling about Natchez, Mississippi, and he might be happier there.[29] (This from the private letters of the two men who were supposed to be scheming on how to filibuster Texas.) Now together again, Houston discovered the perfection of his timing, for Jackson had had a savage falling out with Calhoun over matters both official and personal. Jackson had learned, in that Southern gentleman's way, that Calhoun had tried to have him disciplined for his actions in Florida, and then the degree of offense was trebled when Calhoun and his wife refused to receive John Eaton's new bride, the former Peggy O'Neal, because of the common knowledge of their relationship before they married.

The Cherokee business required several weeks of letters and meetings, during which Sam Houston found himself again in society; the *Cherokee Phoenix* reported on March 4 that the Raven now "mingles in social intercourse and gaiety as freely as formerly." Houston renewed contacts with New York friends, and unsure how much traveling he would do, friends supplied him with letters of introduction to important people in Boston.[30] However, the year 1830, which began with such optimism, soon soured in a terrible way. One of the issues under discussion was the removal of the remaining Cherokees from the Appalachians. When they went west, these people would require rations, which meant that contracts must be bid. Houston, having witnessed the appalling scale of agency corruption already existing in the Indian Territory, decided he would bid on the contract to see that the natives were adequately and fairly fed. Arranging the money through a New York friend, financier John Van Fossen, Houston bid to supply the Cherokees at thirteen cents per ration of beef. It was neither the high nor the low of the thirteen bids received— they ranged from seven up to eighteen cents—but Houston's involvement touched off a furor. What he had done was rap the same kind of hornets' nest of entrenched grafters that he had disturbed as Hiwassee subagent in 1817. John Hamtramack was perhaps only the worst of the five crooked agents whom the Indians, through Houston's influence with Eaton, managed to get fired. When the corrupt agents used their connections to color Houston as a cheat and profiteer, it was something he had seen before, and he handled it in the same way: he kept his papers in order and let them come.

Hamtramack had an ally in the administration in the person of Duff Green, who went to see Jackson and "warn" him of Houston's swindling. The Indian beef ration, said Green, could easily be filled at six cents per ration. Even Jackson was wise to this sort of deceit by now and asked sharply, "Will *you* take it at *ten*?" Green declined, and the president sarcastically upped the bid to twelve cents; it was the beginning of the end for Duff Green's influence with Jackson. The irony was that the contemplated new treaty was never ratified, and no contracts were let to anyone, so Houston found himself embroiled in a huge controversy over nothing and at great embarrassment to the administration.[31] The year got worse from there. Houston left Washington in mid-spring; once it became common knowledge that he intended returning via Tennessee, and having been quoted that he could defeat Billy Carroll if he reentered politics there, the Carroll faction, including the Allens, were terrified that Ulysses was returning to claim his house. In their anxiety to keep Houston in his political grave, and though it had been a year since the awful separation, they decided to resurrect the Eliza issue. The Allens hustled Eliza off to relatives in Carthage, thirty miles farther up the Cumberland from Gallatin, just in case Houston tried to see her. They then formed a committee of gentlemen who were proud to say that they had known Eliza since her infancy, had investigated the circumstances of the marriage's collapse, and, having found in her favor, were bound in honor to vindicate her—as though the issue was ever in doubt with them:

> It appears that very shortly after the marriage Gov. Houston became jealous of his wife. . . . the committee are not informed that he made any specific charges, only that he believed that she was . . . void of the affections which a wife ought to bear toward her husband. The Committee cannot doubt that that he rendered his wife unhappy by his unfounded jealousies and his repeated suspicions of her coldness and want of attachment, and that she was constrained, by a sense of duty to herself and her family, to separate from her infatuated husband and return to her parents . . . since which time she has remained in a state of dejection and despondency. . . .
>
> The committee have no hesitation in saying that he is a deluded man: that his suspicions were groundless: that his unfortunate wife is now and ever has been in the possession of a character unimpeachable: and that she is an innocent and injured woman.

The committee of gentlemen went on to attach the complete text of Houston's desperate "What is to be done?" letter to John Allen begging the family's reinstatement. The committee had not the nerve to publish their findings until after Houston left Nashville, even though his departure was delayed more than a week by chills and fever. But once released to the public, the members enjoined every newspaper within beckoning, in justice to Eliza, to publish everything, which many did in late May, to Houston's further humiliation as he returned to Wigwam Neosho.[32]

And still the year got worse. No sooner was he back home than he began exchanging poison-pen articles with detractors in the *Arkansas Gazette* over the rations contract that never actually materialized. Although the commandant at Cantonment Gibson, Matthew Arbuckle, gave Houston credit during the summer for again preventing Cherokee and Creek hotheads from going to war in Texas, the two men got into a rancorous dispute over whether Houston's Cherokee citizenship allowed him to circumvent regulations that governed other whites who wished to import liquor into the Indian nations.[33] Houston had placed an order for four barrels of Monongahela whiskey and one barrel each of corn whiskey, cognac, gin, rum, and wine. Houston declared he was importing the spirits for his own use, and Arbuckle, believing that no one man could need the amount contemplated, was sure he meant to sell it. The argument reached Asst. Secretary of War P. G. Randolph, who danced around the issue with a decree that Houston was not to use his "citizenship" to evade trade regulations. Randolph allowed him to import the liquor, but he had to fill out an application and post a bond first. While Arbuckle may have been right in his suspicions, it is certain that by the end of 1830, Houston's personal consumption of alcohol was disgusting to even the Cherokees, whose tolerance for souses was well known. Even Houston's Indian name, the Raven, which he always carried so proudly, was occasionally replaced by a taunt less flattering: Oo-tse-tee Ar-dee-tah-skee, Big Drunk. Adding a little insult, the name was not even Cherokee but Osage, thus not only belittling him but also denying his Cherokee identity as well. Through it all, left to run the trading post and manage the house and garden and orchard and nurse him, was Diana Rogers, who seems never to have complained.

In mid-December Houston reopened contact with Jackson, the vehicle being, curiously, an occasion to go back on his word. "When you were elected President of the U. States, I assured you, that I would not annoy you with recommendations in favor of persons who might wish to obtain office, or patronage from you." In reversing himself he was moved by the plight of Capt. Nathaniel Pryor, who had crossed the continent with Lewis and Clark and had fought under Jackson at New Orleans. He had lived as a trader among the Osage Indians the past ten years and was their acting subagent. The secretary of war had assured Houston when he was in Washington that Pryor would be considered for a permanent appointment there, but officials awarded the job to someone else. Pryor, Houston urged Jackson, "has done more to tame,—and pacificate the dispositions of the Osages . . . and has done more to promote the authority of the U. States . . . than any person could have supposed." He was a man of honor and bravery, impoverished when Indians stole his stock of furs. "A vacancy has lately occurred," he informed the president, "and I do most *earnestly*, solicit the appointment for him."

The interesting thing about Houston's intercession for him goes beyond the parallel of Pryor's posture as a beleaguered subagent. He died before Houston's recommendation bore any result and was later characterized as "a man of fine character and great ability, but he yielded to the fascination of free life among the Indians and made no effective use of his talents."[34] One wonders if Houston perceived the same thing about Pryor and saw himself headed down the same road. While 1830 began with such promise, it had been a rotten year for Houston. Even his mail became irritating. One Jonathan Stump, whose letter addressed "Sam Houston, Arkensaws Territory," miraculously found its destination, briefly expressed his sympathies but then went on to his real need, to know whether Houston had heard any stories of gold deposits on "Sinkin Creek," where "Your cenceare friend" was thinking of removing.[35] If he was in any mood to reply I have not found it. Speaking of "cenceare friends," Houston was relieved at year's end to receive a newsy letter from his cheerful New York friend Nicholas Dean, who demanded of him, "in the Shelter and the Solitude of your wigwam,—place your writing materials before you, and devote an hour to one who is now, as always, your . . . sincere friend."[36]

During 1831, profiting by Pryor's example, Sam Houston realized that he was wasting himself, and he set about shaking off his melancholy. Jackson, however, was still not persuaded of Houston's stability. If it was not the president's men who had been snooping in Houston's letters in 1829, they began to now, for in the same week that Houston sought help for Pryor, Jackson wrote anew to the Arkansas territorial secretary, William S. Fulton, to keep watch over Houston, and several years later Fulton acknowledged to Jackson that he had made "personal and confidential investigations" into Houston's affairs and found no evidence of Texas filibustering.[37]

This latest round of surveillance took place subsequent to Jackson's receiving a third story of alleged Houston machinations against Texas. One Dr. Robert Mayo, a social gadfly on the Washington scene, had lodged at Brown's Hotel the previous

February (1830) on the same floor as Houston. Mayo, seeking to "do him justice . . . relative to abandoning his family . . . readily became intimate" friends with Houston, so he claimed, and Houston divulged his nefarious plan to wrest Texas from Mexico, even offering Mayo a surgeon's post in the expedition.[38] Marquis James accepted the Mayo account in its most salient points to help him conclude that Houston was indeed up to something. Llerena Friend thought it suggestive of a hoax.[39] Aside from the premise being a tall one—that Houston took Mayo into his inmost confidence concerning a matter from which he had excluded his most trusted friends— Mayo's letter to Jackson itself reads like a bad melodrama ("Ah, says he, that is a secret"). Mayo deserves little credence as an honest source.

President Jackson, however, was sufficiently worried about all the smoke that he wondered if there could be no fire and had the watch on Houston renewed. Yet there was even more smoke. Some had wafted to Missouri as early as August of 1829, motivating Thomas Hart Benton, Houston's old colonel from the Thirty-ninth Infantry and now a U.S. senator, to write his former subordinate to "call upon me freely if I can be of service to you. I do not know what your plans may be, but . . . our South Western boundary . . . and the public lands, are the two levers to move public sentiment in the West. If you have ulterior views your *tongue* and *pen* should dwell incessantly on these two great topics. Write to me."[40] In this instance, it appeared to be Benton who was doing the agitating, for he enclosed to Houston two pamphlets of his own authorship on the boundary subject and enlisted Houston's aid in getting them published in Houston's locale.

As an issue of historical investigation, there are ingots in both pans of the balance regarding Houston's interest in Texas during his western Cherokee sojourn. Even in his long, wretched letter to Jackson of May 1829, Houston did not specifically disavow any idea of Texas; in fact, the name "Texas" did not appear. He protested that he intended nothing dishonorable or that would involve or endanger the United States; in his mind that would have left room for a Texas scheme. Then there is the account of a man named Morrell in Tennessee, quoting Houston's own assertion that he intended to lead his Cherokee and Tennessee friends in establishing a "little two-horse republic" in Texas and be its first president.[41] This account, however, was not contemporaneous with the events. Houston apparently said this many years later to a Baptist deacon in Nashville at a time when Houston's capacity to embellish his personal résumé was well known.

But from John Wharton, who was supposed to be intimate to such an enterprise, there is a letter to Houston: "I have heard you intended an expedition against Texas. I suppose, if it is true, you will let your Nashville friends know of it." John Wharton was the brother of William, who according to Daniel Donelson was Houston's advance man for starting a revolution in Texas. If Houston had anything afoot, John Wharton would probably have heard of it from William. A second letter from John after he arrived in Texas and had a chance to consult with William, however, shows no greater hint of plotting: "You can get a grant of land," he urged Houston to relocate, "be surrounded by your friends, and what may not the coming of time bring about?"[42]

The John Wharton letters may be the last word on how much forethought Houston gave to the "conquest" of Texas: his destiny was there, somehow. He had investments there, having put money into Texas colonization plans after Mexico began inviting American empresarios to organize settlements. Several friends had resettled there, and Cherokees returning from Texas had alluded to pending rebellion, which he doubtless interpreted as opportunity.[43] He was finished in Tennessee, and it was only a matter of time before his Wigwam Neosho could no longer contain him. Where else but Texas could he go and see what the coming of time might bring about?

But the time was not ripe. Houston had further to sink in self-pity and drink and failure before he could rise and find a destiny. He sobered up long enough to sign as witness to a treaty between the Creeks and Osages that he had negotiated, but when he ran for a seat on the Cherokee National Council only ten days later, to his shock he was defeated. Crestfallen, he talked about relocating among the Choctaws. Consideration of that idea was delayed when in August 1831 Houston received news from his family that his mother was dying, and he hastened to East Tennessee to be with the remarkable woman with whom he had always had such a strained relationship. He arrived timely and was at her bedside when she passed away.

Word of Houston's return to Nashville spread like wildfire among his former partisans, several of whom wrote out on June 30 a florid welcome and testimonial. Referring to his exile as his "immolation," they wished to offer "a humble token . . . of our undiminished confidence and esteem for your character as a private citizen, our gratitude and veneration for your signal services . . . permit us for ourselves and in behalf of a large portion of your fellow citizens, to request the pleasure of your participation in a public dinner."

"Gentlemen," the former governor responded the following day, "your favour of yesterday has been received, and I thank you for the invitation so kindly given." He reciprocated their regards with equal flower, but still unable to face Nashville society, he declined the honor without explanation.[44] While in town he did, however, pose for a portrait to be painted of himself, clad as Gaius Marius in the ruins of Carthage. And, in a gesture of magnanimity worthy of a Roman consul, on July 13, 1831, he took out an advertisement in the *Nashville Banner* and *Nashville Whig* in the form of a sarcastic proclamation:

> Now, know all men by these presents, that I, Sam Houston, "late Governor of the State of Tennessee," do hereby declare to all *scoundrels whomsoever*, that they are authorized to accuse, defame, calumniate, slander, vilify and libel me to any extent, in *personal* or *private* abuse. And . . . I will in *no wise* hold them responsible to me in law, or honor. . . .
>
> Be it known for the especial encouragement of all scoundrels hereafter, as well as those who have already been engaged, that I do solemnly propose, on the first day of April next, to give to the author of the most *elegant, refined and ingenious lie or calumny*, a handsome gilt copy (Bound in sheep) of the Kentucky Reporter, or a snug plain copy of the United States Telegraph (bound in dog) since its commencement.

Given under my hand and private seal (having no seal of office) at
Nashville, in the State of Tennessee.
SAM HOUSTON[45]

The two journals mentioned had been particularly active in their cooperation
with Carroll and the Allens.

After another stint at Wigwam Neosho, Houston left the Indians again in mid-
December 1831 bound for Washington via New Orleans, again on Cherokee business. His friend, the Creek chief Opothleyahola, gave him for the trip a hunting
knife and a buckskin coat with a beaver collar. When the Mississippi steamboat
churned up to the landing at the mouth of the White River, Houston was seen
mounted on an impressive stallion. There happened to be on board the French
essayist and social critic Alexis de Tocqueville with a traveling companion. Tocqueville had lately been in Memphis, where the sight of David Crockett convinced him
that "when the right of suffrage is universal . . . it's singular how low and how far
wrong the people can go." News of Houston's presence on board raced through the
boat, and Tocqueville listened to a run-through of his misadventure, which solidi-
fied the impression first created by Crockett. "This man was once Governor of
Tennesse," he wrote. "Since, he abandoned his wife after making her suffer, so they
say, very ill treatment. He took refuge with the Indians, married among them, and
has become one of their chiefs. . . . He had reason to complain of his wife, others
say he acted very badly towards her. What's certain is that he left Tennesse, crossed
the Mississipi and retired among the Creeks in the district of Arkansas. There he was
adopted by one of the chiefs, and is said to have married his daughter. Since then
he has been living in the middle of the wilderness, half European and half savage."
He avoided Houston for four days before his curiosity got the better of him.

Without putting it in so many words, the Frenchman rather brazenly asked
Houston how a man like him had ever managed to be elected to office. Houston
answered evenly that the people recognized him as being one of them who had risen
by his own exertions. One imagines that Houston put him at ease with pleasant
memories of Lafayette. Tocqueville decided that Houston's greatest contribution to
his diary would be his observations on native customs, and quizzed him accordingly.

"Have you often seen Christian Indians?"

"Seldom," he answered curtly. "My opinion is that to send Missionaries among
them is a very poor way to go about civilizing the Indians." Tocqueville was probably unaware that Houston had been embroiled in controversies with missionaries
to the Indians ever since taking up residence in Wigwam Neosho. His principal difference with them was over education. The more tight vested of the missionaries
wanted to educate the natives to emulate white people, and Houston, who was a
friend of Sequoyah and had told him that his Cherokee alphabet would be worth
more than a double handful of gold to every person in the tribe, agreed with chiefs
who wanted native traditions taught in native tongues. It was a stunningly modern
view (but one that gains him little credit with revisionists who are invested in
depicting him as a racist).[46] Houston might have taken the opportunity to lash

out at the whole missionary endeavor for Tocqueville's benefit, but he did not. What he had come to realize was that ministers, like all Christians, come in two kinds. There are those who are narrow, pinched, and legalistic, like the two Allen family beadles who had denied him communion during his despair over Eliza, and there are those who convert with good works and elevated example. His Cherokees were exposed to missionaries of both kinds. Houston was very cordial with Dr. Marcus Palmer of the Fairfield Mission, whom he characterized as "a useful and intelligent Gentleman, and worth all the missionaries in the Nation. . . . If he can be assisted it will be well for the Indians." And on the opposite pole was the more influential Cephas Washburn, who once wrote highly: "We regard the residence of such a man as Governor Houston among the Indians, as a most injurious circumstance. He is vicious to a fearful extent, and hostile to Christians and Christianity. This I would not wish to have known as coming from me, as he has very considerable influence." Indeed, at the very time Houston sat chatting with Tocqueville, Washburn was busy writing letters cutting the ground out from under Houston's attempts to have one of the more obnoxious missions, Union, moved from Cherokee ground.[47]

Cultural advancement, Houston had decided, must take place before belief can have any meaning. "In my opinion," Houston concluded for Tocqueville, "one should first of all try to tear the Indians from their wandering life and encourage them to cultivate the earth. The introduction of the Christian religion would be the natural consequence." The only exception to this he had seen was that some Indians took a shine to Catholicism. "It strikes their senses and appeals to their imagination."

Sam Houston had lived among the Cherokees as boy and man for a total of five years, and while he respected them and their way of life profoundly, he perceived their shortcomings clearly and had no hesitation in imparting his views to Tocqueville. Probably still smarting over his defeat for the National Council, he believed he saw the Cherokees adopting some of the more odious penchants of white politics, favoring birth and breeding over ability, but he commented favorably on their system of justice, which whites viewed as primitive. What interested Tocqueville the most was the future of the American Indians, and he asked Houston's assessment of the removal policy. "There were," he answered, "and are still, in the interior of [the] southern United States several half-civilized Indian nations . . . who are slowing up the progress that this part of the Union is capable of. Congress, consequently, as much in the interest of the southern States as in that of the Indians also, has conceived the project of transporting them all with their consent into a country which would for ever remain essentially Indian. . . . The United States have sworn, by the most solemn oaths, never to sell the lands contained within these limits, and never to allow the white race to work itself in by any means."

This was an honest answer. Houston saw that the government was removing the natives from the Southeast for its own advantage, but he believed that it was in the best interest of the natives to cooperate. He was blinded by his faith in the government's fidelity, conceding as much in the Senate many years later in his outraged speeches on further land grabs from the Indians. But Tocqueville saw what he did not and led him on: "Do you think that this arrangement is not provisional, and that the Indians will not soon be forced to retreat?"

"No," answered Houston flatly, "I believe that the Indian nations of the South will find a refuge and civilize themselves there, if the government wishes to take the trouble to encourage civilization among them." The former agent added that their isolation, to their benefit, would make it more difficult to smuggle liquor among them. "Brandy," he concluded, "is the great cause of destruction for the aborigines of America." He was more right than he knew.

Tocqueville was pursuing a thesis that the American Indian was doomed by the greed and landlust of the federal government, but he could not get Houston to say it and soon changed the subject. He left Houston, more impressed for having conversed with him but still dubious of the efficacy of popular suffrage.[48] Houston reached New Orleans on January 4, 1832, and a month later was in Washington to help lead yet another Cherokee delegation. Almost from the time he ensconced himself in Brown's Indian Queen Hotel, however, events began to carry him in a new direction altogether.

6

FROM STANBERY TO TEXAS

On March 31, 1832, one William Stanbery—one of a grab bag of variant spellings— a representative from Ohio, rose on the floor of Congress to attack the Jackson administration's Indian policy. "Was not the late Secretary of War," he asked at one point during a rather long speech, "removed because of his attempt fraudulently to give Governor Houston the contract for Indian rations?"[1]

The reference to him was at most oblique, but when Houston read of it on April 2 in the *National Intelligencer*, it brought him to the House foyer the next day, mad as a fighting cock, prowling in wait for Stanbery to come out. His fellow Tennesseean James Knox Polk calmed him enough to lead him outside. But shortly thereafter Houston prevailed on another Tennessee friend, Congressman Cave Johnson, to deliver a letter reciting the offensive quote and stating: "The object of this note is to ascertain whether my name was used by you in debate, and, if so, whether your remarks have been correctly quoted. . . . I hope you will find it convenient to reply without delay."[2] The note was less polite than it sounded, and that it was the first stage of a challenge was made certain by Houston extracting Johnson's word that if Stanbery refused the note, Johnson would "not assume the quarrel himself." Stanbery must have been alerted to Houston's proximity. Acting under the complicated etiquette of dueling, Stanbery refused to receive the note; if he did not read it, Houston could not call him out.

Houston fumed for ten more days. On the evening of the thirteenth, he was in social company with Felix Grundy, who finally possessed the Senate seat Jackson had been angling for him; Sen. Alexander Buckner of Missouri; and John Blair, representative from Tennessee. Strolling up Pennsylvania Avenue, Blair recognized Stanbery approaching and vanished. Houston accosted him, "Are you Stanbery?"

Like Houston, the Ohio congressman was a large and powerful man. "Yes, sir."

"Then you are a damned rascal!" Houston whacked him over the head with his hickory cane, cut from the grounds of the Hermitage, once and twice and then multiple times.

Stanbery shouted, "Oh, don't!" He tried to flee but Houston tackled him, striking him repeatedly, though hampered in the struggle because his right arm was useless due to the wounds received at Tohopeka. Stanbery managed to draw a pistol, pressed the barrel against Houston's chest, and pulled the trigger, but it misfired, and Houston gave him a royal caning on the head and body, which ended by Houston lifting Stanbery's legs in the air and striking him (to be delicate) "elsewhere."[3]

In the quiet decorum of Congress the next day, Speaker of the House Andrew Stevenson unfolded the following note: "Sir: I was waylaid in the street, near to my boarding house, last night, about 8 o'clock, and attacked, knocked down by a bludgeon, and severely bruised and wounded, by Samuel Houston, late of Tennessee, for words spoken in my place in the House of Representatives, by reason of which I am confined to my bed and unable to discharge my duties in the House, and attend to the interests of my constituents. I communicate this information to you, and request that you lay it before the House."[4]

This unlawful behavior went beyond simple battery; it was a violation of congressional privilege to call a member to task for words uttered on the floor. And it was clear from the fact that Stanbery had sworn the allegations before a Justice of the Peace that he intended the House to vindicate him. Duff Green could hardly believe his good fortune to have such material for his newspaper. "Most Daring Outrage and Assault!" was his headline. Within the space of five days, the House scheduled a trial; Francis Scott Key, the author of "The Star Spangled Banner," was engaged as defense counsel; and Houston was interrogated by Congress. The trial itself deteriorated into a political show between the Jackson and anti-Jackson factions, with questions being objected to and answers demanded as well as frequent votes taken on how to proceed. Old Hickory was fit to be tied and advanced Houston the money to buy a proper suit to replace the Cherokee garb he habitually wore.

Final arguments were scheduled for May 7; Key's opening statement had been mediocre, and he was too ill—some accounts say hung over—to perform at the summations, which Houston decided to do himself. Throughout his life, Sam Houston was almost never afraid to make a speech, but he was keenly aware of how much was riding on this closing argument: not his guilt or innocence, really, but public perception of him and his standing with the people. After three years in the wilderness, a future—of some kind—could be reinstated if he performed up to his abilities. But everything rode on the morrow's effort, and it spooked him. He sat up late the night before, drinking. For company he had, remarkably, the Speaker of the House, Andrew Stevenson, who was presiding over his trial. Also in on the party were Grundy and, oddly enough, Tennessee congressman Balie Peyton, not yet recruited by Eliza Allen Houston as her champion. James K. Polk was invited, and attended, but being a bit of a schoolmarm where alcohol was concerned, he left early. Houston drank his companions under the table and had a bellboy fetch a barber, for whom he opened a drawer and pointed out a pistol and a purse. He directed the barber to bring his shaving kit at dawn with a cup of coffee. "If the coffee does not stick when I drink it," said Houston, "take the pistol and shoot me and the gold is yours." By one account, Houston threw up the first cup of coffee, but the second one stuck. Freshly shaven and in elegant new clothes, he headed to the Capitol to reclaim himself.[5]

Most Houston biographies content themselves with a quote from the trumpeting oratory of his final conclusion, but a redux of the whole defense summation, windy and repetitive as it was, reveals Houston's intellectual powers undimmed by three years' descent into living as "Big Drunk." He opened with some rather poetic contrition, that while he believed his actions were justified, he blamed no one but himself for his present troubles: "Sir,"

> I seek no sympathies, nor need;
> The thorns which I have reaped are of the tree
> I planted; they have torn me, and I bleed.

It would have been pointless to deny that the attack had taken place, but, the first element in the allegations, that he was "accused of lying in wait," he insisted simply was not true. "The honorable Senator from Missouri [Mr. Buckner] has testified to the House that I was not apprised beforehand of any such meeting—that it was purely accidental, and wholly unexpected—that the action took place under a heated state of feeling, and was prompted by his arraigning me, before this honorable body, and his subsequent outrages upon my . . . character!" Second, he argued, he had been unarmed. It was Stanbery who had pulled the pistol, not himself. "Sir, had I contemplated any such attack, I should have been prepared for the purpose."

In the third place: "It has been said by my accuser that the attack made upon him was for words uttered in this place . . . , but it was not for the words uttered here that I assailed him. It was for publishing in the *Intelligencer* libellous matter, to my injury; such as no member of this honorable court . . . would ever submit to. . . . It is well known that a private citizen has no opportunity of reply to an attack that may be made upon him on this floor." The grounds of Stanbery's attack had been disproved during the trial itself, he alleged, and therefore, "the proof has failed. The proof was on him. I was not called on to prove a negative." He was sensible of Stanbery's congressional privileges, he continued, and days before the altercation, "I therefore addressed to him a note. It was my privilege to do so. However humble I may be . . . it was still my privilege, in common with the humblest citizen that treads American soil, to address an inquiry to the honorable member. I asked of him, respectfully, and in language to which none can object, whether that publication was his, and in what circumstances it had been made. Sir, he did not deign to reply. . . . He said that I had no right." And that, Houston argued, "was assuming a higher ground than that of his privilege." And if he was outside his privilege, his charges before the House must fail.

Moreover, Stanbery had been inconsistent in whether he had actually accused Houston of fraud. "My accuser declared, in reply to the first interrogatory put to him, that it had not been his object to impute a fraud. On afterthought, however, he changed his position." And furthermore, Houston asserted, he was not being allowed a judgment by his peers. "I am arraigned before a court which is standing on its own privileges—which arraigns me in its own case." And still further, what was the nature of privilege? Was it the law of the land or merely a House rule? "If it exists at all, it lies as a little spark deeply covered; not even the smoke of it has appeared. . . . Where is the privilege?" he demanded. "Show it to me, that I may obey the law. If such a discretion is in your hand, . . . and to be regulated by your discretion alone," then the Congress had taken unto itself the powers of Draco or Caligula. He followed this with a lecture on parliamentary history and the evils of the Star Chamber, similar abuses with which the House was toying. "While gentlemen seem so greatly to dread the tyranny of a single individual, and appear to consider it as a matter of course that it must be some Caesar, some Cromwell, or some Bonaparte, who is to overthrow our liberties, I must . . . dissent from that opinion. All history will show that no tyrant ever grasped the reins of power till they were put into his hands by corrupt and obsequious legislative bodies."

The packed gallery followed his arguments eagerly. At one point a young lady exclaimed from the gallery that she had rather be Houston, a culprit at the bar, than his accusers. Houston looked up and noted her, a Miss Smallwood, and later presented her a ring in thanks.[6] Beginning his summation, Houston asserted that while he, unlike his accusers, never sought to place himself above the laws, he did claim no less legal protection than was extended to all. From that point he launched into a window-rattling finale of oratory that became an instant sensation:

> Would it not have been strange that I should seek to dishonor my country through her representatives, when I have ever been found ready, at her call, to do and suffer in her service? Yes. . . . Whatever gentlemen may have imagined, so long as that proud emblem of my country's liberties, with its stripes and its stars [pointing to the American flag over the portrait of Lafayette] shall wave in this Hall of American legislators, so long shall it cast its sacred protection over the personal rights of every American citizen. . . .
>
> So long as that flag shall bear aloft its glittering stars—bearing them amidst the din of battle, and waving them triumphantly above the storms of the ocean, so long, I trust, shall the rights of American citizens be preserved safe and unimpaired, and transmitted as a sacred legacy from one generation to another, till discord shall wreck the spheres—the grand march of time shall cease—and not one fragment of all creation be left to chafe on the bosom of eternity's waves![7]

The applause was tumultuous. As Houston left the hall, America's foremost Shakespearean actor, Junius Booth, rushed up to embrace him. "Houston," he exclaimed, "take my laurels!"[8]

Houston's defense of himself in the Stanbery case was adroit and lawyerly; it made the most of arguments in his favor—and fomented some other plausible-sounding ones as well. The problem was, of course, that he was guilty as sin. It may well be that, as he maintained, he took Stanbery to task not for what he uttered in the House but for what he saw printed in the *Intelligencer*. However, that paper routinely published verbatim the proceedings on the House floor. That he had encountered Stanbery outside his hotel by pure accident was a plausible claim, but in latching on to it, Houston did what any good lawyer would do—challenge, obfuscate, inflame.

The debate in the House spanned four days. Stanbery's partisans tried to pass an amendment denying Houston the floor, a privilege routinely granted former members. James Knox Polk defeated that measure, but he could not prevent Houston's conviction by a vote of 106 to 89. The former congressman was sentenced to be brought to the well of the House and reprimanded by the Speaker on the following Monday, May 14. At the appointed time, Andrew Stevenson summoned Houston, who came, accompanied by Congressman William Archer of Virginia. Houston bowed formally, and let Archer speak for him, requesting Stevenson to allow Houston's protest of the judgment to be entered in the House journal:

> The accused, now at the bar of the House, asks leave respectfully to state,
> That he understands he is now brought before the House, to receive a reprimand from the Speaker, in execution of the sentence pronounced upon him.
> Was he to submit in silence to such a sentence, it might imply that he recognized the authority of the House to impose it.
> He cannot consent that it shall be thus implied. . . .
> That although he believes the whole proceeding against him, as well as the sentence he now objects to, unwarranted by the constitution of his country, yet [he will] suffer in silent patience, whatever the House may think proper to enforce.

The protest made, Speaker Stevenson opened his part by complimenting Houston on his intelligence and character. "I forbear to say more," he intoned, "than to pronounce the judgment of the House . . . which is that you be reprimanded at this bar by the Speaker, and . . . I do reprimand you accordingly."

After weeks of partisan lightning and oratorical thunder, Stevenson provided an anticlimax of stunning smallness. If there was a loser in all this, it was Stanbery, who was still angry as could be, and if there was a winner it was Houston. Technically he lost the case, but he emerged a national figure once more. "I was dying out," he admitted many years later, "and had they taken me before a Justice of the Peace and fined me ten dollars for assault and battery, they would have killed me. But they gave me a national tribunal for a theatre, and set me up again."[9]

Not content with Houston's "conviction," Stanbery and the anti-Jacksonites took another tack. Using congressional hearings to generate hurtful publicity against those who cannot be struck any other way was a weapon no less familiar to the 1830s than it is in the present day, and they moved for, and won, a committee of seven members to investigate Houston and Eaton for fraud in the Indian rations affair; the chairman was William Stanbery of Ohio. As these hearings droned on, it was apparent that 1817 was repeating itself, and Houston defended himself in the same way: his facts were straight and his papers were in order, and he meekly and promptly produced all the documents demanded of him. It became increasingly obvious that Houston and Eaton were innocent and that the hearings would backfire. Almost simultaneously with the committee's resolution of acquittal, the tenacious Stanbery struck yet again, securing a criminal-assault indictment against Houston in the District of Columbia's federal district court.

This trial did not take place until the end of June, presided over by Chief Justice William Cranch, a distinguished jurist (only two of his rulings were ever reversed) who had led the District Court of Columbia since his appointment by President Jefferson. "The old sinner fined me $500 and costs of suit!" Houston griped to a new business associate. "This is *tough* enough, in my opinion." The ruling "was made solely on party grounds, and I will bear it, for the sake of *Party*!" But to be fair, Cranch gave him until the following winter to come up with the money, and Houston did not consider himself seriously discommoded. "I will arrange some money matters and be off for the West." Only one other matter nettled Houston before he could get out of town. Just as he had come to Washington with an angry squint at John C. Calhoun ten years previous, Houston was trying to think of some venue to get in one more shot at him before he left. "It may be," he wrote, "that I will touch [him] off . . . before I leave here!"[10]

He did get in a parting shot a couple of weeks later, but it was not directed at Calhoun. After the House hearings exonerated Houston, one of Stanbery's partisans on the committee, John Leeds Kerr, stated that regardless of the official outcome, he was satisfied that the facts had established Houston's guilt. Houston was so incensed he could have caned Kerr in the street as well but satisfied himself with a savage broadside in the *Globe*. In a defiant editorial, he sneered at his conviction, expressing the sarcastic hope that publishing a letter in the newspaper would not get him tried a second time for acting in contempt of the House or abridging the privileges of its members. He lashed Kerr for expressing judgments "which cannot be sustained, by the testimony to which he refers." Nor could he find any explanation for Kerr's accusations "other than that he has been and is at this moment, writhing under the most galling state of party chagrin." Houston went on to recapitulate his side of the affair from the beginning, concluding that it was Stanbery behind the whole thing. "To a mind that is capable of reflection, or lighted by one spark of honor, it would be needless to offer any suggestions upon the depravity of a heart which prompted, or the head which designed, a course, such as that pursued by the *Hon* Stanbery. Nothing but the blackest malignity can justify the perverseness and vindictiveness of this man! . . . His vices are too odious to merit pity, and his spirit too mean to deserve contempt."[11]

The House, as it had to eventually, grew weary of indulging Stanbery's vendetta against Houston and found him in contempt of the chair. He "has cut more capers today," Houston wrote triumphantly the day his *Globe* article appeared, "and may be expell'd tomorrow. That's next, is it not?"[12] Convicted but vindicated—in national opinion, the contest was a draw.

The Stanbery affair must have left Jackson in a quandary over what to do with his tarnished prince. Three years in Wigwam Neosho had vented Houston's grief and humiliation; he seemed ready once more for enterprise and had even mentioned reentering politics in Tennessee. Jackson's first term was almost spent, and his clumsy rustic diplomacy to acquire Texas by purchase had gone nowhere. If there was a time when Jackson and Houston collaborated on a Texas action, it must have been during these months, and probably the greatest evidence for it is the change in Houston himself. After three years of drunken self-pity and stagnation, at the end of which even the Cherokees rejected his leadership and ridiculed him, he emerged with shattering suddenness under full sail again and with all the wit, will, and constitution lost since Eliza walked out on him. The change in Houston in April, May, and June 1832 was as bold as the new vision he contemplated.

His new correspondent during these months was James Prentiss, a land broker in New York City and the son-in-law of the proprietor of Brown's Hotel, where Houston was in residence. Houston opened contact with him in late March on the subject of gold discoveries on his Tennessee properties, but the Texas issue quickly came to dominate their communications. On April 8, in a letter to Prentiss, Houston declared for the first time on paper his intention finally to visit Texas, and on June 1 he became Prentiss's business partner in the Galveston Bay and Texas Land Company, formed to snatch up all the fallow opportunities of the Leftwich Grant, an American colony in Texas granted by Mexico in 1825 but since fallen into disorganization.[13] Houston had been an original member of the Texas Association, which petitioned for this grant as early as 1822. However, as he was not the association's legal representative, his partnership with Prentiss to increase their holdings probably conflicted with no existing obligation. Nevertheless, six months before ever setting foot in Texas, Houston was strengthening his already considerable personal stake in future events there.

It would have been toward the end of June 1832 when Houston received a new letter from the younger of the Whartons, John, who was tending to his law practice in New Orleans. His first object was to congratulate Houston on weathering the Stanbery affair, about which "much has been said in the papers . . . both 'pro' and 'con,' and from all that I have read, and heard, you certainly have lost nothing, but on the other hand your conduct has been approved by a large majority. . . . so far as I am concerned . . . , I do most sincerely and heartily rejoice at your whipping the puppy." John Wharton's second object was to acquaint Houston with Dr. Branch T. Archer of Virginia—an introduction providing the second tangible link, after the Whartons themselves, between Houston and the growing unrest in Texas. Dr. Archer, said Wharton, "has been in Texas upwards of twelve months, is intimately acquainted with matters and things there, and is in the confidence of all their leading men. He is of opinion that there will be some fighting there next fall, and that a fine country will be gained without much bloodshed, he is very desirous that you should go there, and believes that you can be of more service than any other man; he left for Virginia to day, and should you fall in with him, I expect he will put you in the notion of going." Wharton asked Houston to procure him a passport to visit Texas; according to his brother, "matters there are getting worse every day, and . . . whenever they are ready for action, I will be with them." Texas was, he concluded to Houston with appropriate alliteration, "a fine field for fame, enterprise and usefulness."

If the Whartons sent Dr. Archer to talk Houston into coming to Texas, it was a shrewd choice of emissaries. He was three years older than Houston, both were Virginians, both had fathers who were officers in the Revolutionary War. Archer was well educated—William and Mary followed by medical school at the University of Pennsylvania—and politically active, having served in the House of Burgesses. He had emigrated to Texas only the year before and immediately fell in with the Wharton faction in agitating for independence from Mexico. Wharton very apparently knew nothing of Houston's growing Texas venture, but his was a seed of advice that fell on fertile soil. It is not certain that Houston and Archer met at this time, but it is likely. Houston was in New York the first week of June 1832 to seal his land deal with Prentiss, returning to Washington on the tenth. Archer's home in Virginia was in Fauquier County, only thirty miles from Washington, and Houston forwarded Wharton's letter to Prentiss, adding a note to explain who the Whartons were, "and you know Dr. Archer." A Texas circle was definitely materializing.[14]

If Houston went to Texas on his own now, however, Mexico could not help but regard him as Jackson's filibuster. It was necessary for the president to give Houston some color of duty in going, and it had to be innocuous. Thus, Jackson engaged his aging protégé as an envoy to the Pawnee and Comanche Indians, his logic being that the further removal of the eastern Civilized Tribes would be facilitated by having a peace established between them and the Plains Indians, whom they greatly feared. When Houston did undertake a Texas journey, he did not want to travel alone, and for a companion he settled on Charles F. M. "Fent" Noland, the friend who had found him in Little Rock in the very wake of the Eliza disaster. As soon as he returned to Washington from New York on June 10, Houston made his intentions clear:

> Dear Noland, I have returned from New York, and design going to Texas in a few days—I write you to ascertain whether or not you have any thought of going to that country. It will be necessary for me to have some person with me, and to be candid, I would prefer you to any other person. I wish a companion of intelligence, of means, and of first rate moral and physical courage. In all these attributes, I am satisfied with you.
>
> Write to me if you can't come down, but come if you can—Do nothing in violation of your parents' wishes in order to gratify me. But if we should live, our wealth must be boundless.

Noland did in fact journey to Washington to join Houston in his Texas venture, and his father invested in Houston's and Prentiss's Galveston Bay and Texas Land Company. But as Prentiss began to lag in his end of the agreement, Noland fell from the scene. He did wait around for a month, but whether other business pressed or whether he merely grew weary of waiting, Texas history missed out on an acquaintance with a man of an apparently compelling character.[15]

Houston arrived in Nashville on August 16 to confer with Jackson. To his annoyance, Prentiss was not meeting his part of the financial arrangements, and Houston's letters became increasingly strident on the subject of his being paid. "If you cannot get others to contribute, at present, and shou'd forward me Drafts upon New York for only $660, it will be of importance to me." Of equal importance to their venture, "I have seen several friends here lately from Texas, and all represent it in the most prosperous state.... Thousands would flock there from this country, if the Government were settled, but will not venture without it! ... Several persons have said to me that I was looked for and earnestly wished for by the Citizens of Texas. Dr. Dillard, an highly respected gentleman, was one of the number. The people look to Indians on Arkansas as auxilliaries, in the event of a change."[16]

The next day Houston visited the Hermitage. Historians have disagreed whether Jackson lent Houston as much as five hundred dollars to finance the Texas journey.[17] Jackson probably did lend him the money, since Houston was broke and had asked Prentiss for six hundred dollars the day before. It was not traveling money, though, for Houston was stuck in Nashville for another month trying to get funds out of Prentiss. He could not bring in the sheaves of the Leftwich Grant without it, but by September 15, "All considerations have certainly failed, on your part, which were held out as inducements to me and as your letters will shew upon their face.... The matter of Texas, has to my mortification, not turned out, as I had hoped and believed."[18] Houston's disappointment may have been slightly disingenuous. One cannot help but notice that, far from "not turning out," Houston's Texas prospects had never been brighter; the Wharton brothers, Archer, and others were beckoning him on, and disengaging himself from the Prentiss relationship left him all the more free to wheel and deal on his own.

This August-to-September sojourn was Houston's last visit to Nashville before entering Texas and his fourth since skulking away on the *Red Rover*. Inevitably, stories surfaced about surreptitious meetings with Eliza. One tale had Houston bribing Eliza's slave, Dilsey, to lure Eliza into Dilsey's cabin, where Houston could gaze upon her one last time from a place of concealment. Another had a tall stranger waiting for Eliza in the drawing room at Allendale, affecting a disguise that Eliza saw through instantly, though she pretended not to recognize him. There was even a story that Eliza herself had changed her mind and desired to reconcile with Houston within a year of their separation. If this was true, it is doubtful that her father and uncle would have permitted it, for the family had exhausted their palette in painting Houston every possible color of scoundrel. If after this effort Eliza went flouncing back to him, the family would have been a laughingstock. Oddly, however, this story seems the most likely of the three. Her menfolk had parceled her off to relatives in Carthage during Houston's last visit to prevent their meeting, and Eliza tried twice on her own in 1836 to effect a reconciliation. It seems astonishing, after all that has been written about how Houston "used" Eliza, that more attention has not been paid to the other men—her relatives—who were using Eliza. They, however, were left in possession of the field, so to speak.

Before leaving Nashville, Houston attended a play, but the performance was shattered by the near riot that erupted at the discovery of his presence and the demands that he get out. Nothing could be clearer testimony that Sam Houston was finished in Tennessee.[19]

. . .

In early September Houston rode into Cantonment Gibson to pick up an important document, his passport, which admonished "all the Tribes of Indians, whether in amity with the United States, or as yet not allied to them by Treaties, to permit safely and freely to pass through their respective territories, General Samuel Houston, a Citizen of the United States, Thirty-eight years of age, Six feet, two inches in stature, brown hair and light complexion; and in case of need to give him all lawful aid and protection."[20]

And then it was back to Wigwam Neosho for perhaps the most painful part of the venture. Cherokee custom was that a man who quit his wife was required to leave her sufficient property to care for herself, and Houston left Wigwam Neosho, with its farm, orchard, and trading business, to Diana Rogers. That was the least he could do, since she was the one who had principally operated the place from the outset. Whatever emotions may have surfaced in their parting, Cherokee marriages were decidedly more mutable than those within American society, and Diana seems to have accepted her fate with equanimity. There were stories, of course, that Houston promised to return for her after things were settled in Texas, but if they were true, she grew tired of waiting: three weeks before the battle at San Jacinto, Diana Rogers Gentry Houston married a man named Samuel McGrady. Afterward, she passed into obscurity and died of pneumonia in 1838. Since her death, at least three graves were touted as hers in later years, the best claimant being one at Wilson's Rock. The remains exhumed there in 1904 were of a tall, slender woman buried wearing a large, expensive tortoise-shell comb. The body was reinterred in the Fort Gibson cemetery beneath a headstone reading

TALIHINA R.
WIFE OF
GEN. SAM HOUSTON[21]

As he was laying his old life to rest and preparing for a new one in Texas, Houston made the acquaintance at Cantonment Gibson of Washington Irving, the celebrated writer, who was passing through on his western tour. Irving left a short glimpse of him—"tall, large, well formed, fascinating man—low crowned large brimmed white beaver [hat]—boots with brass eagle spurs—given to grand eloquence. A large & military mode of expressing himself."[22]

Houston and Irving's party spent an evening swapping stories. For most of the previous three years, Houston had been a pathetic, wasted souse, and undoubtedly he hefted a few drinks on this occasion. His frame of mind, however, was totally renewed, and he was apparently not so stewed that he could not recall, many years later in a Senate debate, a story Irving told about witnessing a fight between two Galapagos tortoises.[23] His memory, as Ashbel Smith said, was awful. In short, Sam

Houston had recovered himself in the vision of the prize now before him. But as far as any officials were concerned, his "first and foremost object" in going to Texas was "to obtain all the information possible relative to the Pawnee and Kimanchie Indians."[24]

During the first day of the trek, Houston was accompanied by his friend Elias Rector, a federal marshal and well-known frontier character. As a drinking buddy, Rector's facility with the bottle was no less than Houston's own.[25] Most accounts of their parting have Houston blathering prophecies of his future greatness while wheedling Rector into trading horses with him.[26] Probably the root that taps closest to fact is from Albert Pike, who knew Rector well enough to assert that he got drunk twice a week on whiskey and then sobered up on wine. Houston's horse, Jack, had no tail, and he worried over the pain that the defenseless animal would suffer from the biting flies in Texas, not to mention his own disgrace of riding a bob-tailed nag into a country where pride in owning a fine horse was an important social consideration. Drunk or sober, he talked Rector into exchanging mounts. Rector also made Houston the gift of a razor, at which Houston famously (if apocryphally) replied, "Rector, I accept your gift, and mark my words, if I have luck this razor will some day shave the chin of a president of a republic."[27]

If the Indian business was a smokescreen to get Houston into Texas, he certainly made it look good. His last stop in Indian Territory was Fort Towson, about five miles north of the Red River, and from there on December 1, Houston composed an endlessly voluble preliminary report to the commissioner of Indian affairs, Henry L. Ellsworth, on what he had learned thus far of the plains tribes. Ellsworth just happened to have served as Washington Irving's western guide and was one of the party with whom Houston had spent that hail-fellow-well-met night at Cantonment Gibson. It is doubtful whether the commissioner would have noticed that the wordy report contained very little information that Houston would not have known off the top of his head already, though with one important exception. Whether by a fool's luck or a genius' design, the only way to contact the Comanches in the dead of winter was to enter Texas: "To reach the wild Indians at this season will be difficult, and only practicable, by way of St. Antone. I wish to set out for that point in six days, and proceed as directly as possible."[28]

Sam Houston splashed across the Red River on December 2, 1832, and partook his first meal in Texas just across the river, in Jonesboro, prepared for him by a Mrs. Ibie Gordon.[29] Fittingly enough, Jonesboro was the first organized Anglo settlement in Texas, having sheltered American squatters on Mexican land as early as 1815. Riding at last on Texas soil, Houston headed Elias Rector's horse south some one hundred fifty miles to Nacogdoches, by far the oldest Texas town east of San Antonio de Béxar, and where his old Tennessee friends included the most prominent local politician and recently appointed alcalde (mayor), Adolphus Sterne. From Nacogdoches he traveled southwest another hundred and fifty miles to the settlement of San Felipe de Austin.

Texas at this time was a patchwork of colonies that the Mexican government had, reluctantly, granted to American empresarios for the purpose of populating the vast landscape with people other than its warlike natives. The first colonist, and still the most important and respected man in the region, was Stephen Fuller Austin, lately of Missouri and New Orleans. Shy, methodical, and duty-driven, a veteran of eleven long years in Texas, Austin was only eight months younger than Houston but a man of vastly different habits and temperament—a conservative, retiring bachelor, he remained a loyal citizen of Mexico in the face of growing unrest over Mexican rule among his own colonists. His first settlement contract was for the immigration of three hundred families beginning in 1821. The Mexican government was wary enough of Americans to require Austin to personally vouch for the character of the people he allowed to settle on his grant, but that system quickly broke down as word of new settlements and free land raced across the South. East Texas was soon flooded with squatters whom Austin and the other empresarios were powerless to evict, and even many immigrants who came legally were insensitive to, even contemptuous of, the delicate state of Mexican politics, the subtleties of which Austin had spent years mastering. Many newcomers even began agitating for an independent and Americanized Texas barely a day after they pitched their tents. The constant war-dogging for revolution by these newcomers destabilized Texas' condition a great deal, and one of the deepest thorns in Austin's side was Houston's good friend William Wharton.

Houston could not have failed to be fascinated with the sheer scope of Austin's accomplishment—the transport of American civilization to Texas and then willing it to take root in a wilderness roamed only by wild animals and Indians who were both fierce and unconquered. Yet Houston must have sensed that he and Austin were bound by their very stars to clash. Houston's arrival in Austin's capital, San Felipe de Austin, was anticlimactic, however, for the empresario was away on business. It seems Houston did have a meeting with Austin's deputy, Rhode Island–native Samuel May Williams. Houston may have broached to him some vague idea of settling natives from the Indian Territory on Texas lands, for soon after Williams sent him a letter in his gorgeous handwriting that by coincidence Tadeo Ortiz, the former Mexican consul at Bordeaux, had also come through San Felipe. "He informed me that he had heard a very good report of the Choctau Indians, and intended recommending to his Government, as a matter of policy & benefit to both parties, to designate a section of Country North West of Bexar . . . and invite them to occupy & settle it. . . . You can," he concluded to Houston, "make any use of this information that you may deem proper, withholding my name."[30] In light of Sam Houston's subsequent and varied attempts to settle Indians on Texas lands, for reasons that served a spectrum of motives, one wonders what the Williams letter added to the mental ferment already taking place, especially since the thought of recruiting "native auxilliaries" had already occurred to him some months earlier.

Before leaving San Felipe, Houston applied for a one-league married man's "head-right" on Karankawa Bay, which was in Austin's colony, and the request was granted on Christmas Eve.[31] After becoming a landholder, Houston downed Christmas dinner with a fellow legend: by happy accident he crossed paths in San Felipe with Jim Bowie, the legendary knife fighter with whom, by tradition if not fact, he had bent the elbow in Helena, Arkansas, during his 1829 flight from Tennessee. This dinner in Texas, though, was almost surely their first meeting.[32] Bowie had become an instant legend for his performance in a savage fight that took place in 1827, from which he emerged victorious thanks to his proficiency with a bloodcurdling, over-sized butcher knife of a fashion that came to bear his name, afterward copied so assiduously that it rapidly became a weapon of choice on the frontier. Bowie had made his fortune in the trade of slaves and of Arkansas lands of dubious title, the proceeds of which he invested in Texas lands. He had angled himself into society in San Antonio de Béxar, the provincial capital, and shortly became engaged to Doña Ursula de Veramendi, daughter of the vice governor of the state of Coahuila y Texas. Bowie undoubtedly told Houston much about Texas, and undoubtedly it occurred to Houston that if one like Bowie could recreate himself as a great man in Texas, so too might others.

Bowie escorted Houston another hundred fifty miles west toward the provincial capital of San Antonio de Béxar. Also making the journey with them were the colonial empresario (and Austin's rival) Sterling Clack Robertson and one Caiaphas Ham, who had been a neighbor of Bowie's in Louisiana, had come to Texas with him in 1830, and was a frequent traveling companion. Ham had also lived with Comanche Indians for some five months and had been adopted by a Comanche chief, so Houston opened his official mission by pumping him for information about that tribe. Comanches did occasionally raid far out of their range and into the area in which the men were traveling; thus, probably at Ham's suggestion, a watch was posted every night. Doubtless there was a good deal of convivial drinking on this trek, and Ham remembered a laughing Houston coming in one morning after standing guard. As Houston told the story on himself, at one point during the night he thought he heard the zip of an arrow passing nearby. Upon turning his head he heard another, and every time he turned his head he heard another until he discovered that the sound was actually the scrape of his hat against his collar.[33]

Bowie's social connections proved lucky for Houston's purposes, and when the party arrived in San Antonio, Houston was received at once into the Veramendi Palace. By a further stroke of fortune, the southernmost of the five main bands of Comanches, the Penatekas, or "honey eaters," had evicted the Lipan Apaches from the Texas hill country a generation before, and San Antonio was a favorite place to gather and trade. Houston found enough visiting Comanches in the vicinity to acquit himself straightaway of his official responsibilities. Probably using Caiaphas Ham's good offices to make their acquaintance, he presented Jackson's message to the chiefs, who agreed to trek to Cantonment Gibson for a talk within three months.

Of course, if these Comanches were Penatekas, as they almost certainly were, they probably had only the dimmest notion of the location of Cantonment Gibson. They were insulated from that distant place, first, by the more northerly bands of Comanches and Kiowas; then beyond them by other plains tribes such as the Wichitas and Tonkawas, with whom they were chronically at war; and by the Civilized Tribes yet beyond them. More than likely the San Antonio Comanches were just being cordial to Houston, who came with impressive Indian credentials and,

Veramendi Palace, San Antonio. Apart from the Governor's Palace itself, the residence of Vice Governor Don Juan Martín de Veramendi was the most sumptuous
residence in Béxar. At the time Texas volunteers stormed the city in December 1835,
Ben Milam was killed before the ten-foot-tall portal. Veramendi himself moved to
Saltillo when he was elected vice governor in 1830 and was elevated to governor by
the incumbent's death in 1832, though he himself died of cholera the following year.
The house was demolished in 1902.

Courtesy Texas State Library and Archives Commission

one feels sure, dressed for the occasion. But probably they had as much intention of trying to visit the moon as Cantonment Gibson. Houston must have
known that; indeed, had the emissary been anyone other than the Raven, one
might think that here was an example of yet another white official treating with
Native Americans in ignorant disregard of their regional and subtribal limitations. At least one other officer saw the flaw in Houston's Comanche agreement
instantly. Back in Arkansas Territory, Albert Pike snapped to Secretary of War
Lewis Cass: "Governor Houston . . . will effect nothing with the Comanches. He
goes to treat with the southern portion of them who are already friendly—he
will never meet with one of the northern portion from whom is our only danger, and even should he do so he would be immediately scalped."[34] Pike could not
have been more correct, and the fact that Houston, who knew the Indians even
more intimately than Pike, seemed to feel that he had done his job so easily reinforces the suspicion that Jackson's invitation to the Comanches was a pretext for
getting Houston into Texas.

If Jackson's and Houston's ulterior intention was to create some ferment by his presence in Texas, it worked. The province was already astir over an upcoming political convention. A conclave the previous year had misfired, and its resolutions were never even presented to the Mexican government. Nevertheless, events had evolved considerably since then. Sam Houston's reputation preceded him, and there seemed to be a kind of consensus around Nacogdoches that he should take part in the growing movement. On February 4, 1833, he received a letter from Peter Ellis Bean, a filibustering curmudgeon who had played both sides of the conflict so often that nobody really trusted him anymore (although he was then serving the Mexican government as military commandant in Nacogdoches): "As it apears that it is the wish of the Citizens of this Cuntry that you Should be a member of the Comitty for to form this estern Part into a Stait that has formerly Bin governed by Cuahuela I feel myself willing to Suport you as far as my Millitary orders will admit."[35]

After only two months in Texas, Houston was gratified that he could open a Texas career with some preexisting standing among the citizens. Leaving San Antonio he repaired eastward, and on February 13, 1833, he wrote a long letter to Jackson from the town of Natchitoches, Louisiana. The importance of his recent Indian business occupied a sentence and a half in a missive of several pages:

Gen. Jackson:

Dear Sir:—Having been so far as Bexar, in the province of Texas . . . I am in possession of some information that . . . may be calculated to forward your views, if you should entertain any, touching the acquisition of Texas by the United States.

That such a measure is desired by nineteen-twentieths of the population of the province, I can not doubt. . . . Mexico is involved in Civil War. . . . The people of Texas are determined to form a State Government, and to separate from Coahuila, and unless Mexico is soon restored to order . . . Texas will remain separate from the Confederacy of Mexico. She has already beaten and repelled all the troops of Mexico from her soil. . . . She can defend herself against the whole power of Mexico, for really Mexico is powerless and penniless. . . . Her want of money taken in connection with the course which Texas *must and will adopt*, will render a transfer of Texas inevitable to some power, and if the United States, does not press for it, England will most assuredly obtain it by some means. . . .

Now is a very important crisis for Texas. . . . My opinion is that Texas, by her members in Convention, will, by 1st of April, declare all that country [north of the Rio Grande] as Texas proper, and form a state constitution. I expect to be present at that Convention, and will apprise you of the course adopted. . . . I may make Texas my abiding place! In adopting this course, I will *never forget* the country of my birth.

I will notify from this point the Commissioners of the Indians at Fort Gibson of my success, which will reach you through the War Department.

If Jackson still entertained any timidity about a Texas venture, more of Houston's letter seemed calculated to edge him in the right direction: "I have traveled near five hundred miles across Texas, [and there] can be little doubt but the country East of the River Grand . . . would sustain a population of ten millions of souls. . . . I should censure myself if I were to conceal from you . . . any facts, which could enable you, during your administration, to acquire Texas."[36]

True to his word, Houston was elected one of five delegates from Nacogdoches to the Convention of 1833, which met at San Felipe on April 1. The purpose of the convention was innocent enough: to petition Mexico for Texas statehood in the Mexican confederation separate from that of its conjoined neighbor, Coahuila. Texas had been promised separate statehood in the Constitution of 1824, although the Anglo colonies did not yet contain the requisite population. The ledger of the Texans' growing discontent with Mexico was much longer than this, however. Partly it was economic. When the Mexican government granted the colonial concession to Stephen F. Austin in April of 1823, it recognized the struggle that the American settlers would endure and so granted them favorable exemptions from taxes and import duties for a period of seven years. Beginning in 1832, although Austin's and the other colonies remained in the meanest material circumstances, the central government let the exemptions expire, and attempted to collect the duties—an act that sat badly with many of the colonists, however justified it was in Mexico City's view. The officials who were sent to enforce the tax collection were clumsy and abrasive in doing it, which sat even worse, for two reasons: first, the Americans found the dishonesty and duplicity of these officials disgusting, and second, even when the officials acted within the scope of their duty, the situation highlighted the fuzzy boundary, under Mexican law, between civil and military authority, which the colonists found appalling.

This lackadaisical blurring of responsibilities hinted also at growing social tensions. Anglos in Texas now far outnumbered the Hispanic Tejano natives, and while many of the latter were also disgusted with the central regime, the ethnocentric Americans tended to regard all Spanish-speaking Texans as a lower class of indolent peasantry. The government was aware of these tensions, for they had sent Gen. Manuel de Mier y Terán on an inspection tour in 1828, and he reported his chagrin that so many Anglos had never seen any Mexicans except those of the lowest and poorest class.[37] He also recommended that all future emigration from the "United States of the North" be forbidden, and a law was passed on April 6, 1830, another provision the colonists found unacceptable. All these factors gave the events in Texas a racial complexion that did not, however, mature until well after the revolution. These tensions erupted in shooting at the tiny port of Anahuac in 1832, led by a local hothead named William Barret Travis, but timely apologies from authorities prevented an Anglo revolt from starting prematurely.[38]

Once Sam Houston arrived in Texas, he had to be brought up to speed on all of these events. When he addressed the 1833 Convention on these weighty issues, he asserted that the law of April 6, 1830, had to be repealed. As far as the Anahuac disturbances of 1832, he believed the resistance was against repressive policies more than to who was in power. "Santa Anna," he said, "was only a name used as an excuse for resistance to oppression." On other points, Houston resorted to the question-and-answer rhetoric he had honed during his years in Congress. Why were troops expelled in 1832? Because their oppression was intolerable. Did Travis and the others do right or wrong? They acted upon the principle that oppression was to be resisted. "Can Mexico ever make laws for Texas? *No*. There is no constitution or law in the confederacy. . . . Mexico is acting in bad faith, and trifling with the rights of the people. Plans formed without the assent of Texas, are not binding upon Texas." The remedy, he finally suggested, was to " form a Constitution for the State separate from Coahuila. Then emigration and every advantage will follow."[39] The results of the Convention of 1833 were far reaching, and for Stephen Austin ultimately disastrous. Houston chaired the committee that drew up the proposed state constitution. Austin and two others (including a prominent Tejano who was thought might wield some influence in the Mexican capital) were selected to present the petition to the government, but with travel funds being short, Austin had to set off alone.

Spring shed further light on Houston's Indian mission, which had ostensibly brought him to Texas in the first place. Not surprisingly, the Comanches never showed up at Cantonment Gibson, and Houston explained the failure in a letter to Secretary of War Lewis Cass. He did not escort them personally, he wrote, as he did not wish to antagonize Mexico nor could he guarantee the Comanches' safety in conducting them through the territory of Indians hostile to them. Not to provoke Mexico was a strange excuse to be advanced by a man who, in private, was advocating the American acquisition of Texas and who, in public, had just drafted an outlaw constitution. The hostility of Indians barring any Comanche trek to Gibson was an eventuality of which he was well aware even at the time he met the Comanches outside of San Antonio. His three years at Wigwam Neosho was plenty of time for him to learn the intertribal hatreds and rivalries—indeed, at one of the first councils he attended as Oolooteka's representative in 1829, Houston expended considerable energy arguing the young Cherokees out of riding off to fight Tawakoni Indians in Texas.[40] The arguments to Cass were limp ones, but what matter—now?

Houston's own route was unimpeded enough when he returned to Gibson, and then on to Hot Springs, Arkansas, in May. His vigorous travels had so aggravated his old shoulder wound that "some bones were working out of it," and recuperation was in order. But it is doubtful that his national sentiments reentered the United States with him. While having vouchsafed to Jackson that he would never forget the country of his birth, in July Houston wrote a letter to his Washington cousin describing himself as "now the resident of another government."

"Jack!" he crowed, "Texas is the finest portion of the Globe that has ever blessed my vision."[41]

7

A MUCH DEEPER GAME THAN FARO

Houston tarried at Hot Springs through the end of July 1833, when he departed and left a forwarding address of Crows Ferry, Louisiana, where he would stop on his return to Texas. As he had written Jack, he was enamored of the Texas countryside, but the beauty of the geography was not the only thing that caught his eye. Another of Houston's old Tennessee acquaintances living in Nacogdoches was Henry Raguet, in whose household he met a soul who was to be his heart's beacon for the next several years. Raguet's daughter, Anna, was seventeen, gorgeous, and spoke four languages. Houston requested her to teach him Spanish, and on November 30 he filed for divorce from Eliza.

Divorce under Mexican law was all but inconceivable, and Houston's petition was a baroque progression of arguments based less on any law than on vaguely alluded principles of the Enlightenment. He conceded he was at a loss to explain why most civilized countries had adopted the "fopperies and quaint conceits" of canon law on the subject, by which the priesthood had "added to their nauseous and repulsive practise of taking confessions . . . and [were] continually inventing fresh absurdities for their ambition and cupidity to feed upon. And thus the sanctuary of Hymen has been polluted by the carnival of rant and jargon. . . . [But], happy for Texas, she is yet untrammeled and unbound by the fetters of precedent. . . . The law givers of the most enlightened communities now look upon the contract of marriage in no other light than a civil contract."[1] Houston also provided a smattering of public policy arguments—that a liberal divorce law would give Texas "cultivated farms, frequented roads . . . crowded habitations and enlightened seminaries," although the nature of such cause and effect remained vague. He also posed the example of the United States, where in all states a divorce might be sought based on the length of separation. In Tennessee, where he had married, the term was two years, and he and Eliza Allen had been apart for nearly five years.

Houston's divorce petition was presented by Jonas Harrison, an elderly lawyer and former alcalde of the Nacogdoches District township of Tenehaw, which he represented at the Convention of 1832. Harrison was a peculiarly appropriate choice, having himself abandoned a wife and children in New York during the financial panic of 1819, within a year had remarried in Georgia, and had, as the saying went, "G.T.T."—Gone To Texas. While Harrison presented the petition, the style of the writing certainly seems to be Houston's. Presumably, the Mexican authorities knew a "carnival of rant and jargon" when they saw one, and Houston's divorce petition gathered dust in the Nacogdoches courthouse until its discovery many years later.[2]

About the time the divorce petition was filed, travelers on the road between Nacogdoches and San Augustine encountered "a gentleman . . . riding a fine horse and wearing a broad brimmed hat, which he touched politely as he passed the ladies. Late in the evening the same man was met returning, and the same gentlemanly deference shown by him." One recorded that her "Mother asked one of [their group] if he knew who that gentleman was whom they had just met. 'That,' said he, 'is Governor Houston, and he says that there is going to be a war in Texas before long, and he means to figure in it.'"[3]

In mid-December Houston was back in Austin's colonial capital, San Felipe, working his contacts and monitoring the political situation. There he may well have made the acquaintance of William Barret Travis, a principal of the near-rebellion at Anahuac in 1832, who noted in his diary, "Genl. Houston is in town." Houston witnessed events in Texas moving at a quicker speed than he had anticipated, and if he was to have resources to help guide those events, he must find them soon. He headed for New York to reestablish contact with James Prentiss and try to squeeze his retainer out of the land investors who had been so resistant to part with their money before. With the motif of an Indian "auxilliary" already part of his mental architecture, it is possible that Houston journeyed by way of Cherokee country, for travelers near Cantonment Gibson found a white man over six feet tall, dressed in buckskin, in the company of several hundred warriors.[4]

Houston left accurate word with his contacts of his route and where he might be reached, and in Washington, D.C., a letter from A. C. Allen overtook him with momentous news. The Convention of 1833 had dispatched Stephen F. Austin to Mexico City to try to get reforms enacted, but Allen wrote Houston at the end of February 1834: "Col. S. F. Austin has been taken for treason against the Gov on account of the letter which he wrote to Bexar last summer. It is thought however that he will get clear."[5] Austin was a collateral casualty of another turn of the kaleidoscope of Mexican politics as well as the victim of the only political blunder he ever committed. The Bustamante government had been driven from power by an ambitious general, Antonio López de Santa Anna, who took office on April 1, 1833, the same day that the new convention met in San Felipe. He had fought his way to power as a liberal federalist, but immediately upon his swearing in he took a leave of absence, leaving Vice President Valentín Gómez Farías to implement the reforms Santa Anna claimed to support. This also left Gómez Farías, as Santa Anna well knew, to face the criticism from Mexico City's powerful and conservative upper class. When Austin arrived in the capital, Farías seemed cordial but would not be led into substantive discussions, fearing to be seen countenancing a liberal stance toward Texas. The two eventually quarreled, and when Santa Anna returned he pronounced the reforms a failure, the country in crisis, and assumed dictatorial powers, which had been his aim from the beginning. "If I were God," he once said, "I would wish to be more."

The normally patient and unflappable Austin saw right through the dictator and wrote an indiscreet letter home admitting that Texas might as well proceed to organize a state government without permission from the new centralist regime. But then Santa Anna granted him an audience and, while refusing separate statehood for Texas, gave enough ground to send Austin home with a compromise victory. Austin attempted to tiptoe out of the country, but when his seditious letter home fell into the wrong hands—loyal Mexicans on the *ayuntamiento* of San Antonio— they betrayed him to the government. He was apprehended in Saltillo in January 1834 and sent back in irons to the capital, where he was held incommunicado.

In New York, James Prentiss heard the news as well and dashed off a hasty note to Houston: "By late account from Mexico Col Austin was in close prison—and much excitement about him—. . . I repeat my regret at the meanness and stupidity of many persons interested as I am in Texas—about contributing something to secure your services—and I am yet in hopes that ere long they will bee glad to employ you." Houston had been tied up in an errand for Lewis Cass, inquiring whether it might be possible to recover an officer who had been captured probably by Pawnees, which makes it likelier that Houston did indeed spend time in the Indian Territory in January or February. When he was finally able to break free and get to New York, he felt himself out of time and gave Prentiss an ultimatum: "If any Company should choose to employ my services in its behalf, it must advance me $2000; and at the end of six months, I must have $1000.—At the end of 12 months, one thousand dollars more, and at the end of 18 months, $1,000. . . . This is the only proposition that I have to make." Four days later Prentiss expressed his "chagrin at the result of my effort to obtain the retaining fee necessary to engage your attention" and relied on their friendship in asking Houston to hold himself free to resume their relationship in more flush circumstances.[6]

Houston assumed an attitude that came to be typical for him when confronted with failure: flip nonchalance. The loss of fees, he wrote, "has not disappointed me much. They will give some $15,000 or $20,000 to some man, who will tell them fine tales, and promise fine things—but this will be their own lookout!" From all developments it was high time for Sam Houston to get himself back to Texas. His tone to Prentiss was still cordial, if only for one reason—he departed New York in such a hurry that he left his map at the City Hotel. "I came off, and forgot it—Fold it up handsomely,—enclose it in a letter to me; and enclose the letter to Mr. Felix Grundy of the Senate—. . . I can't do without it." Back in Washington, he appealed to Jackson to remit the fine levied by Chief Justice William Cranch in the Stanbery case, which the president later did.[7] This was well, for Houston could ill afford the fine because the vouchers he submitted for reimbursement of the Indian mission undertaken for Jackson were met with considerable incredulity. Houston was obliged to hang on in Washington waiting for his map and used the opportunity to make a few final social rounds, sometimes in the company of fellow Tennesseean David Crockett, with whom he signed the autograph book of Octavia Walton on April 24.

Houston received his map from Prentiss that day, which he acknowledged in a hurried letter. He made his peace, of a sort, with Prentiss and agreed not to break off relations with Prentiss's investors, but in future, he scolded, "take my word for it, they will *need* me more than I will *want* them!"

> I do think within one year that it [Texas] will be a Sovereign State and acting in all things as such. Within three years I think it will be separated from the Mexican Confederacy, and will remain so forever—. . . Still, if Mexico had done right, we cou'd have travelled on smoothly enough.
>
> You need not hope for the acquisition (if ever) by this Government of Texas during the Administration of Genl Jackson—If it were acquired by a Treaty, that Treaty, would not be ratified, by the present Senate—!!!
>
> Texas, will be bound to look to herself, and to do for herself—this present year, must produce events, important to her future destiny.
>
> Keep my predictions, and see how far they are *verified*!
>
> —The course that I may pursue, you must rely upon it, shall be for the true interests of Texas.[8]

This was a letter from Houston at his most energized, his awareness bristling, and for not the only time in his life, he showed himself a seer of deep forecast. But from the time he avowed this to Prentiss in high spring until the end of the year, Sam Houston virtually disappeared.

It is certain that he returned by way of Virginia, where he stopped to visit branches of the family tree that had remained in the East. There was presented to him a young cousin, Narcissa Hamilton. Houston was engaged in catching up with other relatives as the schoolgirl handed him her autograph book and asked if he remembered her. In later years she recalled that he hardly slowed his conversation with the others as he composed lines for her book:

> Remember thee?
> Yes, lovely girl;
> While faithful memory holds its seat,
> Till this warm heart in dust is laid,
> And this wild pulse shall cease to beat,
> No matter where my bark be tost,
> On life's tumultuous, stormy sea;
> My anchor gone, my rudder lost,
> Still, cousin, I will think of thee.

Narcissa Hamilton gleaned enough from the conversations to assert that Houston had been in Washington "making plans for the liberation of Texas."[9]

After this, what Houston did during 1834 has remained an aging yellow blank in the chronicle of his life, and his sphere of activity, in Flanagan's phrase, was "contained in the curve of a question mark."[10] Probably his Indian dealings played some role in the missing months. There was that possible Houston sighting at the head of several hundred warriors near Cantonment Gibson during his eastern swing.[11] And then in May, when Houston was on his return trip, his friend and sometime trading partner Benjamin Hawkins, a mixed-blood Creek, wrote that Houston intended to hold an Indian conference on June 20 at either the Brazos River or the Trinity. But of definite sightings or knowledge of Sam Houston's activities, there is none.

In December of 1834, a British travel writer with the felicitous name of G. W. Featherstonhaugh (pronounced "Fanshaw"), who was in the United States gathering impressions for his *Excursion through the Slave States*, unearthed Houston in the hamlet of Washington, Arkansas, twenty miles northeast of the Texas border and only ten miles from the nearest bend of the Red River. The famous Tennesseean-turned-Texan was, Featherstonhaugh wrote,

> leading a mysterious sort of life, shut up in a small tavern, seeing nobody by day and sitting up all night. The world gave him credit for passing these . . . hours, in the study of [cards]; but I had been in communication with too many persons of late, and had seen too much passing before my eyes, to be ignorant that this little place was the rendezvous where a much deeper game than faro or rouge et noir was playing. There are many persons . . . in the village from the States lying adjacent to the Mississippi, under the pretence of purchasing government lands, but whose real object was to encourage the settlers in Texas to throw off their allegiance to the Mexican government.[12]

The obscurity of the town of Washington, Arkansas, in later years belies the fact that in 1834 it held a position of rather greater prominence. Originally the site of a Methodist camp meeting in 1822, it was more densely settled by 1824 and was the first city incorporated after the formation of Arkansas Territory. The seat of Hempstead County, it boasted of having produced more lawyers and political leaders than any other Arkansas town to that time. More to Houston's purpose, however, Washington had grown up at the intersection of five erstwhile Indian traces and in 1834 was the hub of all the important roads in that part of the country. The U.S. Army recognized its strategic importance; Indians removed from the southeastern United States during the Jackson administration were funneled through Washington, and in later years it was a staging area for troops marching to the Mexican-American War. If there was one thing Sam Houston could do well, it was read a map.

The tavern where Featherstonhaugh had spied Houston's curious behavior was the Travelers Inn, located in the center of the town and one of its most prominent buildings. Two stories high with twelve rooms, it was constructed of heart-of-pine and walnut timbers, the virgin forest yielding massive planks eighteen and even twenty inches wide. It was an important stagecoach stop, and broad verandas across the front and sides sheltered disembarking passengers; mail was routed to local residents through the inn, and a large second-floor ballroom was a favored gathering place. Jim Bowie had been in residence here while local smithy James Black custom-tempered the steel and crafted his fearsome "Bowie knife." Stephen F. Austin had stayed here often before his Texas days; David Crockett and his Tennessee boys rested here on their way to the Alamo in 1836.[13]

A researcher on Houston's 1834 trail cannot read Featherstonhaugh's notation without the hackles rising. Was Houston making certain that, once war came, the lines of supply and volunteer reinforcements would be clear? Can the hand of Jackson be seen in these preparations? With whom exactly was Houston sitting up all night? Who were some of those "many persons"—acquaintances from the old days? What would Featherstonhaugh have known about all of this unless somebody told him? Surely he had none of the motives of Duff Green or the Donelsons in accusing Houston of furtive filibustering. One can almost conjure a smug speculator, a little tipsy on the whiskey Featherstonhaugh had bought him, bragging by the fireplace to the wide-eyed English dandy on the mighty future they planned for the huge province Mexico could never hold. In just how deep a conspiracy were they toward their "real object"? Had they met by concert, and if so, who called them together; Houston? And if Houston, what better place than this well-traveled staging area.[14] Who would Houston have met there? Elias Rector is one possibility. Houston had written Jackson the previous July that Rector and a Major Armstrong were "efficient officers engaged in the business of emigration in this quarter. . . . [Rector] will do his duty, whenever it is assigned to him."[15]

Sometimes in following the trail of Sam Houston, one discovers him leaving the telltale moss of the bank and plunging thigh-deep into the swamp of intrigue, safe from scrutiny. The researcher can only prowl the edge and find where he emerged again. As 1835 dawned, Houston was busily attending his law practice in Nacogdoches, shuttling out to San Augustine on legal matters and, presumably, studying Spanish with Anna Raguet.

Certainly, the circumstantial evidence is that Houston was plotting during those mysterious months of 1834, for only after his return to Texas from the United States did his own political position swing from conservative to radical. As late as the Convention of 1833, Houston had sided with Austin against the growing clamor of the Wharton faction for independence. Austin, however, now lay in a dungeon in Mexico City, and a letter from prison counseling quiet and patience prompted Houston to begin to break from his camp. Indeed, it was in a letter to John Wharton in April 1835 that Houston made a famous reference to Austin as a "viper without its fangs," among other derogatory remarks about the Father of Texas.[16] Other aspects of this important letter, however, suggest that Houston was not defecting from Austin entirely but skillfully treading water, testing the current. That John Wharton now held Houston's entire confidence is doubtful, as Houston prattled that from Wharton's brother, William, he had just "learned the news of the Colony, and of its politicks, for really, I was ignorant of them, as no one sends me, either papers, or hand Bills." Not likely. Then too, some of the harsh anti-Austin tone of the letter may stem from the fact that the addressee had recently fought a duel with one

William T. Austin, and Houston may have wished to appear sympathetic in a Wharton quarrel with what he assumed to be an Austin relation.[17]

During the spring of 1835, Houston was not so wrapped up in his machinations that he neglected his personal circumstances. When in residence in Nacogdoches, Houston took to boarding with his old friends, the alcalde and his wife, Adolphus and Eva Catherine Sterne. He had come to Texas early, probably in 1824, and was a war dog for independence almost from the beginning. During an abortive uprising known as the Fredonian Rebellion in 1826, Sterne had smuggled arms to the insurgents in barrels of coffee from New Orleans. Condemned to death and imprisoned, Sterne was paroled through the influence of a Masonic connection, married Eva in Louisiana in 1828, and upon their return built the house in which Houston stayed with them during his visits.[18]

Although it is possible that Houston's true personal opinion of Roman Catholicism was reflected in the emphatic terms of his divorce petition, he was far too pragmatic to let such distaste stand in the way of his personal advancement. Up to this time, he had not observed the provision of Mexican law that required all landowners to be Catholic, so with Eva Sterne standing as his godmother, Houston submitted and was received into the Church in the parlor of their house. The Sternes' daughter recalled late in life that Houston gave her mother a diamond ring as a christening present.[19] Apparently, he took the baptismal name of Paul, and for a short time thereafter signed a few legal documents as Paul Sam Houston in conformity to Catholic custom, though this was a rule not strictly enforced in Texas.[20] His certificate of good character, one of which was required of every resident alien, bears the name Samuel Pablo Houston (which earned an unexplained but exclamatory "[sic!]" from James in *The Raven*).[21] To most Texans during the colonial period, the required conversion to Catholicism was a purely legalistic formality undertaken to get titles to land; by and large they retained a healthy suspicion of clergy and rituals. Most colonists practiced no religion at all, and the Texas Declaration of Independence made prominent mention of the evils of state religion, characterizing the priesthood as the ready minions of tyranny. Such formalities as were observed received little care; there is no record, for instance, that Adolphus Sterne served as Houston's godfather, although biographers usually have assumed so, and Houston himself lightly referred to Sterne as his "God Father" on at least one occasion.[22]

Becoming a Catholic enabled Houston to own property, and he applied for a second land grant, this one in Burnet's colony, where he received a third of a league (about 1,480 acres) for having come without a family. Of course, he had already the grant—a married man's portion—in Austin's colony, and in later years he apparently got in some legal trouble for this double dipping. He tried to wiggle out of it by claiming that his land on Karankawa Bay was not a headright but a purchase and that Stephen Austin had understood it as such notwithstanding the form of the conveyance.[23] However, Austin's adherence to legal forms and method were notorious to those who desired shortcuts, and his endorsement of Houston's petition, wherein he provided for title issuance to follow the usual survey, contains no hint of such an irregular arrangement. Perhaps Houston felt that in the fast-coming

Adolphus Sterne; Eva Catherine Rosine Sterne; the Sterne House, Nacogdoches. Adolphus Sterne first came to the United States on a forged passport as a draft dodger from his native Germany. He became friends with Houston in Tennessee, and on arrival in Texas, Sterne agitated for independence almost from the start. He met his wife in New Orleans and built this house in 1828. Sam Houston was baptized into the Catholic Church in the parlor; He referred to the Sternes informally as his godparents, but while Eva did stand as his godmother, Adolphus, born a Jew and only a nominal Catholic, declined the office of godfather.

All courtesy Special Collections, Ralph W. Steen Library, Stephen F. Austin State University chaos nobody would notice that his thick fingers had slipped back into the cookie jar of land grants, and once Mexican authority was deposed, he expected that all colonial titles would be ratified *en masse*. No matter how favorably one might construe Houston's other Texas dealings, he was, at least in this instance, probably trying to pull a fast one. There are two defenses of Houston's claim that he had come *sin familia* when he was still legally married to Eliza. One was that he had at least instituted divorce proceedings, first in Tennessee and then in 1833 in Nacogdoches. The second relies on the kind of ambiguity that Houston himself could seize and insist upon, the fact that having come to Texas "without family" was not necessarily inconsistent with the fact that he was still married. He simply had not brought his wife with him.

It seems possible that Houston rode out to inspect his new holdings, for after May his prolific pen fell silent but for his signature on a receipt from Judge John M. Dor, who had signed his character certificate. Houston entrusted all his possessions to Dor until he should return for them, and the inventory of his worldly goods provides insight into his economic state and priorities: one table and four chairs; one wash stand and three pans, small, medium, and large; a fireplace set of andirons, shovel, and tongs; a candlestick and snuffer; a sauce pan and lid; a sword and scabbard; and nearly fifty books. The library embraced religion (a Bible, two hymn books, and *Pilgrim's Progress*), the law (*The Federalist*, the Louisiana Code of Practice, a volume of military law, and Valet's *Law of Nations*), and general reference (physiology and Walker's dictionary.) Featured most prominently were the classics: ten volumes of Shakespeare, eight of Plutarch, plus Burns, Byron, and, of course, his two-volume *Iliad*.[24]

• • •

As Texas drifted toward war, Houston prepared for it in his own crablike fashion. Moseley Baker, a prominent member of the war party, had sent Houston captured documents of impending military rule by Mexico; then in August Baker visited Houston in Nacogdoches to reinforce the urgency of his concern. Houston counseled him to remain quiet and stir up no trouble, for radicals, he warned, were in disfavor in that sector.[25] And certainly Moseley Baker, nodding in agreement to keep mum and not antagonize the peace party, had no clue what wheels were really turning in Houston's wily mind, for to the end of his days Baker considered "Big Sam" a timid and disgusting figure who deserved no share of credit for the revolution.

Houston, however, was attempting to take matters into his own hands in an entirely different way. On September 11 the Nacogdoches Vigilance Committee, with Houston as a member and signatory, petitioned President Jackson to prevent Mexico from breaking its 1831 amity treaty with the United States, which she was about to do by encouraging an "incursion" of Creek Indians from the United States into Texas.[26] What Houston and the others desired of Jackson is unclear—the best guess is that they were handing the president a legalism to justify moving troops to the border and, perhaps, clear his way for a forceful American annexation of

Texas. The "incursion"—and interestingly the word is underscored every time it is used in the petition—complained of by the Vigilance Committee had to do with the envisioned settlement of five thousand Creek Indians on part of the Filisola Grant under a shady and inconclusive empresario contract. This was probably beyond the contemplation of the 1831 treaty, which mentioned nothing against movement of Indians from one country at the invitation of the other. (If that did come within the purview of the treaty, then so might Houston's invitation to the Mexican Comanches to visit Cantonment Gibson.)

The Nacogdoches Vigilance Committee was preparing for war far more actively than Moseley Baker realized. In August they called on Houston and selected others to meet with Texas Cherokees and insure their neutrality in the coming conflict—an errand that Houston ultimately tended to, but not until the following February. But Baker would have really been surprised at the depth of Houston's war planning from the Indian angle, for one of the would-be empresarios in the Creek settlement scheme was none other than Benjamin Hawkins, Houston's friend who had reported on his Creek council the preceding summer. Did Houston set up Hawkins with encouragement for a Creek immigration, having as his real object a pretext for justifying American intervention over such a hostile "incursion"? Such a hunch is reinforced by a contemporaneous complaint from José María Carbajal. Surveyor to the de León colony, he reported Houston to the authorities for attempting an illegal settlement of Creek Indians in Texas and warned that he should be arrested. Of proof there is none, but certainly the use of Creeks as pawns in Houston's Mexican policy was a motif that resurfaced during the first year of independence, when Houston met a delegation of chiefs from this same tribe with a view toward settling them on the Rio Grande, from where they would have a free hand to raid into Mexico—if they could be prevented from killing women and children![27]

If Houston was indeed attempting to play an Indian card in his faro game for Texas independence, it calls into question his posture as the perennial friend of the Native American. Or, rather, it would if he was merely using the Indians to justify U.S. intervention. However, it was a hallmark of Sam Houston's life and politics to pursue an object with the grimmest tenacity, but if it proved impractical, to refashion its salvageable aspects into a new and more workable frame. He was the ultimate pragmatist. In this light, the likeliest explanation for invoking the fear of the Creek Indian incursion is this: Even at the time Houston quit Tennessee in disgrace in 1829, he may possibly have envisioned himself at the head of an army of Indian warriors in a fight to separate Texas from Mexico. If Ben Hawkins was correct in asserting that Houston met with the Creeks during the summer of 1834, no purpose for the meeting comes to mind but to encourage their immigration to Texas—almost surely with the object of having them at hand and in alliance with the Texas Cherokees when the revolution came. Afterward, the victorious new nation would thank the Cherokees and Creeks with its friendship and secure land titles for them, on which Andrew Jackson's United States had repeatedly stiffed them. It was only when Houston's Creek scheme had progressed far enough to have to go public with the intended purchase of part of the Filisola Grant that the other players had a chance to react, and the Texas Cherokees and the Anglo settlers around Nacogdoches, both of whom would have been the Creeks' neighbors, reacted with equal outrage.

Llerena Friend found Houston's behavior in this episode "somewhat anomalous."[28] It makes perfect sense, however, in light of the above scenario. First, it seems likely that it was other members of the Nacogdoches committee who approached Houston about their petition to Jackson on the Creek matter—one John Forbes was the chairman. A thirty-eight-year-old Irishman who had arrived in Nacogdoches only that year, Forbes's forceful personality quickly made him one to whom others in the community looked for leadership. Sam Houston, who often assayed people with an uncanny clarity after only minimal contact, also took Forbes into his circle almost from the start, and Forbes served him ably throughout the war. It would not be wholly surprising if Houston became willing to abandon his Creek scheme after Forbes weighed in against it. At any rate, seeing that his Creek enlistment plan could not possibly succeed, there was no harm in recycling it with a more sinister air as a way to encourage American involvement.

Second, the intensity with which Houston fought for secure land title for the Texas Cherokees during the first three years of independence persuades one that had his initial Creek scheme succeeded, he would have treated them with equal liberality. What he had not reckoned on was the bigotry and duplicity of his Anglo colleagues, to say nothing of the Texas Cherokees' opposition. Third, it is also consonant with his consideration in 1837 of settling Creeks along the Rio Grande, by which he would kill two birds with one stone: giving the Indians a secure land grant while using them as a buffer against Mexican invasion. If this theory is correct, then Houston's demeanor toward the Native Americans remained honorable. His apparent desertion of Ben Hawkins certainly seems to indicate that that friendship was expendable, and the petition to Jackson of September 11, in which Hawkins was referred to only as "a quarteroon Creek Indian," contains no hint of what had theretofore been a cordial relation between Hawkins and Houston, who were partners in a gold mining interest.[29] This matter, however, could have been privately reconciled, but for Hawkins's mysterious death soon after. He was probably murdered on the road returning from Mexico—just possibly, though not probably, with the Creek land grant in his hand. There was a subsequent rumor that Houston had him killed,[30] but the Texas Cherokees are far likelier suspects—they were furious with Hawkins, and bushwhacking was not an unknown mode of execution in that nation.[31]

As meticulously as Houston labored to be prepared for revolution, it was circumstances far removed from him that set the rebellion in motion. In June of 1835 the hated customs house was reopened at Anahuac; a gathering of citizens at San Felipe seized dispatches intended for its commander and learned not only that a force of regulars was being sent to enforce the levies, but also that the state government of Coahuila y Texas had been suspended and Santa Anna's brother-in-law, Gen. Martín Perfecto de Cos, installed as military commander. Worst of all, they learned that once Santa Anna had crushed resistance to his dictatorship in the state of Zacatecas, he intended to personally lead a punitive expedition into the

Old Stone Fort, Nacogdoches. Originally built in 1779 as a mercantile and warehouse, the Stone Fort soon acquired quasi-public status. Filibusters made it the capitol of their abortive republics, and the building had served as a courthouse since 1834. Built with an adobe-brick interior and blocks of iron ore for its exterior, the fort was later pulled down but the materials saved for still later rebuilding.

Courtesy Special Collections, Ralph W. Steen Library, Stephen F. Austin State University

American colonies in Texas. This outraged the settlers, who initially routed the Anahuac garrison before it could be reinforced but then thought better of it and apologized to Cos. When they refused, however, to deliver up their leader, William Travis, to Mexican summary justice, Cos placed himself at the head of an army and marched on San Antonio de Béxar.

Before his arrival, the commander of the San Antonio garrison sought to disarm the surrounding countryside, recalling from the settlement of Gonzales a small bronze cannon that had been lent them for protection against Indians. It was a sorry little piece of ordnance, probably an old swivel gun that had already been spiked and repaired once. The citizens of Gonzales did not believe for a minute the pretext that this shabby little cannon was needed in San Antonio's already bristling armory at the Alamo. Thus, they sent a letter to San Antonio stalling for time while appealing to all the other settlements for volunteers. Numerous units of local militia were already *en route* to San Antonio to oppose Cos, but now they altered their march toward Gonzales. When one hundred Mexican dragoons showed up across the Guadalupe River from the town to reclaim the cannon, they were met by one hundred fifty volunteers and a six-foot white cotton flag sporting a likeness of the cannon, subscribed by the legend: COME AND TAKE IT. In the dawn fog of October 2, 1835, the spitting boom of the Gonzales cannon opened the Texas Revolution.

Sam Houston, thus, had nothing to do with triggering the rebellion, but his sly maneuvering in the Redlands had timed to perfection his entrance onto the stage. And on October 5, as soon as there was news that the shooting had started, he put out his own call for American volunteers. In San Augustine he handed a letter, "To Isaac Parker, Esq. present."

> *War in defence of our rights, our oaths, and our constitutions is inevitable, in Texas!*
> If *volunteers* from the United States will join their brethren in this section, they will receive liberal bounties of land. We have millions of acres of our best lands unchosen and unappropriated.
> Let each man come with a good rifle, and one hundred rounds of ammunition, and come soon.[32]

The discovery of any authority on Houston's part to offer land bounties on behalf of Texas at this time would prove a major find. But Parker must have jumped on the fastest horse in the county, for only two days later the headlines in the *Red River Herald* screamed, "HIGHLY IMPORTANT FROM TEXAS!!!! WAR IN TEXAS—General Cos landed near the mouth of the Brazos with 400 men."[33]

On October 8, against the backdrop of the historic Old Stone Fort in Nacogdoches, Houston was placed in command of the assembled volunteers. "Our actions are to become a part of the history of mankind," he stoked them in general orders two days later. "The work of liberty has begun. . . . The morning of glory is dawning upon us."[34]

And upon himself.

8

THE MORNING OF GLORY

Texas and her impending struggle had become an enormous *cause celebre* in the United States irrespective of the effort of any one individual. Whatever labor Houston was up to during those long lost months in Arkansas, however, bore stunning fruit as soon as the fighting started. Offers of aid poured in, sent not to the Texas government but addressed personally to Sam Houston.

"The cause of Texas flourishes in every quarter of the U.S.," one Angus McNeill wrote him from Natchez, Mississippi, the same week. "You will be overrun with volunteers. 30 or 40 leave in this Boat." The same courier that brought McNeil's letter also carried one of the likeliest offers for help, this from Felix Huston (no known relation), a wealthy lawyer also in Natchez. "I believe and hope that your contest will soon be ended—if it is not by this time—but should it be protracted—You will find that the chivalry of the South will not slumber." Felix Huston certainly had not been slumbering. He had chaired a pro-Texas meeting as early as the previous July and was spending thousands of his personal fortune outfitting a whole regiment of volunteers, which he would march to Texas in company with Jim Bowie's brother, Rezin P. Bowie. "We are alive to the importance of the contest in relation to its immediate and prospective effect on the whole Southern Portion of the United States," Felix Huston continued. "If need be we may renew our acquaintance in more active times." Sam Houston folded the letter from the Natchez lawyer and along its outer crease wrote, "Very Well." He had no idea the grief that acceptance would cost him in future years.

Recent academic advocates of the so-called Southern conspiracy, the idea that the Texas Revolution was fomented and supported only by Southerners looking to the extension of cotton and slavery, might find dry powder in Felix Huston's alertness to the possibilities for the American South that a free Texas would represent. However, the issue of democratic liberties suppressed in Texas went genuinely deeper than that. Ira Davis, a surgeon living in the abolitionist environs of Norwich, Vermont, wrote Houston on November 7: "The struggle of freemen against tyranny & usurpation awakes the flame of liberty in the breast of every true American. Although the theatre of action & the scenes of distress is so far removed from our vision, yet we feel that our brethren are there, the cause of liberty is there, and the hand of the oppressor is there." Davis confessed to Houston that he was himself of too delicate a constitution to undertake such a journey, but nevertheless, "if 20 effective young men will enlist I will go with them."[1]

Houston had expended much thought over the years in how to involve Texas' Indians in the upcoming struggle, but now in the press of trying to place the fast-developing revolt in some kind of harness, he had less attention to spare for the native angle. Just at this time Jim Bowie suddenly materialized in Nacogdoches, saying he was on a mission to Chief Bowl's Cherokees. Bowie had just escaped from trouble in Monclova, and his horse was now broken down. As witnessed by Bowie's frequent companion, Caiaphas Ham, Bowie said, "Houston, I want your horse."

"You can't get him," Houston answered. "I have but one and I need him."

When Bowie remarked that he was going to take him anyway and left the room, Houston turned to Ham. "Do you think it would be right for me to give up my horse to Bowie?"

Ham answered, "Perhaps it would be proper under the circumstances."

"Damn him," said Houston, "Let him take the horse."[2]

At first blush it seems odd that Bowie and not Houston should be sent to shore up relations with the Cherokees; certainly Bowie did not command any greater respect from them than they felt for the Raven. Probably there was something shrewder afoot. Bowie was in the van of the war party; Houston was not. On the lam from Monclova, Bowie's first act in Nacogdoches was, accompanied by several men he had enlisted, to raid the armory of military commander Peter Ellis Bean. Bean had long since communicated his separatist, if not revolutionary, sympathies to Houston, but Bowie's precipitate act so outraged him that he reported Bowie to Texas' military commander in San Antonio, Domingo Ugartachea, and requested instructions; Bowie himself was surprised that his move generated no groundswell of support. Next, Nacogdoches's jefe politico, Henry Rueg, sent Bowie to San Augustine to intercept Mexican dispatches intended for their consulate in New Orleans. When Bowie read the papers to an assembly in Nacogdoches, including orders for the arrest of William Travis, Travis himself wrote Bowie that the time was not yet ripe for a general conflagration. When Rueg had Judge John Forbes send Bowie on the mission to the Cherokees—and Forbes was a close ally of Houston's—it was likely a way to keep Bowie active in Texas' behalf but get him out of town; public sentiment in Nacogdoches was not yet solidly behind a war effort (as indeed Houston had told Mosely Baker), and Bowie was not helping matters.[3]

·   ·   ·

When Houston finally did depart Nacogdoches, it was not to the front of battle but to a "Consultation" of the people's representatives at San Felipe. He had been elected a delegate in mid-October. This was not a difficult accomplishment, since he had chaired a mass meeting as early as September 14 to debate the merits of holding such a gathering. As Nacogdoches' leading citizen, he was an obvious choice anyway, but it would not have escaped his notice that the surest guarantee of his election to the center of the action would be to preside over—and be seen to preside over—a convocation of the populace. (Bowie also stood for election to be one of Nacogdoches' six delegates to the Consultation but came in ninth with only sixty-eight votes.)

It had been a year and a half since the Convention of 1833 dispatched Austin to Mexico City to petition for statehood, and the rapidly changing events—to say nothing of the empresario's imprisonment—had made a new general meeting urgent. One had been advocated for several months by the Wharton radicals, who saw such a meeting as little more than a convention to produce a declaration of independence. Without Austin to block him, William Wharton called the Consultation to meet early in the fall, but an unexpected event set the calendar back: Stephen Austin suddenly returned late in the summer. He had spent over a year being tossed from jail to jail, as no real charges were ever filed and no court would take jurisdiction of whatever "offense" he had committed. He was a changed man, sick and bitter, as convinced now as anyone that war was Texas' only recourse, and with his sudden presence and agreement that the Consultation was necessary, the meeting was scheduled for October 15.

Texas colonists were now so wary of the Mexican government's intentions that its couriers were more than once waylaid and lightened of their dispatches. One of them yielded a letter from Santa Anna announcing an imminent punitive raid through Texas and the arrival in San Antonio of the army under Cos. Such developments made a Consultation of the people very urgent indeed. Sam Houston arrived in San Felipe on time but discovered that no quorum could convene because most of the delegates were with volunteers swarming toward San Antonio to resist Cos, and Houston rode out to fetch them. Those volunteers, acting as local companies under popularly elected leaders, had defeated the company of dragoons sent out to seize the Gonzales cannon. Taking the offensive, the Texans then routed Mexican army units at La Bahía and Mission Concepción and had now laid siege to Cos himself at San Antonio. Stephen Austin was with them, ostensibly as their leader but probably, in his own mind, as much their hostage to prevent him from reforming the peace party or bargaining some compromise with the Mexican government.

The volunteers were camped on Cibolo (locally pronounced "Sewilla") Creek, just outside the city, when Houston joined up with them. Among their number was Noah Smithwick, a blacksmith who had repaired the Gonzales cannon to usable condition. "I have a vivid recollection in my mind's eye" of Houston, he wrote in his memoir. "He rode into our camp alone, mounted on a little yellow Spanish stallion so diminutive that Old Sam's long legs, incased in the traditional buckskin, almost touched the ground."[4] (Caiaphas Ham recorded that Houston owned a splendid horse. Bowie must not have returned him.)

If Houston's Tennessee days had left him suspicious of militia, what he beheld on the Cibolo must have filled him with an acute sense of *déjà vu*. "Words are inadequate to convey an impression of the appearance of the first Texas army," according to one of its veterans. "Nothing short of ocular demonstration could do it justice . . . . Buckskin breeches were the nearest approach to uniform, and there was a wide diversity even there. . . . Boots being an unknown quantity; some wore shoes and some moccasins. Here a broad-brimmed sombrero overshadowed the military cap at its side; there a tall "beegum" rode familiarly beside a coonskin cap, with the tail hanging down behind . . . ; there the shaggy brown buffalo robe contrasted with a gaily checkered counterpane. . . . In lieu of a canteen, each man carried a Spanish gourd . . . a fantastic military array."[5]

Still, this was the army he meant to command. Unable yet to give any orders that would be obeyed, though, Houston remonstrated hard at a called gathering of the volunteers. He wanted two things of them. They were, he insisted, too ill trained and equipped to take on regular troops, and they should fall back to Gonzales and forge themselves into a real army. Second, political organization was imperative, and those of them elected to the Consultation must go there and organize a government without delay. As much as the men distrusted the conservative Austin, they wanted to hear his views. So ill that he was barely able to sit on his horse, Austin disagreed with any notion of retreating back over ground they had already won. He did, however, support Houston on the issue of putting a government together. Mosely Baker, who had taken Santa Anna's captured intentions to Sam Houston and saw no need for other persuasion, began nursing a disgust with Houston that never abated to the day he died. Eight years after the argumentative speeches on the Cibolo, he penned an accusation that Houston was so despondent at the men's refusal to retreat with him that he sat up that night, drinking himself into such a stupor that, around midnight, he began wailing for a pistol with which to kill himself but was prevented from doing so by Bowie. It was an outrageous lie told in a pamphlet full of lies so outrageous no one would publish it, but it is occasionally cited as fact by current writers who are less than careful about the toxicity of their sources.[6]

Austin was discovering for himself the problems inherent in leading militia yahoos. The two subordinates he depended on most, Bowie and Georgia slaver James Walker Fannin, listened to his orders and then did as they thought best.[7] Whatever tension there may have been between Houston and Austin quickly passed, and Austin now looked to Houston as a confederate on the issue of organizing the government. At Austin's urging the delegates, reluctantly, followed Houston back to San Felipe. The rank and file, however, refused to let either Austin or William Wharton leave, and Austin sent a letter after Houston underscoring their accord. "The country must have organization," he wrote, "Promptness and energy in the Consultation is all important. All depends on it."[8] Thus when the quorum did gather in San Felipe on November 3, neither opposing principal was present to make his own argument. Wharton's radical stance was made by his brother, John, and Austin's more conservative tone was carried by Don Carlos Barrett and, notably,

Thomas Jefferson Rusk. A native of South Carolina, Rusk began his career as a protégé of John C. Calhoun. His father was one of his tenant farmers, and Calhoun sponsored young Rusk in the study of law. He was appointed secretary of war ad interim by David Burnet, but on his arrival at the army's headquarters provided Houston with invaluable support. Their friendship later cooled over the Cherokee war, but they cooperated in the Senate on several issues. They broke again over the Kansas-Nebraska Bill—Rusk voted in favor—and in 1857 Rusk became president pro tempore of the Senate. Distraught over the death of his wife and himself ill, he committed suicide that year, shortly after reconciling with Houston.

Courtesy Chicago Historical Society

Sam Houston.[9] According to Smithwick, Houston had stoked the volunteers on the Cibolo with the need for independence, "otherwise we could expect no assistance from other powers." Either the rustic smithy's colorful memory had misconstrued Houston's remarks or else Houston postured a bold stance for the men while tacking a more moderate course in the council chamber—behavior well within his parameters.

Houston, as both militia commander of the Nacogdoches volunteers and a political delegate to the Consultation, had adopted a curious pose in which to overthrow a government whose chief offenses had included the commingling of civil and military authority. His strategy and his work at the Consultation, however, show the summation of all that he had learned in the past—from Jackson, from the Tennessee militia, from political enemies, from everything. By returning to San Felipe instead of staying at the fight, Houston not only influenced the course of events and hobnobbed with leaders from all across Texas (and so ensured a future political base for himself), but he also got himself created major general of the army on November 12, a post that carried with it at least the possibility of unifying the disparate volunteer units and turning them into an effective (like Jackson's) fighting force. The parliamentary brawl over whether to give Houston the job did not prevent the acting government, once the matter was decided in the affirmative, from making something of a show of his commission. Only recently discovered, the paper measures some eighteen inches square, across which a large and Spencerian hand flows, not horizontally but diagonally. The document, however, also hints at the controversy of the appointment. While touting the "special trust and confidence" that the government reposed in Houston, it contains detailed admonitions adverting even to his personal habits and sobriety. Houston, bowing to the ceremony of the occasion, penned his oath of allegiance on the reverse side, also writing on the diagonal.[10]

Many in the forming government mistrusted him, and his opinion of fighting a real war with amateur militias was low—a sentiment returned by many of the men with equal warmth—but from the leaders in the field, Houston received welcome support of his insistence that government and military be organized. In addition to Austin, Houston received a letter from one of the prominent officers, Thomas Jefferson Rusk, who had raised a company of volunteers in Nacogdoches, marched them to Gonzales, and now was taking part in besieging Béxar. Two days after Houston was named commanding general, Rusk dashed him a quick letter containing both good news and a warning. The siege was going well, as "I marched a detachment of forty cavalry within 300 yards of the wall & remained there 20 minutes they were afraid to come out they fired their cannon but done us no damage all we want is two or three hundred reinforcements . . . & some thing like organization. Much depends on you & what you do must be done quickly or it will be too late all that can be done shall be done here but you know we have no organization. Make one forceful appeal to the Convention . . . & make the war bear on all alike & whatever may be our fate [we will not] give up the ship."[11]

That war was inevitable was obvious, since the fight was already under way, but the Consultation in San Felipe had to decide whether to declare for independence, as the Wharton faction urged, or to limit their goal to the restoration of the Mexican Constitution of 1824, which Santa Anna had abrogated. The former course meant going it alone unless help could be obtained from the United States; the latter held the possibility of sympathy and perhaps even aid from other Mexican liberals opposed to Santa Anna, of whom there was no shortage. The radicals were not without effective voice; at one point Mosely Baker even moved to disband the Consultation, forget all this folderol, and get on with the fight. At this point Houston stood. With government organization itself hanging in the balance and with an urgent need to shut Baker up, Houston made a rare resort to *ad hominem* attack. "I had rather be a slave," he thundered, "and grovel in the dust all my life, than be a convicted felon!" It was a reference to Baker's emigration to Texas; he had fled Alabama and "G.T.T." over the matter of a forged five-thousand-dollar check. Houston's strike helped keep the Consultation together, but it confirmed an enemy for life in Mosely Baker.[12]

Houston, who had probably spent more time actually preparing for war than any other present, and for all his husbanding of resources from within his former country, identified himself with the more cautious wing. On November 6, by a vote of 33 to 14, the Consultation proceeded through its "Organic Law" to organize a provisional government formed as a Mexican state, separate from Coahuila, and insist upon restoration of the 1824 constitution. One does wonder at this point whether, if Houston had been successful in his attempt to settle the Creek Nation and its several hundred fighting men on an East Texas land grant, his stance would have been so timid. But the wisdom of his omnipresent pragmatism is now evident: the fight was about to begin, and there was no need to alienate European powers and Mexican liberals by declaring it to be for independence instead of Mexican statehood. The justification for violence could easily be shifted later, as indeed it was on the following March 2. Still, the Wharton minority that favored immediate independence was strong enough that one of their number, Henry Smith, was elected governor, which made for endless bickering between him and the "General Council," which was the provisional legislature.[13]

The most colorful memoir of Sam Houston at the Consultation dealt not with his contending for Austin's stand against independence but is rather a distempered accusation from Dr. Anson Jones that he was kept awake one night by a drunken "orgie" at which Houston railed viciously against Austin. The story became a fusebox that powered different anti-Houston stories: one that he schemed to have the volunteer force taken away from Austin, another that he turned Fannin into his spy to subvert Austin's command, and still another that he even plotted the defeat of the force at Béxar to justify his own demand for power. Actually, Anson Jones did not arrive at the Consultation until its work was nearly done. With the perils of immediate independence averted and his appointment secure as commanding general of whatever army he could raise, Houston had little motive to excoriate Austin. It was not his nature to pick fights he had already won, anyway. Moreover, Jones did not write this until 1849, when his hatred of Houston had eaten away most of his reason. Austin's best recent biographer found little to support the story of Houston machinations against Austin, but revisionists repeat it with approval.[14]

By December 3 the volunteer companies about San Antonio succeeded in ousting General Cos from the city, and they paroled him and his men back to Mexico on the promise that they would not reenter Texas under arms. The volunteers were flushed with victory, never noticing that the defeated Mexican units were only the unmotivated conscript fringe of what was in truth a formidable military power. Heedless, many of the Texans began returning to their homes, believing that the Mexicans had been taught their lesson and the war was over. The rest made plans to march south and "liberate" the Mexican town of Matamoros. The latter envisioned scheme was really little more than a pillaging excursion, and Houston's opposition to it was loud and immediate. What was imperative was to unify and discipline the hodge-podge of militia companies and brace for the arrival of Santa Anna. In fact, he had been trying to effect just such an army organization since at least a month before, when he had advised Capt. Wylie Martin that if his ill-clothed and poorly supplied men began to suffer from the winter elements, it would be best to "retire in good order" to the towns of Gonzales and La Bahía for that purpose.[15] Houston also besought the General Council for a unified military command, but instead they authorized a patch-quilt organization of cavalry, militia, rangers, auxiliary volunteers, and an army of reserve, whatever that was.

They also authorized the invasion of Matamoros, but fortunately for the revolution named two different men to lead it, neither of whom would submit to the other. Matamoros, it seemed, was safer than Texas, as Houston's long-dreaded nightmare of warfare-by-amateurs began to materialize before his eyes. Even Fannin, who was one of the Matamoros-bent commanders, agreed with Houston on the subject of conquest by mob. "If a 'Regular Army' be organized," Fannin wrote him, "I would glad receive some honorable appointment in it.—. . . I have not time to give my views on the [current] 'modus operandi.'"[16] Revisionists who now generally depict Houston as acting alone in a monomaniacal drive to mold government and military in his own image could have benefited by this newly uncovered correspondence, which demonstrates beyond argument that Houston, while he was genuinely unpopular with many of the volunteers, when he insisted on organization did so not just with the agreement but at the beseeching of Austin, Rusk, and even Fannin.[17]

And that organization was no easy job. As Houston later lamented, "I very soon discovered that I was a General without an army, serving under . . . a pretended government, that had no head, and no loyal subjects to obey its commands."[18] But whatever the army was, Houston was its commander in chief, and he set to organizing what he could. He departed San Felipe for the makeshift provisional capital of Washington-on-the-Brazos, about thirty-five miles due north, where he arrived on Christmas Day, 1835. To Sam Houston's understanding of the map, most crucial to Texas' defense was not San Antonio but instead a more interior line, from the tiny port of Cópano on the central coast, north through Refugio to the old Mission La Bahía at the town of Goliad, and farther north to the town of Gonzales. And it was upon the latter two places that he began issuing orders for troops to concentrate. While Houston was in Washington, a company of volunteers lately arrived from Alabama and Kentucky was dispatched to Cópano to protect it, and he addressed a circular to American volunteers: "I now recommend to come by sea . . . . The time employed will be less than one-fourth that which would be needful to pass by land." Perhaps with an eye to how much easier it would be to impose his will on infantry than on roving bands of mounted rangers, he concluded the call for aid, "bring NO HORSES, unless for teams, or for packing."[19] He then wrote James Powers, also in Washington-on-the-Brazos, requesting his assistance in forwarding the Alabama and Kentucky recruits to Cópano, concluding, "Say to our friends that, by the rise of the grass, we will be on the march."[20]

Also of great concern to Houston as 1836 opened was ensuring at least the neutrality of the Cherokee Indians in East Texas. Offshoots of the Arkansas Cherokees had arrived in several stages in the area north of Nacogdoches and now numbered about four hundred. In former years the Mexican government had encouraged their settlement as a buffer against American immigration—thus seeming rather like Houston's Indian scheme, only in reverse. If the Mexican government should now offer them secure land title in exchange for aid in putting down the rebellion, the Cherokees could create havoc behind the Texan fighting lines. This was one role in which the government was anxious to benefit from Houston's abilities, and he arranged a treaty council to take place after he had himself visited the front and begun organizing the army.[21] He rode out on January 8, 1836, bound for Goliad to take command of troops he had ordered to concentrate there. And in Goliad he came to recognize, if he had not done so before, just how unpopular a choice he was among the men he was expected to command. Mosely Baker, for instance, had raised the largest unit—Company D, First Regiment—in what would become Houston's army, and the fact that Houston had insulted their elected leader in front of the whole government got him off on a very bad foot.

That was the smaller problem. The larger problem, as he knew it would be, were the volunteers themselves, undisciplined and surly. They expected to elect their leaders popularly, fight when and where they chose, and disband when and where they chose. For them to fight a war to be free from taking orders and have to take orders to do it was beyond their comprehension. In Goliad, Houston knew he had to think fast and talk hard, and to his credit, he managed to talk most of these men out of the Matamoros business, arguing less the politics of the situation than the fact that they were too ill supplied for such a venture. That he remonstrated against the intended expedition is certain, but his exact words have been lost. The speech attributed to him there, with its breathtaking racial slurs ("Nor will the vigor of the descendents of the sturdy north ever mix with the phlegm of the indolent Mexicans"), has been used against him in recent years in his revisionist remolding as a racist. The speech is now known, however, to be not of Houston's authorship but that of a purported amanuensis, German immigrant Herman Ehrenberg.[22] It is far more likely that the general took a quartermaster's hard look at food and ammunition, which he did every time he had to stomp out the Matamoros groundfire subsequently; that argument was what stalled the volunteers, at least for the moment, and bought him time to deal with other matters. Many of the men he was addressing had evacuated from San Antonio, which left the place too poorly defended to hold, so now Houston sent Jim Bowie with orders to the commander there to remove the artillery from the Alamo, blow the fortress up and retire to Gonzales.[23] The commanding general then departed for Refugio, near Cópano and the coast.

Henry Smith knew that the council was hot for the Matamoros venture and, while seeming to endorse it, tried to give his embattled general the cover of allowing his discretion: "You will adopt such measures as you may deem best, for the reduction of Matamoros."[24] Houston knew in a heartbeat that "as you deem best" meant that he did not have to do it at all. The General Council would have none of it, however, and at Refugio on January 20, Houston was stunned to see Francis Johnson and Dr. James Grant arrive with fresh orders from the council, reaffirming the Matamoros scheme. Partly this was intended by Houston's political enemies—among them the chairman of the Military Committee, Wyatt Hanks—to divest him of his command. As they had been unsuccessful in opposing his election, they now reassigned soldiers from under him. Houston had complained of Hanks to Governor Smith as early as December 17, as the council's secretary, Elisha Marshall Pease, later wrote Hanks disgustedly: "Smith continues to act whenever he has an opportunity, and is embarrassing the Government by every means in his power. Houston aids him so far as he dares."[25] Much of the opposition to Houston was based on his reputation as a drunkard. He knew that and took steps to mend the damage. "I am most miserably cool and sober," he wrote his ally Don Carlos Barrett on January 2, "so you can [say] to all my friends, instead of egg-nog I eat roasted eggs in my office."[26] This dogged sobriety lasted throughout the campaign.

For the moment undone by Francis Johnson, Grant, and the planned looting party across the Rio Grande, Houston returned to Washington-on-the-Brazos, telling Governor Smith that with "all available resources of Texas . . . directed against Matamoros," he had "but one course left, to return, and report myself to you in person."[27] The general was now certain that there were intrigues against him, but what he found in Washington shook him to a far greater depth than personal insult. With war commenced against the formidable power of Mexico and with Santa Anna assembling an army of invasion, the supposed government of Texas had dissembled into a convocation of bookslamming pettifoggery. Governor Smith and the General Council were locked in a vicious power struggle like children playing at democracy, who understood its rules but not its reason; they certainly seemed unaware of the perils of their own situation. Smith had tried to dissolve the council, which returned the compliment by trying to impeach him, while the affairs of the fledgling state languished. At least one of Smith's windy rebukes the council handed over to its secretary, Marshall Pease, to file away without the document even becoming part of the governmental record.[28] In Sam Houston's swelling catalog of lessons learned, this was a new and chilling twist, to realize that civil government, no less than a military venture, could be wrecked by relying on walleyed, posturing amateurs. And they had proved it, if in no other way, by appointing a commanding general of the army to fight for their very survival and only weeks later stripping him of his men to indulge a desire to pillage a town of no military value three hundred miles away. It was less than three months since he had opposed his friends the Whartons in voting against independence, but what he saw in Washington-on-the-Brazos hit Sam Houston like a bucket of ice water.

Nor was the Washington sideshow harmless; amateur government was materially damaging Texas' ability to defend herself. Lt. Col. Henry Millard, having been dispatched to Nacogdoches to recruit volunteers, found it slow going, as he fumed in a letter to Houston, because "the government having no credit and the genl council having neglected to furnish me either with credit or funds after promising in the most solemn manner to do so and I have only been able to raise $250.00 by Col. Forbes & myself pledging ourselves for the repayment. . . . I have paid no attention to orders from Gov. Robinson or the council since their disolution with Gov Smith under whom and yourself I can only acknowledge the right to command operations." A couple of days later, he sent an even hotter message to the commanding general: "We have now about 40 men and almost without the means of support, badly clad and in fact I know not what to do unless we can have some assistance from government if their is any government left in Texas. I had reason enough to curse the Dmd council before I left them but their late acts I believe justly brought down the curses of the country." In addition to all this, now a Colonel Sherman of Kentucky had arrived and demanded some of Millard's new recruits, whom he was not disposed to turn over without Houston's approval.[29] The Matamoros business eventually broke up in disarray, as Houston knew it would. Those volunteers who felt cocky enough for action trekked as far south as San Patricio, where Dr. Grant and a party of fifteen foragers were wiped out by cavalry belonging to the southern column of Santa Anna's army, commanded by Gen. José Urrea. After a couple more bloody defeats the others thought better of their rashness.

Texas' image abroad was also suffering. Once the council began functioning, after a fashion, the volunteers released Austin and Wharton to travel to the United States and drum up aid. The former rivals shelved their differences and, in company with Branch T. Archer, headed for New Orleans. The new commissioners found it a slow go, however. Wharton reported to Houston from Nashville in mid-February: "When we arrived in N.O. the cause of Texas was perfectly flat. She had not credit for 25 cents. This was mainly affected by the Insurance offices & Commission houses having commerce with Mexico," and who were fearful that a strong Texas granting letters of marque to privateers would damage their investments in Mexico—surely not the last time that business interests imposed their effect on American foreign policy. With diligence and luck, however, the Texas commissioners were able to negotiate a quarter of a million dollars in loans from Texas' American friends. Since then, Archer, Austin, and Wharton had been beset by foul weather, were snowed in at Nashville, and had no idea when they might be able to proceed to Washington, D.C.[30]

In an endless raging torrent of a report to Governor Smith, whom he considered an ally, Houston cited articles and paragraphs of the Organic Law that had created the General Council in impeaching their conduct, concluding that he no longer considered "the council as a constitutional body, nor their acts lawful. . . . I am not prepared to violate my duty or my oath, by yielding obedience."[31] With John Forbes, his new ally from Nacogdoches, as his fellow Indian commissioner, Houston galloped out of Washington in less than a week, on February 5, for East Texas and the Chero-kee treaty council. But now he had a second objective as well: with the government paralyzed, he determined to expend energy building support for a new convention to declare independence and organize a permanent government.

There was no doubt that the hour for a total break with Mexico had arrived. Even if there had been no definite information that Santa Anna was gathering his army of retribution to march through Texas, it still would have been the only prudent assumption to proceed on, and once the dictator entered Texas with troops, a peaceful compromise into Mexican statehood would have been impossible. More immediately, government by buffoonery might well destroy Texas' chances of sur-vival without Santa Anna ever having to touch off a cannon. The only way to depose the General Council was by convening another meeting of people's representa-tives, which could only result in the declaration of independence that the Consulta-tion had avoided. Any way one looked at it, the moment both sought and dreaded had arrived. A new plenary convention was organized in record time, elections were held on February 1, the delegates convened in Washington-on-the-Brazos on March 1—Houston was accompanied by Forbes—and declared independence from Mexico the next day, which by coincidence was Houston's forty-third birthday. In freezing weather in an unfinished building, they proceeded to draw up a consti-tution, organize a government "Ad interim," and elect leaders.

Formation of the new government was interrupted with the arrival of Colonel Travis's famous plea from the Alamo for assistance. Santa Anna had arrived. Described traditionally as one of the most heroic documents in American history (and described in revision as exemplary of the blustering, filibuster-minded, idiotic bravado of the whole revolution), its contents were intoned to the hushed little assembly in Washington:

> COMMANDANCY OF THE ALAMO
> Bexar, February 24, 1836
> To the People of Texas and All
> Americans in the World
> FELLOW-CITIZENS AND COMPATRIOTS:
> I am besieged by a thousand or more of the Mexicans under Santa Anna. I have sustained a continued Bombardment & cannonade for 24 hours, and have not lost a man—The enemy have demanded a surrender at discretion; otherwise the garrison is to be put to the sword, if the place is taken. I have answered the summons with a cannon-shot. . . . Come to our aid with all despatch—The enemy are receiving reinforcements daily, and will no doubt increase to three or four thousand in four or five days.[32]

A week earlier, Travis had written Houston his own harried endorsement of the general's visceral mistrust of commanding citizen-soldiers. "Militia and volun-teers," he admitted, "are but ill suited to garrison a town."[33]

Three days after the vote for independence, the convention confirmed Houston as commander in chief of the army.[34] The only vote against him was cast by Robert

Potter, a short, posturing duelist and former North Carolina congressman. He had resigned his seat and "G.T.T." after serving time for castrating a fifty-five-year-old Methodist minister and seventeen-year-old boy whom he accused (without evidence) of "violating the sanctity of [his] marriage bed."[35] Personifying as he did the virtues of Southern manhood—chivalry, oratory, bigotry, and bloodlust—he attracted many powerful friends in the Texas government, and from a succession of political offices nettled Houston for the next six years.

During December, Houston had repeatedly predicted that the fight would open on the first of March. His vision proved farsighted by a week. Santa Anna had arrived in force, ready for battle, news that should have occasioned the darkest consternation on the part of the convention. Their response was typical, as the members almost stormed in a body to the defense of San Antonio. Houston, however, having been sent once into the field by a half-cocked government, checked them and insisted that they get on with their organization of state. He would himself take the saddle to collect the troops from Gonzales and ride to Travis's relief. He set out at once, dispatching his trusted Forbes to the coast to round up what recruits and supplies he could find at Velasco, then sortie by water no farther south than Dimmit's Landing, then return to the army with whatever men he had.

It took Houston five days to reach Gonzales, and this has become a point of contention among historians in recent years, especially since Houston left the government with the impression that he was riding straight to the relief of the Alamo. Speculation has ranged from his being in a drugged stupor to the possibility that he was cynically waiting for the Alamo to fall so he could stride onto the stage without competition. "Genl. Houston shew'd no disposition of being in a hurry to the Army," stated one W. W. Thompson in a sworn affidavit four years later, "much to the surprise of myself & others; he remain'd at Capt. Burnum's all night, & all that day, and all night again before starting for Gonzales." The possibility of Houston indulging in either drink or drugs is out of the question; his sobriety on the campaign was admitted by even his worst enemies in attendance. The Thompson affidavit was sworn to an official of Mirabeau Lamar's State Department at a time when government minions were always looking to swear in somebody to say something defamatory about Houston. Thompson also swore that Houston insisted of the siege of the Alamo, "that he believed it to be a damn lie, & that all those reports from Travis and Fannin were lies, for there were no Mexican forces there and that he believed it was only electioneering schemes on [the part of] Travis & Fannin to sustain their own popularity." The Thompson affidavit loses its little credibility there. Houston had predicted the arrival of Santa Anna within a week's accuracy since the first of December, had repeated it many times, and then published a broadside to the people announcing Santa Anna's arrival on March 2.[36]

The main issue to Houston for not being in haste to join the army at Gonzales was that there was no army at Gonzales. He had sent Sterling Robertson to the United States to round up recruits, and closer to home he had sent Forbes to South Texas to muster more, and had sent a courier ordering Fannin to join him in Gonzales. But the only "force" already in Gonzales were a few armed citizens whom J. C. Neill himself gathered to reinforce the Alamo.[37] As word spread over the next few days that the army was to organize in Gonzales, when Houston did reach there on March 11 he found only about three hundred men—"unorganized," he wrote— waiting for someone to tell them what to do. Had he arrived on the seventh or eighth, he would have found a fraction of that number, not enough to mount an effective relief of the Alamo, even had it not already fallen, but plenty to generate the mass stupidity to stampede into Santa Anna's waiting lancers. By the thirteenth, however, with the army finally having a rallying point, with the Alamo in ruins, and with the Matamoros lunacy quiet, at least for the moment, thanks to the Grant and Johnson debacles, Houston's force increased. At first he estimated it to be nearly 500; an accurate count mustered 374. If Houston's calls to fall back and organize had been heeded from the first, Santa Anna would have been in possession of a militarily useless San Antonio, and the Texas commander could have mounted an effective defense of his preferred line with at least a thousand men. But it was not a time to look back.

It was virtually upon his arrival that Houston heard reports, unconfirmed, of the disaster at the Alamo. He sent instructions to Fannin for the defense of Victoria and on the thirteenth sent a trusted scout, Erastus "Deaf" Smith, toward Béxar to ascertain the truth of the Alamo stories. They were confirmed when Smith returned with Susanna Dickinson, widow of Travis's artillery commander, with her infant daughter in arms. The Alamo's defenders had been killed to the last man, and Santa Anna had sent her eastward to warn any others who would resist that they would meet the same fate. About twenty deserters bolted Houston's camp at first revelation of the Alamo calamity; Houston ordered their arrest and return, though he was powerless to prevent the spread of pandemonium in their wake. The disaster at the Alamo and the subsequent loss of other units near San Patricio at least strength- ened Houston's hand against the Matamoros scheme. That "projected expedition, under the *agency* of the council, has already cost us over two hundred and thirty- seven lives, and where the effects are to end, none can foresee." One effect, however, he did foresee: "I fear [Fannin] is in siege."[38] Fannin had in fact started to the relief of the Alamo but was forced by transport breakdowns to turn back, and Houston had lost touch with him.

With Houston on the road to take command of the army, the convention organized a provisional government, and if Houston thought the step would end the intrigues and pettifogging of the General Council, he was bitterly disappointed. Delegates elected as ad interim president of the Republic of Texas David Gouver- neur Burnet and a prominent Mexican liberal, Lorenzo de Zavala, as ad interim vice president. Burnet was formerly a principal of the Galveston Bay and Texas Land Company—one of Prentiss's people who never would come up with Houston's retainer to buy up the Leftwich lands. He was also a confirmed and passionate Houston hater. Fortunately for the commanding general, the man to whom he would report most directly was James Collinsworth, chairman of the ad interim government's Committee on Military Affairs. The convention appointed Potter, a man after Burnet's own heart and who shared the ad interim president's loathing of Houston, secretary of the navy. Potter's naval experience amounted to six years' adolescent sea duty on various vessels, where he gained his reputation as a duelist and liberty-call lothario, but he was still the most qualified man present.[39]

Down in Gonzales, Houston sequestered the Alamo messengers as soon as he heard their news, but the disaster left the people of the town numb with grief. Only fifty miles east of San Antonio de Béxar, they had been the only settlement to send volunteers, thirty of them, in response to Travis's first call for aid. With that whole command now massacred, no defense whatever stood between Gonzales and Santa Anna's pennant-fluttering legions. Houston estimated, too generously, that Fannin had seven hundred men under him, but even if Fannin was safe, he was in Goliad, fifty miles to the south, and in no position to help him. Houston had under his command 374 men, and they were not soldiers but armed civilians, mostly unprovisioned and some without ammunition. Once Santa Anna ordered the resumption of his eastward sweep, Houston's course seemed clear, and he reported to Collinsworth: "We could have met the enemy, and avenged some of our wrongs; but, detached as we were, without supplies for the men in camp, or either provisions, or ammunition, or artillery . . . , it would have been madness to hazard a contest. [The troops] had not been taught the first principles of the drill. If starved out, and the camp broken up, there was no hope for the future. By falling back, Texas can rally, and defeat any force that can come against her."[40]

Many of Houston's undisciplined yahoos, however, were outraged at the thought of retreating. Maddened and goaded by the pathetic plight of the Gonzales families, they never forgave the general for falling back. One such malcontent was a volunteer named Creed Taylor, only fifteen years old but already a veteran who had defended the Gonzales "Come and Take It" cannon, fought at Concepcion, and gone into San Antonio with old Ben Milam. "Let other historians rail and prate as they may," he said later, "but be it known to all future generations of Texans forth that if [another] had been in command, [we would] do as we had done before— whip ten-to-one the carrion-eating convicts under Santa Anna." That of course was twaddle; Santa Anna's disciplined regiments would have atomized them in a battle, but just as Houston could not tell them anything then, historians could not tell them anything later. Strategic considerations flew unseen over their heads. Creed Taylor, at least, did not stick around to nettle Houston further; he left the army and shepherded his family safely east.[41]

The commander in chief was as affected as his men were by the sight of the Gonzales widows, many of whom were hysterical and helpless. While he was desperate to collect all possible supplies for his army, he allowed some military baggage to be burned so the wagons could be used to transport the refugees eastward. With these civilians thus in tow and with the flames of the burning town licking the night sky behind them, Houston retreated into the predawn gloom of March 14. Only a mile or two east of Gonzales they entered a post oak forest so dark that Pvt. J. H. "Hamp" Kuykendall of McNutt's Company remembered they had almost to feel their way as they went. They groped along for ten dispirited miles—made the more miserable by the prevalence of measles—before stopping to rest at

McClure's on the east side of Peach Creek. They had scarcely caught their breath when they jumped at hearing explosions in the direction of the town, and there was a brief terror that Santa Anna had overtaken them with artillery. Calmer heads realized that powder stored in some of the houses had been touched off, but nonetheless they soon took up the trek again toward the Lavaca.

"Immediately after the march was resumed," one recalled, "Gen'l. Houston rode slowly from the front to the rear of the army, pointing towards the ranks with his finger, evidently counting the men. Having numbered his host, he returned to the front, proclaiming . . . in his peculiar deliberate and distinct utterance, 'we are the rise of eight hundred strong, and with a good position can whip ten to one of the enemy.'" That was to encourage the men. If pressed to fight, he would have been lucky to muster half that number. The general's own frame of mind was much more frayed than he let show, but he betrayed his anxiety at Santa Anna's breath on his neck in an incident shortly after crossing the Lavaca. Houston was riding far back in the ranks when the whole procession ground to a standstill, and he galloped to the front of the column to demand the cause of the halt. He was told that a private named Rhodes, in fording a small creek, had stopped for a drink, blocking the line behind him. "Knock him down, God damn him," he roared, "knock him down—standing there and impeding the march of the whole army. God damn him, knock him down!" Rhodes, who was already on Houston's bad side for falling asleep on guard duty the night before, wisely got out of the way. Houston later reprimanded him but, despite having threatened to have him shot for napping, forbore further punishment.[42]

All of Houston's misgivings about going to war with undisciplined militia were proving well founded. These were yeomen who were used to fighting when and how they pleased and voting on what officers to obey. For Houston to not just order them about but cuss them out in doing so, while perhaps standard fare in a real army, generated deep bitterness in a certain number of them. One was John Holland Jenkins, only thirteen years old, whom Houston spied trudging along near collapse beneath the weight of his rifle. The general procured him a mount but warned him not to ride ahead of the army. The horse was spirited, however, and young Jenkins was soon far in the van. "God damn your soul!!!" Houston bellowed after him, "Didn't I order you to ride right here?" Publicly humiliated, Jenkins got off the horse and declared he would die before mounting again. "With those few harsh words," he recalled later, "General Houston completely changed the current of my feelings toward him, and my profound admiration and respect was turned into a dislike I could never conquer."[43]

Some two thousand Mexican troops came after the Texan column apace, covering twenty-four miles in one day's march. "Upon this statement of facts," Houston wrote Collinsworth, "I deemed it proper to fall back and take a position on the Colorado, near Burnham's."[44] Unlike the swift, shallow rivers of the hill country around San Antonio, the Lower Colorado was wide, deep, and swift. With much of his army sapped by the measles and heavy rain on March 18 threatening a rise in the water, Houston saw his men and the families safely across, then ordered the ferry torched. At Burnham's, Houston's continuous effort to instill some discipline in his soldiers began to bear fruit, although in a way he had not anticipated. Houston had occasion to venture beyond the camp's perimeter, and on his return he was challenged by a sentry. Impatiently, Houston demanded whether the sentry did not know the general had a right to pass unchallenged, but the sentry held his ground. He had strict orders from the officer of the day to let no one pass without written permission. "Well, my friend," said the general with some satisfaction, "if those were your orders, you are right." He then seated himself on a stump until the officer of the day arrived to pass him into camp.[45]

Behind the shield of the surging Colorado, Houston had a chance to rest his men and take stock. A party of scouts under Captain Karnes had killed one Mexican spy and brought another one in as a prisoner. Houston adjusted his position thirty miles downstream to Beason's Crossing, near Columbus. He wracked his brain over the chessboard of his maps and rifled communiqués across the countryside, trying to impose some sense of cohesion—to Fannin again, to hold a position on Lavaca Bay and stay ready to join the main army; to Collinsworth again, that Texas' little three-schooner navy give them some cover from the sea. "Keep the navy busy. To it we must look for *essential aid*." His close to the letter was a telling comment on the state of both his army and his office: "We want arms, and need stationary."[46]

9

THE RUNAWAY SCRAPE

By now, a curious trend began to appear on the map of Houston's retreat: delay was strength. At Burnham's, his army increased to six hundred men, more than two-thirds effective. At Beason's, the two hundred fresh Kentucky volunteers under Col. Sidney Sherman arrived. From early on in the muddy "Runaway Scrape," it was unmistakable to a soldier of Houston's experience that every day and every mile he could delay the inevitable showdown, the stronger he got. Conversely, the deeper he could draw Santa Anna into Texas, the more the dictator's supply lines were stretched like rubber and the greater the possibility that any error he might make would prove fatal.

Nor did Houston judge his own men ready for battle—raids, skirmishes, and ambushes, perhaps, but not a real battle against disciplined troops. With the specter of his youth and the Tennessee militia haunting his psyche, Houston utilized the days of March 19–26 at Beason's drilling his army and training them to maneuver by companies, hoping to fashion them into a force that could be depended upon. Their training went well, but once again events began slipping out of Houston's control. Some of the deserters who had fled the army at Gonzales whipped through Washington-on-the-Brazos, prompting the ad interim government to decamp and rumble in disarray toward the coast. Thomas J. Rusk had been made secretary of war, to whom Houston protested: "All would have been well, and all at peace on this side of the Colorado, if I could only have had a moment to start an express in advance of the deserters; but they went first, and, being panic struck, it was contagious, and all who saw them breathed the poison, and fled. It was a poor compliment to me to suppose that I would not advise the Convention of any necessity which might arise for their removal." Even as he penned the letter, Mexican scouts were captured and they divulged that the force now in closest pursuit was less mighty than the general had feared, which made the flight of the government seem even more precipitate and silly. "Oh, curse the consternation which has seized the people!"[1]

That force, six or seven hundred men under Gen. Joaquín Ramirez y Sesma, faced Houston on the other side of the Colorado. Their number was the approximate equal of Houston's own, perhaps even some fewer. His own men pressed him to fight, the ad interim government now ordered him to stand and fight—inspiring example that they were, in mid-stampede to the coast—and Houston critics ever since have insisted "that San Jacinto should have been fought at Beason's Crossing."[2]

Houston knew better. His militia rowdies were not yet a match for regular troops who could wheel and fire by companies and stand fast in the thick of battle. In the unlikely event that they did best Sesma's infantry, there would be further battles: perhaps Sesma again; or Sesma in combination with Gen. Antonio Gaona, now in Bastrop with a thousand troops; or with Santa Anna himself, in Sesma's rear with another thousand; and somewhere to the south, José Urrea was advancing with two thousand more. And if all those were beaten, Juan José Andrade remained in San Antonio with a reserve of fifteen hundred. To win the revolution here, Houston would have had to win not just this fight but also every fight, using the same winded, underdone volunteers, facing in every battle fresh Mexican regulars, seasoned and ready to fight. It would have been suicide.

The mood of the Texan army, however, demanded a taste of battle. Houston had bolstered their morale ever since abandoning Gonzales by promising them a fight and not to provide one now might cost him control of the men. Given some margin of safety by the arrival of Sherman's two hundred Kentuckians, Houston ordered a limited engagement: a small force showed themselves to Sesma's troops, drew fire, and retreated, hoping to lure the Mexicans into an ambush. It was an ancient ruse; not surprisingly, it did not work.[3]

With a little steam thus vented from the army and with Santa Anna's pincers closing, it was time to retreat farther. Houston knew it would be an unpopular order, and thus he had been saving up a piece of grievous news that he had kept from the men until the time was right. No help would come from Fannin; Urrea had beaten him and now held the entire force prisoner at Goliad. Houston had learned of this by a courier three days previous and, in reporting the bad news to Rusk, supposed that Fannin must have attempted to "retreat in daylight in the face of superior force." Then he added, "He is an ill-fated man."[4] Houston was right on both counts. Not only had Fannin attempted the retreat as Houston had suspected, but he ended it by digging in to a defensive position on an open prairie, literally within sight of thick woods from which he could have mounted an effective defense. Fannin had once assessed his own military ability as modest, which was accurate.

Fannin's arrival would have increased the size of the Texas army by some 50 percent, but now that would never happen. Houston assembled his men and told them they were "the only army in Texas now present. . . . There are but few of us, and if we are beaten, the fate of Texas is sealed. The salvation of the country depends upon the first battle had with the enemy. For this reason, I intend to retreat, if I am obliged to go even to the banks of the Sabine."[5] Uncharitable biographers later interpreted this statement as evidence that Houston was willing to abandon Texas entirely; the general himself was satisfied for the moment to have the soldiers understand that he would retreat them as far as he had to in order to fight with advantage. What he could not share with them were plans already in motion to give Santa Anna a rude surprise at the border, if battle could not be joined before then. On this day, the only encouragement to reach the camp was John Forbes's return from the coast. At Velasco he had discovered two companies of volunteers newly landed, and he raised a third company from among the locals. Upon hearing of Fannin's capture, Forbes took it upon himself to modify his orders; he had impressed a schooner to carry out the southward sweep Houston had directed but, considering it more important to join the army at once, decided to set off over-land. Thanks to his enterprise, Houston's men were suddenly buoyed by the arrival of three fresh companies and a large influx of supplies and ammunition.

The next day, March 27, Palm Sunday, as Houston's army trudged to a new camp a mile west of San Felipe, James Walker Fannin and some four hundred of his men at Goliad were lined up and shot; those who survived the first volley were put to the sword. Urrea would have saved them if he could, and, indeed, he exempted several useful men from execution even after being personally rebuked by Santa Anna for such treasonable mercy.

On the morning of the twenty-eighth, the Runaway Scrape resumed upstream along the west bank of the Brazos, though not before Houston's mistrust of militia came starkly to the fore. Two of his company commanders, Wiley Martin and, predictably, Mosely Baker, positively refused to budge any farther.

In retrospect, it seems natural that army resistance to the general should have coalesced in these two. Houston, of course, had been on Baker's bad side ever since Nacogdoches and certainly since vilifying him at the Consultation, but Wiley Martin had more of a history with his commander. Martin was sixty years old to Houston's forty-three; both had fought under Jackson at Horseshoe Bend, where Martin had been a captain to Houston's rank of a mere lieutenant, and he perhaps found it difficult to obey a man who had been his junior, especially since he had heard nothing but "retreat" from Houston since November 25. Neither Baker nor Martin considered Houston their political superior: Baker had been speaker of the Alabama House of Representatives, and Martin had been one of Austin's "Old Three Hundred" and, in fact, had served as alcalde of Austin's colony. Thus, both had cause to view Houston as something of a usurper. Baker and Martin did have some differences between themselves—Martin had joined with Houston in the peace party, while Baker had long agitated for independence—but once on campaign they had no difficulty finding common cause in their vituperation against the general.

If Houston had tried to deal with Baker's and Martin's insubordination in the traditional way, he would probably have lost control of the army. It was a situation of immediate urgency, and Houston's response was a multifaceted stroke of cunning that, over subsequent years, he gained the reputation of being able to call upon. He dispatched his rebellious captains to remain behind and guard the river crossings—Baker here at San Felipe and Martin downstream at Fort Bend. In doing so, he got the two most factious dissenters out of his camp and away from the other men, whom they might influence, and he gave them duties to perform that they could hardly refuse, considering the demand they were making to fight. He got them, at least in this instance, to take an order from him, and he protected his flank while retreating. Moreover, these two companies had been recruited from the farms along the Lower Brazos, and Houston knew if they got into a fight, the men would have the motivation of fighting literally for their homes. The stroke proved as lucky as it was shrewd, for the presence of Mosely Baker and Wiley Martin at the Brazos crossings forced Santa Anna to spend valuable time probing for some other safe place to cross, buying time for Houston to get the rest of the army ready for battle.

So with Baker and Martin safely detached, Houston knew it was time to say something to the rest of the men or risk losing them. "My friends," he said without hint of irony to the volunteers who were furious with him: "I am told that evilly disposed persons have told you I am going to march you to the Redlands. This is false. I am going to march you into the Brazos bottom near Groce's, to a position where you can whip the enemy ten to one, and where we can get an abundant supply of corn."[6] The general rode slowly with the men as they retreated through sheets of rain, his black dresscoat waterlogged and cold. The new refuge that beckoned was the plantation of Jared Groce, one of the richest planters in the country, who had already been generous in his support of the revolutionary cause and who had the means to feed and rest Houston's army.

The blow-up with Mosely Baker and Wiley Martin, the sudden exigency of recasting his plans to both accommodate and defuse them, and his artful oratory to the troops took a toll on the commander. "I hope I can keep them together," Houston confided darkly to Rusk, "I have, thus far, succeeded beyond my hopes." The men suffered another shock when the citizens of San Felipe, seeing the army march by with only a day's pause, burned the town and fled without any orders from Houston. Stephen Austin had founded San Felipe on the west bank of the Brazos without any thought of utilizing the river as a defense; indeed it could not be defended from the west, and Baker's men took up positions on the east bank to keep Santa Anna from crossing. Torching the settlement was probably Mosely Baker's doing, but he said later that it was a "result" of Houston's orders, which Houston denied, deepening their enmity.[7]

Not all the citizen-soldiers in Houston's army shared Baker's contempt for him. Many, in fact, appreciated the general's manically detailed watchfulness over his men. From the moment he had assumed authority, Houston's style of command was close and meticulous, delegating little. Even in the rout from Gonzales, he had detached a special courier thirty miles to fetch a blind widow, whose husband had died in the Alamo, and her six children. According to fifteen-year-old recruit William Zuber: "A respectable number of our men reposed unlimited confidence in General Houston, . . . his inflexibility, confidence of success, and courtesy to his soldiers. Also he kept no bodyguard. When we were encamped, the door of his tent generally stood open, and any soldier who wished could enter at liberty. General Houston never exchanged compliments with a man, however, or conversed with him unless on business, at which time he courteously answered necessary inquiries and gave needed advice and encouragement. . . . When marching, he rode beside one of his teamsters, as is the custom of wagonmasters in regular armies, so that he might be near during their troubles." In camp, those who called for him at his tent found him, when not at his letters or studying maps, whittling, a habit he had developed from his earliest years.[8]

Now, opposite Groce's, Houston's mania for detail had become so ingrained that when he implored Rusk for supplies, he specified: "Don't send by wagons; and let the pack-horses be well hobbled at night. My horses and baggage-wagons in camp give me all the care I have." He was still furious at the panic sweeping the countryside. "For heaven's sake," he begged Rusk, "do allay the fever and chill which prevails in the country. . . . the fame of Jackson could never compensate me for my anxiety and mental pain."[9]

Houston did at least have one piece of good news. The navy, whose aid he considered so essential, had delivered a prize. The Texas ship *Invincible* had captured the Mexican brig *Pocket*, loaded with foodstuffs and munitions for the Mexican army, and brought her into Galveston. Houston parlayed the event into a brave broadside "To the People," combining a pep talk and a call for reinforcements to gather about his camp. "My intention never has been to cross the Brazos," he asserted, "and the false reports spread are by men who have basely deserted the army of Texas." He declared further that the Mexican army was not so large as once feared. "Let the people not be any longer in dread of danger, if the men will turn out like men. . . . *We will whip them soon.*"[10]

In light of subsequent events, historians have long debated whether Houston actually meant not to carry the fight east of the Brazos. East or west of the river was not the issue in his own mind, however. He was doing what he always did best, biding his time, gathering strength while stalling, riding out events until a situation presented itself where a decisive stroke was possible. Prudently, though, he impressed into government service the rugged 130-foot, 144-ton high-pressure steamboat *Yellow Stone* for the purpose of getting the army across the Brazos if it became necessary. Although he had no specific authority from the ad interim government, he also "assured and guaranteed" the captain of the boat, John E. Ross, that the republic would indemnify him for any damages and promised land bounties for the services of her crew. Ross cooperated fully, answering Houston that the ship was half loaded with cotton bales that could now be used for protection. "I have four cords wood on board," he wrote, "& Every thing ready to '*go ahead*.'"[11]

Houston's redeployment had reduced his main army to just over five hundred troops. The men, as ever, spoiled loudly for a fight, but Houston still judged them unready and drilled them for several days, seizing upon the excuse that he was waiting for the artillery to arrive. Citizens of Cincinnati, Ohio, had cast two cannon, along with shot, for the Texas cause and sent them down to New Orleans and thence to Brazoria. Probably the first Houston heard of their arrival was a letter from Edward Harcourt, the German ex-Santanista whom he had appointed chief engineer of the army. Harcourt had been constructing breastworks at Velasco "with the aid of some citizens and sixty Negroes from some plantation" when Potter ordered him to Galveston, where "I found two complete field pieces with

David G. Burnet. Five years older than Houston, Burnet was from New Jersey and came from a more distinguished family; his father had sat in the Continental Congress. Unlike Houston, he never made a success at any career. At the age of eighteen, he went as a filibuster to Venezuela with Miranda; after various business failures, Burnet traded goods to Comanche Indians and lived with them for six months, ending in 1820. He was not a delegate to the Convention of 1836 but attended anyway and won election as president ad interim. After his term as vice president under Mirabeau Lamar, Burnet's life began a long and depressing decline that ended, as a pauper, in Galveston in 1870.

Courtesy Center for American History, University of Texas

ammunition . . . on board of the Pensilvania. I could easier find means to send them by Harrisburg, than from Brazoria," where they had been unable to find a single team to haul provisions. Houston sent for the guns and they were now, he heard, coming overland. Both their expected presence and their delay were godsends to Houston in keeping his men on the string.[12]

The commanding general used the lull to catch up on his correspondence, writing Rusk on the third that eighty recruits had arrived from East Texas and were on the opposite bank. The river was rising, he said, and if his camp flooded he would have to remove either onto an exposed prairie to the west or cross his army on the *Yellow Stone*. "You may rest easy at Harrisburg; the enemy will never cross the Brasos." He added a dispatch the following day with the news of the Fannin massacre.[13] Rusk himself arrived in camp that day with a personal rebuke from President Burnet to stick and fight where he was. "Sir:" the president wrote him, "The enemy are laughing you to scorn. You must fight them. You must retreat no farther. The country expects you to fight. The salvation of the country depends on you doing so."

"I have kept the army together under most discouraging circumstances," Houston protested to Burnet in return, "and I hope a just and wise God, in whom I have always believed, will yet save Texas." In sarcastic humility he continued: "I am sorry that I am so wicked, for 'the prayers of the righteous shall prevail.' That you are so, I have no doubt, and hope that Heaven, as such, will . . . crown your efforts with success in behalf of Texas."[14]

The remarkable thing about Rusk was that he managed to enter Houston's camp with an open mind. The secretary of war had been getting a daily diet of anti-Houston polemic from Burnet and the rest of the cabinet, and he had been fielding letters from other officials and even common citizens who were upset with the choice of Houston to lead the army. One Jesse Benton wrote to Rusk the day after Burnet penned his laughing-to-scorn letter, vilifying Houston while proposing his own strategy, which was exactly the course Houston was following: "But the most discouraging of all things," Benton complained, "was the appointment of Sam Houston commander in chief. I have long considered him unsound in mind and unsound in his heart or will as his head. My plan of defence for Texas has been . . . the very same which enabled the Russians, in 1812, to defeat & destroy Napoleon and his 600,000 men."[15]

Houston, encamped at Groce's, was as much under attack from his own government and army as from the Mexicans, and when Rusk arrived, Houston sat him down and told him, in frontier parlance, how the cow ate the cabbage. Rusk had written Houston from the siege of Béxar in November, endorsing his views on the necessity of getting the revolution organized, and Houston had probably marked him since then as one man in the government whom he could trust with his plans. The substance of their talk is lost, but Rusk went over to his side and from that time shielded him from further governmental interference. Certain of the troops were dismayed by this, muttering that Houston had put some Cherokee spell on him, but from early April, Rusk's alliance with Houston was a crucial factor in the success of the campaign.

The commander in chief used the breather at Groce's also to produce a smattering of personal messages, including a polite lie to the Raguets: "There is the most perfect harmony in camp. . . . Don't get scared at Nacogdoches." To his venerated Colonel Bowl of the Cherokees he wrote: "I am busy and will only say, how da do. . . . give my best compliments to my sister, and tell her that I have not wore out the Mockasins which she made me."[16] But mostly his pen was busily regulating the details of the war: to Mosely Baker, commanding the contingent at San Felipe, to see to it that there was no more looting; to an otherwise unidentified "Major," fine-tuning the deployment of spies in the countryside; to David Thomas, acting as secretary of war in the absence of Rusk, arranging the delivery of supplies; to John

Forbes, ordering tents, but from whom he received not just supplies but three whole companies of new troops.[17] And the men drilled and grumbled.

Actually, a couple did more than grumble. A court-martial convened on April 2, presided over by Anson Jones and Henry Millard, to try Privates John Garner and A. Scales for mutiny and desertion. They were convicted and sentenced to death by firing squad, the sentence to be executed the following day between the hours of ten and three. The court also recommended clemency. Houston was no fool. He knew the army would have exploded if he had tried to shoot the condemned men, but he could not very well acknowledge this openly and had to come up with other reasons to spare them. On the last page of the court-martial proceedings, Houston ordered clemency for Private Garner in consideration of his contrition as well as clemency for Private Scales "in consideration of the peculiar state of mind in which the prisoner is known at times to be, [as] certified" by the army surgeon. The commanding general did not specify whether he meant that Scales was insane or merely ornery. He must, however, have intended his clemency orders to be read to the soldiers, for the paper quickly evolved into a homily on discipline. While the general, as he referred to himself in third person, was disposed to be merciful in this instance, "he is compelled to assure the army, that this is an exception to the general rule, which he is resolved to preserve. Subordination can only be maintained by a strict observance of the rules & Articles of War. This, being the first instance, is directed as an admonition, the next *must* be an example." As an infantry lieutenant, Houston had witnessed Jackson order the execution of men in similar circumstances, and in that case there had been no reprieve. Scales did not hang around to test Houston's mercy a second time. He deserted three days later.[18]

John M. Allen was now en route to him with the cannon, but with the river continuing to rise, it was time for Houston to prepare the public for what he had promised not to do. "Assure the inhabitants generally," Houston wrote Allen, "that the army will not cross the Brasos, unless to act with more effect against the enemy." Those who failed to rally to the army, he threatened, would have their property confiscated and be regarded as deserters.[19] The inevitable finally happened on April 7, as the Napoleon of the West trod the charred ruins of San Felipe and reached the west bank of the Brazos. The president-general ordered a flatboat to be loaded to begin a crossing but abandoned it under fire from Mosely Baker's riflemen; Santa Anna returned fire from his two cannon and positioned his own snipers to engage Baker's. The firefight continued for two days until the dictator realized he was letting his army be pinned down by a mere rear guard. He left Sesma with seven or eight hundred men to finish Baker while he headed downriver to find another crossing.

The Mexicans arrived at Fort Bend, which was defended by Wylie Martin, on April 12. Demonstrating a short learning curve, this time Santa Anna approached the ferry warily, concealing himself and others in brush while putting up Colonel Almonte, who spoke fluent English, to hail the black ferryman on the opposite bank to come across. The trick worked without incident, and Santa Anna had his army across the Brazos before Martin could fire a shot. With the dictator and his army finally on the east side of the river, Martin's current posting was as dangerous as it was useless, and Houston ordered them, as well as those he had deployed along the Colorado, to rejoin the main army. This was one order from Houston that both Baker and Martin obeyed with alacrity.

"It was impossible," Houston rightly concluded, "to guard all the river passes for one hundred miles, and . . . guard any one point effectually."[20] But the Texas commander was not the only one poring over his maps and making assessments. President-General Santa Anna had been making plans too and concluded that if he could collar the rebel government, the revolution would collapse. The local inhabitants, Santa Anna later reported, "uniformly asserted that General Houston was retiring toward the Trinity by the pass of Lynchburg. . . . To block this pass for Houston, and to destroy at one blow the armed strength and the hopes of the revolutionists, was too important a thing to let slip."[21] Now that he was across the Brazos with seven hundred infantry, fifty cavalry, and a 12-pounder, the dictator raced like an arrow for the town of Harrisburg on the mainland opposite Galveston. He also dispatched a courier to Cos, whom he had compelled to reenter Texas in violation of his parole, with instructions to join him with a force of five hundred reinforcements.

Houston, once he realized that Santa Anna's crossing was inevitable, was compelled to cross the Brazos to meet him. Using the *Yellow Stone* and a small yawl, he began ferrying his army to the east bank on either the eleventh or the twelfth, the task requiring more than two full days to accomplish.

With his men stoked for a fight and Santa Anna now stalking the same turf, Houston's worst nightmare was of some premature trigger or disruption in command destroying what little discipline he had been able to instill, and it very nearly came to pass. After dining with some of his officers at Groce's the evening the river crossing was completed, Houston pulled aside Regimental Surgeon Anson Jones, who had achieved some political prominence in Brazoria before joining the army. As Jones wrote in his memoirs, Houston "said there was a 'traitor' in the army among the officers, and asked me to guess who it was." Jones guessed, correctly, that it was James Hazard Perry, a volunteer aide who was really an anti-Houston mole who had joined the army only a few days earlier. "The General said, I have intercepted a letter of his to the Cabinet; he is endeavoring to have the command taken from me, and wants it himself. I told him I have no confidence in Perry, and thought him a reckless fool." Nevertheless, Jones warned him, "there was a deep and growing dissatisfaction in the camp, and that Perry's conduct was but an index of that feeling . . . . I told him the men were deserting, and if the retreating policy were continued, he would be pretty much alone."

It is not surprising that Houston would have taken Perry into his staff; he was a twenty-five-year-old New Yorker with three years at West Point under his belt and had resigned from the academy to come to Texas and join the fight. Houston was ever open to helping young men of ability and promise and patriotism, but something about Perry did not add up. The fold of Perry's letter to the cabinet has a curt endorsement from the commander in chief, who seized it: "I was aware that Perry was a spy sent by Potter and was a fit associate with him. H." That Perry's letter was addressed to Houston's worst enemy in the government, Robert Potter, was even more offensive than his denunciation of the general. Perry allowed that Houston "has entirely discontinued the use of ardent spirits," but then started an even worse rumor. The "general, either for want of his customary excitement . . . or, as some say, from the use of opium, is in a condition between sleeping & waking which amounts nearly to a constant state of inanimity. . . . In a fight the command of this army would as a matter of necessity devolve upon men who are qualified to conduct it."

Still, for the moment, Houston limited his response to a reprimand. Only later, when Perry rode ahead of the army toward Harrisburg in disobedience of orders, did Houston have him arrested, restoring his arms only just before the battle at San Jacinto when he needed every man he could muster. In retrospect, Houston's handling of Perry was prudent, but it created in Perry an enemy for life who returned to haunt him more than once.[22]

The only possible defense that can be offered for Perry's allegation that Houston used opium is that he might have seen him snorting smelling salts. Hamp Kuykendall, who incidentally also vouched for the general's sobriety, had observed that Houston "carried in his pocket a small bottle of salts of hartshorn, which he frequently applied to his nostrils." This was a commercial patent compound of ammonium carbonate, to which the general's frequent resort to ward off colds was understandable and harmless. The medicine had been given him by Chief Bowles's granddaughter, Mary, the same who had made the pair of moccasins he wore when he was not wearing his boots.[23] Perry's tattling of this habit and spreading of the opium rumor, however, were offenses that Houston might well have punished more summarily.

On the thirteenth, as Houston was still engaged in his own Brazos crossing, he issued another broadside to the people, informing them that the Mexicans were east of the Brazos, "treading the soil on which they are to be conquered." Again he blamed popular panic for the fact that the enemy had not been beaten already.

> Reflect, reason with yourselves. . . . The force of the enemy does not exceed nine hundred men. With a semblance of force sufficient to meet him, his fate is certain. If, then, you wish your country saved, join her standard. Protect your wives, your children, your homes, by repairing to the field, where alone, by discipline and concert of action, you can be effective. . . . Come and free your country at once; and be *men*!
>
> Those who do not aid Texas in her present struggle, but flee and forfeit all the rights of citizens, will deserve their fate.[24]

On the east bank of the Brazos, the Texas army was greeted by John Allen and the two cannon from Cincinnati, which the men at once dubbed the "Twin Sisters." Houston placed the guns under command of Col. James C. Neill, whom Travis had relieved at the Alamo, and called for volunteers to become the artillery company. Encouraged by this turn of events, forty men stepped forward, although each cannon required a crew of only nine. With the Brazos crossed, Houston took his men into camp at Donoho's farm, only three miles from Groce's, to pause to allow his scattered units to form up. Donoho was apparently not bashful about his Tory sympathies. He protested the army's camping on his farm and complained of their cutting his trees for firewood. The harried general had had just about enough; he stopped his men from chopping Donoho's trees and let them use his fence rails instead, which were already dry. After this, Donoho made himself scarce. Houston's standing orders had been that the property of the citizens must be respected, but with the general's sentiments about Donoho thus known, the soldiers that evening felt no hesitation in calling upon the gaggle of refugees, who were never far from the army, rounding up several ladies, putting Donoho out of his house, and having a dance.[25]

Mosely Baker and Wiley Martin rejoined the army on the fourteenth with their 350 men, and then their news that Santa Anna had crossed the Brazos in spite of them received an odd confirmation. Scouts brought into camp on a mule the black ferryman from Fort Bend, who said Santa Anna had released him to come to Houston with a message, which he handed over. It was in English, the handwriting was Almonte's: "Mr. Houston: I know you're up there hiding in the bushes. As soon as I catch the other land thieves, I'm coming up there to smoke you out."[26] It was a taunt of breathtaking arrogance. It was also suicidal, telling Houston plainly his plans and expectations. Further captured dispatches showed that the president-general, in his personal sortie to capture the rebel government, had raced ahead of the rest of the Mexican army with just his picked escort of several hundred men. Houston's haste to move immediately was fueled by the knowledge that Santa Anna had finally committed a mistake that could prove fatal. For a few days only, the Mexican commander would be supremely vulnerable.

By the fifteenth, Santa Anna was in Harrisburg; Houston entered Harris County the following day, driving his men relentlessly. All knew that their line of march would soon carry them to a fork in the road, the right one to Harrisburg and a showdown with Santa Anna, the left one, eventually, to Nacogdoches and the United States. All during these weeks, part of Houston's attention was drained by still having to shepherd the stream of civilian refugees fleeing the war, and his intention was to send them up the Nacogdoches fork until the fighting was over. He had ordered an early march that morning, but Wylie Martin refused to move his men until they had their breakfasts. One would think that after all they had been through, Baker and Martin would have behaved with somewhat better discipline, but they were unreformed. Furiously, Houston ordered Wylie Martin to feed his men as fast as he could and then detailed them to escort the refugees out of harm's way. Martin could obey this order or go straight to hell, but in either case he was to clear out of camp. The captain found it an order he could obey.

After so much contention, Houston must have been grateful the men thought to include him in a practical joke, the idea for which probably occurred to them when they saw the general at the forge supervising the chopping up of horseshoes and scrap iron into grapeshot for the Twin Sisters. Two of the men who had escorted the cannons from the coast were Nacogdoches volunteers, S. F. Sparks and Howard Bailey, who had lately been detailed by President Burnet to round up horses and arms in the Harrisburg area and press them into army service. (Of course, one of the horses they pressed happened to be the president's, which despite Rusk's intervention they did not release until Burnet procured them a bottle of whiskey—hence their motivation to accompany the artillery to the army and get beyond Burnet's wrath.) Bailey and Sparks canvassed the camp until they found their fellow volunteers from Nacogdoches and proceeded to trade stories. Just then a new recruit arrived in the camp, complaining that his gun was broken and asking if there was a blacksmith. There was only one tent in the camp and that was Houston's. The others pointed out that tent as the blacksmith's quarters, and the man gave his piece, an old flintlock, to the commanding general and asked him to fix it.

> Houston knew at once that some one had sent this fellow to him just to have a little fun. So as soon as the man left, he took the lock off, cleaned it and put it back. The news spread all over the army, and after a while a man told the owner of the gun that he had taken his gun to General Houston, and that he heard that Houston intended having him shot for insulting him. The poor fellow was nearly out of his wits, and said, "What shall I do? They told me he was a blacksmith, and I did not know that he was General Houston." Finally some one told him the best plan was to go to Houston and ask forgiveness. So he went, and with hat off, he tremblingly told his story. General Houston said, "My friend, they told you right, I am a very good blacksmith," and taking up the gun, he snapped the mechanism two or three times, and said, "She is in good order now, and I hope you are going to do some good fighting."[27]

At Harrisburg, Santa Anna barely missed snagging the government, as Ad Interim President Burnet and his cabinet escaped to New Washington and clambered into boats for Galveston Island at the last moment. Indeed, they were still within musket range as the Mexicans clattered up, but Colonel Almonte, seeing the president's wife in one of the boats, declined to open fire.

Houston had whipped his men the final fifty-five miles in only two and a half days through appalling weather. The road forked on the farm of Abram Roberts in the northern limit of Harris County (near the later site of the town of Spring). The split was marked by the presence of a distinctive tree whose gnarled limbs seemed to point out the alternatives: Harrisburg and battle, or Nacogdoches and retreat farther into the Redlands, perhaps even to the United States. The assistant regimental surgeon was Nicholas Labadie, later a confirmed Houston-hater. By his account, the grumbling among the army was now on the point of mutiny, and all eyes were fixed on the "Which-way Tree" to see whether Houston would take the Harrisburg fork. As the general rode up, Labadie wrote, "Several of us desired of Mr. Roberts, who was standing on his gate, to point out to all the road to Harrisburg. Houston was then close by when Roberts raised his hand and ... cried out, 'That right hand road will carry you to Harrisburg just as straight as a compass.'"[28]

While Houston calmly ordered "Columns right," his detractors have insisted ever since that only a sure mutiny prevented him from retreating all the way to the United States. About the only real evidence to justify this belief was an incident that

happened shortly after passing the "Which-way Tree." With the roads nearly impassable from constant rain, either Houston or his wagonmaster, a Pennsylvania
Dutchman named Conrad Rohrer, had conned one of the refugee women, a Mrs.
Pamela (sometimes Pamelia) Mann, into the loan of an ox-team to haul the
artillery, apparently on the assertion that he was marching to Nacogdoches. Upon
hearing that the army was instead headed for Harrisburg, Mrs. Mann, a frontier
woman of frontier speech, overhauled them and, blowing Houston's hair back with
her vocabulary, concluded, according to the recollection of one of the astonished
bystanders, "Sir, I want my oxen." Houston protested that his artillery could not get
along without them. "'I don't care a dam for your cannon,' she insisted, 'I want my
oxen.' She had a pare of holster pistols on her saddle pummel & a very large knife
on her saddle. She turned a round to the oxen & jumpt down with the knife & cut
the raw hide tug that the chane was tide with. The log chane hook was brok & it
was tide with raw hide. No body said a word. She jumpt on her horse with whip
in hand & away she went in a lope with her oxen."

Houston himself took it lightly. Conrad Rohrer was a big, burly man whose
own command of Saxon idioms was famous, having been honed by coaxing balky
stock animals. Soon after Mrs. Mann departed, Rohrer appeared. One of the Twin
Sisters was stuck in mud and he had come for the oxen. Upon being informed
what had happened, he set up the Nacogdoches fork after her, leaving a blue vapor
in his wake. Houston stood in his stirrups and called out after him, "Rohrer, that
woman will fight!" (Or, by another account, "Rohrer, that woman will bite!")[29] The
general himself dismounted and applied his good shoulder to help free the bogged
cannon; Rohrer rejoined them in camp that night, livid, his clothes torn, but Pamela
Mann's oxen were nowhere to be seen.

The stew over Houston's alleged intention to flee to the United States, which
began during the Runaway Scrape itself, only intensified during that later time when
Texas politics framed itself as for him or against him. His troop dispositions while
in camp at Groce's suggest strongly that he meant to defend the Brazos, although
the number of men he posted at San Felipe and Fort Bend was largely a function
of his desire to get Mosely Baker and Wylie Martin out of his hair. But whatever
his original intentions—and there is other evidence that he was planning a surprise
for Santa Anna in the Redlands—once the dictator crossed that river at Fort Bend
and raced eastward in an attempt to capture the government, Houston knew
instantly that he had him. Santa Anna had divided his force and doomed himself
in the battle that suddenly became inevitable, as indeed Houston declared in his
broadside to the people, beseeching all possible recruits to join the army at once.
If safety was his object, there would have been no need to whip his men fifty-five
miles through sucking mud to be in a position to strike while the enemy was vulnerable. And safety, if by that one means American territory, was not even that close
at hand; from Harrisburg it was another hundred miles east through the pine
forests to the Sabine River and the United States, and more than double that if he
went via Nacogdoches. There was that surprise he was preparing on the Sabine if
he needed it, but before then, most considerations of the map and the evidence of

Houston's own pen militate the conclusion that he meant to fight and fight savagely—if and only if the men were ready, if and only if he could engage with advantage.

Revisionists intent on proving Houston a cant and coward have since seized upon Labadie's rendering of the Pamela Mann incident as proof of their position.[30] What they have less luck explaining is why Houston would confide his strategy to some homespun virago when he kept his counsel away from even his own officers (for good reason, as some of his aides were conduits straight back to Burnet and Potter). Of course, the noncombatant refugees were indeed heading up the Nacogdoches fork, and it is possible that Houston told Mrs. Mann that her animals would accompany that group. It is equally likely that he would have told her anything to get his hands on her oxen.

Aside from Surgeon Labadie, another in Houston's army who left a memoir was James Washington Winters, a nineteen-year-old infantryman who had none of the later political pretensions of the general's detractors. After Deaf Smith captured Santa Anna's courier and Houston knew where and when to strike: "we were then ordered forward with all the speed possible that we might intercept Santa Anna at Lynch's ferry. I never heard any talk as to Houston's not designing to fight; or of officers or men insisting on his taking the road to Harrisburg; or of any one doubting his intention to do so. We went as straight as we could go toward Harrisburg." As far as the incident with Pamela Mann's oxen, Winters wrote that it was true that she unhitched them from the ammunition wagon herself and led them away, and after Conrad Rohrer returned empty-handed from his back-up-the-road confrontation with her, "the boys had a good joke on the wagon master, and did not forget to use it."[31] One of the men demanded to know why Mrs. Mann had torn his shirt, and then speculated she must have needed it for baby rags.

Hamp Kuykendall later weighed in on the retreat-or-fight controversy with a comment that, as far as he knew, the army took the right fork without orders from the general. But then, the order was not given to Kuykendall. As the army marched toward the "Which-way Tree," the unit in the lead was Company K, First Regiment, under Capt. Robert James Calder, a twenty-five-year-old Kentuckian. "To the best of my recollection," Calder wrote later, "after a short halt at that point [the Nacogdoches-Harrisburg fork] I received an order to take the right-hand road. I do not recollect to have seen or heard of any altercation, nor do I think there was any mutinous conduct."[32] One aspect upon which the informants were unanimous was that if Houston had retreated farther, the army would have mutinied. There had been open talk, but only talk, of mutiny since the encampment at Groce's; the men knew it and Houston knew it, and his month-long retreat across the breadth of the country had tried them to the limit of their frontier patience. But indefinite avoidance had never been his plan, and for Santa Anna to have blundered just as Houston's army reached its peak of rage and bloodthirst has to be counted as an important link in his lifelong chain of luck.

One final pea on the balance of the general's intention to fight: There is a story that during the race to Harrisburg, the general stopped by to visit—and perhaps slept the night, although that seems doubtful—at the Oyster Creek plantation of his friend Willis Nibbs, a law partner of the late Colonel Travis. Even as Sam Houston, when he entered Texas, was reluctant to do so on a shabby horse, even so he was now loath to enter battle on one. When he spied a magnificent white stallion in Nibbs's corral, he offered to buy him, but Nibbs deferred to his wife, Ann, who owned the animal. Houston made out a promissory note to her for three hundred dollars, and rode into history.[33]

10

THE LAURELS OF VICTORY

When Sam Houston turned his army toward Harrisburg at the "Which-way Tree," the refugees who had been dogging him turned north up the Nacogdoches fork, escorted by Wylie Martin in his quasi-exile of detached duty. Martin took with him as many as four hundred men, less an indication of the defensive needs of the citizens and more an indication of the number of soldiers who simply refused to follow Houston any farther, even to a fight.[1]

This was a considerable force to siphon from the army on the eve of battle, but in outward appearances the general seemed unconcerned. He turned his attention instead to giving his soldiers a good meal and rest before engaging the host of Mexico. Ever since Gonzales, provisioning his army had been a chronic concern, although it was not his gravest problem as the number of cattle in the countryside, both owned and "public," meant that beef was always at hand. Most other supplies during the long retreat were either scarce or completely unobtainable, but Houston was stern in his instructions that the settlers' homesteads were not to be ransacked for other staples. After making the Harrisburg turn, Houston sent half a dozen men to drive some beeves on ahead of the army to a man named Burnett, who was to have them butchered by the time the army arrived to camp. The detail set off, and on arriving at Burnett's found it deserted, but with an amply stocked kitchen and a yard full of chickens. Houston's strict standing orders were that none of the colonists' property was to be molested, but as the men had eaten nothing for days but beef without bread or even salt, one of the detail, S. F. Sparks, decided to make a real meal. By the time he was done,

> The yard was covered with feathers, and the men said to me, "Ain't you afraid Houston will punish you if you don't take those feathers away?" I said, "No." Well, we all did justice to that dinner.

It was getting late in the evening. . . . Houston, Rusk, Burleson, Sherman and some of the other officers came up and dismounted. I opened the gate, and said, "Gentlemen officers, I wish to see you in the house. . . ." I saw Houston knit his brows when he saw the feathers in the yard. When they were all in, I closed the door, and addressed General Houston in the following way, "General, I have disobeyed orders; when we arrived here, I found everything deserted and we were hungry, for we have had nothing to eat, except beef; so I killed some chickens and baked some bread, and we had a good dinner!" He looked at me as if he were looking through me, and said, "Sparks, I will have to punish you. You knew it was against orders; I will have to punish you." I said, "General, I saved you some," and I took the lids off the vessels that contained the chicken and the bread, and told them to help themselves. Rusk drew his knife first, and all the others followed suit, except Houston, who had not taken his eyes off me all this time. . . . Rusk, said, "General, if you don't come on we'll eat all the dinner. We have not had such a dinner since we left home. Sparks is a good cook."

Then the General drew his knife, and attacked the dinner. After he had eaten a short time, General Rusk said, "General Houston, it is a maxim in law that 'he who partakes of stolen property, knowing it to be such, is guilty with the thief.'" General Houston replied, "No one wants any of your law phrases." After the meal General Houston said, "Sparks, I'll not punish you for this offense, but if you are guilty of it the second time I will double the punishment."[2]

The Texas army reached Harrisburg on April 18 and found that Santa Anna had left it a smoldering ruin, at which Houston let his men have a long look. They then continued another two miles and crossed Buffalo Bayou, an effort that took most of the day, for an old ferry had to be fitted with flooring ripped from the nearby house of a Mrs. Batterson in order to get the cannons across. Surgeon Labadie remembered that the general lined up his army during these preparations and stoked them a little more: "'The army will cross and we will meet the enemy. Some of us may be killed and must be killed; but, soldiers, remember the Alamo! the Alamo! the Alamo!' . . . After such a speech, but d——d few will be taken prisoner—that I know."[3]

Racing toward Lynch's ferry on the San Jacinto River, they resumed their march until the wee hours of April 19, when Houston allowed his men a little rest. Thomas Rusk was with him, and during the lull the general and the secretary of war issued a joint appeal to the people for a last influx of volunteers before the imminent battle. Three Mexicans had been captured, from whom they learned that Santa Anna was "within the sound of the drum" with an escort of only five hundred men. "Are you Americans?" wrote Rusk to the citizenry. "Are you freemen? . . . I look around and see that many, very many, whom I anticipated would be first in the field, are not here. Rise up at once . . . a vigorous effort and the country is safe!"

"We are nerved for the conquest," Houston added in a postscript, "and must conquer or perish. . . . Rally to the standard. . . . Be men, be freemen, that your children may bless their fathers' names!

"Colonel Rusk is with me," he added, "and I am rejoiced at it."[4] Indeed, the presence of Thomas Jefferson Rusk on the march and the complete harmony and concert with which he and Houston acted ought in itself to have impeached the later insinuations alleging Houston's ambivalence to battle.

Houston also took a moment to write a more personal message to Miss Anna's father, his friend Henry Raguet. "This morning we are in preparation to meet Santa Anna. It is the only chance of saving Texas." The country, he complained, "could have started at least four thousand men," but the flight of the government had spread such panic through the countryside that "we will only have about seven hundred to march with, besides the camp guard. We go to conquer. It is wisdom growing out of necessity to meet the enemy now; every consideration enforces it. No previous occasion would justify it. The troops are in fine spirits, and now is the time for action." Sam Houston had himself once lain too near death to have any illusions about his own immortality: "I leave the result in the hands of a wise God, and rely upon his providence."[5]

At dawn on April 20, Houston's scouts discovered a flatboat loaded with flour—a welcoming gift for Santa Anna courtesy of local "Texas Tories." The flour was quickly seized and patted into dough cakes, which with slabs of roasted beef was the best breakfast the men had seen in some time. The meal was hardly begun, however, when more scouts raced in and reported they had skirmished with Mexican scouts near Morgan's Point. At the general's direction, the men grabbed their cakes and chunks of roast and pulled back three-quarters of a mile to a stand of timber along Buffalo Bayou. This gave them command of Lynch's ferry and placed them directly in Santa Anna's path. Houston then ordered Col. James Neill to position the Twin Sisters outside the edge of the forest, where they could be easily seen. Then the Texas army ate, and waited.

As Houston anticipated, Santa Anna spied his position, formed up his men, and probed his artillery placement with long-distance fire from the Mexican 12-pounder. Houston ordered Colonel Neill to return fire, and in their first volleys of grape and canister, the Twin Sisters destroyed an ammunition crate, wounded an officer, and killed a horse and two mules. Annoyed by their accuracy, Santa Anna ordered infantry to seize the rebels' cannons, but they were driven back by more good shooting. Several Mexicans were seen to fall, although Neill was badly wounded in the hip and Houston replaced him with his chief of staff, George Washington Hockley, one of his best friends from Tennessee days who had followed him to Texas in 1835. The artillery duel sharpened; as Houston rode through the ranks to encourage the men, his own horse was hit and had to be destroyed. Twice during the day, Santa Anna commanded playing of the "Degüello," the dismal fanfare of no quarter that had wafted over the Alamo the previous month.

After Mexican fire ceased and the waiting game resumed, the Texans observed the enemy moving their brass 12-pounder back from the island of trees where it had been positioned. The Kentuckian Sidney Sherman interpreted this as a retreat and sought permission to lead cavalry out to capture Santa Anna's gun. Houston refused but, after being indignantly pressed, consented to let Sherman lead a

Jesse Billingsley. A native of Tennessee, Captain Billingsley raised his company of volunteers from the settlement of Mina (later known as Bastrop). Although a San Jacinto wound left one hand crippled for life, in later years he rode actively with various ranger companies, served one term in the Congress of the Republic, and won election to two terms in the state legislature. He lived until 1880.

Courtesy Center for American History, University of Texas

reconnaissance through the trees, though under no circumstances should his force break from cover or precipitate a general engagement. Once he had sixty cavalry behind him, including Secretary of War Rusk, Sherman speared straight for Santa Anna's ordnance. His men, however, were not "cavalry" at all but militia infantry riding horses; they had to dismount to reload their guns, at which point Mexican dragoons swarmed around them. A plea came in for infantry support. It was completely the wrong time and wrong posture to have the main battle, and Houston refused. The men watching were furious; Capt. Jesse Billingsley marched his "first company" of the First Regiment out to help Sherman, passing directly in front of the commander in chief as they did so. The regimental commander, Gen. Edward Burleson, felt compelled to follow with the rest of his command. Houston bellowed at them to countermarch and return. Billingsley's men sneered at Houston as they passed, telling him to countermarch himself. He hoped that he had instilled enough discipline in his yahoos to get them through just one pitched battle, but now it appeared he was wrong. Uncoordinated militia taking on Mexican dragoons on an open battlefield was precisely what had doomed Fannin, and this was an extremely dangerous situation. Sherman's "cavalry" managed to extricate themselves and were already on their way back to cover, having lost one dead and two badly wounded men as well as several mounts. When they regained the timber, Houston gave Sherman a bawling out that, as he was capable of doing, created not just an enemy for life, but one who encouraged later stories of Houston's cowardice. The commanding general did find one man worthy of praise, a peculiarly dressed, poetry-spouting Georgia private named Mirabeau Buonaparte Lamar, who had saved Rusk's life and brought another dismounted and wounded soldier back to safety on his own horse. Houston promoted Lamar to the rank of colonel in front of the men. That night, the soldiers talked only of Sherman's gallantry, not of his stupidity, and some muttered he would be a better general than the one they had. Mosely Baker, who had stayed with the army when Wiley Martin departed with the refugees, was pleased to hear some of them reorganizing themselves to fight without Houston.

The general habitually stayed up later than any of the men; he was an insomniac anyway, but this night he left charge of the camp to Hockley and, making sure the guard was posted, went to bed; he slept on the bare ground, having given his saddle blanket to the men to cut up for powder cartridges for the Twin Sisters. To the army's amazement, the general slept late and soundly. When he rose, Col. John A. Wharton and Hockley informed him that the officers requested a council, to which he agreed. From noon until two o'clock he asked for their views; Rusk, whose opinion of militia was the equivalent of Houston's own, said that to assault seasoned soldiers with barely trained militia, and without even bayonets, would be unprecedented. The field officers voted five (including Sherman and Lamar) to two to receive an attack rather than make one, and Houston dismissed them. The general noticed something that Rusk and the others had missed, though. His men were too walleyed angry to be easily killed.

April 21 crept by until the men began to think there would be no action at all. Santa Anna was satisfied; he had Houston trapped against the bayou, and Cos, marching in violation of the parole he gave at San Antonio in December, reinforced him during the morning, increasing the Mexican force to about 1,350. He could destroy the rebels at his leisure. Within the trees, Houston ordered assembly and roll call, finally, at three in the afternoon, finding 783 men able to fight—more than he expected, but his and Rusk's broadsides to the public had caused more volunteers to slip in by ones and twos. The lie of the battleground was this: Buffalo Bayou flowed in a northeasterly direction behind them, bending ninety degrees to the southeast as it joined the San Jacinto River at Lynch's ferry. From the line of timber that shielded Houston's army, the Mexican position lay southeast across the grass prairie before them; with their camp hemmed in by an impassable marsh called Peggy Lake behind them, their only possible escape route was to the southwest. Santa Anna's officers had warned him against camping there, but he would not listen.

The dictator fortified his camp during the night. The breastworks lay about five hundred yards from the Texans, and their camp at least that distance beyond. As the day wore on, it appeared to the Mexicans that the Texan force would not stir from cover, and they let down their guard. The dictator napped, and there were stories that he was dallying with a woman in his tent.

In disposing his troops for battle, Houston left an unusually strong camp guard of 150 men—principally the young and the sick—which increased to about 200 during the day as more volunteers arrived. He could not be certain of Gen. Vicente Filisola's whereabouts, but if he suddenly appeared with reinforcements while the Texans were engaged with Santa Anna, the Mexicans would most likely arrive via Vince's Bridge, allowing them to rampage through the camp. The formidable guard, entrenched in the thick woods, had a good chance of keeping Filisola occupied.[6] Houston's worry on this point was alleviated by a novel suggestion from the ranks. As the men formed up to attack, Deaf Smith's company found itself on the edge of the line. The left file leader, one John Coker, surveyed the layout and said, "Boys, I believe it would be a good idea to go and burn down that bridge, so as not only to impede the advance of reinforcements of the enemy, but it will cut off all chance of retreat for either party." The idea found unanimous support; Smith knew Houston well and offered to go over and offer the suggestion. The general considered it and asked, "Can you do it without being cut to pieces by the Mexican cavalry?" Smith said that if Houston would detail him six men, he would try.[7] The general made a parting remark that has been rendered in several different versions, the most common being that if they did not hasten, they would find the prairie changed from green to red when they returned.

The two weeks of drilling on the Brazos gave some of the men facility in the jargon but did not lessen their annoyance with the commander. In preparing to advance, Sgt. Lyman Rounds wrote later, "although an admirer of Gen'l Houston, I think he made a rather unmilitary movement in making the attack be formed in double file, marched at a right angle on the enemies left until within musket range, filed to right by flank, so that our Co (A) had to march the entire length of the Mexicans line under fire, before we could face to the front."[8] Houston formed his men into a thin line, two deep and nine hundred yards across. He took the cavalry away from the humiliated Sherman and gave it to Lamar, positioning them on his right to cut off any Mexican retreat. Houston took his position in the center, in front of the Twin Sisters. Looking to his left, there were two infantry regiments, Burleson's next to him and Sherman's farther out; and to his right were two infantry regiments, Rusk's and Millard's, and then Lamar's cavalry. He also had in his ranks one company of Tejanos, led by Col. Juan Seguín. Well aware of the men's hatred of Mexicans, Houston detailed them to the camp guard, which Seguín angrily protested. They had more reason than any to hate the dictator; most of them lived in San Antonio and had no homes to go to until Santa Anna was defeated. "Spoken like a man," Houston conceded, and he had the Tejano infantry insert scraps of cardboard into their hatbands, so they would not be mistaken for the enemy, and then join the assault force.

Ben McCulloch. Although he was a Tennesseean, McCulloch's connections to Sam Houston were a bit removed. His father served with Jackson in the Creek campaign, and two of his older brothers had attended the school near Maryville, of which Houston was the proprietor. In command of the artillery at San Jacinto, only McCulloch's alertness prevented one of the guns from being inadvertently discharged as Houston's horse plunged into the line of fire. After the revolution, McCulloch carried on a distinguished career with the Texas Rangers. Houston and Rusk tried to win him a colonelcy in a Texas cavalry regiment but were frustrated by the Pierce administration. McCulloch was active in the effort to win Houston a presidential nomination, but then they split over secession. McCulloch seized the federal installation at San Antonio, became a Confederate brigadier general, and was killed during the battle of Pea Ridge.

Courtesy Texas State Library and Archives Commission

Houston had by him their only battle flag, depicting a bare-breasted, Roman-nosed goddess hoisting a ribbon reading LIBERTY OR DEATH aloft on her sword; Sherman had accepted it from his ladies' auxiliary in Kentucky. There was a drummer, who could beat time but not roll, and on being informed that there was a fifer in the ranks Houston sent for him. He only knew one tune, an off-color barroom ditty called "Will You Come to the Bower?" It would have to do.[9] At about four in the afternoon, Houston slipped his sword from its scabbard and ordered, "Trail arms, forward!" and rode several yards in front of them, near where the cannons were being wheeled along. The army advanced in near silence.

One of the Twin Sisters was commanded by Ben McCulloch, a twenty-four-year-old Tennesseean and protégé of Davy Crockett. The advancing artillery stopped and Houston gave the order to fire. There was a brief hitch in handling the guns and nothing happened. "God damn it, aren't you going to fire at all?" Houston roared. The Twin Sisters then thundered to life two hundred yards from the Mexican line. "We advanced after each discharge," recalled McCulloch, "keeping in advance of the infantry, until we were within less than one hundred yards of their breastworks." Houston rode about thirty yards ahead of his line, "at which time I had aimed the gun, but was delayed in firing it for a moment by General Houston, who passed across." McCulloch noticed the general just in time and snatched the brand back from the touchhole; one more second and there would have been a change of Texan command before the battle ever started. "After this, I saw him advancing upon the enemy, at least one-third of the distance between the two armies, in front of Colonel Burleson's regiment, when it was not more than seventy or eighty yards of the enemy's breastworks. About this time, the enemy gave way, and the route became general."[10]

Within the Mexican camp, one of Santa Anna's staff officers, Col. Pedro Delgado, while amazed at how thinly the advancing Texan line was stretched, was more concerned with the deadly effect of grapeshot from their two cannons. After the first volley, Houston ordered the men to halt and reload, but at this point there was no more penning up of that much hatred. Screaming "Remember the Alamo!" and "Remember Goliad!" the men raced forward in what could be charitably called open skirmish order. Those who reloaded, fired; most clubbed guns and pulled out fearsome Bowie knives. As they breached the Mexican barricades, it was astonishing how fast the battle raged and then was over. Houston's horse was shot from under him; he was helped in mounting another. A musket ball then shattered his left ankle, but still he advanced with his men.

When he finally made a report on the battle to the Mexican government nearly a year later, Santa Anna, who by one account was interrupted while with a mistress, stated: "I was in a deep sleep when I was awakened by the firing and noise; I immediately perceived we were attacked, and had fallen into frightful disorder. The enemy had surprised our advance posts. One of their wings had driven away the three companies posted in the wood on our right, and from the trees were now doing much execution with their rifles. The rest of the enemy's infantry attacked us in front with two pieces of cannon, and their cavalry did the same on our right." Unable to stem the debacle, Santa Anna said he remembered that Filisola was only a few leagues distant, and the president-general determined to try to reach him. Delgado had a different memory of the moment: "Then I saw His Excellency, running about in the most excited manner, wringing his hands and unable to give an order."[11]

It was a total rout and a gruesome disaster for the Mexican army. Once resistance was over, Houston attempted to regroup his men but was unable to stop the slaughter. In pain and bleeding from his boot, Houston reached the margin of Peggy Lake, where he happened to meet up with Rusk. "At the bog, or quagmire," Rusk remembered, "after the Mexicans were defeated and in full retreat ..., the men were entangled and in confusion; the General ordered a halt to form the men."

That order to halt and regroup later formed the basis of another count in the cowardice accusation, that Houston had timidly ordered a halt before the battle had barely begun. Mosely Baker, one of his worst political enemies, said that fewer than a hundred Mexicans had been killed when Houston tried to break off the action. Of course, that was ridiculous, but the truth was that the army was utterly out of control. When the commanding general ordered his junior officers to instruct the men to begin taking prisoners, one of them transmitted the order this way: "Boys . . . you know how to take prisoners, take them with the butt of yor guns, club guns & remember the Alamo, remember Labaher, & club guns right & left, & nock their God damn brains out."[12]

Along with Rusk, Private Winters also recalled Houston trying to get the army to regroup, but the men's blood was up and they would not be ordered about. "After the fight was ended Houston gave orders to form in line and march back to camp, but we payed no attention to him, as we were all shaking hands and rejoicing over the victory. Houston gave the order three times and still the men payed no attention to him. And he turned his horse around and said, 'Men, I can gain victories with you, but damn your manners,' and rode on to camp."[13]

Houston was not the only one trying to get the stampeding soldiers to heel. After pursuing the routed Mexicans for several hundred yards, Capt. Amasa Turner heard a command to halt but paid it no mind. "I did not order my command to halt until [Col. Henry Millard] came up and called out, 'Captain Turner, halt your company, sir!'" Turner complied, with considerable difficulty, but before Millard could give further orders, Colonel Wharton galloped up, demanding, "Regulars, why have you stopped? On, on!" Millard belayed the order and had just started to discuss the situation with Wharton when General Houston, having damned his men's manners and departed the butchery, joined them. According to Captain Turner, "At this time I saw General Houston with some of his staff walking their horses slowly . . . from the direction of the battle field." As all the officers gathered to confer, Houston spied a line of Mexican regulars, marching in column in the distance. Believing Filisola had arrived, and with his army vulnerable to attack during the indulgent carnage he had tried to stem, Houston for a moment despaired. The others were jarred as the general suddenly "threw up his hands and exclaimed, 'All is lost; all is lost; my God, all is lost!'"

What the others knew, that Houston did not because he had been in the thick of fighting, was that Secretary of War Rusk had managed to round up several hundred Mexican prisoners and was conducting them to the rear. One of Turner's nearby lieutenants joked, "Rusk has a very respectable army now." Houston asked Turner,

"Is that Rusk?" and Turner replied, "Yes, certainly, that is Rusk with the prisoners." Turner then handed Houston a telescope to see for himself.

Satisfied that his scattered army was not in imminent danger from Filisola, Houston finally took some care for himself. "Colonel Wharton," he declared, "I am wounded; have I a friend in this world?" Wharton replied that he hoped Houston had many friends, and the general was helped back to camp.[14]

Houston's cry of "All is lost!" finally made Wharton realize how important it was to get the army to regroup, but he had no more success than Houston in getting his men to desist. "General Wharton tried to get us to cease," wrote Private Winters, "and grabbed a Mexican and pulled him up behind him on his horse, but Jim Curtis shot the Mexican."[15] Another of the men said, "Colonel Wharton, if Jesus Christ were to come down from heaven and order me to quit shooting Santanistas, I wouldn't do it, sir!" Sgt. Moses Austin Bryan, nephew of the great empresario, saw Wharton reach to draw his saber, but when "one of the men took a few steps back and cocked his rifle, Wharton, very discreetly (I always thought) turned his horse and left."[16]

Houston's spent troops made their way, some leisurely and others with a little semblance of order, back to the camp to shake hands and celebrate. Houston was worried—Filisola was still out there somewhere, Santa Anna had not been captured, there might well be another fight, and in their present condition his men were useless. (He was right. The remaining Mexican forces were in fact coordinating further action, and it was a fortunate mix of weather, circumstances and the later capture of Santa Anna that possibly prevented San Jacinto from being followed by a very different slaughter.)

On the day after the battle, the entire camp jumped when the powder magazine blew up. Houston sent to learn what had happened, and soon there was led before him a bewildered seventeen-year-old private named John Farrell. It seemed that immediately after the fight, captured Mexican arms were dumped near the magazine, and Farrell had seen lying on the ground an antique scopet, a kind of short-barreled blunderbuss, which he picked up to examine. Curious of the mechanism, he pulled the trigger to test the flint and a cascade of sparks showered to the ground, which was thickly strewn with powder from the previous day's operations. The sparks caused a flash that quickly ran to the magazine and touched it off.

Perhaps it was the old thespian in Houston who judged that after the preceding day's butchery, a little comic relief was in order. He told Farrell that he would be shot at nine in the morning and ordered the guard to bring the boy before him at half past eight.

When Farrell was produced Houston greeted him, "Well, young man, how did you rest last night?"

"Not much, General."

"Did you think that I would have you shot?"

Farrell stammered that he was not sure.

"Well, sir, young men are too scarce to be shot like dogs." He then ordered the boy released. Practical jokes on the frontier were often brutal, as Houston himself had occasion more than once to suffer. Farrell in later years resided in Washington-on-the-Brazos during Houston's second presidential term. The two were described as good friends, and Farrell put the best face on the incident by saying, "Hell, I did not know but the darned old fool would be as good as his word." It was said, however, that the childhood stammer that Farrell had otherwise outgrown reasserted itself whenever he was reminded of the incident.[17]

Early in the day after the battle, a detachment of Sherman's Kentuckians left the camp on a sweep for prisoners. When they neared Vince's Bayou, the company's color bearer, James Sylvester, split off from the group, apparently with a few others, to go hunting and soon thereafter witnessed a Mexican wearing a private's blouse sprinting toward the remains of Vince's Bridge. When the Texans gave chase, the soldier attempted to hide himself in the long grass, but when discovered he surrendered without struggle.

Houston's trusted Irishman, Maj. John Forbes, was tending to duties near the Mexican prisoners at the guard fire when he saw two men approaching through the tall grass along Buffalo Bayou. One was a very young-looking Texan with a gun on his shoulder, marching the prisoner before him. When the soldier announced that he was taking the prisoner into camp, the Mexican stepped forward and a couple of times said, "Sam Houston!" motioning his intent to be taken to the general. He then reached into his pocket and produced a letter whose salutation Forbes understood: Don Lopez de Santa Anna. Forbes asked the prisoner if he was Santa Anna and received the affirmative answer. At this point they were joined by Hockley, and together Forbes and Hockley, with Santa Anna between them, headed toward the command tent. As they passed by the prisoners, the excited murmur arose, "El Presidente! El Presidente!"

Passing through Burleson's quarters, they found Houston stretched on a mattress placed beneath the boughs of a large oak tree, lying on his left side. According to Forbes:

> I put my hand on his arm to rouse him. He raised himself on his elbow and looked up, the prisoner immediately addressed him, telling him who he was and surrendering himself to him, a Prisoner of War. General Houston looked at him intensely but made no reply, turning to me, requested me to proceed to the Guard fire and bring . . . before him a young man who was reported to be the private secretary of Santa Anna and who could talk English fluently. I did so, and on my return found the Prisoner seated quietly in a chair beside the General's mattress. The young man on seeing the prisoner assured Genl. Houston that the prisoner then before him was truly Genl. Santa Anna.
>
> General Houston wanting additional evidence sent me again to the guard fire to bring Genl. Almonte before him. In bringing down Genl. Almonte, I met Genl. Th. J. Rusk and Lieut. Zavalla. . . . They accompanied me with Genl. Almonte to where Genl. Houston was, when the Prisoner was fully recognized and identified.[18]

With all the commotion of witnesses and interpreters coming and going, the exact words of the interview between Houston and Santa Anna have been lost.

The gist of their rather baroque exchange, however, has been redacted and para-phrased so often that a kind of homogeneity exists among the sources. In Houston's own memory, the dictator was seated not on a chair but a box, Almonte was sent for to interpret, and it was Santa Anna who broke the tense silence after surrendering. "The conqueror of the Napoleon of the West is born to no common destiny," he said, "and he can afford to be generous to the vanquished."

"You should have remembered that, sir, at the Alamo," Houston countered sternly.

Santa Anna tried to evade responsibility, first on the grounds that the Alamo was taken by storm, which allowed him to kill the defenders to the last man. When Houston refused to accept this, the dictator claimed he was acting on orders from his government.

"You are the government yourself, sir," Houston snapped, also refuting Santa Anna's claim that since Texas had no recognized government, he was correct in treating insurrectionists as pirates. And no grounds whatever existed, said Houston, to excuse the slaughter of Fannin and his entire command after they had surrendered to Urrea. Santa Anna said highly that Urrea had no authority to accept their surrender on any terms, and he would execute Urrea himself if he ever got hold of him.[19]

A few sources depict Santa Anna losing his nerve under Houston's steely inflexibility and requesting his box of opium.

Another of the suffering Houston's visitors was Peggy McCormick, the lady on whose land the battle had been fought. One can almost imagine Houston straightening himself to receive her thanks and homage. What she came with, however, was a demand that the Mexican dead be disposed of.

"Madam," he countered grandly, "your land will be famed in history as the classic spot upon which the glorious victory of San Jacinto was gained! Here was born, in the throes of revolution, and amid the strife of contending legions, the infant of Texas independence! Here that latest scourge of mankind, the arrogantly self-styled 'Napoleon of the West,' met his fate!" Houston's long career of oration about San Jacinto was auspiciously begun.

"To the *devil* with your 'glorious history'!" snarled Peggy McCormick. "Take off your stinking Mexicans!"[20]

In the relief both real and comedic, one rather important job was being neglected. "Sir," Rusk sent a brief note to Houston, "There are between four and five hundred prisoners and four men as a guard. If the guard have not been sent over immediately there ought to be fifty men at least ought to come over." The Mexican prisoners, while behaving in an orderly way, took it very ill that no effort was made to bury or burn their dead, an attitude that gained little sympathy among the Texans, who soon discovered that the troops under Urrea had treated Fannin and the four hundred other victims of the Goliad massacre with equally little regard.[21] Texan dead from the Alamo had been cremated, but a half-hearted effort by some to burn the Goliad bodies resulted more in a barbecue than a cremation. Still, Peggy McCormick had a point; there were so many bodies on the battlefield that when the tide of Texan refugees reversed itself and headed back west, their progress over the San Jacinto plain was impeded by the sheer number of corpses. "Father pulled one out of the road so we could get by without driving over the body," remembered a wide-eyed little girl named Dilue Rose, watching from her wagon seat. "We camped that night on the prairie, and could hear the wolves howl and bark as they devoured the dead. We were glad to leave the battle field, for it was a grewsome sight." McCormick never did manage to get the Mexican dead disposed of in a sanitary way; they decomposed where they lay. Only after the bodies were reduced to skeletons did local citizens bury them in mass trenches, and then only because their cows took to chewing the bones, which "imparted such a sickening odor and taste to the beef and milk that neither could be used."[22]

The conduct of Houston's army in the moments after the battle provides ample evidence of his correctness in doubting the reliability of militia. Once their blood was up, anything like discipline was entirely overthrown. During the few weeks of the Runaway Scrape, his drilling of them had infused the men with just enough coherence to start one full battle, but luckily for him and for Texas, that was enough. The new revisionists cite this behavior as evidence of the disrespect in which Houston was held by his own army. And, from the standpoint of many of the undisciplined yahoos in his camp, they are correct. Where the modernists go awry is in arguing that, therefore, Houston was a poor choice to command the army. The fact is that if any other figure in Texas had commanded the army, the revolution would have ended in disaster.

That Houston was a reluctant warrior was a charge first leveled by his enemies when the war was barely over. The first volley was fired by one Robert Coleman, who had been one of Houston's aides-de-camp since April 1 and continued in that capacity until July. In 1837 he wrote and had privately published a scurrilous booklet entitled *Houston Displayed: Or, Who Won the Battle of San Jacinto? By a Farmer in the Army*. In it he attacked Houston's conduct of the battle and especially his handling of Coleman's fellow aide and Potter's spy, Hazard Perry, and it provided a gospel for Houston's enemies to hang their faith on. In it, a balky Houston was forced to fight by his own army, even the order at Peggy Lake to halt and regroup evidenced his timidity. Coleman drowned in the Brazos that summer and never lived to enjoy the grief his little pamphlet caused Houston from then on.

The general had already told his men from their bivouac on the Colorado River that in order to fight Santa Anna with something like an advantage, he intended to retreat even "to the banks of the Sabine," and many years later Houston said in a speech that he had "determined to retreat and get as near to Andrew Jackson and the old flag as I could."[23] The editors of Houston's correspondence note that if this is an accurate transcription, it was "the nearest that Houston ever came to an admission that he planned to retreat to the boundary,"[24] and latter-day grinders of the axe of revisionism cite it as "compelling evidence" that Houston intended flight into the United States.[25] One aspect of this speech that has escaped commentary, however, is that it was made in a folksy, jesting context; it was the summer of 1845, and Houston had taken to the stump to promote annexation.

Naturally, he seized upon any opportunity to allude to Old Hickory and Old Glory. This attitude did not even approach defining Houston's state of mind or intentions on the eve of San Jacinto.

But what if Santa Anna had not blundered? What if, in that green April in the arching live oaks on Buffalo Bayou, Santa Anna had, by the grace of whatever evil totem he bowed to, managed to face Houston with his entire legion? Would Houston have taken him on with his seven hundred spitting, cussing volunteers? It was both the genius and luck of Houston's career to be able to stall for the most favorable circumstances. But if the entire Mexican army had been on hand, he would not have thrown his army into a useless sacrifice. Houston was too practical and had refused to do so too many times before. The sympathy aroused in the United States by leading the sick and hungry refugees of the Runaway Scrape across the Sabine would have been enormous. Even if President Jackson had contributed no regiments, Houston himself could have raised masses more volunteers, trained them, and reentered Texas on much more equal terms. And if Santa Anna had pursued him into Louisiana to break up such an operation, then America's entry into the fray would have settled the matter altogether. Given a choice between suicide and Louisiana, Houston would have chosen the latter.

It is a moot question, of course—but it would have been moot in any case, for the wily Houston had one last ace up his sleeve. Samuel Price Carson had been a congressman from North Carolina before removing to Texas just in time to sign the Declaration of Independence. He was a workhorse in drafting the republic's constitution and almost became the ad interim president of Texas; Burnet defeated him by only six votes. Burnet made him provisional secretary of state and dispatched him to the United States to press for aid. Carson and Houston had been friends for years, and Houston had recruited him into his Texas land speculation as early as 1832. At the very time Houston's columns paused at the "Which-way Tree" to see whether he would fight or run, Houston opened a letter from Carson reassuring him that if he found it necessary to retreat to the Sabine, he—Carson—had "plenty" of volunteers there ready to join the fight.[26] Moreover, the U.S. commander in Louisiana, Edmund P. Gaines, with whom Houston was on the friendliest terms, had also advanced troops forward to the Sabine on the pretext of Indian troubles around Nacogdoches. Gaines had been moved to this act by a deputation of Nacogdoches citizens headed by Houston's intimate friend Phil Sublett.

Indeed, a couple of contemporary sources asserted that Gaines himself looked the other way as soldiers from his command shucked their uniforms and crossed the Sabine to fight in Texas.[27] This probably did happen on a small scale, but there is no evidence that Houston's army was ballooned by an influx of American regulars in the week before San Jacinto. There is further evidence, however, that Houston, Carson, and Gaines collaborated in preparing a piney woods Waterloo for the Napoleon of the West, if that became necessary. Burnet had instructed Carson to go to Washington, D.C., not the thick forests along the Sabine, but before going east, Carson decided to visit his Red River plantation via Natchitoches and tarried actively in western Louisiana.

Gaines himself made no secret of his sympathies, reporting to the U.S. secretary of war that Jackson "has been pleased to direct my immediate attention to the western frontier of the State of Louisiana in order to preserve, if necessary, by force, the neutrality of the United States." Further, "should I find any disposition on the part of the Mexicans or their red allies to menace our frontier, I cannot but deem it to be my duty . . . to anticipate their lawless movements, by crossing our supposed or imaginary national boundary, and meeting [them] wherever they are to be found." To that end, he made arrangements to be joined by "the fine legionary brigade commanded by General Planche, of the City of New Orleans," plus other local forces to the number of eight to twelve thousand men—doubtless the "plenty" of volunteers about which Carson advised Houston. Gaines communicated his intentions to Carson, who passed them on to Burnet. (The president ad interim appears not to have received the letter, at least not by the time he wrote Carson on May 23 lamenting that he had not heard from his own secretary of state since he was dispatched to the United States.) "It is only necessary," Carson wrote Burnet, "to *satisfy* Genl Gains of the facts . . . in which case he will cross and move upon the aggressors."[28] Nor was this Carson's only reassurance to Burnet on the point of American intervention. "Jackson will protect the neutral ground, and the beauty of it is, he claims to the Nesches as neutral ground."

Carson wrote this letter on the way out of Texas, and upon seeing the panic in the country fretted that Houston must fight soon and successfully. Ten days later, after meeting with Gaines, so certain was Carson of the plan's success that he wrote Houston: "My view is, that you should fall back, if necessary, to the Sabine. I am warranted in saying that volunteer troops will come on in numbers from the United States. . . . You must fall back, and hold out, and let nothing goad or provoke you to a battle, unless you can, without doubt, whip them."[29]

Moreover, Carson reported to Burnet that Gaines had sent a call for auxiliaries not just to Louisiana but to Mississippi, Alabama, and Tennessee as well. At least a portion of them would be commanded by Gen. Richard Dunlap, another Houston intimate from the old days, who had sent Houston encouraging correspondence during his exile in Wigwam Neosho. "I joined the volunteers," Dunlap later explained to Carson, "with a full conviction that we would not be detained long in the service of the U.S. and in that event I could take the whole volunteer corps with me to Texas."[30]

If any of General Gaines's men crossed into Texas to help in the cause, they would have come over on Gaines ferry, where the Camino Real reached the Sabine, at which point perhaps three-quarters of all overland immigrants had entered Texas. The proprietor of Gaines ferry was old James Gaines, born in 1776, who had been hauling back and forth on the Sabine for seventeen years. The first alcalde (1824) of the District of Sabine and later postmaster, Gaines knew every path and trace through the woods. He was a firebrand revolutionist, a signer of the Texas Declaration of Independence, and he also helped draft the Texas Constitution, which brought him into cordial relationship with none other than Samuel Price Carson. Burnet did not timely receive all of Carson's letters, but James Gaines did send

Burnet a letter on March 28 that must have driven the president near mad, wondering what on earth was transpiring in the deep forests east of Nacogdoches, but probably unable to decipher Gaines's henscratch hand: "Our Good People have turnd out Liberally among them is My Cousin EP Gaines & the greater part of the arms & amunition & horses is Gone But many more is falling out To leave in a Few days."[31]

Clearer than old James Gaines's grammar and syntax was the fact the he was the first cousin, on both his father's and mother's side, to Gen. Edmund Pendleton Gaines, whose troops were encamped across the stream. Sam Houston, in making plans to meet Santa Anna on the Sabine, was not just being strategically prepared, he was also being prudent, for James Gaines was in possession of information he considered reliable that indicated the dictator planned to carry the war to the border in any case: "I calld in Mrs. Dill She Without Interogation inform me that [illegible] Jose Elias has Told her that he conversd with St Anna and that he Told him he meant to March his army To Sabine And Teach Old Jackson To keep his people at home And make them behave themselves." Gaines ferry was the most prominent crossing point on the border, and it is unthinkable that the old postman-ferryman-revolutionist was not active in organizing a defense. "Genl. Gaines & the troops are near. Their purpose," he wrote coyly to Sam Houston, "is to be guessed at."[32]

Santa Anna sealed his fate when he raced ahead of his army; Houston then knew he had him and thereafter had no other intention but San Jacinto and battle. But, if the dictator had marched into East Texas with his full force, Houston still had the option to continue to lure him farther eastward into ambush along the Sabine. If such a fight had opened, it is not hard to imagine that many of Gaines's men would have missed roll call for a day or two and aided the massing Louisiana volunteers. It was a fight that would have taken place in the middle of nowhere, Jackson would have secretly exulted, and no one else in Washington would have been the wiser, at least for a while. When Houston had assembled his army at the end of March and informed them of Fannin's capture, he told them he intended to retreat, even "to the banks of the Sabine," a tantalizing hint of a plan he could not reveal. Ultimately, it was a card he never had to play.

Others suspected, however. Andrew Jackson's position that Texas was originally included in the Louisiana Purchase was well known, as was the long controversy over whether the boundary was the Sabine or the Neches River. Anson Jones, Houston's emotionally unstable secretary of state during his second administration, perceived in a lucid moment both the scheme and its justification:

> The retreat of Gen. Houston to the country between the Sabine and the Neches . . . would have been considered an invasion of the territory of the United States, by their President, and by the Taylor of that day, Gen. E. P. Gaines—a conflict would have ensued between some of his troops and some of those of Santa Anna—blood would have been spilled upon (disputed) American ground—and "war commenced by the act of Mexico!" Then General Jackson

would have accomplished what Mr. Polk subsequently did; Gen. Gaines would have been the "second Cortez" instead of Gen. Scott, and the Treaty of Guadalupe Hidalgo would have been signed in 1838, instead of 1848.[33]

At the end of the day, it was certainly remarkable how quickly the Texas Indians, whose threatening demeanor caused Gaines to move troops to the frontier, became quite suddenly peaceable after San Jacinto was safely won. In fact, Houston's own chronicler, Henderson Yoakum, had to admit in his *History of Texas* that "there was much that was not true in regard to the reports of Indian movements in eastern Texas."[34] Did Houston and Sublett exaggerate the apparent Indian danger to provoke American intervention and then use Carson to make sure that American troops were in place and in time? Houston's very first call for volunteers the preceding August, with its promise of reinforcements from General Gaines, suggests that this was in his mind all along. In sum, to the extent that Sam Houston bears revisionist blame for not galloping Brunnhilde-like onto the pyre of the Alamo, and for the subsequent Runaway Scrape, he must also be given credit for orchestrating what would have been an overwhelming and fatal bushwhacking of Santa Anna in the old Neutral Ground.[35]

All this was sub rosa, of course. Officially, General Gaines prepared lengthy formal communiqués to both the Texan and Mexican commanders, adjuring them not to breach the frontier into U.S. territory. In the letter to Houston, before the dispatch of which news of San Jacinto had reached the American camp, the Spencerian hand of the adjutant is followed by a postscript in Gaines's own Arabic-looking scrawl offering to "extend . . . any act of kindness in my power, not incompatible with the laws governing neutrals." He also had some thoughts on what Houston should do now that he had Santa Anna and his army cooped up. "An old soldier of your acquaintance has often taken occasion to say to young officers who were liable to be rendered inefficient by the very natural exultation which usually follows the achievement of a signal victory—be *vigilant*—be magnanimous—be just—and be generous, to the vanquished foe:—but above all, *be vigilant*."[36]

It seems the modern intellectual fashion to treat the Texas Revolution as a felony committed against the dignity of the Mexican nation by a besotted gaggle of slave-smuggling American land speculators and to humbug any voice that there may have been a kernel of justification for it.[37] One must concede that for generations the topic of revolutionary and frontier Texas history basked in such a rosy glow of uncritical hero worship that some contrary reaction was not only inevitable, but justified and even overdue.[38] This new wisdom, however, has entrenched itself by glossing over the fact that it was Santa Anna who abrogated the Constitution of 1824, which envisioned full Mexican statehood for Texas, and that the Anglos who fell at the Alamo died contending not for independence but for restoration of the Mexican constitution. Nor does it have much luck explaining why so many Hispanic Tejanos supported the revolution with their whole hearts nor why Texas was not the only state in rebellion against Santa Anna. Nor does it explain exactly how much of the dictator's gothic, vanity-driven brutality Texans should have endured

before a resort to arms would have been justified nor why the Mexicans themselves shook off his enlightened despotism in no fewer than three separate coups
d'état.

Santa Anna was righteously defeated, and it was the patience, sagacity, determination, and—as is the case in all war—luck of Sam Houston that effected it.
But the vigilance that General Gaines pressed upon him Houston needed not on
account of the whipped Mexicans but against his own government. No sooner was
victory won than the Houston-haters in Burnet's cabinet began rummaging for
some way to get rid of the general. Navy Secretary Potter, for instance, suggested
making a charge of Houston's distribution of Santa Anna's treasure among his
troops. The low point in their scheming came during the first week in May, when
Houston's ankle wound became dangerously inflamed and Surgeon General
Alexander Ewing recommended his removal to New Orleans for expert treatment.
The *Yellow Stone* stood ready, but Burnet refused Houston permission to leave the
army. When the *Yellow Stone*'s captain defied Burnet and declined to leave without
Houston, Burnet relented, but when Ewing accompanied the patient, Mirabeau
Lamar, rapidly quickening as a Burnet partisan and now the newly minted secretary of war, stripped Ewing of his commission for desertion. From Galveston, an
increasingly fevered Houston thought he would sail on the Texas warship *Liberty*
to New Orleans and decent doctors, but again Burnet refused him permission to
leave, hoping to charge the commanding general with abandoning his post—an
act of such stupefying meanness that even Burnet's statesmanship in surrendering
the government to Houston the following autumn hardly atones for it.

Eventually, Sam Houston reached New Orleans on a shabby little schooner
called the *Flora*, but the jubilant throng that bellowed its welcome was none the
smaller. The general rose and tried to thank them but fainted in the arms of his
friend William Christy. In the crowd on the wharf, a violet-eyed Alabama schoolgirl ten days past her seventeenth birthday, in the city on a holiday, witnessed his
landing. Margaret Lea maintained ever afterward that when she saw him, she felt
the eerie sensation of destiny sweep through her.

Houston's recuperation was cheered as he began receiving laurels, some forwarded by just plain folks, from his former country. He and Christy had a mutual
friend, George William Boyd, city marshal of Lafayette, Louisiana. "My dear Houston," Boyd wrote on June 6, "I feel a deep, a profoundly deep, interest in your triumphant success in this war of human rights." He sent a sword and sash, not for the
commanding general, but for him to present to some officer whom he felt deserving,
"it being the most valuable article I possess adapted to your present vocation."
Along with the sword he sent a sympathetic warning that Houston's hardest times
still lay ahead: "There will be jealousies, persecutions, treacheries starting up
among little men of narrow minds, who will endeavor to cast a slur over your
brightest acts.... Such ever, from time immemorial, has been the case and you cannot hope to escape." Houston had already survived one encounter with Burnet's
and Potter's crowd, and he was sure to have appreciated the sentiment. Others
offered advice more political. "Sir: You have possession of Santa Ana," adjured

William Johnston of Pinckneyville, Mississippi, "by all means hold him until you *finally* dispose of the whole question—You have immortalized yourself—But take care of the country—Your Hardest Battle is to come."[39]

In total, the revolution had claimed up to six hundred fifty Texans' lives. Expressed as a percentage of all those who had enlisted, the freedom of Texas was one of the most dearly purchased revolutions in history. The reporting of casualties was inconsistent at best, nowhere worse so than with the horrifying Goliad massacre. The families in the United States whose sons and brothers had disappeared into the Texas maelstrom were now frantic about them. Sam Houston was the only name that many of them knew to associate with Texas, and most now knew he was in New Orleans. The commanding general lay with his foot in bandages, opening letters beseeching his help in finding lost loved ones: Francis Mahan of Philadelphia was seeking his son Phineas, who at last word was to be taken to Matamoros and executed. "With the deepest anxiety I have sought to learn of his fate, but in vain. If he perished in the cause of Texas and died like a brave youth[,] as a father I can't help but mourn his loss & premature death, but it certainly will be a proud consolation to my sorrows that he died in a good cause and will hereafter in a better world receive his reward. . . . But Oh my Dear Sir, the agony of suspense on this subject to a Father you may well imagine." From John G. Stewart of Monticello, New York: "I would be thankful if you will be so kind as to inform me if my friend Martin Hammond is alive and in your army or murdered by Santa Ana when Col. Fanning's regiment was slaughtered butchered by the Mexicans."

When Houston was well enough to begin the journey back to Texas, their letters trailed him like grieving camp followers, the postal clerks dutifully striking through "New Orleans" and inserting "Natchitoches," then the postmaster there striking through "Natchitoches" and replacing it with "Fort Jessup," then stricken through again and forwarded to San Augustine. From Charleston, South Carolina, H. K. Grimker inquired into the fate of Cleveland Kinloch Simmons—he had fallen at the Alamo. From Wilmington, North Carolina, Samuel Mabson asked after George Fennell—he had died with Fannin. Letters came from as far north as Penobscot County, Maine, each more piteous than the one before.[40]

Interspersed among these dolorous letters, and following the same trail of postal forwards, were other packets that raised his spirits, as news of the victory spurred some old acquaintances to get back in touch with him. John D. Bowen, who had been his aide during his term as major general of the Tennessee Militia, had established himself in Charleston, South Carolina. "Although it has been a considerable length of time since I have seen you," he wrote, "yet I think and talk of you daily, and can never cease to love you. . . . immediately upon hearing the account of the battle, I illuminated my house and had all the citizens to rejoice with me." Houston's fame in Tennessee soon gained even more luster when he remitted some spoils of the battle to his favored cousin Robert McEwen. "I take pleasure in forwarding to you as a present," he wrote, "the saddle & Bridle rode and owned by Gen'l Santa Anna, at the battle of San Jacinto. It was presented to him by Gen'l Siesma, and is said to have cost $850.00. You will find the stirrups Gold, embossed with Platina. [They] ... were sold as spoils after the Battle ... and were purchased by a friend for me, without my wish or knowledge."[41]

In San Augustine, Houston stayed at the home of Phil Sublett, one of his closest friends, who was the son-in-law of the town's founder, Elisha Roberts, whom Houston knew from his days with the Tennessee Militia. It was a congenial place to recuperate. Other resident Houston friends included William Kimbro, a company commander at San Jacinto; James Bullock, who was prominent in the Texas troubles of 1832; and his brother-in-law and Houston's aide-de-camp, Alexander Horton. The ailing general recovered enough to accept an invitation to deliver a July 4 Independence Day oration, where he was, to local amusement, outshone by old Jonas Harrison, Houston's erstwhile divorce lawyer.[42]

Meanwhile, Ad Interim President Burnet's turmoil with the army continued. A new figure began to gain prominence on that front, who came to occupy much of Houston's attention during the next year: Felix Huston, the lawyer from Natchez who had offered his services the year before. As he had promised, Huston marched from Mississippi into Texas with a whole regiment of between five and seven hundred men, but not until July, well after the shooting had stopped. The existing Texas army was thoroughly impressed by his arrival—the fact that he was accompanied by Rezin P. Bowie, brother of the late Jim Bowie, did not hurt his standing, either—and the ranks began looking to him for leadership. At the time Houston departed for New Orleans, Rusk was left in acting command of the army, but Ad Interim President Burnet soon attempted to foist his new protégé, Mirabeau Lamar, onto the soldiers as his replacement. The army was already furious with Burnet for not executing Santa Anna, and while the ad interim president had every right to name Lamar to command the troops, they regarded it as interference and resented it. A group of officers formed a committee to consider what to do, and named Felix Huston to chair it. Huston's committee confirmed Rusk in his command, which was heartily ratified by a vote of the troops; Lamar was galled and continued issuing orders as commanding general until Huston and the others persuaded him to step down.

The Mississippi generalissimo opened a correspondence with the convalescing Houston on August 2 in the spirit of a willing friend and admirer, amused that the soldiers, because of the similarity of their names, would not be persuaded that they were not related. "The men are anxiously asking me when you will be here— and altho told to the contrary ... they still insist that we are Brothers, or cousins. They therefore think that I ought to know when you will be on." He then urged that a victorious Texas turn and invade Mexico. "It is apparent that even if [the Mexicans] do not intend to re-invade Texas it will be their policy to threaten to do so from time to time.... Texas will be worried to death." That much Houston had heard before and probably conceded the premise that phantom invasions would become Mexican policy. However, Huston gave a second justification that raised warning flags in Houston's mind, that the men "need the excitement of expected battle or they will disperse." Such a man needed to be watched.

Felix Huston had high praise for Rusk and expressed the hope that he would one day become president of Texas, but he scorned Burnet and blamed him for citizen contempt for the army, which he characterized as rampant: "I have refrained and shall refrain from interfering with the *politic* or polosy of this community . . . but I have *seen* with great alarm an attempt by many politicians of Texas to rase dissentions from selfish motives between the citizens and Volunteers." By and large, according to Huston, the citizens were a bunch of ingrates. "I have seen a wealthy Texian refuse to furnish a bowl of buttermilk to [my] men, when he milks 60 cows, and throw it by pailfuls to the hogs. . . . I can trace this too true a picture to the head of this Government. . . . *They had better beware.*" Houston was sympathetic toward the army's difficulties, but any officer serving a democratic government who could issue such a threat doubly bore watching.

Burnet and Lamar were not through with plotting yet either, continuing to argue that Sam Houston had forfeited his station by leaving the country. "I have by rumor heard it suggested," Huston wrote the recovering commander, "that the plan was when you reported yourself to the Secretary of War for service that no orders should be given you. There are a precious set of scoundrels in Texas. Accept my best wishes for your speedy recovery and soon join the army."[43] Houston resolved to return as fast as he could, partly to try to gain control of the conditions that Felix Huston outlined, but more importantly to try to gain control of Felix Huston himself.

Nor was Huston the only rambunctious officer anxious to carry a war of punishment into Mexico. Texas brigadier Thomas Jefferson Green had come to Texas as a land empresario earlier in 1836 but quit the scheme and joined the army. Even more of a hotspur than Huston, Green also showed himself to be more interested in the politics of their fresh-won independence. "Wm H Wharton came into camp a strong Austin & *negociation man* & left full of fright," he bragged to Houston from Coleto headquarters on August 10. Green and his men had roughly persuaded him "of the falacy of *negociation—Powder & Ball* are our arguments—Pen & ink with Santa Anna . . . are delusions." General Green, assuming Houston to be as hawkish as himself, desired to know who the commanding general supported for President. "Austin is the negociation candidate . . . who is to the be fighting candidate?— our first choice here was yourself & Genl Rusk, we understand you refuse & Rusk is too young—who next?—Let us know soon, some one in the name of God *firm & honest* who will fight us out of this difficulty." Sam Houston quickly understood that Felix Huston was not the only firebrand he had to keep an eye on.[44]

As autumn began to cool, the commanding general got his strength back. "When I parted with you last, I really thought you could not live long enough to reach Texas," wrote his friend I. M. Glassell from Louisville. "Rest assured that to find myself deceived . . . has been no little gratification to your old & constant friend." The letter was to introduce the bearer, his nephew George A. Smith, who had come to Texas to buy land, to Houston's consideration. Gradually, the correspondence from the east offering to raise troops, which had cropped up in his letterbox all year, began to take on a different complexion, such as one written by P. P. Harney of Giles County, Tennessee. They had volunteers ready to strike out for Texas, but then news arrived of San Jacinto and they stayed home. However, "should the enemy again dare to show his face, Giles Cty will send a respectable force to your aid."

The letter was to introduce the bearer, W. J. Kyle, to Houston's consideration. It seemed that Sam Houston was not only stronger, he was once again the man to know.[45]

The lionization of Sam Houston was shared in by a huge preponderance of the new nation's new citizens, and in Texas' first election, the choices for president were Sam Houston and Stephen F. Austin. Houston received 5,119 votes, and Austin only 586, fewer than former governor Henry Smith, who withdrew from the contest. Typically for Houston, once he felt fit, some of his first thoughts were of Texas' Indians; the Cherokees had stayed out of the fight and now would want the land titles they had been promised. And Houston met with others as well; during an autumn council with Indians at Nacogdoches, friendly Delawares brought in a Mrs. Elizabeth Kellogg, a survivor of the Parker's Fort massacre the previous May. The Delawares had paid $150 for her to her Comanche captors, and Houston reimbursed them the same figure.[46] The incident is a small vignette, but a telling one, in examining Houston's Indian policy, for in it he struck his practical middle ground between demanding her return *gratis*, as Indian haters would have done, and giving the Delawares a reward above their own expenditure, which might have encouraged the ongoing trade in white captives. Elizabeth Kellogg, however, was the only woman that Houston freed that autumn. A letter borne by a private messenger arrived from Washington, D.C., dated October 6 from a distant Allen family cousin named John Campbell: Eliza seemed to desire a reconciliation. Seven years in lonely reflection through the paned windows of her house was a long time to realize she had thrown her life away. Had she chosen differently, she now would be the first lady of a new nation. The magnitude of her error was too great to bear, and she repented. According to Campbell:

> Mrs. Houston was [at my brother's] about the time the news that you had gained the victory over Santa Anna, and his Mexican forces, reached that place, and it is said that she showed great pleasure at your success and fairly exulted: she spent part of her time at my Brothers, and his family says that no sbject could be touched on, that was so interesting to her, as when you were the subject of conversation, and that she shew evident marks of displeasure, and mortification, if a person was to say any thing unfavorable of you in her presence. I heard that some of her friends wanted [her] to git a divorce; and she positively refused . . . —She has conducted herself with great sircumspiction . . . and prudence and with great dignity of character so much so that she has gained the universal respect of all that knows here.

The missive not being from Eliza herself, it does not prove beyond doubt her desire to reconcile, but coming from an Allen cousin, it would only have been sent with her approval. It seems doubtful that Houston replied to the letter.[47]

Not all communication from old acquaintances that autumn was so painful. Family friend J. P. Clark wrote him from Nashville, sending greetings from Houston's cousin McEwen, who said, "Remember [me to] him, and if any opportunity occurs of your aiding him in any way do it, & charge it to the Firm of Wife, Children &

Friends." Clark informed Houston in detail that Nashville had gone delirious when news of San Jacinto had arrived, far, far outdoing the demonstration got up for Jackson after the battle of New Orleans: "Houston, it would have been worth the Battle if you could have witnessed the illumination of the city . . . and seen the busy throng, men, women & children, 'black spirits & white' parading the town and huzzaing Houston and Texas. I never witnessed a more magnificent spectacle. . . . Grundy's house and the whole of Cedar Hill was in one burning light. It was splen-did and I say, if you could have seen it, it would have been the proudest night in your life! My better half, and the Boys, oh, how they rejoiced! the little rascals were out nearly all night." Clark allowed that Houston still had enemies in Nashville, but "it was gall and wormwood to [them, but] your real friends have made the most of it."[48]

Ad Interim President Burnet had his own cup of wormwood to quaff, and faced with continued unrest in the army, he resigned suddenly on October 22. Houston was taken by surprise. Burnet's demeanor toward him had always been malicious, petty, and mean-spirited. But for Burnet to have first refused to resign when the military demanded it and now to quit once a legal transition was assured, transfer-ring power to a man who could control the army, did much to preserve democracy in the new republic. Such statesmanship from a man like Burnet sucked the wind out of Houston's sails. He learned of his imminent inauguration only four hours before the ceremony, not enough time to puff them back out again and prepare a suitable address.

11

THE BARNYARD REPUBLIC

I, Sam Houston, President of the Republic of Texas, do solemnly and sincerely swear, that I will faithfully execute the duties of my office, and to the best of my ability, preserve, protect, and defend the Constitution of the Republic.

Sam Houston, Town of Columbia,
Representative Hall, October 22, 1836

For once in his life, Sam Houston was stuck for a speech. "As yet our course is onward," he vamped. "We are only in the outset of the campaign of liberty. Futurity has locked up the destiny which awaits our people." Delicately aware that it was Austin who deserved the presidency, but that Austin, because of his too-long-held loyalty to Mexico, no longer commanded the people's affection, Houston expressed gratitude that in his election he had been "preferred to others, possibly superior in merit to myself."

Finding some oratorical stride, he fought San Jacinto again—he was always safe with that—and counseled peace with the Indians on the frontier. And, aware that many in the Texas Congress would be squinting at him from this day on, he made a remarkably humble call for their counsel and cooperation. If he should fail to realize his great vision for the country, he said, they should "correct my errors and sustain me by your superior wisdom." Much of that vision was occupied by the subject of annexation to the United States, and in a technique used by many chief executives since, he introduced the subject by directing the attention of the gathering to a special guest, William Christy of New Orleans. "He was the first in the United States to respond to our cause. His purse was ever open to our necessities. His hand was extended in our aid."[1]

However extemporaneous the speech was, its printing in the United States carried the news of the accession of constitutional government in Texas. Houston's New York friend Samuel Swartwout read it there and sent congratulations, averring that the only fault he could find with it was that he was not present to hear the address.[2] Throughout America, people watched to see what Texas' next move would be, for the same vote that carried Houston into the presidency also had on the ballot a referendum whether to seek union with the United States or maintain Texas' status as an independent nation. In the whole country, only ninety-four men voted to go it alone if annexation were offered.

Nothing could happen until Houston learned the actual condition of the government's finances, and he fired a quick undated note to learn "the amount of contingencies of the Cabinet of the Government 'ad Interim,' and the items contingent or otherwise charged by the President besides his salary." Four days after the inauguration, the president named his cabinet—Rusk to the War Department, S. Rhoades Fisher at Navy, and Henry Smith at Treasury. While the people had rejected Stephen F. Austin as president, Houston knew very well that the respect that the great empresario commanded abroad would render him indispensable to the upcoming tasks of peace with Mexico and either independence or annexation. Austin was tired and sick, but Houston prevailed on him to take up the portfolio of the infant State Department, where among his first duties he arranged the exchange of prisoners of war with the Mexican consul in New Orleans. In his haste to get the cabinet list to the Texas Senate—or perhaps in his anxiety that the confirmations be swift and smooth—Houston neglected to include his choice for attorney general, James Collinsworth, an oversight he remedied the following day.[3] The most odious of Burnet's provisional cabinet to be rid of was Navy Secretary Robert Potter, and Houston wisely did not take him head on. Rather, he combined the secretariats of the army and navy, thus streamlining the administration, saving money, and getting Potter out of the way without making it look personal. The new president was more magnanimous in the minor appointments, as he named as comptroller of the republic Marshall Pease, who had been so critical of him when secretary to the General Council.[4]

The first order of business was the army. Felix Huston assembled his troops on October 29, announced to them that their greatest advocate, Sam Houston, had been inaugurated president of the Republic of Texas, and that the president urged them with all possible energy to be patient in bearing their privations a while longer. "The President requests me to say," Huston addressed them, "that you shall have ample justice done you and at all times rely on him as your friend, that he has received more cheering intelligence in relation to supplies from New Orleans, and he thinks they will soon be on. . . . He urges the necessity of discipline and order." A week later, though, Huston sent the president a very strict letter on just how bad things were: "I have no cavalry—. . . Not over one half the army are reported fit for duty—there are a great many who have been sick who have not proper sustenance to recruit their health, only beef to eat. . . . At the time I took command the camp was flooded with whiskey and retail shops made of the tents—and quarrelling and fighting & noise was heard all over the camp. This however I have put a stop to." Worst of all, the enlistments of between three and four hundred of them were about to expire, "and I find them little disposed to do duty." None of this, he protested, was his fault.[5]

The Texas Army might well have overthrown Ad Interim President Burnet had he not resigned and handed the problem off to Houston, and now Houston needed to do something. He had already dispatched the army's quartermaster general, Almanzon Houston (again, no relation) to the United States to drum up support, happily with some success. He reported home that he had raised forty thousand dollars to buy supplies, although there were some aspects of his doing so that apparently gave him some pause. "I have a great deal to communicate to you but not time to spread it on paper and some of it would not look well even if it was spread on paper." The president sent another message to the army, of which Huston reported: "I had a very good general parade today. . . . I made them a speech and read them part of your letter . . . ; they Cheered in the liveliest style—, I am become jealous of your unbounded popularity." (If Felix Huston had joined the army before San Jacinto was fought, he likely would have felt quite differently.) Things, he said, were somewhat better.[6]

Taking up the reins of power required attention to a myriad of other important details, and Houston was in almost daily communication with Texas' agents in New Orleans, Thomas Toby and Brothers. "Congress will greatly need the supply of Stationary recently ordered by my predecessor," Houston wrote Toby, "and in addition you may send 1000 large Wafers for impressing the Seal of this Republic, and also a quantity of good sealing wax." To this requisition was added a few days later an urgent request for bound record books and journals.[7]

The business of state waited upon no such formalities, however; as late as November 12, Houston was subscribing official documents, "Given under my hand and private seal there being no seal of office at Columbia."[8] Nor was this lack of an official device any harmless deficiency, for the United States was about to use it as an excuse to postpone having to consider anything about Texas. Whatever his other shortcomings, President Ad Interim Burnet had made a good choice in James Collinsworth as commissioner to the United States to seek annexation. Burnet grimaced at Collinsworth's friendship with Houston—it was he who had nominated him to be commander in chief of the army and then served as his aide-de-camp—but more to the purpose, he was a Nashville native and a good friend of Andrew Jackson. Burnet dispatched him to Washington in the company of a second commissioner, a former Kentucky legislator of the Jackson party, Peter W. Grayson.

Shortly after his sudden inauguration, Houston received Collinsworth's report on how things went: not well. At the time they arrived in Washington, the commissioners found Congress adjourned and Jackson packing up for the Hermitage. (However, the Texas debates that had lately taken place in Congress, according to the outgoing commissioner Sam Carson, had been extravagant in praise of Texas and of Sam Houston. The "*marked* respect with which *Your name* was treated, and the eulogies bestowed by some of the most distinguished debaters . . . were most generous, and kind," Carson wrote Houston. "Many were the tears that fell in the Senate on that day.") But having missed Congress, Collinsworth and Grayson, "Impressed with the importance of an interview with [Jackson] previous to his departure," made straightaway for the White House. Old Hickory received them correctly, but coolly for someone who was by repute so anxious to welcome Texas into the Union. "He briefly informed me that nothing could be done until he heard from an agent despatched from the government of the U. States to the government of Texas to inquire into the civil and political condition, . . . [and] refered us to Mr Forsyth Secretary of State for all further communication on the subject. We saw

Mr Forsyth and presented our credentials, they were formally objected to for the omission of the seal of the State being affixed to them." With the government recessing, Collinsworth and Grayson shrewdly agreed to split up, Grayson to stay in Washington to do what good he could, and Collinsworth to tag along with Jackson to Tennessee, where he might be able to use their friendship to advantage. Jackson had to be nice to him, and Collinsworth "Saw him frequently while there." He could not, however, get anything more out of Jackson privately than he could officially, and the American president even adjusted his grounds for keeping his distance from Texas. "He informed me in substance that nothing could be done until the Congress of Texas met and organized a more formal and regular government, than that then in existence." Collinsworth did venture the opinion that Jackson favored the acquisition of Texas, but "I cannot too forcibly impress upon [you] the necessity of despatching some one forthwith vested with plenary powers to the court of Washington, as in my opinion much may be endangered by delay to bring these matters before the approching session of the Congress of the United States at an early period of its session." Annexation, which Texans had once taken almost for granted, was off to a slow and chilly start.[9]

The press of work in Columbia was such that President Houston began delegating oversight more liberally to his cabinet, at one point advising Toby to stop inquiring of him on a number of topics at once. "I would remark that it would be most convenient in future to receive distinct letters upon the different subjects, whether Civil, Military, Naval, or Financial addressed to the appropriate Departments, and that would render the business of each Department more intelligible." And still the office supplies had not come. "I cannot omit again calling your attention to the list of books wanted for this office. They are of the utmost importance and I hope you will leave no measure untried to procure and forward them. Our stationary, too, is reduced to the scantiest allowance, you will therefore see the importance of a speedy supply."[10]

The little town of Columbia, near the lower Brazos, was as rude a frontier village as ever hosted a national capital. One early visitor was Francis Richard Lubbock, a South Carolinian just turned twenty-one, who had come west in search of his brother Tom, who had disappeared into the maelstrom of the revolution. To defray the costs of the trip, Lubbock brought with him a boatload of merchandise, and when put off at Bell's Landing—the new Rome's new Ostia—with his goods, he saw in an instant that he had landed on opportunity's shore. Frank Lubbock, merchant (and future governor), opened for business. "The circumstances were favorable, the little town being filled with people, so very promptly my goods were all sold at a fine profit." Columbia had a tavern, Fitchett & Gill, where meals could be bought, but its sleeping accommodations were limited to the ground beneath a nearby live oak, "the lodging place of many," including young Lubbock.[11]

Congress had impressed most of the few buildings for government use, including a two-story frame house for the House of Representatives and a smaller single-story house for the fourteen-member Senate, whose committees met in attached sheds. The town's nearest neighbors were scattered plantations and woods "filled

Texas Capitol, Columbia; Francis Richard Lubbock. The Merchant who carried the first boatload of merchandise up Buffalo Bayou to Houston city, Frank Lubbock became Sam Houston's close friend; Houston later left his wife in the care of Lubbock and his wife when he had to trek inland to Austin to attend the government. Later the men split politically; Lubbock opposed the Know Nothings and chaired the convention that nominated John C. Breckenridge for president in 1860. He was elected lieutenant governor when Hardin Runnels defeated Houston in 1857 and lost the office in the turn-about two years later. Their friendship endured, however. Lubbock continued to serve his state in many different capacities until his death in 1905.

Texas Capitol courtesy Austin History Center, Austin Public Library; Francis Lubbock courtesy Texas State Library and Archives Commission with bear, Mexican lions, deer, turkey and game of every kind." The government quickly decided that the rudeness and remoteness would not do for the capital of a republic, and almost from the start consideration was given to where to locate the permanent seat of government.

But more urgent matters required the president's attention, and Mexico was next in line. Seeking to normalize relations as quickly as possible, one of his first official acts was to lift the blockade of Matamoros, and a few weeks later he rescinded Burnet's letters of marque and reprisal. Copies of the proclamations were sent to Agent Toby in New Orleans with instructions to make certain they were printed in Mexican newspapers. (He may also have had an eye to the New Orleans papers, remembering how the insurance companies' and brokerages' hostility to the revolution had dampened Texas' prospects of obtaining credit.) But the greatest difficulty was simply keeping Santa Anna alive. Three days after he took office, Houston wrote the Mexican minister in Washington, D.C., suggesting that the best way to implement Santa Anna's desire to go there would be for him to make application to Jackson, who could dispatch an American ship that would ensure his safe journey. In any case, "I pledge myself *most solemnly*," he wrote, "to do all in my power . . . to obtain the release and restoration of General Santa Anna, and his countrymen to their homes."[12]

That, however, was easier said than done. Since his incarceration at Orozimbo plantation, the president-general had already survived one drunken assassination attempt, and many in the army and government were loud in their insistence that he be shot, or hanged, or burned at the stake, or worse. Houston remonstrated forcefully that under the constitution the disposition of prisoners was his executive responsibility. The Senate, many of whose members had campaigned on a promise to execute Santa Anna, passed a resolution on November 11 concurring that the president had power to release most prisoners but declaring Almonte and Santa Anna to be exceptions. Houston returned the resolution five days later with a lengthy message full of policy arguments. "I now regard our national standing as connected with the preservation of his life," he wrote. How would Texas be looked on by the world's great powers if the chief of state of a great power was strung up? The conditions of his confinement already were such that Santa Anna's health was faltering. "Would Texas, as a people escape the imputation of having poisoned him?" Besides, the dictator was worth far more alive, and in Washington. "Faithless as Santa Anna may be, if he were to renew his pledges to Texas through the Government of the United States, he would not dare to violate them; nor could he do so without . . . calling down the indignation of the United States and ensuring their zealous aid in our behalf, should it ever be required. . . . So far as I have been enabled to regard this subject, I have been guided by what I have esteemed to true policy of the country, and with a desire to promote its true interests. A matter of so much importance to the country, does not admit of personal or individual feelings. It should in my opinion, be looked at on the ground of policy alone."[13]

The frontier senate of the Republic of Texas did not like being told what to do and often overrode Houston's vetoes with ease. In this instance the president engaged in a bit of what later became known as reverse psychology: he returned the resolution to the Senate, not with a veto, but with a request that they reconsider it and offered to bend to their will if they insisted. It was a calculated risk, but it worked, and for once the Senate reversed itself. Houston drew up safe-conduct passes for Almonte and Santa Anna and took them to Orozimbo himself, where he house-guested for the night. Santa Anna was packed off to the United States, escorted by Bernard Bee, Houston's former aide-de-camp Maj. William Patton, and Houston's own trusted Hockley, with instructions to avoid towns and crowds that could place the dictator's life at risk. "We escaped recognition and detention most wonderfully," Hockley reported back to the president from the Mississippi riverboat *Tennessean* on December 13, "but two or three instances having occurred—and they unimportant." In their flight eastward, the party had spent so much time splashing through swamps and bayous that Santa Anna remarked they would have made better time sailing on the *Independence*. The dictator was, however, just glad to be alive. "Gen'l. S.A. is in fine spirits and speaks of you often," Bee reported home. "Your kindness to him you may be assured will not soon be forgotten."[14] (Bee was wrong on that count; the dictator's gratitude was used up by 1842.)

With the president having determined to keep Santa Anna alive and try to make a reliable peace with Mexico, the general of the Texas Army continued beating his drum for more war. Felix Huston clanged his alarm bell on November 10 that, according to an Irish informant, "an army of 24,000 are to march soon. . . . San Luis Potosi is to furnish 8,000 and New Leon 4,000." To meet this threat, Huston dispatched Col. Juan Seguín to San Antonio with a garrison of 80 men, but he doubted that Seguín could control them, for "they have no American officer." Four days later, he reversed course and suggested abandoning San Antonio, since Seguín did not even speak English. General Huston's own facility in English, however, did not prevent the troops under his personal command from disorderly conduct; he had been compelled to break up another grog shop and asked the president for instructions on "how to handle officers who have overstayed their furloughs. I have thought to sending and arresting the whole of them." At least a supply ship from Mobile finally arrived and disgorged sugar, coffee, clothing, and blankets for the army.

In requesting on November 26 that President Houston come out to head-quarters for a conference, Felix Huston repeated his fear that the enemy would swarm again before Texas could prepare. Houston wrote him on the same day, which cheered the general enough to reaffirm his loyalty to the president, but he could not forbear expressing his contempt for the Congress: "My God, could it be supposed that at this time when every patriotic pulse should be beating with care and apprehension for the welfare of the country, there would be little and grovelling spirits who would sow dissension, and prostrate the energy and power of the country?" Two weeks later, his lack of cavalry to keep an eye on the countryside prompted General Huston to conceive a new plan to forestall the expected invasion: he wanted to expel the Mexican population from San Antonio. "Whilst the Mexicans from Bexar are permitted to reside there and haul things from Dimmitt's Landing, spies under cover of them will be continually among us. . . . Yesterday a party of 15 armed men were seen near the camp at a distance by a waggoner and by some of the guard. And I could not raise a single horse to ascertain who they were and it is a mistery to me." But, while maintaining the necessity to "remove all Mexicans in front of the army," Huston also noted that his men now had no flints or cartridge paper. "The waste paper of the printing office," he wrote, "would be gratefully received." The president, if not his general, readily appreciated the incongruity of reconciling the army's destitution with Huston's desired campaign. In response, Houston did what he always did so well: he stalled for better circumstances, sending General Huston replies that were encouraging but noncommittal.[15]

As Santa Anna made his way toward Washington, his escort bore two letters from President Houston to President Jackson, the first one introducing the Mexican dictator as a soldier and gentleman and asking Jackson to accord him a dignified reception, notwithstanding the mood of the times, which "might be injurious, to the reception, which I claim to solicit for Genl. Santa Anna in Washington." Far more interesting was the second letter, marked "Private," whose tone may have been at least partly occasioned by Felix Huston's weekly and sometimes twice-weekly stream of appalling army news and raising the alarm that the Mexicans were about to invade again. And its tone was reinforced by Houston having in hand James Collinsworth's bleak report on the prospects of annexation. Though Texas had been angling for recognition, Houston confided to his revered mentor, and while

> It is policy to hold out the idea (and few there are who Know to the contrary) that we are very able to sustain ourselves against any power . . . yet I am free to say *to you* that we cannot do it. . . . My great desire is that our country Texas shall be annexed to the United States on a footing of Justice and reciprocity to the parties. . . .
>
> [This] is a matter of great distress. . . . To witness the fairest portion of the Globe cast on the hazard, more uncertain than "a Die" must awaken . . . sensations of the most lively and painful character. I look to you as the friend and patron of my youth and the benefactor of mankind to interpose on our behalf and save us.[16]

One aspect of this much-quoted letter strikes one as very odd: if Jackson and Houston had in previous years colluded as tightly as some scholars think they did, then Houston should have been able to presume with confidence Jackson's vigorous backing on the annexation issue.[17] But that is not the tone of the "Private" letter.

Nor was Jackson's behavior unequivocal. Certainly, he favored acquiring Texas, and during the preceding summer, as he told Collinsworth in stalling him, he had dispatched to Texas one Henry M. Morfit, a minion of the U.S. State Department, to investigate conditions in the new republic. Morfit, while generally impressed with Texas' thirty thousand or so Anglo-Americans, felt the Mexican threat too great to encourage recognition, let alone annexation.[18] In Jackson's last annual message to Congress on December 8, he allowed that sympathy on the part of Americans for their compatriots in Texas was understandable, but for the United States to act in any regard toward Texas would cause their character to be questioned.

"There are already those," he wrote, "who . . . charge us with ambitious motives and insidious policy," concluding that great caution was called for lest national policy be governed by partiality. The administration, for the time being, let the matter rest.[19]

Along with the two missives for Jackson, Houston sent a third letter to Washington with the dictator's escort, this one for his favorite cousin, Jack. It was a scattergun of exhaustion, affection, and loneliness for family attachments and perhaps bears something of the flowing bowl in its emphases. But he did not forget to solicit the Washington Houstons' hospitality for Santa Anna, and "By all means get Texas annexed to the U. States—I wish to retire, and spend the balance of my days in peace, and to review the past, as a Philosopher shou'd do—See all *our* old friends, and tell them it is my soul's desire.—I never was ambitious, but *fortune* has given a semblance to my actions which my soul never *desired*! My life has been one of agitation, and it is time that I should be calm and meditate upon the future. Oh write to me every day! Make it your daily business—Yes your task!! Give my love to dear Cousin G. . . . Kiss Mary, and tell her of me. Kiss all for me!"[20]

Texas took the final step of nationhood on December 10 with the adoption of a flag—a single golden star set on an azure background—and the Lone Star seal, for which the wax was ordered six weeks previous.[21] There was some sparring with the Texas Congress over issues of serious substance. They passed an act providing for a post office department, but one whose head was to be elected by Congress. Houston pointed out that this would hold him responsible for an executive department whose head he could not control, and he vetoed the measure. His argument was that the constitution was framed so as to prepare Texas for admission to the United States, where postmasters served at presidential pleasure. As the Texas Constitution was itself silent on the subject of postal regulation, the American model, he said, was the one that should be followed. He did not mention the fact that the post office was a major asset of presidential patronage.[22]

Not every measure to stem from Houston's first term was the result of surefooted statecraft. It was important to act and act vigorously to get the country going and not overly fear making mistakes. On those occasions when he did believe he made an error, the president acted with his usual pragmatism to correct it. One such example was the chartering of the Texas Railroad, Navigation, and Banking Company. Houston, no less than his Tennessee political mentors John Rhea and Joseph McMinn, was a constant champion of internal improvements, which Texas plainly needed, and the petition for the company's charter bore many signatures of the galaxy of Texas leaders: Stephen F. Austin, Branch Archer, James Collinsworth, J. P. Henderson, and the revolution's banker, Thomas McKinney. President Houston approved the bill when it emerged from Congress and signed in on December 16, but upon reflection, his Jacksonian suspicion of creating such a powerful corporation sided with loud public criticism of the measure and he changed his mind. With the charter already issued, however, some cleverness had to be exercised to get rid of the company. What Houston seized on was the provision that a deposit of twenty-five thousand dollars in gold or silver be paid to the government within eighteen months of the charter's issuance. The company's founders came up with the required cash, but it was in paper notes. Treasurer Asa Brigham, doubtless with Houston's approval, refused payment, and the scheme folded.[23]

As winter deepened, pressure weighed ever more heavily on Andrew Jackson to speak on the issue of bringing Texas into the Union. The lopsided result of the Texas referendum was widely known, Houston's commissioners were buttonholing Jackson's ministers, and there was enormous public agitation about it. But annexing Texas would fracture the slave-sensitive Congress and probably cause a war with Mexico. With the pressure on, Old Hickory did something that was, for him, startling: he played for time, and he used Houston's own words to do it. With the private letter of November 20 fresh in hand, in which Houston admitted that Texas could not be counted on to sustain herself against Mexican determination to keep her, Jackson sent a message to the U.S. Congress on December 20. It had ever been the policy of the United States, he said, to withhold recognition in cases of contested independence until there was a clear and permanent winner. That had been the policy with European revolutions and in the western hemisphere that had been the policy toward Latin America. The United States had not recognized Venezuela, Ecuador, or New Granada until their contests were well settled. Thus, it was "known to the world that the uniform policy and practice of the United States is to avoid all interference in disputes . . . and eventually to recognize the authority of the prevailing power, without reference . . . to the merits of the original controversy. Public opinion here is so firmly established and well understood in favor of this policy that no serious disagreement has ever arisen among ourselves in relation to it." Yet, Jackson acknowledged, the issue of recognizing, let alone annexing, Texas was "a matter of peculiar delicacy, and forces upon us considerations of the gravest character." Acting in too great haste to recognize Texas might allow the world to construe, "however unjustly," that the United States had been behind the revolution. Prudence, he concluded, "dictates that we should still stand aloof and maintain our present attitude" either until Texas was recognized by other powers (and preferably by Mexico herself) or until "the course of events shall have proved beyond cavil or dispute the ability of the people of that country to maintain their separate sovereignty."[24]

This news would have fallen as a heavy blow on Texas' secretary of state, but he never heard it. Stephen F. Austin retired with a chill on Christmas Eve, 1836, and the drained empresario quickly sank into fever and delirium. Raising himself from his hearth pallet to proclaim, "Texas is recognized! Did you see it in the papers?" he gave up his exhausted ghost shortly after noon on December 27. "The Father of Texas is no more!" Houston informed the country. "The first pioneer of the wilderness has departed! General Stephen F. Austin, Secretary of State, expired this day." In homage to Austin's "high standing, undeviating moral rectitude . . . untiring zeal and invaluable service," the president ordered a thirty-day period of mourning with all civil and military officers to wear crepe on their right arms and every post and garrison to fire a twenty-three gun salute—one for each county.[25] Texas' ship of state, however, sailed on without Austin. Attorney General Henderson took up the state portfolio, and only four days after Austin's death, William Wharton and

Memucan Hunt were accredited as agents to the United States to relieve Collinsworth and Grayson and make another run at recognition.[26] The president still did not have a Great Seal of Office to affix to their credentials. One small compensation for a classical scholar like Houston: the wax on the surviving commissions bears the faint outline of what appears to be a signet ring, a certification usually associated with Roman caesars.[27] (Another imperial gesture that Houston employed to exasperate his enemies was his deliberate—as historically alleged—separation of the "S" from the "am" in his signature, causing it to read "I am Houston," in imitation of the Spanish kings who traditionally signed documents "Yo, el Rey." If so, then at least he kept his capacity to have fun in even the gloomier times.)[28]

"I have read General Jackson's Message," Houston soon wrote with some resignation to his New Orleans agent Thomas Toby, and while he tried to spin it favorably, he was at least a little incredulous at Jackson dragging in the Latin American precedents regarding recognition—again, not the words of a co-conspirator. He found Jackson's report "politic, but not unfavorable. . . . How the U. States can get over our recognition I can not conceive. None of the S. American States ever had higher claims, and surely Mexico, to the present moment has not fairer claims to recognition. Spain up to the present moment has not been willing to recognize her Independence. When Santa Anna would arrive at the City of Washington, and the whole matter was presented to that Government, I do hope that justice wou'd be done to our cause." Until then, he was committed to doing what was best for Texas: "We must be up and doing, to the last moment!"[29]

If President Houston had not by now divined for himself the cause of American unwillingness to even look in Texas' direction, Wharton clarified the issue for him in his first dispatch.

> I will now tell you the whole secret of the reluctance of Congress to act on this matter. . . . Some of the members have openly avowed to me their reasons for wishing to postpone our recognition until the next Congress . . .—that the North will be opposed and the South in favour of annexation;—and that Mr. Van Buren of course will have the support of either the South or North in mass accordingly as he favors or opposes annexation. The fear then of throwing Mr. Van Buren into a minority in the next Congress induces his friends to desire a postponement. . . . Be it understood also that many of those same individuals are in favor both of annexation and recognition, but they wish Mr. Van Buren to have his own time and select his own mode of bringing them about.

His opinion was that the only remedy was to convince Jackson to act, and to that end he obtained an audience with the president. Wharton, who had been a Texas independence radical since 1832, must have been crestfallen as Jackson soothed him that all would come right, and that he believed Santa Anna sincere in his assurance that upon his return home he would normalize relations with an independent Texas, which would remove any impediment to recognition. Jackson must have been providing his politically puny successor some additional cover by snowing

Wharton; it is unthinkable that a man as shrewd and cynical as Old Hickory could have been taken in by Santa Anna's sudden slathering of sincerity. Annexation, it seemed, was proving a harder job than any in Texas had imagined.[30]

On the day Austin died, the president lost another friend, but one he could well do without. The relationship ended, not by death, but in a bitter and sarcastic resignation from good feeling and rapport: Felix Huston had had enough. Throughout the autumn, his constant stream of letters to Houston on army conditions and pestering for the Mexican invasion increased, each one more than the previous, in their expressions of regard. "Your Obedient Servant" warmed to become "Your Friend," and as the letters became more familiar in tone, Huston took it upon himself to offer opinions on state matters. He expressed his approval of Houston's handling of Santa Anna, pressed for a conference to clarify the Mexican plans, and himself submitted a bill to Congress approving the invasion. When the president finally clipped his wings, Felix Huston's brittle presumptions were shattered.

> I have been deluded into the impression that a strong personal attachment had sprung up between us and that in you I would always find a friend and defender from malevolent aspersions. I was justified in this by all our personal intercourse and correspondence. I have awakened somewhat suddenly from my *romantic* dream of friendship. . . .
>
> The good of the country requires that there should be harmony in action between the President and the Commanding General—
>
> I shall not use your name except with respect till this campaign is over— and require of you to do the same towards me. If you do not wish to accede to this proposition let me know, and if things here come to the worst, the sooner the better. I have my opinion of you, that you and I can understand each other as *enemies* if we have not as friends.

What touched off this astonishing tirade, in addition to the president's lack of support for Huston's bill to authorize the invasion of Mexico, was that, allegedly, Houston was overheard telling certain senators that General Huston had retained a mule belonging to an aide, a Major Morse, because he might want it himself to come to Columbia. One can almost hear the president wryly asking the senators what chance an army had of success invading Mexico when it was so ill equipped that its commanding general had to steal a mule just to get to the capital to lobby his bill? It was a quintessentially Houston stroke, but the perceived mockery left the Natchez caudillo beside himself.[31]

Apart from Felix Huston's pouting and the fact that the government in Columbia remained rough around the edges, by New Year's Day of 1837 the business of governing proceeded at least with a kind of routine. Gone were the vague and gusty directives from Burnet, although subordinate officials turned to Houston for a time to clarify or reissue some of the more confused of them. Maj. George Styles of the Third Infantry, for one, was stranded in New Orleans scratching his head over orders received "in the usual style of Mr. Burnett" and asked Houston for new ones.[32]

With the presidency, inevitably, came petitioners seeking a smorgasbord of opportunities and favors. Houston's letterbox during these months included a communication from William Patterson of New Orleans announcing that he had perfected an improved rifle capable of twelve to eighteen shots in half a minute and desiring to know when might he demonstrate the new weapon for the Texas Army. (He seemed blissfully unaware of Texas' payment history on its debts.) Ambitious parents asked the president to advance their sons in the military. "I write you in behalf of a meritorious youth," wrote John H. Wallace diffidently from Fredericksburg, Virginia, "of seventeen years of age, William F. Maury." After going to Texas for love of liberty, he "is now, (as his Mother so feelingly expresses it) 'in the ranks as a common soldier, unknown, unnoticed, uncared for.'" He hoped Houston would find it in his power to promote him.[33]

And there were office-seekers, men of adventure who presented themselves and their services unbidden or, perhaps more cleverly, who gained letters of introduction from Houston's myriad acquaintances back east. His New Orleans friend William N. Hill forwarded so many that by February, Hill wrote apologetically, "You must pardon the liberty I take, in so often recommending individuals to your Kind attention and consideration,—for, when I meet with a honorable and inteligent gentleman, whose very soul is devoted to the cause of your adopted Country, I cannot forego the pleasure of making him known to you[.]" Not that Hill was ready to desist at this point. "Such an one," his letter went on, "is the bearer of this, my friend, George E. Boswell whom I beg leave to recommend to your especial attention."[34]

And so it went. Houston's frequent Nacogdoches host, Adolphus Sterne, recommended people for government posts. One would-be Texian diplomat in Lexington, Kentucky, shrewdly obtained an introduction from Mary Austin Holley, Stephen Austin's cousin and, recently, author of an immensely popular travelogue entitled *Texas*. A Dr. Harral of New Orleans volunteered himself to be surgeon general of the army. And Captain Karnes of the "Whip-handle Dispatches," in a letter underscored *Private*, went so far as to lambaste his local district attorney for "conduct . . . reprehensible in a sworn officer of the government" and recommended a friend of his as a suitable replacement. Karnes seemed unaware that the official he complained of, John Ricord, had until lately served Houston as private secretary and had been promoted to D.A. of the Fourth District as a reward for meritorious service.[35]

With peace, of a sort, restored, interest in immigration from the United States was on the upswing, and Houston, who personified Texas to many there, received inquiries about land and conditions from prospective settlers, some of whom he knew and most of whom he did not. Often their petitions were mixed with further congratulations on the San Jacinto victory. One Tennessee postmaster, David Gallaher, with whom the president seems to have had some acquaintance in his previous life, wrote him from "Houston PO Wayne County Tennessee" and bragged: "I called my PO after you and also my youngest son I call Sam Houston I named him some months before your victory at San Jacinto. I felt confident in my mind that you would conquer Santi Anna, but the most of the people in this country hissed at me, but [now] they say I was a wich to guess, and called My Son for one of the Bravest men on Earth. I tell them I always knew that." He went on to request Houston to open him a subscription to a Texas newspaper so he could decide whether to relocate.[36]

The president, wishing to "avail myself of a moment to say 'happy new year,'" found time to send a freshly completed poem to Miss Anna. "I feel some hesitancy," he averred, "to forward to you a few lines for criticism," but the effort was another "part of the return for placing on my *armour* when we parted."[37] The poem itself, eight stanzas of Ivanhoe-ish military allusions, was entitled, "March, Chieftain." If poetry ever provides a window into the soul of the poet, Houston's stamp is there— so grandly and smoothly brought off that you almost forget it is childishly simple in structure. It concludes:

Lady, thy mandate I'll obey
And make it good in mortal fray
Or ne'er survive the battle day
To greet thy smile again.

Should I return from well-fought fields
I'll bring again thy warrior's shield
And at thy feet I'll proudly yield
The laurels won for thee.[38]

The president had already presented Anna Raguet with a more literal set of San Jacinto laurels—magnolia leaves taken from the battlefield, and his pursuit of her was unswayed by further news from Tennessee: Eliza was trying again to take her chair as first lady. With the message from her cousin John Campbell having had no effect, a new letter arrived from Houston's cousin Robert McEwen. The latter had by now received Santa Anna's gold-and-platinum-bedecked saddle, and Houston was even more the talk of Tennessee. McEwen's letter of December 13, featuring now-illegible strikethroughs in his jagged hand to get the wording just right, interceded for her as far as a cousin permissibly could: "I feel satisfied from what you say that your intention is now to reunite yourself to your wife, at this many of your friends are of opinion you will, it is quite evident that your wife much desires such an event. I am told she often speaks of you & seemed gratified to hear of your success, always manifesting the highest respect for you."[39]

Whatever Houston might have said to make McEwen believe that a reconciliation was in the offing, Houston set the record straight and declared impossible a reunion with the woman from whom he had now filed for divorce—twice.[40] His life's brightest prospects seemed now immediately before him, and this was not a time for looking back when all he could survey was so much pain. And Eliza, having spent months publicly showing all of central Tennessee how ardently she was now devoted to her husband and being scorned for her trouble, was now left with more egg on her face than her family had ever pelted Houston with. Up to this time her comments on the separation seem to have been limited to family members and confidantes and were mild in tone. Her vilification of him as an insanely jealous, superstitious wildman, as later told to Balie Peyton, may very well have been brought on by this final rejection.

President Houston had been planning an inspection tour of the army at least since his New Year's letter to Miss Anna, but his sense of urgency about it was growing. The troops were as rowdy as they were disheveled. Only a few days after polishing off his poem for her, he received a vitriolic letter from a Daniel Elam of China Grove, alleging that a detail of soldiers guarding Mexican prisoners "passed my house to day not asking me for suplies of any kind passed on by . . . & drove off a parcel of Cattle & among which was my *Oxen*. . . . they killed one without giving me any notice of the same—or giving me any thing to show for the damages they had done. Believing as I do that you for one will not suffer such depredation . . . Committed on private property when at the same time there is a plenty of public Cattle in the Vicinity," he demanded Houston's attention to the problem.[41]

The situation was indeed bad; the troops were hungry. At Camp Independence, Houston accompanied General Huston on a scout of the countryside near army headquarters. The expedition produced not protein but a letter, which in his anxiety President Houston neglected to date, to Capt. Andrew Neill at Casey's Ferry, "— [Send] any word that you can to the people in Bay Prairie to forward Beeves to the army. I wish it done speedily. I will pay them in cows and calves in sixty days! If there can be no other cattle furnished, let the public cattle be sent." General Huston seems to have found some better mount than Major Morse's mule, but lost him. The army commander "is out hunting his horse," he concluded the letter to Neill, "or he would give you this order."[42] While trying to supply the army generally, Houston also acted specifically on Daniel Elam's complaint of army confiscations, sending Capt. B. J. White to scour the Brazos "as high as Leckeys or even higher, should it be needful . . . to ascertain what amount of Beef and Pork could be obtained if needful and at what price." The president's anxiety manifested itself in the repetition of the word "needful" as well as in his instruction that anyone who supplied beef to the army would be allowed to keep and use the hides and tallow in addition to payment for the meat. "My object," Houston declared, "is to have the Army supplied regularly, and prevent all *future* impressments of supplies or any thing else which may belong to the citizens."[43]

Such frankness, however, was for confidential exposure only. Apparently, Houston determined to present a different posture for public attention. While in the field, the president received a letter from Gail Borden, editor of the Columbia newspaper, asking, "What shall we say of the army?" The subsequent edition described the troops as hale, hearty, eager, and in good spirits.[44] Houston repeated the fib in reply to a letter from Catherine Duane Morgan, who had inquired after her two sons, distant relatives of Benjamin Franklin who had come to Texas with volunteers from Pennsylvania. "I have visited the army," Houston soothed her, "and met with your noble sons, and I really think if asked for your jewels you might well give the answer of Cornelia and point to your boys. I was much pleased with both, but felt a peculiar interest in George, he being so young an adventurer in our cause. . . . The

Army was in fine health and improving in discipline daily. The troops at this time have abundant supplies and so far as we can learn the enemy are not yet on the advance."[45] Surely it was neither the first nor the last time in military history that reality had to be made over for public consumption.

Upon his return from this depressing progress, Houston sought escape in a long and chatty letter to Miss Anna; he thanked her for kind words about his poem and then boxed her with a flurry of banter: "Report says that you and Capt. Edwards are to be united—is it so? Bye the Bye, I am told it is reported that I am married to Mrs. Long! I never saw her but twice, and I don't think she wou'd marry me, and besides she has one or two pretty Grand Children, which wou'd argue that she was older than I am! I will not marry until I can once more go to Nacogdoches and see how my matters are there! and if my tenants have erected me comfortable cabbins; why then I may look out for a 'spare rib' to appropriate to myself."[46] With "spare rib" set into quotations, Miss Anna would have surmised that Houston in his playful way was referring not to barbecue but to Genesis, and womanhood, and that he meant to find his wife—her—in Nacogdoches. (He had used almost the same phrase eight years before—"may it be that I will splice myself to a rib"—shortly before the Allens announced his engagement to Eliza.)[47]

Such presidential daydreaming about future bliss was a temporary respite, for he had a grim business to perform. Army morale and conditions were so bad that the president reorganized the command structure. The exact timing of events is no longer certain, but apparently Houston let it be known during his tour that he was thinking of placing the army's quartermaster general, Albert Sidney Johnston, in overall command. One soldier, James Allan, took it upon himself to write the president on January 25 that, while "your visit, has done much toward soothing the unquiet," he questioned the capability of certain officers, "men of prominence opposed to Genl Johnston taking command—these men court popularity like demagogues more than officers." In Houston's own mind, he could not exculpate Felix Huston from the frequent camp disorders and desired to place him in a position of less influence with Congress. On January 31 he named Johnston, a Kentuckian who graduated from West Point in 1826, as senior brigadier general in command of the army to be served by Felix Huston as junior brigadier. There was no way Houston could have foreseen the consequence. Johnston arrived at army headquarters, Camp Independence, on February 5; Huston, scalded, challenged Johnston to a duel, which was fought two days later. Huston retained command, at least temporarily, by shooting Johnston through the buttocks.[48]

News from the army continued to worsen. In early March from Camp Preston, Col. Henry Teal, the unlettered but reliable rustic whose company had guarded the gathering at Washington-on-the-Brazos as they declared independence, wrote to Houston, "for to state to you our Situation. of our army we have not one mouthfull of bread Stuffs, nor hav not had for ten days and beef is verry Scears and hear to get and when got verry pore and bad. . . . I think that my letters must lay in the Post Office at Columbia . . . or the mail not in operation. I am adoing of evry thing in my power for to disiplin my command . . . [but] it is verry hard for to command

men that is bear footed and naked and hongry."[49] Strangely, Houston seems never
to have replied to this or any of Teal's numerous letters, each more plaintive than
the one before, on Houston's neglect to correspond as he had once promised.
Rather, each bears the endorsement "Referred to the War Department." Teal had
seen Houston as recently as January 29, when he delivered the president the letter
from Anna Raguet that prompted the chatty reply about spare ribs. From their
tone, Teal sounded as though he needed a friend more than he needed instructions,
and why Houston would have withheld something as easy to give as his paternal
reassurance was a mystery, certified two months later when Teal was murdered in
his sleep.[50] When Houston heard of Teal's killing, he sent a message to troops in
the field saluting their bravery and their service in such difficult circumstances,
but he condemned the murder in the strongest terms and appealed for order in the
camps until adequate supplies could be sent them.[51]

About a week after receiving this particular letter from Teal, Houston ordered
Texas' New Orleans agent, Thomas Toby, to tighten the requirements for allowing
more volunteers to sail: "no more troops are to be sent to Texas, but such as bring
good arms, two months provisions, and six months clothing, all to be provided
at their own expense. . . . We do not want naked men, nor men unarmed, nor
starving." The fact that Houston ended his instructions to Toby with Teal's own
words (although he did substitute "starving" for "hongry") might have given that
lonely yeoman some comfort.[52]

Felix Huston had complained to the president during the fall that some citizens
had been abusing his soldiers, but the Elam letter seems to be the first complaint
that Houston received from an aggrieved citizen. Still, such tension between army
and people was not the only reason Houston needed to ride out and eyeball the
soldiers: throughout the early weeks of 1837, rumors of the Mexican reinvasion
came so thick and hot that for a while it seemed that every ship docking in New
Orleans after a Mexican port call was met by one of Houston's contacts, who questioned the crew on the state of Mexican preparations.

The most detailed information yet from New Orleans came from Houston's
private secretary, John Ricord, written on January 26; when the president saw it,
his jaw must have gone slack. Ricord provided a detailed accounting of 1,335 Mexican infantry from eight different battalions, supported by 670 cavalry, 400 recruits,
and thirty pieces of ordnance, "all in good order," in Matamoros. They were presently
expecting reinforcements of 150 cavalry, 200 infantry, and two more cannon. A
northern force of 2,300 men under Gen. Nicolás Bravo, of which Ricord knew no
details, were in Saltillo, and a 150 cavalry garrison in Laredo.[53] Houston no sooner
observed the grim condition of his troops at Camp Independence than he wrote
Colonel Seguín at San Antonio: "I need not suggest to you the necessity of sleepless
vigilance and increasing caution. You know the enemy you have to guard against."
Actually, Seguín had another enemy closer at hand: Felix Huston had issued orders
that the colonel interpreted as relieving him from his command in favor of an
Anglo, a Lieutenant Colonel Swytzer. "*As to my having confidence in you,*" Houston
wrote Seguín in confirming him in command, "I solicit you to rest assured that I

entertain for you a *high regard*, and repose in your honor and chivalry the most *implicit* confidence. . . . I well know how you bore yourself in the conflict. I shall always be proud to reward your merit and require your services."[54]

After receiving Ricord's report that General Bravo was in Saltillo organizing, Houston heard from an independent source that this northern army was on the move, but the Texas Army was still hungry and unprepared. The president had already activated several different schemes to get food to them. But as he ever did in an emergency, Houston believed that actuating one more plan could not hurt and if any man in Texas could make things happen, it might be crusty old Capt. Randal Jones, a veteran of the Creek War and a participant in James Long's fili-buster. "Dear Sir," Houston wrote him on February 7, "I wish you to be in instant preparation to forward Beef to the army. I have just received Express and the Report is that Bravo is at Matamoros. Forward Beeves, and tomorrow I will send you the bond of the Government. For Gods sake be up and doing. Let those who can be spared turn out as spies."[55]

As if a starving army and massing enemy were not trouble enough, Ricord's letter from New Orleans wedged a new, completely different burr under Houston's saddle: affairs at the Texas agency in New Orleans were in a disarray that went beyond the weakness of Texas' juvenile economy. Ricord had ascertained, he wrote, that Agent Toby "is personally little esteemed in New Orleans, where many look with suspicion, upon the movements of men who belong to the sect of Jews. That he is surrounded by men of the same persuasion who are his Factors, Brokers, Clerks and patrons; and into the hands of such men, most if not all the Land Scrip passes for goods at an exorbitant price, and by means of cunning management, becomes a source of private emolument."[56] This presented Houston with a dilemma, for Thomas Toby had been a friend to the Texas cause since the revolution opened, and he was the owner of the *Yellow Stone*, which he had placed in the service of the army. But the ingrained anti-Semitism aside, the charge was a serious one. Toby and his cabal, Ricord charged, managed Texas' business affairs in such a way that confidence in the land scrip became depressed; the same men then bought the scrip at prices far below their realistic value. Texas' credit was taking a battering while the agent and his friends made a profit on it.

The jury on Toby was still out, though, for Houston received a better report of him through another of his New Orleans informants, R. H. Smith. The city, according to Smith, was crawling with ne'er-do-wells posing as volunteers on their way to Texas but who had no intention of actually serving. To get an accurate picture of the situation, he told the president, "do as I done stay about two or three days and listen & not let it be known you ever saw Texas then you would hear things stated for facts that would astonish any man on earth." Some of the imposter volun-teers had been sniffing about for land scrip or other Texas emoluments, but "your agent and his spies are too smart for them."[57]

The Toby matter would have to be dealt with in its turn. Right now the perceived Mexican threat required action, and Toby would have to be relied on. For months Felix Huston had been forwarding every wild rumor he heard about astronomical numbers of Mexican regulars poised to pour over the border. The president knew he was trumping up a case to invade Mexico and discounted his reports by an appropriate amount. John Ricord, however, had been working the docks in New Orleans and talking to sailors fresh out of Mexican ports; the numbers he forwarded, unlike Huston's, were very plausible and could not be ignored, nor could information from still other sources. "In the holy name of God," Houston beseeched Toby on January 27 (and before he could have received Ricord's accounting) Toby should send the Texas warship *Independence* back home for duty and locate the captains of the *Invincible* and *Brutus* and get them embarked as well. (The *Invincible* had been lately in New York, and when she returned to Texas she bore a small cargo for the president and a note from his friend William M. Price: "My dear friend, I send to you by the Invincible four Boxes containing a general assortment of *comforts* for The hero of Texas—I congratulate you with all my heart upon the success of your . . . valiant efforts in the emancipation of Texas.")[58]

Perhaps a courier delivered Ricord's letter by the first of February, for on that date the president wrote Toby again: "For God's sake fit out the *Independence* and send her to sea! Don't fail, & no matter about the cost." Throughout Texas' revolution and the early months of struggling to maintain herself, many men, both public and private, had hazarded their personal fortunes for the sake of their country, and in the present emergency, no less should be expected of the president of the republic. Fearing that the *Independence* was being detained for debt in New Orleans, Houston wrote Toby a second time on February 1: "Send out the Independence & if necessary, I authorize you to pledge a first rate League of land on Red River at Port Bolivar, belonging to me of undoubted Title. I refer to Christy."[59]

Arranging Texas' little navy in a picket line along the coast was one line of defense. At the very same time, a second possible defensive bastion of a completely dissimilar nature presented itself to Houston quite unbidden. When he returned from his gloomy army inspection, he found a letter from Rusk marked *Private & Confidential*. It seemed that Creek Indians north of the Red River, whose treaty with Osage Indians Houston had negotiated in 1831 and whom Houston had tried and failed to settle on a Texas land grant in 1834, were interested to learn whether the Texas land offer was still good. They desired a settlement on the frontier between Texas and Mexico, where "to the number of five thousand [they would] engage in an active war against Mexico." Rusk cautioned that "this is a delicate & highly responsible business," but one he generally endorsed. "I am thoroughly convinced that we need not expect permanent peace with the Mexican nation until they are fully convinced of our ability to do them great harm at home & I would like to see five thousand Indian warriors turned loose upon them west of Rio Grande if they can be prevented from killing women & children." Still, Rusk said he would defer to Houston's "greater knowledge of the Indian character."

Such an offer was tempting. A buffer of several thousand Indians friendly to Texas would answer a great security need, but he also remembered the Cherokees' opposition to the 1834 scheme, and he could not trust Congress to give the Creeks a secure land title. So, he did what he always did so well: he tread water. Houston wrote the Creeks' emissary, Lt. Peter Harper, to tell the Creek chiefs that they would be welcome to visit him on the first of May after the capital had been moved to a permanent location. "Tell them I will take them warmly by the hand. They will be welcome!" However, "I find on reflection that it will not be in my power to come to any conclusion on the subject," as he would have to lay the matter before Congress. In the meantime, he suggested Harper ascertain where exactly the chiefs desired to settle.

The Rusk-Houston plan of Creek settlement failed, but not at the Texas end. Through Harper, Houston sent his reply to his old Creek friend Opothleyahola, the same who had given him the buckskin coat in which Alexis de Tocqueville had beheld Houston at the end of 1831. A copy of the letter, however, fell into the hands of William Armstrong, acting superintendent of the Indian Territory agencies, who touched off a firestorm of indignation when he sent copies of it to the commissioner of Indian affairs and the Arkansas federal district attorney. "The Creeks as well as the Cherokees," he warned, "have a great disposition to engage in the contest between the Texians and the Mexicans, and there are those among them . . . who are secretly encouraging such a design. . . . I have and shall continue to use my efforts to check anything of the kind."[60]

Overarching all these difficulties was the fact that, as Houston ceaselessly pointed out, there was never a dollar in the treasury. At one point, the president was even reduced to issuing a letter to "Any Captain of a Steam Boat, or Vessel" asking cabin passage on credit for an aide traveling to the United States, "and the same will be paid out of any monies in the Treasury." That was a phrase familiar to American appropriation bills; what Houston left out was the part that there never was any money in the treasury. Having once authorized Toby to hazard a league of his personal lands in procuring supplies, as spring wore on and the Mexican threat seemed to intensify, Houston sent the army's commissary general in New Orleans, A. S. Thruston, an order even more sweeping:

> I wish but a word. I wrote you officially the other day. I write now to inform you with *great* urgency of our situation. There are 500 men in Camp without arms. . . . Only four days provisions are in camp—forward supplies (send Mr. White at Mobile. I have written him). Do all that you can. Run in debt to get supplies for the army . . .—Some people will advance to us—and go on *Tick* if our agents do not furnish cash, or supplies! . . . We must have them, and you are authorized to hypothecate all my lands amounting to 50,000 acres of the best land in Texas, of undoubted titles. . . .
>
> You must attend to this. . . . If you can send 3000 shirts (substantial) 2000 prs. shoes, and as many suits of clothing, do so.
>
> I pray God that you may succeed!!!

And as irritated as the president was becoming with Felix Huston, his vexsome general still knew people of influence, and he would have to be relied on. "Genl. Huston will render you all the aid in his power & no doubt can assist you much!"[61]

Ultimately, even his friend and government printer who had disseminated the Texas Constitution, Gail Borden, came after him for money. During the war, Mexican troops had burned his press, which he had replaced by using a personal line of credit in Cincinnati and mortgaging his land on the Brazos. He had been faithfully executing his contract to print the government's laws and proclamations, but having never been paid, his creditors were "hot upon us for payment of the goods."[62]

In sum, the spring of 1837 might have been depressing beyond redemption, but for the fact that, as the president had alluded to in his letter to Harper and touted more grandly in a letter to his old friend Swartwout: "In a few days the Government will remove to ... Houston, as they call the new City. ... the Government will remove to that place, and be stationary for some five years." Relocating the Texas capital had been contemplated since the early days of its establishment in Columbia. The construction of an entirely new town, named in the president's honor, was the enterprise of the Allen brothers, two young stockbrokers from New York who had bought a half-league of land on Buffalo Bayou upstream from San Jacinto. During the revolution, both Augustus C. Allen and John Kirby Allen had proven themselves financial patriots of the first order despite government arrears and citizen ingratitude. Their plan to move the capital from Columbia succeeded when they offered to raise a new capitol building at their own expense. The idea to name the city after the president was said to have originated with Augustus' wife, Charlotte, and a two-room dogtrot was constructed next to their own home to serve as an executive residence. The Allens also conveyed some town lots to President Houston—a favor that would surely raise eyebrows today, but at that time no one thought it anything more than a courtesy.

Houston was duly flattered to have a namesake capital, but he was not long distracted from the next goal: annexation of Texas to the United States. "We see that 'Uncle Sam' has recognized our Independence," he continued to Swartwout, then finding one of his opportunities to mimic Lafayette: "This is pretty well, and if we are annexed next session, 'I will die appie.'"[63]

12

HOUSTON, AS THEY CALL
THE NEW CITY

And life in the new town was sure to be gay. President Houston never lost sight of his position as the most eligible bachelor in the republic, and the removal of the seat of government to Houston city at the end of April 1837 picked up the pace of his social whirl. It also doubtless increased the frequency with which he was seen in public wearing the wonderful clothes to which he had always been so partial. Samuel Hewes, Texas' commissioner of purchases in New Orleans, had sent him a batch in March: "I think they are handsome and I [know?] they will please Your Excellency. . . . the Hat corresponds to the clothes, [but] is not as I requested it should be. . . . [The hatter] suited his own taste and I trust has suited yours."[1]

Not everyone was impressed. Vice President Mirabeau Lamar was temporarily out of Houston's hair, vacationing back in Georgia, but one Lamar partisan wrote derisively to his principal, "I find the President extreamly courteaous when he out for general inspection, this seldom oftener than once in sunshine, between eleven & two, he . . . dresses himself gaudily in self peculiar taste viz. black silk velvet gold lace crimson vest and silver spurs." By taking a stiff drink, Houston "makes himself again *Hector* upon his feet and no longe the wounded Achilise of San Jacinto . . . and with a tread of dominion in his aroganic step strides . . . across his own nominated metropolis . . . to the barkeeper."[2]

The latter charge was certainly true enough: Houston was drinking too much. In addition to Mexico, the army, Toby, and his other problems, the campaign for Anna Raguet was not going well. He wrote Miss Anna more frequently and at greater length than any other of his correspondents of the time, and she could not help but enjoy the status of being courted by the president. Early in March, Houston's friend John Roberts wrote him of "one little joke, General, I must tell you—The other day I dropped in at Col R's and the pretty and lively Miss A had a letter in her hand which She said was from you—I advanced with due reverence, touched the corner of her cape, remarking at the same time that I must have the pleasure of Kissing the cape of the Presidents future . . .—and pressed it to my lips—an agreeable scene and a hearty laugh. Well General was this not tolerable gallantry for a backwoodsman on his debut at *Cort*."[3]

But, while drawn to his fame and his luster, the virtuous girl of twenty could not wish away Houston's wife still living, his Cherokee liaison, and his drinking, and was polite to him. Shortly after Roberts's visit, the Raguets left for a month's sojourn in the United States. Miss Anna's sometime detachment eventually caused Houston's eye to wander (if indeed he needed any encouragement), and he paid a small attention to a Miss Barker of New Orleans. Sam Hewes, who had sent him the clothes, gave her a letter from Houston enclosing a ring.

On Anna Raguet's return journey to Texas, she happened in New Orleans to meet Miss Barker, resulting in a contretemps that sent Houston into something of a tizzy. He wrote Miss Anna—perhaps a bit lamely—that Miss Barker had been kind enough to visit him while he was recovering from his San Jacinto wound, confessing that he had "sent to [Miss B.] a trifling evidence of respect, which I dare not offer Miss Anna. . . . If I admired Miss Barker, it was because I admired others to whom she bore a striking resemblance!"[4] When all else failed, he could still count on his war wounds to get some consideration.

The first anniversary of the battle of San Jacinto was celebrated in grand style. The residents of the new capital were treated to the sight of a tall flagpole being erected in the middle of town, which was then fitted with a splendid new flag in finest silk of the golden Lone Star against its dark blue background. And in a salute that only Sam Houston could have arranged, several hundred Indians who had been camping in the surrounding pine forests, trouped into the city and performed a massive circular dance around the flag, hailing the republic and—here was the point—respectfully demonstrating their worthiness to a just land settlement.[5]

That, however, was small doings compared to the ball planned for that evening. From the account in the *Ladies' Messenger*, it must have been held in the capitol, for it described a large two-story building, almost finished. The ceiling was of exposed beams, but wooden chandeliers were produced, each fitted with six or eight sperm candles. Revelers came from up to sixty miles away by carriage or horseback, or by rowboat from Harrisburg, each wearing finery, some of which was undoubtedly worn for the first time since being packed to move to Texas. There were more than enough cotillions to fill the twenty-by-fifty-foot room, but all withdrew to the perimeters when the orchestra—a fife, a fiddle, and a bass viol—struck up "Hail to the Chief."

Sam Houston's protestations of fealty to Miss Anna did not prevent him from opening the 1837 San Jacinto Ball in a ruffled shirt, a scarlet cashmere waistcoat, and gold-corded black velvet suit. His consort at the ball was, of all people, Mrs. Mosely Baker, whose husband now sat in the Texas Congress representing Austin County. After all the grief her husband had given him, from trying to break up the Consultation of 1835 to his recalcitrance during the Runaway Scrape to a recent bill of impeachment, Houston was still playing with him. Eliza Baker wanted to attend the ball, Mosely was out of town and could not take her, so the president would get an evening with her to make a favorable impression and the galled Baker would be in his debt. Besides, as Houston was quick to tell her, he was dancing with the most beautiful lady in the room, which by common consent she was, resplendent in white satin with a black lace overdress.[6] This was one hand with Baker in which Houston took every last trick.

He was still in considerable pain from his San Jacinto wound; in fact, where all the other dancers had performed the ritual of exchanging their street shoes for dancing slippers, the president wore boots with short red tops folded over and laced to support his weakened ankle. The dancing continued until midnight, when supper was announced at Benjamin Fort Smith's nearby hotel. A dirt-floored eave ran down one whole side of the hotel, where tables were laden with venison, turkeys, wine, cakes, and coffee. After supper the ball resumed, cotillions giving way to Virginia reels that continued until dawn. Without doubt the first San Jacinto ball was the most glittering affair ever staged in Texas up to that time, and the exhausted guests were persuaded that Texas, socially, had arrived. All they had to do was figure out how to avoid the sizzling sperm oil that dribbled from the candles overhead.[7]

On May 5, Houston addressed Congress on the subject of Texas becoming part of the United States, which was supported by the vast majority of people in Texas. He treated the occasion as a kind of State of the Union address—or in this instance, the State of the Republic. He was escorted into the chamber by a joint committee of the Congress along with the cabinet heads, and the president was seated between the Speaker of the House and the president pro tempore of the Senate.[8] The most interesting aspect of his speech opening Congress shows the fruition of one of the lessons Houston learned as long ago as Tohopeka: lead, but not too far in advance. The subject was the African slave trade and the common knowledge that human chattels were being stockpiled in Cuba for export to Texas. "This unholy and cruel traffic has called down the reprobation of the humane and just of all civilized nations," the president told the Congress, several of whose members gritted their teeth. Continued traffic, he noted, was against the policies of the United States and Great Britain as well as Texas, but as the Texas Navy was not strong enough to interdict it, England and America should feel welcome to intercept slavers on Texas' behalf. Such a policy "will at once arrest the accursed trade and redeem this republic from the suspicion of connivance, which would be as detrimental to its character as the practice is repugnant to the feelings of its citizens."

This was shrewd. He attacked not the institution of slavery but its continued traffic, an aspect that was a long established part of the public debate and thus not too dangerous domestically to broach. The United States had sidestepped annexation, and at least for the time being, Texas must go it alone and independent. That required British friendship—the British loathed slavery—and it was no accident that seated with Houston and the other dignitaries before Congress was Joseph Tucker Crawford, the British consul at Tampico, now accredited to look after his nation's interests in Texas as well. In this speech, Houston placed Texas in a favorable international light without hopelessly alienating Texans to whom slavery was an entity of unquestionable rectitude. There is no question who was doing the leading here.

Nor was Houston mouthing platitudes for Crawford's benefit while otherwise winking at the practice; he meant what he was saying. A couple of weeks later, he instructed his minister in Washington, D.C., Memucan Hunt, to ask the U.S. government for aid in putting down the traffic. (A peculiarity of the Texas law was that slaves could be imported into Texas if they had been legally owned in the United States, a loophole that prompted slavers to discharge their cargos secretly in Louisiana and bring them overland with false papers. At Houston's request, the United States agreed to station a warship off the Louisiana coast to discourage this practice.)[9] Houston's action in suppressing the slave trade, without moving against slavery itself, demonstrated the state of Houston's own thinking on the "peculiar institution." He disliked it and was ambivalent toward it, and shared Lafayette's opinion of its eventual demise, but he also recognized it as a fact of life to be dealt with justly, with cognizance of the owners as well as the owned. By this measure, Sam Houston's thinking in 1837 was fully consistent with, if not as fully formed, as it was in his momentous slavery speech in Boston nearly two decades later.

Regarding annexation itself, it had, he admitted, been offered to the United States "in the most frank and undisguised manner." Uncle Sam had given them the cold shoulder, but for now Houston was willing to make excuses for them. "The period at which the congress of the United States was compelled to adjourn," he said, "prevented any action of that government."[10] Actually, there was a good deal more to it than that, for the U.S. Congress was deeply divided on the point of even recognizing Texas. Houston had lately received a letter from cousin Jack, dated March 2, informing him that the Senate had passed a resolution in favor of recognition by a vote of twenty-three to twenty-two. "The House will act on it tonight or maybe tomorrow, but I dread everything." Politics was first even on Jack's mind—and he intimated that he was considering buying Texas bonds and removing there— and the family news that Houston always awaited eagerly from Jack and Gertrude, in this instance his god daughter Mary's progress at dancing lessons, was pushed to the end of the letter.[11]

Congress might speak on the issue or not, but the conduct of American foreign policy was the province of the president, and in his last official act, Andrew Jackson extended diplomatic recognition to the Republic of Texas. Having preferred annexation, Houston was disappointed but not surprised. Texas' admission as a slave-holding state would teeter that delicately preserved balance in the American Congress between free and slave states, a circumstance that the powerful northeastern states simply would not countenance. Texas was now a nation and had to look after her own interests. Recognition and trade had to be sought from the European powers, and "Texas," he lectured its Congress later in the year, "with her superior natural advantages must become a point of attraction, and the policy of establishing with her the earliest relations of friendship and commerce will not escape the eye of statesmen."[12]

Numerous other functions of nationhood had to be mastered. To protect those relations of commerce, Texas needed a navy, and Houston ordered suitable vessels. To regulate the national finances, paper currency was devised, bonds were issued, and Texas' financial condition appeared to stabilize. At Houston's behest, the reliable J. Pinckney Henderson laid aside his portfolios as attorney general and acting secretary of state and took up diplomatic credentials as Texas' minister plenipotentiary to Great Britain and France. Passing through New Orleans on his way to Europe, he was happy to report back to the president that "we find Texas rather in better credit here than we expected to find it." And Henderson was able to ease Houston's mind about his vexsome New Orleans agent. "That Mr. Toby has done some things wrong I have no doubt but truly I believe he has done as well as any other person could have done under the circumstances and certainly better than any other agent which has come within my knowledge. Therefore allow me to request you *not to curse him any more until you hear all,* however a *dam* occasionally may do no harm."[13]

The Cherokees and other Indian tribes of East Texas had still to be pacified, and a delegation of natives paraded into Houston's spartan residence early in May 1837 for a smoker with the president and his cabinet. Houston hoped that the Indians' homage to the Texas flag on San Jacinto Day had helped their standing with the townspeople, and he arranged another meeting with the Cherokee chief, The Bowl. "Don't forget to bring [the treaty]," Houston cultivated him. "It has ribbons and a seal on it."[14]

Houston received another distinguished visitor during this same week, the great naturalist John James Audubon, who left an indelible picture of the executive residence:

> We approached the President's mansion wading in water above our ankles. This abode of President Houston is a small log house consisting of two rooms and a passage through, after the Southern fashion. The moment we stepped over the threshold on the right hand of the passage we found ourselves ushered into what in other countries would be called the antechamber. The [dirt] floor, however, was muddy and filthy; a large fire was burning, and a small table covered with paper and writing material was in the center; campbeds, trunks and different materials were strewed around the room. Here we were presented to Mr. Crawford, an agent of the British minister to Mexico, who has come on a secret mession. The president was engaged in an opposite room on some national business and we could not see him for some time.

Audubon and his party used the delay to tour the Allens' capitol building, whose bough ceiling had not kept out the day's downpour. They encountered Houston on his way home, observing from a distance "a scowl in the expression of his eyes that was forbidding and disagreeable." Houston was wearing the black velvet and gold lace suit, "and around his neck was a cravat somewhat in the style of '76." Whatever it was that clouded the president's visage dissipated, and "he received us kindly, was desirous of retaining us for awhile, and offered us every facility in his

Executive Mansion Houston 1837–3[?]
Republic of Texas
Sam Houston, President

Texas Capitol; the Executive Mansion (both in Houston). The city of Houston served as Texas's capital for only two years before the Lamar government removed to the interior village of Austin. The Allen brothers' capitol was expanded and later converted into a hotel. The first Texas White house was very different from the one that Sam Houston saw in Washington, D.C.

Both courtesy Texas State Library and Archives Commission

power. He at once removed us from the anteroom to his private chamber, which by the way was not much cleaner than the former." Audubon found Houston's cabinet huddled in the bedroom, working, but time was taken to drink toasts to the republic.[15]

With Henderson off to Europe, Houston needed a secretary of state, and he settled on Tennesseean and Nacogdoches resident Dr. Robert Anderson Irion. One of those educated frontier jacks-of-all-trades, the widowed Irion came to Texas, practiced medicine, became a surveyor, was a militia commandant during the revolution, and most lately had won election as senator from Nacogdoches. He was one of Sam Houston's closest friends—and a deeply secret rival for the affections of Anna Raguet. Sending Henderson to England would probably mean that Texas would have to express herself on the slavery issue again. Houston had favorably impressed Consul Crawford, but in England proper his attack on the slave trade would not be enough to outweigh the fact that slavery itself was still legal in Texas, which would be a high hurdle to clear for British recognition. Houston's instructions to Henderson, via Irion, on this point were the best he could do under the circumstances: "On the subject of slavery you can speak with candor and truth, admitting that its institution was cruel and impolitic, [but] that under existing circumstances, owing to the . . . nature of the climate, the habits of the people and the locality of the country, it *must* continue as provided by the constitution and laws." England would have sense enough to know that if she wanted to circumvent American tariffs with Texas cotton, she would have to accept Texas as a slaveowning nation. Nevertheless, Henderson should remind them "that the condition of slaves in this Republic is far more tolerable than in the U. States," which might have been an acceptable card to play in diplomacy, but this assertion was not in fact the case at all, whether Houston believed it so or not.[16]

Another important concern for the national security had little to do with Indians or the Mexican threat. Despite the measures Houston had taken in March and April, the army was still too large, too restive, and headed by filibusters still full of fight. In May, Felix Huston arrived in the capital to persuade the government to let him lead a punitive expedition against Mexico—at which point newly discovered papers indicate a radical departure from the history that is traditionally related. As universally minstreled in every Houston biography since *The Raven*, the president saw in Huston an ambitious martinet who was a greater threat to Texas' hard-won democracy than to Mexico, and he loosed one of his multifaceted strokes. It was Sam Houston's habit when entertaining a distinguished visitor such as Felix Huston, as a matter of courtesy, to surrender the presidential bed and sleep on the floor.[17] On this visit, however, acting in dead of night on May 18, President Houston hissed awake War Secretary William S. Fisher and dispatched him to Camp Independence with secret orders to furlough the soldiers by companies to various ports on the coast. The furloughs were liable to revocation at any time, and those men not responding within thirty days would be tried for desertion. As Houston knew they would, the unwanted johnnies-come-lately began hopping aboard vessels bound for the United States. By coming to Houston city, General Huston separated himself from his command, and the president now ensured that Huston had no army to return to. Precious money was saved, the threat of military dictatorship was averted, and the army was reduced to a manageable six hundred men. Felix Huston, relieved of command, outmaneuvered, and hopelessly bamboozled, went back to New Orleans.[18] President Houston's standing among the citizens increased after this display of "Indian cunning." Frank Lubbock, the New Orleans merchant who was one of the very first suppliers of goods to the new capital, called the feat "one of the most marked evidences of statecraft I have ever known."[19] Foxing Felix Huston has become one of the best-loved Houston legends.

Recently examined documents, however, place a different complexion on the episode. In truth, General Huston had requested of President Houston a personal furlough of ninety days to allow him to return to the United States and arrange his personal affairs, as early as March 16. He presented his request in person, and general orders in Houston's handwriting appear on the same paper granting the furlough, but then Huston delayed his departure until he felt the army could better spare him. Since their February duel, Huston and Albert Sidney Johnston had made up and now presented common cause to the president, lobbying for the Mexican invasion, which if nothing else, dramatized Houston's virtual isolation in opposition to the silly scheme. It was, astonishingly, Huston and Johnston who recommended furloughing the army in a joint petition to Houston, which is undated but noted as received in the presidential office on May 24. Their idea was to furlough all but three hundred of the army until the first of November, by which time they, Huston and Johnston, would have raised six *thousand* volunteers to invade Mexico on the first of December.[20]

But the president had already decided to act. Furloughing the army was a good enough idea, and he wrote Fisher on May 18, asking him to "ascertain whether it would be proper to furlough such officers and men as have been long in service." He countermanded that directive on the next day, May 19, and if he sat up by silent candlelight while Huston was asleep, it was to write this letter: "I have come to the conclusion as there is no prospect of an active campaign that one half or two thirds of the army may be furloughed for their time of service. . . . They will be entitled to their monthly pay and bounties as though they had been in service all the time. . . . this policy is just and generous to the brave men who have embarked on our cause."

Fisher then rode out to the army with discretion to furlough them or not as he thought best, and if these doings were a surprise to Huston, they were less so to the men under his command. "The report that those of the army who had been longest in service were to be furloughed, had preceded me," Fisher reported to Houston on May 24, "and my arrival had been anticipated anxiously since sunrise, and I have been assailed by crowds of applicants for furloughs. . . . Those who have arrived lately do not expect any indulgence of this kind—and I think it would be good policy to furlough all but, military men, and Wigginton's command, which are new recruits. This would leave in the field a force of 600 men." And this, ultimately, was what was done.[21]

The proceeding seemed no less a coup to Felix Huston, however, who learned of it on June 3, and he wrote a letter to the president in handwriting nearly twice as large as his previous missals: "Sir:—Having received certain intelligence that the Honl. Secretary of War Wm. S. Fisher has furloughed and is engaged in furloughing a large part of the army *indefinitely* I cannot, but think that such a decided step a rejection of the proposition made by Genl. A. Sidney Johnston and myself."

The president received Huston's letter the same day it was written, and he decided to play dumb. "General—Your views on the subject of furloughing the army are appreciated. When the Secretary of War was ordered to the army, it was for the purpose of obtaining information. . . . I am not advised by the Secretary of War now in camp that any portion of the army has been furloughed." It was a lie, of course, but the president saw no need to pick a fight that he had already won. Houston did point out the impracticalities of a campaign against Mexico during the summer: there was not a dollar in the treasury (one of his favorite phrases) with which to outfit an expedition, and some of the men were already without shoes; the south Texas brush country was in an acute shortage of water and the soldiers would suffer terribly; and the prospect of impressing supplies in Mexico herself were dim. The president did not rule out a campaign in fall or winter, as Huston and Johnston had suggested, when the conditions both logistical and financial might prove more favorable. But there would be plenty of time to discuss that when Huston returned from his furlough to the United States, which had been deferred to this point, and Houston wished him a pleasant journey. What he undoubtedly hoped was that the whole business would have blown over by then. "The army will be curtailed," he swore in a letter to Miss Anna, "as it ought to be for the good of the country—We will never have another *Volunteer Army*." This was one instance of forecast, however, where his skills let him down.[22]

A second letter from General Huston followed five days later, asking somewhat lamely that, if he could not invade Mexico with six thousand, might not Houston let him do it with one thousand? "I find that the opinion prevails that your Excellency is opposed to the expedition—if so I will at once withdraw the proposition."[23]

The discrepancy between the legend begun in *The Raven* and the actual facts is one more of dramatic timing than of effect. If Marquis James's account of Houston slipping out of the house as Huston snored is a bit hyperbolic, the president acted with no less shrewdness. Talk of furloughing the army had been bandied about for weeks, and for Houston to have taken another's idea, improved it, and capitalized upon it shows him acting even more centrally within his personal parameters than James depicted. One might also note that this was almost exactly the same stunt that Wyatt Hanks had pulled on Houston early the previous year when he assigned Houston's army to the Matamoros venture, and Felix Huston himself had complained for months about the number of enlistments that were continually coming due. But, as usual when Houston recalled a stratagem from his or another's past, he put his own unique stamp on it. Frank Lubbock's admiring remark on Houston's "evidence of statecraft" was still not misplaced.

If his handling of Felix Huston was not evidence enough of "Indian cunning," Houston gave a second display of it at about the same time. It is less well known than the Huston affair, but the president's roommate Ashbel Smith was privy to it and remembered it in his reminiscences. At some point, Maj. Thomas G. Western, a frontiersman and Indian agent two years older than Houston, was placed in command of the garrison in San Antonio. Western had formerly been in business there until he was ruined by depredations committed by both sides in the revolution. He did not much care who knew of his scorn for the Houston administration, and the president wanted to relieve him. Béxar was much farther from the center of government than Camp Independence, however, and Houston feared that an order relieving Western would be flouted. The president buttonholed Col. William Patton, who was soon to serve as part of Santa Anna's escort to Washington but who was just then headed to San Antonio on other business. Pretending to draw Patton into his confidence, Houston mentioned the necessity of appointing a minister to represent Texas' interests in England. "He spoke of Major Western, lauded his polished manners, his courtly address, his diplomatic ability, [and] asked Col. Patton what he thought of the appointment of Major Western for this mission. All this he begged Col. Patton to hold in strict confidence." Houston waited until he was certain Patton had reached Béxar and then sent orders to Western to report to the capital. Patton, of course, had blabbered everything he knew to Western, who showed up in Houston primped for his elevation into the diplomatic service. By the time he learned, several days after his warm welcome from the president, that the appointment had gone to Henderson, his replacement was firmly in charge of the troops in San Antonio. It was a sneaky way of doing business, to be sure, but necessary in a small army "where there were very few above the rank of captain who did not aspire to be commander-in-chief."[24]

American recognition was long since achieved, but autumn brought word from Houston's commissioners in Washington that annexation was still beyond their grasp. "I have called on several members of the Cabinet," Peter Grayson wrote him on October 21, "among others Mr. Poinsett, whose warmth on the subject seems equal to our own, but was met by him with the *Cabinet suggestions* of a little delay for the present!!" There was a rumor that Henry Clay would come out in favor of acquiring Texas, and if he did he could bring enough Northern votes to join with the South, and they would win, but "upon the whole . . . according to the views I take of the subject, I look *upon the result, as exceedingly doubtful.*"[25]

Still, Texas' first steps toward nationhood were completed, and the bucolic republic began to gain favorable international notice, and not just from England and France, important as they were. In July the president sifted through the usual letters of introduction and paused over one from John C. Williams of Velasco, introducing Charles, Comte de Farnese, who had come to Texas to see what good he could do. A following letter from the count himself presented Houston a lucid, twelve-point proposal to separate Catholics in Texas from the archbishopric of Monterrey, which he judged would speed Texas' recognition by Catholic countries. He also outlined the provision of land grants to establish parochial schools. The count

President Sam Houston. Various dates have been ascribed to what appears to be the earliest known photographic image of Houston, dating possibly to the time of Margaret's honeymoon daguerreotype of 1840. His dress and Washingtonian queue suggest the costume that he wore to the inauguration of Mirabeau Lamar in December 1838.

Courtesy Daughters of the Republic of Texas, the Alamo

requested Houston's permission to present the matter in Rome, where he believed he could use his court connections to good effect.

The count's abundant good sense and discretion impressed Houston. He replied in barely a week, though still apologizing that he had been too ill to correspond more quickly. He wrote that land grants were the domain of Congress, not the president, but "it does rest with the president to express his profound veneration for the true religion and for sound education . . . , and if it pleases the Holy See to use your talents for the good of Texas, it will give great pleasure to, Your most respectful servant." The letter was rendered into French and dispatched on August 5. The count did take the matter to Rome, but he was not successful in getting an archbishop consecrated to the Texas flock.[26]

As Houston city took root and flourished, visitors of the breeding of the Comte de Farnese were vastly outnumbered by those who came in more humble circumstances. But all considered Houston the man to apply to when they needed particular help. One of the more unusual requests was from T. W. Ashton, a newcomer who had arrived to go into business with Captain English. "In New Orleans I had the misfortune to lose all my cloathing and my situation compels me to ask that which I would fain ask of any one else . . . : a letter to some merchant . . . that will let me have such things as I am in want of until I can get in business." He promised not to run up a tab of more than a hundred dollars.[27]

Whether addressing the Congress in Houston or courting Anna Raguet in Nacogdoches, Sam Houston during that winter of 1837–38 was probably more in his element and closer to happiness than at any other time in his bachelor life. December afforded the opportunities to wear many costumes: Masonic regalia to preside over the first convocation of the Grand Lodge of Texas (he had transferred his own affiliation to the Holland Lodge No. 1 in Houston on November 13) then buckskins and turban, no doubt, to treat again with his Cherokees near Nacogdoches.[28] But it was his role as a leader of frontiersmen that he relished most. In all his capital, there were only three stoves, so a public fire was often made on the street before the saloon. To the horror of Lamar and the other stuffed shirts, Houston passed away cold evenings consorting with commoners, downing hot toddies and regaling the ruffians with his oratory.[29] If the weather was too inclement for the public fire, resort could be had to the Mansion House, a tavern of exotically dubious repute whose proprietress was none other than Pamela Mann, she of the Twin Sisters, the oxen, and "Rohrer, that woman will fight." (Or "bite.") When the capital was established at Houston, Mrs. Mann abandoned her Harrisburg digs to locate where the commerce was and opened a boarding house at the corner of Milam and Congress. With a downstairs stocked with whiskey and an upstairs stocked with "fawn-necked damsels," controlling her clientele required a constant exercise of her frontiersmanship. She was frequently prosecuted for assault and larceny, but that did not prevent her and President Houston from becoming good buddies and undoubtedly sharing some good-natured amusement over their muddy confrontation on the Harrisburg fork.[30]

Yet there was Houston's other side, tender and cultured, which he hid, fastidiously, from all but his most intimate associates. One of the few privileged latter was his roommate, Dr. Ashbel Smith, who happened to own perhaps the finest book collection in Texas, a kaleidoscopic library that tumbled from military tactics to phrenology to Confucius. The Roman orators were there, as were the Greek philosophers, Houston's beloved Homer, and the Enlightenment—Racine, Descartes, forty-one *volumes* of Voltaire. In the Executive Mansion—such as it was, with no fireplace and only a small clay stove to warm their fingers, Indian style[31]—"four nights out of five" in their shared bedroom in the "quiet hours after midnight," Houston liked to have Smith read to him from these classics. And, if some friendly rabble invaded the hour for a little late carousing, they were welcome—after Smith first stuffed the book under a pillow.[32]

This intimacy with Smith lasted—despite some strain in their later years—until Houston died, and the relationship is worth a closer look. In appearance, the contrast between the two men could not have been more complete. Houston was now forty-four years old, his fleshy leonine countenance was beginning to wear, but his stature of six-feet, two inches was as commanding as ever. Ashbel Smith was twelve years younger, a full eight inches shorter and then only spindly built, and homely almost to the point of cruelty, though fastidious to the point of vanity. He was subject to illnesses of the chest as well as to woeful depressions that were probably more Byronic than physiological in nature. This unimpressive frame, however, jailed a mind that radiated brilliance. A Connecticut Yankee graduated from Yale Medical School, his mastery of classical literature rivaled Houston's own. Years spent in schoolteaching and then practicing medicine in North Carolina gave a sternly Southern turn to his gentlemanly character. Only once, apparently, did he falter, that being in a paternity affair from which he disengaged himself with two thirty-dollar payments to the wronged girl's father.[33]

Ashbel Smith arrived in Houston city on May 9, two days after Houston met Audubon. Smith was recruited into Texas service by both Memucan Hunt and J. P. Henderson, and among the parade of would-be worthies who came armed with letters of introduction, Smith's dual sponsorship got Houston's immediate attention. He and the president took an instant liking to one another, so much so that Houston took the remarkable step—perhaps he saw the trunks full of books— of inviting Smith to live with him. And Smith's abilities, coupled with the city's appalling lack of sanitation, made for an instantly busy medical practice. After only a month of living together, Houston cemented their relationship when, with Smith doctoring out of town, Houston nominated him surgeon general of the Texas Army, confirmed by the Senate on June 7.[34]

Their living arrangement gave Houston the best of both worlds—he could spend the day cavorting with rustics in their own terms and then come home at night to a companion who knew mathematics, geology, and philosophy; who had won a prize at Yale for his mastery of Greek and Latin poetry; and who wore a Phi Beta Kappa key as part of his daily apparel. Scholars who have interpreted Houston as a cynic, an aristocrat who was not one of the crowd but who knew how to manipulate the crowd by aping them, misunderstand him. Houston craved both rustication and refinement as surely as man needs food and shelter: a vivid, full-blooded venting of his homespun passions was his food; Ashbel Smith was his shelter.

It was no accident that Houston had himself painted as Gaius Marius; those who view that toga-wrapped portrait of him as evidence of patrician leanings could use a dose of Houston's own classical training: Gaius Marius rose as a man of the people, who near the close of his life snatched Rome, in the name of the people, from the grip of Lucius Sulla and his abusive senatorial snobs. (It was also Marius, not coincidentally, who recognized the potential disaster of relying on a citizen militia and professionalized the Roman army for the first time and, not to overextend the analogy, paid his soldiers in land bounties.) Houston knew precisely why he wanted to be painted as Marius even if his logic leaves his biographers behind. Houston, like Marius, moved among patricians and, like Marius, had married among patricians but, like Marius, never befriended them to the detriment of the common citizens. At the Mansion House or by the public fire, these were Houston's true people. This vacillation between bawdy ballads and quietly recited poetry was not the ultimate expression of his personality, but it was a mode of living he could get by on until something, or someone, came into his life that could bestow the fulfillment he lacked. Ashbel Smith probably understood something of this; one thing he got out of his friendship with Houston was a chance to study a brilliant, troubled spirit other than himself. Quite apart from his own episodes of melancholy, Smith's fascination with the murky depths and malfunctions of the mind was professional. He had once considered making a medical specialty of lunacy and wrote of the patients he had observed in asylums with both a chilling clarity and a personal empathy, betraying his own strange awareness of what a thin line separates the truly brilliant from the truly mad. And Houston fascinated him.

Smith, for his part, made himself indispensable. He doctored Houston when he was sick and, perhaps more importantly, sobered him up when Congress tried to take advantage of a temporary incapacity. Smith attributed some of the president's habitual drinking to an attempt to remain popular with the hard-drinking frontiersmen who were his core of support. But he knew there was more to it than that; he believed that in other part it was Houston's way of spiting opinion. That winter, particularly, there were other grounds on which to rationalize Houston's excessive drunkenness. He was lonely, and he was making no progress with Anna Raguet. He was grieving: "My Friend Deaf Smith," he wrote Miss Anna, "and my stay in darkest hour, Is no more!!! A *man, more brave*, and *honest* never, lived. His soul is with his God, but his *fame* and his *family*, must command the care of His Country!"[35] The further fact was, simply, that he was and long had been an alcoholic. That realization lay some few years in his future, but he did know his drinking was getting out of hand, and he opened 1838 by giving himself some incentive to improve: he bet A. C. Allen a five-hundred-dollar suit of clothes that he would "not use any ardent spirits, wines or cordials" until the end of the year, signed, sealed, and endorsed before a witness.[36]

However, it was exactly in January of 1838 when Houston made the acquaintance of Hamilton Stuart, a Kentucky emigrant only twenty-four years old who, like so many others, came with letters of introduction and the ambition to find his fortune. He was already an accomplished newsman, having founded the *Kentucky Gazette* two years previous. He had been warned of Houston's intemperance and, being a young man of delicate sensibilities, worried about the impression he would make on the president if he declined to drink with him. The boat took a week getting from Galveston to Houston, hanging on snags, grounding on sandbars, and tangling on overhanging branches, but when he arrived he found the city celebrating the arrival of a barrel of ice from New Orleans. It was "probably the first" to be seen there, and Stuart found the president of the republic indulging in iced champagne. He presented his credentials, and as he feared, Houston invited him to drink. Stuart declined and then apologized if he had given offense. Houston, he recalled, put his hand on Stuart's shoulder. "Young man, I never insist upon any one drinking with me. I sometimes think I drink too much myself. Probably it would have been better for me if I had never acquired the habit."[37]

For purposes of the wager with A. C. Allen, though, it should be noted that it was not made until January 7, and if the iced champagne incident took place before then—if for instance the ice had arrived for a New Year's Day celebration—there was not yet a bet to violate; indeed, it is tempting to suspect that the Allen bet might even have been occasioned by the hangover Houston acquired by getting snockered, not on frontier rotgut, but on iced champagne.

When the president finally heard from his minister plenipotentiary to England and France, Henderson still could not be very encouraging about recognition from the European powers. He had put the very best possible face on Texas' conditions and prospects for the British prime minister, Lord Palmerston, whom he was certain was sympathetic, although the rest of the cabinet was not. "How different business is done here from what is the practice in our plain, candid Republican style." England, he wrote, probably will not recognize Texas as long as they are having trouble in Canada, and France probably will not recognize Texas because she is expecting war with Russia and needs to keep on England's good side. France, therefore, could not be expected to take any action regarding Texas that England might interpret as an attempt to sneak an advantage there. Geopolitics, the frontier rustics were discovering, could be thorny. "I feel disappointed," Henderson wrote the president, "mortified—mad—but one must keep cool and be prudent in such cases. The time is most unpropitious for Texas, and only requires more firmness, and perseverence." Henderson would shortly leave for France, and if he made no progress there would return to London and await instructions.

On February 23, Houston finally received a generous settlement from the government for his revolutionary services—a total of $5,905.27 including a salary for himself of $200 per month; salary, clothing, and rations for four servants; forage for seven horses at $56 per month; his own rations; and a "per diem" of ten cents a mile. The account was submitted by Houston, audited, and issued by Comptroller Frank Lubbock on the same day—perhaps to keep Congress from meddling in it.[38] Of whatever regularity, the money came at a welcome time, for Houston had just bought a tract of land at Cedar Point, a prominence overlooking Galveston Bay, which he intended as a summer retreat. He loved the place, with its lush coastal grass and open glades of large trees, some like heavy ghosts leaning inland, sculpted by the sea winds. He rhapsodized in letters to Miss Anna over his "splendid purchase [of] . . . a Fairy region . . . beneficial to my health." During all his thirty years in Texas, Sam Houston bought, sold, and traded many parcels of land, but Cedar Point held his heart until he died. It was not a clean purchase, and it took ten years of legal battle before the Texas Supreme Court finally rested title in him. He won it dearly and never let it go.[39] A neighbor described the house Houston had built there as a log cabin of one room about fourteen feet square.[40]

The acquisition of a quiet retreat was fortunate for him, for his relations with Congress became downright ugly at times during 1838. They had far less sympathy for the Texas Cherokees than Houston did and spurned the treaty he had negotiated with them. Houston vetoed a land-office act, but Congress enacted it over his objection. They also wanted to issue more paper currency, even though the existing money had depreciated to 65 percent of par. And Texas' most valuable resource, her vast, vacant public domain, was of limited use: so much of it had been granted away in veterans' bounties or to immigrants that the remainder could not be sold for any realistic price. On the international front, Houston seemed resolved that since the United States had rejected Texas as a state, the republic should take her place in the family of nations. Secretly, he sent instructions to the minister in Washington, D.C., to withdraw the annexation offer and concluded a trade agreement with England. Mexico, of course, still rattled her rusting saber but did not act.[41] Nor were things on the personal front much more promising. In his pursuit of Anna Raguet through spring of 1838, Houston maintained his jolly pretenses, their correspondence often carried, John Alden–like, by the suffering Irion. In truth, Houston was making little progress with her.

As he was fond of saying, there were other fish to fry, though, and another young lady was quietly stalking him. There was a ball in Houston to celebrate George Washington's birthday, and Dilue Rose, whose father had driven over the "grewsome sight" of the San Jacinto battlefield, was now a wide-eyed debutante of nearly thirteen. She was about to realize "the height of my ambition" by dancing with the president when she was politely elbowed aside by an ambitious widow named Boyd. The wily Dilue bided her time until April 15, when she was to be the bridesmaid at the Mansion House wedding of Flournoy Mann, son of the redoubtable Pamela. President Houston was to be best man and as such would be her escort. Her goal was almost within her grasp when at the last moment another managing widow, a Mrs. Holliday, intervened, suggesting that Dilue was too young and timid for such a duty, and took the president's arm herself. The town of Houston, Dilue Rose committed snidely to her memoirs, "was at that time overrun with widows." She was left stewing, "without escort," until she was introduced to Ira Harris, whom she wed the following year.[42] At one point during 1838, Houston also paid some court to Frances Trask, aged thirty-one and lately a Massachusetts schoolteacher, offering his carriage to take her to a party. If she agreed, "Genl. H—— assures her ladyship that the steed, as well as the carriage, shall be of the first order in appearance and qualities."[43]

It is doubtful that his intentions toward any of these ladies were serious, for during the spring Houston plotted a more determined campaign for Anna Raguet. With the success of the revolution, his petition in Mexican court for a divorce from Eliza—the "carnival of rant and jargon" one—was rendered a dead letter, and under the Texas Constitution the power to grant divorce was vested in Congress. For his own case, however, Houston transferred jurisdiction to a district judge, who heard the matter in chambers. The divorce was granted, and his freedom was completed with the death of Diana Rogers, who had since remarried anyway, in Indian Territory.

Another grand ball was got up for San Jacinto Day, which the Methodist missionary and lately elected Senate chaplain Littleton Fowler observed was attended by "about fifty ladies, and two or three hundred *gentlemen*." His sarcastic reference to "gentlemen" was occasioned by the event being, in his view, little more than "a fine time for Big Bugs to get drunk without reproach." Fowler did not single out Houston as one of them, but when the president invited Fowler to dinner two days later, the minister said he was too ill to accept. Three weeks later Fowler did accompany Houston and several members of Congress on a boating excursion to Galveston. There, the missionary who had laid the cornerstone for the first Protestant church in Texas (in San Augustine) at about the time Houston was recovering from the iced champagne "saw *great* men in *high* life. . . . If what I saw and heard were a fair representation, may God keep me from such scenes in the future. On our return on Sunday afternoon, about one-half on board got mildly drunk and stripped themselves to their linen and pantaloons. Their Bacchanalian revels and blood-curdling profanity made the pleasure boat a floating hell. . . . I relapsed from this trip and was brought near to the valley of death." Frank Lubbock was one of those on board. He was less a prude than Fowler but admitted that the revels may have gotten a bit out of hand. Still, "much is to be overlooked in these old Texans who carried with them . . . their unquenchable love of liberty."

Neither Lubbock nor Fowler singled out Houston as one of the inebriated, although the missionary had been made keenly aware of Houston's weakness and had heard him savagely attacked in Congress. It is doubtful Houston would have invited Fowler into his company just to make a spectacle of himself, and Fowler would have surely noted it if he had.[44] In fact, Houston was probably buddying up to him so that good reports of the president might reach Nacogdoches, where Fowler had only recently made prominent connections and organized a church. Such a good report would not fail to reach Houston's beautiful but elusive siren. On June 4 Houston wrote Miss Anna with news that he planned to visit her and persuade her of the legality of his divorce. He was upset that people unfriendly to him had induced her "to believe that I had presumed to address you at a time when I must have [known] that legal impediments lay in the way of my union with any lady." When he came, he promised, he would bring legal opinions that would persuade her otherwise. That was the major business; the Nacogdoches visit was to be a multipurpose trip, however, for he needed to spend time monitoring the Cherokee situation. To that end, Houston appointed a young protégé as new chief clerk in the Indian Department. He was John Randolph Ross, a descendent of the distinguished Ross family of Virginia. He probably came to Houston's notice in January upon receipt of a letter from the youth's father, Randolph Ross of Lynchburg, offering to raise troops from Tennessee if the Mexicans invaded again and inclosing a letter for his son that he asked Houston to pass on. Young Ross was at that time an aide to Felix Huston, from whom the president rescued him with the appointment to the Indian Department, and now Houston intended Ross to accompany him on the trip.[45] The final business to attend before leaving town was satisfying: publishing the terms of the Treaty of Amity and Commerce with Great Britain.

Houston departed his capital on July 5 or 6, but almost immediately the trip went awry. Young Ross took desperately ill, prompting Houston to send back for Ashbel Smith. "Mr. Ross has been unwell for three days. He was first attacked with Diarrhea, and was not bled until the third day. He mends none, his discharges are bloody and dark. His tongue is furred, and a constant pain in his bowels. . . . 'Dr. Houston' feels satisfied that this case is over his hooks. I will hail your arrival. The distance is great to visit a Patient—but the Youth is far distant from the widowed Mother, and the relict of a Gallant man." On the outer fold of the letter he penned EXPRESS!!! and set the rider on his favorite saddle horse, Sam Patch, whom he seldom allowed anyone but himself to ride.[46]

Houston nursed young Ross for a week, and after Smith's arrival the patient seemed to improve. Houston resumed his journey, but his worry over Ross was little eased. "I am most effectually broken down as a medicine man," he wrote Irion, "and feel the want of science and skill. . . . There is something hidden, and to me mysterious in these dysenteries that I do not comprehend."[47] Houston was in Nacogdoches by July 21, having been conducting the business of the republic virtually from horseback: his proclamation of July 11, calling the national elections for September 3, did not close with the usual "Done at the City of . . ." but rather a hasty "In testimony &c. / Sam Houston."[48]

Congress's repudiation of the Cherokee treaty cost much of the good will of those tricked and cheated people. It was a situation that Houston had seen before in East Tennessee during the winter of 1817–18, which he had defused by convincing John Jolly's people to move west. The situation was more complex now—there was no justification for forcing The Bowl's people to vacate, and as president as well as the man who had guaranteed them justice, Houston felt personally responsible that justice be done. As president he should have had the power, but he found arrayed against him a large majority of the people, who wanted the Cherokees gone. Some were itching for a chance to exterminate them; Houston received a windy declaration from Francis W. Johnson that ridding Texas of natives was the only security for her future, and offering himself as head of the strike force. Noting that this was the same loser who had led a chunk of the revolutionary army off to Matamoros and gotten nearly all of them killed, the president buried the paper in his files. From mid-July to October, Houston was constantly among the Cherokees trying to salvage the peace, sending repeated warnings to The Bowl not to countenance Mexican overtures. On August 12: "I have given an order that no families, or children of Indians shall be disturbed or have trouble, but that they shall be protected and even the Mexican families, and property shall not be troubled." On August 14: "When I wrote to you last I hoped that trouble would have ended. It has not been so. . . . [The Mexicans] must not stay in your country or it will make trouble. . . . Gen. Rusk says if you are peaceful that you shall not be hurt nor your people. Remember me and my words." On August 15: "My Brother, be at peace, and tell my red brothers to do so. Tell the women & children to be happy. The white warriors will not hurt their friends. . . . Genl. Rusk will protect you. Look to him as a great friend."[49]

Not that Houston was flailing in any romantic miasma about his hearty red yeomen. They were angry and there were Mexicans among them, egging them on. War might erupt, and however sympathetic he was to the injustices worked upon The Bowl's Cherokees, Houston could not have an Indian war in East Texas. During the very same days he was laboring to save the situation with their aged chief, he was also writing to Rusk, who was now wearing another hat by commanding the militia, that if there was an attack, "you may look for it at night, and from several points. Don't let your lines be broken at night. . . . Let strict subordination be maintained in the army—no firing without orders." Houston, of course, was an old Indian fighter and fussed at Rusk constantly: "Don't be drawn into an *ambuscade*, by any means and be careful, about chasing spies when they show themselves."

Nevertheless, Rusk was not to do anything to provoke the Cherokees. "I pray you to suppress firing in camp only when needeful, and let silence be preserved." As long as they were at peace with the Cherokees, "treat the Indians and their property, as its guardians, preventing all injury to every specie of property."[50] He particularly requested Rusk not to provoke the Cherokees with some deliberate display of force. Thus, Houston's posture was unchanged from the dilemma he had struggled with under Joseph McMinn so many years before. He was still trying to convince natives to yield to white authority while also trying to guarantee native rights under that white authority, all the while trying to keep undisciplined, Indian-hating, land-hungry whites at arm's length. In sum, he tried to procure some semblance of justice for all concerned.

The Cherokee business took up so much of his attention that not until August 3 did he get around to the personal matter that was, to him, of equal moment: "Gen'l. Houston has the honor of sending to Miss Raguet some papers which may afford her Ladyship some amusement." The divorce papers were accompanied by a testimonial from Irion as to their genuineness.[51] News of the irregularity of the divorce leaked, however, scandal was whispered anew, and the spotless Miss Anna kept her distance.

Houston was barred by the constitution from a successive term, and it appeared likely that the people would spurn his candidate in favor of Mirabeau Lamar. Since Houston had promoted him from private to colonel on the field of San Jacinto, Lamar had turned on him completely and gone bag and baggage over to Burnet; if anything, he had become even more of a pompous bombast—albeit an educated one—than his principal. Houston closed out his presidential term striving mightily to steer the ship of state, but Texas would not answer the helm. It confused him. Not unpredictably, he confided his heart in a letter to Andrew Jackson, describing Texas' prospects as "not worse previous to the day of San Jacinto." The letter contains the Houston turns of phrase, but it is unsure and muddy, at once self-important and falsely modest. "Unimportant as my career has been thus far," he wrote, "or what it may hereafter be, I am aware it must pass the present and be subject to the scrutiny of after time."[52] In September, Lamar did win the election, largely by default. There were in the contest two candidates friendly to Houston, by coincidence they were James Collinsworth and Peter Grayson, the co-commissioners who had spent most of Houston's term in Washington trying to get Texas noticed by the United States. The Burnet-Lamar faction, out to win at any cost, mounted "terrible calumnies" against the emotionally fragile Grayson, who repented that he had allowed himself to be talked into running at all and shot himself on July 9. Two days later Collinsworth, after a week's bender, drowned in Galveston Bay; he was also rumored a suicide, but that was never certain.[53]

For all these reasons, of Houston's many sojourns in Nacogdoches, this one was the most stressful, because with everything else going wrong, he still had to be on his best behavior in his losing campaign for the affections of Anna Raguet. This particular stay, therefore, is most likely the one during which Houston accompanied several lawyer friends on a hunting excursion of several days on Neal Martin's property outside of town. While the other men were out in pursuit of the panting deer, Houston, attended by his bodyservant, also named Sam, stayed behind at Martin's cabin, drinking—or as the informant put it, the president "looked upon the wine when it was red." This got to annoy his companions, who determined upon an appropriate revenge:

> The general had a horror of ticks; he would strip off his clothes and make Sam tick him every night before he went to bed. One day his legal friends, assisted by Martin's children, picked a cap box full of ticks—deer ticks, dog ticks, seed ticks and every other kind of tick. There must have been a million of them in that box. That night, just as General Houston was getting into his bed, one of his friends surreptitiously emptied the box of ticks into his bed. Exclamation points are needed here. !!!! He called for SAM in capital letters. The reader may conjure his most expressive language . . . and it won't begin to do justice to General Houston's vocabulary. He himself had to resort to the Injun tongue.[54]

By the time the president returned to his capital in October, he was beaten down and depressed. Young Ross had died. After having been left in Ashbel Smith's care, the surgeon general's ministrations rendered Ross well enough to return to Houston city, but he relapsed and hovered near death for weeks. Mindful of his duty even in his condition, Ross wrote Houston that if a carriage could be provided, he felt he might be well enough to rejoin him and resume his responsibilities. Houston was deeply affected by such loyalty and composed a letter of condolence to Ross's mother in Virginia. "You may be assured, Madam," he wrote, "that while you are bereaved of a noble son, I am deprived of a valued friend—one whom I had marked as an associate in my retirement, where his situation would have been that of a son. His fine intelligence, his nice sense of honor, his manly pride, and excellent discretion, as well as the purity of his habits had endeared Mr. Ross beyond all others who have stood in the same relation of life to me."[55] The same station in life, one should note, in which the youthful Houston had stood in relation to Andrew Jackson. One of the most remarkable but least remarked on facts of Sam Houston's life is that he habitually collected about him young protégés and informal wards, even as Jackson had done. Probably it was not conscious imitation; probably it had to do with his own keenly felt lack of a family, for this practice declined somewhat after the births of his own children. But it was a peculiarity that observant friends noticed. "Houston was always kind to young men," wrote merchant Frank Lubbock, "most certainly he was in a great degree to me. Yet I had no reason to expect any great favor."[56]

Nor was young Ross's death the only trial of the journey. While passing through Menard's Mill, the wife of Houston's friend Michel Menard died of a hemorrhage. "He is inconsolable in his grief at her loss," Houston wrote Irion. "He loved her much, and only the other day I saw them both so happy. They had no care—joy sat upon their countenances!!!"[57]

It was raining when the president returned to Houston in this dour state of mind, but what he found there surely set him up again. A theater troupe, the first professional repertory company to perform in Texas, had entered Houston during the summer, and at the president's arrival a state dinner was got up to fête them. There was no time for the president to change out of his mud-spattered clothes before being seated next to the theater's star, a Mrs. Barker. After the dinner there was to be a performance of a piece that had gained especial favor in Houston, a fluffy farce entitled "A Dumb Belle, Or, I'm Perfection," but as the assemblage made their way to the theater, it became clear that the etiquette of gala performances still lay a bit beyond the ken of the townspeople. As one observer recalled:

> As the president and his escort entered the orchestra played "Hail to the Chief," but there were no seats vacant to accommodate them. The stage manager ... came out and requested the men in front, who were gamblers and their friends, to give up the seats. This they refused to do.
>
> Then the manager called for the police to put them out. They became enraged, and drawing weapons, threatened to shoot. The sheriff called upon the soldiers to arrest and disarm them. . . . The president got on a seat, commanded the peace, asked those in front to be seated, ordered the soldiers to stack arms, and said that he and the ladies would take the back seats. This appeared to shame the gamblers. One man acted as spokesman and said that if their money was returned they would leave the house, as they had no desire to discommode the ladies. He said that they would have left the house at first if the police had not been called.[58]

Count on President Houston to know the best way to handle his rustic rowdies— but Mrs. Barker soon proved no less adept herself at finding her way into their chivalry. At the conclusion of the performance, her husband drank a toast to her with a gill of laudanum and died, throwing his widow and three orphans onto the mercy of the community. Houston immediately vacated the Executive Mansion for their comfort until the family could situate themselves, and various subscriptions were undertaken to provide for Mrs. Barker and the children. At the last one, at which Mrs. Barker performed Shakespeare's Juliet, local saloonkeeper Tom Hoffman proposed marriage and was accepted. Hoffman then advanced his bride a thousand dollars to visit her family in England, and she disappeared at the end of April. She never returned, although she did marry again, in Georgia.[59]

By early November the cares of the year had taken their toll. Thomas F. McKinney found Houston "nearly all the time drunk," and the January temperance wager with A. C. Allen for the five-hundred-dollar suit of clothes long forgotten.[60] He did pull himself together long enough to approach Congress again about the Cherokee question, on November 19, with a lengthy remonstrance urging them "to tranquilize and conciliate the tribes yet friendly on our northern frontier," but he got nowhere.[61]

Turning over the end of a calendar year always seemed to have particular importance for Sam Houston, a time when he could shirk off the weight of the old year and begin, bravely, anew, and 1838 was a good year to be rid of. In wrapping up his term, Houston forgave one old score, certifying an honorable discharge to

Wylie Martin, whose insubordination had given him such headaches during the Runaway Scrape and who had left the army in such a huff three weeks after San Jacinto that he never received discharge papers. What service he did render qualified Martin for a veteran's land bounty, which he now applied for, and Houston acknowledged the claim as good. Martin went on to serve three terms in the Senate.[62] Lamar too benefited from Houston's end-of-term magnanimity. In the capital, government contractors had been busy sawing and hammering on a new Executive Mansion, which President-elect Lamar would find decidedly more appropriate than the muddy dogtrot that Houston shared with Ashbel Smith. Seeking a smooth transition, Lamar inquired through an intermediary whether the furniture in the existing presidential quarters was the property of the republic or Houston's personally and, if the latter, whether he might buy it, offering to use his own money if Congress did not act in time. The furniture was indeed the president's personal property, and he agreeably sold it to the newcomer for cost plus freight.[63]

The president's enemies, however, were less forgiving of him, as an item in the *Telegraph* of November 24 mentioned: "two or three individuals have recently been boasting that they intend to challenge Gen. Houston immediately after his present term of service shall have expired. We advised these disappointed aspirants to devise some more rational method of exhibiting their chagrin and hatred." Houston, who "has proved his courage on the battlefields of his country, and who, whatever his faults, will be revered while Texas exists," would never degrade himself to duel with "blackgammons" such as them.[64]

While Houston closed his tenure with generosity, he had one last personal gesture for his rivals of rather a different sort. Mirabeau Lamar succeeded to the presidency on December 10 and was nearly in a fit that his elevation should come off perfectly. Houston arrived dressed as George Washington, in a suit of federal knee breeches and his hair tied in a queue. According to one observer, the departing president "dressed himself so much like Stuart's portrait . . . with powdered hair and elegant fitting garments, that he really looked more like the picture than ever Washington did himself." Protocol allowed him a valedictory of his administration, and with Lamar waiting to deliver his inaugural address, Houston prattled on for three or four hours—no great challenge that, but Lamar was so undone that his secretary had to read his speech for him.[65]

13

INTERREGNUM

The year 1839 opened with further personal tragedy. A week after losing his office, Houston lost his close friend John A. Wharton, who succumbed to a fever, and then his brother William followed three months later, having accidentally shot himself while dismounting from a horse. As always, sadness begat drink, and as at the beginning of the previous year, when he made the sobriety bet with A. C. Allen, Houston gave some reflection on the progress of his personal weakness. And again he made a start at reform: at the first temperance meeting ever held in his name-sake capital, in February, it was Houston who offered the temperance motion. He did not himself take "the pledge," however. "Do as I say," he intoned during a long speech, "not as I have done."[1] There was rationale for this curious behavior, perhaps even wisdom, in not appearing to be too perfect in the eyes of men, who could vote—the unpopularity of Aristides, Ashbel Smith called it, and he and Houston would have known. Houston city was nowhere close to being a civilized place yet, and the preponderance of its frontier-type residents bent the elbow with something approaching ferocity. But its domestication was inevitable. By acknowledging his faults honestly and endorsing a positive social development, though swearing no vow he could not keep, he lied to none, lost ground with few, and held the floor so long that the preacher who was slated to follow him on the platform, who might well have exhorted him to try harder, was bumped from the night's program. For a method of cashing genuine sincerity into popular sympathy, nothing could have been more typically Houston.

During this time, he was planning an extended trip back to the United States, contracting before he left for a house to be built for him in Nacogdoches during his absence. He wrote of his impending journey to Anna Raguet on February 8, and the letter contains a curious mixture of hints on the state of their relationship. He had forborne writing for a month because of the "general report . . . that you are to be Mrs. D——. Today I learn it was not so, and I feel more at liberty to write." He commented on his greatly improved health, which he attributed to "a total change of habits"—perhaps a reference to his newfound temperance—and he looked forward to having a new residence near hers: "I will select a fine lot, Miss Anna! I still regard Nacogdoches as my home." He would have preferred to spend the summer with his friends there, but his youngest sister, Eliza, had borne children whom he was anxious to see, and he was compelled to the journey east. Apparently, Houston still strove to present himself to her consideration in the most favorable light, but just as apparently, they were not as close as in former years. As he closed he let her know that "Doct. Irion sends all love."[2] No longer secretary of state—Mirabeau Lamar booted him out the day he was inaugurated—Irion was almost as good a catch as the president and in some respects better. He was thirteen years Houston's junior, had graduated doctor of medicine from Transylvania University in 1826, had emigrated to Texas in 1832, and after an interlude as a trader and land speculator had settled down to the practice of medicine in Nacogdoches. Elected a senator in the First Congress of the Republic of Texas, he served until Houston appointed him secretary of state in June of 1837. During that tenure of public service, Irion had carried numerous letters from Houston to Miss Anna, discreetly awaiting her final denial of Houston's suit before instituting his own. It is unclear whether at this point Houston yet knew that Irion was a serious rival, but he teased them both about it endlessly.

Freed from the fiduciary restriction of office, the former president also turned his attention to shoring up his personal affairs. He opened 1839 by taking on a law partner, John Birdsall of Houston, a brother-in-law of the Allens whom he had appointed attorney general of the republic in August of 1837 and who, like himself, was sure now to be out of a job, for the Congress had refused to confirm him as chief justice.[3] Then in May, Houston along with George Hockley, Phil Sublett, and four others founded the Sabine City Company to develop a town at Sabine Pass near the Gulf of Mexico on the Louisiana border. Most biographies treat the proposed City of Sabine as a minor endeavor, but Houston was more than a silent partner, and at first it occupied a good deal of his time. The company's director, Niles Smith, receipted him for twelve hundred dollars to buy twenty thousand feet of lumber with which to build a house, specified as twenty-four feet square with a ten-foot gallery, and Houston later put a tenant on his land, rent-free, to keep out trespassers. The company issued scrip for town lots, some of which were conveyed to Houston as a partner in the venture.[4]

In San Augustine to help organize the Sabine City business and in the wake of finally losing Miss Anna, late spring of 1839 is the likeliest time that one of the well-known events of the Houston legend actually took place. His once-hopeful sobriety forgotten, late one night in a booming thunderstorm, a roaring drunk Sam Houston presented himself at the door of Phil Sublett's house. He was one of Houston's closest friends, in addition to his City of Sabine partner, and would have been one to whom Houston could complain of his snakebitten love life. Sublett, according to the story, got Houston quiet by the fire, then sat by him and said: "Sam, you know you can trust me. Why did you quit Eliza?" Houston stood up, suddenly cold sober. "Sir, you violate the laws of hospitality by seeking to tear from my bosom its secret." He rode off into the storm, leaving Sublett calling after him to come back. Whatever injury he carried from Eliza still ran as unhealed as his Tohopeka wounds.[5]

Further preparing for his journey, Houston obtained from the State Department a passport good for travel not only to the United States but to Canada, England, and France as well. Curiously, the document is neither signed nor dated, but Houston did take sufficient umbrage at being described as "a citizen of the Republic of Texas" to have the words "a citizen" stricken through and the words "late President" inserted. (As a further note on Houston's physical bearing, this passport, like his American passport in 1832, assesses his height at six feet, two inches.)[6] Then, he was off to the United States to shill for Sabine City.

At the end of May, Houston was in New Orleans, where he pitched the project to William Christy. The land prospects were interesting, though not, in some observers' eyes, as interesting as the spectacle the former president was making of himself. Memucan Hunt wrote back to Lamar that Houston's "coat was burned off him whilst he was drunk on his journey."[7] Gaunt and funereal looking, Hunt was the former minister to the United States who had fallen out with Houston and in with Lamar, and he seems now to have been Lamar's eyes and ears during Houston's vacation. Apparently in Houston's entourage as a member of the Texas–United States Boundary Commission, Hunt wrote another clucking letter on July 13. He was "surprised to find how favorable an impression [Houston] had made" on a visit to Columbus, Mississippi, but Hunt seemed sure that the people he talked to, at least, now had a correct picture of the "ridiculous" and "contemptible" hero of San Jacinto. A more immediate cause of his animosity is also revealed in the letter, as Hunt bristled that Houston had engaged in conversation "a young lady, who he knew I would shortly visit with," and lavished his charms on her first. Gnats, as Houston might have said, are for swatting.[8] It was the first indication that Houston was hunting for more than investors. Winding his way toward the Hermitage and Andrew Jackson in no particular hurry, he left the plats for Sabine City with Christy to show to potential investors there in New Orleans and proceeded to Mobile. There he made the acquaintance of businessman Martin Lea, who advised him that as Houston traveled inland, he should discuss the plans with his brother-in-law, planter William Bledsoe of Marion, Alabama, and perhaps his widowed mother, Nancy Moffette Lea, who had just sold her plantation and had funds to invest.

On July 20 William Christy sent a letter after Houston, scolding that he had received "not a line from you since you left Mobile." It was an early sign that Sam Houston had found an even better friend.[9] Martin Lea invited him to a garden party at his estate outside Mobile so he could meet Nancy Lea. Upon being introduced around, Houston mistook Nancy Lea's daughter, twenty-year-old Margaret, for his host's sister-in-law, Antoinette Bledsoe, and remarked to one of the guests, "If she were not already married, I believe I would give that charming young lady a chance to say no."

Antoinette Lea Bledsoe. It was Margaret Lea's younger sister Antoinette
who introduced her to Sam Houston. Margaret was twenty; Antoinette,
who married the day after she turned eighteen, was afraid her sister
was going to become an old maid.

Courtesy Sam Houston Memorial Museum

Antoinette, who was younger than Margaret and fearful of her sister becoming
an old maid, pulled Houston out of a conversation, interrupted her sister as she
was passing a dish of strawberries, and introduced them. Margaret was a violet-eyed
beauty with wavy brunette hair, accomplished, well connected, and deeply religious. Houston spent no longer explaining Texas' prospects to Lea, her son, and her
son-in-law than it took to win their interest. Back at the party, he presented Margaret
with a carnation plucked from the garden. She put it in her hair and they took a
walk. Margaret imparted that she had seen him on the dock in New Orleans three
years before; he pointed out a brilliant star and asked her whether that might be
their star of destiny, and after he was gone, he hoped she would recall him and the
Lone Star of Texas whenever she saw it. After the former president of Texas departed,
Margaret was so overcome that she fled to her room and commenced writing
poetry.[10]

With an itinerary to keep, Houston departed Mobile on the rest of his business. Margaret Lea was only the first well-bred filly, so to speak, to catch his eye in
Alabama: at the end of August, he expended six thousand dollars of his Sabine City
land scrip to purchase seven blooded horses from Hickman Lewis of Limestone
County, four valued at six hundred dollars each, two at eight hundred dollars, and

the prize, a chestnut filly named Proclamation, "by Arab dam Lady Hamilton by Balls Florazelle," for two thousand dollars.[11] Then it was on to Tennessee to visit the other former president, Andrew Jackson. Then he continued east, back to Maryville to visit kin, but even in the bosom of his family, his past continued to haunt him. In a vacant moment while reclining on a couch, perhaps daydreaming about Margaret Lea, someone made a snide remark about his first wife. "Houston got up with eyes flashing. 'Whoever dares say a word against Eliza shall pay for it.'"[12] Houston's mind, however, was less on his past than his future. Whether jawing politics with Jackson or lounging about with relatives, he could not long take his thoughts off Nancy Lea's daughter, by now back home in Marion, Alabama. There was no route back to Texas but through there.

When they had parted in Mobile, Margaret had removed the carnation from her hair and set her contemplation to paper:

> Why have I sought thee out, loved flower?
> To gaze upon thy radiant bloom?
> Or doth some tranquilizing power
> Breathe in thy rich perfume?
>
> He placed thee in my hand, that friend
> Who now doth distant roam,
> I took thee, little thinking then
> How dear thou would'st become.[13]

It was far more than a land booster's spirit that prompted Houston to visit Marion and invite William Bledsoe and Nancy Lea to Texas. He had proposed marriage to Margaret, and she had accepted, to the consternation of her mother, who doubtless was more familiar with her prospective son-in-law's reputation.

While Houston was wooing Margaret Lea and sipping refreshments with Andy Jackson, the Lamar government back in Texas went to its duties like a bull in a china shop. While Sam Houston invariably outshone Lamar as a clotheshorse—whether to his glory or to onlookers' chagrin depended who was doing the observing— Mirabeau Buonaparte Lamar was not without his own eccentricities of appearance, a man, according to one observer, "of the French type, five feet seven or eight inches high, with dark complexion, black, long hair, inclined to curl, and gray eyes. Lamar was peculiar in his dress; he wore his clothes very loose, his pants being of that old style, very baggy, and with large pleats, looking odd, as he was the only person I ever saw in Texas in that style."[14]

The administrative housecleaning was to be expected with any change in administration, but with Lamar it was more personal. According to Frank Lubbock, who was turned out of his office as comptroller general, even at this early date "the country was divided into the 'Houston Party,' as all adherents of Sam Houston were called, and the 'Anti-Houston Party,' for in those days there were no Democratic or Whigs in a party sense in Texas, and elections turned as to the policies advocated by Houston and those opposed to him."[15] Some of Lamar's acts seemed merely vindictive. The nation's flag was changed from Houston's beloved gold Lone Star

Mirabeau Buonaparte Lamar. His valor in the skirmish of April 20, 1836, earned
Lamar an accolade from the Mexican line—a gallantry he did not return, for
he was among those who would have put Santa Anna to death. As president of
Texas, his plan to set aside public domain to benefit education put Texas schools
on a solid financial footing. His schemes for Texas' imperial expansion, however, ruined the feeble economy.

Courtesy San Jacinto Museum of History

on a field of royal blue, to a white star on a red, white, and blue tricolor; Lamar and
Burnet had collaborated on the design. (They wasted no time in getting rid of
Houston's flag, either. Lamar took office on December 10, 1838; artist Peter Krag's rendering of the new banner, for which he earned fifteen dollars, was dated January 25,
1839.) The official seal was also changed, and a commission was appointed to select
a site and lay out an entirely new city to replace Houston as the nation's capital.

Lamar's administration was not without its successes, principally in the field
of public schools, which were put on such a good footing that Lamar has always

borne the title "Father of Texas Education." In contrast, though, the actions of the Lamar government upon the international stage were bound to yield wicked results. An imperial dreamer, Lamar had resumed a belligerent attitude toward Mexico with a view to extend Texas' frontiers to the Pacific. First, the new naval vessels that Houston had ordered arrived, and Lamar loosed them into the Gulf under command of a kindred spirit named Edwin W. Moore with orders to aid Mexican rebels in the Yucatan. Second, he began scheming to assert Texas' sovereignty over New Mexico east of the Rio Grande, but Congress refused to go along. An implacable Indian hater, Lamar ordered war to the death against the Plains Indians with whom Houston had sought to treat and the expulsion from Texas soil of Houston's gently cultivated Cherokees. This was accomplished in the bloody Cherokee War, at the culmination of which Houston's revered eighty-four-year-old chief, The Bowl, crippled by gunshot wounds in the back and thigh, ordered his people to retreat, dragged himself to a tree, and reclined against the trunk. There, Capt. Robert Smith, taking cognizance, as he later defended his action, that The Bowl did not specifically ask for mercy, put a pistol to his head and blew the gasping old man's brains out. (A more plausible explanation of this behavior—invariably omitted from the general histories—is that Smith was the son-in-law of Jesse Watkins, a peace commissioner whom The Bowl's Cherokees had executed.)[16] Later comers scalped the chief; one flensed a razor strop from his back. Most galling of all, at the head of Lamar's army was Thomas Jefferson Rusk, now chief justice of the Supreme Court.

Sam Houston had followed all these developments at a distance, and by the time he returned to Texas, his rage was positively Jovian. Ashbel Smith once wrote that the ex-president "appeared not infrequently carried away by bursts of tremendous, tumultuous, uncontrolled passion—to be fairly beside himself. But this . . . was all pure judgment and calm calculation."[17] This time, however, he was in deadly earnest. He blistered a Nacogdoches audience with a speech that left people muttering. His friendships with Adolphus Sterne and Henry Raguet chilled—although now with the promise of his own personal bliss, he continued to write chatty letters to Miss Anna. His rift with Rusk, however, was complete. Sam Houston was too close a student of *The Odyssey* not to have seen something Homeric about his return to Texas, and like Ulysses, he had now to rid his house of pretenders. And like Ulysses, he had help, this from the people of San Augustine who had elected him *in absentia* to the Texas Congress.

When the government convened it was no longer in Houston. Lamar's commissioners, trying to divine the intersection of future trade routes, had hewn a new village out of raw wilderness some eighty miles northeast of San Antonio, naming it Austin. Houston called the exposed hamlet "the most unfortunate site upon Earth for the Seat of Government." There was not a house, he wrote Miss Anna, between there and Santa Fe. But at least many of his friends were there with the government, and they welcomed him with an invitation to a public dinner on November 11.[18] In this lugubrious place to begin work, he sighed of national affairs, "I might have been happy in ignorance at home had I not known the full extent of Lamar's stupidity."[19]

In December he raged at the House for two days about what had been done to the Cherokees, whose only real sin was that they had "received a pledge [of land] from the provisional government of Texas . . . and were *dupes enough to believe it!*"[20] When the Congress adjourned without acting on it, Houston swore that so far from giving up, his pursuit of the Cherokee issue would, as he had said, "stick like a blister!!!" (The locals, however, were more interested in his comments about the location of the capital in Austin, which they intended to hold against him, and got their hands on the written record of his remarks. As the recorder of the House journal noted in his entry, "The manuscript of . . . of Mr. Houston's first speech having been lost, or carried away from the editor's room by some person, we are compelled to give a brief sketch of it from recollection.")[21] Having failed to win any relief for the Cherokees on December 2–3, Houston came back with a new Cherokee bill on December 22; a portion of the land that the revolutionary government had promised to the Cherokees spilled onto land otherwise granted by the Mexican authorities to men now friendly to the Lamar government. Much of the land scrip had been passed to speculators, who now stood to become land barons at bargain prices. To prevent at least this much of the scheme from reaching fruition, Houston introduced a bill providing that money from Cherokee land sales go into the treasury, not to the speculators.[22] This effort also amounted to nothing, and the former president's rage over the Cherokees' fate was fueled even more a couple of weeks later when one of the leaders of the Cherokee War, Hugh McLeod, sent him The Bowl's cocked hat as an insulting present.[23]

Public sentiment was against him on the Cherokee matter, but a new issue soon presented itself to Congressman Houston. The Kingdom of France recognized the backwoods republic in the fall of 1839. The foreign ministry dispatched as an informant on Texas affairs a cocky and dubiously titled underling, Jean Peter Isidore Alphonse Du Bois, Comte de Saligny, although he probably was not really a count. Upon the establishment of relations, he was appointed chargé d'affaires; arriving in Houston in January of 1840, he headed inland to the rude new capital of Austin, where he quickly made a bad name for himself. During a stay at Bullock's Hotel at Congress and Pecan Streets, Du Bois grew increasingly appalled by the city and its inhabitants and began constructing a comfortable residence on a hill east of town, into which he eventually retreated with his servant, Eugene Pluyette. The "count" had already made a hard name for himself in the frontier capital by refusing to pay the bill from his stay at Bullock's Hotel, which he claimed was padded with extra charges. The dispute escalated when pigs, nominally owned by Bullock but running wild, broke into Du Bois' room, destroyed bedding, and chewed up several diplomatic dispatches. Ultimately, Bullock bloodied Du Bois' nose, and a couple of the pigs wound up on the chargé's dinner table.

Although he paid his official respects to President Lamar, Du Bois knew that the real man to see in Austin was Sam Houston, and local lore celebrated their meeting for years.[24] The French emissary was a dandy and a clotheshorse, an affectation with which Sam Houston was not unfamiliar, but when the count called upon the former president wearing his sash and medals, Houston greeted him wearing an Indian blanket wrapped around his bare shoulders. He let the blanket slip away, revealing the bandages from his old Creek Indian War wounds, as he proclaimed something to the effect of "a humble republican soldier, who wears his decorations here, salutes you." The citizenry haw-hawed, but the joke was really less than fair, for Du Bois was a veteran of the street fighting that had put his king, Louis Philippe, on the throne.

After having his little bit of fun with the French chargé, Houston perceived a way to use him against Lamar. Du Bois was heavily promoting a French immigration scheme, which became known as the "Franco-Texienne Bill." Under its terms, Texas would grant three million acres to French empresarios who would settle some eight thousand families on the frontier and maintain a picket of forts for twenty years in exchange for a tax abatement. Lamar and Burnet opposed the scheme, which was reason enough for Houston to endorse it. It was introduced into the Texas House on January 12, 1841, and passed that body eleven days later. Lamar had awarded himself a furlough and returned to Georgia for a visit, leaving the government in the care of the vice president, David Burnet, whom Houston considered no improvement. The acting president vowed to veto the measure, and the Senate, knowing that a two-thirds vote to override could not be mustered, never considered it. There was little in the Franco-Texienne Bill to merit Houston's support, but quite beyond giving him an issue other than the Cherokees on which to battle the administration, Houston stood to gain from supporting the French proposal. If and when he returned to power, French friendship would prove a very useful card to play against the United States in the annexation game, and supporting a bill that had no chance of becoming law was an inexpensive insurance policy to guarantee French amity in the future.[25]

(Unwittingly, the Lamar government played right into Houston's hand, alienating France with amazing celerity. When the State Department declined to consider Bullock's beating a state crime but rather let the matter proceed as a simple assault case, the French chargé left Austin in a fury. Although the citizens made rude comments about the "No-account de Saligny," he was the brother-in-law of France's finance minister, and Lamar's government lost out on a five-million-dollar loan as a result of the incident.)

Du Bois was far from the only one who sensed that although Mirabeau Lamar was the president of Texas, Sam Houston was not finished, he was only dormant. It was a feeling that pervaded from the highest to the lowest.

From Paris, Texas' minister plenipotentiary, J. Pinckney Henderson, wrote letters to Houston keeping him as fully informed of diplomatic maneuvers as if he had never stepped down from the presidential chair. "I am now daily expecting this Government to recognize Texas. I have since the receipt of Saliney's report been urging the matter in the strongest terms." France's foreign minister was favorably disposed and awaited only a report from an Admiral Bodon on Texas' apparent security as a nation to proceed. Once the report arrived, "The Duke of Orleans (the heir apparent) told a diplomatic gentleman the other day that . . . he believed that Mexico has more to fear from Texas than Texas from Mexico." And a common citizen, Maria McManus, the wife of one of Houston's spies during the Runaway Scrape, wrote to Houston from New Orleans. She was taking her son to Europe for schooling and requested of Houston "a simple letter to Our Minister in France and on to his Holiness the Pope. . . . I cannot ask Gen. Lamar and were I on terms with him that would justify the request, though he is for a time head of our republic, would not give the influence yours would command. The name of the victor of San Jacinto . . . is known in every saloon in Europe."[26] Houston certainly would have agreed with her assessment of Lamar; his presidential performance up to this time struck Houston as so bleak that he wrote to Irion at the end of January 1840 that "the veil of futurity will disclose scenes of extravagances . . . that will strike the mind with horror." He did send more cordial New Year's greetings to Miss Anna, although now he did it through his friend Irion.[27] She and the former secretary of state were to be married on March 20. There is perhaps no more genuine measure of a man's character than how he comports himself when his friend becomes a rival for the affections of a woman, and Houston lost Anna Raguet with a smile and a bow, with grace that went beyond the contentment he expected to find in the arms of Margaret Lea. And undoubtedly he did so with a whole heart; in fact, Houston's letters to Anna Raguet made favorable mention of Irion as a competitor at least since summer of 1838, when at one point he teased her, "I don't say he is courting [you]—but—he has some matters in hand of importance—He is a noble gentleman!!!"[28]

Houston went on to tell Irion that he expected his own marital "frolic," as he called it, to occur by mid-February, and he even bantered with Miss Anna about it: "I am anxious to visit Nacogdoches again! I would then see my friends, and be happy." It would, he said, be the last of February or the first of March before he could come, but when he did arrive: "It is reported that I am to take home with me, a clever wife! This is the Report, and may be so, in truth! Shou'd such be the fact, you will see her, when she goes eastward."[29] Learning of the impending arrival of the Leas and Bledsoes, Houston repaired to Galveston. When their ship anchored, the former president boarded a small boat and was taken out to her, and he had arranged for the shore battery to boom a salute as he approached. On deck he greeted Nancy Lea and the Bledsoes and inquired after Margaret. "General Houston," said Nancy Lea dourly, "my daughter is in Alabama. She goes forth in the world to marry no man. The one who receives her hand will receive it in my home and not elsewhere." If Sam Houston had entertained any doubts before as to what kind of woman he was getting for a mother-in-law, he certainly had none after this.

Nancy Lea had put her foot squarely down on the prospect of a wilderness wedding for her daughter, and the nuptials were exchanged, with faultless propriety, in Marion, Alabama, on May 9. The only small hitch was quickly disposed of. One of Margaret's protective male relations drew Houston aside and said as bravely as he dared, that "the family would appreciate it if he would tell them why he left his first wife." Houston was marrying Margaret, not the whole family, and now it was his turn to put his foot down; if the wedding depended on their knowing everything about his first marriage, he said, they had better call their fiddlers off.[30] They backed down.

Margaret Houston, 1840. After her Alabama marriage, Margaret arrived in Galveston with her husband and her trousseau of three dresses—this appears to be the purple silk one—her slave companion Eliza, and a cargo of personal treasures, including her rosewood piano. Other than the retreat at Cedar Point, it would be several years before she had a home she could call her own.

Courtesy Sam Houston Memorial Museum

The newlyweds disembarked in Galveston with Margaret's trousseau—one white satin dress, one purple silk, and one blue muslin—and her rosewood piano. To mark the occasion, a daguerreotype was taken of Margaret in her finery before the couple proceeded inland, and Houston showed his bride the thriving little city named in his honor—though he could no longer say that it was the capital of the republic. In Houston, they houseguested a good while with Frank Lubbock and his Creole wife, Adele. The town's first merchant had prospered and now lived in a two-story house across the bayou from the noise and clutter of the town. A recent advertisement for his mercantile had touted the arrival of various items: "a few dozen Choice French Wines per French Brig Fils Unique. Hardware, Groceries, Boots and Shoes . . . Tools; 40 to 50,000 feet Lumber; 12 bbls. Sugar; 30 sacks Salt; Hams; Havana Segars," and twenty sacks of Coffee direct from Havana.[31] With Margaret's effort at his moral reform having just commenced, it is easy to picture him gazing with mixed emotions—now confidently, now piteously—at the few dozen choice French wines.

Even with his bride on his arm, however, Houston still cast an angry eye at Lamar and elevated his attacks to an all-out assault. At the end of August, the Houstons received an invitation from Philip Sublett to attend a public dinner to be held in their honor in San Augustine. The former president declined because the "unusual sickness prevailing" rendered festivities inappropriate. He felt it his duty, however, to "designate Thursday (Sept. 3) as the day on which I will meet with my fellow citizens" in San Augustine to discuss the affairs of the country. He then loosed a broadside against Lamar's administration, concluding after listing a catalog of particulars, "It is vain to attempt concealment of our situation any longer from the public eye,—the depression of every class of the community proclaims that there is rottenness at the core!"[32]

Inevitably, the wedding of the former president occasioned much discussion throughout Texas. Bernard Bee, who was Lamar's minister to the United States but impartial enough in his views to serve all administrations and keep everybody's respect, confided darkly to Ashbel Smith that Houston was "totally disqualified for domestic happiness." Margaret, for her part, was not unaware of the mass consternation on the part of well-bred people in Texas. She confided her own feelings to the family scrapbook that not only had General Houston won her love, but, every inch her mother's daughter, she intended to turn him around.[33] However, Sam Houston, known drunkard, reputed womanizer, and confirmed wildman, was a spirit whom no power on earth could have broken to the traces unless he willed it to be so. But, after his reelection to Congress in September of 1840, it was apparent that he had put himself—had chosen to put himself—under Margaret's subjection. Congress may have met in the distant village of Austin, but the mail brought him frequent messages from her. "My Love," he cooed in answer to one of her admonitions, "I do sincerely hope that you will hear no more slanders of me. . . . if you hear the truth you never shall hear of my being on a 'spree.'"[34]

The missal is one of the earliest of their many lengthy separations and set a pattern for the next two decades. Margaret had been ill—her health was never robust—but even when she was healthy, she never followed her husband to the seat of power. In an era in which society women doted over their prominence and place at table, it can only have been deliberate that Margaret planted herself in the background. And her husband, while over the years penning endless variations on the theme here established—"Every hour that we are apart, only resolves more firmly not again to be separated from you"—did endure repeated separations of months at a time.

There were many who, like Bernard Bee, predicted that the Houstons' union would end in a kind of marital Armageddon. What they failed to see was that the marriage was an extraordinary alliance of two powerful spirits, she no less than he, who complemented each other with a perfection that would have been impossible had they not been so utterly dissimilar. Margaret knew perfectly well that she had married a titan, and she did not confide herself idly to her scrapbook; she meant, with all conceivable grimness, to reform Sam Houston. But clever woman she who knew that he was best governed with love, patience, only occasional firmness, and above all, distance. And his letters, filled with tenderness and yearning to be with her, made it clear from his very absences that, while she was first in his heart, she was second in his mind and career. But curiously, it seems as though the fact that Houston had entrusted the care of his soul to Margaret, that he had no more war to fight within himself, left him the more energy to wage political battle. There were many victories yet to be won before the reality of Texas could match his vision of it. Instinctively, he knew that he could not attain those victories if so many of his mental and emotional forces were forever to be diverted to the containment of his spiritual turbulence. That, of course, is speculation to which no footnote can readily append. Yet the evidence is there, in abundance, both in the tranquility of his home life and in the zeal and cleverness of his political jockeying during 1841. The next presidential election was now less than a year away; there would be wins and there would be losses, but victory, he now knew, was ultimately possible.

As it happened, 1841 opened with a loss: in December he had sought an appropriation of money to give effect to his earlier Cherokee Land Bill, which, he declared, would "rip up fraud to its foundations" by selling the former Cherokee lands to keep speculators from cashing in on them.[35] A House-Senate Conference Committee killed his bill. Cherokee rights and their lands were dead issues as far as Congress was concerned, and Houston knew it, but it was a point from which to attack Lamar and Burnet and their allies. "Congress meets too often," he fumed in a letter to Jackson's erstwhile Mexican envoy, Anthony Butler, "and does too much . . . and when it is done the country has paid for a beautiful patch of lawsuits!"[36]

Congress was much more interested in President Lamar's promotion of a military expedition to Santa Fe. One of the more florid contributions in favor of the scheme was delivered by Isaac Van Zandt, a twenty-seven-year-old failed storekeeper who had turned to the law when he discovered his flair for oratory—a résumé not dissimilar from Houston's own. He was from Franklin County, Tennessee, southwest of Houston's old Hiwassee haunts; still more reason for the former president to consider luring him into his circle. Van Zandt was a latecomer to Texas, settling in Harrison County and starting a town that he named for Chief Justice John Marshall, which locale he now represented in Congress. As the debate over the Santa Fe expedition droned on, Houston sat, whittling, on his backbench. What they were proposing, he said when he finally rose, was to send an isolated column of soldiers across six hundred miles of unexplored territory to a city that would receive them as enemies and provoke Mexico into new hostility. It was folly. Coming to Van Zandt's youthful spouting for it, Houston said: "A Tennessee neighbor once stationed his negro, Caesar, with a rifle at a deer drive, and told him to shoot when the animal broke cover. The deer sprang out, but the rifle made no sound. When Caesar was cursed for not shooting, he replied, 'Lord a mighty, massa, dat buck jump so high, I think he break his own neck.' So with my young friend Van Zandt; he jumps so high in his speech that he breaks his own neck, and it is not necessary to shoot at him." His partisans roared and the bill was defeated, but his swipe at Van Zandt was sufficiently good natured to preserve a rapport with him that later proved quite valuable.[37]

When Congress adjourned in February, Houston repaired to his namesake former capital, where Margaret had been ill. It was widely expected that Houston would enter the fray for president, and the geography of the contest would prove interesting, for Houston's continued savaging of Austin as the country's capital had cost him much of his support in Texas' western districts. To ascertain Houston's demeanor toward them, the vigorous young congressman representing Gonzales sat down and wrote the general a letter: "You are represented by many of your opponents, as being inimical to the interests of the West . . . , as deeming us unworthy of governmental consideration, or even mercy—as partial to the East because of its strength and hostile to the West because of its weakness—et id omne genus. I have not been able to bring myself to believe that . . . I will not believe it. Am I right?"[38] The letter's author was Washington Daniel Miller, just turned twenty-six, unmarried, and a one-time aspiring professor of mathematics who emerged from the University of Alabama with a degree in engineering followed soon after by a license to practice law. Wash Miller was the very kind of intelligent, bantering blade who had always energized Houston's paternal instincts, and in this case he could make further claim to the general's interest as a friend of Margaret's brother, Vernal Lea, who had decided to relocate in Texas with his sister and mother. Houston wrote Miller a defense of his stance; Miller's assumption that Houston would run for president was only a tad premature; he was not actually nominated until April 8, but when it happened, it was in the manner Houston preferred: by a convocation of citizens. The vote by a gathering in his San Augustine district was unanimous.[39] He would run in opposition to the former provisional president, that tight-vested font of morality David Burnet, and the campaign promised to be personal in its viciousness.

Houston gave speeches in Nacogdoches and San Augustine, and after this brief round of campaigning, he took Margaret off to his "fairy land" at Cedar Point to spend the summer. The weather turned hot and sultry, but their months together on the shore of Galveston Bay were idyllic and the closest they ever came to a proper honeymoon, alone in the country and deeply in love. Bernard Bee had considered the match doomed, but those closer to the couple quickly believed otherwise. "My dear Friend," Judge George W. Terrell wagged at him in midsummer, "Having an hours leisure . . . I have concluded that I could not spend it more agreeably to myself at least, than in writing a line to my old friend . . . , probably it may amuse you for a few minutes, and thereby dispel the enui with which you maybe be beset this hot weather in your *solitary retirement.* But ANGELS AND MINISTERS of Minerva defend me . . . it entirely escaped my recollection that that incomparable wife of yours was with you—who, if report be true, would have kept Goldsmith himself cheerful."[40]

And Margaret Lea Houston had some need of a sunny disposition, for her husband was not the only one who had to endure ribbing about his earlier reputation. The previous January, Houston had teased Anna Raguet that she would meet the new Mrs. Houston when he brought her to Nacogdoches. When that visit took place, Margaret was also introduced to local raconteur Nat B. Walling, who asked her ebulliently if she had ever been to Shelby County. When Margaret replied that she had not, Walling said she must do so, for Houston had some forty children there. After a stunned silence, Walling explained that Houston was so popular there that at least forty little boys had been named after him. Houston took on his droll look. "In future, my friend," he said, "I will thank you to connect your sentences more closely."[41]

And when not occupied with Margaret, there was always politics. Lamar's military adventures had been expensive, and with neither coinage nor sufficient customs receipts, Lamar had met the cost of empire by printing more and more paper money, which by now was trading at appalling discounts—sometimes over 90 percent. The worthless cash, however, made excellent fuel for Houston's campaign. The country's finances were so bad, he wrote his Tennessee friend Gen. William G. Harding, the irony was that whoever won the election, recovery would take so long that Lamar's reputation would not be embarrassed by any rapid change. Lamar himself "wou'd no doubt be impeached, but the poor soul is too contemptible to incur hatred."[42]

Lamar was well aware of the evaporating finances of the nation and cast his glance afresh at the tariff revenues to be gained if commerce on the Santa Fe Trail were diverted from the Mexican economy to Texas. That trade represented hard cash, for which Texas was desperate. He had desired the previous year to send a military expedition to Santa Fe to assert Texas' claims to New Mexico east of the Rio Grande, but Congress—wisely, for once—declined to back the scheme. But where trade goes, sovereignty often follows. Lamar therefore recast his Santa Fe plan as a "trade expedition," issued a call for merchants to load wagons of goods and for volunteer troops to protect them, and entrusted his proclamation "To the Citizens of Santa Fé," extolling their projected union with Texas, to five civilian commissioners. The whole expedition, twenty-one heavy ox-drawn wagons hauling some $200,000 worth of merchandise protected by five companies of volunteer infantry and a small battery of artillery, an aggregate of more than three hundred men, rumbled out of Kenney's Fort near Austin on June 19, 1841. They headed vaguely northwest, poorly guided and underprovisioned, but stoked by the cocksure bravado that was the hallmark of the Texas volunteer. The rolling plains engulfed them, and nothing more was heard of them for the remainder of Lamar's term.[43]

Houston still fought the charge that he felt no regard for the interests of Texas' western districts. In answer to a rampant story that if he were elected he intended to depopulate Austin, Houston wrote his refutation to the Austin newspapers. He did not back down from his stance that the exposed hamlet was no advantageous site for the capital of the republic. "My opinions and feelings in relation to the subject . . . have been expressed by me, and are published to the world. They were candidly expressed; for I have nothing to disguise on the subject." But, he went on, "it is not true that *I did ever* 'say in San Augustine, or Nacogdoches, or somewhere else,' that if I were elected President, that 'Austin should be desolate, and the grass should grow in its streets.' If I had said so at any place, it could easily be established, but to charge a man with having said a certain thing *somewhere*, or *somewhere else*, shows that it is just as *false* as it is *ridiculous*!" Of Lamar's excesses and the trappings of empire, Houston added in a closing barb, "Our motto ought to be, *fewer officers and more cornfields!*"[44]

Gonzales's congressman, Washington Miller, who had written Houston on the same subject in February before Houston's actual nomination, wrote him in July: "I am happy . . . to say, that your remarks are entirely satisfactory to us in this region. I was told to beware—that the people of *this* section of the country at least could never support . . . an individual who was known to be inimical to their interests." Miller informed Houston that he had decided not to seek reelection to the Congress himself but rather use his energies to get Houston elected president again, notwithstanding the opposition in his own area. "I think I can come up to the polls on the 6th Sept next, if not with a majority, at least with a noble minority for him whom I love to esteem the *Novissimae Reipublicae Faben*. At any rate, 'I'll try.'"[45]

Houston was rapidly becoming enchanted with Wash Miller, who wrote his letters in a style of lucidity and playful wit that bore a startling similarity to his own, and Houston marked the bright young bachelor for advancement. The campaign issues of this election were valid—some, such as the charges of fraudulent land grants, were actually important, but they cast relatively small shadows over the public consciousness. In the perception of the people, the real contest was between the personalities of Houston and Burnet, and things got dirty. Houston was portrayed as a relentless, blaspheming drunk, and he in turn took to referring to Burnet by an Indian name, Wetumpka, which he claimed meant "Hog Thief" (although his new friend Wash Miller, before leaving Alabama for Texas, had been employed in a corps of engineers for the "Wetumpka and Coosa Railroad," an interesting coincidence).[46]

A series of inflammatory letters were published and widely disseminated— subscribed "Publius," for this was the age when Roman orators were regularly resurrected as the authors of scurrilous pamphlets—accusing Houston in high scorn of being a drunken reprobate unworthy to hold elective office. The author could only have been Burnet or someone close to him. The blast that Houston prepared in response to "Publius" was a cool and political calculation. At a personal level he was unfazed. According to one acquaintance of the time, "General Houston seemed to no more feel the keen sting of his enemies' darts than the thick skin of a rhinoceros. . . . it was well known that when General Houston so desired, he could crush any of his opponents."[47]

But even if he took "Publius" not personally to heart, his barrage in response was no less withering. Ensconced in the serenity of Cedar Point, Houston wrote a series of five replies to "Publius" (two of which survive) in August and September that were positively inspired in their ferocity. Addressed not to the orator but "To the Honorable David G. Burnet," thereafter referred to contemptuously as Davy, Houston identified the former provisional president as the author of "Publius" and proceeded to call him out for every insult, injury, inconsistency, lie, deception, and hypocrisy committed since their names had first been linked with Texas. Rather than enlist the name of a Roman orator to subscribe his own work (although one is confident that if he wished to do so, he could have picked a fine one), Houston subscribed his invective "TRUTH" and lit into Burnet first for his colonial land speculations and then for charging personal expenditures during his term as ad interim president to the credit of the republic. Did Houston do the same during his term? "Houston paid for his own! and out of his salary he lived in a miserable hut." Burnet, while vice president and acting as president in Lamar's absence, "rose in the Chair of the Senate, and begged for the addition of *Six Thousand Five Hundred Dollars*, to be added to his salary, and the Senate, in pity, gave it to poor Davy . . . because he cried in the Senate—while crying Poverty—Poverty, I am so poor— and screwing up his mouth. Let those who think him poor, look at the Auditor's books, and see what cash he has down and compare it with his expenses and his services. His Brandy was purchased by the people's money; so that the heaviest item, fell on the people."

And on the subject of liquor, on which the "Publius" numbers indicted Houston repeatedly, the general responded with enumerated and witnessed occasions of Burnet's own public spectacles, and added moral hypocrisy to boot.

> Will you, Judge Burnet, or will your friends for you, deny that after the battle of San Jacinto, when you went to Galveston on board the steamboat Yellow Stone, that you were so deeply inebriated, that though you attempted to make a speech abusive of Gen. Houston to the soldiers and spectators present, that you failed, but not until the soldiers gave you the d——d lie for calling Gen. Houston a coward?
>
> Nor will you deny that at Austin, during the first session of Congress . . . following you were so deeply intoxicated that you went sound asleep in your seat and snored away your time until you were awoke by Mr. McLeod, Secretary of the Senate, by orders of the members. When you were disturbed by being well shaken, you raised yourself up with an ineffably *idiotic* smile and hiccoughed out, "Gentlemen, I believe—hic—I was in a doze." Now, Sir, you are the man who prates about *sobriety*, morality and religion. Oh, shame, where is thy blush! . . . You political brawler and canting hypocrite, whom the waters of Jordan could never cleanse from your political and moral leprosy.[48]

Houston was proud of the work. He sent a draft of the first installment to Ashbel Smith for some highly confidential editing. "It is just from the pen, and no time for correction . . . have it copied by all means. . . . Wetumpka will feel it, if feel he can. Don't let my name be known, or traced.—If you think they will not publish it in Galveston, send it back by Frank.—I will go to Houston soon, I think."[49]

Houston's inspiration, one might note, was of the moment and the issue. None of it came from the bottle. "Things move on with me pretty coolly, and very dryly," he wrote Samuel May Williams while working on the "TRUTH" letters, "drily because we have had no rain for the last nine weeks, drily because we have no liquor, and I do not taste one drop of it." Then he added, perhaps with pride, or in self-persuasion, "nor will I do it!" His temperance did not spare him from the wrath of Burnet, who dispatched Branch Archer with his challenge to the field of honor. "What does he predicate the demand upon?" Houston inquired closely, and Archer replied that it was for the abuse he had suffered. "Has n't he abused me to an equal degree?" Houston responded calmly. "He has done so publicly and privately until I am

compelled to believe that the people are equally disgusted with both of us." Archer
returned the note, unanswered, to his principal.

In the rough and tumble of Texas politics, Houston was often challenged by
lumps who had no other argument to offer, refusing one with a snap that he never
fought downhill and giving the challenge of another to his secretary with instructions to mark it number fourteen, file it away, and tell the aggrieved gentleman he
must wait his turn. "I thought you were a friend of mine!" Houston exclaimed in
shock to still another, and he valued friendship as much as any man alive.

"So I was," came the answer, "but I do not propose to be abused by you or anybody else."

Houston saw the necessary tack in an instant. "Well, I should like to know, if a
man can't abuse his friends, who in hell can he abuse?" This challenge and others
ended in a laugh, as Houston successfully negotiated the coterie of antebellum
blowhards and did it with such élan that cowardice was only seldom mentioned
in the same breath as his name. To the end of his days, the only duel he ever fought
was the William White affair on the Kentucky line.[50]

During the campaign the newspapers of course chose sides. The *Houstonian*
proudly printed the viperine "TRUTH" letters. The *Austin Centinel* was one of the
majority that supported Burnet, saying Houston would "*blaspheme his God*, with
the most horrible oaths, that ever fell from the lips of man."[51] Margaret had begun
working her change on Houston, but they had not been together long enough to help
his reputation. Not all the brawling was of the verbal variety between the principals. B. J. White later wrote Houston from Texana: "Previous to your election I was
nearly alone in your support for sometime in Jackson County. Still I stood up
against the current . . . until it enraged [one] gentleman so much. He came to town
to give me a public cursing as he said. He commenced it by abusing you & praising
Burnett until I was forced to contradict it, he struck me with a large hickory stick,
however I sent him home with my mark in his eyes—and an eternal hate existing
between us." During the heated campaign, Houston did receive one interesting
endorsement in his opinion of Burnet. During the latter's tenure as acting president,
he tapped Houston's friend George W. Terrell to serve as secretary of state. Terrell,
to Houston's chagrin, accepted, but toward the end of July admitted to Houston:
"I recollect you said to me that Burnett offered me the appointment . . . for the purpose of bribing me, that if I accepted it I would not hold it a month—that he would
require of me, such partisan subserviency that I would resine the office in a fit of
indignation—and that if I did not accept he would be my enemy always. This at
the time I attributed to your prejudice against the man, which prevented you from
doing him justice. . . . You knew the man better than I did."[52]

The majority of Texas newspapers were predicting Houston's defeat. He, however, seemed to be brimming with confidence; indeed, Houston was already planning to be sworn in wearing attire that would make the Federal knee breeches he
wore to Lamar's inauguration look like sackcloth. In mid-August, an incredulous
Du Bois de Saligny reported home to the foreign minister that Houston had
requested him to order an inaugural ensemble of clothes from Paris: "This costume

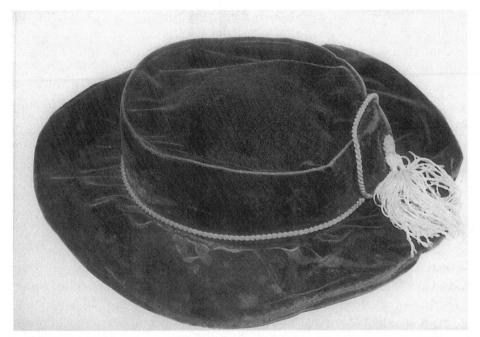

French Velvet Cap, 1841. Confident of a second presidential triumph in 1841, Houston requested the French chargé d'affaires, Alphonse Du Bois de Saligny, to order him a Plantagenet suit in green velvet for his inauguration. Du Bois was horrified, and Houston never had the nerve to wear it, but the cap survives.

Courtesy Sam Houston Memorial Museum

is to be composed of a complete suit of green velvet all embroidered in gold; a little Spanish-type cape also of green velvet and covered with rich embroidery, and in addition a hat á la Henry V, hidden by an immense plume of three colors. It is in this strange outfit that the true head of the Republic of Texas intends to take his seat in the presidential armchair." Du Bois considered Houston's taste in apparel a holdover from his life among the Indians.[53]

The election was held on September 6, and when the ballots were counted, Houston garnered 7,508 votes, Burnet only 2,574. Memucan Hunt, the Lamar partisan whom Houston had once outmaneuvered for the attentions of a young lady in Mississippi, lost the vice presidential contest to another plain-spoken populist, Ed Burleson, one of Houston's regimental commanders at San Jacinto. With victory, the past and future president was free to celebrate, which he did—but soberly. Edward Winfield, a locally prominent politician and Texas Ranger in Washington County, attended a barbecue that was got up in the Houstons' honor a couple of weeks after the election. "Strange to say," Winfield marveled to Ashbel Smith, it "was a cold water *doins*. The Old Chief did not *touch*, taste or handle the smallest drop of the *ardent* during his stay in this county."[54]

Winfield's phrasing was not random; the recitation not to "touch, taste or handle" were from the temperance oath, and words that became regular fare in

Houston's correspondence with Margaret. His sobriety, however, did not transmute itself into spiritual generosity toward the vanquished; the campaign had been ugly, and Houston was not a magnanimous victor. "I appreciate [your] feelings of indignation . . . in the slanderous, base and unfounded reports circulated against me during the late canvass," he told a gathering in Crockett shortly after the election. "The *result* has shown the contempt of a free people for the wicked and base originators of falsehood."[55]

When the new first couple returned to Houston on November 6, it was to band music and peals of artillery followed by a reception at the home of Mayor John and Mrs. Eugenia Andrews and a ball at the City Hotel. Then it was off to Cedar Point to rest and settle his affairs before making the journey to Austin and the inauguration. In his coastal "fairy region," Houston was in a high frame of mind, dashing off a note to Ashbel Smith, "We will be happy if you will come and eat Ducks with us!"[56]

The president-elect accepted an invitation to address a crowd in Houston on November 25, although that festivity began with a faux pas. The orator who introduced Houston alluded in his welcoming remarks to the recently published *History of Texas and Texans* by Henry Stuart Foote. Houston disapproved of the book, mostly on the grounds that Lamar had been a primary source of information, but he treated the offense lightly, remarking that he expected the book to be "more footed than eyed." Houston went on to vow not to do as Lamar had done in appointing officers to govern the country "whose very actions savor of iniquity, and stink in the nostrils of the Almighty." He deplored "our money depreciated, our credit sunk, our political institutions and laws disregarded or suspended." He blamed the Lamar government for the failure of the anticipated loan from France, although he had to consider it a kind of disguised blessing: "I thank God! . . . [for] we should not have been able to pay it when demanded." He also faulted Lamar for doing nothing to quell a vicious feud in East Texas, since known as the Regulator-Moderator War, that was spreading mayhem and claiming lives by the dozens.

Mostly, the November speech was pretty standard Houston fare, but it has a curious anomaly in the middle, an elegiac tangent from which it was apparent that the president-elect's Alabama belle was beginning to work her influence. "Oh, it is the woman who makes the hero," he asserted of the Texan character, proceeding to wax not only poetic but even a little King Jamesian: "It is she that instills the fire of patriotism—it is she who inspires every noble purpose, that animates the bosom of man. . . . may she take care with all diligence that she forget not the little leaven of patriotism that leaveneth the whole lump. . . . What is it that guides the soldier's hand, and nerves his arm in battle, but the anxious desire to defend the near and dear? . . . Oh, gentlemen, it is woman who blesses her country." Texas, he admitted, had begun as a frontier land with few women, and that was the reason that "it has been too usual among us to have recourse to the grog shop . . . or, still more demoralizing, to resort to the faro bank." As the country settled down, however, and with the advent of more women, "we must expect many evils to be corrected."[57] The words undoubtedly sounded strange coming from him, in this city, to this crowd, many of whom could tell tales of Houston's evening revels in Pamela Mann's Mansion

House. Margaret was seldom amused by allusions to—or persons from—her husband's wilder days. She did once express a certain pity for Pamela Mann, but by then she could afford to. "My Love," she had written her husband almost exactly a year before, "you will hear of the death of poor Mrs. Brown (formerly Mrs. Mann)."[58]

Houston departed his city, worried about leaving Margaret behind while she was suffering malaria and complications from a miscarriage at Cedar Point. Although a new presidential house was available, he entrusted her to Mayor and Mrs. Andrews, whose mansion on Austin Street was one of the largest in the city— public rooms downstairs and five bedrooms above. There, her perceived conditions worsened from melancholy at his absence, and she did not venture downstairs for over a week. A steady stream of callers who came to greet the new first lady were turned away with thanks, but for two exceptions; she came down once to see a doctor to treat her cyclical difficulty, and once to see Pizene Edmonds, who was departing for Austin.[59] The country's mail was in chaos, and letters were usually carried by friends of the correspondents; Margaret felt it ungracious to have him call at the door for her letters to her husband without thanking him.

The president was scarcely out of town before he began writing a stream of solicitous letters. Referring to Margaret as "my dear 'Dulcina'" (and thus oddly casting himself as Don Quixote), Houston compared the desolation of the prospect of weeks or months without her against the season they had shared at his "fairy region," Cedar Point, a time "of more inestimable value than [all] my past existence. The recollection can never fail to awaken in my bosom the purest happiness, and inspire a feeling of gratitude to our God for his matchless kindness. They were hours of bliss to me because you seemed happy."[60]

One of Margaret Lea Houston's most remarkable attributes was her intuition; many times, during nearly a quarter century of correspondence, their letters crossed in the mail with thoughts on the same subject. Cedar Point was now much on her own mind. "Dearest do you ever think of our sweet woodland home! Oh what happy days we have passed there! I remember in one of our evening rambles when we had paused to survey the grandeur of the scenery I looked up and beheld in your countenance a reflection of the joy that filled my own soul and oh my brain seemed almost oppressed with a sense of happiness."[61]

The president was also sensible of the role that his newfound temperance had played in their relationship. From Montgomery on November 30: "I appreciate properly the influence of sobriety upon our happiness, and the necessity of my adherence to a principle which can place us in possession of every earthly blessing. . . . Affection for *you*, my love, had produced this change. . . . *In all things* rely upon my devotion to your dear self and be happy." From Washington on December 2: "my Maggy! I need not tell you that my arch enemy never dares to approach me! I mean 'Grog' in any shape or character." It was a pun referring to both alcohol and his new pet name for the defeated Burnet.

In Houston's retinue on the Austin journey was Maj. James W. Scott, who had served as paymaster in his first administration. The road was dotted with "stopping places," farms whose families made extra money by sheltering travelers overnight. Arriving at such a house after a long day's ride, Houston suggested that they stay over. His staff had been warned that the proprietor was a Burnet partisan virulent to the point of having sworn to kill Houston if they should ever meet. "Well," said Houston, "this is the right place at which to stop." His aides were dubious but had to go along, deciding among themselves not to address Houston by name. As the staff bedded down the horses, Houston engaged the owner's children on the porch, telling them stories until the parents joined the audience. As the proprietor prepared to serve them dinner, Houston put his hand on the man's arm and said: "My friend, although I do not profess religion, still I always ask God's blessing when I partake of His bounty. Allow me to ask a blessing."

Margaret's habit of bedtime Bible study also served well; the lady of the house produced a Bible, and Houston selected, read, and discussed a passage with the others before retiring. After breakfast, the aides packed belongings and saddled the horses, when one of them slipped up: "General, we are ready to start."

"General who?" demanded the owner.

The president-elect answered: "General Houston. Houston himself."

"Are you General Houston?"

"I am, sir."

Undone, the innkeeper said, "Well, I have always said I would kill you on sight; but, sir, any man that can talk to my wife and children as you have talked, ask such a blessing on the meals, read the Bible, and comment on it . . . is always welcome to my house." Payment was offered but refused, and the innkeeper, Scott reported, was a staunch Houston supporter after that.[62]

The citizens of Austin were faced with the delicate prospect of welcoming as president a man who many believed was poised to ruin their town by removing the government. Accordingly, a delegation met him bearing a flowery script of welcome, extolling the country's wisdom in electing him again, proclaiming their willingness to let bygones be bygones, and offering him a gala dinner or a ball—his choice.[63] The president-elect received them graciously when he arrived in Austin on December 8, but in his correspondence he was still spewing about Lamar, "too base to be respected and too imbecile to be trusted!" he wrote Margaret. "He has made several overtures to me for friendship, thro his friends, or rather an effort at reconciliation. . . . Pity can only save him from impeachment"—as though impeachment were even a possibility four days from the end of his term. Margaret offered sensible counsel to go easy on Lamar, reminding Houston "that it is an easy matter for us to be generous when it costs us nothing." But he would have none of it. Such an effort "wou'd be at the cost of my honest pride of heart," and Houston allowed himself a quick smile that a retrenchment bill slashing government expenses, reducing salaries, and eliminating minor positions had made it to Lamar's desk with only four days remaining in his term. Ordinarily, it could become law in five days without the president's signature, but in this circumstance, Lamar must either sign it and take the blame for it or see Houston deal with it on his first day in office.[64] While Houston attacked the bill in a letter to Margaret, he knew perfectly well the country needed it and must have seen the irony that Lamar, who had spent the national debt up to about seven and a half million dollars, signed it two days before leaving office.

Upon his arrival in Austin, the president-elect was escorted to and fêted at the Eberly House, a boarding establishment whose proprietress, a recently widowed (for the second time) Angelina Eberly, was a well-connected Tennesseean who had been among Stephen Austin's "Old Three Hundred."[65] In fact, it is possible that she and Houston had known one another in Tennessee: Mrs. Eberly's brother was Congressman Balie Peyton, the gentleman to whom Eliza Allen whispered out her confidences over her failed marriage. It was a small world, indeed.

Frontier accommodations being what they were, not even the president-elect could be guaranteed a bed to himself. At least one night he slept with George W. Terrell, another Tennessee crony whom Houston had appointed district attorney when he was governor. But it was Margaret who was in his dreams, and he wrote her: "Judge Terrell was my bed fellow last night, and is one of the most profound sleepers that I have known. When he rose at day break, I fell into a profound and delightful sleep. I fancied that you were in my arms, and that we were felicitating ourselves . . . and that we were as happy as mortals can be! My heart beat high, and my bosom swelled with joy and delight! My delightful vision was . . . annihilated by a call to 'Breakfast.'"[66]

To the concussion of cannon, the swearing-in ceremony took place in Austin on December 13, 1841, at the log capitol overlooking the Colorado River at Guadalupe and Live Oak (now Second) Street. Frank Lubbock remembered the weather as gorgeous. "To accommodate the sightseers, who swarmed on the ground at an early hour, a staging had been erected, and seats prepared under a beautiful awning spread in the rear of the capitol. These seats were occupied by both houses of Congress and a brilliant assemblage of ladies and gentlemen. President Lamar and President-elect Houston were escorted in military style by the Travis Guards from the President's house to the capitol. President-elect Houston and Vice-President-elect Burleson, attended by committees, made their appearance at 11 A.M. Prayer was offered by Judge R. E. B. Baylor, and the Speaker of the House administered the oaths."[67] Houston's summertime vision of his inaugural as a Plantagenet fantasy in green velvet with a plumed cap "á la Henry V" seems to have evaporated. His actual attire presented a much more homespun symbolism; the audience of a thousand beheld him in pantaloons, a fur hat with a wide brim, and a "linsey-woolsey hunting shirt," according to Josiah Gregg, who personally found the frontier outfit as redolent of vanity as anything more baroque could have been.[68] Mirabeau Lamar bore the spectacle with fortitude but, remembering his own humiliation three years before, declined his prerogative to address the crowd. As Sam Houston completed his oath, he kissed the Bible and a brand was touched to one of the Twin Sisters.

After the ceremony the new chief executive invited the members of Congress to dine with him at the Eberly House, and then all rested up for the inaugural ball to be held that evening. The ballroom was the Senate chamber, decorated for the occasion with a Texas flag—changed into a tricolor by Lamar, an American flag, and the Mexican banners captured at San Jacinto. The centerpiece was an arrangement of muskets and a Lone Star formed of burnished bayonets framing a transparency hailing "The Laws and the Constitution."[69]

While Margaret Houston's absence was noted with general regret, the *Daily Bulletin* reported that at the ball, "various persons of distinction participated in the dance, and visitants from all parts of the country." While the president and vice president were on hand for most of the evening, "I did not dance," Houston wrote Margaret, "tho' importuned by all to do so." He gave the excuse that he could not enjoy himself while knowing his wife was ill in Houston, although he just received her letter that she was improving. The real reason, he confided, "is simply that you wou'd prefer that I wou'd not."

Moreover, the poll had been "that I wou'd get into a 'spree' before all was over—but they were wide of the mark. I 'touch not taste not, and handle not (and want not) the unhallowed thing!'"[70]

14

NOT A DOLLAR IN THE TREASURY

With the festivities done, President Houston set straight to work; there was a flurry of letters, all of the same date as the inauguration: "The President requests Colonel George W. Hockley, at his earliest convenience, to take charge of the Department of War and Navy of the Republic of Texas." "The President requests the Honorable Anson Jones, at his earliest convenience, to take charge of the Department of State of the Republic of Texas." "The President requests Washington D. Miller, Esquire, to proceed at once to the discharge of his duties as Private Secretary to the Executive." Only one of the cabinet appointments was delayed, and that by only three days—his choice of Asa Brigham as secretary of the treasury.[1] Judge Terrell, Houston's bedpartner at the Eberly House, was appointed attorney general. It was a comfortable appointment for Terrell, who had served in the same capacity when Houston was governor of Tennessee.

Burnet, during his period as acting president, had created almost as much confusion as he had as ad interim president, and it took a while for the air to clear. Immediately after the election, for instance, Houston received a petition from sixty-four citizens in the Collectoral District of Calhoun urging the reinstatement of George M. Collins as collector, who was removed by the preceding administration for reasons "frivolous . . . and unjust." I. F. Winfred wrote to him at Cedar Point disavowing anything Houston may have heard about him: "I am very sorry to see my name mentioned with D. G. Burnett and others concerning confiscations providing the Mexicans took the country. I assert to you on the honor of a man that there was no plans laid between me and any others mentioned."[2]

Houston had already decided to maintain his residence at Angelina Eberly's establishment, eschewing the large President's House built for Lamar. Located on a hill near the corner of San Jacinto and Hickory (now 8th) Streets—which in any other context would have been an unusually auspicious location for a Houston dwelling—

the President's House was the largest in Austin, appearing from the surviving drawings to have had a second-story balcony and exterior staircase. In Lamar's haste to get it erected, however, it was built of green lumber, and although only two years old, had already begun to pull apart as the timbers dried. The interior was largely ruined, and one of Houston's first orders was to inventory the damaged furniture. "Congress may sell it," he wrote Margaret, "for I will never use it. 'Tis nearly all destroyed $8,000 worth." The sofa was still suitable to sit on, but the astral lamp was broken and the marble tops were broken off the tables. The two maple bedsteads were in better shape than the moss mattresses; in the whole house, the only undamaged items were dining-room pitchers. Furthermore, as he informed Congress: "There are no locks on the President's House, and . . . what remains there is exposed to pillage, which has already commenced. The building itself is in a ruinous and dilapidated condition, and not in a situation to be tenanted with any degree of comfort to the occupant."[3]

Houston found the presidential office in somewhat better shape. The pine table, desk, and three Windsor chairs were only slightly beat up, and most of the office equipment—a patent letter press, wafer stand, tin paper cutter, two lead paperweights, two cards of steel pens, and a short shelf of legal books—were in working order. And so work began.

Houston's trusted Hockley was the only choice for army and navy. Brigham was an obvious choice for treasury; he had served in that post in Houston's first administration, and Lamar, finding no objection to his conduct of the office, continued him there until Brigham retired in spring of 1840. Houston found him amenable to recall.

The other appointments were more interesting. John Ricord, Houston's private secretary from his first term, had left Texas in 1837, and the appointment of Washington D. Miller to that same office in 1841 bears odd parallels. Houston had first asked the young ex-congressman to consider the job as early as October 12, a full six weeks before mentioning the State portfolio to Anson Jones because he had heard that Miller was seeking the post of chief clerk of the House of Representatives. Houston urged him stridently to forego that job "with a *very sincere wish* that you wou'd *accept the situation*" in the cabinet. Like John Ricord, Wash Miller was an experienced secretary who was rootless and vaguely dissatisfied with the world. A bachelor, he was an engineer by training and had once intended a career as a mathematics professor, but he came to Texas late in 1837 and situated himself as a clerk in various government departments. Houston's anxiety to employ him, and whether Houston saw something of Ricord in their similar disaffection, are mysteries, but as with John Ross, Frank Lubbock, Ricord, and others, the president continued his penchant for helping undirected young men. Miller, for his part, was brilliantly suited to this post—letters he received even when in college were all docketed and the date of reply noted. Once he arrived in Austin, he quickly grafted himself to the president as an indispensable right hand, discerning and meticulous. And Houston's pleasure with Miller's acceptance shows in his signature on the appointment—more than six inches across and, counting the rubric, three inches high.[4]

Dr. Anson Jones. Like David Burnet, Massachusetts-native Anson Jones turned to Texas opportunities after multiple business failures in the United States. Between Houston's later basking in public acclaim and Jones's bitter attempts to reclaim credit for annexation, ending in his suicide on the steps of the Capitol Hotel in Houston, their respective roles can now probably not be precisely delineated. Houston, however, did begin angling for European friendship before sending Congressman Jones on his first diplomatic mission to the United States in June of 1838. This rare photo image of the last president of Texas was among the effects of his widow, Mary Jones, a founder of the Daughters of the Republic of Texas.

Courtesy Republic of Texas Museum

If another run was to be made at annexation, the choice of secretary of state was crucial, and Houston selected Dr. Anson Jones of Brazoria, a gifted but difficult man who brought to the post great assets, mostly intellectual, and great liabilities, mostly emotional. Much of his cross nature undoubtedly stemmed, first, from the fact that he had never in his life been allowed to follow his own interests and, second, from the fact that until he came to Texas, he had made repeated failures of the ventures he had been talked into. Born in Massachusetts in 1798, in his youth Jones had desired to be a printer but was pressured to enter medicine. Both his practice and his apothecary failed, and he was arrested for debt; he removed to New Orleans to begin another business, which also failed. At the urging of others, he visited Texas, did not like what he saw, and almost literally turned on his heel and sought return passage on the same vessel that brought him, but then at the urging of others, he stayed. Jones settled in Brazoria, where fortune finally smiled and he became a man of property, but by then his sour disposition was too fixed to be sweetened. Yet he had the elements to attract Sam Houston's notice: he was educated, a founder of the Philosophical Society of Texas, and for many years before entering Texas had been a prominent Mason. More importantly, he possessed a genuine streak of Cincinnatus: before the war he had moved resolutions for independence but preferred not to be nominated to the convention; he was surgeon of the Second Regiment at San Jacinto but preferred to retain the rank of private. Sam Houston had always been attracted to such virtues. When he finally stood for and was elected to the Second Congress, Jones's legislative record was solid, and Houston had sent him as minister to the United States in 1838 to withdraw the annexation proposal. During the Lamar years, Jones found himself increasingly allied with Houston, and they saw eye to eye on annexation.

Sam Houston would have been amazed, therefore, by a peep inside Anson Jones's hefty diary. During Lamar's term, Jones was in agreement with Houston about the then-president, who "may mean well . . . but his mind is altogether of a dreamy, poetic order, a sort of political Troubador and Crusader and wholly unfit for . . . his present station." But the shrewd Dr. Jones also saw exactly the kind of hay Houston intended to reap from Lamar's ineptitude: "I fear that Gen. Houston does not care how completely L——r ruins that country, so that he can . . . say, 'I told you so; there is nobody but old Sam after all.'" In Jones's estimation, Houston's strength and popularity were not intrinsic. He "is not so strong in what he does himself, as in what his enemies do: it is not *his* strength, but *their* weakness—not his *wisdom* but their *folly*. Cunning, Indian cunning, is the secret of his business. Old Bowles, the Cherokee Indian chief, learned him all he knows, and . . . he learned *Indian* well." He had already sized up Houston as a master "of the art of appropriating to himself the merit of others' good acts."[5]

Anson Jones's diary displays a curious chemistry of perspicacity colored by an acetic ambition that no one else suspected. Jones was civil to everyone, but only to curry future advantage; he recorded the shortcomings of all at length in his journal. In his estimation, no one could rule Texas as ably as himself, and he must rightfully inherit the presidential chair at some time. That no one else seemed to share this sentiment was a repeated bruise on his sensitive ego. Houston did not consider Jones a political rival, so the fact that Jones secretly hungered for a share of Houston's glory, as revealed in Jones's later insistence that he had been the real architect of annexation, and then his evolution into a passionate Houston hater, probably shocked him. From Houston's view, what he got in Anson Jones as secretary of state was a good, reliable beast of burden, a kind of camel of state who would bawl and spit but who, in the end, would pick up his load and carry it safely. But for now, annexation was still a goal to be achieved, and if properly managed, the two men could make an effective team.

Before reaching for such a lofty goal, smaller matters had to be gotten in hand, but at least he was back in a position where perhaps he could do something. To address Congress on December 20 again from the lofty chair of the presidency gave Houston peculiar satisfaction. Describing himself as having been "elevated a second time by . . . an enlightened . . . people to the Chief Magistracy of our country," he outlined his program. Lamar's "trading expedition" to Santa Fe had been betrayed to Mexican officials of the city, and some of its members had, in the Mexican fashion, been massacred after placing themselves at the mercy of the authorities. The rest were clamped in irons and herded in a death march almost as far as Veracruz, where survivors were locked in the Perote prison, and diplomatic efforts were needed to free them. Lamar's entire grand scheme had crashed down, but Houston knew it was impolitic to fault him more than the Mexicans. "Overtures have been made by my predecessor," he allowed, "for the purpose of securing amicable adjustment of existing difficulties; but, as often as made, they have been rejected. . . . Therefore, until a disposition is evinced on the part of Mexico herself to solicit friendly relations, the present Executive of Texas will neither incur the expense nor risk the degradation of further advances." There were other ways, however, to be moderate. "Aware of the Mexican character . . . I would recommend the kindest treatment of her citizens;—so far, at least, as they might be disposed to engage in commerce with ours." And he had already made up his mind to recall the Texas Navy from its harassment of Mexican shipping—although this proved to be a drain on his time and attention that swelled to a political hemorrhage before it was done.

The money would have to be resuscitated, for by the end of Lamar's term it was trading as low as 3 percent against the U.S. currency. "There is not a dollar in the treasury," he told them flatly. "The nation is involved from ten to fifteen millions. The precise amount of its liabilities has not been ascertained." One thing, however, was certain: "We are not only without money but without credit; and, for want of punctuality, without character."[6] He recommended a new issue of currency, receivable for specie, instead of the promissory notes that Lamar had flooded the country with.

On Indian relations, there was not a soul in the hall who did not know how he felt, but instead of the expected broadside, he expressed his views with the patience of one resigned to beginning again. "Our Indian relations are far from being satisfactory. . . . The hope of obtaining peace by means of war has, hitherto, proved utterly fallacious. It is better calculated to irritate than to humble them.

Neither can we pursue with the hope of exterminating them. Millions have been expended in the attempt, and what has been the result?" He intended to renew attempts to make peace.

It was a speech calculated to offend none and promote something in the way of national unity. There was much work to do, but also much to be thankful for. Texas had now survived just short of six years as a sovereign nation, and Houston proclaimed that March 2, Independence Day (not to mention his forty-ninth birthday), be set aside as a day of "devotional exercises," recognizing that "the Texian people have been objects of the peculiar care . . . of a Divine Providence."[7] His assertion did not apply to one part of Texas, however, that had become an ungovernable hell and required Houston's immediate attention. The Regulator-Moderator War, a feud centered about Shelby County in the eastern Redlands, had claimed dozens of lives in four years. Houston had been apprised of the difficulties a few months before in a bloodcurdling letter from Judge Terrell, who at the time was living in San Augustine, in the center of the mayhem:

> It really appears to me as if society were about to dissolve itself into its original elements. . . . At a called session of the district court in Sabine a few days ago, for the trial of Means for murder a man was shot down at the door of the courthouse, if not inside of it. . . . I was sent for last week to try (as examing court) twelve men in Nacogdoches who was charged with hanging a horse thief. It was represented to me that the *regulators*, as they were termed were the strongest party, and they and their friends were determined they should not be tried. . . . I went, and when I arrived there found . . . at least two hundred armed men in the courthouse."[8]

The famous Regulator-Moderator War began as a dispute arising out of the prevalent trading in land scrip, much of which was fraudulent and known to be so but traded in anyway. Its causes by that time were a dim memory, and the conflict merely lurched from one act of revenge to the next. Beleaguered citizens browbeaten to join one faction or the other had appealed to the government for years for aid, but only after Houston's return to the presidency was there a response, he ordered Gen. James Smith to raise a militia force, which, amounting to five hundred volunteers, cowed the militants into lying low, if only for the time being.[9]

While Houston may have restored domestic tranquility in East Texas, the people's foreign outlook was more surly. Trouble in the east was little compared to the trouble looming in the west. Lamar's rental of the Texas Navy to rebels in Yucatan and his "trade" mission to Santa Fe, with its subsequent capture and the brutalization of its members, inflamed anti-Mexican sentiment in Texas. Indeed, although the revolution had begun on Mexico's own legal grounds—maintenance of the Constitution of 1824—feelings against Mexicans on the part of Anglo Texans had since degenerated into ethnic prejudice of the most deplorable kind. Even in centers of Hispanic population such as San Antonio, leading citizens such as Col. Juan Seguín, a hero of the revolution, were forced to flee to Mexico for their personal safety.

Even after Houston's accession, Lamar's faction in Congress was strong enough to pass a bill purporting to annex all of northern Mexico. Houston vetoed the thing as a "legislative jest," pointing out that Texas as she lay was greater than the republic could usefully occupy. "We may regard Mexicans as we think proper," he admonished the congressmen, "but still they are men and entertain . . . some sense of shame and injury," which the proposed bill would only inflame.[10] It was now known that the survivors of Lamar's filibustering "trade mission" were languishing in irons in Perote Castle near Vera Cruz, having endured a horrific march from Santa Fe all the way to the prison. Houston expressed sympathy for the men in a private letter to Robert Irion, his first-term secretary of state. Houston had maintained their friendship after Irion won Anna Raguet, and the regard was returned in such measure that they named their first son after the president. "You know the fate," Houston wrote, "of those poor fellows who went to Santa Fe, but the effects of that silly and vicious project, are not yet passed from us. I think that we will be annoyed, if not invaded, by that very act. . . . Shou'd we be invaded this spring will not surprise me! We may, at all events, look out for a demonstration." The events of the following weeks proved him, once again, a seer of formidable insight. "Mrs. Houston was quite well," he continued, "but again has the chill, as she writes me. I am crazy to see her! I hope to do so as soon as Congress adjourns. I pray you to commend me, with great regard, to Mrs. Irion, and be assured of my undying esteem and friendship."[11]

There was much work to do, however, before he could even think of visiting his wife. He submitted for Congress' consideration correspondence concerning King Leopold of Belgium, whose country was only five years older than Texas. Having settled his quarrels with the Dutch, Leopold was on the lookout for good investments for his country and was interested in extending a loan to the cash-starved republic if he could gain certain commercial privileges.[12]

Houston issued a proclamation on January 31 condemning the vigilante justice visited upon the notorious murderer and Negro stealer Thomas Yocum (or Yokum) the previous October, but it turned out that the president needed to exercise his own vigilance over Congress.[13] Having failed in their bid to legally annex northern Mexico, the Lamarites passed a bill setting a more modest goal, to erect a string of frontier "military colonies" beyond the present line of settlement and populate that country. In his veto message, Houston conceded that the proposal sounded good, but he pointed out that the envisioned forts would be too far out to protect from Indian attack and too far apart to help each other, not to mention the fact the government had not a dollar to equip or arm them. Far better, he advised, first to make a dependable peace with the Indians and then there would be no need to defend them. He vetoed a succession of other bills—some would have created new counties in ways he considered unconstitutional; others would have caused the government to violate existing contracts with empresarios who were attempting to settle parts of the public domain.

Vetoing their bills was one way to keep the Lamar partisans in line, but one particular situation arose stemming from the previous administration that demanded an exercise of that Indian cunning Houston was so famous for. In 1840 the Lamar government had enacted an outrageous law that gave free blacks in Texas two years to remove out of the country or face enslavement. With time running out, Houston was receiving petitions, signed by lengthy lists of white citizens, asking an exception for this or that free black whom they considered a valued member of their community. The president did not judge it likely that Congress would repeal the law. However, the constitution gave him the power of reprieve. Therefore, he quietly waited, and on the day Congress adjourned, he issued a proclamation:

> And WHEREAS, it has been represented to me that there are a number of honest and industrious persons of color, who have been citizens of this country for a number of years, and have always heretofore conducted themselves so as to obtain the confidence and good opinion of all acquainted with them, and are now anxious to be permitted to remain in the Republic. . . .
>
> THEREFORE, be it known that I, Sam Houston, President of the Republic of Texas . . . issue this my proclamation, remitting the penalty of the law that otherwise might attach against them for remaining in the Republic."

February 5, the day Congress adjourned, was the second anniversary of the passage of the act and the day that Texas' free blacks would have been liable to seizure. Persons thus spared were required to post a bond, and though there was a time limit on the remission, the proclamation operated to kill the whole wicked idea, just as Houston knew it would.[14]

Throughout these weeks Houston learned to rely heavily on Wash Miller, his private secretary, eventually permitting his advice on subjects where he would probably have admitted no other. At one point the president, who prided himself on being a connoisseur of fine horses, let Miller persuade him of the superiority, for some purposes, of mules, and on Miller's advice he purchased a large, shaggy, chestnut-colored lop-eared riding mule whose fancied resemblance to a bear prompted Houston to name him Bruin. When Congress adjourned on February 5, Houston gave him a try, saddled him up, and headed east to Houston and a visit with Margaret. He found her in fine health again, surprised and delighted by his early arrival. "My dear Miller," Houston wrote when he had the chance, "I made the trip in two hours less than four days. So you see the *mule* did me honest service. I left and passed all company on the way. I was in sight of Wynnes on his arrival, tho' he had started one day sooner than I did!" From that time, Bruin did much more honest service for his owner.[15]

With an administration now functioning, Houston had time to consider the country's foreign affairs. Anson Jones huddled with him over the choice of a chargé d'affaires to send to Europe; they settled on Houston's old roommate, Ashbel Smith, who was polished and cultured, spoke fluent French, and could be trusted. Houston and Jones journeyed to Galveston, conferring with Smith over long dinners at the Tremont Hotel before he sailed on March 15. Ashbel Smith, despite Houston's warm and constant friendship, had never felt fully appreciated or believed that his talents were advantageously utilized until now. His appointment to the royal courts of Britain and France, however, elevated his self-esteem to the point that he now began referring to himself, Houston style, in the third person.[16]

France's profile was less than it was formerly. Du Bois de Saligny had moved, having stormed out of Austin after the Pig War and seeking refuge in New Orleans, from where he was of only limited effectiveness in looking after his country's interests. He did utilize the good offices of James Hamilton, the former South Carolina governor who had been his legislative point man during the Lamar years, to speak well of Houston. "Of my respect and extreme regard for the present Executive you are fully sensible. . . . Indeed, I look to him as the only man who can save the Republic from her most excruciating embarrassments." He was, however, still smarting from his bloody nose, and France would not help Texas, he warned Hamilton, until his personal honor had been vindicated. Embarked for England, Ashbel Smith stopped off in New Orleans to see him, and for his first diplomatic success reported that Du Bois had agreed to return to Texas by the next ship. At least, he made it as far as Galveston; he was never again induced to return to Austin.

A new British chargé had arrived, Sir Charles Elliot, like Du Bois a diplomatic journeyman with an already checkered history. In his first posting, as trade superintendent at Canton, he was widely held responsible for the outbreak of the Opium War. During the previous three years, Lamar's visions of imperial grandeur and his government's utter disinterest in annexation to the United States had lulled the European powers into a frame of mind that Texas, as a freestanding country, was here to stay. Houston's election reignited the annexation debate in the United States, and the solicitous cordiality that France and England extended to the new republic made it obvious they preferred to keep her independent. Their success would depend in part on their ability to keep Mexico at bay, and Elliot, for one, tried to reassure Houston that things with Mexico were not as bad as they seemed. Writing from one of the better-stocked kits in the country, Elliot wrote on neatly trimmed stationery of laid gray watermarked paper, dipping into a small pot of bright blue ink. "I have a private letter from Lord Aberdeen," he confided to the president, "in which he says, 'we shall do all in our power to bring them (the Mexicans) to a more conciliatory policy, notwithstanding our mediator has been refused, and I have some reason to hope that it will not be very long before a change shall take place in this respect.' Lord Aberdeen's words, my dear General, are very *weighty things* indeed. He never says more than he means." Houston had wasted no time in making a friend of Elliot, who subscribed himself, "Attachedly yours."[17]

Nevertheless, rumors of hostility continued to emanate from beyond the Rio Grande, and as usual when war threatened between Texas and Mexico, inquiries began to arrive from prospective American volunteers. Houston discouraged them. "To conquer Mexicans in Texas is one thing," he counseled one, but "to battle Mexicans in Mexico is a different kind of warfare."[18] By now, however, Santa Anna had had quite enough of Lamar and the Texas warhawks and was determined to reestablish his claims to Texas. But of the dictator's movements no definite news reached Texas, and rumors of Mexican invasion ran high and low as regular as tides. While Houston was home with Margaret, he left Wash Miller in Austin to review his correspondence and forward to him those items that Miller believed merited his attention. On February 16, Miller reported that apart from some Indian raids: "Austin is very dull. . . . As yet all here is quietude and peace. The battalions of the *redoubtable* Santa Anna have not yet made their appearance on our confines. Let them come. . . . God and the friends of freedom will smile upon their funeral march." The talk of the town rather was on preparation for Independence Day: "heavy *preparations* are being made to *keep fast* on the Second of March! Eggs are in demand!! It is said they are to be *drunk—not* eaten!!! . . . so the world wags, and we wag with it." A week later Miller reported that a group of idle congressmen and other worthies had just returned from an excursion to San Antonio: "The party were well pleased with their visit. They were feasted, fêted and fandangoed in fine style. The report of invasion, I learn, is generally considered in that quarter as all humbug. Major Whiting arrived last night from San Antonio. No news, no invasion."

Not everyone felt so sanguine. George Hockley warned Houston at the end of February that a train of nine Mexican traders had been murdered outside San Antonio and their wagons looted of as much as three thousand dollars in goods. "It is now reported that a Mexican force is daily expected at Bexar, to avenge the death of the murdered . . .—that citizens are barricading the streets."[19] The sentiment around Austin was, Miller reported, all for carrying a war into Mexico, and there was enormous impatience and recrimination against Houston for not doing so already. A resolution was being got up censuring the president for not pursuing a declaration of war, and "our friend W. E. Jones is in the field with cudgel in hand, against you and all opponents of immediate war measures."[20] Their rationale was that the various Texan prisoners in Mexico were either dead or were never coming home, and there was no sense trying to appease Mexico with a weak policy when there were no lives to be saved by it. Rumors of a Mexican incursion picked up again on March 2, but Miller in his Independence Day greeting said he no longer gave them much credit. Four days later he ate his words: "Since closing my letter last night, highly important intelligence has been received from San Antonio. Rodriguez arrived early this morning, and reported that a large force of Mexicans was advancing upon the town. . . . About three hours after the arrival of Rodriguez, Mr. Generas . . . reports that previous to his departure about five hundred of the enemy had arrived near the town, and were in view of observers stationed in the top of the church."[21]

The news soon rolled like a shock wave that not just San Antonio but also Refugio and Goliad had all fallen to Mexican armies. War Secretary Hockley wrote to Houston in haste from the exposed little capital of Austin that he was burying the archives of the various departments beneath their respective offices so that, in case the town should be captured and burned, "the valuable papers will be comparably safe."[22] Miller did not help the president's frame of mind any when, along with the March 6 express, he sent three large packets of his personal papers for safekeeping.

Houston, who was just then in Galveston, sent Hockley orders to remove the archives to Houston city. It is doubtful Houston believed that Austin or its archives were in imminent danger of destruction. He had never really accepted the outpost as the seat of government and, indeed, had lectured Congress more than a month before that the archives were not secure in the frontier hamlet, that their loss "would be irreparable injury to the country."[23] Thus, while Houston probably figured that the Mexican incursion was intended merely as an annoyance, the invasion lent the color not just of reason but also of emergency to his scheme. Still, that annoyance had to be dealt with, and on the same day that he directed Hockley to remove the archives, he issued orders to Brig. Gen. Alexander Somervell to take the field and "defend our liberties to the knife."[24]

To the surprise of virtually everyone, within a week the emergency passed as the Mexican troops retired beyond the Rio Grande as suddenly as they had appeared, and Houston's orders to Gen. Edwin Morehouse directed him to "communicate to the troops who have so spiritedly rallied . . . that . . . *the farmers will return to the cultivation of their fields*."[25] Houston's trusted G. W. Terrell was able to learn from local Hispanic residents that the Mexican army had invaded in the hope that they would be joined by the Tejano population around San Antonio. "In this they were disappointed," Terrell reported, "and the evening before they left here they were informed by some of the Mexicans that a large force was concentrated . . . which would attack them immediately, and that induced them to evacuate the town." Despite the Mexican withdrawal, Terrell added his voice to the chorus that Houston must allow the volunteers to pursue the invaders back across the Rio Grande. "All the troops here will be greatly disappointed if they are ordered back—if you order them to proceed it will more than counterbalance the removal of the Archives. . . . We calculate upon being able to overtake the Mexicans and give them a severe drubbing."

Houston had heard such language before, from Felix Huston, and it awakened in his mind nightmares of unreliable militia amateurs that dated back through his first term all the way to Tennessee. "They will get cool too soon," he now confided to Robert Irion. "Fervor is short lived. This we will keep to ourselves." Besides, he added, "we can't be broke up in crop time." The president had no intention of letting men fight just because their blood was up. And in a second curious parallel from the Felix Huston period, bogus "militia" bands again began pillaging the citizens: a petition from the settlers around Refugio complained to Houston that "many of us have had our cattle taken by men professing to be officers under orders emanating from your Excellency, but there conduct is at such utter variance with [your] proclamation, that we are led to believe many of said inforcements are without your orders."[26] The more things changed, it seemed, the more they stayed the same.

There was not one thing in the Felix Huston period that President Houston was anxious to relive. The invaders were gone, and he could now put his feet up for a while. "War does not press upon us," he wrote Wash Miller. "We will be in no hurry . . . . Fools only pursue phantoms & children will chase butterflies."[27] This more relaxed state gave Houston time to consider which attitude toward Mexico would yield the best result, and the strategy he adopted was typical but nonetheless fascinating: a curiously chimerical shadowboxing of bluff and feint, of braggadocio and timidity, focusing the attention of everyone on the Mexican question while using the respite to labor toward that other object—the removal of the government from Austin.

The people in the hamlet capital were alert to him, however. As early as February 8, right after Houston left town at the adjournment, G. W. Terrell wrote him a stern letter. "I found a good deal of excitement on the subject of the removal of the archives. . . . It is said you have *threatened* to remove them; and *they threaten* to arm both here and at Bastrop to prevent it. . . . The only bad consequence I fear from [removal] is that it will prejudice the people throughout the Republic against your Administration—that it will make Austin more popular and will prevent their being retained at whatever point they are removed to. . . . [But] if the order is given Hockley & myself can and will execute it."

The next day, February 9, Washington Miller echoed Terrell's warning in "my first epistle" as private secretary that the citizens were exercised on the point. "Judge Brown of Nacogdoches called on me this morning and requested me to say to you, *in his name*, that he would prefer witnessing the *destruction* of the archives, to their being removed by Executive order without the approbation of the people." And even their friends, Miller urged him, advised not to move the archives unless and until a real emergency threatened. "When the danger is apparent," Miller quoted them, "and the people see it, then the time has arrived to remove them, and not before," and the people would know it if he was trumping up an excuse.[28]

It is remarkable that Houston would have overruled advice that was as cogent as it was strident from two of his closest associates. But, to his thinking, invasion by a foreign power must surely be reason enough, whether or not he thought the invasion would stick. As Terrell and Miller predicted, Houston's first orders to remove the archives from Austin created a mighty stir. Five hundred of its citizens turned out to sign a petition asking him to rescind the directive. He held firm: "[T]he present confusion in the country," he replied, was part of the reason things had gotten in such a fix, "and so long as the seat of government remains detached, the country will be liable to similar evils."[29] The argument was specious, but it sounded good.

His rhetoric to and about Mexico, meanwhile, took more turns than a corkscrew. He sent a vituperative epistle to Santa Anna on March 22, recalling the terrible retribution of San Jacinto and threatening its like again. "Ere the banner of Mexico shall triumphantly float on the banks of the Sabine," he wrote, "the Texian standard of the single star, borne by the Anglosaxon race, shall display its bright fold in liberty's triumph on the isthmus of Darien." Houston's declaration was widely published to enormous acclaim in the United States; indeed, only one week after he wrote the letter, the elegant phrasing prompted the Nu Pi Kappa Literary Society of Kenyon College in Gambier, Ohio, (whose president was Guy M. Bryan, Stephen F. Austin's nephew) to make Houston an honorary member.[30] But in the end, the president proved more sensible than zealous. He postponed calling Congress to consider the matter, confiding to Treasury Secretary William Henry Daingerfield, "I cannot trust their wisdom in our present situation."[31] What he meant was, Congress might force his hand with a declaration of war. Then he had the nerve to claim that

Congress had not granted him the "requisite means" for such a war, much as he might be in favor of it. But, turning again, he cautioned citizens that Texas should not wage any war for conquest or plunder and should only attack if the war would be "one which the civilized world would justify."[32] But within a few weeks his tone was again menacing. The president sent to the Texas agent in New Orleans instructions, made public and reprinted, to let the volunteers come ahead, for the "bright beams of the single star will soon be reflected from the rushing tide of the Rio Grande."[33]

With Mexico's actual menace—soldiers—having retreated beyond that rushing tide, the republic's real difficulty—poverty—surfaced with a vengeance. Bookkeepers submitted bleak balance sheets of Texas' debts with a range of options, varying from delayed payment to default. On May 16, Treasury Secretary Daingerfield handed over a box containing $120,000 of a new issue of paper money, but with nothing to support the bills, the president dispatched Daingerfield the next day to the United States to negotiate a million-dollar loan. Until that ship came in, even Texas officials sailing to the United States had to beg their passage: "To Captain Rollins, of the Neptune, or Captain Wright, of the New York: The bearer ... goes on public service of importance to the Republic. You will confer a private and public favor by facilitating his passage to New Orleans. His passage, of course, will be a charge against this government, which will be liquidated with pleasure at the earliest moment possible. Sam Houston."[34] Another necessary ocean passage required more direct action. The late Mexican invasion had come across the Rio Grande, but just in case another force decided to duplicate General Urrea's 1836 route up the coast, Houston thought it prudent to station soldiers at Corpus Christi. The overland route was extremely arduous, and the only ship then in port capable of conveying the troops there was the American brig *Retrieve*, newly arrived in Galveston with a cargo of lumber and whose master, Capt. Thomas Means, gallantly offered to take the charter on credit if the government could not come up with the twenty-five dollar-per-day charge. But when the original consignee objected on the grounds that it would negate the insurance policy on his cargo, Means sought to cancel the bargain. "The President," explained the acting secretary of state to the American chargé, "not being disposed to ask security for the Govmt., offered to pledge his watch or any other personal property he had for the payment ... but, perhaps through delicacy the Capt. declined the offer. ... [As] a last resort (though with great reluctance) the President deemed it an imperative duty to order the Brig to be taken for that purpose; and would now be happy to have it in his power to remunerate Capt Means ... for the services of his vessel." Houston's commandeering the *Retrieve* created a small diplomatic incident with the United States at a time when the two countries' relations were already on a decline.[35]

The republic's grinding poverty was also stinting the progress of Texas' newest diplomat, who had the delicacy to makes his needs known only after plying the president with a good story. Houston appointed James Reily, an Ohio lawyer who had settled in Nacogdoches and who later served as Rusk's aide-de-camp, chargé d'affaires to the United States. At New Orleans, before Reily and his wife embarked

on the steamboat *Grey Eagle* for Cincinnati, "we . . . found many of Mrs. Reily's
Lexington & Kentucky friends & relations. . . . You would have been both flattered
& amused to have heard Mrs. Reily's vindication of yourself & the loud praises of
yourself & lady. If Sam Houston is not known throughout . . . the Exchange Hotel
as a fine patriot—a moral man—a most exemplary husband and a great man, it
is not for want of an advocate. . . . Please do not forget that [Washington] and my
station is an expensive one & let me have funds when convenient."[36]

The president greatly desired to open an effort at pacifying the Indians who
roamed central Texas, but there too the lack of funds crippled the effort. In mid-May
he dispatched his trusted G. W. Terrell to talk two men skilled in Indian dealings,
Joseph Durst and Leonard Williams, into visiting the tribes and making peace with
them, though he mentioned nothing of presents or inducements to show good
faith to the natives—a fatal shortcoming that Houston was, for the moment, powerless to remedy. Col. L. B. Franks, who had commanded a company of spies during
the Runaway Scrape, was now serving as Indian agent, operating under some color
from the government. When he reminded Houston that he needed funds to carry
out his duties properly, the president was reduced to replying:

> Your exertions thus far have been characterized by patriotism and a lively
> regard for the reciprocal welfare of both the white and the red man. . . .
>
> I am very sorry to inform you, that it is utterly *impossible* to furnish you
> at this time with any pecuniary assistance. There is not one dollar in the Trea-
> sury. . . . We are all in great straits for the want of means; but, for the sake of
> saving our . . . currency, under existing embarrassments, we cannot venture
> to throw any more into circulation. In the meantime we shall have to suffer
> and do the best we can. . . .
>
> Accept my best wishes for success in your efforts to benefit the country
> and the Indians, and believe me, Very truly yours,
>
> Sam Houston

When he was sixteen years old, Houston put himself in debt because he knew the
importance that natives placed on presents and a material show of regard. At twenty-
five, inducements had been a keystone of his success in getting the Hiwassee Cherokees to accept removal to the West. To write such a letter as this now could only
have made him sick, especially if he ever learned that his message was possibly the
cause of Colonel Franks's ruin. Stranded among Indians without money, and then
having his horse "impressed" into government service by a company of rogue
rangers, Franks a few weeks later was charged with murder, perhaps the result of an
attempt to recover his horse. He escaped custody during a storm and disappeared
from history.[37]

Talk of renewed war between Texas and Mexico was still all the rage in the
United States, but accepting whole regiments of impoverished new volunteers was
unthinkable. To one of his procurement agents, in sending him to the United States
for supplies, he wrote: "I command that all persons engaged in forwarding troops
to Texas, shall not permit them to embark, without the requisite supplies for six

months. . . . If the emigrants come without means, Texas must be destroyed. It will be more fatal than an invasion by fifty thousand men from Mexico." Felix Huston and the army chaos of 1837 were still vivid in his memory, and army encampments along the coast were already suffering severely from lack of water.[38]

Sam Houston's mixed signals about his intentions toward Mexico confused Texas' friends in the United States, who did not know whether they should send aid or not. Texas' consul in New Orleans informed the president: "up to this time nothing is talked of but Texas and Mexico. Last evening a meeting was held at Bank's Arcade in favour of Texas. Gen'l Foote presided. About 3000 to 4000 persons in attendance. . . . Influential and intelligent men say, 'Houston don't want men or any thing else if he did he would say so in a manner not to be misunderstood.' Now all I have to say to you Genl is this. . . . Only say you really want men &c &c and all can be had. This you may rely on it is so. Many gentlemen have said to me, They will at any time give large sums if Houston wants it. . . . Everybody here of influence looks to you." President Houston's refusal to authorize aid from the United States was also grating the war party at home. The day after the consul wrote him from New Orleans, B. J. White wrote him darkly from the town of Texana: "I have just returned from camp where I have been in the midst of friends & foes to you, and . . . heard all manner of speculation relative to your movements & motives. . . . You are represented as being afraid some man will rise to be as great as you are, also that your plans at aiming to be the dictator of Texas . . . has so far rought on your feelings that you will not agree to receive any ade from the U S. . . . *Now my once* adored friend look at the things as they are."[39]

War with Mexico, however, was not Houston's end; using the threat of war with Mexico as a card in his hand of international poker was his goal, but sometimes he seemed to forget that he was not the most experienced player at the table. The man some were beginning to call the Talleyrand of the Brazos was crafty, but he had governed Texas for a total of just over two years, matching wits with countries that had perfected their tricks over centuries. The congeniality of his correspondence with Sir Charles Elliot must have deepened his concern to receive a letter from his New Orleans consul, outlining numerous circumstances that lent credence to rumors that Britain was secretly encouraging and even aiding Mexico in the latest hostility. A Texas weakened and embattled, though not in danger of being conquered, might prove more malleable to British will. Houston's chargé in Washington, James Reily, wrote him on the same topic, saying that President Tyler concurred in the opinion that Britain was somehow implicated. Reily requested Henry Clay to take up the matter with the British minister in Washington, and Clay was able to satisfy Reily that there was nothing to it. Still, even as the citizens of New Orleans held back from sending aid because Houston was not aggressive enough, Daniel Webster confided to James Reily that, while in his opinion Mexico should have recognized Texas long ago, the young republic's present hostile posture made it impossible for the United States to intervene in the dispute. The only certainty for Houston now was that he could not be certain of anyone but himself.[40]

After so much dreary business, Houston doubtless smiled at Reily's relating of an earlier and much happier connection, although it came with a threat:

> Last Tuesday I attended a ball given Mr Clay on his retirement from the Senate. It was a brilliant assemblage. . . . I was introduced to several ladies & many enquired about *Governor* Houston. One in particular & I don't intend to tell your lady at all. A Mrs. Addison, but formerly a Miss—Shall I tell you General? Well then a Miss Smallwood, asked most affectionately after the hero of San Jacinto—spoke of his manly appearance—his majestic bearing—his warm heart . . . & pulling off from a hand like ivory a silken glove, showed me a ring prized above all, a gift from Sam Houston, long worn & deeply valued. She is the young lady who seated in the gallery & listening to Houston's defence remarked that "She would rather be Houston a culprit at the bar than his accusers." I gratified her by telling her I had heard you mention the subject in the wilds of Texas. We have become sworn friends, & altho she is now somewhat faded, yet is a fine dashing & showy woman. She spoke [also] of Dr. Anson Jones. I tell you what it is General both you & your Secretary of State had better keep me here & *pay me well* & promptly for staying, for if I come home in a bad humor with both or either I shall be armed with facts enough to ruin your peace with your families.[41]

As was his habit, Reily was warming up Houston with an agreeable anecdote before introducing his serious, and repeated, theme. "My terms just now," he continued, "are one thousand dollars as I wrote before placed in the hands of James Erwin Esq. in Orleans." James Reily simply would not understand that *no one* in the government was getting paid.

The president finally called Congress to meet—in Houston city, one might observe—on June 27. There had been some attrition from their numbers since their last meeting, and as Houston called a special election to fill the vacancies, two of the casualties mentioned were not without meaning to him: Wylie Martin, senator from Brazoria and the oldest man, at sixty-five, serving in that body, whom he had known since Tohopeka, had died. And likewise Robert Potter, the vulgar runt who had sniped at and slandered him throughout the revolution, died as he had lived, violently—murdered during a flare-up of the Regulator-Moderator feud.[42]

When Congress assembled in Houston they declared war on Mexico, naturally, but Houston vetoed the act, complaining that his powers as commander in chief "are useless" on the grounds that there was "not a dollar to commence operations with."[43] With Congress meeting and international affairs pressing, Houston had need of his able but querulous Dr. Jones, whose return from a leave of absence was delayed by sickness. "That you were unwell, I knew," Houston wrote him, "but until Mr. Johnson informed me yesterday, I was not apprised of your extreme illness. I was glad to hear that you were 'able to shave'—these shaving times." The letter, doubtless intended to cheer and welcome the gloomy Jones, is peppered with other puns and plays. The president did explain himself on vetoing the declaration of war—"Had I sanctioned the war bill, I could not have commanded any means within twelve months, and the ardor of our people while it is restrained, is most impetuous." His chargé in Washington, James Reily, whose wife had informed the entire Exchange Hotel of the president's virtues, had suddenly resigned. "The Major thinks his case is a hard one," Houston wrote Jones. "His mind seems to have fallen into a queer snarl about money matters; he cannot understand them." And of his agent Memucan Hunt, he chuckled: "Poor Hunt, I am half angry with him; but he is so amiable a simpleton, that I really pity and forgive him. If . . . he would only let me alone. . . . Now I will close *that*. When you can in safety come, I will be very happy to see you."

As usual, it was a mistake for the president to try to be friendly with Jones, who endorsed the effort darkly: "There is much mystery and double-meaning in this letter." Jones never understood that Houston was punching and pulling at Mexico, and he believed to the last that only his influence had kept Houston from mounting an invasion. A couple of years later, Jones dug the letter out of the file and endorsed it a second time: "I took, and *maintained* the ground, that nothing since the days of the Crusades was more absurd than offensive war with Mexico. The President adopted this view of mine, and expressed it, at my special instance . . . but abandoned it soon after. . . . I wash my hands of them entirely and altogether."[44]

While restraining his forces and vetoing Congress' declaration of war, Houston, in his private correspondence, further absolved himself from any blame for the lack of a campaign. "Those who wish to embark in a war against Mexico," he wrote Richard Roman on August 10, "will find that the President has done everything in his power to give it forwardness. If the people wish to fight, they have [his] authority and . . . his sincere wishes for the most perfect success and glory in the proposed campaign."[45] Houston did indeed lend his authority to at least one private enterprise against Mexico at this time. At the same time he wrote Roman, he received a letter from his good friend William Christy in New Orleans, outlining a tantalizing proposition:

> There is here at this moment a young man, Charles A. Warfield Junr. just from the Rocky Mountains . . . whom I have known from a boy (he is now 26 years of age) and whose father resides in this City:—he came here to tender his services to you, as Colonel of 300 Mountain Boys. . . .
>
> How is this to be done?—I can think of but one way:—let Mr. Warfield be commissioned as Colonel, furnish him with a sufficient number of blank commissions to officer his regiment [and] . . . give him explicit orders. . . . The Regiment will be organized within Mexican Territory in so quiet a manner (for the men are now ready to march) that the Enemy will be taken by surprise wherever they meet them.—Mr. W. says that he will ensure the taking of Santa Fé and all intermediate posts between that and Texas. . . . he is fully aware of the difficulty of keeping such a Border Corps . . . from degenerating into a band of robbers, . . . and pledges his honor to prevent such an occurrence, and I will pledge my word for him.

Houston so far had resisted war to the knife against Santa Anna, but the prospect of harassing him, without expense, in a region where the dictator had felt himself secure, was too tempting to pass up. Hockley issued young Warfield his commission on August 16, and his Mountain Boys headed northwest. Warfield, however, soon learned the same lessons about the reliability of militia forces as Houston had long ago; his regiment of three hundred melted away under the prospect of real action and probably never numbered more than a couple of dozen, but they actually did manage to annoy New Mexico in a small way.[46]

The president saw no harm in indulging such little harassments, but if Houston did seriously consider a full-scale invasion of Mexico during these days, he quickly dismissed the idea for its obvious impracticality, just as he had since the Matamoros business in 1836. But the flap and confusion allowed him to accomplish his other goal: the government was meeting back in Houston. In fairness, there was more in the balance than just moving the capital. Throughout the rumbling of war, Texas had maintained a blockade of Mexican ports, a policy to which both the United States and Great Britain objected. To maintain a warlike posture while moving, crablike, toward peace might well have been useful to Houston in negotiating the three trade agreements that were concluded with the British in 1842. After their consummation, and after a meeting on September 10 at which both the American and British chargés pledged their governments to renew their efforts to win Texas recognition from Mexico, Houston withdrew the warships on September 12.[47] The style of it all was quintessentially Houston: using the same set of circumstances to advantage on different fronts at the same time but taking the counsel of none and letting his true goals be revealed only as *faits accompli*. Thus, his energetic shadow-boxing avoided war with Mexico while mollifying his own hawks, carefully making enough of a show of truculence to expedite major trade agreements with a great foreign power, all the while getting the capital moved out of the hated Austin. The Talleyrand of the Brazos was at the height of his powers.

But his apparent vacillation, which so exasperated Anson Jones, finally unhinged George Hockley as well, who on September 1 sent the president a windy and vituperative six-page resignation modeled vaguely on the Declaration of Independence. It was an act that bruised Houston badly, for the two had been close confederates since the revolution. By return note Houston asked Hockley to reconsider, "influenced by the friendly personal feelings which I have long cherished for you, without the least guile." The president then prevailed on their mutual friend, G. W. Terrell, to convey to Hockley a second voluminous letter defending his naval policy, which had been Hockley's principal grievance. Terrell delivered the paper to Hockley, who declined to read more than two pages of it before dismissing it "with some other remarks not necessary . . . to repeat." Had Hockley read the letter, he might have been moved, for never before had Houston gone so far to reclaim a friend he genuinely loved: "We have been together much in life—we have been intimate. You have possessed my full confidence . . . whenever circumstances have thrown us together. . . . A matter of law has lawfully separated us in our official relations; but it has produced no estrangement of that respect which I have cherished. . . . I sincerely wish you a full measure of happiness."

If Hockley had "placed the same estimate upon my *regard*, which I have long done upon his *friendship*," Houston grieved to Terrell, the incident would not have gone so far. But, "occasional jars will test the solidity of a building: And Heaven knows that my poor Wigwam gets several."[48]

Historian Sue Flanagan attributed Hockley's alienation to Houston's strange penchant for making enemies of longtime friends. Indeed, that trait does represent a curious trend throughout his life, which Ashbel Smith analyzed as "acting on one of Talleyrand's strange maxims: 'Would you rise, make enemies.'"[49] In this instance, however, Hockley—like the other people around Houston—simply had little idea what the "Old Chief" (his friends had appropriated Jackson's title for Houston, at least in Texas) was really up to. Hockley was of the faction demanding war against Mexico, and he did not perceive that, to Houston, Mexico was not an end but a means. He did recognize that Houston was being coy about the limits of his executive office. The president, he charged rightly, had allowed most of the navy to "sink and rot" for lack of a specifically conferred power but had no difficulty ordering Somervell to invade Mexico without any specifically conferred power. While Hockley saw the inconsistency, he did not see that there was a method in it.

Hockley's miscue was understandable, for Houston's smokescreen about war was a particularly dense one, even by his standard. Just as Hockley was disgusted with him for his lack of action, Margaret lived in fear that he would act. She had been ill again—asthma—and was to have spent the first half of the summer back in Alabama, but she balked at leaving. "She is reluctant to go," Houston wrote Treasury Secretary Daingerfield, "she has some fears that I may take a fancy for the Rio Grande and 'dodge' her until the war with Mexico is ended. Now, this is groundless, so far as my intentions are concerned."[50] But nobody, not even Margaret, really knew. Certainly, Houston did not "dodge" her too completely, for sometime around the end of August Margaret conceived the couple's first child.

Oddly, it was Santa Anna himself who settled the question of hostility between Texas and Mexico. On September 11 an army under a French mercenary and Santanista, Gen. Adrian Woll, struck north across the Rio Grande and retook San Antonio. This time, Houston's "Orders to the Country" called not only for their eviction but also pursuit into their homeland.[51] Although this new incursion into Texas turned out to have little more substance than the one in March—Woll pulled his troops back to Mexico after occupying San Antonio for nine days—it had more serious consequences. At the first alarm, a militia company of fifty-three men under Nicholas Moseby Dawson from the town of La Grange attempted to reach the main body of Texas troops outside San Antonio. They were surrounded by Woll's soldiers, whose artillery killed about half of them. Most of the rest were, in the Santanista tradition, shot down while attempting to surrender. When Woll pulled out of San Antonio on September 20, he took with him as prisoners the dozen survivors of the Dawson massacre as well as the judge, jury, and witnesses of a San Antonio courtroom he had surrounded while it was in session. With dozens of Texas citizens dead and others held in bondage, it was impossible for Houston not to act. Back in Mexico with his hostages, Woll tried to arrange an armistice on September 26, but it was too late.

Ten days after Hockley quit, the presidential directive about the location of the capital finally came down. Congress had been meeting in Houston, anyway, and Austin's exposure, remoteness, and rotting condition "render it utterly unsuitable for purposes of government."[52] Houston city, however, was as remote from the new hostilities as Austin was exposed to them, and moreover the nearly bankrupt government was being bled at the rate of five thousand dollars per year rent on the capitol. Then came a godsend: the city fathers of Washington-on-the-Brazos approached the president through William Y. McFarland with an offer to make Washington-on-the-Brazos the new capital: "to provide and furnish comfortable rooms for all the [government] officers, to provide and furnish suitable buildings for the honorable Congress in which to meet and hold its sessions. All of which was to be done without cost or expense to the government."[53] Such an offer was a powerful incentive, and the president acted before they could change their minds. He accepted their offer on September 10 and arrived in the city on October 2, on his riding mule, Bruin, beside Margaret in the wagon with her harp, piano, and her housekeeper and companion, Eliza, who had been bought for her as a playmate when she was a girl. The government was left to follow them as best it could.

Houston ordered Somervell to the Rio Grande on the following day, and five days further on, with all eyes turned southwest, he ordered the commissioner of the land office, Thomas William "Peg Leg" Ward, to prepare for the removal of the national archives from Austin, over the Brazos-Colorado divide, and to Washington. The government could not function without its papers, and if they could be spirited out of the town quietly, Austin would be decapitalized before the residents knew it had happened. Houston trusted the job to two stalwart San Jacinto veterans, John W. Hall and William Albert "Uncle Buck" Pettus, both older than himself, to engage wagons and fetch the state papers, but they let him down. The hundred-mile journey posed a serious Indian risk, and the two opted to reach Austin on good, fast saddle horses. Pettus, a fifty-five-year-old Virginian and man of property, owning four town lots and some eight thousand acres of farmland, borrowed his wife's treasured favorite, Old Ball (who once shied from entering a grove of trees seconds before a Comanche raiding party broke from the cover and chased her all the way home). Pettus and Hall found two wagons to hire in Austin, which were then loaded in full view of the residents and prepared for an early start. Any remaining vestige of secrecy evaporated that night over drinks and cards in a local saloon. When Hall aroused himself in the morning, he was confronted by a clot of angry villagers who had trained the town ordnance on the wagons, all led by a woman with a match in her hand who swore to blow them to kindling wood at the first sign of movement. Hall found Pettus in the hotel, who advised him: "See here, Hall, I know that lady, and she will shoot. She is as brave as Julius Caesar." The two concluded to return to Washington-on-the-Brazos and report to Houston; Pettus sent a slave to the stable for his horse, and Old Ball was presented to him, tail, mane, and ears shaved clean.[54] The first round of the "Archives War" went to Austin.

The encounter left Houston's land commissioner stranded in Austin in the most hostile imaginable surroundings, and eventually Peg Leg Ward, after suspending the business of the Land Office because of the invasion, had to join the chorus of government employees pleading for relief: "I am situated in the most awkward predicament, opposed to the interests of the people through my official station, and am compelled to ask of them favors so that I could remain at my post. I have no money and being here on the frontier have no opportunity of collecting any. Now with the suspension of payment in the Treasury has left me poor indeed and leaves me open to insult at every moment. . . . For your present of tobacco I am much obliged and if possible I would be more obliged if I could obtain the amount due me by the Republic."[55]

With or without its papers, the government was now back in Washington-on-the-Brazos. Lacking rent for their own accommodations, the president and first lady were taken in by Judge J. W. Lockhart and his wife, Eliza. Margaret had been looking forward to having a household of her own at last and now, pregnant and sick, she again found herself being a frontier houseguest. It did help her considerably when she learned that the Lockharts were from Union Town, Alabama, only twenty miles from her native Marion, so there were old times to talk over.[56] Eliza Lockhart responded gallantly, providing the first family with a room of their own, furnished with a great heavy clothespress, her own prized mahogany four-poster bed, and she even cooperated when the president wished their bedroom to have a new door cut to the outside.

The president made a polite houseguest, except on the score of chewing tobacco. Mrs. Lockhart was a fastidious housekeeper, and Houston, receiving visitors while taking his ease on the front porch, exercised the carelessness of expectorating on the freshly swept porch, "when he could just have easily spit over the rail." Mrs. Lockhart was greatly provoked. Houston, however, had cemented a special friendship with his hosts' son, John Washington Lockhart, a strong, intelligent, and malleable young man of eighteen years; if Houston had married when he first felt the call, he might have had a son of his own this age. John Lockhart was awestruck by the president, and Houston virtually adopted him. He gave the boy the run of his office, where he nosed through affairs of state, remarking at one point on the boldness and grace of Queen Victoria's signature on a newly arrived navigation treaty.

By various accounts, Washington's population had now swelled to between 250 and 400 citizens, of whom four were doctors and four lawyers. One of the latter, W. Z. McFarlin, turned his law office over to the government for use as Houston's office. It was a one-room affair, with the door in the west wall opposite the fireplace in the east wall, with windows on the north and south sides. The center of the room was taken up with a large table, at which was the building's only chair, but there was a couch under the north window. Once ensconced, Houston engaged a local carpenter to make a half dozen sturdy chairs of ash, with the peculiarity that they be seated in pure white cowhide—"without blemish," insisted the president. When they were delivered and one of them proved to have a small imperfection, Houston's protégé looked on wide-eyed as the president flew into a rage and ordered it replaced. "I suppose he had been considerably irritated previously," wrote the incredulous Lockhart, "or he would not have noticed the defect. He was usually kind and affable." But he was all business these days; there was not even time for pleasurable reading. "If he had any books in his office I failed to see them, and I was in his office many times."[57]

The State Department, from which Dr. Anson Jones would carry out the annexation campaign that Houston masterminded, was housed in a made-over carpenter's shop across the street from the two-room Postal Bureau. Even more open to the weather than the president's office, chinks in the State Department walls were stuffed with rags to keep out the wind. Caesar's touchy horse did not enter such a stable without complaint. A couple of weeks before removing the capital from Houston, the president wrote Jones requesting him to return to his duties from a leave of absence, and the note contains only the merest hint of disapprobation: "During your absence, business has greatly accumulated in the Department of State. There is much of high importance that should be tended to immediately. Not a single member of my cabinet is present, and events are thickening and pressing upon me. I regret that you have not been with me since your health was sufficiently restored.... My health is so bad that I have to employ an amanuensis." On receipt of the letter, Dr. Jones penned an angry memo—to himself, for he often wrote angry memos to himself—that "I have done everything necessary in the Department of State, though a good deal absent from Houston during the summer .... General Houston promised when I took the office I should be paid in par funds. This has not been done, and I *have been obliged* to do something for a support aside from office."[58]

Of course, Houston had not been paid his salary either, and he was in tighter straits than his secretary of state, though he was less given to complaint. Obligingly, Dr. Jones headed for Houston city, only learning en route that the capital was being removed to Washington-on-the-Brazos. Never one to forget an injury, Jones pulled Houston's letter from his papers three years afterward to add an additional barb: that during the entire tenure of the government in Washington, "I have not been absent from the seat of Government except on public business.... The President and all the other members of the Cabinet were frequently absent, and I have been consequently for months left to administer the Government 'solitary and alone.'"

With such primitive infrastructure, no single building was at hand that could accommodate the Congress. The House of Representatives, therefore, convened in the large, drafty frame building where the Declaration of Independence had been signed in 1836. The Senate's arrangement was cozier. There were in Washington-on-the-Brazos two principal saloons, which for delicacy's sake were usually referred to as "groceries." The more respectable, and therefore less busy because the owner did not extend credit, was the enterprise of San Jacinto veteran B. M. Hatfield. Upstairs of Hatfield's "grocery" was a large open room that usually served as a gaming hall and whose principal item of furniture seems to have been a billiard table. This room, when Congress was in session, Major Hatfield rented to the Senate, to whom he even extended a special courtesy: rather than force the members to pass by the bar on their way to conduct the nation's business, he constructed an outside staircase and boarded over the indoor stairs when they were in session.[59]

Porcelain Teapot, Gift of the Empress of China. The opulence of the tea service sent by the Chinese Empress may have unnerved Houston; in January 1843 he ordered a coffee service from the coast, underscoring that it be plain white.

Courtesy Texas Memorial Museum

As Texas' importance came to be recognized around the world, young Lockhart saw other royal signatures, including that of Louis Philippe of France, whose hand he considered small and effeminate. Houston signed his own documents with a goose quill—"he would use nothing else," observed Lockhart—and his signatures of this time are among the largest of his always-large subscription, indicative of his brimming confidence.[60] Goodwill presents began arriving from foreign powers, even those of whom Texas had no present need of recognition; among them was a dazzling porcelain tea service from the Empress of China. The most magnificent gift was a heart stopper—a suit of clothes in crimson silk from the sultan of the Ottoman Empire, complete from fez down to yellow leather curled-toe booties sewn onto the bottoms of baggy red zouave pantaloons. The Arabian Nights outfit was said to have caused even the gloomy Margaret to peal in laughter, but not even she could induce Houston to try on the pantaloons with the yellow booties. Surrounding the whole costume, however, was a blazing crimson silk robe with which Houston fell in passionate love. Lockhart remembered that he wore it all summer, reclining on his office couch while dictating to Wash Miller; he even wore it to meet with Indians who rode in for talks and handouts. As fond as he was of his robe of state, Houston would never wear the fez, preferring instead his favorite white beaver hat with the half-inch nap.

This was the glamorous side of Texas' national affairs, but two more mundane issues pressed with great urgency. There was the Mexican hostility to have to conclude, but even more immediately there were the Indians. The Brazos Valley was roamed by a patch quilt of native tribes—Wacos, Keechis, Anadarkos, Kickapoos, Delawares, Tonkawas, and others. They were not as unremittingly hostile as the Comanches farther west, who also posed a danger, but they were impoverished and often had to resort to raiding to supply their needs. In addition, they were suspicious of the Texas government, which under Lamar had massacred the mostly peaceable Cherokees, butchered Comanche chiefs who entered San Antonio for a council, and pursued every other possible avenue of bad faith toward them. Houston knew that the Brazos Indians had to be pacified and at once. It would be a useless exercise to remove the capital from Austin because of the danger posed by the Mexican invasion and place it where there was an even greater danger from angry Indians.

Indeed, Houston began work on Indian pacification before the government ever left Houston city. On September 26 he instructed the Indian agent, L. B. Franks, to find the Tonkawa and Lipan villages on the Upper Brazos, treat with their headmen, and persuade them to send representatives to the Waco village for a council on October 24. "You are authorized to supply in a judicious manner the necessities of the two tribes, during the absence of their warriors."[61] To treat with the natives, the president appointed commissioners whom he could trust to carry out his bidding, including Attorney General Terrell, whose health, although he was only thirty-nine, had begun to fail, and Houston believed that an excursion onto the drier plains of the Upper Brazos would restore his vigor.[62] In addition to the official agents and commissioners, Houston also knew the value of having operatives working behind the scenes, and during autumn of 1842 he engaged the services of (among others) a remarkable man named Jesse Chisholm, one of Houston's oldest intimates, whose mother had been a Hiwassee Cherokee from Tennessee and whose aunt had been Diana Rogers. Chisholm was an active horse trader with virtually all the Indians of central and eastern Texas and the Indian Territory, who spoke perhaps a dozen of their languages fluently and at least a smattering of twice times that many. The natives trusted him, and when Chisholm began talking up Sam Houston's character and Indian credentials, they listened.[63]

In a still separate effort, Houston began trying to round up Indian captives taken by various Texas militias during the preceding few years. An earlier agreement obligated both Texas and the natives to exchange prisoners, and while Houston put out the word that Texas commissioners would have Indian captives in tow for the October 24 council, collecting them would be no easy task, considering the extent of their dispersal, the attitude of the authorities who held them, and the short time allowed. Shrewdly, Houston addressed himself to John Henry Moore, the most celebrated Indian fighter in the Brazos Valley. From his homestead near LaGrange, Colonel Moore had raised militia companies and fought both Brazos and Comanche Indians with equal zest and success. Houston had great respect for him, having entrusted the defense of San Antonio to him in 1840, but the two could not have been more different. Houston was a classical scholar, whereas Moore had originally "G.T.T." in 1818 as an adolescent fugitive from Latin lessons.

Four days after arriving in Washington-on-the-Brazos, Houston sent a remarkably respectful and diplomatic letter to Moore, who was recovering from a spate of dire health, and Houston hoped to find him tractable. In the treaty, Houston explained:

> It was agreed by both parties, that all prisoners heretofore taken from either should, at the time and place designated . . . be restored to their own people . . . . There are a good many prisoners in your part of the country, taken by yourself and others, in 1840, and 1841. I must ask the favor of you to interest yourself in the delivering of these prisoners to our commissioners, for the purpose of being returned to their people. . . .
>
> Be so good as to have all the prisoners sent up to Mr. Stroud. . . . I have great confidence if we comply in good faith with our agreement, a general peace may be concluded with the tribes bordering upon our frontier, which will give permanent security to our border settlements. . . . the time is growing short.

Houston explained that the only reason he did not appoint Moore himself as one of the commissioners was that word reached him the colonel intended raising a company for service against Mexico. To free Moore for this laudable duty, Houston indicated he would send Maj. John Chenoweth down to take charge of the Indian captives and free Moore to his more important work.

Chenoweth, however, was another one who would have to be worked on, as he had only recently written Houston for permission to raise a company of volunteers for action against the Indians. Houston answered him on October 8 in a voice as deferential as that used with Moore. "Your suggestions have received my earnest consideration—knowing as I do the importance of securing the frontier settlements from Indian alarm and depredation. Under perhaps any other circumstances . . . your proposition would have met with my ready acceptance." Houston then explained the arrangement to Chenoweth and requested him to have the captives ready to hand over by the October 20. "I wish you to interest yourself in the matter, and see that all if possible are delivered. . . . Fair compensation will be allowed you for your services."[64]

The following day Houston drafted out the treaty terms for the commissioners: peace, mutual friendship and assistance, repatriation, and no liquor trading among the Indians—he even spelled out penalties for settlers who raised unauthorized militia companies to prey on the tribes. A further memo a week later included more specifics: no violation of white flag, no molestation of women and children, Indians visiting the capital to be subsisted by the government, and (interestingly) peace among the different tribes would be undertaken as well as peace between whites and natives.[65] The president was not so taken up in the rosiness of the moment that he ignored the volatility of the October gathering, instructing Eli Chandler, a reliable ranger, to accompany and protect the commissioners and also to prevent meddling

Indian-haters from disrupting the council. However, "Your force should be small—some ten or fifteen will perhaps be sufficient. A large force would be more apt to excite among the Indians distrust and suspicion."[66]

On the very same day, Houston addressed the other side of the ledger, sending letters to the Indian chiefs through the commissioners, explaining that he was unable to come himself because the Mexicans had come into Texas for war and reminding them that the trouble between Texans and Indians had started with Lamar. "My red brothers, who know me, will tell you that my counsel has always been for peace. . . . A bad chief came in my place, and told them lies and did them much harm. His counsel was listened to, and the people did evil. His counsel is no more heard. . . . we are willing that your women and children should be free from harm. . . . If the Big Mush is in council he has not forgotten my words; and he knows that my counsel was always that of a brother; and that I have never deceived my red brothers, the Cherokees."

In final preparation, Houston placed five hundred carefully husbanded dollars at the disposal of G. W. Terrell for presents to the Indians. He had intended to send a hundred blankets and other trade goods, but the ship that was bringing them from New York "was shipwrecked off the Bahamas, and the vessel, cargo, and every soul was lost. . . . Do the best you can" and invite the chiefs to visit Washington-on-the-Brazos in the spring.[67]

Sam Houston dispatched the hopeful convoy and waited, but for weeks he remained frustrated as no precise information arrived from any quarter. November was half gone before he learned that, as diligently as he had labored to stage a productive treaty council, events conspired against him. At the initial contact on the Red River, the Indians misunderstood the intended time of the meeting and were late. The commissioners understood that the Waco village was on the east side of the Brazos, which was flooding, but learned late that it was ten miles above the Bosque on the opposite side. Other high water on the Colorado, "higher and more difficult of crossing than has ever been known at this season," prevented the Indian captives he had sought to sweep together into one place from being delivered as promised.[68]

Although the mission Houston sent up the Brazos did not accomplish all he hoped, the Brazos chiefs were impressed by the flurry of conciliatory gestures and had seen and heard enough of Houston to give his word a chance. Few in Washington-on-the-Brazos even knew that the president had sent a mission up the river, but its effects were felt. "These men were sent secretly and their mission was not known until their return, which was after several months," wrote Lockhart. "A decided change was, however, noticed on the frontier. Hostilities in a measure ceased among all the warring tribes that these men visited, except the Comanches."[69] Houston used the breather provided by the Brazos mission to begin laying groundwork for a much grander and more formal convocation of the Brazos tribes at the Texas capital during the spring, and then he turned more of his attention to the Mexican problem.

Down on the border, Brig. Gen. Alexander Somervell's campaign opened with some success. His force of seven hundred volunteers captured both Laredo and

Guerrero, but then that venture too veered off course. With the army composed of militia, Houston should have foreseen it. The object was to rescue from Gen. Adrian Woll his fifty-three Texan hostages, but most of Somervell's force had only volunteered for the excitement and profit of some fast border pillaging; two hundred of them went home after Laredo. Once it was obvious that the prisoners could not be retaken and equally obvious that he could not sustain a campaign in the Mexican interior with five hundred ill-equipped yahoos, Somervell ordered a general retirement on December 19. About three hundred troops, however, elected to follow two men who had come along to nurse anti-Houston political grudges: William S. Fisher, Houston's secretary of war from his first term, and Thomas Jefferson Green, a turbulent and dissatisfied man who had made a life out of false starts never carried through. Much evil mischief would follow.

This unauthorized group continued down the Rio Grande to the important Mexican garrison town of Mier, where predictably they were trapped by a Mexican army under General Pedro de Ampudia that outnumbered them ten to one. After their surrender, Santa Anna, naturally, ordered them all shot, but they were saved once by Ampudia and again, after a failed escape, by Coahuilan governor Francisco Mexía. Seventeen of the prisoners—10 percent of the remaining total—were executed by lottery at Salado in the notorious "Black Bean" episode. The rest were taken deep into tropical Mexico and plugged into Perote Castle, whose dripping casemates were crowded with the survivors of Lamar's Santa Fe expedition, then with Woll's hostages, and now with the Mier bunch.

As usual when state affairs consumed all of Houston's time, his personal business was going to ruin. He and Margaret had left their affairs in Houston in the care of Thomas Bagby, only twenty-eight years old but already a successful merchant and cotton broker. Now they were desperate for money, and when Houston could spare the time to write Bagby, the letters were scattergun shots of raising a few dollars:

> Pray do help me by renting my house. . . . That fellow Kelly has lied to you out and out. There is not a word of truth in his statement. I wish you would rent the house to some good man for $15 or $20 per month, and by the month.
>
> Do pray prevent my being cheated if you can. Every body who can will rob me, &c because I can't attend to my private business. . . .
>
> Please see if you can sell my papers for anything—Make Earl pay his note. It will help me some.[70]

Margaret, unhappy as she was, at least gave her husband a breather on the temperance issue, albeit on medical advice. "I wish you to save me all the Orange Peal you can with convenience," he included in a letter to Bagby. "I need it for bitters. The doctors commend it. I don't drink hard, but what I do take, I wish it to be palatable."

Houston's relations with Congress soured even more. He had called a special session to meet in Washington-on-the-Brazos on November 14, but the members ignored him, showing up instead for their regular session on December 1. On the subject of removing the capital from Austin, Houston complained to them of the "acts of the most seditious and unauthorized character . . . perpetrated by persons styling themselves the 'Archives Committee'" in refusing to deliver up the government's papers.[71] Sam Houston, however, was not one to miss a trick; at least once during this period, notwithstanding his bellyaching, he managed to turn the archives confusion to his own advantage. When the British chargé d'affaires lodged a protest concerning the Mexican blockade, Houston used the archives, the primitive mail system, and his own labyrinthine grammar to produce a jewel of obfuscation. The misunderstanding, he soothed Elliot, "was owing, I presume, to a misapprehension . . . on the part of the Acting Secretary of State, as I feel pretty well assured, that, as the Archives had not arrived, that he could not refer to the [document in question], and I am not certain, as he had been absent, that he had ever seen it; as we had no Mails to the Eastward, where he was at the time it was promulgated."[72]

Houston did have allies in Congress, especially in its leadership. Vice President Ed Burleson presided over the Senate above Hatfield's saloon, and even more importantly, Richardson Scurry, Speaker of the House over in Independence Hall, proved himself a powerful ally on annexation, among other subjects. Like many other Houston confederates about the capital, he had fought at San Jacinto, as a private in the artillery company, and now replaced the thunder of the Twin Sisters with that of his oratory, as he often descended from his chair to take the House floor himself in defense of Houston and his policies. He was assisted by Isaac Van Zandt of Harrison County. The leader of the anti-Houstons in the Senate was Brazoria planter William Jack, who had served in the administrations of both Burnet and Lamar and was a confirmed partisan of theirs. However, he was also virtually the only one of that camp whom President Houston actually respected, first for his valor in the revolution, and second for Jack's making it clear that his differences with Houston were political, shying away from attacking the president personally.[73]

At the end of the year, Houston finally took the archives matter into his own hands, and this time he went about it with the thoroughness he should have used the first time. After the abortive attempt to sneak the papers out of Austin during the fall, he had left Land Commissioner Peg Leg Ward on station there since his department could not possibly conduct its business without reference to its records. Ward was unpopular in Austin and lived under constant derision and threats. Houston knew that Ward was a man who could get things done; before his days as land commissioner, Ward had been the Allen brothers' contractor to build the hurry-up capitol in Houston; not begun until April 16, 1837, Congress met there on the first of May with tree branches for a roof. T. W. Ward did not carry great style, but he knew how to make things work. "Though I have not often written you," Houston communicated with him on December 10, "yet have I often thought of you, and your unpleasant position, surrounded as you are by so many difficulties and disagreeable circumstances." But help, he wrote Ward, was on the way. By a letter of the same date, the president directed two rough frontier rangers, Eli Chandler, recently returned from guarding the Indian commissioners, and Thomas I. Smith, to raise a company of volunteers and fetch the archives from Austin. "Do not be thwarted in the undertaking," he ordered them curtly. "You are acquainted with the condition of things at Austin, and the exasperation of feeling pervading those who are directly interested in that place. You will govern your movements so as to suffer no detriment, either to yourselves, or the property you may have in charge. Be prepared to act with efficiency." He suggested that the totality of government records would fill perhaps fifteen wagons, and they should recruit a sufficient force to handle the teams and protect themselves from either Indians or Austin citizens. He directed Smith and Chandler to communicate secretly with Ward and let him know when they would descend on the town, but to move with secrecy and see that none in Austin were warned of their coming. Houston then issued a presidential proclamation legalizing their raid and adjuring that "all persons are hereby enjoined, and especially commanded, in the name of the constitution of the Republic, in no wise to interfere with, obstruct or impede" the removal of the archives.

"May heaven favor your efforts," Houston wrote Smith and Chandler in a separate letter with their orders. "Promptitude and despatch may save the records of the nation, and even the nation itself!"[74] It took a couple of weeks for Smith and Chandler to organize the expedition, and in the dead of night of December 29, 1842, Smith, Chandler, and some twenty men rumbled their wagons into the city and reported to Ward. The next day they commenced loading the wagons.

The citizens of Austin at this time kept a cannon primed in a public place for any citizen to touch off as an alarm of Indian attack, and Angelina Eberley, Houston's erstwhile landlady, not about to see her business ruined by Austin's depopulation, spied the undertaking and touched a brand to the ordnance.[75] A charge of grapeshot raked the land office and sent the rangers diving for cover, as Ward heard a mob gathering with shouts of "Blow the old house to pieces!" Peg Leg Ward was not unfamiliar with cannon, having lost his right leg to a Mexican ball at the siege of Béxar and his right arm the previous year to an errant San Jacinto Day salute. Not waiting around to sacrifice any more body parts for the republic, he and the Texas archives—as much as had already been loaded—were well on the road out of town by the time a posse formed and moved out after them.

The president had to wait a week before receiving Ward's report. The commissioner had sent the wagons eastward, not on the Bastrop road but by an upper trace near Brushy Creek "because of the people living on Brushy not being so violent against the removal as the people living below." The heavy wagons were quickly overhauled and surrounded by the Austin posse, and there was a brief firefight before the archives were surrendered to prevent blood being spilled. "The archives were forcibly taken from them and lodged in Mrs. Eberly's house. . . . I have employed all the exertion I could to have them restored to this place, but in vain, and what the result may be, Providence alone can determine. Many threats have been made against me . . . but however dangerous or unpleasant my situation may be I will not complain if I can do a service to the Republic."[76]

The so-called Archives War, of which this was substantially the end, really says less about Sam Houston than it does about the nation that elected him president. Assertions of the virtues of Texan plainspoken forthrightness and their ability to defy political abuse were not mere rhetoric. Sam Houston had desired to lead a proud people, vigorous and free, and now, for better or worse, that was exactly what he got. That it was he who now tried to impose an unacceptable fiat on them was an irony he was compelled to recognize, and he admitted defeat.

The president's last fight of the year with Congress was over the navy. Before his death, Robert Potter, who had been Burnet's ad interim secretary of the navy, sponsored legislation throwing more money at a branch of service that was breaking the treasury. The high-maintenance vessels were in New Orleans for repairs, and the administration had sent the fleet's commander, Commodore Edwin Moore, cash from the new issue of currency to pay bills with the understanding that he would not float it all at once and depress the exchange rate. He did exactly the opposite. Conditions aboard the ships were awful; there had been a mutiny aboard the schooner *San Antonio*, one of the officers was murdered, and Houston requested the crew's extradition from Louisiana governor A. B. Roman.[77] His disagreements with Commodore Moore had erupted into a full-blown feud; against orders, Moore sent the *San Antonio* down to Yucatan to try to collect some of the rent due for services under the Lamar government, but instead she was lost at sea in a storm. Three days before Christmas, 1842, Houston sent a secret message to Congress noting that the builder had indicated an interest in buying back the vessels Texas had purchased, and suggesting that the nation would be better served by selling the fleet. This was one matter in which it seemed the president let his personal animosities sway his policy too much. It was true, as he informed Congress, that he had withdrawn the blockade, but peace with Mexico was too dim a vision to dispense with an arm of service that acquitted itself admirably and might yet prove of more value diplomatically. The Texas Navy was anti-Houston and always had been, and there is little doubt that Houston's animosity toward it reflected his unwise rancor toward Potter and Moore.[78]

Overall, 1842 was a political draw for President Houston. Ending the Regulator-Moderator War was a win, the Archives War a loss, while the navy business dragged on in Congress. Mexican armies were at least out of the country, but the prisoners in Perote had still to be bargained for. Complicating that situation, one cannon on the ship of state broke loose and had to be quickly lashed down: South Carolinian James Hamilton, Texas' perennial tinker, tailor, investor, and speculator, opened out-of-the-box negotiations with Juan Almonte, taking a view toward Texas' cession or sale to the United States. "I have assured [Almonte]," Hamilton wrote eagerly to Houston, that if Almonte could get Santa Anna to license him to deal, "that I would write to you, requesting you without any public appointment challenging the smallest degree of publicity, to authorize me *privately* to treat as a secret agent." The plan was a disaster in the waiting; the mere mention of an American Texas was Santa Anna's panic button, and if Hamilton acquired color of authority for it, any chance at Mexican recognition would be lost and hostilities renewed, to say nothing of Almonte probably being stood to a wall and shot. Houston and Jones acted vigorously through the Christmas holiday to ensure that no representatives would entertain Hamilton's proposition. In the more regular field of diplomacy, shuttling between the Courts of St. James's and St. Cloud, Ashbel Smith proposed a tripartite mediation wherein Britain, France, and the United States would jointly pressure Mexico to recognize Texas. His idea met with only partial approbation. Given Mexico's continued truculence, Lord Aberdeen and M. Guizot concluded that joint coercion would only make things worse, and it would be better that the three powers "should act separately, but in strict concert with a view to . . . effect an accomodation between Mexico and Texas."[79] Sam Houston therefore did what he did best, he monitored the situation for the most favorable augury. His tightrope act of provoking annexation to the United States by Texas' increasing coziness with France and England had been inconclusive to this point, but he was rapidly acquiring a mastery of the situation that allowed him to move more aggressively the following year.

15

THE TALLEYRAND OF THE BRAZOS

President Houston opened 1843 in distraction, but politics were not uppermost in his mind. He did send blustery messages to Congress on the subject of the archives, of which he ceremoniously washed his hands—"If the archives are not preserved," he snorted, "the blame cannot attach to the Executive"—and the navy, which he was still trying to rid himself of.[1] But what really had him in a dither was, at the age of nearly fifty, his impending fatherhood. Margaret was now five months pregnant, and the president of the republic was positively aflutter with delicacy and discretion over her condition. The pregnancy was not an easy one, and Margaret had already miscarried once during their first year together at Cedar Point. Moreover, away from her native Alabama, she displayed a propensity for asthma, which the grass plains around Washington-on-the-Brazos exacerbated to an alarming level. (In later years he wrote a friend that Mrs. Houston was not well, and "I am satisfied never will be [well] out of a Pine Country. . . . The Prairie Country don't suit her disease.")[2] Shortly before Christmas 1842, Nancy Lea alighted from a stagecoach.

Margaret was only one of her six children, and when the matriarch removed to Texas, the rest of her brood cast their lots with the new country as well. They settled, more or less grouped around the sugar plantation of Margaret's younger sister Antoinette and her husband, William Bledsoe, at Grand Cane, some twenty miles north of Liberty. Mrs. Lea had been in residence there when, alarmed by the news of Margaret's difficult confinement, determined to remove her expectant daughter from the frontier back to Grand Cane, where she could nurse her. Houston had desired Margaret to stay on in Washington-on-the-Brazos, but plowed under—not for the first time—by his mother-in-law, the president was left now on his own. "You may have conquered Santa Anna," Nancy Lea was fond of telling him, "but you will never conquer me."[3]

While he was devoted to his wife, Houston's temperance had not been tested in some time by a prolonged separation. At some point in the low ebbs of official crises and personal loneliness, Maj. B. M. Hatfield, saloonkeeper and the Senate's landlord, collared the president and placed in his hands a bottle of fine Madeira from a shipment lately arrived. At first Houston declined the gift, but at length accepted it, in his unique calculus, as a gift for Mrs. Lockhart, who hosted the president in her house. Had the lady been at home, that would have been the end of the story, but she was not. When her return was delayed late into the evening, the president retired to read in Mrs. Lockhart's great mahogany four-poster. However good his intentions may have been, he was unable to resist the savory Madeira leering so closely nearby. In his earlier drinking days, Madeira seems to have been one of Houston's favorites, and once the cork was out, he proceeded to get presidentially ripped.[4] In this state he imagined that one of the bed's four posts was stifling his breath, and he fetched his slave, Frank, who was housed in a nearby lean-to, to bring an ax and ordered him to chop it down. The Lockharts burst through the door just in time to see the mahogany timber crash to the floor.[5]

In a curious way, the famous bed-chopping incident speaks in Houston's favor. Drunks get out of practice, and for an alcoholic of Houston's legendary proportions to get that loaded on a single bottle of Madeira, this episode testifies to a long abstinence. Some accounts, however, attest that the "bottle" was a gallon jug. The exact amount that Houston consumed is unknown; all that is certain is that the he got snockered. There was only one source from whom Margaret could hear such unspeakable news, and once he sobered up, the president of Texas slouched up on the saddled Bruin and headed for Grand Cane to confess. Margaret, wisely, accompanied the president back to Washington-on-the-Brazos, but they paid a price: Nancy Lea came with them too and lived with them until the pregnancy was safely completed. Returning to the Lockharts was out of the question, and a simple but suitable dwelling was found to rent. The impoverished president now found himself with an entire household to furnish and entrusted a huge order for foodstuffs and supplies to William Bryan, now Texan consul in New Orleans: two barrels of flour, two barrels of sugar, barrels of mackerels, herring, buckwheat, and apples, kegs of lard and butter, two sacks of Java coffee, and a box of tea, specified as Young Hyson. Perhaps finding the empress of China's porcelain tea service too florid for everyday use, Houston ordered "1 Sett neat *white* china for Coffee" plus dry goods—socks, handkerchiefs, a bolt of linen diaper ("*for towels*," the father-to-be underscored in too much protest), and furniture calico: "but take care to select none such, as will exhibit Turkey Gobblers, Peacocks, Bears, Elephants, wild Boars or Stud Horses!!! Vines, Flowers, or any figure of taste; you can select." The combined worries of home and country seem also to have taken a toll on the president's whittling: the final item in the order was "1 Handsome pocket Knife (pretty large.)"[6]

With the Madeira forgiven and peace in his house restored, January also brought a Treaty of Amity and Friendship signed by King William of the Netherlands. However, another of Houston's diplomatic maneuvers at this time later backfired. Thinking, as he always did, to fell as many birds as possible with one stone, and with the issue of annexation ever turning in his mind, he sat down on January 24 and composed what he thought was a shrewd letter to Capt. Charles Elliot, the British chargé d'affaires to Texas. His first point was to solicit British intercession for the Texans taken prisoner at Mier. "It is true the men went without orders," he admitted, "and thereby placed themselves out of the protection of the rules of war. This much is granted. But the Mexican officers, by proposing terms of capitulation to the men, relieved them from the responsibility which they had incurred." Once they surrendered, Houston urged, they became prisoners of war, not mere brigands, and were entitled to humane treatment and repatriation.

Houston next pressed on Elliot a number of particulars, some dubious and some not, designed to show why the temper of the United States was more in favor of annexation than at any previous time. After ever so gently alluding to the British interest in Oregon, which would be jeopardized by annexation, he suggested that the British could counter this annexation mood by convincing Mexico to recognize Texas' independence. Santa Anna, Houston assured Elliot, would find it much in his interest to do so. "In all these matters I may be mistaken," he wrote, "but I am honest in my convictions that Texas and England would both be beneficiaries by this course. Time will tell the tale."[7] The missive was sealed and sent off, and its effect was awaited.

While he defended the status, if not the mission, of the Mier prisoners, Houston elsewhere showed himself capable enough at winking at more genuine brigands when they could be enlisted to harass Mexico. Young Charles Warfield's Mountain Boys "battalion" had never amounted to much, but in January the government was approached with a similar project by a man whose abilities were more tested. Quartermaster of the Army Jacob Snively was a Nacogdoches surveyor who had proven his abilities as an infantry officer in the revolution; Houston had used him as an operative among the Indians during his first term, and he had served Albert Sidney Johnston well. When Snively approached the government with a plan to capture Mexican trade on the Santa Fe Trail, it dovetailed nicely with Houston's needs. If the United States ultimately showed no better interest in annexing Texas than they had thus far, and Texas was required to go it alone indefinitely, then Houston meant to enforce Texas' authority to the last extremity of its territory, which under the Treaty of Velasco extended as far north as later Wyoming. Trade passing between the United States and Mexico passed through Texas' sovereignty, and a useful purpose could be served by reminding the other two parties of that fact. Snively was authorized to recruit a force of as many as three hundred men (although it never actually exceeded two hundred). Houston gave himself the out of denying government responsibility for them by having them operate as privateers, with Mexican trade interdicted in Texas to be divided between them and the government. Designating themselves the "Battalion of Invincibles" with Snively in command, aided by Eli Chandler of the late "Archive War," they sallied west from Fort Johnson on the Red River in late April, hoping for better luck than Lamar's losers had.

Such Machiavellian puppeteering was becoming increasingly difficult to manage, less for its intricacy but more for the sheer lack of time Houston was getting alone. With the door to the one-room presidential office standing open to the street, it seemed everybody and his buddy felt free to drop in on the chief executive. That, of course, was a key component of Houston's popularity, but in early 1843 so many people hallooed and entered that the president probably began to repent of having those six "unblemished" cowhide chairs made. "Some call on business," he complained to his friend Bagby back in Houston, "some through curiosity, and others, as they say 'to spend the time.' Now this last is cruel to me. If they choose to waste their own time, why that is all right; but they ought to reflect when they are consuming mine that it is of some value to me and to the country. I can't say [that] to them—that wouldn't be kindness—so . . . I have to endure the 'auger' and I may screw and twist as much as I please! Oh! what charming wretchedness—who can wonder at my happiness."

When she was feeling well, which was not often, even Margaret nosed in to make a bid for presidential attention, interrupting even the above letter. "Mrs. H. says, 'do ask Mr. Bagby if he sent the Cambric Linnen.' . . . I say—'No, Madam, but I will request him to read over my last three letters'—Please do peruse them, Bagby? I make this request, merely that you may see how much I am in want of everything!!!"8

One group of visitors Houston unfailingly made time for were the natives, who felt welcome to descend on the capital and be treated to food and presents at any time. Houston pampered them with certificates of friendship, and the sight of Indians camping on the outskirts of Washington-on-the-Brazos was common enough to incite little public curiosity—although there was occasional consternation, as when a bony old Indian woman was observed plucking and devouring vermin from the hair of a companion. With Houston's previous council out on the Brazos having been a partial misfire, he was deep in preparations for a much larger, multitribal council to be held there at Washington-on-the-Brazos in April. But for now the natives' freeloading sojourns were getting out of hand, and the president began looking for ways to keep them out, without hurting their feelings, until he was ready for them. At one point he was compelled to order the Indian agent, another old San Jacinto veteran named Benjamin Bryant, to "communicate to the Chiefs of the Lipans and Tonkeways that, without leave of their agent and a passport, none of their people are to visit the seat of government. If needful at any time, the agent can . . . permit a few of the chiefs to come in on business."

There were two reasons for this. One was concern for their safety; as the Texas capital grew, it became crowded with more men who were unsympathetic to Houston's friendship with them. "There is some hazard to [the Indians] in coming among the whites . . . and considerable danger to a single one." This reason was spelled out to the natives. The other reason, of which they were not informed, was that they were eating the government out of house and home. (Saving money by cutting back on the natives' visiting rights was a precedent Houston would have remembered from his Wigwam Neosho residency as early as 1830.) "While they remain at a distance," Houston explained to Bryant, "they cannot know how poor the government really is. If they know our poverty, they will entertain less respect for us."9 The incident that prompted this presidential directive happened the same day he penned the order to Bryant. A Tonkawa chief named Yonsey visited the town, and Houston had to finagle government finances merely in order to make the chief a small present of two pounds of lead, a pound of gunpowder, and four twists of tobacco.[10]

With only a couple of weeks left before the Washington council with the Indians, Ben Bryant sent word that one of the Lipan Apaches' two leading chiefs, Flacco, was dead, along with a plaintive note from the chief's aged father of the same name asking Houston for any information he had about his son's death. Houston responded that he knew nothing, "only it is said that Mexicans from the Rio Grande killed him. Maj. Hays has written to me on the subject. When I get new particulars of his death, I will write you and you can inform his father of the facts." Houston knew perfectly well that pointing the accusing finger at Mexico would incite revenge raids across the border, and Houston instructed Bryant that if the Lipans and Tonkawas headed for the Rio Grande "to take satisfaction for his death, tell them by no means to harm women and children. The warrior . . . only fights with men. I will never shake hands with a red brother who has stained his hands with the blood of women and children."

In a more compassionate addendum to this rather incendiary response, Houston sent Old Flacco four plugs of tobacco and several shawls for his wife and composed a lengthy ode to the valor of the dead chief, which he instructed Bryant to translate to them carefully, as it would comfort the old man. On that same day, March 28, Houston very practicably curried some favor with the Lipans' other chief, Castro, by issuing him a certificate of friendship. The next day he drew on the Indian Department for seventy-eight dollars' worth of trade goods for his commissioners as further inducements to the tribes to come to Washington-on-the-Brazos, and a couple of days after that dispatched a personal emissary, Stephen Z. Hoyle, to Houston city with a five-hundred-dollar shopping list of presents to be distributed at the council. The president even selected the merchant, J. F. Torrey and Company, throwing out the bait that if the Torreys would furnish the goods on sixty days' credit, they would be rewarded with further Indian purchases by the republic. The two hundred pounds of lead and fifty pounds of tobacco one would expect to see, but of the more particular items that Houston judged would make the best impression on the natives he knew so well, he was emphatic in his detail, and if Hoyle could not find them in Houston, he should go on to Galveston to get them. Among this list were: "20 butcher knives, lignum vitae handles, with brass rivets; 4 doz flashy red hdkfs, or shawls; 8 ps. inch, or half inch ribbon—red, blue, green, yellow and white."[11]

Brazos Indians began arriving in the Washington vicinity about April 9, and they were directed to a pleasant campground in a spring-fed glade about a mile south of the town. Observers thought it odd that the president did not ride out to greet them. Instead, Houston, knowing what would make them comfortable, let them acclimate and mingle with the townspeople for some days before getting down to business. "They behaved themselves very nicely," noted an observer, "not molesting anything and I only saw one who was under the influence of fire water, and he was a young buck, who would sing snatches of religious songs and clap himself on the breast and say, 'Me missionary, me heap missionary.'"

When the president finally appeared with his aides, he cantered up in full general's uniform, dismounted, and walked the entire length of the camp to embrace the chiefs, "one arm over and one arm under." When leaders of both sides were seated in a circle, "a huge calumet made of stone with a cane stem was placed in the center of the circle." Houston had it filled with aromatic kinnykanic, a mixture of tobacco and sumac. "General Houston was the first to draw smoke, which he did with great solemnity—as much so as if he was partaking of the Lord's supper."

Houston had prepared so ably and laid so much groundwork that the actual business of the council, hearing what all the chiefs had to say and concluding the terms of the agreement, went quickly. Wash Miller sat by him, taking notes in pencil of all that was said, writing so rapidly that his normally careful hand slurred in places into an unaccustomed, but still legible, scrawl.[12] Everything the natives had to say pleased the president. At one point in the ten-day sojourn, however, Houston was required to exercise some of his Indian savvy. One of the Caddo chiefs, Red Bear, was proving slow to accept white people as friends, and when Houston presented him with a percussion rifle, Red Bear scornfully rejected it for being not as fine as the flintlock presented to a rival chief, Aquaquash. About an hour later, the president, accompanied by several men both white and native, entered Red Bear's dwelling. According to one witness,

> in one corner of the room was Red Bear lying on a scaffold used for a bedstead, covered up head and ears, the maddest Indian that I ever saw. . . . The general . . . paid no attention whatever to him, but . . . took a seat among half a dozen Indians sitting around and commenced talking about Red Bear, heaping abuses on him. . . . At last General Houston told the other Indians that Red Bear was a squaw. At this he leapt out of bed as if on springs, made his way to where the general was standing and embraced him, and . . . promised to accept the gun and be friends forever.
>
> In an emergency like this I reckon there are few men who would have known how to act.

This was not the recalcitrant Red Bear's first attempt at accommodating the whites, for his mark appeared as well on a treaty signed the preceding August.[13] Such testiness was not the rule at the conclave, however, and in response to the government's hospitality, the Brazos Indians held dances at night and, perhaps conveying a message along with the fun, demonstrated their archery for their hosts, piercing a yard-square swatch of buffalo hide from a hundred yards distance.

As the council drew to a close, Houston asked his former landlady, Eliza Lockhart, to prepare a dinner for fifteen or twenty of the headmen. As recalled by her son, "The menu consisted of beef and corn-bread. The beef was boiled and cut into chunks about the size of a man's fist, put into trays and tin pans. . . . When dinner was announced [they] marched in and took their seats. Long benches had been prepared for them as seats. . . . When shown how to use their knives, forks and plates they made an attempt to imitate, but finally laid them aside and pitched in with their fingers. In this way of feeding they were perfectly at home and did ample justice to what was set before them, except the corn bread, which they did not quite understand."[14]

If earlier in the spring President Houston discouraged too many natives from visiting the town, it was only because he was saving up to subsist them, if anything lavishly, during the council. During the ten days that natives were in residence about the capital, their board bill came to $163.35, including 88 pounds of bacon, 48 pounds of pork, 602 pounds of beef, 20 pounds of coffee, 32 pounds of sugar (Indians were notorious for their fondness of sweet coffee), 12 1/2 bushels of cornmeal, 1/2 bushel of peas, and 1/2 bushel of salt. And this was in addition to the generous disbursement of presents—overall a huge bite out of the struggling treasury.[15]

With the Indians of the Brazos Valley ostensibly pacified, Houston lost no time in casting his attention farther out and set about organizing another council for late summer at Bird's Fort on the Upper Trinity, near the later site of the city of Fort Worth. This council was to include even Comanches, and Houston shrewdly restored two Comanche female captives (who did not want to return to their people, by the way) through the offices of a Delaware Indian intermediary, Jim Shaw, whom the Comanches knew. In his communication Houston recalled the Council House massacre that had enraged the Comanches and announced: "the man who counseled to do this bad thing is no longer a chief in Texas. His voice is not heard among the people." A further gift of fifty-two dollars' worth of trade goods attested his earnestness that the chiefs should meet with him at Bird's Fort in August.[16]

No sooner had the president looked far afield than he discovered a groundfire to be extinguished at home. The very day after the Washington-on-the-Brazos council broke up, word reached him that a party of Waco Indians had stolen some two hundred horses belonging to Lipans and Tonkawas. The latter tribes were hopping mad but, having just signed a treaty, deferred taking matters into their own hands and instead presented themselves to their agent for justice. Houston wrote a counseling letter to the Waco chief, Aquaquash, who had signed the agreement, saying he understood the offense to have been committed by a party of about thirty wild Wacos who were not at the council, and he knew that Aquaquash could not have known of it. But the treaty having been signed, Houston looked to Aquaquash as chief to see that the stock was recovered and brought into the Delaware trading house, where the Lipans and Tonkawas could claim them. "I have told them you would have them returned," wrote Houston, "for I had all confidence in your words." There followed one of Houston's hallmark compressions of multiple meanings: the desirability of peace, the formidability of Tonkawas as enemies, and his own awareness of just how savage the natives could be not just to whites but to each other: "By returning the horses it will help make peace with all the red brothers, and the Toncahuas will not wish to fight or ever again eat people."[17]

Houston's confidence in Aquaquash was not misplaced. He and other friendly Indians accompanied the commissioners, including G. W. Terrell, on the Comanche mission. When the latter proved disinterested in peace with Texas and held a council to decide whether to kill Houston's emissaries, it was Aquaquash who rose and declared that if they killed the white commissioners, he and the other Wacos and

Delawares were ready to die with them, and the Comanches backed down.[18] (At the Washington-on-the-Brazos council, when doubt was expressed whether Aquaquash would really vindicate the government's position to the Comanches, the old chief had responded, "I'll go home & bring Comanches to your house & see what you'll say then.")[19]

Thus, it was old Aquaquash who spared Houston's Indian policy a calamitous setback in spring of 1843, but it was Houston's meticulous forecast, preparation, and execution of Indian policy that quieted the frontier for at least the next few years. The middle course that he steered in dealing with the Brazos Indian tribes in 1842 and 1843 was in every element as consistent as the course he had undertaken as Cherokee subagent under Joseph McMinn in 1818 and with the Texas Cherokees during his first term: Take no advantage of them and do not let them take advantage of the government; live up to the government's obligations and insist that they do the same; protect them from white encroachment while ensuring that plunder of Anglo settlers ceased. There was another element of consistency as well, although perhaps less noble. Houston saw no harm in managing Indians affairs in such a way as to increase native hostility toward Mexico. In 1832 Samuel May Williams watered a seed that probably already lay in his head of the advantages of cultivating friendly Indians on the border; in 1837 Houston schemed to settle five thousand Creeks on the Rio Grande; in 1843 he let Old Flacco know that his son, the chief, had been killed by Mexicans on the border. Moreover, to Old Flacco he even repeated his 1837 admonition to spare women and children during their raids into Mexico. To Houston, anything that could slip a burr under Santa Anna's saddle was all to Texas' advantage.

Meanwhile, the Houston mercantile of J. F. Torrey and Company accepted the government's Indian business on the terms Houston had proposed. They were probably jarred, however, when the president used the deal as a bookkeeping breather, bypassing his beleaguered treasury and issuing warrants directly on the store to pay friendly Indians in merchandise, charged net sixty days to the government. Sam Houston had never been one to miss a trick.[20]

The president's Indian attentions were necessary, but they were a drain on his time that he could ill spare from the complicated faro he was playing in international geopolitics. Still pending was that artfully incendiary letter to Charles Elliot, the result of which he was hoping "time would tell the tale." What Houston thought he did was, first, procure a helpful and probably necessary ally in securing the release of the Mier captives by, second, holding out to England the hope of preserving a sphere of influence in Texas, knowing all the while, third, that the alarm would be raised in the United States if the Americans thought for a minute that Texas was serious about going British. The Talleyrand of the Brazos should have been proud of himself, but this particular artful incendiary device suddenly blew up in his face.

Elliot forwarded Houston's request to Richard Pakenham, Britain's minister to Mexico, with a request to render assistance in the matter. Pakenham brought the American minister to Mexico, Waddy Thompson, into the deal, and he was sure to report news of the British-Texan rapprochement and possible Mexican armistice to Washington, D.C., all of which was just what Houston hoped. But then, whether by diplomatic snafu or by design of partisan press in Mexico, it was in all the news-papers that Houston had repudiated and abandoned the Mier prisoners as outlaws. He had, of course, done no such thing, but the anti-Houstons swarmed on the issue like angry hornets.

But at least the Americans were taking notice. "My dear Judge," Houston wrote the American chargé Joseph Eve in mid-February,

> I find, as news reaches me both from the United States and Texas, that the sub-ject of annexation is one that has claimed much attention and is well received. I find that even the *oldest settlers*—even some of the original "Three Hundred," are as anxious for the event to take place as any that I met with. How the project is to ultimate, it is impossible to divine. The democracy of the United States is in favor of the measure; and if it should become a political *lever*, both of the political parties will sieze hold of or grasp at the handle. But of these matters you can judge better than it is possible for me to do. You have more sources of information than I can have. Truly thy friend,
>   Sam Houston

Having spent so much time thinking about his native people, it seems the presi-dent had also been polishing his timing to know when to lie low and play the Indian with the Americans.[21]

The need to settle this international intrigue took an urgent turn on February 11, when the Texan volunteers captured at Mier, being marched to prison in the capital, attempted an escape in the town of Salado in Tamaulipas. Santa Anna, true to form, ordered all 176 fugitives shot, but Coahuila governor Francisco Mexía dodged the order until diplomats had a chance to work on the dictator. Their efforts were only partly successful: Santa Anna would still have his blood, but the death sentences were reduced to one man in ten. On March 25 the prisoners were forced to draw beans from a pottery jug—159 white ones for prison, 17 black ones for the firing squad.

News of the "Black Bean" episode hit Houston hard, especially after word reached Texas of the pluck and courage of the condemned. The first black bean went to Maj. James Decatur Cocke, a pro-Lamar newspaper editor who had repeatedly attacked Houston for being too soft on Indians and Mexicans. Cocke held up his bean and said, "Boys, I told you so; I never failed in my life to draw a prize." Houston's young protégé, John Lockhart, happened to be in school at Groce's when the farewell letter of one of the victims, Robert Holmes Dunham, was delivered to his mother. When Houston learned of this, he sent young Lockhart back to Groce's to request the grieving mother to lend him the letter. The convulsed woman "drew the missive from her bosom," recalled Lockhart, "and with many admonitions to be careful and not lose it ... gave it into my keeping."[22] The president, already taking a beating in the press for allegedly selling out the Mier prisoners, ground his teeth over it for several days before returning it.

Just at this time, as fate would have it, the faro with Santa Anna took a turn that can only be described as bizarre. Among the captives that Woll herded out of San

Antonio Lopez de Santa Anna. Known to history mostly through a romantically retouched early daguerreotype in full uniform, Santa Anna did not age well. He lost a leg in battle defending Tampico from a French invasion and in his subsequent regimes confirmed his early penchant for brutality. In attempting to keep his country together, however, he proved no more able a diplomat than a general.

Courtesy Library of Congress

Antonio was Judge James W. Robinson, an abrupt and irascible man of fifty-three years, who at the Consultation of 1835 had been among the loudest advocates for declaring immediate independence and who, when the "Permanent Council" impeached Governor Smith, was made acting governor and as such feuded with Smith over executive authority. As a ringleader of the rebellion, he stood in imminent danger of being shot, and where a reasonable man might have attracted as little notice to himself as possible, Robinson began addressing obsequious letters to the dictator, assuring him that the vast majority of Texans desired to return to the Mexican union and would do so if honorable terms could be offered them. Stunningly, Santa Anna believed him, and Robinson, rather worse for wear, appeared in Galveston at the end of March with the dictator's terms: that in return for Texas' recognition of Mexican sovereignty and laws, amnesty would be extended to the rebels, no Mexican troops would be stationed on Texas soil, and Texans would be given a kind of internal autonomy. Robinson also made good a pledge to Santa Anna to lobby the issue and, upon his arrival in Texas, point out that the Mexican tariff would place a twenty-five-cent-per-pound floor under Texas cotton. As the terms were published in Galveston, Robinson made his way inland to Washington-on-the-Brazos and reported himself to President Houston on April 6.

Robinson told the president that he was honor-bound to report some response to Santa Anna but was unsure what to say. The wily Houston, while hardly able to believe his good luck, knew exactly what to say. Whether he dictated the response to Robinson or wrote it out and had him copy it in his own handwriting is not known, but the document is a delight of subterfuge and twenty-four-karat Houston.

> I find that your Excellency and myself were mistaken when we suspected that Texas was torn to pieces by factions. It is not so. . . . I found the people much engaged in the cultivation of their farms, except those who are very anxious for an invasion of Mexico, and many who are in favor of an invasion are improving their farms and planting their crops so as to be ready. . . .
>
> I would think that Houston would prefer peace. . . . He has always been opposed to an irregular warfare between the two countries; but he has now succeeded in making peace with the Indians, and, as that will relieve the northwestern frontier of much embarrassment, it is possible that he may unite all the influence he may have with those in favor or prosecuting the invasion of Mexico. . . .
>
> The last Congress passed a law favorable to what war spirit there is in Texas; and the President has the authority to accept the services of forty thousand volunteers. . . .
>
> I would most respectfully beg to submit to your Excellency, in gratitude for your kindness to me, a few suggestions, which your Excellency can take into your distinguished consideration.
>
> The first is, that if your Excellency had thought proper to have released all the Texian prisoners and let them return to their homes, and declared an armistice of some months, until the people of Texas could have time to think of your propositions . . . , it would have had a good effect upon the people.

One can almost see Sam Houston smirking to himself as he closed "Robinson's" letter: "I will endeavor so to manage as to get my dispatches to your Excellency through some safe channel. Your Excellency will be aware of the discretion with which I have to act" lest their communication be discovered.[23]

Frank Lubbock considered the "Robinson" letter "one of Houston's ablest state papers."[24] As diplomacy, it was a delaying tactic worthy of the first Elizabeth, and as it played out over the following several months, it worked to perfection. The next step was to send another letter to Charles Elliot, the British chargé d'affaires, suggesting vaguely that it was a good time to have a talk with Santa Anna and then giving him an incentive to do it with a unilateral declaration that Texas would take no further action against Mexico except in response to further aggression. At this point, however, another danger arose, one of greater moment than James Hamilton's fancy to play secret agent. Just as during the Runaway Scrape, when insurrection in his own ranks might have spelled disaster, it nearly happened again. In spite of Houston's proclaimed ceasefire except in self-defense, the Texas Navy's Commodore Edwin Moore, a Lamar appointee who had carried out that administration's alliance with Yucatan rebels, sortied in the six-hundred-ton *Austin*, accompanied by the *Wharton*. Moore had himself raised some thirty-five thousand dollars to keep the ships operational; he did receive Houston's orders to return to Galveston, but fearing (with considerable justification) that the president would sell the vessels, Moore renewed his alliance with the Yucatecans, who paid for the ships' new fitting out. Thus, while Houston was trying to convince Mexico of his peaceable intentions, the commodore of his navy engaged Mexican ships on April 30, May 2, and May 3. As soon as he heard of Moore's insubordination, Houston dashed off hurried a disclaimer to the American chargé d'affaires, Joseph Eve. The commodore's crime, he allowed, "is one of great atrocity, and I have availed myself of the first moment to take the only corrective in my power." That corrective was to issue a proclamation branding Moore and his ships as pirates and invoking the aid of any vessel of any flag to assist in their arrest. Houston sent a virtually identical letter the same day to Elliot and also apprised France's acting chargé d'affaires, the Vicomte de Cramayel.[25]

The president's personal affairs, at least, took a happier turn, as Margaret was safely delivered of a healthy boy on May 25, 1843. Houston wanted to name him William Christy in honor of his and Texas' friend in New Orleans, but Margaret would not hear of it. He was named, instead, Sam Houston Junior. Answering congratulations from Elliot, Houston wrote proudly: "Mrs. H. and the boy are doing well. He is stout and I hope will be useful to his kind. May he be anything but a loafer, an agitator, or in other words, a demagogue," which brought to mind the Mier prisoners. Houston felt sorry for them, but British friendship, he wrote, if it could arrange a peace with Mexico, would leave them without a cause. "I can only sorrow for our heroes. Poor fellows! they have great cause to hate 'John Bull.' He has by his interference blighted all their hopes of immortal fame, and now they will have to *leave, loaf, steal, starve*, or make an honest living by honest means."[26]

Sam Junior was allowed to be an idler for a while, but Margaret found nursing him difficult, for the pregnancy had inflamed a small breast tumor, and Houston had already written a doctor friend in Houston city to please "obtain 'Nipple guards' for Mrs. Houston. She has indications of a 'sore breast' and expects soon, to have to 'Nurse.'"[27] Nancy Lea, who had helped the family repeatedly from her substantial purse, now purchased a milk cow to allow Margaret to wean the baby as soon as possible. Houston was grateful for this intervention but humiliated at being unable to provide for his wife and child himself. His mother-in-law insisted with a snap that he could starve for his country if he wished, but Sam Jr. was "not old enough to undergo . . . Valley Forge." They reached a face-saving compromise: the president would repay her out of his salary, which he must surely eventually receive. If this incident indeed reflected Houston's financial condition in May and June, he must have felt it all the more keenly for having in his desk a warrant for two thousand dollars, paid him in January, which the treasury apparently was unable to honor.[28]

The president never let his poverty stint his hospitality, however, nor his penchant for picking promising young men out of a crowd for his notice and favor. Years later, one such project recalled:

> I had come to Texas from Alabama, and was at Washington on the Brazos . . . in 1843. One morning I was approached by Houston's negro boy Tom, who was his cook and body-servant, with an invitation from the President for me to dine with him that day. I was then only about twenty years of age, and was naturally a good deal flustered by the unexpected honor, which I was unable to account for, as I had never spoken to the President. The dinner was at one o'clock. I found the President at the double log-house which was his residence. He received me with a kindly and hearty welcome, which put me at once at my ease. The dinner consisted of wild turkey, bread, and black coffee. Houston said that but for the kindness of a neighbor, who had sent in the bird, the dinner would have consisted of only bread and coffee.

Sam Houston was a master practitioner of the Southern art of getting acquainted by comparing kin until some connection was found, and in this instance he stunned the young stranger. "He told me all about my family and relatives in Tennessee, and in fact a great many things that I did not know myself."[29]

According to a Tennessee friend, Houston made it "his constant study to know every man by name whom he happened to meet. If he did not know the name he would make the man believe he did, which accomplished the same end." During his visit to Jackson in 1839, he and a friend met a man on the Gallatin road, whose name was found to be Hale, the brother of a soldier killed at San Jacinto. "The General, who had never seen him before, hastened towards him and exclaimed: 'How are you, Mr. Hale? I am glad to see you again—how well you are looking.' Remembering the General as Governor of the State years before, Mr. Hale expressed his satisfaction at being recognized, and wondered that the General should have remembered him. 'Remember you,' said Houston, 'how can I ever forget you, sir, or any member of your family? Did not your gallant brother die in my arms on the bloody field of San Jacinto?'"[30]

Two months after his naughty "Robinson" letter, and having given Elliot a chance to work, Houston judged it was time to sweeten the pot for Santa Anna. While admitting to his Secretary of State Anson Jones that the people decidedly favored war with Mexico, he found the country's interest better served by inviting the mediation of friendly governments to negotiate their differences. This he did on June 15, declaring Texas' unilateral armistice with Mexico as evidence of the republic's good faith toward el Presidente's propositions to bring Texas back into his fold. The newspapers, which had no idea what he was up to, shrieked their outrage that Sam Houston was actually considering Santa Anna's offer. What he was really doing was buying time.[31]

Other diplomatic ground shifted during the summer of 1843; Joseph Eve was recalled to the United States, and he took leave of President Houston in a long letter on June 10 packed with private as well as official compliments. Officially, Eve was sacked for financial irregularities, but those were innocent—he had merely sought an advance on his salary to cover loans he had made to friends. The real issue was that he was becoming entirely too friendly with Houston and Texas, and U.S. Assistant Secretary of State Fletcher Webster, who opposed annexation in the most earnest way, used the opportunity to try to damage Texas' prospects for admission by firing Eve. It was a wasted effort, for Eve was soon to be replaced in any case. He was nearly sixty, consumptive, and fevered, and died in Galveston only six days after penning his affectionate farewell to Houston. He was supplanted by Gen. William Sumter Murphy, who was as warmly espoused to annexation as Eve had been and with whom Houston quickly forged a cooperative working relationship.[32] And the Texas guard in Washington, D.C., changed also. After James Reily resigned in a snit, Houston replaced him with Isaac Van Zandt, the windy but promising young representative from Marshall, at whose expense Houston had had some fun in the Texas Congress. He would be steadied by the more experienced J. Pinckney Henderson, who had performed well as Texas minister to Britain and France.

(No sooner did Van Zandt arrive in Washington, of course, than he wrote home to the president: "I have been truly unfortunate in not receiving a dollar from the government and consequently feel like any thing but . . . free and independent, cramped as I am. . . . I hope relief may come in time yet.")[33]

By September Houston decided it was time to lure Santa Anna further into his trap, on the fourth ordering the release of any and all Mexican prisoners held in Texas in exchange for the release of Texan captives in Mexico. He also appointed Hockley and Samuel May Williams commissioners to treat with Mexico, in Mexico, on the terms of a permanent armistice. Still working, ever crablike, to get Texas into the United States, his scheme nearly collapsed when Santa Anna learned that Houston, while negotiating with him, was also negotiating an annexation treaty with the United States. The jig was very nearly up, but by affecting a public posture of indifference to annexation, Houston kept the dictator guessing.

By December, the president was back in Washington-on-the-Brazos, awaiting the arrival of the Eighth Congress, which he had called to meet on the fourth but, for want of a quorum, missed the call by several days. On December 2, 1843, a remarkable editorial appeared in the *National Vindicator*, the town's weekly newspaper under the somewhat bored title "ANNEXATION AGAIN":

> It is urged by some that the bulk of the people of Texas are in favor of annexation to the United States; and while that opinion is only expressed by a few, the editor of the Telegraph, and others hostile to the Executive, they do not seem to advance any good reason for forming such an opinion. . . .
>
> In the first place, the United States rejected us with scorn when we first made the overture. Her policy was not deep enough to foresee when she might have use for us. . . .

In the event of a war between Great Britain and the United States, Texas, if annexed, would be the weak point, and the most likely to suffer by the war. . . .

If we remain as we are, in case of a rupture between the United States and Great Britain, which, however much to be deprecated may not be far distant, England will give us a high price for our cotton, and induce thousands of planters to leave the United States and come to Texas to raise that cotton which she will not take from the U. States, and . . . we can then supply the United States and Mexico with European goods, and receive their gold and silver in return; and thus engross the business of three distinct nations. This would do more for Texas in one year, than one hundred years of annexation to the United States would do. Let the people of Texas look to it; and while the golden apple is held out to them, let them not cast it aside.

A TEXIAN[34]

Who was "A TEXIAN"? The logic, structure, and vocabulary are all Houston's. While others spoke of "the President," he habitually referred to himself as "the Executive." The various shorthands ("U. States") and expressions ("however much to be deprecated") were among his stock phrases; the classical allusion to Atalanta and the golden apples needs no amplification. And, to sway public opinion by planting letters in the press from fictitious citizens was a tactic perfected by Andrew Jackson's "literary bureau."[35] It seems probable that while Houston stood tapping his foot waiting for the Eighth Congress to assemble, he used the time profitably to augment his diplomatic maneuvering with a little surreptitious editorializing. And the piece he generated was one he could then produce as an anonymous expression of public sentiment, intended to encourage the British and further worry the Americans.

Whether or not the "TEXIAN" editorial was a product of his own pen, Houston was certainly deep in the hand of playing his British annexation card. His opening address to the Eighth Congress on December 12 echoed the editorial in its sunny comments on the friendly attitude of "Her Britannic Majesty's government." The United States government is prominent only in being snubbed; its only mention in his whole address was to American interdiction of the Snively Expedition. The "Battalion of Invincibles" had proven themselves only slightly less woeful than Lamar's "traders." Instead of being captured and either shot or imprisoned by Mexicans, they were instead captured and disarmed by U.S. soldiers protecting a Mexican train on the Santa Fe Trail and were given the choice of either accompanying the dragoons back to Missouri or returning disarmed through Comanche and Kiowa country to Texas. The incident may have occurred on Texas soil, and the president seized on it as "an infraction of our revenue laws by citizens of the United States attended with circumstances of a very unpleasant character."[36]

These public hisses at the United States began to have an effect. Infirm and in pain at the Hermitage, Andrew Jackson was sufficiently worried over Houston's willingness to let Texas get on without American solicitation that he was prompted to expend some personal capital in a private letter to him, "You know my dear General, that I have been & still am, your real friend." And Santa Anna was prompted to take enough bait to begin releasing some of the Texans held in Perote Castle—not the Mier prisoners yet, but Lamar's Santa Fe survivors and Woll's San Antonio hostages were, in stages, set at liberty. When they began arriving back in Texas, most felt they were due some kind of compensation for their service and subsequent confinement, but they ran headlong into the financial realities that Houston had been daily living with. One group of rangers taken about the same time as the Santa Fe expedition—who had thus been longest in prison—took their claims all the way to the president in person. "All we could get out of presadent Houston," recalled one named William Rozier, "was by the eternal god boys there is not a dollar in the trashery I have to get my grog on a credit those claims are as uceless as brown paper. So we scattered to the places we called our homes."[37] Houston by now had stopped drinking, except for the orange bitters that Margaret allowed him, so he was not expending credit for grog, but he still retained the power to soften bad news with the common touch.

On February 18, 1844, Houston's commissioners finally signed an armistice with Mexico. Of course, he was not particularly interested in an armistice with Mexico and utilized Texas' description in the document as a "Department" of Mexico to let it die quietly and allow the Mexicans to wonder when it might be ratified. He was much more interested in the pending annexation treaty with the United States, but then in March he was sidetracked when he found himself required to fight an old battle again. James Hazard Perry, the rogue aide who had entered Houston's camp opposite Groce's in April of 1836 as a plant for Burnet and Potter, had taken to the lecture circuit on the topic of San Jacinto, giving a version of events less than flattering to the former commanding general. Once the revolution was over, Burnet had rewarded Perry with a colonelcy in the regular army, with attendant land bounties, but as soon as Houston was inaugurated Perry decamped back to New York, where he became a Methodist minister. The president sat down and composed a lengthy column, presumably for distribution to the New York newspapers. In angry defenses of his career, Houston habitually referred to himself in third person, and he did so here while citing chapter and verse of Perry's repeated disobedience, rumor mongering, and suspected collusion with the enemy.[38]

Andrew Jackson was chronically ill during February and March, but he doggedly bombarded Houston with letters on the necessity of annexation to the point that it seemed Houston's British card might be working too well. He dispatched Wash Miller to the Hermitage with a private assurance that Texas was still willing to join the United States, although he maintained the posture even to his "Venerated Friend" that, at this point, the United States had more to gain from it than Texas. Jackson grilled Miller, who replied that if Texas were spurned by the mother again, "she may look to a better reception from the grandmother." The words could only have been Houston's. It had been just over a year since the Texas president hinted to Elliot that a British sphere of influence in Texas would help them hang on to Oregon. It was an argument that struck home with Jackson, who wrote Houston in agitation in March that if England held sway in Texas, "she would form an iron Hoop around the United States, with her West India Islands that would cost oceans of blood, and millions of money to Burst asunder." He pledged himself to promote the annexation treaty and to try to keep it secret until presented to the Senate to keep "that arch fiend, J. Q. Adams" from starting an effort against it.[39]

Texas and the United States finally consummated a treaty of annexation on April 12, 1844, signed by John C. Calhoun for the United States and J. Pinckney Henderson and Isaac Van Zandt for Texas. However, Sam Houston had not even received his copy of it on June 28 before the nosecounters in the U.S. Senate realized it would fail ratification, and Houston began to worry that he might have fundamentally miscalculated Texas' chances of admission to the Union. Texas, it seemed, might genuinely not be wanted. With the entire world aware that the treaty was signed, however, Texas was left with insufficient diplomatic cover to protect her from Mexican wrath. "If negotiation fails," Houston wrote his ministers in Washington, D.C., the morning after he read the document, "our file is uncovered, the enemy may charge through our ranks, and we have no reserve to march up to our rescue." He chastised Henderson for not pressing for American protection until the deal was final, but "'tis well enough, we cannot go back, and therefore we must march forward with decisive steps." One of those steps was to gird themselves for perhaps permanent existence as an independent nation. "If from any cause, we should be rejected," Houston continued, "we must redouble our energies," and he now must "express to you decisively what my purposes are. Texas can become Sovereign and independent, founded upon her own incalculable advantages of situation, and sustained by European influences without the slightest compromittal to her nationality. If the present measure of Annexation should fail entirely, and we are to be thrown back on our own resources, fix your eye steadily on the salvation of Texas. . . . I again declare to you that every day which passes only convinces me more clearly that it is the last effort at Annexation that Texas will ever make, nor do I believe that any solicitation or guarantee from the U.S. would at any future day induce her to consent to the measure." Houston was satisfied that his armistice with Mexico would fail; he excused his commissioners for signing it, even with its reference to Texas as a Mexican department, for "by signing it they obtained a safe convoy out of the country, which might not have been the case if they had refused their assent to the conditions. They were both well acquainted with Mexican faith and Mexican perfidy."[40] On his own side of the diplomatic faro table, Santa Anna saw the Texas Senate reject the armistice he had offered and then learned that Texas and the United States had signed an annexation treaty. Sam Houston was not the only one gritting his teeth over someone else's perfidy.

Two weeks later Houston wrote his Washington ministers again, stating that the diplomatic rumor mill was beginning to spin out stories—one that Waddy Thompson, whom the United States had dispatched to Mexico, was sent for the purpose of purchasing the Californias and with authority to "settle the boundary of Texas to suit themselves"; and a second one that eight or ten Mexican soldiers were killed at Corpus Christi, having been landed at that place to break up a ring that smuggled goods into Mexico. "Thus you see," wrote a droll president, "our people must be doing some little mischief. We must always enjoy some agreeable excitement, or things will not go very well." After another week, American rejection of Texas annexation seemed a foregone conclusion, and Houston angrily ordered Henderson home; Van Zandt "will remain at that Court, wait upon the Executive, Mr. Tyler, and assure him that this government, relying upon the pledges given by that Government will confidently expect that no molestation to Texas by Mexico will be permitted." He sounded much like a bride left standing at the altar, not just in tone but in asserting that the other party had more to gain from the match: "And though the advantages presented to the United States were incalculably greater than those resulting to Texas, she was willing to stand the hazard of the adventure. The statesmen of that country appear to be united in opinion adverse to our admission. . . . It would be unpleasant for us to enter into a community as a member, where we should be regarded ungraciously by either of the political parties. Texas, alone, can well be sustained, and . . . we will be compelled to assume such attitude toward other countries as will certainly look to our independence. . . . Texas can now command interests which will require no such sacrafice."[41]

Sam Houston had good reason to believe that Texas, as he claimed, could well be sustained. England was public in her solicitation of Texas' welfare, despite rumors of her also encouraging Santa Anna, and the French, who had been playing the game only at a distance since the disaffection of Du Bois de Saligny, was showing closer interest. The president had in hand a new letter from Ashbel Smith: "I was at the Palace of the Tuileries last evening and had the honor of a conversation with the King about our country. He inquired particularly in relation to annexation to the American Union. I replied . . . that could we have our option we should undoubtedly prefer a separate existence with peace. The King appreciated most highly your policy in reference to a war with Mexico etc., and expressed himself most decidedly in commendation of . . . your efforts to obtain peace. I made a suitable answer adding that we place much reliance on the continuance of the friendly offices of his Gov't. to bring the present negotiations to a favorable termination." Ashbel Smith also wrote of a favorable meeting with the papal nuncio in Paris and that he had his eye on the Spanish government, which had been in too great a turmoil to be of much benefit, but they seemed to be settling down. Houston's overall conduct, he concluded, "has been extremely well received."[42] With France and England both in play and a possible Spanish card still in the deck, Houston and Texas could afford to raise the stakes for the United States.

The next few scenes in the geopolitical drama were not Houston's to act, however, as during the summer he fell into chills and fever—perhaps malaria—and had to slow his pace. As all expected, the U.S. Senate rejected the annexation treaty on June 8. The British minister in Washington, D.C., discounting rumors of Britain's aiding Mexico against Texas, had assured Reily through the State Department that England thought it really more likely that Texas would conquer Mexico than the other way around, but that did not entirely quash the feeling that Britain had an interest in keeping the pot boiling for the time being. In July, Houston received an urgent letter from General Murphy, the sympathetic American chargé at the U.S. legation in Galveston, renewing that fear. Murphy had just received word from the

American legation in Veracruz "that active preparations are making by Genl Santa Anna to invade Texas with a large force, at the earliest possible moment. That a large body of Troops have been secretly despatched, to reinforce the Army of the North .... Mr. Green further adds that 'Santa Anna calculates on some 'foreign aid.'"[43]

None of that, including the hint of British duplicity, was anything Houston had not heard before. Nor was the information of Mexican troop movements any great shock, for he already had in hand a rather baroque declaration of war from Santa Anna, which he answered in a high and insulting style on July 29. Dripping verbal acid, Houston catalogued Santa Anna's massacres of 1836, the brutality of the death march from Santa Fe in 1842, and the decimation in Salado. "Eight years ago you were a suppliant," Houston reminded the dictator,

> obtained your liberation without ransom, *and acknowledged the government of Texas.* If Texas existed *then* as a nation, her recognition since that time by other powers, and her increased commercial relations, would well excuse your recognition of her sovereignty *now....* If you ... intend to prosecute [war]— do it presently.... Present yourself with a force that indicates a desire of conquest, and we may respect your effort. But the marauding incursions which have heretofore characterized your molestation, will only deserve the contempt of honorable men. I have the honor to embrace you with salutations of the most affectionate regard.
>
> Sam Houston[44]

The president had already extracted from Murphy a promise that American warships would protect the Texas coast—a pledge given without authority, which landed Murphy in hot water at home and led to his recall. But Murphy, like Joseph Eve before him, was broken down by Texas service and died only a couple of weeks after warning Houston of Santa Anna's preparations.

As if the failed annexation treaty with the United States was not enough, and now with the dictator rattling his saber again, a new challenge erupted. The Regulator-Moderator feud, which Houston thought he had dispensed with in 1842, flared anew, and during the summer Houston was barraged with pleas from citizens in and around Shelby County to somehow put an end to the bloodshed. Since the last armistice, a Mississippi sociopath with a hunting horn named Charles W. "Watt" Moorman had assumed control of the Regulators and established a kind of feudal barony under his own rule. It was only a rumor that he was plotting a coup against the central government, but it was a certainty that some three hundred citizens in the Redlands were under arms.

Houston might not be able to control Santa Anna, but he certainly could control Shelby County, and, somewhat improved from the chills and fever, he took to the saddle for East Texas. His call for militia brought out six hundred volunteers organized by San Augustine merchant and postmaster Travis Broocks, operating cooperatively with regular troops under Gen. James Smith. On August 15 Houston and Rusk entered the town to quell the trouble. Houston, who had represented the district in Congress during his presidential interregnum, sat on a stack of firewood, whittling, while local officials recounted the recent horror of murders, lynchings, and cabin burnings. When he had heard enough, the president issued a proclamation, wiser and more subtle than the one two years' previous. Noting that the citizens were "arrayed under different leaders, in opposition to each other, and to the great terror and alarm of peaceful inhabitants," he declined to assign any blame. "It has not been in my power to possess myself with all the causes which led to this condition of things. Therefore, I abstain from making any decision as to the merits or demerits of the parties. . . . This is a mild and advisory course."[45] The document went on, however, to warn the partisans that if they continued with their carrying-on and he had to sic the gathering militia on them, they would not like the result. Houston then instructed Marshal of the Republic Alexander Horton to arrest ten leaders of each faction and bring them in. The Moderators came eagerly; Watt Moorman first tried to negotiate. "You speak of negotiations which are going on with those who have not yet surrendered," Houston admonished Smith. "I am unable to comprehend what character of negotiations can be concluded between the offenders against the laws and the laws themselves." If talks were ongoing, it was desirable that he should see them through, but "no officer of the government who is sent for the maintenance of laws" could strike a deal outside the course of justice. Watt Moorman finally came into town under compulsion.

The president, in what was described as a "fatherly talk," mediated their differences, persuaded them to make a treaty, and proclaimed the war ended. Amazingly, it stuck.[46] Houston's "fatherly talk" was, of course, backed up by Travis Broocks's militia, which remained on guard even though provisioning them worked a hardship on this impoverished section of the republic. "Dear General," Broocks wrote the president on August 23, "I find the citizens in this Country most generally *eaten out*, It seems hard to take the last they have without paying them, Consequently I have promised the government will pay for what we get, or I will pay them myself. . . . if some provision is not made we will be Compelled to leave for home, Please give me authority to draw on the Custom House, or the Sheriff of San Augustine County for some amount."

"I have the honor to acknowledge your dispatches," Houston answered him on the same day, but "I can only assure you, Congress made no appropriation for [the present] service, and I dare make no expenditure not sanctioned by law. Considering the scarcity of corn for the inhabitants of Shelby County, the horses should be grazed on grass, but not fed with corn—or it may greatly distress the community." He then referred Broocks to his regional commander, General Smith, whom he cautioned, "the greatest care and economy should be used in sustaining the troops, lest the scarcity of supplies should produce great want in the community." Not leaving circumstances to chance, Houston stayed in San Augustine until the end of the month, reducing the force to one company of mounted rangers as the danger faded. His orders were meticulous in their insistence that brute force was to be a last resort. "You will be careful to secure all who may surrender," he instructed Smith, "their persons and property inviolate from any indignity."[47]

Houston's role in ending the Shelby County conflict, while it was timely and successful, would be easy to overstate. In the first place, both sides of the conflict were exhausted by five years of fighting. Second, and more importantly, historians of the frontier have long noted that it was in the nature of a feud to dissipate once the government asserted its authority, for it was "not lawlessness. It [was] an appeal to a law which is felt to be a reasonable substitute" in the absence of actual jurisprudence.[48] Houston himself showed an awareness of this phenomenon, explaining almost paternally in his "Open Letter," "If persons in society have rendered themselves obnoxious to the laws, it remains with the laws to punish them—but not for citizens to . . . assume to themselves powers which belong to the constituted authorities."[49]

Back in Washington-on-the-Brazos, meanwhile, the momentum in favor of annexation was rumbling downslope despite the fact that the United States would have to be dragged into it. The following poem appeared in the *Houston Telegraph and Texas Register*, tantalizingly subscribed to the authorship of "H******."

THE PLEA OF TEXAS
Admit us—we would deem it shame,
Of other lands such boon to claim,
    For we are free and proud—
But we a mother's love may seek,
And feel no blush upon our cheek
    Before her to have bowed.

We are their children; doubt it not
We've proved our birth on many a spot,
    Where cannon thunder pealed—
'Twas Saxon heart that dared the fight,
'Twas blood of yours that gave us might,
    Upon Jacinto's field.

We love your flag, your laws, your land—
Wishing to worship, see we stand
    At freedom's Temple door—
Admit us now for it may be,
That lost on Time's tempestuous sea,
    We part, to meet no more.[50]

Again the fingerprints are there—the reference to San Jacinto, the allusion to the tempestuous sea. Was "H******" Houston? When the poem appeared, the president was in Shelby County arbitrating the Regulator-Moderator War, but the *Vindicator* was a Houston-friendly paper, and its editor, Thomas "Ramrod" Johnson, was a pal with whom Houston and Wash Miller had colluded on other occasions.[51] As with "A TEXIAN" the year before, and doubtless in other anonymously published tracts of the period, one feels safe in saying that Texas's wily president was a busy man, propagandizing below decks as energetically as he steered the ship of state.

The Houston house at Grand Cane was a short ride from the conflicts in Shelby County, and the president reached home on September 2, where his health broke again, relapsing into the summer's suffering, and, he wrote Col. J. C. Neill, "the most violent attacks of chill and fever that I have ever experienced."[52] Nevertheless, Houston was anxious that the coming treaty council with the Comanche Indians should come off without a hitch. Most of them had ignored his commissioners at Bird's Fort, so he authorized Neill to make whatever contracts might be necessary to subsist the Indians who came this time, and, advising Neill of his—Houston's— slowed itinerary in making his way back to Washington-on-the-Brazos, he should keep the president informed of the results.

The most important of the Southern Comanche chiefs, Po-chee-naw-quo-he-ep (literally, Long Time Erect Penis, known however to whites as Buffalo Hump), had refused to treat with anyone less than Houston himself, and his presence at the council was imperative. The president was well enough to make the journey, held at the falls of the Brazos at Tehuacana Creek on October 7, 1844, where he made his apologies again for the mayhem of the Lamar years. "I made a peace with the Comanches," he asserted. "That peace was kept until a bad chief took my place. The chief made war on the Comanches and murdered them in San Antonio. He made war, too, on the Cherokees and drove them from the country. Now this has to be mended. War can do us no good."[53] In two days of negotiations, Houston talked the Comanches into a treaty of twenty-two articles, but he had to give ground on one front: the free-roaming Comanches would not countenance any restriction on their movements nor recognize any line they could not cross. Pragmatically, Houston struck out that article and inserted one that Texas would allow no bad men onto the Comanches' hunting grounds, but if the Indians found one there, they would deliver him unharmed to the government agent. This Buffalo Hump found accept-able, and he and his subchiefs put their marks to the paper, giving Houston some hope that the wicked mischief of the Lamar administration was finally put to rest.[54]

In the United States, the demise of the annexation treaty failed to dampen the issue of Texas admission to the Union. Quite the opposite, in fact: it made Texas annexation the dominant issue in the 1844 presidential campaign, so much so that the contest between Henry Clay and Houston's old Tennessee friend and congres-sional colleague James Knox Polk became a virtual referendum on the topic. Until his pied destiny of ruin and triumph intruded, Sam Houston had been regarded as Jackson's political heir, but in his absence it was Houston's friend Polk who began to be referred to as "Young Hickory." Indeed, it may be said that Polk had trod Houston's road not taken. He had served seven terms in the U.S. Congress, the last two of them, from 1835 to 1839, as Speaker of the House. As the aging Jackson found it increasingly difficult to keep his own minions in line over his choice of Martin Van Buren as his immediate successor to the executive office, Polk stood by the Old Chief. Van Buren's first two years in the White House were Polk's last two in Congress before being elected governor of Tennessee in 1839. He only served one term, being defeated in 1841 and 1843 by ascendant Whigs. Thus, by the 1844 Democratic Convention, Polk had been five years out of public service.

Van Buren was succeeded in 1841 by William Henry Harrison, who died only one month into his term, and the office was assumed by John Tyler, a Virginian sympathetic to U.S. expansion, especially of the southern boundaries. Van Buren intended a second run for the presidency in 1844, but when he published a letter shortly before the Democratic convention repeating his opposition to annexing Texas, his party rebelled. Through eight ballots the Democrats refused to renominate Van Buren, after which he withdrew his candidacy. Polk, who had been vocal in his support for the acquisition of both Texas and Oregon, was nominated on the ninth ballot. The Whigs put up Clay, who opposed an American Texas with as much energy as Polk supported it, and the issue got a vigorous airing during the campaign. When all was said and done, Polk defeated Clay by thirty-eight thousand votes and claimed an electoral majority of 170 to 105.

Seeing in Polk's election a mandate for territorial expansion, President Tyler enacted a stratagem for Texas annexation that would break the Senate deadlock. (At least, Tyler set the plan in motion; the idea may well have been Jackson's.)[55] Because Texas and the United States had been negotiating as separate, sovereign powers, the issue was submitted in the form of a treaty, and under Article 2, Section 2, of the U.S. Constitution, ratification required a two-thirds concurrence of Senators. However, the restrictions specified in Article 4, Section 3, regarding the admission of new states were limited to preserving the integrity of existing states. Previous states had been admitted by joint resolution, and nothing prevented Texas from following the same path, which required only a simple majority in both houses.

Genuinely spooked at the prospect of Texas as a British satellite and how that would complicate the map of North America, the Tyler administration made certain to make Texas an offer that could not be refused. The terms of the joint resolution were a vast improvement over the previous treaties. Texas could enter the Union directly as a state, although she might if she wished split at a later time into four additional states. Texas had to keep her national debt but also kept her trackless public domain to defray it. The joint resolution passed the House of Representatives by a comfortable margin, but it was in the Senate where the balance between free states and slave had been so carefully nursed, and debate there teetered acrimoniously. Both Northern and Southern cohesion collapsed, and when the poll was taken, votes were cast by individual senators for individual reasons. The final tally was twenty-seven to twenty-five—in favor. The offer was good until the end of the year, and a new U.S. chargé d'affaires to Texas, Andrew Jackson Donelson, was hustled westward with the documents and instructions to press the issue vigorously with Texans.

This was the same A. J. Donelson who, as Andrew Jackson's private secretary, had relayed his brother Daniel's marital gossip about Sam Houston to Old Hickory.[56] Now, on his way to Texas, A. J. Donelson stopped again at the Hermitage to deliver the happy news to Jackson, who rose to palsy through a three-page letter to Houston: "I now behold the great american Eagle with her Stars & Stripes hovering over the loan Star of Texas, with cheering voice welcoming it into our glorious Union and proclaiming to Mexico & all foreign Governments in Stentorian voice, you must not attempt to tread upon Texas—that the United Stars & Stripes now defend her—Glorious result, in which Genl you have acted a noble part."

Even now, Jackson could not refrain from still giving Houston advice—the new state constitution must forbid banks and corporations, Texas must close its borders to further foreign colonization—but at last he felt their relationship had come full circle, fully restored. "If providence spares me, to next summer of which I have great doubts, I hope to see you, your amiable lady & charming boy at the Hermitage, where you will receive a hearty welcome, not on your way only to see your relatives, but on your way to the Senate of the U. States, to take your seat with the sages of our Union."[57]

Jackson was not the only man in the United States brimming with confidence that they had made Texas an irresistible offer. Polk's secretary of state was, of all people, John C. Calhoun, Sam Houston's oldest and bitterest nemesis—but even he became caught up in the Texas fever. "I am happy to inform you that the course you have pursued has met with the entire approbation of the executive," he encouraged Donelson early in January 1845. "The important points were to secure the confidence of the government of Texas and to keep open the question of annexation in both of which your efforts have been entirely successful."[58] If Calhoun had known how Houston played the United States like a fiddle for the English and the French, he probably would have had a stroke.

Anson Jones finally realized the destiny to which he believed himself born, sworn in as president of the Republic of Texas on December 9, 1844. In his campaign he never committed himself on the subject of annexation—his support from Houston was lukewarm at best—nor was there a syllable about it in his inaugural address. Not that anyone much cared what Anson Jones thought about annexation. It was Houston's opinion that everyone sought, and his smokescreen was so dense that two continents were in confusion over his intentions. Ashbel Smith had returned from an arduous duty in Europe, and Houston, in taking leave of Washington-on-the-Brazos in February 1845, suddenly appeared in Smith's lodging, "booted, spurred, whip in hand. Said he: 'Saxe Weimar (the name of his saddle-horse) is at the door, saddled. I have come to leave Houston's last words with you. If the Congress of the United States shall not by the fourth of March pass some measure of annexation which Texas can with honor accede to, Houston will take the stump against annexation for all time to come.'" With that he gave Smith his accustomed bear hug and left without another word. Even though Smith himself later wrote of Houston's penchant for melodrama and his ability to play for effect, this almost spectral materialization left the shocked Smith with the impression ever afterward that Houston did not favor annexation.[59]

Donelson was sufficiently buffaloed by Houston's feints and lunges that he made a trip to Iberville, Louisiana, to seek advice from one of Houston's oldest friends, E. G. M. Butler, in whose youth Houston had dragged around Washington, D.C., in search of the right hat to open his congressional career. Donelson "read to me his correspondence with the Texan Government," Butler recalled, "of its apparent indifference; of his visit to Houston, in the interior, and his indignation toward Van

Buren, and consequent opposition to the proposed treaty." Butler advised Donelson to worry less over Texas's leaders and be less bashful about pitching annexation directly to the people. It was brilliant advice, for Texas was still a rude and direct democracy, and where the people were inclined, the leadership would have to follow. After packing Donelson back to Texas, Butler repaired to the Hermitage for a last visit with the Old Chief, who had entered his final decline.[60]

Washington-on-the-Brazos, unlike Paris or London or Washington-on-the-Potomac, was not a big enough town to conceal much intrigue, and at one point the British Elliot and the American Donelson found themselves contending for their respective positions at opposite ends of the same hotel supper trestle. When Elliott began getting the upper hand in volume, Donelson called coldly down the table, "Captain Elliott, I think you are making a fool of yourself."[61] The author of the storm was no longer at its center. His official duties finished, the former president and first lady left for a triumphal tour of the United States, intending to travel from Galveston to New Orleans to Tennessee to visit the venerable Jackson.

In New Orleans at the end of May, Houston was greeted as a hero and invited to a public fête, where the sponsors hoped to hear a speech explaining Houston's annexation tactics. What they got was a surprise. Donelson was with him part of the time. "He declined the dinner," he wrote,

> but . . . he delivered a temperance speech yesterday evening, gratifying a large audience by an elocution and sentiment that would have commanded applause before the best critics. The truth is Houston is a reformed and improved man. Fortunately married to a lady of fine endowments, combining religion with an amiable simplicity of manners, natural goodness of heart with a romantic taste, he realizes . . . the fruits of a happy union.
>
> Chastised by deep affliction, and wonderfully preserved by Providence from the wreck which usually overtakes those who embark on a sea of wild adventure, Houston comes back to his native land with a renovated constitution, and a mind greatly enlarged. He seems determined to atone for the disappointment of his friends, when he exiled himself, and sought asylum in the hospitality of old King Folly. . . . There never was a man more popular than he is now with his countrymen. . . .
>
> He goes to the Hermitage to carry to its venerable tenant . . . the homage that is due to him.[62]

Considering that the author of this letter was one of the Jacksonian protégés whose tale bearing had sharpened the pain of that exile to King Folly, it might not be too much to observe that it was Donelson whose mind seems to have been enlarged by a better acquaintance with Houston. But Donelson was adroit in identifying the creator of this new and greater man. "You will find Mrs. Houston a most amiable, pious and cultivated lady," he wrote ahead to Jackson at the Hermitage. "When they arrive let Mrs. Donelson know it, to whom I have written requesting her to open her house to the General and suite. . . . My great wish is to see you again. May Heaven bless the wish, and save your life yet longer."[63]

What neither Donelson nor anyone else in Houston's party knew was that Andrew Jackson already lay dying. Houston was to address an annexation meeting one evening at the Arcade, when he was handed a letter by a Captain Hart, whose timing was managed by the letter's author, E. G. M. Butler: "My dear General, allow me to recall myself to your remembrance by informing you that I have just returned from a pilgrimage to the 'Hermitage' to take a final and sad leave of our dear old friend; and his parting inquiry of me, in regard to annexation, was, 'Edward, what will Houston do?' It is owing to my inability to answer that question that I now address you; and it can not be possible that a native of Virginia and a citizen of Tennessee can have so far forgotten what is due to himself and his country as to lend himself for an instant to the representatives of England and France."

That night there were various speeches at the Arcade advocating the joining of Texas to the United States; when Houston was called for, he said, "My friends, I have been accused of lending myself to England and France; but, I assure you, I have only been *coquetting* with them." It pained him, he said, "to weary your patience in listening to matters personal to myself," but he felt compelled to answer back to some of the worst of the newspaper editors who had been abusing him for the alleged sale of Texas and U.S. interests to Europe. "Will my fellow citizens forgive me for lowering myself sufficiently to notice these creatures?" The crowd roared its approval. Willard Richardson of the *Galveston News* he characterized as too mean to steal. "That is fortunate," he allowed, "for the inmates of the penitentiary are not likely to be disgraced . . . by being his associate." Francis Moore of the *Houston Telegraph* "is a one armed man. You never would forgive me for abusing a cripple, but I must confess that that one arm can write more malicious falsehoods than any man with two arms I ever saw. His one arm is more prolific for evil than the traditional bag that had seven cats and every cat had seven kits.

"These men," he admitted, "in retailing their slanders, are compelled to tell some truths. I did direct our minister at Washington to withdraw the application of Texas for annexation and commence paying court to England and France, for reasons that public policy has heretofore forbid an explanation." Now, however, he would explain it to them. Annexation, he said,

> did not meet with a respectful consideration. . . . To my great surprise, it met with a decided and insulting rebuff. . . . I admit that I have recommended that treaties of reciprocity be made with England, squinting even to the future extinction of slavery in Texas. When at the same time my only object was to turn public opinion in the United States in favor of annexation. I can justify myself by the suggestion of a very natural supposition.
>
> Supposing a charming lady has two suitors. One of them she is inclined to believe would make the better husband, but is a little slow to make interesting propositions. Do you think if she was a skillful practitioner in Cupid's court she would pretend that she loved the other "feller" the best and be sure that her favorite would know it? [Laughter and applause.]

Andrew Jackson and Sam Houston (both in 1845). Andrew Jackson had been in failing health for years as he fretted over the success of Texas annexation. He did not live to see it, but he did live to know it was a certainty. He is seen here propped up on pillows for a last pose. His death on June 8, 1845, occurred only hours before Houston's arrival with his wife and son. Ironically for a man who gave impetus to the idea of popular sovereignty, his administration also fostered the convention system that Houston found so revolting. Sam Houston was a man whose appearance altered dramatically with changes in dress and grooming. Seen here as the "Talleyrand of the Brazos" at the height of his powers, this photo was taken in Kentucky shortly after the funeral of his mentor and former president.

Jackson courtesy Library of Congress; Houston courtesy Center for American History, University of Texas

> If ladies are justified in making use of coquetry in securing their annexation to good and agreeable husbands, you must excuse me for making use of the same means to annex Texas to Uncle Sam. [Laughter and cheers.][64]

After New Orleans the Houstons hastened to Tennessee, the two-time former Texas president hoping against odds that they would be in time to receive Jackson's benediction. They were informed on the road just outside Nashville that Jackson was dead. Admitted to the death chamber, Houston held up his two-year-old son and told him to try to remember the man he once looked upon. He then laid his head on Jackson's chest and wept.

Old Hickory died in the confidence of annexation, but he did not live to see the fact, and the Europeans were far from ready to give up the game. Before Anson Jones heard of the joint resolution, the French and English chargés d'affaires persuaded him to give them a final ninety days to convince Santa Anna to acknowledge Texas independence, during which he would make no move toward the United States. The popular momentum to join the Union was now so overwhelming that when Jones agreed to the delay, he was threatened and burned in effigy. Elliot and Cramayel hastily organized a conference of "umpires" and returned with the dictator's promise— for what it was worth—that he would recognize an independent Texas on the condition that she never join with another country. Anson Jones played his final role well. By delaying the call of a convention to vote on annexation until July 4, he was able to lay before the people of Texas both documents, giving a clear choice: a treaty of peace and recognition by Mexico, or the joint resolution of the U.S. Congress making Texas part of the Union. Jones's motives were now so suspect that for his trouble the convention censured him and briefly considered deposing him. Instead, they contented themselves with rejecting the Mexican treaty—unanimously—and accepting the American resolution—with only one dissent. The members then quickly set to drafting a state constitution.

Donelson's messenger, a General Besancon, was admitted to the White House on the evening of July 27 to give President Polk the good news.

16

THE BARBARIAN SENATOR

Having wrought a heritage for his Texas, Sam Houston now evinced a curiosity about his own heritage. Late in November of 1845, he wrote his cousin William Houston Letcher of the Virginia branch of the family, seeking news of their ancestry. "There is one matter which I wish to learn something about, and you are the only person, who can satisfy me on the subject. It is our family. Aunt Gillespy often wished me to write down our genealogy, but I always neglected it, until her death. Now I know only my Grand Father Houston name, if it was Robert. . . . I am equally ignorant, of my Mother's stock, and can only trace back by the Mother to my maternal Grand Mother, (a Blair). You can let me know much, if you have not become lazy."

The latter sentence sounds more curt than it is, for the tone of the lengthy missive is amiable and jocular; it also contains a tongue-in-cheek assessment of the state of the five-year Houston marriage. "You have, I doubt not, heard that my wife controls me, and has reformed me, in many respects? This is pretty true, and I tell her, that I am willing that she should have the full benefit of my character, but it so happens, that she gets all the credit for my good actions, and I have to endure, all the censure of my bad ones. Thus you see that I am bankrupt, in all good reputation. Well, so long as a good name remains in the family, I will be satisfied."[1]

Margaret, unsurprisingly, was keen on encouraging her husband's domestic curiosity. Ever since they married, she had shared him with his country, endured countless separations, and taken a back seat to his endless preoccupation with Texas's affairs. She had taken the rank of first lady of Texas even while enduring the grinding poverty of depending on her mother to provide for them; perhaps now, she fancied, he was hers for a while, and family would come first. On the occasion of Anson Jones's inauguration—and more importantly, Houston's retirement—she presented him with a poem that voiced her hopes:

Dearest, the cloud has left thy brow
    The shade of thoughtfulness, of care.
And deep anxiety; and now
    The sunshine of content is there.

Thy task is done; another eye
    Than thine must guard thy country's weal;
And oh! may wisdom from on high
    To him the one true path reveal!

This task is done. The holy shade
    Of calm retirement waits thee now.
The lamp of hope relit hath shed
Its sweet refulgence o'er thy brow.

He found the poem on his desk.[2] Her meaning was clear, and indeed she had even more reason for encouragement. Knowing that Margaret's health suffered at Washington-on-the-Brazos and desiring more privacy than could be afforded by staying in the Lea family compounds at Grand Cane, Houston bought and began improving a plantation fourteen miles east of Huntsville. The terrain was elevated, scenic, and seemed healthful, and the augury was wonderful, for the tall trees were full of ravens that cocked their heads to eye him below. The place seemed a bit too lonely to Margaret, but, thrilled at the prospect of being neither a houseguest nor a tenant for the first time in Texas, she established her household at Raven Hill in 1845. But if Margaret truly believed that her husband's lot now could be that of gentleman farmer and father, bitter must have been her disappointment.

In a way, the death knell for such bucolic hopes had already begun to toll. U.S. president James K. Polk had long since written to his envoy to Texas, A. J. Donelson, that if Texas entered the Union, "Nothing could give me more pleasure personally, and nothing I am sure would give a vast majority of our people more pleasure, than to see my old friend Houston bring her constitution in his hand as one of our Senators, [and] take his seat in the Senate of the United States next winter. Surely he will not, cannot, hesitate. Make my kind respects to Houston and tell him that I hope to soon welcome the young republic of which he was the founder, into our confederacy of States, and to see him the representative of her sovereignty in our Senate."[3]

As required by the federal joint resolution, the article of annexation approved by the Texas convention in July, along with a state constitution, was submitted to a referendum of the people in October. It was hardly a contest. President Polk dispatched U.S. troops to Corpus Christi to keep Santa Anna from getting any ideas. Houston enjoyed his rather Elizabethan progress through the United States before returning home in October; Margaret stayed away an extra month to visit family in Alabama. For Christmas in Houston city, he was happier than perhaps he ever had been. He received a gift of "a fine Durham" and was fascinated with the prospect of crossing that breed with Texas's native wild cattle, hoping to blend the hardiness of the longhorns with the superior meat and milk of the blooded cattle. His intention now, he said, was "to carry out the object that first induced my location to this country—that of stockraising."[4]

It was not the only time that Houston's history changed complexion to suit his mood; his enemies, certainly, showed no awareness that his ambition had always been to be a cattleman. Outraged by the common assumption that Houston would take some high post in the new state government, they were training their sights to discredit him. The former president sighed in speeches and newspaper columns: yes, he had always favored annexation; no, he had never abandoned the Mier prisoners; and the like. His most hysterical detractor for the moment was Anthony Butler, Jackson's testy and bullying one-time minister to Mexico. In the stable of Jackson protégés, he was one of the less savory, and Houston had written of him a dozen years before, "Such men as he, would destroy a country, but take my word for it, he will never gain one!" Butler fired a scorching letter to him, threatening to expose to the world proof that he had long possessed that Jackson never had thought much of him. Houston's disposition was too sunny to take him seriously. "Noble Sir:" he replied on Christmas Day, 1845, "Your favor of the 15th inst. reached me quite opportunely. I am compelled to regard it as a gift of the season, although it is characterized by a warmth which only belongs to your generous nature." Houston then relied on his "awful" memory to produce a lighthearted résumé with dates and documents and witnesses of Butler's own shady career. "As to the object of your address to me, I cannot arrive at any conclusion. It may be that you wish to extort hush-money from me. If so, you had better rely—" at that point the surviving document is, tragically, torn, although the subsequent reference had something to do with demons. "Col. as I cannot suppose you to change your tone to pleasantry nor I my opinions of your character in any respect, I think you had better agree with me in one thing only, and that is to drop our correspondence [although] you write beautifully. . . . Wishing you may live a thousand years or at least until you become an honest man, or get in a better humor, or do some good thing and have it certified to, and put into the Newspapers, and the autograph left with the printer . . . Adieu, Colonel."[5]

The former president was in Austin on February 19, 1846, for the official transfer of authority. Anson Jones read a speech, intoning: "The final act in this great drama is now performed. The Republic of Texas is no more." He lowered the Lone Star tricolor from the flagpole into Sam Houston's waiting arms. The legislature had convened its initial meeting three days previous; there was a brief scramble to see who would support whom for U.S. Senate, and the first governor, Houston's former minister to Europe, J. Pinckney Henderson, was satisfied with the foregone conclusion that Houston would be one. The former president, ever demure when it came to claiming an office, couched his desire in terms of allowing his friends to run his name, and he would serve, if elected. When the votes were taken on the twenty-first, Houston and Thomas J. Rusk were the overwhelming choices.

Anson Jones had assumed that one of those Senate seats would be his, and the recently censured president's failure to receive even a single vote marked his passing from Texas affairs. He retired to Barrington, his estate near Washington-on-the-Brazos, where he became a wealthy planter and spent the next several years milling his papers and poison-pen diary into a combative anti-Houston memoir. The book's failure to interest a publisher, combined with personal disappointments, finally overtaxed his brittle mind. A few days short of his sixtieth birthday, he mounted the steps of the old capitol in Houston—since become a hotel—ranted briefly, and blew his brains out. Dr. Jones had played a pivotal role in the annexation of Texas to the United States, although not perhaps the splendid and indispensable role he had imagined for himself.

The prospect of a move to Washington, D.C., hit Margaret as a major calamity. She once entertained the hope that she would have Houston to herself as a gentleman farmer and Cincinnatus at Raven Hill. Losing him to the country again was bad enough, but to leave everything of life she had known for a hive of intrigue like the national capital filled her with a dread approaching terror. She made a little effort at packing but then seized upon her newly realized pregnancy to stay put. They parted on March 8, and Houston sailed from Galveston on the twelfth. For company at Raven Hill, Margaret had Eliza, who had served her since she was a girl, and Joshua, a very able slave whom she had also brought to the marriage, to run the farm, which was tended by a handful of others. Then there was Sam Junior to care for, as well as someone new in their household. Before removing to Texas, her brother Vernal had adopted a child, now eight years old, named Virginia Thorn; when Vernal was widowed, he asked his mother, Nancy Lea, to care for the girl, and then she passed to the Houstons. The new senator was cognizant of the example Jackson had given him of raising wards as though they were part of the family, but Houston was suspicious of Virginia; she was, in country parlance, "not right." Characterizing her at one time as "a fearful child," he warned Margaret again, "Beware of Virginia. There is no telling what the little *monster* may do!" Unwilling to go and not happy to be left behind, Margaret adopted a posture not uncommon in this situation: the martyr. "Alas, what has always been my decision when my own happiness or the good of the country was to be sacrificed? . . . I wish you to be governed entirely by your own judgment, and though the decision may bring misery upon me beyond description, I will try to bear it without a murmur."[6]

On Sunday evening, March 29, 1846, Houston paid a call on his old Tennessee friend James Knox Polk. It was a great distance—and not just in miles—from the log-pen dogtrots of Texas to the drawing rooms of the White House. Polk greeted him warmly, first because they were friends, second because Houston had announced his political affiliation as a Democrat whom Polk could rely on for support, and third because G. W. Terrell had written Polk a warning. Houston, he said, was disposed to return to the Democratic Party, "but I know him well and know that he will fly off sooner on . . . some personal insult . . . than any other in the world."[7] The new member was escorted to his seat in the Senate the following day; to preserve Senate regularity that only one-third of the body stood for re-election every other year, he and Rusk drew blindly from a box containing ballots marked two, four, and six years. Rusk drew a six-year term, Houston, two.

Senator Sam Houston. Seated with his walking stick, favorite white beaver hat, and Cherokee blanket surmounting his dress suit, this photo by Frede-ricks's New York studio shows the visage Houston presented at the time he entered the U.S. Senate. Houston was a frequent and popular speaker in New York, which formed the core of his support for the presidency in the late 1850s.

Courtesy Sam Houston Memorial Museum

In this chamber of gravely clad senators, Houston undertook his duties, his suit surmounted, often as not, by a great Cherokee blanket—a magnificent barbarian, one observer called him. One can almost see him arranging it, glaring with satisfac-tion at Calhoun, for joining Houston in the Senate, turning up again like a bad penny, was John C. Calhoun of South Carolina, whose distaste for native wear he had once made clear. Calhoun was as incendiary and focused as ever. During his tenure as secretary of state, his great interest in annexing Texas was the extension of Southern slaveholding territory, and with that goal accomplished, his home legislature returned him to the federal Senate to continue twirling the whetstone of states' rights and slavery. Houston felt otherwise quite at home, reunited with Henry Clay and Daniel Webster and Thomas Hart Benton.

The first issue of importance arose on April 15. President Polk desired the United States to withdraw from its condominium agreement with Great Britain in the Oregon Territory. Polk had run on the slogans of "Texas and Oregon" and "Fifty-four forty or fight," a reference to the northernmost latitude of Oregon to which many wanted to press American claims. As he promised Polk he would do, Houston rose from his chair to be recognized. Other senators stared in amazement; it was tradition that no freshman senator rise to speak on any subject. Not every freshman, however, was a former two-term president of an equal and once-independent republic or made chairman of the Military Affairs Committee upon his arrival. Houston wished to be understood, he said, as supporting the president's position. "If England designs to negotiate, the notice will not exclude her from that privilege. The way to negotiation is as open to her as it ever was. But . . . England has proposed arbitration—she has not talked of negotiation. Are we to wait on the nods and becks of England to determine our own policy?" If he ever saw the text of the speech, one can only imagine the reaction of Capt. Charles Elliot, who was once persuaded that Houston and Texas were England's friends. Nor could he have failed to recall Houston's suggestion three years previous how British influence in Texas helped England keep a grip on the Pacific Northwest. England perceived her vulnerability as well and averted war by agreeing to split the vastness of Oregon with the United States. A spectacular addition was made to the United States, which Houston had been one of the first to foresee, and which was one result of the annexation of Texas.

No blood was spilled to acquire Oregon, but Santa Anna had followed Texas events with growing feelings of rage and betrayal. Polk moved the army in Texas under Zachary Taylor south to the Rio Grande, the boundary agreed to in the somewhat coerced Treaty of Velasco, which had ended the Texas Revolution, although Mexico now claimed the Nueces River as the border. A Mexican army crossed the Rio Grande into the "Nueces Strip" and fought—and lost—two engagements. A week after Houston's speech on Oregon, the president-general of Mexico declared war on the United States. No one was surprised; it was the other great reason, apart from slavery, that the Whigs had used to oppose the acquisition of Texas. Polk asked for fifty thousand men and ten million dollars to prosecute the war, which Houston warmly espoused. Finally, power was at hand to carry a war deep into Mexico and, he hoped, impose some stability in the Southwest. Down in Texas, volunteers flocked to the standard. Ever one for internal improvements, Houston pointed out to the Senate, as a matter of defense policy, that by dredging a total of only thirty-three miles through coastal marshes, the United States could send ships via Texas's coastal lagoons from Louisiana all the way to Mexico, invulnerable from both storm and blockade. No action was taken on his idea, but even as Houston in 1827 anticipated the Tennessee Valley Authority by a century, he now anticipated the Intracoastal Waterway by a generation.

If Houston had desired a military commission to go fight in Mexico, a general's billet was his for the asking, and Margaret was sadly resigned to it. He repeated himself numerous times that he would not join the army if she did not freely consent, and this she did, although like any well-bred belle, she knew the art of consenting without consenting. Appeals to guilt had never restrained him from action before, but when Congress adjourned on August 10 and Houston hightailed it home, it was not for the Rio Grande with a sword in hand. It was for Raven Hill, just in time to greet a daughter, Nancy Elizabeth—the impish and irrepressible Nannie—who was born September 6 and named for Margaret's mother. Barely pausing to kiss the baby, he was off again for speeches and barbecues. Margaret's isolation at Raven Hill and her husband's long absences caused her to slip into a chronic depression, relieved only by attending church in Huntsville, where she often stayed the weekend as the guest of the minister's wife, Frances Creath. Margaret slowly came to terms with the fact that she was married to a figure of national importance and must either establish a residence in Washington, and thus make them both miserable, or resolve to maintain the Texas household as a hospitable refuge that Houston would want to return to as often as possible. She wisely chose the latter course.

Returning to the Senate for the session that commenced in January 1847, his performance wavered. He had differences with the administration and his relationship with Polk cooled, which the president, probably wrongly, attributed to Houston's failure to receive an invitation to join the army as a major general. It was the only explanation he could give for Houston's introduction of a bill to federalize state militias and have army officers elected by the ranks—a policy that had been nothing but disastrous in Houston's own experience. Also, it was possible that, while supporting Polk and the war against Mexico with his hawkish position, he was trying to increase the presence and prestige of Texans in the campaign. Houston was busy, receiving on the order of thirty letters a day asking his attention to some concern or another, and he tended the business of his constituents, but he was no longer the one making policy and no longer the center of the action. He was a senator and major celebrity, but he was discovering that the passage from president to senator was a step down. Houston had been a man of large deeds done in large causes, and an examination of his early career in the Senate shows his mind active and engaged, though to lesser purposes than he was accustomed to. Sifting through the political hubbub about him, he saw only one issue that weighed on the scale of great issues, and that was the deepening sectional hostility, brooded over by Southerners like Calhoun and exacerbated by abolitionists from the North. In the inflexibility of both camps he foresaw the breakup of the Union itself, the one calamity that he had believed, ever since he discussed the matter with Lafayette, must be avoided at any cost.

In her lonely eyrie at Raven Hill, Margaret's concerns were of smaller scale but no less moment. A cancer had been discovered in her breast, and in February of 1847 she endured Ashbel Smith's excision of the tumor. A teetotaler even in this exigency, she endured the operation unstupored by alcohol—the silver coin she bit during the procedure is still in the family. After the close of the spring session of 1848, the

Woodland House. Sam Houston loved the place he designed at Huntsville, which was always Margaret's domain. Surviving grounds plans reveal extensive flower beds, gardens, and orchards. Her creation of a bountiful, retreat was an important weapon in her campaign to keep her husband's ambitions in check. The couple later also purchased a much larger farm in Independence, seventy miles west, where Nancy Lea relocated her household.

Courtesy Sam Houston Memorial Museum

last of his term in office, Houston headed home to tend his plantation and take up his legal practice. Margaret's isolation at Raven Hill, made the more nerve wracking by her health, prompted him to find his family a place in town. Raven Hill's manager owned a tract in Huntsville a short drive south of the business district located in a broad vale with a spring and cabin. Characterizing it as a "bang-up place," the senator traded for it and began enlarging the cabin into a unique house. From the time he entered Texas to the time he died, Sam Houston occupied eleven different residences for a span of at least six months each. During one period, his expansive affairs required the maintenance of no fewer than four different seats for his household.[8] But apart from his summer retreat at Cedar Point, Woodland was the only one to which he developed any great attachment. In 1848 he moved his family from Raven Hill southwest to Huntsville, just across the Trinity River, into this house that he designed himself, for which reason, if for no other, it is worthy of examination.[9] Just as the airy but practical elegance of Monticello and the sobering self-assurance of the Hermitage came to reflect the spiritual visages of their creators, perhaps Sam Houston too left an abiding shadow in the clever modesty of Woodland.

In the early 1980s controversy raged—no other word serves—over restoration of the structure. Original records are lost and early photographs offer nothing dispositive of its first appearance. No one today knows whether the gracious outlines and neoclassical portico were part of Houston's conception or were a later addition. The tidy white clapboards, which Houston may have intended, were nailed at some unknown later date onto the hewn-log framework that was certainly Houston's creation. The debate over restoring the house mirrored the divergent perceptions of Houston that simmered for generations after his death. Those who see him as a Lincolnesque rustic in a Cherokee blanket argued that the clapboards should be removed and the house shown in its original log exterior. Those who view Houston as a clever patrician who knew how to "play the Indian" insisted that the neoclassical refinements remain. To strip them away, they said, would merely help Houston perpetuate his own cynical charade. None of this is particularly surprising, but that Sam Houston should still have such an effect today on otherwise reasonable and scholarly people is a meter of the charge his aura still carries. The "pro-rustics" won, as contractors removed the clapboards as well as much of the interior trim, piled the boards into windrows, and not to make too fine a point of it, burned them.[10]

Actually, if the white clapboards were indeed nailed over the logs at Houston's direction, the idea would not have been original with him. It was a technique not uncommon, and he had seen such a treatment himself when a guest at Holland Coffee's Glen Eden mansion in Grayson County, built three years before Woodland.[11] All that, however, is beside the point. With his beloved house, as with his politics and with his life, Houston's stamp lies not in the veneer but in the design: the house is fundamentally common but large for the genre and enhanced by turns of imagination that improve and clarify its functions. (Recalling Houston's 1837 New Year's poem for Anna Raguet, this assessment of his dabble in architecture is consonant with his dabble in poetry.) Woodland House is a dogtrot, dual log pens separated by an open breezeway. Because of its practicality, it was the most popular style in Texas at the time; such a house could begin as a single-room log cabin and then be expanded virtually room by room as one's family grew until, by the time it was finished out, it presented a front that was gracious but solid and well suited to the climate.[12] Stone or sawn lumber might also be used where they were plentiful, but most dog-trots began as log cabins.

Houston's own personality can be found in an upstairs breezeway he designed and his separate outbuilding law office—the former maimed and the latter destroyed in the later "restoration." (The ingenious breezeway was rendered useless when the portico was removed and replaced with a more rustic-looking eave porch.) He and Margaret christened the house "Woodland," an echo of the name once given to the house at Cedar Point during their first blissful summer together. But if she had an expectation that their separations were to end and that she would settle in as the wife of a busy town lawyer, she was disappointed. By Christmas 1847, the family learned that Sam Houston was going back to Washington, D.C., for a second term in the United States Senate. Margaret was resigned to delivering their third child, second daughter Margaret Lea Houston, without him on April 13, 1848.

Houston had been spoken of as presidential timber from the time he led Texas into the Union, but publicly he expressed his disinterest in the 1848 election and advised other senators to tend to business. He did chair the caucus that selected Baltimore as the site of the Democratic convention, and in his private correspondence he considered his chance at the presidential nomination as good as anyone else's; certainly, he did not write off any thought of the White House in future. "As it is," he wrote Margaret, "my name is used with good effect, and . . . and will insinuate itself among the people & there will settle down to a decided bias in my favor, and should I at some future day be brought before the nation, it can be done successfully. The feeling in all parts . . . is in favor of my name being used in 1851." Margaret was always nervous for his soul when he began speculating about more powerful office. "My dear Love," she wrote him on May 8, "I fear that you are suffering your mind to be drawn off from the subject of religion, by the political excitement of the day. . . . Oh, when I think of the allurements that surround you, I tremble, lest they should steal your heart from God." For the present, at least, she could console herself that he "had to refuse the Vice Presidency most positively."[13]

That Houston was bored with Senate routine was revealed in his participation in the debate on the Oregon bill, at one point during which he rose and said, "I propose, with the view of bringing this unprofitable, if not injurious discussion to a termination to offer the following amendment." This bill was one that did get his attention, however, because Calhoun and the other Southerners were using it to whip up the slavery issue. Ultimately, Houston supported the admission of Oregon as a free territory; Thomas Hart Benton voted with him, and the bill carried, leaving Calhoun to seethe that the South had been beaten by Southerners. Houston was quite clear, however, in his reasons for supporting the bill: "I have no idea that slavery will ever be extended to that portion of the United States; nor do I have any idea that any person from the South . . . would desire to emigrate with his slaves to a region as inclement as that is, and incompatible as it is with [slave] labor." To impose the question of slavery on the admission of a territory in which slave labor would never make sense anyway, he said, was silly. "I would be the last man to wish to do anything to prejudice the interests of the South, but I do not think that on all occasions we are justified in agitating this mooted question." Commenting on Calhoun's tantrum, he said evenly, "I am not one of those who feel disposed to croak, and who feel alarmed whenever this question is alluded to, believing that a crime is at hand, and that the Union is about to be dissolved." He knew even as he said it that he was whistling through a graveyard.

And he had to do it again ten weeks later, when Calhoun and his allies raised their usual threat of nullification and, if that failed, even secession over the Oregon issue. Houston rose and recalled that the first time nullification was threatened was during his residence at Wigwam Neosho. The cry, quoted the *Congressional Globe*, "reached him in the wilderness . . . but it rung in his ears, and wounded his heart. But now he was in the midst of such a cry, and he was bound to act as a man conscious of [his] solemn responsibilities." Again Houston fought down Calhoun. "It could not be the interest of the North to destroy the South. . . . And he thought the South—and he was a southern man—should make some sacrifice for the purpose of reconciliation with the North. . . . He protested against the cries of disunion, and against every attempt to traduce the Union. He was of the South, and he was ready to defend the South . . . , [but] the Union was his guiding star, and he would advise his friends of the South and of the North to pursue measures of reconciliation. . . . He regretted that the Senator from South Carolina had used any menacing language against the Union."

Calhoun denied that his tone was menacing, but still the South should have a convention and decide what to do. Houston was unruffled. He had seen Southern conventions before, he said, and "he had seen a much more respectable convention of buffaloes."[14] Such exchanges were his daily fare in the Senate, and his vigorous and frequent defense of the Union increased talk picturing Sam Houston as president of the United States. On the evening of February 7, 1849, the Polks gave one of their last receptions in the White House, which Houston attended. The president escorted the grand dame of Washington society, the eighty-one-year-old Dolley Madison. "I made some display," Houston wrote Margaret the next day, "by asking Mrs. President Polk to take my arm, and we walked around the 'East Room.' . . . I only regretted, that you were not upon my arm, in lieu of Madam. I would rather have you there, if we were private folks, than any one on earth. . . . There are a vast crowd of people there, and . . . I suppose that not less than one hundred persons of both sexes, spoke to me on the subject of bringing you to the White House, & living there! It may be so!!"

If there were any single subject upon which Sam Houston could have written his wife and made her blood freeze, he had just done it. Margaret did not fear society. Everything in her history shows that, when she was not in maternal confinement (which was often) and was otherwise well, she was a gracious and easy hostess. She did live, however, in mortal dread of society's corruption. Her entire credibility with her husband lay in her devotion to religion and family while living in hope of the hereafter. Margaret was a woman of great intuition, and she had already begun to fear that power was turning his head. She had hinted to him on this subject many times, but now she had not even received his letter when she felt it necessary to declare herself clearly on the subject: "My dear love, I cannot enter into the schemes of wordly greatness, which your friends are planning for you. Should the Lord have work for you to do, I know he will direct you, but the praise of man is an empty thing, and one year of domestic quiet is worth all the laurels of earthly heroes fame." That was all she said about it before turning to farm and family; she had hit him with the stick and now held out the carrot: "Our crop will be planted late, owing to the quantity of rain that has fallen. The tobacco arrived from New Orleans today, and Mr. Gott seems quite delighted. . . . Sis tells me that her boy is said to be singularly like yourself. Well I am willing that all the handsome children should be like you. . . . If the Lord in his mercy should unite us again on earth, I believe there are happy days for us."[15] Their letters crossed in the mail.

Margaret Lea Houston's genius was that she cared for her husband's soul more than she cared for his fame, and she knew that unless someone undertook that

Pres. James K. Polk; Dolley Madison; the White House (all c. 1840s). With Texas safely annexed to the United States, President Polk gave his last reception in the White House in February of 1849, at which he, Dolley Madison, Sam Houston, and Sarah Polk comprised a foursome. Both Polk and the eighty-one-year-old widow of founding father James Madison died soon after.

All courtesy Library of Congress

responsibility, he would end as the emotional derelict she first met, great man though he may have been. Intuitively, she knew that she could not keep that hold over him if she went to Washington to soiree and entertain, and be no better than the women he knew there. Senator Houston's presence in Washington society was measured, genial, and—from Margaret's tutelage—sober. He did attract the notice of women, who approached him for the best of causes: "Respected Sir," wrote Mrs.

John L. Norton of New York, "It may surprise you to receive a letter from a stranger. . . . But why cannot those who are strangers today be friends tomorrow—American Union No. 10 Daughters of Temperance are making arrangements to hold a public meeting at the Broadway Tabernacle as soon as practicable & they have instructed me to request you to be present on the occasion & deliver for them and a New York audience a Temperance address. . . . Ex-Mayor Harper will preside." Not even Margaret could object to that.[16]

John C. Calhoun, at age sixty-eight, entered his final illness late in 1849, and Washington slowed in the deathwatch. Poised to assume leadership of the Southern cause was Jefferson Davis of Mississippi, while Calhoun's loud and perennial vindication of South Carolina herself was taken up by James Gadsden. Once an aide-de-camp to Andrew Jackson, Gadsden followed Calhoun in deserting Old Hickory over the nullification issue, an act that Houston considered unforgivable. In his position as a member of South Carolina's Democratic party executive committee, Gadsden attacked Houston's Senate performance as inimical to Southern interests; Houston answered him in a letter that was widely published and remarkable less for its hot and insulting tone—although it was, especially in recounting the history of Calhoun and nullification—than for the clarity with which Houston expressed his opinion that the growing sectional acrimony was the fault neither of the North entirely nor the South entirely. The fault lay with the unreasoning extremists of both camps. The safety of all Americans' rights depended "upon the inviolability of the Union. . . . And whatever is calculated to weaken or impair the strength of that Union,—whether originating at the North or the South,—whether arising from the incendiary violence of abolitionists, or from the coalition of nullifiers, will never meet with my unqualified approval. . . . In my humble judgment, the course pursued by Mr. Calhoun, and the *Abolitionists*, tend to the same end. So far they are co-workers." Calhoun's hysteria that a rabid North was arrayed in monolithic hostility against the South was, said Houston, "conjured up by [his] distempered fancy. . . . None in the North, excepting a comparatively small class of agitators . . . ever speak of interfering with slavery," and the nullifiers in their ravings were hastening a crisis "more rapidly and certainly than all the abolitionists of the North, that ever raved in the impotence of their fanaticism." Sam Houston's attempt to strike a balance of reason and compromise within the framework of the constitution was a theme he repeated with ever-growing urgency for the rest of his life, but it was already hard to hear him in the extremists' clamor to fight it out.[17]

In the opening session of 1850, one other voice of reason rose above the din. Henry Clay of Kentucky, a one-time enemy of Jackson's but who over twenty-five years' acquaintance earned Houston's respect, submitted an omnibus compromise by which slavery would be prohibited in the District of Columbia, and California admitted as a free state, but, in exchange, federal interference in interstate slave trade would be barred and fugitive slaves who reached the North were to be returned to their owners. Texas also gained by the measure; abolitionist army officers had intervened to prevent Texas from organizing Santa Fe as a Texas county, and the annexation marriage was threatened by this serious quarrel. Clay's bill reduced Texas's territory by a couple of hundred thousand square miles but in exchange for ten million dollars to settle the former republic's remaining national debt. Territories created from the remainder of the American western lands were to be organized without reference to slavery. It was statecraft of shattering brilliance.

In opposition to Pres. Zachary Taylor and the Southern radicals, Houston took the floor to support Clay. His passionate advocacy of the Compromise of 1850 and the indivisibility of the Union filled twenty-five typeset pages, which he had printed in advance as pamphlets and widely distributed. This was his chance to be heard nationally on the one subject that he considered of overarching importance. He admitted that he was not himself as religious as he ought to be. "I cannot offer the prayers of the righteous that my petition might be heard. But I beseech those whose piety will permit them reverently to petition, that they will pray for this Union, and ask that He who buildeth up and pulleth down nations will, in mercy, preserve and unite us. For a nation divided against itself cannot stand." The applause was deafening. (Across the capitol in the House, there had been a change in the delegation from Illinois. A disappointed Whig, an outgoing one-term congressman named Abraham Lincoln, was so disgusted with events that he had not even sought reelection. But one of Houston's pamphlets must have found its way to him.)

"I wish, if this Union must be dissolved," Houston concluded, "that its ruins may be the monument of my grave, and the graves of my family. I wish no epitaph to be written to tell that I survived the ruin of this glorious Union."

The senator from Texas was lionized, but he was nowhere to be found, and invaluable political capital was sacrificed as Houston raced home to deal with a domestic crisis. His and Margaret's troubled ward, Virginia Thorn, had run off with Woodland's overseer, Thomas Gott, who managed to get himself appointed as her legal guardian. As if this was not scandalous enough for a girl of fourteen, she filed suit against Margaret for assault and battery—to which it was strongly believed she was advised by Houston's proliferating enemies at home. For Margaret's defense, Houston settled on Henderson King Yoakum, who was not just a lawyer but a historian and writer as well. The two were warm friends, and they both consented to serve on the board of Huntsville's Austin College when it was chartered in 1849.[18] During this sojourn, Houston at least had the opportunity to gauge the reaction of his constituents to his "nation divided" performance and discovered that his support had eroded only to the extent that growing Southern extremism had managed to win a few converts. His loudest critic at home was the state representative from Marshall, Louis Wigfall, whom Houston quickly sized up as a spiritual heir of David Burnet and who believed that the world revolved around cotton, slavery, and dueling. The governor, J. P. Henderson, had joined the "anti-Houstons," but only to hedge his bets on the outcome of the growing controversy over Texas's boundaries. Ashbel Smith had his ear to the ground on Houston's behalf and was able to report: "Everything is going on well here—the people will not respond to the course suggested by Gov. Henderson and Mr. Wigfall in their published letters. I have received several letters from the North and West, in which your course is highly lauded and approved."[19]

There was also evidence nationally that Clay and his moderation were having an effect. One of Calhoun's last projects was the assemblage of a convention of Southern fire-eaters in Nashville to articulate their demands and, if they were met, to advocate Southern secession from the Union. After Calhoun's death and the likely passage of Clay's compromise, this Nashville Convention misfired. It did convene, but only nine states sent delegates. Henderson was the only participant from Texas, and he was only interested in rounding up support for Texas on the boundary question.

On his way back to Washington later in the spring of 1850, Houston stopped in Knoxville to visit his sister, Mary Houston Wallace, known to the family as "Polly." He had worried over her mental instability for many years. In 1829 her doctors had suggested that H. Haralson not deliver Houston's letter from exile to her; in 1848 he asked his trusted Ashbel Smith, whose medical studies had included lunacy and who was then traveling in the East, "to go by East Tennessee, and to stay as long, as needful, or as you can, if thereby, my poor sister can be relieved." This visit during 1850 was an interview of deep pain for Houston, as the once-beautiful Polly had lost her mind and been once confined to an asylum, and the stricken Houston had to concur that she had become a "confirmed lunatic." In earlier years, Polly had married Matthew Wallace and on being widowed wed his brother, Gen. William Wallace. Marquis James believed her insanity was the result of a "tragic marriage," but Houston blamed not Wallace but the combined effects of the "change of life," a brain abscess, and worst of all his own youngest sister Eliza, who he believed had driven Polly mad with recriminations over her remarriage and recruitment of other family members against her.[20] It was a family horror and schism that caused Houston wretched grief. He did not write Margaret of the visit until he reached Blountville on the Virginia border a hundred miles away. "As I intended, I visited my poor afflicted Sister. She knew me, and was very glad to see me. She embraced me just as she had always done. For hours in general conversation, she was as rational, and her style, and language, as good as ever. You would suppose that it could not be possible, that she was insane." Polly fluctuated from the most genuine awareness to morbid vapidity. "She has not been confined in a long time," Houston wrote, "and sits in the parlour, but has a dislike to sit on a chair. She desires to sit on the floor. They have great trouble to keep shoes, & stockings on her, and she will not wear any thing on her head. The day that I spent there, she wore her clothes without trouble, and consented to go, and sit at table, but we could not prevail upon her to eat." Nevertheless, during the visit she continually recalled events from their childhood, like Sam's once stealing cream from the spring house on their farm, and otherwise "seemed disposed to plague me! in kindness. She never smiles, but looked pleasant, but never cheerful!"

What affected Houston most deeply was the fact that Polly, in the tangle of her mind, knew how brutally her sisters had acted toward her and forgave them. "She is even yet charitable to Eliza, & Isabella. She speaks of Phebe Jane and Mary with great affection. . . . She never uses any expression, in company that is misproper, but is perfectly delicate, in every thing. These facts will gratify you," he continued to Margaret, "tho' the subject is the most melancholy, that I have ever contemplated. The deep reverses of my own past life, never, so much called into action my sympathies . . . as that of my poor Sisters afflictions. . . . She is now a wreck of a noble mind, and the most foully & cruelly slandered female, on earth, in my opinion. I further, my Love believe, that she was a converted christian. To this I will add my most fervent prayers, that God when he calls her home, may restore her, to reason."[21]

With such enervating Houston family matters on his mind during the Tennessee traverses of his senatorial years, there are almost no references to his ever inquiring after his first wife. Once, however, in Nashville, while guesting with his old friend John Shelby, he was besieged as usual by callers. Among them was Judge Josephus Guild, once a friend, and then one of the "committee of gentlemen" formed to restore Eliza's reputation. "I did not know how he would now receive me," Guild wrote, but "extending my hand as I approached him, he rose and greeted me in the most cordial manner, and expressed much concern as to my welfare. We spent an hour chatting about men and events of the 'long time ago.' At one time during the interview, when not interrupted by visitors, he took me cordially by the hand and said, 'Guild, you did a noble thing in vindicating the character of Eliza.' . . . It was too delicate for me to press the interview further." After so many years, he still did not blame Eliza Allen, only the family that forced her into a loveless marriage.[22]

After he arrived in Washington in the spring of 1850, Houston learned of his sister's sudden death—not Polly but, to his amazement, Eliza. In his letter to Margaret, he numbly repeated the same word: "I could not at first realize the news of Sister Eliza's death. The shock I could feel, but all the reality I do not yet realize." And the worst blow was that Eliza had perished without restoring peace in the family. "These visitations are admonitions, which we ought not to disregard, and I will try and be ready for the summons which none can avoid."[23]

But grief was followed by joy. The calendar of Houston's shuttle between Texas and Washington was such that, while he was home long enough to father a child, he was almost never around to welcome one into the world. The same letter relaying the news of Eliza's death also acknowledged his satisfaction at the birth of a third girl, Mary Willie, on April 9. "Well, I am happy to hear that it was a little daughter, tho' I would have been equally gratified if it had been a son. Poor Sam, he will feel the apparent injustice, I fear, and think he is not treated with . . . fairness! But he is magnanimous." Sam Senior had once promised Sam Junior six little brothers, but it did not appear he was making good headway. Rather, "it appears something like the 'six little sisters.'"[24]

As it did after every visit home, the straitjacket of Washington business soon enveloped him, the more urgent now for the growing sectional clamor. "The difficulties connected with the slavery question," wrote a solicitous editor of the Harrisburg, Pennsylvania, *Keystone*, "occasion much anxiety in this quarter, and it is to such as you we are looking for their amicable adjustment. Our people value the Union above all . . . and would make any sacrifice for its preservation. Nothing with us, can weigh in the balance against it. . . . May God give you at Washington, who have the authority, wisdom to avert the danger which hangs over us." It was a letter after Houston's own heart, and Harrisburg became a regular stop on his lecturing trotline.[25]

Throughout the summer, he supported Clay ardently and blasted Zachary Taylor repeatedly on the Texas boundary issue, while from July through September the different parts of the Compromise of 1850 became law. Washington moderates were jubilant when the whole package was enacted in September. Houston found himself gaining in national stature and did not hesitate to use his far-flung extended family as his eyes and ears and to give him opportunities to disseminate his views. His cousin Narcissa Hamilton of Virginia, whose schoolgirl autograph book he had graced years before with the poem about his bark being tossed, sent him some remarks she thought he should see, mixing politics with a renewal of affection from that branch of his family he did not get to see very often: "The enclosed communication is a reply or whatever you may call it, to a most unwanton assault upon you, in [ex-Governor McDaniel's] Richmond speech. . . . Could you steal any possible chance, slip away from the City and spend a few hours with us." At the opening of 1851, Senator Houston received an inquiry from a young congressman-elect from Virginia, John Letcher, who just happened to be his cousin. Elements in Virginia were considering a proposal from South Carolina to host a convention of other Southern states with a view to organizing a national convention to amend the constitution to strengthen the South's, and slavery's, position. Letcher solicited Houston's views on the subject, and the senator responded at length. He said enough harsh things about the abolitionists to mollify Southern opinion, but that movement seemed to be waning and was "fast falling into the exclusive hands of the thread bare white fanatics like Garrison . . . and those of the negroes who belong to the Fred Douglass order of runaway patriots." For Virginia to host a convention of Southern states just now "could secure no good end, but to protract agitation, and furnish a sort of safety-valve for the over-charged patriots of South Carolina and Mississippi to let off their *extra gas.*—This can just as well be done in town meetings . . . , Fourth of July orations, and on other suitable occasions for these pyrotechnic displays."

It was a pity Calhoun was no longer alive to hear Houston light off on South Carolina, which had "coquetted with Mississippi, and produced that unlucky nondescript, the Nashville Convention. She courted Georgia, and offered the lead in the great enterprise to her, but that noble state contemptuously rejected it. She is now coaxing the Old Dominion to join her mad scheme. . . . I believe she will spurn it with disdain. . . . Surely Virginia will not confess that her star is on the wane and that of the Palmetto State in the ascendant. Virginia is, as she has ever been, her own mistress, and can say to South Carolina, 'Be still! We want no family jars.'

"We are admonished by the highest wisdom," Houston concluded, that "sufficient unto the day is the evil thereof. Let us give up to croakers and prophets of ill the task of trampling on the constitution. . . . The employment is congenial to their feelings, and affords them the only chance they have to attract public attention." Houston's letter soon found publication.[26]

Such political probity, however, and his dark contemplation of looming disaster and how to stem it were for the newspapers, the Senate chamber, and his political intimates. For his public image Houston shrewdly decided to show a lighter countenance. Only four days after the Letcher letter, Houston embarked on speaking tours, and while visiting all the right cities and all the right people, he made certain that all of his appearances were charitable, not political. For now it was necessary that people like him and turn out to hear him; the bitter pills he could feed them after they were accustomed to flocking to his table. On January 28 he delighted a crowd at the Musical Fund Hall in Philadelphia, playing the extemporaneous raconteur in a lecture, "Trials and Dangers of Frontier Life," that was a fundraiser to rebuild the Southwark Church. He opened with a factually flexible history of Texas and then fought the revolution and San Jacinto again, referring to himself in his wonted third person as the commander in chief. The effect was one of modesty, but it was surely no bad thing to get people thinking again of "Sam Houston" and "commander in chief" in the same breath—while not, of course, giving a political speech.

He allowed that he was aware that some persons in the United States had opposed annexation on the grounds that Texas was populated by ruffians of the worst element. "I know very well that Texas had a very bad reputation," he wagged. "If a man lived in the United States, and perpetrated a mean outrageous act, cut his stick, and took his kit on his shoulder, and it was asked, 'Where has he gone?' the answer was, 'Sloped for Texas.' They located all the rascals in Texas; didn't send any of them to Arkansas. . . . But I will wager you have never taken into consideration . . . that Texas is indebted for all the vagabonds, rascals, and scoundrels she has got, to the old States of the Union. Did you ever think of that before?"

There was no improvement for such men in frontier Texas, he claimed, because Mexican tyranny had suppressed preaching of the gospel, a topic from which he segued into a homily on Texas's ongoing spiritual elevation. Noting the number of ladies in the hall, he took the opportunity to crow that Texas took a back seat to no other in advancing the legal standing of women: "I will tell you what it is. Texas was the very first State that took up the great subject of homestead possession to the ladies. Our laws are that, if a lady marries, her husband has no control, without her consent, over her estate; he cannot dispose of any portion of it, nor can it be taken for the satisfaction of his debts, incurred either before or after marriage. She is entitled to half that is produced during the time of their marriage; and if he dies owning the whole estate, and she owns nothing, she has her homestead, and improvements, and farms, protected to the amount of two hundred acres, or two thousand dollars, that cannot be attached. Now, if you can beat that, I will give up." Houston's bantering Philadelphia lecture was not without its purpose, as he concluded that while Texas was America's youngest and most liberal daughter, her experience was seasoned by nearly ten years of independent nationhood. If the United States found herself in difficulty, as she clearly did, Texas may be looked to first for loyalty and sympathy and leadership—he did not have to get more specific than that. The crowd loved it.[27]

During the last week in February he was off again, this time to York and Harrisburg in Pennsylvania. In the state capital he spoke at a fundraiser for a ladies' group seeking to buy a parsonage for their church—and was only coincidentally given a hero's welcome by the Pennsylvania legislature, where he addressed the state House of Representatives. "I need not tell you, that they were pleased," he wrote Margaret, "and to that effect, I sent you a paper today. I have not seen the local Paper, but suppose they puffed me." His effort for the parsonage did raise three hundred dollars.[28] Then it was on to New York to give a temperance speech—and was only coincidentally made a member of the Tammany Society and was fêted by the political elite of America's largest city.

To listen to Sam Houston's speeches in the opening weeks of 1851, one would think that the presidency was the last thing on his mind. Not much, it was not. "The city authorities have tendered me the hospitalities of the city," he wrote Henderson Yoakum, the family trusty who was representing Margaret in the Virginia Thorn business, "and old Tamany has elected me a member of the Tamany Society. You need not, my Dear Friend, suppose that I will play the Simpleton in the midst of all these demonstrations." One of the meetings he made certain to arrange in New York was with Texas veteran Robert Wilson, who seemed to have a strong interest in Houston's elevation to the White House. And when he was back in Washington, Houston spent time huddling with his Boswell, C. Edwards Lester, on the production of an autobiography that would better acquaint the public with his life and passion.[29]

Houston reported to Margaret of the New York visit that it had poured rain for three hours that evening before his speech, and when he entered, he had expected to see the large hall mostly empty, but "to my astonishment, I found the most brilliant audience, that I had ever seen. . . . So soon as I was seen, the applause began, and continued, for many seconds." He spoke for an hour and a half. "When I was done, the applause was renewed, and when that ceased, three hearty cheers were given. The handkerchiefs of the Ladies, were flourished with great spirit." Houston was particularly pleased that the crowd was said to be as large as the one that greeted Jenny Lind. "When the meeting was over, two carriages were in waiting to take me to Balls . . . , [each Room] contained six to eight hundred persons! I was introduced to both assemblies by the Presidents of the respective associations. At each Ball, as I entered the Band played 'Hail to the Chief.'"

"Well my Love," he finally concluded, "I declare to you, that all this display, and all the manifestations of approval, or admiration, did not afford me as much pleasure, and joy, & felicity, as to press you to my heart. . . . So you need not for a moment suppose that any thing on earth can seduce my affections from home." It was a rather puny afterthought, and Margaret doubtless drew little comfort from it.

With the close of the session imminent, Houston was anxious to get home, not just to see the family but also because the Virginia Thorn trial was expected to start at any time, and Margaret was a nervous wreck. His last couple of letters to her before departing Washington were full of happy chatter about having to stop by the milliner and pay for the dresses and bonnets he was bringing home. "If I stay another day, I think I will get another dress for you! I wish by all means, not only to see you smile, but to keep you smiling." Still, his mind was not entirely on home: "There would not be one single State of the whole *South*, but S. Carolina, that would not go for me, if I am the Democratic nominee. They could not go against me. If they do, it would be an unaccountable freak, indeed!"[30]

Virginia Thorn's complaint against Margaret resulted in a mistrial, and if Houston's enemies won a battle by dragging his wife through court, his friends won the war: the records of the First Baptist Church, which Margaret considered of greater importance, were cleansed of any mention of the affair; the church minutes of the period now appear recopied in a single hand.[31] The Walker County Courthouse is similarly missing a transcript of the legal proceedings, although the event itself was recorded. The only surviving account of the trial seems to be that in Henderson Yoakum's diary.[32] Still, the ordeal seemed to sharpen the dread that Margaret had felt for a couple of years, the dread of a public life, the dread that the prospects of further fame and power would indeed seduce her husband from the righteous path. In February of 1849 Margaret had vowed never to take part in her husband's public life in Washington, but after two years of enduring his long absences and sensing her hold over him slip, she wavered in this resolve. Once again, her intuition prompted her to act in advance of the situation becoming unmanageable. On February 8, just as he was confirming appointments for his New York visit, she wrote him a hint that if they could procure lodging in "a pleasant boarding house for us about 8 or 10 miles from the city" where their family could maintain some semblance of privacy, she might be induced to bring the children to the capital.[33] By April 2 the senator was back home, however. The passage of a long summer together deepened their Texas contentment, and the subject of removing to Washington seems not to have surfaced again. What Sam Houston might have gained by Margaret's presence in Washington, both in social capital and in campaign time not lost in endless treks home, we can never know.

But his presidential prospects did follow him home to Huntsville. One of the first letters he received on this sojourn was from Nicholas Dean, one of the sponsors of his New York visit, whose warmth had expressed itself in the dark days of Wigwam Neosho. He and Houston had been friends for thirty-five years, and now Dean made certain of Margaret's friendship as well by dispatching a nurse named Isabella to help with the children. "She is the person, that we needed," Houston thanked him, "and you may feel assured, that Mrs. Houston is happy to acknowledge herself under a thousand obligations to her husband's long tried & highly valued friend, Mr. Nicholas Dean of the Empire City." After such salutations he got down to business: "You wish to know, how you can serve. Well, really you know best, [but] if you wish to open a correspondence with gentlemen in Texas, I would name Hon. H. Stuart of Galveston, and Col. H. Yoakum of this place as two gentlemen quite suitable. Also, Col. Ebenezer Allen of Galveston."

They were men who could be trusted to organize the Texas end of a bid for a presidential nomination. Margaret had him back on her turf now, though, and she made certain that this visit was blissful. "My friend, I assure you," he admitted to Dean, "when I am at home, in my woodland residence, with my wife and brats, I feel no disposition to return to scenes of official conflict. . . . I am farming in a small way, and am busy as a 'bee in a tar barrel,' planting peas, corn, rice and millet —all in a small way! I love milk & butter and they are fine for children, so I wish to have what will produce them in winter."[34] In this instance Houston was not being coy. Margaret was able to work on him all summer, by the end of which his biographer Lester was chastising him, "the nomination will be between you and Douglas. . . . it is necessary for you to shew yourself throughout the United States, in order that you may come personally into intercourse with some hundreds of thousands. . . . Your friends are all anxious for you to travel through the country and they wonder why you do not do it. . . . they seem to think you are more insensible on the subject than they themselves."[35] And then thrown into the balance, letters arrived in September, informing him that Houston clubs had been formed in Hartford, Connecticut, and in Thomaston, Maine.

One incentive not to tour the nation was that Houston was feeling his age, having just turned fifty-eight. In a month of farming in that "small way," he wrote cousin Jack, "I have injured the old wound in my right shoulder. So much so, that I can only write with difficulty. I must take a rest, I find, from necessity, or I may make myself a cripple!"[36] That was in May; by October Margaret found her challenge renewed. "Jack!" Houston wrote his cousin, "if I live, this winter, I will make 'old Tammany' ring!! . . . because I am to go there . . . and accept my election as a member of the *order*! Foote, Douglas and others have had their day and mine is to come!"[37] As good as his word, Houston was in New York at the end of the year and absent from the birth of their fourth daughter, Antoinette Power Houston—Nettie—on January 20, 1852.

Houston's currying favor in the North led him to expand his trotline of lectures to embrace Ohio as well as New York and Pennsylvania, but his presidential chances fell prey to events that were moving beyond him. Abolitionists were ascendant in the North, sectional radicals were gaining again in the South, and the management of the political conventions, which he historically regarded with suspicion, were passing under factional control. Thus, while Rusk recognized his ambition ("It will nearly kill him if he fails," he wrote)[38] and while Texas democrats passed a resolution recommending him to the notice of the national party, Houston saw cracks in his Texas standing. David Burnet and Mirabeau Lamar still railed periodically about his bloated mass of iniquity, and the influential J. P. Henderson had now defected and gone over to the radicals. Nationally, shrewd party operative Andrew Johnson of Tennessee conceded that "all agree that if [Houston] could receive the nomination . . . he could be elected by a greater majority than any other person now spoken of." New England senator Charles Sumner would have gone over to him in a minute: "With him the anti-slavery interest would stand better than with any man who seems now among the possibilities. He is really against slavery, and has no prejudice against Free Soilers. In other respects he is candid, liberal, and honorable. I have been astonished to find myself so much to his inclining." The convention, which was again in Baltimore, was so badly fractured that on the first

C. Edwards Lester. Houston chose C. Edwards Lester to write his "authentic memoir" and assisted in the effort, knowing the book could be helpful in the public exposure necessary to gain a presidential nomination. As the last Jacksonian exponent of popular sovereignty, however, Houston's ardor for the presidency cooled once he realized he could not obtain it without the party dealing that had become part of the political landscape. It was a stance that flummoxed and frustrated his young Boswell, who was of the new generation that took such management for granted.

Courtesy Library of Congress

ballot no one was even close to a majority; Lewis Cass and James Buchanan were the frontrunners, but each had opposition so solid the proceedings became deadlocked. Houston drew only eight votes on the first ballot and threw his support to a dark horse, Franklin Pierce, who won the nomination and later that year, with help from Houston's campaigning, the election.[39]

By his next visit to Huntsville, the senator discovered more incentives to stay closer to home. One was that he discovered that his son and heir could use some masculine rearing. Sam Junior was nearly nine; Houston was proud of his preco-cious intelligence but had mixed emotions about the fact that Margaret had him composing poetry—simple couplets like "Texas is my native home / Where I love to live and roam." Houston forwarded this to Wash Miller in an undated note marked "Private" under the title of *Sam's Impromptu*! along with "Another to his new sister Antoinette Power: 'The first violet of the year / I give, to my little sister dear.' . . . I send you these to amuse you," he joked to Miller, "for you know, I have great contempt, for second rate Parts, and I would not wish Sam to be a second Byron. Jno. Quincy Adams, & M. B. Lamar, you know wrote Poetry. Think of that! A son, any thing but a Poet, or a Fidler, or a song singer." If Margaret was campaigning to get her husband to spend more time at home raising his son, she found a light but effective goad.[40]

One thing that did reassure Margaret of her husband's life in Washington was that he had found a friend and spiritual advisor of the first quality. During his first summer in the city, he had attended services at the Baptist church on E Street. "To day I went to hear a Baptist preacher, (the Revd Mr Sampson.) He is a young man, but one of the most able divines, that I have any where heard. . . . [He] gave us a rich feast on the spiritual and practical duties of the followers of the Lord Jesus Christ. I have never heard any thing superior—extempore, or written. That he is a pious man, I have no doubt. It is my determination, while we are detained here, to attend his church, as often, as he preaches." The impressive cleric was George W. Samson, and over time the senator and the pastor developed a trusting friendship. Accord-ing to Samson, he was even moved to inquire of Houston the circumstances of separating from his first wife, a question that from many others for many years had prompted vehement refusals. The senator relented and told Samson that he judged from Eliza's behavior before and during the wedding that all was not well with her, "which convinced him," Samson wrote later, that "some secret had not been revealed. Before retiring, he frankly told her of his suspicion, asked a frank confession and pledged her that he should work her no injury. His frankness and firmness led to the confession that her affections had been pledged to another . . . and that filial duty had prompted her acceptance of his offer."

Historians have split over the credibility of this account. Marquis James accepted its salient points in *The Raven*; others have doubted that Houston would have broken such a habitual and manic silence.[41] Such an exchange probably did take place. In Margaret's absence, Houston had placed his spiritual contests into Reverend Samson's care, and since 1846 their friendship had become robust and mutual. A pastor's geniality notwithstanding, this was an era in which Baptist churches could make very particular inquiries into one's private life before deciding whether to extend fellowship.[42] Samson was Baptist enough to ask such a question and compas-sionate enough to accept such an answer. It would be quite possible that Houston would finally open himself enough to repeat to a pastor whom he trusted something that he had doubtless imparted to Margaret years before.

On his way to Washington, D.C., in 1853, Houston stopped in Knoxville to visit again his dear but deranged sister, Polly. While there he stayed, not with relations, but at the Lamar House hotel in a large corner room on the second floor where Andrew Jackson had once held court. Here he was surprised by touching evidence of the kind of enthusiasm with which he was regarded by at least one segment of the population. While Houston was engaged with eight or ten of Knoxville's prominent citizens, fourteen-year-old John B. Brownlow marched up the stairs and knocked on the door.

"Excuse me, General Houston, for interrupting in this way, but as soon as I heard you were here, I wanted to see you. It will be a source of pleasure to me in future to remember that I had the honor of shaking hands with the hero of San Jacinto."

The gentlemen present smiled at that, and the old General smiled and said: "Then you have read of San Jacinto?"

I said, "General Houston, any Tennessee boy who is as old as I am, who has not read of San Jacinto, ought to be ashamed of himself. . . ."

He spoke deprecatingly, and said: "There have been a great many battles fought, my son, where there were a hundred times as many people engaged as in that."

"Yes," I said . . . , "but you made such a clean job of it, General. . . . You only had a few men, and Santa Anna had thousands, and you captured every Greaser you did not kill, including Santa Anna; you came mighty near wiping them out."

I started to leave then, and he gave me a very cordial invitation if I ever was in Texas to be his guest, to call and see him.[43]

The youth of the yeomanry did not always greet him so cordially. Senator Houston loved to tell the story that on these journeys to Washington, he would disembark from the riverboats at Cairo, Illinois, and stay three or four days to enjoy the fishing. One time he was trying his luck from the stern of a wharf boat a few feet away from a youngster whose line took a bite just as Houston cast his out, and they became snarled. "Sonny," said the senator, "go elsewhere and fish, and then we'll avoid entangling alliances."

"You blasted old short-coat," the boy snapped, "go elsewhere yourself and fish." When Houston remarked on the boy's sauciness, he erupted that he knew Houston was really a horse thief named Sam Dawson who had fled to Texas ahead of the law. "Now you're putting on a big shine, you old thief, and calling yourself Sam Houston." With that the boy snatched the astonished senator's fishing pole and cast it into the river. "I have met men in debate at the bar," Houston said, "on the stump, and upon the floor of Congress, but never was I so completely discomfited. The boy decidedly had the best of me."[44]

Returning home after the close of the 1853 session, Texas' senior senator was importuned in Nacogdoches by a deputation of religious leaders who sought his aid in the passage of legislation that would prohibit selling or consuming alcohol on Sundays. The temperance movement nationally was on the ascent; Maine passed the first state prohibition statute in 1851, and a dozen other states either had or were preparing to follow suit. The preachers' request struck a deep chord in Houston, or perhaps, discord. His personal reform had begun with his marriage to Margaret, and he had now been sober for ten years since that humiliating incident with Mrs. Lockhart's bedpost. Margaret, and not unimportantly Reverend Samson, had made enormous strides with his growth in faith, and he was long since one of the Sons of Temperance. But to the depth of that enlarging soul he was also a libertarian, a believer in freedom of choice and the fundamental right of people to live without any governmental interference not absolutely required by the public good. Margaret was sure to be all for the proposal. Sam Houston the master politician could have easily buried the conflict—either joked it away or pled lack of authority or supported it publicly while privately doing nothing; all those were in his repertoire. But he did not. He looked the issues, including his own weakness for alcohol, hard in the eye and elaborated his thoughts in a kind of position paper that was stunning in its moderation and foresight.

"I have given the matter some thought," he wrote, and he concluded that he could not go along with them. In the first place, such a prohibition was impractical and unenforceable. "So long as the soil produces fruit and grain, ardent spirits will be manufactured and used as a beverage. . . . If you prohibit the sale of intoxicating liquors in one country, the article will be obtained from the adjoining one; if the state abolished traffic of ardent spirits; importation of the same from neighboring states will be resorted to." And if importation were banned, Houston used the example of the British Opium War in China as the probable result—and that was a conflict he was somewhat familiar with, as the man who caused it, his friend Capt. Charles Elliot, had been British chargé d'affaires to Houston's capital at Washington-on-the-Brazos.

In the second place, history was against the very concept. The U.S. Constitution mandated that Congress make no law respecting the establishment of religion. "That clause was placed there by wise men," he wrote the ministers, "by men who had been careful students of history. . . . When tyrants ask you to yield one jot of your liberty, and you consent thereto, it is the first link forged in the chain that will eventually hold you in bondage." By example, he recounted the history of the Irish, "that noble race . . . whose bravery immortalized every battlefield . . . , permitted the English lords to be centuries in forging their fetters, inch by inch, here a little, and there a little until today they are in helpless bondage." And the laws of Mexico, "intended to prescribe and regulate a person's religious belief, were the first moving cause that inspired the Texas patriots to draw their swords. . . . History teaches us that men composing all denominations of religious faith, when clothed with ecclesiastical and temporal power combined, have been tyrants."

In the third place, such a law would work injustice on minorities who enjoyed the same constitutional guarantees as everyone else. "Let us suppose that the Quakers, the Jews, the Seventh day Baptists, and others, that believe that Saturday . . . is the day God set apart, should get control of the legislative branch of the government" and decree Saturday to be the holy day. "What do you suppose the religious people who believe that [Sunday] is . . . the day that Christ ordained, would say?

Would they not all proclaim that such a law was a violation of the constitution? . . . We must remember that this is a land of equal rights to the Jews as well as to the Gentiles." America, further, was a land of immigrants, and he drew upon Texas's experience in populating the Hill Country. "Our friends, the Germans, are a class of immigrants I have made exertions to secure. They purchase our lands and pay us cash. Some of them have settled on land that was considered unproductive without irrigation, but through their skill and industry this dormant soil blossoms . . . and brings forth immense treasures of wealth. When, in our distress, we beckoned these peaceable, intelligent and hardy pioneers to our shores, we promised them an asylum of freedom. I can never give my consent to the passage of any law intended to regulate the manner in which they, or any other class of people shall observe Sunday."

In the fourth place, the real issue was not drinking per se but drunkenness. "To declare it to be a crime to . . . drink wine in moderation would, in effect, accuse Christ and the holy apostles of a sinful practice. The first miracle of our blessed Saviour was the manufacture of wine out of water. It was performed at the request of His mother at the wedding of her niece, His cousin. The object of the miracle was to furnish a stimulant . . . to prolong the mirth and joy of the wedding party. We must presume, therefore, that Christ and his disciples made use of wine as a beverage." Christ also, he pointed out, distributed wine at the Passover and instituted Holy Communion.

In the fifth place, morality cannot be legislated. "I am a sincere Christian," he protested, but "nowhere in the New Testament can we learn that any agency save moral suasion was invoked to make people religious or moral."

Senator Houston concluded with an honest reference to his own personal struggle with drink, invoking the verbal talisman recited so many times to Margaret. "I do not object to total abstinence. I believe that total abstinence is the only way by which some intemperate drinkers can be saved. I know it from my own personal experience. When a person's appetite for stimulating beverages becomes uncontrollable, he should 'touch not, handle not.' If I cannot indulge in the use of the same in moderation, it is my misfortune. To undertake to prescribe rules for conduct for others more fortunate, by legislative enactments, is a species of legislation that will not be tolerated in a free land."[45]

Back at Woodland with his family and surrounded by its bountiful gardens, Sam Houston had time to reflect on his eight years in the United States Senate. He was a man of action, one who would ride to battle with a feather in his cap. The Senate was stultifying, and, even worse, the men who arrogated to themselves the position of vindicating the South, were men he could not stand. Calhoun was gone at least, but so were the Senate's great sea anchors, Clay and Webster. The country seemed on its way to ruin, and by the beginning of summer 1853, he concluded that if anything good was going to happen, he would have to make it happen. He decided to enlarge his profile and enhance public awareness of him with a speech in Austin, but that required an invitation from someone to speak, and with the current ascendance of the sectionalists, such an opportunity did not seem likely to materialize.

As usual, that was no barrier, and as usual, he began in a jocular tone. "My dear Miller," he wrote his old friend and former private secretary on June 10, "As you are not inclined to come, and see me, I am inclined to go, and see you. Now you can get up a mutiny, and invite Rusk and me to Austin, and I wish to go there, if possible. I would say sometime in the month of July, say about the 15th or 20th would be about the time. On the 4th of July I expect to be at Palestine, and speak there. This matter is *privately suggested and for your own eye*, and when you have read the letter, *burn it*!!!" It was hardly unusual for Houston to desire not to be discovered as the author of his own invitation, but Miller, ever the clerk, instead of burning the letter endorsed it, answered it, and filed it away. Miller, who was then living with his sister and family near Austin, seemed dubious that a gathering could be organized on such short notice, but in any event he did reply, half jokingly, that Houston might need troops to protect him in the state capital.

"I was amused at your great *caution*," Houston then teased him on June 30, "and your notion about auxilliary forces, which you wished me to have, should I go to Austin. No risk, no merit! Well. I may, if spared, be at Austin in the fall, and hope Rusk will be with me." Corresponding with Wash Miller was a tonic for Houston. Washington was full of constraints and struggle, and Margaret, though he adored her, was no match for his own racing intellect. ("My ever dear Love," she had written him once, "I am so poor a politician, that an argument that would comfort me entirely could probably seem like the prattle of a babe to you.")[46] But in this exchange Houston also had to relay some bad news. Miller, along with former legislator Peter Gray, had been angling for a federal appointment, and Houston had failed to secure it for them. Miller was one man to whom Houston felt safe in opening his mind, and he used the topic as a springboard for a polemic against Franklin Pierce, in whose election he had taken considerable part. "Not an auditor or permanent Clerk at Washington, could we get appointed, out of the many hundreds in office! I did too much for Pierce, and he is jealous of me. *If God wills I will make him more so.* Ah! Miller, a mint for one days talk with you! The wish, and effort, will be to crush me between Disunionists & Freesoilers. Well, let him try the game. I am for 'old time Jackson Democracy.' It has no chance now, you may rely on it. . . . I have not known a weak man to come into place, by a large majority, but what he disgraced himself or ruined his party. Now I will not be surprised to see Lamar come into favor, and get a good appointment from Pierce. It would not be worse [than] the appointment of Gadsden to Mexico!" The senator then caught Miller up on family matters. Sam Junior had taken up the study of Latin "& bids fair to become a scholar. Nannie now nearly seven years old has also commenced Latin. She has a great passion for learning, and a remarkable genius. You may say, the children have a right to make up for their Father's omissions."[47] (The difference in Houston's handwriting between the former and latter topics is dramatic—fast and sloppy and angry when discussing Pierce, serene and flowing—though still as difficult as usual—on the children.)

One other topic merited Houston's fury in his June letters to Wash Miller. His old friend and ally Thomas William "Peg Leg" Ward, land commissioner during the "Archive War," had found himself in acute need. Houston lent him a sum of money—apparently several hundred dollars—and lent his influence in getting President Pierce to appoint Ward consul to Panama, a position worth some twenty thousand dollars per year. Now, Houston was, as he often was, strapped for cash, and Ward declined to repay the loan, and, to Houston's mind, sought to make other friends in the administration. Houston was livid. "I had recommended him for his present situation, because he was mutilated, and I pitied him. . . . Now you see the poor dog. Many persons are anxious to get [his job] . . . and he will play the fool so soon, his life of glory will be very short. I want you to let some friend of his know what I say, that he may hear of it!!!"[48]

Ward had managed to repay some $375—Houston allowed it might have been $475, but he did not think so—of the loan, leaving a small enough sum that in other circumstances Houston would have overlooked it, but to be in Houston's debt and then attach himself to Pierce was unforgivable. "Now tell Carruthers, (my cousin) if he is sober, to call on Col. Ward and ask him if he will pay me what he owes me. He said to me in presence of Genl. Rusk he would pay me if it was not paid. . . . If he don't pay me he must be sued, and I care not about the *Statute of Limitations.* Can I not rely on my friends? Who is a good Collecting Lawyer on whom I can rely? Write to me by *return mail* and let me know."

The storm of such correspondence played out in the senator's office, which occupied a log outbuilding in a corner of Woodland's front yard. If it was a season of repaying debts, Houston was soon reminded of an old one of his own. One Sunday, upon the family's return from church, they were hailed outside the hotel by its proprietor. A traveler had stopped in that morning, deathly sick, and inquired where in Texas Sam Houston lived. On learning that he was at that moment attending church nearby, he took a room, instructing the proprietor to stop them as they passed and tell General Houston that "a Golladay of Tennessee is lying sick here." Houston at once dismounted and entered. According to the patient: "I knew from the description that I had had of him, that it was General Houston, although I had never seen him. I called him by name. He asked if I was the son of his old friend, Isaac Golladay, of Lebanon, Tennessee. I replied that I was. He then asked me which one. I told him I was Frederick. He said he knew my elder brothers, but he had left Lebanon before I was born, but added, 'If you are the son of Isaac Golladay I recognize you.'"

At Houston's insistence and over Golladay's protest, the senator returned in the morning in his carriage and fetched him away for nursing at Woodland. "He placed me in a room in his yard [the law office], saying that Mrs. H. was confined to her room with an infant at that time." Golladay's fever rose and Houston sent for a doctor. For nearly two weeks Houston had a servant tend him night and day, and he himself looked in on the patient often. "One night, especially, when I was sick, the doctor had left orders for my medicine to be given me during the night, and my feet bathed in warm water. He stayed all night with me. He had the vessel of warm water brought, pulled off his coat, rolled up his sleeves, to wash my feet." Golladay objected that the servant was right at hand, but Houston cited the Bible as his example and did it himself.[49]

It was a fine autumn at the Woodland house. The feeling that he was slipping the bonds of the Senate and forcing the action put Houston in high spirits, and he enjoyed some cuffing banter through the mail with Wash Miller. "Write to me soon and see if you cannot rake up something to quarrel with me about, as I love controversy." Just in case Miller was not up to the task, the Senator put a topic of his own on the table: "Miller, you let *Wilcox* take off Mary Donelson, because you *would* not. Bah! Miller, this was a naughty act of yours." When Miller, by now a confirmed bachelor, pled overwork for his lack of social presence, Houston refused to excuse him: "Who cares if your work is not done! No one will blame you. Get married, Miller, while young!!!"[50]

In October of 1853, Houston rode up to the T. and S. Gibbs store in Huntsville and found a local resident named McKell auctioning off a slender young male slave to pay an overdue liquor bill. "My friend," he said, "don't you know it is against the law to block the plank-walk in this way? If you want to put on a show, why don't you move the slave-block back to the courthouse square where it belongs. . . . This little Negro isn't old enough to have any sense, and these white boys are scaring him."

Upon learning that the boy had already been sold to a notorious local slave driver named Moreland, Houston made a show of angrily buying the boy himself, on the condition that McKell also sell him the rest of the family so they could stay together. The boy was Jeff Hamilton, thirteen years old—McKell had passed him off as eight—who became Houston's personal servant and, later, driver and office boy. The senator took Jeff into Gibbs's store and procured him a sack of candy and a white straw hat with a red ribbon. To Sam Houston the proper headgear was ever important. "Don't get scared and cry anymore," Houston told him, "as no one is going to hurt you. I have a little boy almost as old as you with whom you can play."[51]

The practice of white parents buying a playmate for a child was common enough among the well to do, even as Margaret's father had bought Eliza for her. But Jeff recalled his ten years of servitude to the Houstons, lasting until the general's death, with enormous affection.[52] Houston returned home, dispatching Joshua in the wagon to return and fetch this latest addition to the household. Soon after, during a family trip to Independence to see Nancy Lea, Houston conveyed some land and collectible notes to his nephew, Martin Roysten, with instructions to procure the remainder of Jeff's family from McKell. As Houston feared, the family had been sold piecemeal.[53] He finally did make it to Austin for a speech expounding his views and had the satisfaction of reconciling with T. W. Ward. Before leaving for Washington, Houston took Jeff to the house of a doctor named Rawlings, who had agreed to hire Jeff for nominal wages while teaching him the duties of a house servant.

While Houston was sojourning in Texas, feuding with Peg Leg Ward, buying Jeff Hamilton, and getting Margaret pregnant with their sixth child, the dual call of Congress and celebrity were pressing him from afar. "We notice that the list of Lecturers for Franklin Lyceum at Providence embraces your name," wrote the Library Association of Pawtucket, Rhode Island. "Our Village is situated four miles south of Prov with hourly communication either by coach or car. Can you not, Sir, before you return, accommodate [us] with a lecture also?" As the event was a fundraiser, they regretted they could only offer a thirty-dollar speaking fee.[54]

Senator Houston made his customary New York visit as January closed. There, he received his usual hearty reception but learned after he returned to Washington that he had left some hard feelings in his wake. His New York presidential boosters were alert to his interests, however. James Auchincloss warned him that one A. A. Cargill was angry over feeling Houston had given him the cold shoulder. "Now I do not want you to lose a solitary friend," Auchindort chided, "particularly at the present picture. You will gratify me if you will rectify this matter with C, and get all straight as a *loon's leg* with him, for although C does not mingle much in political circles here ... still he might damage us some what by giving vent to his grievances in connection with your name."[55]

No sooner was Houston back in Washington than he was engulfed in senatorial business—letters seeking appointments to patronage offices, letters thanking him for appointments to patronage offices, and the like.[56] They were not sufficient to distract him from a new issue of awful moment that loomed before him. The Senate's chairman of the Committee on Territories was Stephen A. Douglas of Illinois, ambitious for the presidency and a political knife fighter. Needing to win Southern support for building a northern transcontinental railroad and anxious to be seen as friendly to Southern interests to further his chances at the White House, Douglas introduced a bill organizing land west of Missouri and Iowa as the Kansas and Nebraska Territories. The bait for the South was that the territories would be allowed to decide the slavery question for themselves. This seemed simple to Douglas, believing that slavery would never prosper there anyway because the land was unsuited to plantation agriculture. He miscalculated Southerners' willingness to flood the area with sectionalist immigrants, though. Worst of all, his bill required the repeal of that part of the Missouri Compromise that barred slavery north of the thirty-six degrees– thirty minutes line, which had served as the glue that had held the nation together for more than thirty years. The reaction Douglas received rocked the country.

Houston rose on February 7 to reserve time to himself for a major exposition on the Kansas-Nebraska controversy. He allowed that he expected the bill to pass, but "I think it is ... fair that the minority should be heard with some degree of patience and indulgence, if necessary. . . . I deem this a subject of vast importance, and as I am to be one of the actors in it, I must be permitted ... to submit such views as I have." With debating time scheduled, Houston went into his prebattle quiet, saying little from his chair in the Senate—whittling, as he still whittled endlessly—and rising occasionally to make a little joke. On the following day, he offered a consent motion to admit ladies to the floor of the Senate. While he had, he admitted, opposed such indulgences in the past, the galleries were full, the weather was inclement, and "there are several hundred of them at the door."

The amanuensis of the *Congressional Globe* recorded the reaction of, "SEVERAL SENATORS: Oh, no!"

Well, conceded Houston, maybe there were fifty. The motion failed.[57]

Houston was scheduled to speak on February 13 but was too ill to do so, and although still sick, he took the floor the following day, spoke until he gave out, and then took the floor again on the fifteenth. Territories, he said, are incipient and by definition cannot make these decisions for themselves, and the lands west of Missouri were promised to the natives in perpetuity anyway. Southerners reacted with universal indignation, to which Houston protested that he was acting in their own interest as well. "No event of the future is more visible to my perception than that, if the Missouri Compromise is repealed, at some future day the South will be overwhelmed." He brought law books; he brought visual aids. Where his speech on behalf of the Compromise of 1850 filled twenty-five pages, his effort against Douglas and Kansas-Nebraska filled more than thirty, but it was a futile struggle and he knew it.

The vote was slated for March 3, and in the last-minute debate, Stephen A. Douglas spoke well into the evening, during which he yielded to Houston for a moment. "It is now half-past seven o'clock," said the old Texan. "I cannot see any particular necessity for going on tonight, and therefore we might as well adjourn." He was summarily shouted down. "Then I give notice that I shall take the floor after the Senator from Illinois gets through." Douglas ranted until after eleven.

Senator Houston's last redoubt against the Kansas-Nebraska bill was to return to the Indian angle: that its enactment meant breaking up and settling tracts of territory in violation of treaties that guaranteed the land to the Indians forever. At once he was pounced on by unsympathetic Midwesterners who wanted to see the Indians either broken or exterminated. Houston had no difficulty making answer, and while he did it in faultless senatorial courtesy, the censure in his voice may be perceived almost as plainly now as in 1854:

> The honorable Senator from Indiana [MR. PETTIT] says in substance that God Almighty has condemned [the Indians], and made them an inferior race; that there is no use in doing anything for them. With great deference to that Senator . . . , I must be permitted to dissent from his opinions. . . . Sir, it is idle to tell me that. We have Indians on our western borders whose civilization is not inferior to our own. . . . They have well-organized societies; they have their villages and towns; they have their state houses and their capitols; they have females and men who would grace the drawing-rooms or salons of Washington; they have a well-organized judiciary. . . . The Indian has a sense of justice, truth, and honor that should find a responsive chord in every heart. If the Indians on the frontier are barbarous . . . , who are we to blame for it? They are robbed of the means of sustenance; and with hundreds and thousands of them starving on the frontier, hunger may prompt to such acts to prevent their perishing. . . .
>
> We should be careful if it were with a power able to war with us; and it argues a degree of infinite meanness and indescribable degradation on our part to act differently with the Indians, who confide in our honor and justice, and who call the President their Great Father, and confide in him.

Stephen A. Douglas. The "Little Giant" had been chairman of the Committee on Territories in the House before taking over the same duties in the Senate. He was an expansionist without apology, opposing compromise with the British over Oregon and advocating the annexation of Cuba. He did win the Democratic nomination in 1860, but even his history of pandering to the slaveocracy could not prevent the party from splitting, which handed the election to Abraham Lincoln; Douglas won only twelve electoral votes. After the Civil War began, he supported theUnion and died of typhoid contracted during a tour to encourage popular support of the war effort.

Courtesy National Archives

Corruption in the management of Indian affairs was the first political subject with which Houston had ever become familiar. "Not less than one hundred millions of dollars . . . since the adoption of this government, have been appropriated by Congress for . . . benevolence toward Indians; but I am satisfied that they have never

Charles Sumner. For Senator Sumner to have deferred his attack on Stephen A. Douglas and yielded the floor instead to Houston was a remarkable show of respect, for Sumner was one of the body's leading abolitionists. His radicalism later earned him a near-fatal caning on the Senate floor at the hand of Congressman Preston Brooks of South Carolina. Nevertheless, Houston's disapproval of slavery, which was more measured and pragmatic, won him Sumner's support for the presidency.

Courtesy National Archives

received fifteen millions beneficially. . . . It is in the power of the Congress . . . to do some justice to the Indians by giving them a government of their own, and encouraging them in their organization and improvement. . . . If you will not do it, the sin will lie at your door, and Providence in his own way . . . may at some day avenge the wrongs of the Indians upon our nation."[58]

Sam Houston ever characterized himself as being too unrighteous to put forth religious arguments for his positions, but in this instance those arguments were made for him. In one of the first attempts by religious leaders to organize for political effect, over three thousand pastors from across the North signed a petition against the Kansas-Nebraska bill. On March 14 Edward Everett of Massachusetts presented the document for the consideration of the Senate. No sooner had he done so than South Carolina's Butler and Virginia's Mason leapt to their feet to protest what they viewed as a leap beyond the bounds of religious office. But it was Douglas of Illinois, sensing political hay to gather, who took up the cause for the Southerners. Vituperation defined Stephen Douglas's style of argument, and he let fly at the New England churchmen with a vengeance. The petition, he said, "is presented by a denomination of men calling themselves preachers of the gospel, who have come forward with an atrocious falsehood and an atrocious calumny against the Senate, desecrated the pulpit, and prostituted the sacred desk to the miserable and corrupting influence of party politics."59

The packed gallery was heavily salted with movers and signers of the petition, and to vindicate them, Massachusetts senator Charles Sumner rose with fire in his eyes.

Abruptly, Houston cut him off. "Sumner, don't speak! Don't speak! Leave him to me!"

Sumner had sense enough to realize that for a Southerner to flense Douglas would be doubly effective, as Sumner would be perceived as merely sticking up for his own abolitionist crowd. "Will you take care of him?" he asked Houston.

"Yes, if you will leave him to me."60

When Houston took the floor, his first point in defending the ministers' petition was as simple as he thought it dispositive: the Kansas-Nebraska bill passed the Senate in the early hours of March 4; the petition was dated March 1, *ergo*, it could not have had the object of attacking the Senate for passing the bill. But, more fundamentally, "I certainly can see no more impropriety in ministers of the Gospel ... memorializing Congress, than politicians or other individuals. I do not believe that these ministers have sent this memorial here to manufacture political capital. ... Sir, it comes from the country. I told you that there would be agitation, but it was denied upon this floor. Is not this agitation? Three thousand ministers of the living God upon earth ... send a memorial here upon this subject; and yet you tell me that there is no excitement in the country!"

Ministers, he insisted, have no less right to petition the government than any other citizens. "No man can be a minister without first being a man. He has political rights; he has also the rights of a missionary of the Saviour, and he is not disfranchised by his vocation. . . . He has a right to contribute, as far as he thinks necessary, to the sustentation of its institutions. He has a right to interpose his voice as one of its citizens against the adoption of any measure which he believes will injure the nation. These individuals have done no more. They have not denounced the Senate, but they have protested, in the capacity of ministers, against what I and other Senators on this floor protested. They have the right to do it, and we can not take that right from them."

Having only recently rebuffed Baptist preachers who desired his help in writing Sunday prohibition into law, Houston was perhaps more sensitive at this time than at any other to religious meddling in state affairs. It was a boundary he had surveyed already, and he did not perceive that the petitioning ministers had crossed it. "I do not think there is any evidence that the gentlemen who have signed the memorial have any disposition to establish theocracy in our country, or that they wish to take the Government into their own hands, and exercise a controlling influence over it. We find that those who have signed this document are of different sects and various denominations. I think there is no danger that such an amalgamation of . . . opinions will take place as to . . . endanger our liberties."

Houston readily admitted that "it is true that the memorialists speak of the measure as immoral. Surely that ought not to insult Senators. They are not such paragons of morality that they cannot bear to have their morality questioned. . . . Is their morality of such a delicate texture as to be affected by a memorial coming from 'the land of steady habits'?"

Senator Douglas had charged that the ministers presented the petition to create agitation and to insult the Senate. Houston further readily acknowledged agitation in the country, but "the cause is not the clergymen who have signed this memorial. The memorial is the effect of a cause brought forward and presented in the Senate." The real cause, he argued, was the attempt to repeal the Missouri Compromise, "which I predicted would have this influence upon the community. . . . If we wish to avert calamitous effects," he concluded, "we should prevent pernicious causes."[61]

Throughout the North, for his opposition to the Kansas-Nebraska Act and further for his defense of three thousand Yankee ministers who attacked it, Sam Houston was almost universally lionized. From the villages of Maine southward he was asked to send copies of his speeches.[62] In the South he was almost as universally vilified.

• • •

From his boyhood roaming the Hiwassee River banks with the *Iliad* under his arm, to his shared smoky bedroom with Ashbel Smith in the "Executive Mansion" in Houston, to his elegantly accessorized years as Texas senator in Washington, Sam Houston never tired of hearing great classics ably recited. It was, after all, an age when florid expression and powers of rote memory entertained and uplifted people for blocs of time later supplanted by motion pictures and television. It was the pre–sound bite age, when the beauty of language was allowed to roll unhurried. One evening, while receiving friends in his suite at Willard's, Houston asked if none of the company could recite Sprague's oration on the disappearance of the Indian, and as it happened, one of them did know it:

> Not many generations ago, where you now sit, circled with all that exalts and embellishes civilized life, the rank thistle nodded in the wind, and the wild fox dug his hole unscared. Here lived and loved another race of beings. Beneath the same sun that rolls over your heads the Indian hunter pursued the panting

deer; gazing on the same moon that smiles for you, the Indian lover wooed his dusky mate. Here the wigwam blaze beamed on the tender and the helpless, the council-fire glared on the wise and daring. Now they dipped their limbs in your sedgy lakes, and now they paddled the light canoe along your rocky shores. Here they warred; the echoing whoop, the bloody grapple, the defying death-song, all were here; and when the tiger strife was over, here curled the smoke of peace. Here, too, they worshiped; and from many a dark bosom went up a pure prayer to the Great Spirit. He had not written His laws for them on tables of stone, but He had traced them on the tables of their hearts. The poor child of Nature knew not the God of revelation, but the God of the universe he acknowledged in everything around. He beheld Him in the star that sank in beauty behind his lonely dwelling, in the sacred orb that flamed on him from His mid-day throne, in the flower that snapped in the morning breeze, in the lofty pine that defied a thousand whirlwinds . . . and in his own matchless form, glowing with a spark of that light, to whose mysterious source he bent in humble, though blind, adoration.[63]

As the guests in Houston's sitting room listened respectfully, it is easy to imagine the "Barbarian Senator" leaning back in his own chair, his eyes closed, alone with memories that none present could possibly share. Houston foresaw clearly the doom of the western Indians in the passage of the Kansas-Nebraska Act, and it was only natural that in his mind's eye he should relive the free life of "measuring deer tracks" one last time. But, in a way, it was a personal farewell not just to them but also to their uncomplicated spirituality, for Margaret had been pressuring him relentlessly on the state of his unredeemed soul.

The past couple of years had been manic ones, from flying high in the presidential assay of powerful men to enduring the walleyed tantrums and the monolithic rejection of his policies in his own section. This wild and passionate ride had led Houston into considerable soul searching, and he had been steadfast in his personal journey toward salvation. His friend and Texas's congressman for the eastern district Lemuel Evans rented the rooms immediately beneath Houston's, and he attested his personal knowledge that the senator prayed on his knees both upon retiring at night and upon rising in the morning.[64] For now, Washington disgusted him, and shortly after defending the ministers, Houston headed home—the family was in Independence—before Congress even adjourned.

Rufus Burleson, the pastor at the Independence Baptist Church, was barely half Houston's age but showed no reluctance to dispute with or even provoke him in their religious discussions. On at least one occasion, Burleson sought an unfair advantage, continuing one of their arguments from the Sunday pulpit, a redoubt from where he figured he could not be gainsaid. But he underestimated the Old Chief, who stood up in his pew and tried to argue back. Houston liked Burleson well enough, but he considered him something of a stuffed shirt and banty rooster; occasionally, the senator exacted his Houstonesque revenge by, for instance, insisting that he had indeed been imparted omens by eagles and ravens, and then he would settle back to enjoy the fit he knew would follow. (Burleson wrote in his memoir that he and Houston once jawed about the "augury of birds" until after midnight.)[65] The boy understood power, however, and Houston knew that as president of Baylor College, Burleson swayed a considerable body of local opinion. Besides, Margaret liked him, and she was warm buddies with his bride of one year, Georgiana, so Houston tolerated him.[66] Occasionally, he even talked politics with the minister, and when he returned beaten down by the 1854 Senate session, he told Burleson gloomily that, though his vote against the Kansas-Nebraska bill was the most unpopular he ever cast, it was also the wisest and most patriotic. Douglas of Illinois had "introduced the repeal of the Missouri Compromise to catch the vote of the South. He is now preparing another bill, called 'squatter sovereignty,' to catch the North, and he hopes that the two will place him in the presidential chair." By doing so he opened the Pandora's box of slavery that had been locked by the Missouri Compromise, and William Seward and the abolitionists were rejoicing. Houston then made one of those predictions that can come only from weary greatness. In 1860, he said, "the Free Soil party, uniting with the Abolitionists, will elect the president of the United States. Then will come the tocsin of war and the clamor for secession. . . . Each section, in profound blindness . . . will rush madly into war, each anticipating an easy victory. But . . . what fields of blood, what scenes of horror, what mighty cities in smoke and ruins—it is brother murdering brother. . . . I see my beloved South go down in the unequal contest, in a sea of blood and smoking ruin." He said a military dictatorship would then be established over the blasted South, for which the North "will herself reap the bitter curses . . . of assassinations."[67] His prescience, in hindsight, was stupefying.

Upset and distracted, he returned to Washington in May 1854, leaving Margaret eight months pregnant. Throughout their marriage, their letters protested their misery at being apart while recognizing that their fate was to be seldom together. But this time it was different. Margaret sensed his depression, and from that, the mood of the country. She did not want him to leave, and she was desolate enough to play rough. These were burdens he did not need just now. His love for her was firm, but for the time being, it must be from a distance. "I am as anxious my Love, to be and stay with you as you are to have me. [But] a work has begun, and if spared, I must go on to its completion. It is not vanity I hope, my Dearest, but this very crisis, I do believe." Margaret's intuition, as it often did, prompted her to reply before receiving his letter, and she still wanted him home. "Dearest," she wrote on May 24, "I must tell you that sometimes a dark thought presents itself to my mind, 'if his affection had been equal to mine, could he have left me?'" She wrote that the dark thought was transient and knew that as soon as he read it, he would know it was anything but. A week later she suggested that he resign from the Senate and come home to stay. "I know the country needs your services, but when we calculate the sacrifices which must be made at home, is it not a question, which has the strongest claims upon you, your country or your family?" And added to all of this was her concern that Sam Junior was growing up without a father. Nor was even that all. She enclosed a letter from seven-year-old Nannie:

Independence May 24th, 1854

My dear papa, I want to see you very bad. How long will it be before you come back? How far are you now? Mama has cut my hair I think it looks better.... Grandmama was very ill the evening you left and had a chill. She was in bed for three or four days. They sing hymns at the school house. I love to sing them. Mammas corn in the garden has roasting ears . . . we have some ripe figs. Mamma has been very sick since you left. Maggie says she wants to see you very bad. . . . Your affectionate daughter Nannie

"My dearest," Margaret penned across the bottom, "Nannie has composed this letter without the slightest assistance."[68] Sure she did. Against all entreaty and attempts to inflict guilt, the senator held firm, and he later learned by letter of the birth of a second son, Andrew Jackson Houston, on June 21. The birth took place in Huntsville before Margaret moved the household back to Independence for what proved to be a very difficult summer. Her sister Antoinette's daughter had succumbed to pneumonia, and Margaret had tried her best to give comfort. Nancy Lea was even more morbid than usual, daily appraising her partially built tomb with jabs of her walking stick. "It is a mournful thing," Margaret wrote Sam in mid-June, "particularly as I think she does not realize . . . she is talking every day about . . . death."[69] Margaret's latest confinement and Houston's long absences made her own "glooms," as she called them, deepen to the point that she settled in her mind that there was no peace for it except in her husband's baptism. He might have evaded her during the summer, but when he arrived home—in Independence—on October 17, he walked right into an ambush.

Margaret knew the time was auspicious. She knew her husband was a hero in the North for his defense of the three thousand ministers from Stephen Douglas's abuse. She knew he had been thinking heavily on religion, and she knew George Samson had been working on him at the E Street Church in Washington. Judge Baylor—Robert Emmet Bledsoe Baylor, the same man who had sworn in Houston at his second inaugural—was planning a four-day revival at Independence in November, at which he had promised to administer his celebrated sermon "Jesus Wept," and the assemblage would be vast.[70] Thus, from the moment Houston hung his hat, Margaret was on him. For nearly a month she read to him incessantly from her Bible and made him discuss the relevant passages. But Houston's refusals were adamant, and he must have been wretchedly unhappy. He had chosen to put himself under her emotional and spiritual care, and he must have known since the day they married that this hour would come. But now, under the fury of the final assault, surrender did not come easily. Surrender was a foreign thing to him.

Margaret wore him down enough for him to admit that he believed, but still he would not be baptized and apparently would not at first discuss why, repeating only that he would consider it. Stymied by this obstinacy, Margaret then fell heir to a stroke of luck—or Providence. There appeared at the front gate Brother George Washington Baines, a favorite family friend, who lived in Anderson but served the church in Brenham, requiring a frequent shuttle. A former Arkansas legislator, Baines

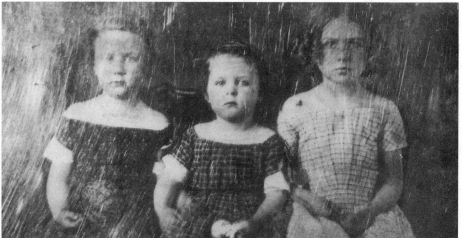

Margaret Houston; Maggie, Mary Willie, and Nannie, 1853. By her early thirties, Margaret lost the baby fat evident in her honeymoon photo and blossomed into a beautiful, though often solemn, young matron. After the birth of Sam Junior in 1843, she had her hands full with the appearances of Nannie in 1846, Maggie in 1848, and Mary Willie in 1850. Nettie followed in 1852. She also had to campaign gamely to lure her husband's attention from national politics; these daguerreotypes, which she had taken late in January 1853, helped keep him focused on home, hearth, and religion.

Both courtesy Sam Houston Memorial Museum

was forty-six, a man of wide experience in life as well as religion, and although he was a Baptist minister he was urbane, clever, and open minded—traits that later cost him some hard feelings in the church but gained him Houston's affection.[71] Margaret flew out to the gate and prevailed on him to help her. "Sister Houston saw me," recalled Baines, "and came out to meet me, evidently excited, and exclaimed, 'Oh, Bro. Baines, I am so glad to see you. Gen. Houston has professed religion, but says he cannot join the church. I want you to talk to him about it, for I know he has the greatest confidence in your knowledge of such things. . . . Communion is his difficulty." Rufus Burleson and others, she said, had tried to sway him, without success. Houston was away from the house, and Margaret and Baines sat up until she prevailed on him to stay the night. Baines met the senator at breakfast, and as the preacher prepared to leave, Houston, to Baines's surprise, asked to accompany him. Brenham lay about ten miles south of Independence, and as the two men walked their horses, Sam Houston, for one of the rare times in his life, sought counsel. "My wife and other friends seem anxious for me to join the church," he began, "and I would do so if I could. But with my present convictions, which I received when a boy, it is impossible."

Of all the pastors in Texas, Baines was the best equipped to talk to Sam Houston. According to one acquaintance qualified to speak: "It always seemed to me that he could see as far into the subject as it fell to the lot of man to do, and that he was wonderfully gifted in seeing the difficulties in the way of reaching correct conclusions. Fortunate was [he] who had him for counsellor when in deep theological waters, or in the midst of fiery trials. I never went to him without getting instruction and comfort."[72] Baines asked him to continue.

It seemed that in Houston's youth, his mother—one of the few times he ever spoke of his mother—took him to a service of their own Presbyterian denomination. Its feature was a fierce sermon by "the great Dr. Blackburn" from Corinthians on the sure damnation of unbelievers who take communion. From this, and surely from the time of his separation from Eliza, when he had been refused communion by two Presbyterian ministers, he had lived in terror of the Eucharist, afraid that if he joined a church and partook of the Lord's Supper, the doubts of his own heart would cost him his immortal soul.

To ministers of the gospel, the proper frame of mind toward communion is not a new issue, nor was it then, and Dr. Baines dispatched it quickly: in the Corinthian letter, St. Paul bespoke the damnation of those who deliberately mock Holy Communion by eating it to satisfy bodily hunger. It had nothing to do with denying communion to believers who were struggling with sincere questions in their hearts. "Thus you see why I said," concluded Baines, "that the great Dr. B. made a fearful mistake." If throughout his life Sam Houston had been more willing to discuss matters of such deep personal moment to him, he would have heard this explanation before. But for him the issue was still entwined beyond extrication in that scarifying episode with Eliza and his having been spurned by the Presbyterian Church—or rather, by two weak-kneed Presbyterian Allen family minions unwilling to provoke their masters.[73] As Houston would not speak of her, he could not speak

Rev. and Mrs. George Washington Baines. Like the Houstons, the Baines family was associated with both Huntsville and Independence, Texas. In addition to his pastoral duties, Brother Baines served a term as president of Baylor University and was the first editor of the first Baptist newspaper in Texas. He was the great-grandfather of Pres. Lyndon Baines Johnson.

Courtesy Texas Collection, Baylor University

of it. Finally, under Margaret's lovingly merciless barrage, he had risked revealing the very depth of his heart and been rewarded. "I see it clearly. Your view is new to me," he said quietly to Baines. "I will return home and read that chapter carefully."[74] This he did, and afterward pronounced himself ready for immersion. (And if the argument that Sam Houston had crudely used his marriage to Eliza as a vehicle to get to Texas needs a final nail in its coffin, his conversion on the road to Brenham is bright and sharp.)

Houston's fear of approaching religion with insufficient reverence was a note sounded more than once during Margaret's campaign to win him to baptism. "You my *dearest*," he had written her several years before, "may rest assured, that I will never trifle with professions connected with the institutions of religion or the adoration of Jehovah!" And Margaret's position as his spiritual guide was more than evidenced by the fact that Houston's bearing toward religion spilled over into his contemplation of *her*. Should he reflect on her beauty and virtue "in derision of Gods attributes, I wou'd be sinful, but I do so with reverence, if not with a 'perfect heart.'"[75]

Margaret's joy approached delirium as she rifled messages to all the kith and kin within beckoning. As word spread and the day approached, the little town of

Independence engorged with people as the event took on as much atmosphere of carnival as conversion. Friends, well wishers, strangers, the amazed, and the merely curious streamed in from as far away as Austin. Although it was Judge Baylor's impending visit that fueled Margaret's determination and Pastor Baines's counsel that carried the day, young Rufus Burleson was not about to be upstaged. Securing to himself the appointment to conduct the actual immersion, Burleson announced his intention to conduct the rite in his own baptistry-like contraption—shaped like a coffin, no less—that in previous times he had sunk in Kountz Creek for the baptism of Baylor students.[76]

"The sexton went down in the morning to see that the pool was in order, and came back very much distressed." Vandals had filled Burleson's coffin-shaped thing with mud and branches during the night. The minister calmly asserted that he would out-general them, and at the morning service announced that the proceedings would be moved to nearby Rocky Creek at the "Baptizing Hole," a gravel-bottomed pool some twenty feet in diameter, fringed with cress and water lilies, just downstream from a five-foot waterfall. On Sunday, November 19, 1854, before an enormous throng, Sam Houston was buried with his Lord in baptism. One witness to the event was a young Baylor student, T. J. Goree, who was boarding with the Houstons; he was stunned when the normally reserved Margaret, unable to contain her triumph, "turned Methodist and shouted a little."[77]

The sunshine was brilliant but cold, and the senator's teeth chattered audibly as he emerged from the water. "Well, General," a friend said later, "I hear your sins were washed away."

The sins, perhaps, but not the imp. "I hope so," Houston wagged, "but if they were all washed away, the Lord help the fish down below."[78]

17

SECTIONAL MADNESS

If it was true that by entrusting his personal turbulence and his soul to Margaret, Sam Houston freed himself to wage ever more fierce political battle, then his ultimate submission in the act of baptism in November of 1854 could not possibly have come at a more critical time for either the man or his country. By the middle of the 1850s, no thinking American could fail to see the country racing headlong and out of control toward the abyss of disunion and probable civil war. Houston shook off his spiritual doubts to find himself the most influential man in the United States, and, obsessed with saving it, he rose from the waters of Rocky Creek, went to Boston, and gave the speech of his life.

On this occasion he was to debate the radical abolitionist William Lloyd Garrison on the issue of slavery, and Boston positively crackled with anticipation. Rumors even spread that Houston would make other appearances as well, a confusion he straightened out as best he could before arriving. The arrangements for the trip were probably handled by his Boston friends, Speaker of the House Nathaniel P. Banks and Dr. J. W. Stone, the latter requesting of Houston a summary of how he intended to approach the subject. This Houston declined. He was acutely aware of the importance of the appearance, but being an accomplished orator, he also knew how to keep an audience in suspense: "If the particular points are not stated [in advance], it will create a greater interest in the community," he wrote. Besides, "I declare to you, my dear Sir, that I cannot designate the Phases of the Subject which I will present, because I do not know myself."[1] Like a good stump speaker, he intended to wing it.

Entrained for Boston, Houston was handed a mysterious letter in New York urging him to desist. Probably it was from Rusk, but the nature of the warning is now unclear. The editors of Houston's correspondence suggest that it might have urged him away from his flirtation with the Know-Nothing Party; Wisehart interpreted it as a plea to call off the Boston speech. Whatever the purpose, the writer urged Houston not to endanger his prospects for attaining the presidency. "Dear General," Houston answered from New Haven, "I appreciate your advice as well as that of our friend Burke, but I must go on. Under like circumstances General Jackson would have done so. To be honest and fear not is the right path. I would not conceal an honest opinion for the Presidency. If I [did], I could not enjoy the office."[2]

The train paused again in Hartford, Connecticut, and Houston called on a politically influential writer, sixty-four-year-old Lydia Howard Huntley Sigourney, who presented him with a book of her poems. Margaret was a great fan of hers, and as Houston wrote her an acknowledgment soon after, "Your Poems, Lady, afford her the purest delight, and . . . had I failed to make my visit to 'Mrs. Sigourney,' while in Hartford, it would have been a cause of . . . a 'Curtain Lecture.'"[3]

In Boston at last, Houston addressed a packed Tremont Temple on February 22, 1855—Washington's birthday—on the issue of slavery: "Unsolicited, I am here—I may say undesired; because it devolves upon me a grave responsibility to vindicate an institution . . . with which I had no election, one that fortune, or destiny, cast me into connection with." Portions of this remarkable *tour de force* assert the usual Southern clichés of slavery, of happy "darkies" having "the care of their masters"; "I never yet heard of a slave that committed suicide" and the like. Its bedrock, however, lay in economics, and the development is vintage Houston, pointing the accusing finger at the proud abolitionist Brahmins, calling them hypocrites, and making them laugh while he did it. Houston's timing and inflection may be inferred from the bracketed notes of the stenographer:

> Let us look for a moment at the condition of the North. The immense improvements you have made I am delighted with; I congratulate the people of the North with all my heart upon their many beautiful, convenient, profitable and elegant improvements. . . . But do you believe that if it had not been for the influx of foreign labor, you would have had these railroads? [Cheers and laughter.] Would the Americans, sons of the revolution, ever have been able to do the digging and all the other work that has been done here? [Cheers.] No. You never could have done it in the world. Well, it is done, and I am glad to see that it is done. [Laughter.] But let us reason a little further. Suppose the railroad projects had taken place before the time when you emancipated your slaves, and no foreigners had come. . . . Do you think that if the railroads had been started then, emancipation would have begun? You would have had negroes at work building railroads to this day, just as sure as the world. [Applause and laughter.]
>
> When foreign labor had been reduced to a standard, at which it was cheaper than that of slaves, with the capital invested in them, you employed foreigners, and turned off your slaves.

To force sudden emancipation upon the South now, he argued further, would create a horde of free blacks, destitute, unemployed, and unemployable. If the slave were freed, "no one would take care of him. His toil would stop, and his recompense, and he would be cast into the streets. . . . You might call him free, but he would be an object of want and wretchedness." It was Lafayette, honed for a new audience. Far better, Houston said, to support the colony of former slaves in Liberia. That was the only chance "that seems to loom up in the distance, by which . . . provision can be made for restoring these people . . . to the land of their origin." To educate and prepare slaves for a free life, in a place free of white men "where they are not trodden down," would be a good outcome. "If the same amount had been spent in building up and colonizing Liberia, which has been wasted in other ways in relation to them, it would have been better."

And who was to say, he argued further, that a forced emancipation now, when slaves were so ill prepared, might not frustrate some greater plan? Here, his long Bible studies with Margaret and Sundays spent whittling through George Samson's sermons, yielded a remarkable point of view. "When Joseph was sold . . . to the Midianites, and when he was transported to Egypt, no one could have divined the subsequent wonders of Divine power. The children of Israel remained four hundred years in Egypt ere they were redeemed, and then it was by miraculous and infinite power. Was this all chance? . . . Here was an act of emancipation. And how do we know by what means, at some future day, if we use our influence to excite humanity towards these beings . . . they may become nations that . . . some day radiate science and religion throughout the continent of Africa?"

After all this, Houston was still not willing to let the Bostonians off the hook, cutting his argument the other way—that in the South, slavery did not, in fact, benefit the slaveowners as much as was commonly believed. And, if there was an influx of cheap foreign labor in the South such as they had in the North, slavery would topple of its own dead weight. Southerners were no hand at building ships, he allowed, but if foreign labor came to the South they would learn shipwrighting and send the slaves straight back to Africa. Houston concluded his speech with a plea for unity. He was now well known as the lone Southern champion for the Union.

> I have told you the truth, and how, by the necessity of our condition, [South-erners] are forced to act as we have done in regard to slavery. . . . I trust, though a misunderstanding may have arisen between [North and South], no deplorable result may arise, such as has been prognosticated.
>
> Our country is too glorious, too magnificent, too sublime in its future prospects, to permit domestic jars or political opinions to produce a wreck of this mighty vessel of State. Let us hold on to it, and guide it; let us give it in charge to men who will care for the whole people, who will love the country for the country's sake, and will endeavor to build up and sustain it, and recon-cile conflicting interests. . . . This can be done, and let us not despair and break up the Union.[4]

Sam Houston's Boston speech was a masterpiece of courage, eloquence, wis-dom, and passion, and by the time he was done, he owned the hall. His mixture of economics and homespun homily, of his fiercely held convictions and his gentle prodding irony, netted thunderous applause and left many convinced that if there was in the United States one man who possessed the guile to navigate the shoals of sectionalism, it was the tall, chiding old senator from Texas. Back home, the state *Gazette* printed an extract and analysis of the Boston speech. As foul as Houston's Kansas-Nebraska treason might have been to the South, it seemed now to dawn on at least a few Texas editors that here was a Daniel who could defend the South in the lion's very den and walk away, not just uneaten, but victorious.[5]

Modern scholars typically place a different spin on the Boston speech, emphasizing Houston's use of racial stereotypes as proof of his inability to grasp the moral dimension of slavery.[6] William Lloyd Garrison possessed a buzzard's visual acuity of the moral dimension of slavery, but this man who publicly burned the U.S. Constitution, espoused the economic ruin of the South, and called even for Northern secession was, as Houston saw with an even harder clarity, every bit as responsible for the eventual horror of the Civil War as was the most intractable, slave-beating Southern planter. Scholars today who use the Boston speech to vilify Houston as a racist utterly misapprehend his purpose. Houston was a realist who saw that the South could never be weaned away from slavery unless they first understood that it could be in their economic interest to do so, nor should they be expected to until some economic alternative was in place to forestall the total collapse of the region that sudden emancipation would bring. To Sam Houston, what was paramount at that time, in that place, and during that crisis was keeping the Union together, and the issue of slavery would have to be sorted out within the parameter of keeping the Union together—a view, not to make too fine a point of it, that came to be adopted by Abraham Lincoln.

Of course Houston's personal racial attitude was a product of his time and his geography. Of course he believed that the white race was superior, and in his writing and in his speaking, of course he made free fun of black attitudes and dialect— no less than Abraham Lincoln. They believed this because they were the products of a culture and a history in which black people were given little opportunity to demonstrate their ability—let alone their right—to assume an equal place.

However distant that equal place was, Houston at least set his servants down the road toward it, and he had no misgivings about their abilities. He told Tocqueville as early as 1831 that he believed the innate intelligence of the slave was equal to that of the Indian—which was to say, very intelligent. "The difference you notice between the Indian and the negro," he told the French essayist, "seems to me to result solely from the different educations they have received." The natives learned to be self-reliant from a very early age, but "the common negro was a slave before being born, without pleasures as without needs. . . . The first notions that he receives from life show him that he is the property of someone else, that the care of his own future is not his concern."[7] Houston saw to it that his people did take care for their futures; when his slaves sought work outside the household, he let them keep the money they earned, which as their master he was not obligated to do. He saw to it that they learned to read, write, and figure simple arithmetic, including interest, so they would not be cheated in business.

His oversight extended also to their personal habits. As Jeff Hamilton recalled: "The General and the Missus saw to it that the cabins were kept neat and clean, and that we had plenty of bed covering during the cold months. We didn't have to run around in our bare feet in the winter-time like many slaves, but were given good shoes and other clothing. The General did not permit his slaves to be whipped. And if we got sick, we had the best care than any one could possibly get in that day and time." Once, Houston appeared unannounced in the slave quarters and discovered the servants gobbling pork, fried sweet potatoes, and crackling bread from two big communal platters and exploded: "Liza! What in the hell do you mean letting these people eat like a lot of hogs? You are not living at the home of a savage!" Immediately he had Joshua drive him and Jeff over to Tom Gibbs's store and bought a supply of new tin plates, cups, and flatware for their use.[8]

Just as did many of the leading writers of the day, Houston often drove home a humorous point in the unlettered speech patterns of the slave. As early as 1826, when he was a member of Congress from Tennessee, he wrote an acquaintance that he was happy to be reassured of his friendship: "I was truly alarmed least some 'snake had come across de Road for to make distarbance.'" In 1838 he had protested his sobriety to Anna Raguet, "I never drinks nothing," and his 1840 speech in the Texas Congress against Lamar's Santa Fe scheme included a slave homily.[9] If in using these and similar expressions Houston was offending the dignity of the race, then no less guilty were some of the most eloquent abolitionists of the day, including Harriet Beecher Stowe herself.[10] One might also note that Houston delighted in mimicking other accents, including French and German, but whether in imitating slave speech Houston was callously making sport of the downtrodden or paying homage to their untutored folk wisdom is a debate recent scholars try to win tenure with. There was no malice in Houston's own heart. To the extent that the modern academic community expects Houston to see the slavery issue through the eyes of our own political correctness, they place on him a burden that is grotesque in its unfairness. Even Frederick Douglass, in evaluating Abraham Lincoln's speed on the issue of emancipation, had the goodness to weigh what was right against what was politically possible. Modern historians might borrow some of his spiritual generosity.

If anything, insofar as the institution of slavery could admit of having a good master, Houston was one. Only once was it recorded that he ever beat one of his slaves, an incident that happened at the Woodland house in Huntsville. He owned a saddle horse, Old Pete, who was quite spirited—Houston referred to him as vicious— and the senator was the only one who could ride him. Jeff Hamilton had been in the family plenty of time to learn that the impish Nannie would do about anything to raise a rumpus; Jeff was watering Old Pete at the spring when he handed Nannie a switch and mischievously told her to strike the horse, which she did—on the nose. In the ensuing fracas, Nannie fell into the deep pool and might have drowned, but Jeff and other servants jumped in and pulled her out. Houston stood by silently as Margaret questioned Jeff and Nannie both. When she was finished, according to Jeff, "the General took out his long pocket knife and cut a good-sized limb from a sapling and pointed to the stable. I knew that my time had come. He took me inside one of the barns and gave me one of the soundest thrashings a boy ever got."

Gibbs Brothers Mercantile; Thomas Gibbs. The Houston family traded at Gibbs Brothers during their residence in Huntsville. Tom Gibbs and Houston became close friends during this time.

Both courtesy Sam Houston Memorial Museum

Jeff remained Houston's driver, and much more typical of their relationship was Jeff's recollection that, on the road, whenever Houston reached for the basket of cookies—he was inordinately fond of cookies—"he gave me a handful whenever he helped himself."[11]

• • •

Houston's newfound peace of soul may have nerved him for the political contests, but still, old habits died hard. Some time after his conversion, he was out riding on a blistering hot day with District Judge John H. Reagan of Palestine, who was prominent in the Baptist church. Houston's horse misstepped and nearly threw him, at which Houston exploded, "God damn a stumbling horse!"

As Reagan later recounted to Alexander Terrell, he asked in shock, "Oh! brother Houston, do you still swear?"

"Well, what must I do," asked the senator.

"Ask God to forgive you."

"I'll do it. Hold my bridle rein." Houston dismounted, knelt in the hot sun, and asked forgiveness. (Houston apocrypha, if not Houston himself, also provided an assessment of his effort: "That," he supposedly told Reagan upon rising, "was a damned good prayer.")[12]

With the political battles heating up, however, and with the stakes growing ever more desperate, not all of Houston's attempts at personal mildness were so lightly disposed of. Soon after his return to Washington, Rev. George W. Samson called on him at his hotel rooms to express his gratification at the baptism. The interview lasted for a friendly but earnest hour after which, Samson recalled in his oddball mix of first and third persons, "the pastor was followed as usual to the door, and, as often happened, the General asked: 'Brother S., is there anything I can do for you?'"

Samson had been somewhat privy to Houston's struggle over the issue of communion—he knew that it was the stumbling block but did not know why—and he pointed out to him that a communion Sunday was imminent, and a leading church member who would also take communion was a political adversary of Houston's. "You will meet at the Lord's supper next Sabbath evening," said Samson.

> You ought not to meet until that difficulty is settled. Now I wish you, after service on Sunday morning, to let me bring you two together, and without a word of attempt at justification on either side, I wish you to take him by the hand, and say with all your heart, that you will forgive and forget and bury the past, and that you wish him to do the same, and hereafter to meet you as brothers in Christ. The fire began to glow in his eyes, his brow to knit, his teeth to clench, and his whole frame shook with the struggle. . . . But in an instant, the man whose passion had been terrible . . . replied, "Brother S., I will do it." And, what he promised was done, and in an air of majestic frankness and nobleness of soul, such as moved every beholder.[13]

In 1852 Houston had campaigned for and helped elect President Pierce, who proved a profound disappointment; his manifest weakness and vacillation left his administration in tatters and so frustrated Pierce's one-time supporters that even the orator Edmund Burke, who had nominated him, turned on him. Burke, a kind of American Warwick, transferred his presidential support to Houston lock, stock, and barrel. For Houston to have acknowledged Burke's advice against giving the Boston speech, but appearing anyway and emerging triumphant, convinced the kingmaker that here was a man worth his time, and if Houston intended to make a run for the presidency, Burke could be a powerful ally. It was unclear, however, whether Houston stood any closer to the White House in 1856 than he had in 1852. Clay and Webster had both died in 1852; the remaining senator whose ambition burned most ardently for the presidency was Stephen Douglas of Illinois, and Houston had shown during the Kansas-Nebraska debates that he could handle the "Little Giant." The political landscape, however, had shifted just as Houston had predicted to Rufus Burleson. The abolitionists and free-soilers did join forces to become the Republican Party, and while the Whigs broke apart, the Democrats fell increasingly under the power of Southern extremists. With the parties in control of the nominating system, there was no place for a nationalist moderate to find refuge.

By default, Houston began an affiliation with a group that became known as the American Party, a quasi-secret society, nativist, antiforeign, and anti-Catholic. He was aware that it was a patchwork affair of disaffected Whigs and other refugees such as himself, and the senator tried to make light of it. "Now, of the Know-Nothings," he was recorded in the *Senate Journal* shortly before the Boston speech, "I know nothing. [laughter]; and of them I care nothing, but if the principles which I see charged to them in many instances are [true] . . . , I can say to gentlemen that I concur in many of them." Still, he was not overly warm in his endorsement. He had long been the staunchest friend of foreign immigrants in Texas and was a bit sore on the movement's nativist bent. "I admit," he said, "that we are all descended from foreigners." Under some attack, he yielded for a question from Sen. Stephen Mallory of Florida:

> [Mr. Mallory asked whether Houston approved "so much of the creed attributed to the Know-Nothings as would make those who profess the Roman Catholic religion ineligible to office."]
>
> MR. HOUSTON. I would vote for no such law.
>
> MR. MALLORY. I asked the gentleman whether he approved that or not— not whether he would vote for it.
>
> MR. HOUSTON. No, sir; I could not approve of such a law. But the proscription charged . . . is no more than formerly existed between Whigs and Democrats. When party discipline was kept up, if a Whig voted for a Democratic candidate he was ruled out of his party and branded a deserter.[14]

In July of 1855, Houston published a letter again repudiating the extremism of the Southern wing of the Democrats and endorsing at least some of the principles of the Know-Nothings. Of the American Order's alleged secrecy, Houston answered sarcastically that the existing national parties lived in glass houses from which they ought to cast no stones. "Are not secret caucuses continually held by the political leaders of both parties in Congress? 'Oh, yes,' it will be answered, 'very true, very true! but there is a necessity for this. We have to take care of our parties, to form plans for the people to carry out. And if we did not make platforms for them, they would not know how to vote upon important subjects.' This explains much of the opposition to the present movement."[15] Houston probably knew how ill suited he was to the nativists and that their movement would soon wither; had he ever been persuaded of their viability he might have joined, but that is doubtful. He was there only because the national parties staked out increasingly extreme positions, and from all his remarks private and public it was clear that Sam Houston held extremists on both sides of the slavery issue equally responsible for the relentless sectional acrimony.

If there was one position of the Know-Nothings that Houston could endorse completely, it was their stance on Indian rights, envisioning eventual citizenship for them and a native state to be formed from territory in the Northwest.[16] The Kansas-Nebraska Act's violation of Indian treaty rights was a keystone of his opposition to that measure, and during this same summer he at least received some vindication on that particular point from a common man who could not have stood closer to the Kansas controversy. A. M. Hunt, a resident of Kickapoo City, Kansas Territory, had ventured to call on Houston at his Willard's Hotel residence the previous year, sending up his card and being readily admitted for a talk. Hunt now wrote him from Kansas:

> This Territory is now distracted by free soil and proslavery factions. The Fireaters and the abolitionists, being mere *guerrillas* on either side. A pro slavery man Malcolm Clark was killed at Leavenworth city a short time ago by one C. McCrea, who narrowly escaped hanging by the proslavery fire eaters. The Missouri men are taking the law in their own hands as you will have seen by the papers of the day. There is a great deal of difficulty among squatters in not knowing where their lines run.
>
> I have only made the acquaintance of some of the Kickapoo & Pottawotmie indians as yet and find your sketch of them . . . to be just as my fancy had pictured it. By a few simple presents of hook and lines now and then . . . and by acting perfectly square with them, they have always met me with a "How" for me and an unsophisticated shake of the hand. . . .
>
> With the best wishes of a squatter in the wild West——
>   A. M. Hunt[17]

Concomitantly, Houston perceived a second threat to native security in bills that were regularly introduced to increase the size of the army, and he opposed them vociferously. At the end of 1855, his politics, from the Kansas-Nebraska issue to his Know-Nothing affiliation, was costing him goodwill, even among his closest friends. In December he dashed off a quick note to Ashbel Smith, who had taken a seat in the state legislature, to keep their relationship from breaking: "My Dear Smith, I write this to say that whatever our political [differences] may be, they will not with me disturb our personal regards. When I reach Austin I will be happy to meet you at Halls House."[18]

Had there been a way for Sam Houston to be politically connected with the people through some venue other than parties and their platforms and conventions, as was possible in the early days of the Texas Republic, he surely would have preferred it. And the fact that the times left Jacksonian populism behind did not go unlamented in other quarters. On April 28, 1856, the *New York Herald* published an article announcing its own impatience with conventions:

> There is a fierce war now going on between the Pierce and Buchanan men, and it waxes hotter every day. It is no uncommon thing to hear the Pierce men denouncing, in unmeasured terms, the Buchanan men, and vice versa. Pierce is losing ground every day, and he is aware of the fact. He informed a friend of his from the South, who is a delegate to the Cincinnati Convention,

that it was his wish that his friends in the Convention, in case he could not succeed, should go for a Southern man. "But," said he, "if you cannot do that, throw your strength to Mr. Douglas." . . .

General Houston . . . has received letters from all parts of the Union—democrats and whigs—urging him to become a national candidate for the Presidency, regardless of convention; the people are getting tired and disgusted with conventions.

A supporter in Baltimore sent Houston a clipping of the article from the *Herald* and asked for comments that could be published in the Baltimore press. The Texas senator had become well known as an enemy of party manipulation and especially conventions; as one of the last surviving Jacksonians, he believed that democracy should be direct and lively participated in by an engaged electorate. Houston had even heard from his cousin Narcissa Hamilton on the subject four years earlier. The timorous schoolgirl whose autograph book he had signed more than twenty years before had grown up into a literate and cheerful correspondent. "I had contemplated writing for some time," she informed him, "but concluded to wait until the adjournment of the Baltimore Convention. I am more and more disgusted with the intriguing politicians that manage the convention, and stifle the will of the people. . . . [But] you must not conclude that I have gone over to the whigs."[19]

When the hated convention season arrived, Houston allowed his name to be put forward nowhere. The Democratic nomination went to James Buchanan, whose friend he had been for more than thirty years. The Republicans put up John C. Fremont. The Know-Nothings too produced a convention and nominated former president Millard Fillmore with Andrew Jackson Donelson as his running mate—possibly an attempt in part to win Houston's support. In this they were disappointed, however. Donelson called on Houston to ask his help, and though they were friendly, the senator refused on the grounds that he could not support the Know-Nothing platform. A New York friend, Mrs. Ana Stephens, wrote to express her chagrin that the system had passed him by in 1856, just as it had in 1852, but Houston comforted her in a long and cheerful letter. "I am perfectly happy, and if I wished to be President, I would much rather take my chances, as a National Candidate, & go before the people without any Platform, but 'the Union & the Constitution,' than to rely on a nomination of the Convention, and accept the platform sent forth." Besides, he added, the Know-Nothings had no chance. When "poor Donelson" asked him to at least not campaign against them, he agreed. "I could have added that dead ducks need no killing!" And it was evident that Margaret was succeeding on one score: the senator was learning to look to home and family for comfort from battle. "And just think of the Addendas," he wrote Mrs. Stephens, "no less than six little Houstons to dandle on my knees, & kiss them and call them dear Children. Is not this worth more than all the honors, now a days, with all their cares and corruptions?"[20]

Houston suffered a grievous loss late in 1854. Henderson Yoakum, the lawyer and writer whose monumental two-volume history of Texas, completed with Houston's help, had appeared the previous year, went to Houston city on legal and Masonic business. After giving a speech, he collapsed and was carried to the house of his and Houston's mutual friend Peter Gray; Yoakum died of consumption on November 30. "The news of my dear Friend Yoakums death has reached here to day," the senator grieved to Margaret from Washington. "Oh, how melancholy it is to reflect on this result. Little, oh, little did I apprehend the end."[21] The senator was not the only one laboring under bereavements. "I could not write to you last teusday," Margaret had written him earlier, "which was my usual day, because Sister Creath seemed to be so near her end, that I thought it best to be with her on that day."[22] It was Frances Creath who had gotten Margaret through the lonely months at Raven Hill.

National politics were followed closely in a Texas that was increasingly Southern in its outlook. In March the U.S. Supreme Court handed down the Dred Scott decision, finding that a slave who had resided for a time in a northern territory lacked standing to sue for his freedom because, in the eyes of the law, he was merely property. Northern extremists began calling for tariff reprisals against the South. The battle for reason and calm really did seem no longer worth fighting, and when Houston gave a hint that he might retire from the Senate, the rumor raced across Texas like a blue norther that he would run for governor. However, Texas anti-Houstons, sometimes referred to as regular Democrats, had now had about enough of their renegade senator. On May 4 at their state convention in Waco, they nominated for governor the sitting lieutenant governor and former Speaker of the State House Hardin Runnels, a burned bachelor of thirty-six who reputedly had never gotten over being shunned by his bride-to-be after building and furnishing a handsome mansion for her on his Bowie County cotton plantation. (Senator Houston, of course, was one man who could have advised Runnels to count his blessings at escaping marriage to a woman who did not want him.) For a platform, they ran on condemnation of Sam Houston and approval of the tide of Southerners flooding across Kansas.

Horrified and infuriated, it took Houston less than two weeks to decide what to do. "Today I have declared myself a Candidate for Governor," Houston wrote to Rusk from Huntsville on May 12. "You will be surprised . . . for you know it was my intention to retire . . . to private life." But it was the regular Democrats in Waco who "make the issue as they declare 'Houston, and anti-Houston.' So now the whip cracks, & the longest pole will bring down the persimmon. The people want excitement, and I had as well give it as any one."

On this particular day, Ed Sharp, a plow salesman, rolled into Huntsville in a buggy advertising his wares. Upon learning that the legendary Sam Houston resided in this town, he inquired at Gibbs's Hotel directions to the senator's house. Woodland was visible across the vale just south of the business district, and when Gibbs pointed it out, Sharp strode boldly off to make his acquaintance. He lost sight of the house briefly in intervening woods, and on emerging from the trees found himself quite near and unexpectedly face to face with a man who could only be Houston.

Feeling embarrassed at the awkward position in which I had placed myself I felt that some explanation was necessary. . . . I inquired if I had the honor of addressing General Houston. His reply was:

"You have, young man. What can I do for you?"

"Nothing, General. If you are Sam Houston the object of my mission has been accomplished, as I only desired to see Sam Houston."

Houston was so flattered that he took young Sharp into the house and introduced him to Margaret, with a remark that he had just received a nicer compliment than ever on the Senate floor. To Sharp he imparted that he had just decided to announce for governor and invited him to walk with him up to Gibbs's; the hotel was also the location of the stage office, and the senator wished to book passage on the next day's coach for Houston to publish his campaign schedule. They learned there that the morrow's Houston stage was already full, and likewise the senator was unable to arrange an alternative conveyance at the livery stable. At this point young Sharp spoke up that he was on his way to Houston and would be happy to have some company.

If Houston had any doubts, they were dispelled when he saw Sharp's buggy—a brilliant scarlet affair with gilt lettering announcing "Warwick's Patent Plow." He was enchanted to discover a young man with a gift for self-promotion as promising as his own had been. Houston in his old age was no less willing to give his friendship to promising young men than he had been with Frank Lubbock or John Ross or Wash Miller or John Lockhart or any of the others. On the way south, they stopped in Montgomery so Houston could deliver a speech, and inevitably the curious gathered around the strange buggy and inquired after Warwick's Patent Plow. Sharp saw in a flash that if he could serve as Houston's driver the whole distance of the campaign, he could, as he later wrote, "see and reach more Texas farmers in a week . . . than he could in a year on his own."[23]

He broached his idea to the senator after the Montgomery speech. "Is it possible, my young friend," Houston responded, "that you could confer so great a pleasure and benefit to me without . . . inconvenience to yourself?" Sharp assured him he would be getting the better end of the bargain, and the deal was amicably struck. The new gubernatorial candidate was sixty-four and a half years old, but so far from conceding anything to age or infirmity, Sam Houston, when they reached his namesake city, published a campaign schedule that would have crushed a lesser man—but never, as he was able to tell Margaret, campaigning on Sundays. As given out to the newspapers:

I propose to address the people of Texas at the time and place hereafter set forth:
Crockett, Houston County . . . . Wednesday, May 27
Alto, Cherokee County . . . . Thursday, May 28
Rusk, Cherokee County . . . . Friday, May 29
Nacogdoches, Nacogdoches Co . . . . Saturday, May 30
San Augustine, San Augustine Co. . . . . Tuesday, June 2

Shelbyville, Shelby County . . . . Wednesday, June 3
Carthage, Panola County . . . . Thursday, June 4
Henderson, Rusk County. . . . . Saturday, June 6
Tyler, Smith County. . . . . Monday, June 8
Gilmer, Upshur County . . . . Wednesday, June 10
Marshall, Harrison County. . . . . Friday, June 12
Jefferson, Cass County. . . . . Saturday, June 13
Daingerfield, Titus County. Wednesday, June 17
Tarrant, Hopkins County. . . . . Thursday, June 18
Greenville, Hunt County. . . . . Friday, June 19
McKinney, Collin County . . . . Saturday, June 20
Alton, Denton County. . . . . Monday, June 22
Birdville, Tarrant County. . . . . Wednesday, June 24
Dallas, Dallas County. . . . . Thursday, June 25
Waxahachie, Ellis County. . . . . Friday, June 26
Corsicana, Navarro County . . . . Saturday, June 27
Fairfield, Freestone County. . . . . Tuesday, June 29
Centerville, Leon County . . . . Thursday, July 1
Madisonville, Madison County. . . . . Friday, July 3
At these several points designated I will be happy to meet Hon. H. R. Runnels,
the nominee of the Waco Convention. I object to all "whippers-in, or teasers."
  Sam Houston

This itinerary comprised an enormous loop through eastern and northeastern
Texas and this was just the first half of the campaign. After spending the Fourth of
July holiday at home in Huntsville, Houston intended another swing, this one through
the southwestern reaches of the state:

The hero of San Jacinto is communing with the people. I propose to address
the people of Texas at the time and place hereafter set forth:
Anderson, Grimes County . . . . Wednesday, July 8
Boonville, Brazos County. . . . . Thursday, July 9
Wheelock, Robertson County . . . . Friday, July 10
Marlin, Falls County . . . . Saturday, July 11
Waco, McLennan County . . . . Monday, July 13
Cameron, Milam County. . . . . Wednesday, July 15
Caldwell, Burleson County. . . . . Thursday, July 16
La Grange, Fayette County. . . . . Saturday, July 18
Bastrop, Bastrop County . . . . Monday, July 20
Austin, Travis County . . . . Wednesday, July 22
Lockhart, Caldwell County. . . . . Thursday, July 23
San Marcos, Hays County . . . . Friday, July 24
Seguin, Guadalupe County . . . . Saturday, July 25
New Braunfels, Comal County . . . . Monday, July 27
San Antonio, Bexar County . . . . Tuesday, July 28

Gonzales, Gonzales County . . . . Thursday, July 30
Clinton, DeWitt County . . . . Friday, July 31
Victoria, Victoria County . . . . Saturday, August 1
P.S. The Ladies are most particularly invited to attend.[24]

The Know-Nothings had little strength in Texas, and had the candidate been anyone but Sam Houston, it is doubtful that the regular Democrats would have taken the bid seriously. But Houston was a formidable stump speaker, and Runnels, by all accounts, was dismal, so the party dispatched not one but three of their heaviest hitters to dog Houston's trail and rebut his speeches: J. Pinckney Henderson, who had been Texas' first governor after annexation, along with Louis T. Wigfall and Williamson Oldham, both of whom later became prominent in the Confederate government. Also campaigning against Houston was the regular Democratic candidate for lieutenant governor, Houston's old friend Frank Lubbock, who made it clear, however, that his differences with the senator were purely political and that Houston still held a place of honor in his personal affections.

Before reaching Nacogdoches, Houston received word that Rusk intended to speak against him and in favor of Runnels. "This appeared to have a very depressing effect on Houston," Ed Sharp recalled, "and I heard him say in camp, 'Is it possible that my dear old friend Rusk has become my enemy?'" From Alto, the day before the Nacogdoches date, Houston penned a quick note to Rusk and sent it ahead: "Dear General—I will be happy to see you before I speak. I only wish 10 or 15 minutes to talk. . . . On Saturday in your Town at 2 Oclk P.M. Thine Truly, Houston."[25] When the time for the confrontation arrived, the audience beheld Houston and Rusk mount the stage from opposite sides. The two old campaigners drew near, and when they embraced, both broke into tears. Rusk led Houston away to his house, and neither one reappeared to address the people. When Sharp called for Houston in the morning at Rusk's home, the two old warriors embraced again, having made their peace. A few weeks later, Rusk died by his own hand.

Their next stop was San Augustine, which Houston had represented as congressman in the Republic of Texas during his presidential interregnum. Rather than enduring these travels as though it were a grueling campaign, Houston seemed rejuvenated and acted like a boy on a camping trip, which, more than not, it was. In sixty-seven days of campaigning, he and Sharp spent fifty-eight nights on the road. "Upon finding a suitable camping place," Sharp wrote later, "we would broil a little bacon . . . and spread out blankets. When this was done the General would commence by relating amusing anecdotes . . . and wind up with a song." Nothing much had changed since rooming with Ashbel Smith, except for the apparent absence of Latin.

After San Augustine there was a speech in Shelbyville, then June 4 found Houston driving the buggy through the woods of Panola County. By now he had given Sharp a pretty thorough recitation of his life and adventures, which stopped abruptly, Sharp noticed, at the time of his first marriage. He almost asked the hated question, but then, realizing what an invasion it would be of Houston's privacy, "checked myself before I uttered a word, but he very readily anticipated my thoughts. He stopped the horses, and looking me full in the face said: 'Go on, my young friend.'"

Acutely embarrassed, Sharp explained that his curiosity was not idle; his interest was solicitous.

"Then you admit, do you, young man, that you were about to ask me why I left my wife in Tennessee."

"I do, General, but I hope you will forgive me."

"I will not only forgive you . . . I will gratify you." Houston then explained in an even voice that "through the advice and influence of relatives and friends she had been induced to marry the governor of Tennessee instead of . . . the man of her choice."[26]

This exchange did not mean that Ed Sharp had become so intimate with Houston that he was admitted into some special emotional sanctum denied others. What it meant was that Eliza was no longer an issue with Sam Houston. His explanation was the same in every respect that he had already given George Samson and, indeed, the same in every respect that he had given Frank Chambers during his acute despair nearly thirty years before. His story had not changed, but Houston had changed; having the security now not just of Margaret but also of the church, he was finally at peace with the subject.

At the speech in Tyler on June 8, his designated opposition for the day was Wigfall, a South Carolina firebrand who had once killed a man in a quarrel without benefit of a duel. He had been in Texas only since 1846 and had publicly attacked Houston regularly since 1850—four separate counts in Houston's personal disdain of him. Ed Sharp recalled that it was the demands of their traveling schedule, making a speech every day or two in towns that were on average thirty miles apart, that prevented Houston from engaging in full debate with his opponents during this junket. Alexander Terrell, an Austin lawyer who was running for district judge as a regular Democrat, claimed rather that it was from pure defiance that Houston would not deign to share a platform with any of them. He seems to have been closer to the mark, recalling that at Tyler, "[Houston] closed his speech by telling his audience that a murderer named 'Wiggletail' would follow him, and he advised them not to hear him 'unless they were fond of lies.' After speaking he sat on the porch of a hotel near the courthouse and when the crowd left at the close of Wigfall's speech, he rose and met them with uplifted hands and shouted, 'Did I not tell you that you would hear nothing but lies?'" The truth was that Wigfall was perhaps the only one of the regular Democrats who could match the senator as a stump speaker, and his 1857 efforts hurt Houston's campaign.[27]

In four days more than a month, Houston and Ed Sharp rolled up more than seven hundred miles in the red and gold buggy emblazoned "Warwick's Patent Plow." The candidate had given some two dozen variations on what was the same basic speech of two to three hours duration. When they creaked into Huntsville at midnight on July 3, the rejuvenated Houston was so far from exhausted that he addressed the Independence Day barbecue the next day. "I have been east," he wrote triumphantly to Ashbel Smith, "and you will see it swept as by a Tornado." The senator did feel he had a fence to mend with his best friend, though. When he had once assured Smith that he did not intend to run for governor in 1857, Smith suggested that he might try it himself, and now Smith might conceivably feel a bit unhorsed. The brilliant scholar-turned-planter, however, regular Democrat though he had become, was unswerving in his personal affections.

For Houston to take his message directly to the people was probably the only way they would hear it because most Texas newspapers were still inimical to him. Judging the eastward trip a success, Houston set out with Sharp for the westward swing. In Austin on July 22, Houston spoke in a grove of trees north of the capitol, as the finishing touches were being put on a barbecue nearby. Many in Austin had had no use for Sam Houston ever since the "Archives War"; among those who denounced him was revolutionary hero and ranger captain James W. Swisher, one of the men to whom Cos had surrendered San Antonio at the end of 1835, a signer of both the Texas Declaration of Independence and the Constitution. He was one source of potential trouble that Houston defused from the start, spying Swisher in the audience and declaring, "Yes, I see many of my old boys before me, and yonder sits Captain Jim Swisher, the bravest of the brave." The accolade brought a tearful reunion from Swisher after the speech.[28] Most in the audience were less moved; the *State Gazette* in Austin was typical in assessing his effort, bemoaning, "the dirty black-guardism, the filthy allusions to mules, etc., and the garrulous abuse of men, are things beyond description! . . . Before he got through . . . with the Waco Convention, Houston imitated the squalling of a cat in pronouncing the word (Waco). . . . The applause was very seldom and very feeble . . . When he had finished there were many empty benches. It was a melancholy picture of imbecility, vindictiveness and hate in old age."[29]

Far from discouraged by his newspaper reviews in Austin, Houston and Sharp pressed on in their Warwick's Patent Plow buggy to Lockhart, where in the audience was Alexander Terrell, who was running for judge in the district that included Lockhart and Austin. It was a stifling hot and humid afternoon, and Houston spoke

> from a long platform erected in a grove near Storey's Spring. A large portion of his audience was composed of his San Jacinto soldiers and their kindred. He was clothed in a long coarse linen duster that reached to within a foot of his ankles, loose pants of the same material, no vest, low quartered shoes, and his shirt collar opened until the audience could see the grizzled hair on his breast a foot below his chin, and as thick as a buffalo mop. I had never before heard him speak . . . , but his erect bearing, the majesty of his appearance, his deep-toned, commanding voice, impressive gestures, and perfect composure made a lasting impression upon me. That impression was deepened when he denounced the executive committee, of which I was a member.

As Houston was speaking, his opponent for the day arrived—Williamson Oldham, lately of Arkansas, where he had served as speaker of the state house and state supreme court justice before his political career there declined. Oldham carried a memory of Houston as a drunk in Fort Gibson, Indian Territory, refusing to speak

English, but Houston knew a couple of unflattering things about Oldham too, largely concerning his implication in an Arkansas financial scandal. He had removed to Austin in 1849 and run unsuccessfully for Congress. He was, to Houston's disgust, the editor of the *Austin State Gazette*, which had just excoriated him. Oldham arrived while Houston was speaking and began removing two large volumes of the *Congressional Globe* from his saddlebags, intending to inflame the crowd against Houston using the senator's own words uttered in support of the Union. The crowd began to buzz. "Be still, my friends, be still," said Houston, "I will report the cause of the commotion." He walked to the rear of his platform and looked over. One can imagine the theatrical gestures that would have accompanied the silence. He returned to his place and said, "It's Oldham, only Oldham, I'll tell you what he's doing." He made another descrying look off the rear of the stage. "He is opening some books, but they are not the bank books he stole and sunk in White River, Arkansas!" Terrell was standing at Oldham's side as the latter bit his cigar in two.

Houston then launched into a tirade against the regular Democrats and the Waco convention, which had denounced him in their platform as a traitor and vowed their intention to handle him without gloves. "Well," huffed Houston, "that paper is too dirty for me to handle without gloves."

> He paused a moment, and took deliberately from the pocket of his duster a pair of heavy buckskin gauntlets and with mock gravity drew them on. . . . Then drawing the paper from his pocket he read that portion which declared that all traitors should be defeated, and in the defeat of Houston "add to theirs a name of fear that traitor knaves shall quake to hear." Throwing the paper to the floor with a quick impatient gesture, he exclaimed: "What! I a traitor to Texas! I who in defense of her soil moistened it with my blood?" Then he took several steps, limping on his leg that was wounded at San Jacinto. . . .
>
> The effect can hardly be described. A wave of sympathy swept over the audience, and red bandana handkerchiefs were wiping tears of indignation from the eyes of his old soldiers. Then he stooped down and after picking up the paper said, "Let me read you the names of that executive committee." He read: "Williamson S. Oldham—though he stole and sunk those bank books in White River and ran away to Texas, he is not yet in the penitentiary.
>
> "J. M. Steiner—a murderer. He murdered Major Arnold.
>
> "John Marshall—a vegetarian; he won't eat meat; one drop of his blood would freeze a frog.
>
> "A. W. Terrell—he used to be a Whig in Missouri. They tell me that the young scapegrace wants to be your judge. A pretty looking judge he would make, this slanderer of a man old enough to be his father."

Out in the audience, A. W. Terrell felt the heat. "I have heard all the great orators of the Republic and State of Texas, except Lamar and the Whartons. Houston . . . before a frontier audience excelled them all."[30]

From Lockhart, Houston and Sharp proceeded to San Marcos for a speech the next day, and the day after that—Saturday, July 25—to Seguin. There, Col. George B.

Sam Houston in Linen Duster. In 1857, a vigorous sixty-four years old, Houston campaigned for the governorship, riding over fifteen hundred miles in Ed Sharp's buggy wearing a linen duster. The closed shirt and cravat were for the benefit of the daguerreotypist; his midsummer stump speeches were noted to have been given in an open collar.

Courtesy Texas State Library and Archives Commission

Hollamon offered Houston the hospitality of his estate, Elm Cove, where he spent the night in an enormous walnut four-poster bed that had been lengthened for the comfort of tall men. The candidate asked with his customary confidence if he might have a duplicate made for the Governor's Mansion and obtained the name of the cabinetmaker.[31] Now on the homeward stretch of his campaign tour, only five more engagements stood between Houston and Huntsville.

In Victoria, Houston spoke for two hours "to an audience of perhaps 500 persons. He wore a long brown linen 'duster,' was tall and portly, and bore evidence of a dignified, well-preserved manhood. He . . . scathed the Waco Convention . . . and . . . occupied much time in proving that he was in full rapport with . . . the 'divine institution,'—averring that he owned as many slaves as his means would admit of." In Austin, Houston had been received with hostility, at least according to the hostile newspapers, but in Victoria, Houston was the guest of honor at a reception and ball in the home of Judge Alexander Phillips, a former congressman of the republic who, upon retiring to private practice in 1850 after three terms in the state senate, built a lavish mansion in the Louisiana Creole style.[32]

In two months, Sharp and Houston covered well over fifteen hundred miles in the scarlet buggy, punished in the final weeks by dust storms and temperatures of well over one hundred degrees. When the election finally came, the returns trickled in for weeks, but eventually the smoke cleared enough to see that Hardin Runnels, the pinched bachelor from Red River, had handed Houston the first electoral thrashing of his life. When all were tallied, Runnels had 38,552 votes, Houston 23,628. The senator, so far from devastated, wrote Ashbel Smith on August 22: "The fuss is over, and the sun yet shines as ever. What next? . . . In the result of the election I am cheered, and were it not for my friends, I assure you, I would rejoice at the result, if I am spared to take my seat in the Senate. I will, as the Frenchman said, 'Have some fish to fry.' Had I been elected, I would have had other 'fish to fry.'"

Other fish, indeed. It would have been uncharacteristic of Sam Houston to enter any contest without a back-up plan, and he was already calculating on a scheme that he wished to pore over with his old friend. "Is there any way we can contrive a pow-wow, that we may unite in trying to draw the veil partially aside, and take a peep into coming events? I want to talk grave as well as laugh with you. . . . Oh, I do want some one who has seen other days in Texas to talk with!" And so typically for Houston, who often clucked over the matrimonial negligence of his bachelor friends, he had some happy chaff to toss in the air to mask the real purpose of their meeting: "We have in our vicinity one of the grandest Girls (a Miss Campbell) said to be in America. Come and see her. You can say that you are going up to see your prospective Ranch on the Navisoto; and 'say you hear the fever has broken out at Houston, and I must return.' . . . If you come to see me, I bind myself to make you laugh." One of the jokes he wished to share with Smith was that Mirabeau Lamar had been appointed United States minister to Costa Rica. "Is [this] not a *funny* thing." He predicted that the victors would not enjoy their spoils as much as they thought, and he believed that the result of the election was poor compensation for what he called the murder of T. J. Rusk.[33]

Shortly after his gubernatorial defeat, Houston received a letter from Alexander Terrell, newly elected judge of the Second Judicial District. He enclosed a newspaper article in which he said that, while he had opposed Houston for political reasons well known, the language in the Waco platform branding him a traitor and knave had been added without his knowledge, and he declared that Houston's patriotic services to Texas were known to all. Moved by such a gesture, Houston wrote him back saying that, in his "long and eventful career," he had never received anything that pleased him more and that he hoped one day to know Terrell personally.[34]

The losing campaign for the Governor's Mansion left Houston so broke that when his treasured Wash Miller needed to borrow some money at the end of the summer, Houston could not accommodate him. "My Dear Miller," the General wrote him, "I have to begin with the usual expressions, or 'I am sorry,' or 'I regret that it is not in my power to [succor?] you.' Truly my friend, I have not the sum at command if it was to save my life. Yesterday, I had to raise a hundred dollars by borrowing." Even worse, his friend Yoakum had died owing him some four thousand dollars, and "I do not know when I will get any part of it. . . . As to the late election," he added, "my dear fellow, I am not chagrined or mortified . . . only on account of my noble friends, who are so strongly Knit to my heart." The people had spoken, and "now I am hands off. . . . Salute my friends with cheerfulness, for I am really so. Miller, come down, and see us."[35]

Houston always hurt when he was unable to oblige his friends when they asked favors, personal or political, and after returning to Washington for the opening of the 1858 session, he sat up late Christmas night to cajole his way back to Wash Miller's good side with one of his playful letters:

> It is . . . more than a year since I have been gratified by a missile from you. This causes me to say, what are you engaged in, that you can't tell me something? Is there any thing that I can try to do for you? . . . If not, write to me and let me know that you are well and about to marry, or to do some clever thing. . . .
>
> Write. Write.
>
> Thy Devoted,
>
> Houston
>
> a happy New Year!!!

If Miller had been able to visit, it would have been one of the last times that the Houstons entertained a guest at Woodland: the 1857 campaign expenses cornered the senator into a move he winced over—selling his beloved Woodland house to whittle down his debt.

The Texas legislature punished Houston for his Unionism by announcing his replacement at the expiration of his current term—an unprecedented insult that led to calls in the press for his resignation. Houston returned to the Senate in good-humored defiance, sporting a waistcoat sewn from a jaguar skin and quoting the Bible that, after all, the leopard cannot change his spots. His thinking had certainly modified since that day in 1829 when he resigned the governorship of Tennessee, declaring he would "hold no delegated power which would not be daily renewed by my constituents." Southern firebrands were gleeful that the Texas legislature had turned him out before the end of his term and taunted him on the Senate floor. "I have this assurance," he answered one, "that I made the State of Texas, but I did not make the people; and if they do wrong, the State still remains in all its beauty . . . and I am a proud citizen of it."[36]

He opened 1858 in the Senate with a tribute to Rusk. His friend had been much respected in the Senate, which had named him president pro tempore during the last session, but personal reverses and the death of his wife had broken him. The two senators from Texas had had a stormy relationship, but their reunion during the late campaign had healed much, and Houston's eulogy was decorous and touching: "As a soldier he was gallant, his chivalry spotless, his honor clear; as a statesman he was wise, conservative, and patriotic; as a friend, he had all the high qualities that ennoble the heart; . . . as a man, he had all the qualities that adorn human nature." His appeal had been not sectional, but national, and Texas, Houston said, "has no material to replace him in this body."[37]

Houston backed up his public remarks with private acts that were consistent with them. Rusk's suicide had left in limbo a Louisiana jobseeker named Clinch who had sought Rusk's patronage, and Houston endorsed his candidacy to a post in the Treasury Department. "I sincerely hope with your kind disposition," he wrote Treasury Secretary Howell Cobb, "it may be compatible with the public interest to give him a situation. . . . If Genl Rusk were living . . . he would have given all his influence."[38]

In commending Rusk's career to the Senate as having been of national rather than sectional significance, Houston framed a thought with material that was already at the fore of his worries. Sectionalism, with all its petty rants, was indeed more on his mind than ever, for the break-up of the Union, of which he warned during the Kansas-Nebraska debate, he now saw more clearly than ever. That regional impudence would triumph over national interest seemed inevitable, with all its apocalyptic consequences. He had to do something; he had to concoct a plan. He would be out of the Senate in less than a year and a half and would no longer have that platform from which to work. It was a time for Houston to retreat deep within himself and think hard.

If any in the Senate had known him well enough, they would have detected the signs, for at any time in his public life, when Houston began to develop plans, he began almost simultaneously throwing up clouds of chaff to disguise what they might be, combining chimerical bantering with periods of deep silence, whittling, and more whittling. He rose in the Senate to offer a motion that volunteers be dispatched to restore order in Utah. Such "animated young men will take wives from amongst the Mormons, and that will break up the whole establishment; it will take away their capital."[39] Then he sat and whittled. He rose to offer a motion abolishing the Senate's night sessions, then sat and whittled. He wagged his tongue at Jefferson Davis on Indian conditions, and after sat and whittled. Not surprisingly, it was Texas that eventually came to the fore of his scheme to save the Union. No fewer than five times he opposed increases in the regular army and pressed for aid for the Texas Rangers to keep order on the frontier: "Give us one thousand Rangers," he taunted, "and we will be responsible for the defense of our frontier. Texas does not want regular troops. Withdraw them if you please."[40]

When he finally spoke what was on his mind, on February 16, he delivered a speech that must have stupefied the Senate. Mexico, he asserted, wracked by twenty-five revolutions in twenty-eight years, ought to be conquered and made an American protectorate. "The chances multiply, from day to day," he urged, "that the country will be turned over to barbarism—. . . Mexico cannot prevent it, because she is never free from civil war or other intestine commotions; and we cannot, short of hermetically sealing our frontier. . . . We have, then, no alternative if we put the slightest value upon our interests . . . but to arrange plans immediately for ruling her wisely, and as far as possible, gently."[41]

Doubtless this was the scheme he had wished to discuss with Wash Miller after his gubernatorial defeat. By April he added new twists to this rhetoric, emphasizing the charitable results to Mexico herself from an American occupation and mentioning that the cost of the venture would be defrayed entirely by Mexico's customs receipts. "Hence it is clear that we have it in our power . . . to breathe the breath of new life into her nostrils; and without incurring the risk of a dollar."[42] In all, Houston broached the topic of the Mexican protectorate six times, but nobody paid any mind.[43] Finally, on June 2, he delivered not an ultimatum but one of those idle prophecies by which he had long since acquired the habit of saying what he really meant: "Men who may have power to accomplish something . . . may undertake such an enterprise. I should not feel myself restrained at any age to interpose on behalf of humanity, and to arrest the cruelties on . . . a defenseless people."[44]

During that spring, he also tended to other Texas interests in the Senate. On April 17 he argued for a southern route of the contemplated transcontinental railroad (which had also been a favorite cause of Rusk's), backing up his call with evidence that along this route mail passed from San Antonio to San Diego in only three weeks.[45] By and large, however, few in the Senate took Sam Houston seriously after the Texas Legislature declared him a lame duck, and more than once he had to fight off Southern taunts, especially over his stand on the Kansas-Nebraska Act. "I was not the enemy of slavery," he defended himself, "nor was I its propagandist." He had fought the bill "to prevent conflict in a future time."[46] On another occasion he answered derision at his having been run out of the Democratic Party by declaring that he had become his own party. "Well, sir, that is a great convenience," he wagged defiantly, "because there is no dissension in my party. . . . I am a unit."[47]

Back home, Margaret was expecting again; Houston's letters to her on May 17 and 19 expressed hope that he would be home for the delivery. He had a dream, he wrote, that the event had already taken place, "but the dream was not *distinct*"; that is, whether they had another son or another daughter. On May 25, without her husband's presence, Margaret gave birth to William Rogers Houston, named for a close family friend.[48] After the end of the session, setting up house at the Independence farm, Houston branched out into areas new to him: he purchased the rights to a patent medicine, Calvert's Bee Gums, and he leased a pasture and purchased three hundred head of sheep—not for himself, but to turn over to Sam Junior. Jeff overheard the senator tell an old army pal that even if the boy got swindled out of the livestock, it would be a valuable lesson to him in looking out for himself. But there was a lot more on Sam Houston's wily mind than these things. For a retired country squire desirous of tending his farm and marketing his patent, Houston gave a lot of speeches in the summer of 1858: August 12 in Washington County; August 14 at Independence; August 17 at Hempstead. At Danville (now a ghost town south of New Waverly) on September 11, a great barbecue attracted five hundred people, who listened to him hold forth for two hours with one of the finest speeches he ever made. He was not selling Calvert's Bee Gums from the back of the wagon, either. Senator Douglas of Illinois was a "prince of humbugs" and his Kansas-Nebraska bill a "firebrand." The Southern League was the mischief of disunionist agitators, no good would come from reopening the slave trade to Africa, and he supported President Buchanan. And Texas, he told everyone, would never have peace until Mexico was pacified as a U.S. protectorate. Sam Houston sounded an awful lot like a man who intended to throw Hardin Runnels out of the Governor's Mansion in 1859, and according to one observer, "the strange thing about Houston is that he speaks better now than he did ten years ago. . . . There is no doubt [he is] mollifying . . . his bitterest enemies."[49]

Returning to Independence after the speaking tour, the senator discovered that Sam Junior, far from losing his sheep or being swindled, had fattened them up, driven them to Galveston, and turned a tidy sum on them.[50] At this point every small income helped the family, for the 1857 campaign had savaged their finances. Ed Sharp had provided the transportation, but the supplies, the barbecues, and the printing bills of his modern-style campaign had left a modern-sized debt. Houston did still have one more session to serve in the Senate, so he could count on his federal salary, but the eventuality of his retirement loomed close enough that, as usual when some chapter of his public life closed, he spent time shoring up his private affairs. Perhaps inspired by Sam Junior's Galveston sheep profit, he decided to establish a flock at Cedar Point, just next door to the Galveston market. Writing Ashbel Smith that he had decided to "go into the *sheperdizing* business," he cajoled him that Smith was away from home too much to give proper attention to his sheep, which were consequently going to the "hogs & dogs. . . . Now, my Dear Friend, don't you get provoked at me, for disparaging you in the way of sheep-husbandry. I admit your universal intelligence, and ability in general matters, but you would not do, *personally*, as a sheep man!" Noting that sheep had been selling in Louisiana at $2.50 a head, and that Smith's animals were already acclimated to the brackish local water they would find at Cedar Point, Houston offered him a generous $4.00 a head. Other text in the letter shows, however, that Houston had not consigned himself irretrievably to the sheep pasture. While avowing that he had no more political ambitions, he yet added ambiguously, "unless I go to Mexico, to take a look at the interior of the 'Halls of the Montezumas'"; the protectorate again.[51]

Early in December 1858, Houston returned to Washington for his final stint in the United States Senate. Rusk's replacement, J. P. Henderson, died in early June after a tenure of only four months, and Houston delivered a eulogy on the floor, unaffectionate but respectful.[52] One of the first items to be considered was, once more, the transcontinental railroad. Political shenanigans had been afoot to define three possible routes to study: a northern, a central, and a southern. Houston picked up immediately on the ruse that the "southern" route was located no farther south than the central plains. Sarcastic and cajoling, Houston's performance during the two-day debate revealed a reserve of spunk: "If this is to be a great national work, give it national character. . . . I have regretted . . . that in the course of this discussion it has been deemed necessary to draw any invidious distinction between the North and the South. . . . You never hear me talk of 'southern rights.' . . . All the states have equal rights." The route that was cheapest and most express, he argued, followed the "natural trough" of the Red River, thence to El Paso, and finally across the southwestern desert to San Diego. "Why rule out this route?" he demanded.

Although it was a southern railroad Houston was arguing for, he came under attack from Alfred Iverson of Georgia, who accused him of currying favor with Northerners now that his fellow Southerners had spurned him and denied him continuance in office. Houston answered Iverson with blandishments that poured out thick as molasses from a tar barrel, but there was poison in it too. "Those who have known [Houston] intimately in Texas," reported an observer for the *Dallas Herald*, "and seen him prepare for the annihilation of an opponent, can readily appreciate [that his] great forte is the adroit mixture of flattery with the most consummate ridicule." And Houston still had his classical literature to call upon.

"The Senator from Georgia pronounces me dead," he said in his most droll voice. "It may be so, and if it be so, it recalls the fable of Aesop, which tells how a lion lay dead in the forest, and a certain animal came and kicked the dead lion. In courtesy to the south, and in deference to the Senator from Georgia, I will not mention the name of this animal that came and kicked the lion." That was merely an introduction; the real salvos came, again, on the subject of national dissolution. "Have gentlemen ever reflected," Houston admonished, "when, where and how they are to begin disunion; and where it is to end? Will they cut the great Mississippi in two? . . . If my advocacy of the Union has caused my immolation, politically . . . I exult and triumph in that."[53]

The necessity of daily arguing in defense of something Houston held as sacred as the Union led him through an emotional *Götterdammerung*. From these debates he would return to his lodging and write Margaret that he was "sick, weary, and . . . disgusted, with all the developments around me. . . . To dine with the President . . . is not a pleasant duty, as it will place me in stays. . . . I do long to throw off the harness and submit myself to the rule of 'petticoat government.' . . . Family, flock, and honest thrift are all I am now interested in." Well, almost all. "At this moment," he wrote on, "I need your society and advice more than I have ever done. . . . I will make no decision until I can see you [on a] . . . matter [that] relates to the 'Protectorate.' I can entertain no proposition, with any pleasure, that even blinks at a temporary separation from you."[54]

Through nearly twenty years of marriage, Margaret learned to take comfort in the General's repeated vows of life's desolation when separated from her, even as she learned to accept endless separation. She had endured whole seasons without him, had borne children without him, and had never taken her place in the high society of Washington, where a woman of her beauty and culture could have been mistress of a household that radiated elegance. But that was the wisdom of her policy, to share her husband with their country but to provide him a refuge from their stupidity and ingratitude, to keep a home for him where he could always return and feel safe. Moreover, it was an impregnable testament to the sincerity of her religious tenets that she considered the honors of the world as dust and rot. Only by turning her back on Washington society could she credibly espouse the moral superiority of piety and simplicity. This she did, and in so doing helped cement the faith that her husband had struggled all his life to find peace in. Margaret Lea Houston had earned her reward, and now at last those interminable separations were about to end.

Sam Houston, on the eve of his retirement from the Senate, deserved to think that, even though great conflict lay ahead, at least his past reputation was now safely harbored. That illusion was shattered when he opened a letter from Westchester County, New York, dated February 24, 1859.

> Reverend James H. Perry, D.D., of New York, delivered in a lecture in the Methodist Episcopal Church, this evening, the most bitter remarks respecting your bravery and honor that ever passed human lips. The subject was "The battle of San Jacinto; its causes and consequences." . . . He said, "I wish it to be understood . . . that the battle of San Jacinto was fought, and the victory was achieved, in spite of General Houston, and the wreath that now encircles his brow as the hero of that battle has not in it one green leaf. . . ."
>
> May I inquire if you remember James H. Perry as your aide-de-camp, and what part he took in the battle?"[55]

What a remarkable testament to the virulence of Hazard Perry's hatred that it burned afresh after thirty-three years. In sadness and disgust, Houston rose in the Senate to refute it one last time. "For . . . years this gentleman has been sedulously engaged in defaming [my] character, or attempting to do it. I was apprised of it before. Gentlemen of his denomination, of high respectability, assured me that a stop would be put to it. I see that he has broken out in a fresh place. . . . I should not have felt it necessary to reply to the attacks that have been made upon me, were it not that I am to leave a progeny, that might, at some future time, be called on to know why a response was not given to these fabrications."

Houston then made a defense of the Runaway Scrape and the San Jacinto campaign that fill thirty typeset pages, including supporting documents and testimonials. At its conclusion, Houston declared that he did not intend to address the Senate again before the expiration of his term and asked the body's indulgence for a closing remark, which turned into a final plea for the Union: "Mr. President, I know the high and important duties that devolve upon Senators, and I have confidence that their attention and their great abilities will be called to the discharge of those duties. . . . My prayers will remain with them, that light, knowledge, wisdom, and patriotism may guide them, and that their efforts will be perpetually employed for blessings to our country; that under their influence and their exertions the nation will be blessed, the people happy, and the perpetuity of the Union secured to the latest posterity. [Applause in the galleries.]"[56] At least he intended these to be his final words, but they were not, quite. Senate debate the following day on a post office appropriations bill, which proposed mail routes, as with the railroad bill in January, that ignored and cheated the South, led him to rise one more time and

Sam Houston, Brady Studio, New York, 1859. Before leaving the Senate, Houston paid a final visit to New York City. "I will not regret my visit," he wrote Margaret, "for I look upon it as my last visit, and I have many warm friends to whom I am much attached." While there, he posed for a series of photographs at Brady's.

Courtesy National Archives

take some brief pot shots. "I could not resist the inclination," he explained, "to do justice to all sections of the country."[57]

Sam Houston left Washington, D.C., on March 10, 1859, never to return. The following day, the *Washington Evening Star* reported that, "Up to the hour of his departure, his rooms were crowded by his friends calling to take leave of him. No other public man ever made more, or more sincere friends here, nor was severance of a gentleman's connection with American public affairs ever more seriously regretted than in his case."[58] It was a regret shared by Houston's friends, and Wash Miller wrote him mournfully about the end of such an era. "I am almost distressed," Houston answered him, "at what you write about my retiring from public life. Why, my dear Miller, I assure you, I have not been so buoyant, & cheerful for 45 years as I have been since I was beaten for Governor. . . . I pray you my dear Miller to be reconciled." His optimism was unfeigned, as borne out by family letters. "Well, to day is beautiful," he wrote Margaret, "and like spring. I presume all our people, I mean the children, are almost crazy to get to 'the Bay.' This I infer from Mary Willie's letter. I would like to know what Master Andrew, with his new pants, has to say on the subject. It will just suit him," because at Cedar Point, "there will be no chance to shut up his dogs, or anything else for awhile." He speculated that Andrew would become quite a fisherman in Galveston Bay, especially if he believed fish eating would make him big and strong—then Houston pulled out of that train of thought. "Whenever I begin to write about home matters," he confided to Margaret, "my feelings are so strong, that I can with difficulty write anything coherent, or sensible."[59]

18

THE LAST ALMOST OF A RACE

As bad as his finances had been at the end of the 1857 campaign, Sam Houston now, for once, ended a stint of public service without being strapped for money. He had drawn his salary for a year and a half, and he left Washington with a cash draft of $2,550.[1] However, that grave leave-taking with which Houston bade farewell to the Senate and his grand departure from Washington two weeks later led to a retirement of exactly ten weeks. If at any time Sam Houston actually believed he was finished with politics, then he was virtually the only person in Texas who did believe it.

Hardin Runnels had proven himself an unpopular governor; frontier events got away from him, and almost from the hour Houston arrived home, the former senator was barraged by a hail of letters from those urging him to run again. One of the most articulate was from an old friend, Swante Palm of Austin, for whom Houston had been lobbying to secure a consular post in Denmark, though without success. In a clear and unadorned hand, Palm excused himself, that as he was "one of those many that wishes at the next election to redeem their last vote against you, I am bold to mention the subject to you. Your friends here are numerous and much encouraged by accounts from all parts of the state. The[y] are anxious to have a chance to vote for you for the Governorship, and are waiting impatiently for your declaration that you will accept the office."[2] His Galveston editor, Hamilton Stuart, agreed that Houston's political stock was on the rise, but believed that he should hold out for reappointment to the Senate. One telling letter arrived from C. B. Way of Waco, a city that Houston had repeatedly disparaged during the 1857 campaign for their hosting the convention of the state regular Democrats. There were still some hard feelings in the town, but Way forwarded a petition from one hundred citizens of surrounding McClennan County urging him to stump for governor again. "We are in earnest. We think Texas needs your services. We don't believe you can refuse her. . . . We can safely promise you a majority in this County larger than in this City." But if Waco could go for him, who would not? Andrew Jackson McGown, a San Jacinto veteran, Huntsville resident, and leading founder of the Presbyterian church in Texas, penned Houston a shaky letter from the steamer *Diana*. "[T]he boats rocking," he wrote, "& They have taken the table from me to set supper. . . . Genl Michaels is on board—was against you before—will now vote for you—says you will be elected."[3]

Sam Houston had long eschewed nomination by convention but held himself amenable to a call from the people, and the momentum of these communications was irresistible. From the house in Independence on June 3, he wrote his friend George Washington Paschal, editor of the *Austin Southern Intelligencer*, that he had "yielded my own inclinations to the inclinations of my friends, and concluded, if elected, to serve the people as the Executive of the State. The Constitution and the Union embrace the principles by which I will be governed if elected. They comprehend all the old Jackson National Democracy I ever professed, or officially practised."[4]

In the effort to unseat Hardin Runnels, new times would call for a new strategy. Runnels was a good states' righter, but in Texas the great sectional arguments that preoccupied the nation had, during his term, become somewhat dislodged by issues closer to home, as the frontier was ravaged by Indians on the northwestern edge of civilization, and turmoil ensued along the Rio Grande thanks to a rampaging bandit-cum-folk hero named Juan Nepomuceno Cortina. Runnels was vulnerable, and Houston had sense enough not to rehash the old Kansas-Nebraska donny-brook. His exhausting canvass in the previous election had resulted in defeat, and this time the less he said, the better. He intended to stand on his stature and let people vote against Runnels. For Houston to open a second campaign for governor and not give some accounting of that earlier defeat, however, would have been unthinkable, and he did it with grace and humor, though without really giving any ground. To a large audience in Nacogdoches he admitted:

> Two years ago you gave me a little the worst skinning that mortal man ever got. It was a regular drubbing. You beat me after the best style, as you had a right to do. I had voted against the Nebraska bill and against Mr. Buchanan. Well that is past. The Nebraska bill has had its day, and the results are to be seen. What they are I will not say, but I will say that Ex-Gov. Hammond, one of the most profound statesmen in the South, and one whom your legislature has fully endorsed, has declared "*The Kansas Nebraska bill was a delusion and deception from the beginning. It was a snare to those at the South. It was rotten with fraud, and those who made it, flinched from its consequence.*" Other members of Congress and statesmen have declared that the South was deceived in the bill. I was the only extreme Southern Senator who voted against it, and for that you whipped me like a cur dog. If I was wrong, I own it and take it all back, and if you were wrong I forgive you. So we will start even again.

Only Sam Houston could in one breath claim to "take it all back" after lining up endorsements that he had been right all along. He did admit rather pridefully to being old-fashioned. "I am a Democrat of the Old School. In politics I am an old Fogy. An old Fogy because I cling devotedly to those primitive principles upon which our government was founded. . . . You may change parties, build up and pull down platforms,—but the principles of democracy will remain intact." This was the launching point for a foray into the evils of party conventions and the platforms they spawned. "If Conventions be democracy, how was it that democracy existed before Conventions? Jefferson did glorious work for the people before their time. He was not nominated by one. I myself am older than platforms. . . . The first National Convention I ever heard of, was to nominate Martin Van Buren upon Gen. Jackson's ticket. Jackson was asked to go before it. He refused and appealed to the people, who sustained him. . . . I have told you that platforms, when they are used to blind the people to the designs of men are dangerous."

Just at this point in Houston's speech, part of the staging around him collapsed, and as the dignitaries picked themselves out of the dust and lumber, the would-be governor never missed a beat. "There!" he wagged, "Did I not tell you platforms are dangerous?"

It would be easy to imagine Sam Houston joining in the roar of laughter he could elicit, and in his early life he may have had his raucous moments, but not so during these later years. "He is the only man I ever knew," wrote Alexander Terrell, "who having a keen sense of humor never indulged in boisterous laughter. When his anecdotes or droll sarcasm excited those around him to merriment, he would remain with features unmoved and only show his enjoyment . . . by opening his large blue eyes as if in astonishment."[5]

Having enumerated the dangers of platforms, Houston proceeded to work over the late Democratic convention in Houston city, whose platform advocated reopening the African slave trade and making it sound like a good thing, when in fact, he insisted, it would be a disaster for the South. Just as he had before the First Congress of the Texas Republic, Houston attacked the slave trade without attacking the institution itself, but the economics of his arguments were now formidably refined:

> Reopen the African Slave Trade and the South will be deluged with barbarians. Your present stock of negroes would fall in value. . . . The Labor market would be overdone. The vast army of slaves would be put to work in your cotton fields, and the vast crop would glut the market beyond all reasonable demand. Prices would fall to four or five cents per pound, and even then, when the demand was supplied, the greater portion of your crop would lie upon your hands for want of a purchaser. Freight would advance to an enormous price, because every sail that the Yankees could raise—these dear Abolitionist gentlemen who love the negro so well—would be engaged in the traffic. . . . The yankees would then get your cotton at four cents per pound, and make it into calico and red handkerchiefs to buy negroes with on the coast of Africa, which they will bring South to sell for your hard dollars. To such a ruinous policy I am opposed.

The talk of the town in 1859 was of an impressive new building that had just been completed at Nacogdoches University, a two-story brick Greek revival temple of learning that had been constructed at much cost and care. Texas had now reached such a state of development that more thought was being given to education, and Houston announced that he wished "to be allowed to present a few ideas." The legislature, he believed, had the duty to provide for the basic education of the masses, and he conceded that the time would come when the state might underwrite a large university, but it could not yet afford one. Besides, history had shown that "a great National or State [school] becomes a receptacle of the sons of politicians and the wealthy. As at West Point Academy, they are drilled and taught—eyes right— eyes left; but if they haven't got the brains, it is impossible to make great men out of them. Unless Providence stamps the man of genius, depend upon it, education will not give it to him. . . . You cannot convert a puddle duck into an eagle. You can make an educated fool,—but you cannot educate a fool into a man of genius." Primitive education, he said, should be as free as possible, but the current system of home universities such as that in Nacogdoches was satisfactory, even though they charged tuitions to maintain themselves. "That's the way to get education— work for it. A man knows the value of it then"—this from a man who educated himself after less than one year of schooling.

The former senator closed his speech—not unusually for him—with compliments to the ladies who had come, even though, "I know that politics are always uninteresting to you." Yet their presence "is a guarantee that their husbands and fathers and brothers are men of intelligence and refinement. . . . All parties desire your approving smile, and therefore all are encouraged by your presence."[6] Houston announced that this Nacogdoches speech would be the only one he would deliver during the campaign—a radical departure from the bone-wearying buggy tour with Ed Sharp two years earlier. Once it was published, he intended to let the people's intelligence be their guide, and if they should call him from retirement, he would answer, and if they did not, he was happily retired as it was.

The anti-Houstons, however, campaigned vigorously, and in addition to the usual bear-baiters, one of the men taking the stump against him was William Read Scurry, a lawyer and legislator who carried negative associations in Houston's memory. He was born in Gallatin, Tennessee, and was eight years old when the town erupted over Eliza Allen's cruel fate. Scurry had settled in San Augustine, Texas, in 1839, and somewhere in Houston's elephantine memory, he had stored away the note that Adolphus Sterne never particularly liked him. As a representative in the last Congress of the Republic, however, Scurry was an effective advocate of annexation, but now he was a regular Democrat and as hot to break out of the Union as he once had been to get in. Houston took his own revenge on this disloyalty; Scurry had a reputation for slovenly dress, and Houston began referring to him simply as "Dirty Neck" (or sometimes "Dirty Shirt") Bill.

In the end, Houston's restrained presence in the campaign carried the day. In the election at the end of August 1859, Houston received 36,227 votes to Runnels 27,500— less than the margin Runnels had bested him with in 1857, but a win nonetheless.

A couple of weeks later, supporters threw him congratulatory barbecues in Huntsville and Montgomery, during which he reprised his one campaign speech, in a moderate tone, to loud applause. Unlike the torrent of recrimination that he heaped on David Burnet after his second Texas presidential election, a newspaper reporter noted that Houston "spoke in kindly terms of governor Runnels, but regretted the company he kept, but said he had no complaint to make, and did not know that Governor Runnels was at all culpable for his frontier policy."[7]

For the new administration, Houston sought to round up old friends, and one of the first letters, dated August 30, carried much hope with it: "My Dear Miller, The report is that I am elected by 8. or 10. thousand votes. Will you be my private Secretary? I will keep the place vacant until I can hear from you. I have only time to say that my family send love to you. Sam is as large as you—nearly. Mrs. H. is not very well."

Wash Miller was visiting family in another Huntsville—Alabama—and his reply, in his carefully schooled hand, survives only as a fragment. Houston must have been shocked. The rampant rumor, which Miller credited, was that once Houston was elected, he would serve only until the legislature convened and reappointed him to the Senate. To the governor-elect, Miller expressed his continued respect and affection, but he really could not come back for so short a need of duty. Besides, it was an office that required a great deal of energy, and he believed Houston would do better to find a suitable younger man. On October 8, Houston dashed off a note on a half-sized scrap of stationery: "Dear Miller—Your letter has this moment reached me. I intend to be, and stay Governor, if I live. So you can come on as soon as possible." But Wash Miller was tired and unavailable, to his mentor's great disappointment.[8]

Houston's strenuous push during his closing years in the Senate to impose an American protectorate over Mexico had gone nowhere, but in between his election at the end of August and his inauguration shortly before Christmas, it looked like the issue would present itself to him on a platter. On September 28, Cheno Cortina, at the head of a mob of banditos, captured Brownsville and subsequently bested first a posse of local guards and then a unit of Texas Rangers under W. G. Tobin. By early November, Cortina was ensconced on his mother's sprawling, inherited ranch six miles north of Brownsville with an "army" of between three and four hundred men, the Mexican flag fluttering above the house. He began issuing windy proclamations demanding the end of mistreatment of Mexicans in the valley on pain of burning Brownsville to the ground. This had become a matter beyond the scope of state jurisdiction, and on November 15 the U.S. Army's department commander, Brig. Gen. David E. Twiggs, sent Maj. S. P. Heintzelman to assume command of the border and put down the Cortina insurrection.

Houston's inaugural took place on December 21 with Margaret in attendance, one of the few times she ever took part in her husband's public life. In his speech, Houston gave the Cortina issue full play. He had failed to have an American protectorate established over Mexico, even though that nation's

history is a catalog of revolutions, of usurpations and oppression. As a neighboring people to us, it is important for the maintenance of good neighborhood,
that law and order should exist in that country. The Mexicans are a mild,
pastoral and gentle people, and it is only by demagogues and lawless chieftains
... [that] disorders in that country are continued. ...

    Should no change take place in Mexico, restraining their disorders, and should
they extend to this side of the Rio Grande, it will demand of the Executive of the
State the exercise of its fullest powers, if needful, to protect our citizens.

Major Heintzelman, meanwhile, had reached the Rio Grande Valley, and
although he considered the lamentations of the Brownsville citizens to be overblown,
his regulars and a force of rangers under Rip Ford routed Cortina's army at Rio
Grande City. Cortina vanished back into Mexico only to reappear in early February
and try to capture a Rio Grande steamboat. The army and rangers were still vigilant and defeated him again. Realizing he may have bit off more than he could
chew, and knowing of Houston's sympathetic feelings toward Mexicans in Texas,
Cortina issued another proclamation, this one placing the cause of the valley Mexicans under the governor's protection. It was true that Houston spoke kindly of
the Mexican people in his inaugural, and he then made good on his words with
one of the first proclamations of his term, demanding an end to the brutal reprisals
that Anglo posses in the valley were inflicting on its Hispanic residents. "I ask those
who have been deluded into this enterprise to abandon it," he wrote. "The laws
are to be executed alike to all our Citizens of whatever tongue, and none need fear
prejudice." A few months later he issued a contract to the publisher of a Spanish-
language newspaper to begin translating the laws of Texas into Spanish so that
everyone could understand them.[9] Such sympathy, however, he did not see as inconsistent with the protectorate, and the governor was already about those plans. The
army assigned one of its senior officers on duty in Texas, Col. Robert E. Lee, to the
Valley to end the Cortina business once and for all. Returning from an eastern
furlough, Lee stopped in Austin and called on Houston both in the mansion and
at his office. Lee was a distant cousin of Margaret's; he and the governor were both
Southern Unionists who had declared their ultimate loyalties to their states. Their
meeting was cordial, and doubtless they exchanged amiable memories of their
days as competing suitors for the hand of Mary Parke Custis and how well things
had turned out for both of them.

    Their business together, however, was more prickly. In person, they probably
reexamined a subject about which they had already exchanged written sentiments
through intermediaries Albert and Pryor Lea. In the event of Houston's election
as president, Houston told Colonel Lee that the extension of an American protectorate over Mexico would be a priority of his administration, and he was curious
whether Colonel Lee might accept the post of governor of Mexico. Doubtless, Houston's phrasing was delicate and subjunctive, but the question was so premature that
Lee very sensibly froze. He could not risk compromising his duties as a U.S. Army
officer and wanted nothing to do with some harebrained filibuster anyway. His

correspondence with Houston's emissaries displayed the same genius for tactical retreat he later showed on the battlefield: "I have no doubt that arrangements will be made to maintain the rights and peace of Texas, and I hope in conformity to the Constitution and the laws of the country. It will give me great pleasure to do all in my power to support both." The governor was unwilling to further disturb such a fine sense of honor, and he let the matter drop.[10]

With office came, inevitably, applications for appointments, one of which provided the new governor an opportunity for some fun. Benjamin Franklin Shumard had been appointed state geologist by Hardin Runnels. He was eminently qualified for the post and was doing a fine job, but with the change in administration he was fearful of being dismissed. Flanked by Houston's friend George W. Paschal and by Andrew Jackson Hamilton, a good Union man, Shumard called on Houston. They discovered the governor busy at his desk in the capitol, but he quickly took charge of the conversation: "O yes, glad to see you, Professor. Few men in Texas are qualified for your office. You call rocks the bones of the earth and tell how old it is by inspecting them. Yes, yes, a rare sort of learning! I wish a test of your skill. Find out and report to me the composition of the dirt on Bill Scurry's neck. If the report satisfies me I may keep you. Good afternoon, Professor, good afternoon." Being Houston, he was not too busy to stand and bow as Shumard and his seconds exited. Soon after, A. J. Hamilton chanced to meet Judge Alexander Terrell, who inquired after Shumard's chances. A bemused Hamilton quoted Houston's satisfaction with him: "He is a remarkable man, sir," said the governor. "He reports that he has found six distinct strata of filth on Bill Scurry's neck, and in the lower strata next to the hide he has discovered the fossil remains of animalculae!"

(Shumard's reprieve was temporary, however. In August of 1860, Houston replaced him with the candidate whom Runnels had rejected, Francis Moore, former mayor of Houston city who was Houston's old friend and Unionist ally. Moore, who had turned to rock study in midlife with work at the New York Geological Survey and the Philadelphia Academy of Natural Sciences, was a gifted but amateur geologist whose credentials were inferior to Shumard's.)[11]

The retention and later replacement of the state geologist was handled rather lightheartedly, and Houston's assumption of the state executive authority seemed barely marked by the wholesale political sackings that often accompanied a change of administration. There was one notable exception. Gen. John Slater Besser, his rank descending from former service in the Missouri militia, had been the financial agent for the state penitentiary in Huntsville since 1853. He was a Unionist, had lived in Huntsville since the year after the Houstons built Woodland, and the two men were well acquainted. Besser aroused Houston's ire by declining to support him in 1859, and when the newly installed governor heard a rumor that the penitentiary inmates were being given bread made from inferior meal, Houston went after him with a vengeance. He issued a proclamation against him, authorized the Walker County sheriff to use force against him, and ordered the penitentiary's board of directors to undertake an investigation that required Besser to produce extensive documentation of his entire tenure.[12]

Houston's disdain for John Besser even extended to his home life, where Alexander Terrell was astonished to discover that "Houston ... directed that a lean, half-starved estray dog that came to the Mansion should not be fed by anyone but himself ... and then while he was eating would beat him with his staff until he howled, and while beating him would say: 'How do you like that, General Besser?'" Terrell explained this conduct as a holdover from Houston's Cherokee days; the Indians believed that they could hex an enemy in the fashion that the governor exhibited. Aside from the nineteenth century being a time generally less concerned with animal welfare, there is one other possible explanation for such appalling conduct. Second son Andrew had acquired the common little boys' habit of bringing stray dogs home, which his parents tolerated to a degree, at least until one of the animals gave Andrew a nasty bite. Margaret regarded the wound lightly until it became infected. Fever and swelling set in, Margaret reproached herself dreadfully, and for a time it was feared that Andrew's leg would have to be amputated. The crisis did pass, but now the suspicion lingers whether this stray dog that bit the one who befriended him was a circumstance too close, in Houston's mind, to his relationship with Besser not to indulge in a little Cherokee witchery.[13]

Houston later admitted that his vindictiveness toward Besser was unjustified, calling it the one mistake of his administration. Much more typical were his attempts to forward the careers of those in need. When he heard that the founder of Corpus Christi, filibuster and perennial hard-luck case Henry Kinney, had been mentioned as a possible minister to Mexico, Houston sent an endorsement to Secretary of State Lewis Cass. "I am not aware to what extent [his] friends ... have interested themselves in his behalf.... [but] Should it please the President to confer this position, or some similar one on Colonel Kinney, I doubt not but he would endeavor to meet the highest expectations of the Government."[14]

As measured by domestic policy, Houston as governor of Texas was energetic and attentive, his exercise of executive authority enlightened and progressive. He remained watchful of the welfare of the inmates at the Huntsville Penitentiary, and throughout his tenure he exercised his pardoning power with astonishing liberality. On one occasion, convinced that justice had miscarried, Houston pardoned a Fayette County slave named Bill of the capital offense of assaulting his master.[15]

Houston's bearing toward Native Americans had never changed. While he continued to pursue a policy of respect and justice toward them, he was still firm about keeping the frontier free of pillage and did not hesitate to order rangers into the field to pursue and punish Indian raiders. He was also, however, wise to the game of ranger companies forming up to answer nonexistent Indian emergencies and galloping off on an Indian-hunting lark at state expense. He meant to have none of this, declaring that rangers who convened without proof of Indian trouble would not be paid or rationed. "Sir," he wrote curtly to a ranger lieutenant in August of 1860, "Reports of Indians being in the Country, committing depredations will not be taken as evidence of the fact, it must clearly be established by positive proof.... In the counties south of you it has been fully ascertained that white men are committing most of the injuries upon the settlers.... The people of the frontier should keep a strict watch upon all suspicious characters as the Executive cannot protect them from *white Indians.*" The very day after sending this letter, he received one from Joseph Cox of Coxville in Hill County warning that just such a cultural cross-dresser was last seen headed for Austin and inquiring whether the authorities there had seen him. "My Dear Sir," Houston responded, "Your truly interesting letter was this moment received. . . . You are aware that I have been charged with befriending the Indians when I would suggest that white men might have a hand in it. . . . [A]ll can now form their own opinions of my suspicions." Cox, said Houston, had neglected to include a description of the culprit, and as soon as one was received, the executive would make certain that the authorities remained vigilant for him.[16]

The gravity of the secession issue and the desperation with which it was agitated had taken much of the fun out of politics. Still, Houston's election as an avowed— and loudly avowed—Unionist went far to restore his hope that the people could be brought to reason. The crisis was growing but not yet critical, and he had time to begin his patented crablike angling to influence circumstances—pressing the federal government for money and supplies for frontier defense, but defense to be under-taken by Texas Rangers, not federal troops. Texans under arms and under his com-mand, not the army's, he could perhaps parley into future leverage for the Mexican protectorate. It was a reprise of his Nacogdoches strategy of 1835, but it was a slow game, which gave him time to enjoy life. Ensconced in the elegant Governor's Mansion with his wife and six of the children, life was rowdy, gay, and deeply ful-filling. The house itself, while ponderous in scale with seventeen-foot ceilings down-stairs and thirteen-foot ceilings upstairs, was far from palatial in accommodation. In fact, the house was furnished largely with pieces salvaged from the erstwhile "President's House" several blocks away, the wrecked condition of whose furniture Houston had itemized to the Texas Congress eighteen years before in declining to live there. He had been governor only three days when a bill was given him for an enormous new four-poster bed, custom-lengthened to accommodate his height— which has been identified ever since with the mansion as the "Sam Houston Bed."[17] So typically for him, he remembered the most comfortable night he had spent during the grueling 1857 campaign, had kept the name of George Hollamon's cabinet-maker in Seguin, and had Hollamon's great walnut four-poster copied in formal mahogany.

There were only seven rooms in the house, excluding the stair halls and the kitchen and servants' areas, which were in a rear addition. The great parlor, a smaller drawing room or family library, and dining room lay downstairs, with four bed-rooms above. The stairs at the rear of the central hall curled up from lower right to upper left. The first door on the left at the top of the staircase opened not into a bed-room but to a secondary corridor that ran privately to the back stairs. The northwest bedroom opened from this little hall, and Houston had the chamber subdivided into two smaller rooms for his still-growing bevy of children.[18]

The mansion was destined for little formal entertaining during the Houstons' tenure. At the time they moved in, Margaret was already four to six weeks pregnant, and this confinement promised to be difficult. Austin society, which had come to

Governor's Mansion, Austin. Built in 1856 for $14,500, the mansion's first tenant was Gov. Marshall Pease. As secretary to the government ad interim, Pease had been critical of Houston, but later in life they shared a common loyalty to the Union. Pease and his wife, Lucadia, established a level of official entertaining that the Houstons, between Margaret's illnesses and the growing hostility of the times, could not match.

Courtesy Austin History Center, Austin Public Library

revolve around the governor, survived two dour years under the bitter bachelor Hardin Runnels and longed for a return to the days of the genial and popular Marshall and Lucadia Pease. Margaret Houston disappointed them, but her lack of public popularity did nothing to dull life within the residence, as the Houston children thundered through the biggest house any of them had ever seen.

The only one of them not living at home was Sam Junior. Soon after the inauguration, the governor accompanied his heir and namesake to Bastrop to enroll him in the Bastrop Military Institute, founded and administered by Col. R. T. P. Allen.[19] On his visit there, the governor was invited to inspect the cadets, which he did with relish, handling every gun. While in Bastrop, Houston boarded at the Nicholson House, whose proprietor, Jimmy Nicholson, was an English immigrant and former Bastrop mayor. Surrounded by friends such as George W. Paschal and A. J. Hamilton, Houston held court there for several days; he was as fond as ever of swapping stories late into the nights, and he regaled his admirers with tales of his eventful life. The state district court was also meeting in Bastrop, and Judge Alexander Terrell, whom

Houston had assailed from the stump in 1857 as one of the Waco Convention and who had touched Houston with a reconciling note, was also boarding with Nicholson. The two became fast friends despite the fact that the governor, while indulging that genteel Southern practice of comparing kin, quickly discovered that Terrell's mother-in-law was Eliza Allen's first cousin.

The new governor was not without enemies in Bastrop, either, and he was warned to be on the lookout for an old ranger named Ham White, who had taken offense to a snap Houston had made during the "Archives War" that the people on the Upper Colorado were horse thieves and nursed a grudge ever since, muttering regularly that he would kill Houston on sight. One night at Nicholson's, the two men found themselves seated opposite one another at dinner. Ham White tried to pick a fight with "a very insulting remark intended for the General. All heard it and expected trouble; no answer was made, but Houston after laying down his knife and fork straightened up in his chair and looked with defiant gaze straight at Ham White who dropped his head and continued eating. Not a word was spoken, but anyone who has seen a powerful mastiff cow a barking dog with a look can understand the scene."[20]

Such altercations were now quite common in Houston's life, and with the political climate becoming increasingly more hateful, Margaret's usual concern for his safety became all-out fear. Houston kept no bodyguards and there was no protection at home, either. It was probably more than a desire for a quiet confinement that led the mansion door to be closed to casual callers beginning in May 1860, which reversed a policy begun with Marshall Pease, and it sharpened Austin's social disapproval of Margaret.

If Houston found himself threatened in increasingly secessionist-minded Texas, his stature as a presidential possibility began unexpectedly to brighten. The Democratic convention assembled in Charleston with the high hopes of Stephen A. Douglas, who felt he could claim Southern loyalty for his having championed the Kansas-Nebraska Act. Before the convention, a group of Galveston Unionists petitioned Houston to let them place his name in nomination. In answer, he wrote a long letter attacking the convention system of nominating candidates. "The grand idea of parties, as maintained by the great men of the past, has been destroyed," he said, but now "the people are ignored entirely by the politicians, when the chances of Presidential candidates are summed up, and he who has at his command, the largest number of clique leaders, is regarded as certain of nomination." He would have none of it and would accept nomination only from the people. "I will not consent to have my name submitted to any Convention, nor would I accept a nomination, if it were tendered me, and procured by contrivance, trick or management. If such a thing were possible, that I could be elected and not in harmony with the voice of the majority of the American people, I would not hold the position a single day, but retire to private station, solaced by self-respect."

Of course, placing Houston's name before the convention in Charleston would have found little sympathy, anyway, but when the delegates assembled, the confident Douglas was shocked to discover that the temper of the cotton radicals had left even him behind. The South split the Democratic Party even as they intended to split the Union, bolting the Charleston convention and settling on John C. Breckenridge as their own candidate. Abraham Lincoln, who was anathema to the South, was nominated by the Republican Party, and as if splitting the Democratic vote was not enough to hand the election to Lincoln, the new Constitutional Union Party still had its convention to meet in Baltimore.

Houston's repudiation of a convention nomination shocked and flummoxed his supporters, who had become savvy to the new style of electioneering. But if he demanded a call by the people, they could arrange it. One mass meeting took place in Austin on March 20, 1860, calling itself the "National Democracy," headed by Anthony Branch and former governor Marshall Pease among others, and on March 22 it passed resolutions calling for a Houston candidacy. A second and more important mass meeting was called for San Jacinto Day, April 21, on the battleground, with twenty-three vice presidents, including eight veterans of the 1836 battle. With equal praise for Houston's heroism and Unionism, the old general was nominated again. Former Texas president Burnet, who was living in nearby Galveston, was distempered by the proceedings. He had long since quit public life and had slowly declined into poverty, obscurity, and cane-whacking anger. Like Anson Jones before them, Burnet and Mirabeau Lamar prepared an anti-Houston "history" of the republic, but it died for want of a publisher, and Burnet was reduced to hiring out his slaves and confiscating their wages to pay his rent. He sent a letter to Ashbel Smith congratulating him on not attending the San Jacinto mass meeting and proclaiming his disgust with "those who hang on to that false man's skirts merely for the vain hope of political advancement."[21]

Once the Constitutional Union Party convention gathered in Baltimore, the two leading names circulated in that group were the only two Southerners who had opposed the Kansas-Nebraska bill, John Bell from the border state of Tennessee and Sam Houston of Texas. The governor had not explicitly licensed his name to be placed in nomination there, but he was curious to test his strength. On the first ballot, Bell polled 68½ votes and Houston received 57: nearly half of Houston's from New York, 7½ from Pennsylvania, and 5½ from Illinois—all areas where he had actively cultivated a following. With the name of Sam Houston now in serious contention at a national convention, however, the northeastern powerbrokers had to take stern stock of his assets and liabilities. There was the matter of his character: Houston had now been sober for eighteen years, but he did have, as the phrase went, a first wife still living, and there was the Indian liaison with Diana Rogers, though no one dared broach these concerns publicly. When support began to shift to Bell, it was for the stated reason that he, better than Houston, could bring old-line Whigs into the party. On the second ballot, Houston had 69 votes to Bell's 125. The Virginia delegation then switched to Bell, followed by Kentucky, and Houston's candidacy folded amid fulsome praise of his leadership and long service to his country.

The wisdom of the Constitutional Unionists' nomination of Bell was questioned almost from the beginning. R. D. Rice, a Douglas supporter from Maine, wrote his candidate that he could breathe a sigh of relief at facing Bell instead of

Houston, who could have mounted a "movement formidable or even reputable in popular estimation. . . . The *people* more than politicians have faith in 'Old Sam,' and will enthusiastically rally in his support."[22] The party convention, according to Rice, who did not even support the Texan, had done exactly what Houston had accused all party conventions of doing. If the people controlled the selection of candidates to appear on the ballots and were not limited to just voting for president, Sam Houston might well have carried all the states north of the Ohio River from Illinois eastward. He would have carried Texas and probably California; he would have lost the Deep South, but they would have accepted him in office as they could not accept Lincoln. The slave states would have waited to see whether he was strong enough to deal with the issue in a measured and equitable way. Thus, Sam Houston was denied the chance to face what would have been the supreme test of both his vision and his political skills. Andrew Jackson Donelson of Tennessee also believed that the better man lost out, but it was left to another Tennesseean, Andrew Johnson, to give the clearest assessment. Johnson was nominated and elected vice president to Abraham Lincoln; unlike Houston, he was still a drunk, but he was one of the shrewdest politicians around. In his view, had the Texas governor been nominated in 1860, Sam Houston and not Abraham Lincoln would have been president of the United States.

Once all the fuss in Baltimore was over, Houston disclaimed any intention of having accepted their nomination if it had been tendered. But his friends were not ready to give up. One of his most active supporters was John Hayward Manley, a lawyer in Houston who had helped draw up the San Jacinto resolutions on April 21 nominating Houston for president. To Manley, the governor expressed his appreciation for the San Jacinto resolutions, for he considered that the only valid process of nomination. "If the independent masses of the country deem my name important, in connection with the Presidency, they have a right to use it." But, "if my name should be used . . . , the movement must originate with the people themselves, as well as end with them. Houston quoted to Manley his previous letters on his objection to nomination by "contrivance, trick, or management" and concluded, "The people alone have the nominating power, as they have that of election."[23]

Houston's presidential possibilities were not entirely extinguished, however. Manley and several others who had been responsible for the San Jacinto gathering, including Ben McCulloch, were now entrained for New York to lay their resolutions before the people there. That, in Houston's book, would pass muster as a popular nomination. Published broadsides invited the people to a Houston rally to take place in Washington Square on May 29. The throng that gathered beheld staging lit with Chinese lanterns and torches, draped with flags, and backed by a portrait of Houston with the legend:

FOR PRESIDENT

GEN. SAM HOUSTON

An honest man no party platform needs,
He follows right, and goes where justice leads.

A brass band was playing and operatives were distributing copies of campaign songs extolling the hero of San Jacinto. A lengthy parade of speakers, including Clinton Roosevelt, took the podium in his praise, advocating, among other things, outlawry of the convention system, the establishment of "Houston clubs" throughout the state, and a mass Houston meeting to be held on July 18. The New York newspapers gave full coverage to the Houston festival the following day, mostly expressing their approbation of a Houston candidacy.

The whole effort was quaint and even moving. However, the United States had become too large for anyone to garner a presidential nomination through neighborhood clubs anymore. It was true that the spark struck in Washington Square did catch in small tinder in Texas and even elsewhere in the South. One Houston man in Georgia suggested that "San Jacinto neighbors get up small meetings in all the states, and run electoral tickets in every state."[24] That, however, was precisely the fatal flaw. The whole process was now larger, and even getting on the ballot was controlled; Lincoln's name did not even appear on ballots in the South. Thus, while Houston backers Tom Carothers and J. Carroll Smith puffed hopefully on the tinder sparked from New York, it eventually, as it could not do otherwise, snuffed out in tiny curls of smoke.

Houston had known for some weeks that his presidential bid had expired when, on August 18, he felt it necessary to send official word to his friends in the North: "I withdraw my name from the list of candidates for the Presidency." He readily admitted that "it may be said that I yield least, as my chances of success are not so apparent. But with four opponents of the nominee of the Republican Convention in the field, the defeat of all is equally certain." By taking himself out of the race, Houston claimed a right to be acknowledged sincere in repeating his oft-repeated warning one more time in the plainest terms possible: "There must be an abandonment of specious dogmas, clap-trap platforms and electioneering cant" or the result would be "a dangerous war of sectionalism, and a reckless spirit of disunion, both North and South." He would not endorse any of the remaining candidates. "I desire to see a union of all national minded men, to defeat dangerous sectionalism; and I leave my friends free to pursue whatever course may appear to them best at such a crisis. I cannot conclude without returning my sincere thanks to those who have in various ways expressed a desire to see me occupy the distinguished position of President. But to remain longer in the field, could be productive of no good, and it might be a stumbling block in the way of those who desire harmony."[25] There was even better reason not endorse anyone else: Houston realized the folly of the multiple candidacies in a second. "What would it avail," he wrote A. Daly, "if I should come out and cry Huzza for Breckenridge, when if he were to get the vote of the United South it would not elect him? Can he get his own state? Doubtful. . . . Can he calculate on getting one single northern state? If so, I cannot tell which one."[26]

On November 6, 1860, Jeff drove the governor to the poll to cast his ballot for president, but this was one instance where exercising the franchise gave him no pleasure. On returning to the office, Houston's secretary asked him lightheartedly who he voted for, only to suffer a withering look. The governor's disgust was over which evil to vote for, probably not over his absence from the ballot. After more than a decade of waxing and waning presidential speculation, Houston apparently took his departure from actual contention in genuine good heart. "I am as easy as an old shoe," he wrote in a warm note to Ashbel Smith, "and have come to the sage conclusion, that if the people can do without my services, I am sure that I can do without their suffrages. So you see I still retain a share of common sense!" While he admitted that "I am with politics as Falstaff was with strong Potations," there could be no doubt that looking after his family's interests provided a more nurturing substitute. "My Dear Smith, You did promise to visit the Point—see the mill, and write to me. Do you recollect the promise?"[27]

It is altogether too easy now to read Sam Houston's claims that he would not accept a nomination from any convention as an expression of sour grapes. In fact, Houston had campaigned for governor twice by excoriating conventions and platforms as antidemocratic. What actually slipped by him were the times. Houston had recently described himself politically as an "Old Fogy." He was proud that his political sentiments hearkened back to Andrew Jackson and torchlit parades and popular sovereignty. He did not see, or more likely he refused to see, that the political game had become slicker and that "management" was now an essential ingredient of political participation at the national level. Politics had sludged into a new era of professional posing, which he found repulsive. If he had chosen to play by the new rules, he might have excelled: his ten years' cultivation of the political machine in Tammany Hall delivered twenty-eight New York votes for him at the Constitutional Union convention. But it was a step he could not take and retain his self-respect. Sam Houston was born at the right time to win Texas her independence and lead her into the Union, but he was born half a generation too early to save that Union.

But as always when politics rankled him, as it did through the whole presidential season, he found solace and even joy in his family. After leaving Sam Junior at Allen's Bastrop Military Institute, Houston bombarded his absent heir with weekly letters of family chatter and fatherly admonition. On April 7: "Andrew is the cleverest fellow in the world if he can do as he wishes. He had been hugging the dogs the other day, and that night I had to get up, take off his flannels, turn them inside out and whip them in the hall, as I think the fleas would have nearly eaten him up otherwise. Since then I think he has not been so familiar with them." On April 14: "The young ladies do not often come to see us, except Miss Rosa. I fancy it is owing to your absence. If you live to return, I presume, if you are as clever as I hope you will be, they will be like a swarm of bees about the mansion." On April 23, when he might have held forth about San Jacinto: "I have been down to Lavenburg's and have purchased the Hat. It has not 'Mexico' in it, but is more beautiful than any I have ever seen. It is perfectly white. . . . You will soil it unless you are very careful. I would advise that you put it on in the evening when the air is damp so as to fit it to your head. You might dampen it around the inside by the band, and it will more rapidly yield to the shape of your head. It is a Mexican hat and has the word 'Sombrero' in it. . . . It will do!!! It cost $4.50. Is it worth it?" On April 30: "My dear son, if I annoy

Sam Houston Junior. In his youth Sam Houston Junior showed as much promise as his father when it came to fancy hats. He never quite lived up to his father's more serious expectations, however. Margaret managed to send him to medical school, and he maintained a practice for a time but preferred a career as a writer, at which he met limited success. He married in 1875 and fathered three children. Upon being widowed eleven years later, Sam Junior moved in with his sister Maggie's family, where he stayed until he died at age sixty.

Courtesy Sam Houston Regional Library and Research Center

you by the frequency of my writing to you, I will not interdict you from retaliating by writing twice as much as I do. I only regret that I cannot interest you more by writing such things as would be of lasting benefit to you, and greatly instructive to you in the affairs of life."[28]

Not that the governor had been slack in the latter department, either. Margaret had desired to send her son a print entitled "The Trapper's Last Shot," but when Houston proved unable to find it in five different establishments, he substituted—surprise!—Gaius Marius in the ruins of Carthage. "I wish you to read the history of Gaius Marius," the governor wrote him. "I think that you will find it in Rollins,' or Gibbon's 'Decline and Fall of the Roman Empire.' If not in one of them, you will find it in 'Plutarch's Lives.' Colonel Allen or some of the Professors can point you to it. You will be instructed and delighted with it, as he was one of the Proudest Romans." Houston then delayed sending the drawing—"you have not told me that you have read his history. Do so, and you will be better prepared for the likeness when you receive it."

The old general was a demanding parent-correspondent. The family had scarcely arrived back in Austin before he was upbraiding Sam Junior for not keeping in touch: "I expected you to write some ones of the family, but to my surprise no letter has come. . . . You have time my son to write and I trust you will not fail to write at least once a week, to some member of the family." When the beleaguered boy did dash off a response at the end of January, Houston lectured him on his penmanship: "Your letters were received, and I am sorry to see them written and folded so slovenly. I would rather see more care taken by you." But in April a carrot was added to the stick: "Be sure, my Dear Boy, to catch your pen far from the end. This I never learned. Had I done so, it would have been a great thing for me. Attend to this direction by all means, & I will be able next year, should we live, to get you in an office. If you write a fine hand there will be no trouble, as I have already spoken to a friend at the head of one of the offices."

Still more instruction followed a few weeks later: "I would . . . commend to your particular attention a Poem of 'Burns.' It is his advice to a young friend, Andrews. In my course of life, I have found [it] one of the most salutary, as well as one of the safest guides that I have met with in life. . . . Memorize it by all means, that beautiful emination of heart, and intellect. I esteem it one of the riches & treasures of memory. Possess yourself of it, my Dear Boy; and act upon its teachings —through life, and you will never have cause of regret. . . . I am glad that you received your Hat, and that it suits you."[29]

The Houston mantle—if not the hat—was a hard one for a cadet not yet seventeen years old to bear, but the father, now sixty-seven, was trying to settle it on the boy's shoulders as gently as he knew how. The praise given the recommended Burns poem was so extravagant that, at whatever age he first read it, it must have struck Houston deeply and abided with him. Yet, curiously, this is the only mention of it in the vast canon of his writings. The piece could only have been Robert Burns's "Epistle to a Young Friend," addressed to "Andrew dear," which dated from May of 1786 and appeared in the bard's initial *Poems Chiefly in the Scottish Dialect*.[30] It does not make an appearance in either *The Raven* or *The Great Designer*, but a study of it provides another startling essay in the workings of the Houston mind—that he did not merely read things and remember them, rather he absorbed them, assimilating them until they became almost part of his biology. His dogged, seldom-broken silence on the subject of Eliza, for instance, walling off many of his closest friends, is weirdly echoed by the fifth stanza of the Burns poem:

> Ay free, aff han,' your story tell,
>   When wi' a bosom cronie;
> But still keep something to yoursel'
>   Ye scarcely tell to onie:
> Conceal yoursel as weel's ye can
>   Frae critical dissection:
> But keek thro' ev'ry other man
>   Wi' sharpened, sly inspection.

One even wonders whether Burns's "Epistle," absorbed and transmogrified into Houston's own chemistry, played some role in that fateful decision to turn himself over to Margaret and be ruled by her in matters of the soul. The tenth stanza is most appropriate:

> When ranting round in Pleasure's ring,
>   Religion may be blinded;
> Or if she gie a random sting,
>   It may be little minded;
> But when on Life we're tempest-driv'n—
>   A conscience but a canker—
> A correspondence fix'd wi' Heav'n
>   Is sure a noble anchor!

Doubtless, once Houston fastened upon Margaret as his own correspondent with heaven, she, if not heaven, did anchor him for the rest of his life. Nor can the fifth line of that stanza—"But when on Life we're tempest-driv'n"—fail to recall the contribution Houston made to his cousin Narcissa Hamilton's autograph book as early as 1834:

> No matter where my bark be tost
>   On Life's tumultuous, stormy sea;
> My anchor gone, my rudder lost,
>   Still, cousin, I will think of thee.

Indeed, this became a repeated motif of Houston's poetry, appearing again in "The Plea of Texas" from August of 1844. One sees the Houston life-pattern assert itself again: absorb it, improve upon it, and utilize it. Once Houston did that—with anything—he lost track of what was his own thinking and what he appropriated from another mind. It was a philosophy itself justified by another stanza of the "Epistle," the last line of which may even have been Houston's first hint of where Dame Fortune might lead him:

> To catch Dame Fortune's golden smile,
>   Assiduous wait upon her;

And gather gear by ev'ry wile
    That's justified by honour:
Not for to hide it in a hedge,
    Nor for a train-attendant;
But for the glorious privilege
    Of being independent.

The stanza recalls yet another echo from early in Houston's life—his letter to Joseph McMinn asking his help in making his first political run, in which "gathering gear by ev'ry wile" became "I am resolved in combining all the might that I can by popularity muster." Burns had apparently been with Houston a very long time.

Back home in Independence, Margaret's mother was suitably proud of her family's restoration to its more familiar standing, but she was mindful of the fact that Margaret and the general were far from wealthy. Thus, she took it upon herself to provide them frequent wagonloads of fresh sausage and produce from her own resourcefully managed household. Unfortunately, she did not reckon the transportation difficulties, leaving Houston the unhappy alternatives of either paying ruinous freight rates for meat and fruit that spoiled on the road or hurting her feelings by requesting that she not bother. Seeking an escape, he wrote family friend Joseph Ellis, "I wish that you and yr Brother would just take a peep at the waggon which Mother has calculated upon as you pass Gen Davis place," hoping they could convince her that the conveyance was unsuitable.[31] Apparently, Ellis failed in his mission, for the Houston family tradition is that the governor was eventually reduced to sending his mother-in-law a note: "For the Lord's sake, send no more food. Thy dutiful son, Sam."[32]

Margaret's new pregnancy was a hard one, and Austin's climate exacerbated her asthma to such a degree that she spent most of her time in bed tended by Eliza and first daughter Nannie, who did her best to keep the house quiet while her mother was sleeping. When Margaret was awake, her fear for the governor's safety in the increasingly mob-swayed capital began to border on paranoia. Her gloomy letters to Independence caused her mother to obsess endlessly about them—and send more food. Her sister, Antoinette, and husband had visited the Houstons in the mansion soon after they moved in, and she knew that Margaret was merely in one of her moods, but it took the combined effort of both Antoinette and elder sister Varilla to prevail on their mother to get in a stagecoach and visit Austin so to persuade herself that the situation was not as desperate as she feared. Nancy Lea was now eighty, having grown mighty in both girth and eccentricity. She did not travel well; the July journey left her hot and frayed, and what she discovered in Austin was insurrection not outside the mansion but within it. The children were running amok.

Austin's geography, situated where the gulf plains rise suddenly into the hill country, leaves it prone to violent thunderstorms, one of which exploded over the city soon after Nancy Lea's arrival. Unknown to the children, their stern, solid, unflappable grandmother was terrified of thunderstorms. As the deluge intensified and the mansion shook from the blast of close lightning strikes, Nancy Lea coasted through the house like a wailing specter, finally flinging herself onto a bed and covering her head. It was a grievous mistake. In a flash the smaller children bounded up after her, bouncing up and down in mocking giggle fits. As the storm subsided, Mrs. Lea's fear turned into biblical wrath, seizing a switch and slashing in pursuit of the little Houstons, who followed six-year-old Andrew Jackson in scuttling under a bed. Nancy Lea, too large to follow and too dignified to get on her knees, lashed blindly under the bed until she was satisfied that justice was done.[33]

Young Andrew was close to incorrigible. His only innocent activity seems to have been playing stick horses with Jeff; he was much more in his element when creeping under a table to pin Nettie's dress to that of a guest or in sliding down the banister to plop in the entrance hall as the governor was seeing a visitor to the door. "I have had to keep him at the office some days," Houston wrote to Sam Junior in the spring of 1860, "as they can't manage him at home." Undaunted by his exile, Andrew became a favorite of Houston's secretary of state, Eber W. Cave, and perched grandly in his office writing "official" letters. One day he even got the better of the tolerant Cave, who barked at him, and Andrew skulked up the capitol stairs bent on revenge. Seeing a key dangling from the door of the Senate chamber, he pushed the door to, turned the key and made off with it. No one was the wiser until the senators began calling for help from their windows to the street below. An amused crowd gathered and began heckling the trapped and increasingly hungry legislators. "Hey, there, Taylor," one called up at Robert Taylor, a Unionist from Bonham, "we got you constitutional pie eaters where we want you now!" The governor had a good idea of the nature of the commotion and had Andrew found, but only the combined threats of a flogging and sending for the sheriff to take him to jail produced the key from its hiding place across the street. Sam Houston had been both the perpetrator and the victim of too many practical jokes not to appreciate the boy's genius, though. With all his powers as governor, he remarked dryly, he had not managed the legislature with anything near the generalship shown by his Andy.[34]

To a good extent, it was a case of like father, like son, and not even the governor managed to stay entirely out of the doghouse. The first daughters all being popular schoolgirls, there were adolescents about the mansion constantly, one of whom, Adele Atwood, offered to demonstrate a new dance step, the "pigeon's wing," to her friends. The governor was within hearing of this, Margaret was safely upstairs, and he had not "cut a rug" in years. Houston was, reportedly, loving his brief backslide into the sin of dancing when a sudden whirl revealed Margaret in the parlor door, staring glacially, and the capers came to a sheepish end.[35]

Such family diversions kept Governor Houston on an even emotional keel, for as the summer of 1860 gave way to autumn, the thunder of approaching secession grew ever louder. "I saw the storm gathering," he told an Austin crowd on September 22, "and strove to arrest it. Would that I could have been successful." He knew now that he would never be president, but his struggle to keep the Union together was not lost yet. Throughout his life he had fought as the consummate pragmatist, surfing the crest of circumstances beyond his control and adjusting to reverses until he sensed that a solution was certain. He had done it in keeping his Tennessee Cherokees out of Jackson's way; he had done it in retreating before Santa Anna in the Runaway Scrape; he had done it in engineering the annexation of Texas to the United States; and now he was doing it to preserve the Union. His attempt to unite the country behind the Mexican protectorate had failed, as did his bid for the White House, but he might still convince Texas not to secede. It was not an unreasonable hope: Unionist sentiment in Texas was strong enough to have elected him governor less than a year earlier. Now he intended to do what he did best, take his case straight to the people, beginning with Austin. Much of this first speech, given on September 22, hearkened back to his earliest and brightest technique of stump speaking, combining grand vision with a Socratic staccato of questions that could lead to but one conclusion. In his long life, he said, he had seen the American people ascend in steady progress.

> Power, wealth, expansion, victory, have followed in [their] path, and yet the aegis of the Union has been broad enough to compass all. Is not this worth perpetuating? Will you exchange this for all the hazards, the anarchy and carnage of civil war? Do you believe it will be dissevered and no shock felt by society? You are asked to plunge into a revolution; but are you told how to get out of it? Not so. . . .
>
> What is there that is free that we have not? Are our rights invaded and no Government ready to protect them? No! Are our institutions wrested from us and others foreign to our taste forced upon us? No! Is the right of free speech, a free press, or free suffrage taken from us? No! Has our property been taken from us and the Government failed to interpose when called upon? No, none of these! . . . I come not here to speak in behalf of a united South against Lincoln, I appeal to the nation. I ask not the defeat of sectionalism by sectionalism, but by nationality.—The Union is worth more than Mr. Lincoln, and if the battle is to be fought for the Constitution, let us fight it in the Union and for the sake of the Union.

The text of the governor's Austin speech runs to sixteen closely typeset pages—quite an oration for a man of nearly sixty-eight who averred that he had arisen from a sickbed to deliver it. But having given his audience stern medicine, he thought it well to give them a spoonful of sugar as a reward. In telling jokes, Houston had always delighted in mimicking accents, and he concluded with a lengthy yarn of "a fine old German named Steinberger, who was a great Whig; and a near neighbor to him lived Judge Johnson, a leading Democrat of the day." Once, when Steinberger had a case pending in that judge's court, he thought it well to mend fences between them, but he outsmarted himself when he exclaimed: "I did not say dot all the Dimmercrats was grand raschals; but I dit say dot all the grand raschals wash Dimmercrats. Dot is vot I said, Shudge!"

It was, Houston explained, his way of assuaging hurt feelings and telling them that he knew that not all Southern Constitutional Democrats were disunionists, for "there are good and loyal men to be found in this party," but they had to allow him that all disunionists were Southern Constitutional Democrats. The governor concluded with a tug at their heartstrings. "I cannot be long among you. My sands of life are fast running out. As the glass becomes exhausted, if I can feel that I leave my country prosperous and united, I shall die content. [But] to leave my country, and not feel that the liberty and happiness I have enjoyed would still be theirs, would be the worst pang of death."[36]

This virtuoso effort drew some sympathy, but the firebrands were not moved. "Old Sam . . . may take the stump and shed tears like a crocodile," wrote secessionist (and briefly a few years later acting governor) Fletcher Stockdale, but "these tricks are stale and no longer win."[37] However, the Austin speech was only the first round in what became an exhaustive speaking tour in defense of the Union. Between October 17 and 29, he reprised in small his whirlwind campaign of 1857; he was now three years older and far less hardy, but he delivered impassioned speeches in Bastrop, Independence, Navasota, Anderson, Huntsville, Danville, and Cold Spring.

This barnstorming across the state was not merely a series of uncoordinated speeches. Typically for Sam Houston, he had a particular object in mind. The presidency was now beyond his reach, but there might still be a way, he reasoned, to save the Union. In each town he visited, Houston, in addition to speaking publicly, privately probed the leading men as to whether they could be persuaded, even in the event of Lincoln's election, to continue pursuing states' rights within the Union. He had hinted at this in the Austin speech, telling the assemblage, "The safety of the Government is threatened; and it seemed to me that the time had come for a renewal of our vows of fidelity to the Constitution and to interchange, one with the other, sentiments of devotion to the whole country." In Independence, seated late at night beneath a live oak, he told Rufus Burleson, whom he had brought closer into his circle because the reverend was a declared Unionist, "I am making my last effort to save Texas from the yawning gulf of ruin." His design was rather Tecumsehian, hoping to coordinate "leading men in all the great centers of influence to meet simultaneously in their different localities and proclaim their unalterable devotion to the South . . . but to declare that our wisest and safest plan is to make our fight in the Union." Houston, said Burleson, assured him that leading citizens he had spoken to approved the idea, and he asked Burleson to lead the meeting in Independence, to which he agreed.

Lincoln was elected president on November 6, 1860, but Houston still had not given up on his Tecumseh-like scheme. Three days afterward he dispatched a note from Austin to Ed Burleson, Jr., son of his old companion in arms and vice president of Texas Ed Burleson: "You will be here on some time during tomorrow, *as early as possible*, with all of the men you can bring, *who are true to the Country* and on whom you can rely in an emergency. When you arrive I will explain everything to you." This much of the letter was dictated to a secretary, but beneath his signature was a penciled postscript: "Dear Colonel, Hurry by all means."[38]

Shortly after the national election, Houston received a letter signed by some sixty-five citizens of his own Huntsville requesting him to set forth his views on the current crisis. Although Houston when he spoke extemporaneously never wanted for cogency in his arguments, the opportunity now to organize his thoughts on paper, which was published and circulated as a broadside, allowed him to flesh out more exactly what the monetary risks were.

> Should Lincoln falter or fail by allowing the laws to be subverted . . . , oppressing the people of the South, he must be hurled from power.
>
> I need not assure you that whenever the time shall come, when we must choose between a loss of our Constitutional rights, and revolution, I shall choose the latter.
>
> [But] if the Union be dissolved now, will we have additional security for slavery? . . . Our treasury is nearly empty. We have near half a million of dollars in the Treasury of the United States. A million of our school fund is invested in U. S. bonds. . . . Are we justified in sacrificing these when they are yet protected and secured?
>
> Here, I take my stand! So long as the Constitution is maintained by the "Federal authority," and Texas is not made the victim of "federal wrong" I am for the Union as it is.[39]

Back in Independence, Rufus Burleson did his part to effect Houston's plan; he led a spirited public meeting on the town square, with two Baylor students leading each side of the debate. "The affirmative was carried overwhelmingly, and the Stars and Stripes were suspended from a liberty pole fifty feet high." They waited to hear of similar resolutions from Texas' other leading towns, but the secession flood in Texas was too strong to resist. "In a few days General Houston sent me word: 'All is lost. When the hour came we could not rally a dozen men bold enough to come to the front and avow their convictions.'"[40] Within a few days, the mayor of Independence, Task Clay, chopped the liberty pole down, and the American flag was left where it lay.

With Lincoln's election the states of the South began pulling out of the Union, but Governor Houston interpreted his own election as a mandate to continue opposing secession. He therefore continued his pragmatic tactical retreat. Houston attempted to get advice from the Texas Supreme Court on the legality of secession, but he quickly learned that Associate Justice Oran Roberts and Chief Justice Royal T. Wheeler were both secessionists. Justice James H. Bell informed him that in his view secession was not unconstitutional, but in a speech Bell gave Houston an opening: only the legislature had the authority to pull a state out of the Union.[41] The governor saw in a flash that the Texas legislature was not then in meeting, and despite loud calls from the secessionists to convene a special session, he had no intention of doing so. The firebrands saw through this tactic immediately and sent a deputation to call on Houston, including among their number his closest friend, Ashbel Smith.

The governor was capable of accepting political differences among his personal intimates; he had proven so with George Hockley and Alexander Terrell, but it cannot fail to have grieved him to see Smith among the group that petitioned him to call the legislature into session. When they failed in their mission, and with Justice

Ashbel Smith. Despite growing political differences, Ashbel Smith's friendship with Sam Houston endured a quarter of a century. An able agriculturalist as well as medical doctor, historian, and writer, he was a judge of numerous national and international expositions. He was a founder of the University of Texas and, as an early advocate of black education, also a founder of Prairie View A&M. Sam Houston respected him deeply, and despite the general's endless heckling to marry, Smith died a lifelong bachelor in 1886.

Courtesy Texas State Library and Archives Commission

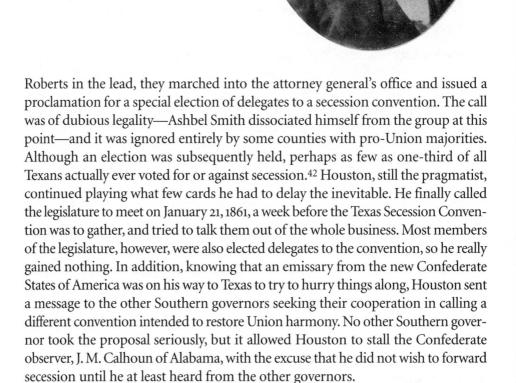

Roberts in the lead, they marched into the attorney general's office and issued a proclamation for a special election of delegates to a secession convention. The call was of dubious legality—Ashbel Smith dissociated himself from the group at this point—and it was ignored entirely by some counties with pro-Union majorities. Although an election was subsequently held, perhaps as few as one-third of all Texans actually ever voted for or against secession.[42] Houston, still the pragmatist, continued playing what few cards he had to delay the inevitable. He finally called the legislature to meet on January 21, 1861, a week before the Texas Secession Convention was to gather, and tried to talk them out of the whole business. Most members of the legislature, however, were also elected delegates to the convention, so he really gained nothing. In addition, knowing that an emissary from the new Confederate States of America was on his way to Texas to try to hurry things along, Houston sent a message to the other Southern governors seeking their cooperation in calling a different convention intended to restore Union harmony. No other Southern governor took the proposal seriously, but it allowed Houston to stall the Confederate observer, J. M. Calhoun of Alabama, with the excuse that he did not wish to forward secession until he at least heard from the other governors.

In a way, it is still painful to see Houston playing such a powerless hand, and the legislature met and quickly swept his barricades aside. When, against his urging, the legislators bestowed their recognition on the upcoming secession convention, the governor had no choice but to acknowledge its legitimacy as well, but he had one more trap to set: he recognized its authority only to withdraw Texas from the Union—"within the scope of the call under which its delegates were elected"—they had no authority to join Texas to the Confederacy. Texas's own secession convention, then—a kind of rump assembly of colonels and firebrands given after-the-fact recognition by the state government—met in Austin on January 28, 1861. It was presided over by Oran Roberts, the state supreme court justice who had called them together. Houston knew him well, for Roberts established his law practice in Houston's own San Augustine in 1841, when Houston represented that district in the Republic of Texas Congress. Houston's antipathy toward him is best related in a vignette left by former governor-for-a-month "Smoky" Henderson. As the convention, meeting on the second floor of the capitol, hurtled toward secession, Henderson stopped to see Governor Houston in his first-floor office. Houston,

> with the deliberation and clear enunciation that characterized his speech, said, "Well—Henderson—what—can—I—do—for—you—my—friend?"
>
> Henderson said, "Governor, I want you to pardon Mrs. Monroe."
>
> "Why should I pardon her? . . . Wasn't she fairly tried?"
>
> "Yes, and given six years."
>
> "And she appealed and the conviction was affirmed, Henderson? Am I right?"
>
> "Yes . . . the opinion . . . was the ablest ever written by Judge Roberts."
>
> "Oran Milo Roberts? That fellow who is presiding over that mob upstairs?"
>
> "Yes, governor."
>
> "Then I'll pardon her. No citizen shall be deprived of liberty by such a fellow."[43]

The governor proved as good as his word. Mary Monroe had served three years of a six-year sentence for murder when Houston, "it being shown to me by petitions and facts presented that there is reason for the exercise of executive clemency," pardoned her on February 11.[44]

Relations between the secession convention and the executive had, in fact, deteriorated to such a degree that they were not even speaking. John H. Reagan, who in earlier years had upbraided Houston for continuing to swear after his baptism, had since been elected to Congress but resigned his seat and returned to Austin in February 1861. "At the breakfast table at the hotel, on the morning of my arrival, I met quite a number of the delegates to the convention, and inquired of them whether any effort had been made to secure the cooperation of the State government with the convention. General Houston was then Governor, and was an avowed Union man. The delegates to whom I mentioned the matter advised me that no effort in that direction had been made; that they feared an offensive reception if they attempted to approach him on this subject." Reagan felt it imperative, for the smooth function of Texas's government through the impending change, that Houston be brought to the table and his cooperation secured. Reagan, as a regular Democrat, had supported Hardin Runnels against Houston in the 1859 campaign, but the governor knew very well that Reagan's stance in Congress had consistently been that of a pro-Union moderate, and their meeting was cordial.

I inquired of him if anything had been said to him about the co-operation of the State government with the . . . convention. He answered that no one had spoken to him on that subject. I told him that was what I had come to talk to him about, to which he said, "You know I am opposed to secession." I answered that I was aware of that, and stated that this matter had reached a point which involved the future of the State, and had passed beyond the consideration of individual interests . . . , that the people recognized his conservatism and the importance of his co-operation with them, and I expressed the hope that they might secure it. He said he had been born and reared in the South, had received all his honors from the South, and that he would not draw his sword against his own people. He continued: "Our people are going to war to perpetuate slavery, and the first gun fired in the war will be the knell of slavery."

Reagan argued the position then current, that if the South showed a united front, the European powers, especially England, would intervene and offer to negotiate a settlement. Houston, however, "said that this was a great mistake; that Great Britain had for forty years pursued a policy favoring the dissolution of the American Union." The main reason for this, countered Houston, was that England would gain from a civil war keeping American cotton off the market by gaining an opportunity to develop a cotton industry in India, even as France would do the same in Algeria. The governor could also call upon his presidential experience in this argument, remembering how, during the difficulties with Mexico from 1842 to 1845, the British found an interest not in who won but in the dispute itself. During the Civil War, when Reagan served Jefferson Davis as postmaster of the Confederacy, "I had occasion at different times to call the attention of President Davis and his cabinet to what Governor Houston had said. . . . I did this because of the noticeable fact that when the Confederate armies obtained a victory the British organs of public opinion encouraged the Federals, and when the Federal armies obtained a victory the same newspapers encouraged the Confederates. . . . It impressed me then, as it has ever since, as indicating his prophetic insight."

Reagan still did not have an answer to his main point. "I asked him if a committee from the convention should call on him if he would meet it in a friendly spirit, to which he answered that he would." Reagan then trudged upstairs to the convention, secured the appointment of a committee of five, including himself, who returned downstairs and conducted a civil but inconclusive meeting with the governor. Jeff, who had driven Houston to the capitol that day, had a somewhat different memory of the meeting. He recalled that the governor went upstairs to meet the committee, a particular he remembered because someone slammed the door in his, Jeff's, face. From a hiding place in the upstairs gallery, he heard his master advise them again to settle matters with the Union peaceably: "I know what war is." He bared his shoulder and displayed the fresh bandages over his 1814 wounds. "I have been in it often and do not want any more of it. War is no plaything and this war will be a bloody war. There will be thousands and thousands who march away from our homes never to come back."

It was too late, however, for such a play for sympathy to be effective. William P. Rogers, a member of Reagan's committee, was a Houston intimate, and the governor had a son named for him. Rogers loathed Jefferson Davis and had been a Unionist until Lincoln's election radicalized him. "Sam," he demanded of the governor, "do you believe that your wife and daughters ought to scrub their clothes at a wash-tub and cook meals in pots over a hot fire? Before I would suffer my wife and daughter to cook and scrub, I'll wade in blood up to my neck!" Hiding in the gallery, Jeff heard his master answer "that no white woman had ever died from honorable work." What Houston did concede to the committee, which he confirmed in a written memo, was that he only wished the forms of law to be followed. "I can assure you, Gentlemen, that whatever will conduce to the welfare of our people will have my warmest and most fervent wishes. And when the voice of the people of Texas has been declared through the ballot-box, no citizen will be more ready to yield obedience to its will, or to risk his all in its defence, than myself. Their fate is my fate, their fortune is my fortune . . . as of old, I am with my country."[45]

Houston invited the committee to meet again with him that evening at the mansion. That meeting also produced no agreement, but interestingly Houston requested them to ask the Committee on Public Safety, which was chaired by Judge John C. Robertson of Tyler, to call on him, and "he could give them some information which might be serviceable to them. I was not advised as to what occurred in that conference," wrote Reagan, "but immediately afterwards the late General Ben McCulloch and others went to San Antonio and demanded and received the surrender of the Federal soldiers there, and took possession of their arms and supplies."[46] Reagan was under the impression that Houston's requested meeting with the Committee on Public Safety was for the purpose of coordinating the surrender of the federal stores in Texas. That seems doubtful, however, because Houston had written to Department Commander Brig. Gen. David Twiggs "through a confidential messenger" several days earlier warning him that "information has reached the Executive that an effort will be made by an unauthorized mob to take forcibly and appropriate the public stores and property to uses of their own, assuming to act on behalf of the State." He asked Twiggs whether he would think it within his duty, in the event Texas seceded, to surrender the supplies of his command to the governor or his representative. When Governor Houston had his earnest but friendly parley with the Committee on Public Safety, he was in all probability fading them, trying to learn their plans for the purpose of getting the federal arms and ammunition surrendered to his own loyal rangers and kept out of the secessionists' hands. Had he succeeded, it would have been the only element of his tactical retreat to which any real leverage would have attached.[47]

Twiggs was in a difficult situation. He had just assumed command of the Texas Department, relieving Robert E. Lee only a few weeks before. Twiggs was the second-ranking officer in the U.S. Army, and his valor in the Mexican War had led Congress to vote him a jeweled sword in a solid gold scabbard. He was also, however, a native of Georgia and was searching for a way to reconcile his sense of military honor with his loyalty to the South. Events, however, overtook them all. Twiggs asked to be relieved of his command in favor of the next senior officer, Col. Carlos Waite, but before Waite could reach San Antonio, the committee sent Ben McCulloch to seize the army property there. Backed by a hastily assembled "militia" of about a thousand, it was McCulloch and the convention, not Houston, who received Twiggs's capitulation on February 15.

The meek surrender of about one-tenth of the army's total assets horrified Robert E. Lee, and Twiggs was stripped of his rank and cast from the army in disgrace. Both Lee and Twiggs, however, were soon accorded Confederate billets. It was Colonel Waite, a New York abolitionist, who was left holding the bag in Texas, faced with the dilemma of evacuating his more than three thousand soldiers and dependents before they could be taken prisoner. Under McCulloch's siege, he pledged to march his men to the coast and embark them for the North. Abraham Lincoln and the army, however, had other ideas.

In Washington, the president and his high command followed Sam Houston's struggle against secession with the liveliest interest. Lincoln was engaged in a fierce struggle to keep the Border States loyal to the Union, and if he could help Houston hold Texas as well, the new Confederacy would be crippled from the outset. Waite received orders countermanding his evacuation and instructing him instead to prepare a fortified encampment at the port of Indianola, manned by at least five hundred but preferably twelve hundred troops, and hold it until further orders. He was to "communicate as freely as practicable with General Houston . . . and comply with his wishes or suggestions if practicable." And if Houston should take up arms against the secessionists, Waite was to "give such aid and support to General Houston . . . as may be within your power." As Waite holed up and wrote to Houston, Lincoln sought to reach the besieged Texas governor through two other mediaries.[48]

Events in Austin, meanwhile, moved on apace. In response to Houston's insistence that the convention exceeded its authority by joining Texas to the rebel alliance, the delegates swore an oath of allegiance to the Confederacy on Friday, March 15, and George Chilton was dispatched to the Governor's Mansion to inform Houston that he would be required to follow suit. Chilton knocked on the door at eight in the evening, met with Houston, and desired an immediate answer. Houston needed time to think over such a momentous decision, and Chilton agreed that he could give his answer at noon the following day—the time that the legislature had already appointed for Houston to appear and swear the oath. The Houstons' supper that night was solemn. "When the negro servants had removed the food and soiled dishes, Mrs. Houston brought out the family Bible and placed it before the General at the head of the table. The negroes brought in their raw hide bottom chairs from the kitchen and the servants' quarters and arranged themselves along the back wall of the dining room. The General then read a chapter from the Bible, made appropriate remarks, and they all knelt in family prayer as was the usual custom." When the children retired for the night, eldest daughter Nannie, now fifteen and of all the children the one who most resembled her father, paused to urge him not to worry.

Nannie Houston at Age Fifteen. Of all the Houston children, none bore greater resemblance to their father, either in features or in flip demeanor, than his eldest daughter, Nancy Elizabeth. Her marriage to Joe Morrow produced six children; she also helped her mother raise her nearly incorrigible little brother, Andrew Jackson Houston. She lived until 1926.

Courtesy Sam Houston Memorial Museum

After the children were in their rooms, the troubled governor limped upstairs to consider what he must do. Margaret, unable to sleep, remained downstairs. "After bidding his family good night the General left positive instructions with Mrs. Houston that he must not be disturbed under any circumstances and that no visitors were to be admitted to the mansion. He then went to his bedroom on the upper floor, removed his coat and vest and shoes and remained alone throughout the night during which he did not sleep. Instead he walked the floor of his bedroom and the upper hall in his sock feet, wrestling with his spirit."[49]

The Governor's Mansion was only sparsely appointed, and the broad upper hall was almost bare—furnished only with an area carpet, two hide-bottom chairs, and a quartet table.[50] In the east wall was the door out to the front balcony, and on the west end the stairs curled down into the gloom of the first floor. The lofty thirteen-foot ceiling made it seem an even lonelier cavern in which to wage the final crisis of his political conscience. He was Sam Houston. He had won Texas her independence in battle and, as president of his nation, had engineered her entry into the American Union. He had represented her in the U.S. Senate for thirteen years. Now he was called upon either to lead her out again or be forced from public life amid the hoots and catcalls of his enemies. He must either swear his allegiance to the dandies and firebrands and slave drivers whom he had vilified during all of his political career, or go into exile and disgrace. Houston had said repeatedly that if it came to secession, he would stand with Texas, but could he bring himself to actually lead her out of the Union?

The family tradition is that Margaret heard the pine floor creaking deep into the night as Houston alternately paced and prayed. When he came down in the morning and faced her, he said, "Margaret, I will never do it."[51] It was March 16, 1861; as the convention droned on, Sam Houston arrived at his first-floor office and awaited the inevitable. A Houston partisan, the Reverend William Mumford Baker, witnessed "the old governor sitting in his chair in the basement of the capitol . . . , sorrowfully meditating what it were best to do. . . . The gathering upstairs summoned the old man . . . to come forward and take the oath of the Confederacy. I remember as yesterday the call thrice repeated—'Sam Houston! Sam Houston! Sam Houston!' but the man sat silent, immovable . . . , whittling steadily on."[52] Since the governor did not appear at the appointed time, Houston's office was declared vacant, and Lt. Gov. Ed Clark of Marshall, a former Texas secretary of state who had slid into office on Houston's coattails, was sworn in as governor of Texas. During the preceding night of agony, and during a mournful watch in his capitol office, Houston had labored over a speech, one last passionate plea to the secessionists to recognize their madness:

> My worst anticipations as to the assumption of power by this Convention have been realized.
>
> It has elected delegates to the Provisional Council of the Confederate States . . . before Texas had withdrawn from the Union, and . . . annexed Texas to the Confederate States and constituted themselves members of Congress. . . .
>
> [It has] appointed military officers and agents under its assumed authority. It has declared by ordinance, that the people . . . ratify the Constitution . . . of the Confederate States. . . . It has changed the State Constitution and established a TEST OATH of allegiance to the Confederate States . . . , [those refusing to swear it to] suffer removal from office.
>
> Fellow-Citizens, in the name of your rights and liberties, which I believe have been trampled upon, I refuse to take this oath. In the name of the nationality of Texas, I refuse to take this oath. In the name of the Constitution of Texas, which has been trampled upon, I refuse to take this oath. In the name of my own conscience and manhood, which this Convention would degrade by

dragging me before it, to pander to the malice of my enemies . . . , I refuse to take this oath.

I deny the power of this Convention to speak for Texas. . . . I PROTEST IN THE NAME OF THE PEOPLE OF TEXAS AGAINST ALL THE ACTS AND DOINGS OF THIS CONVENTION, AND I DECLARE THEM NULL AND VOID!

At that instant Sam Houston held in his own hands the power to begin the Civil War in Texas among Texans. In his heart, though, he had already settled the issue with himself, that if such an awful conflagration ignited, it would not be by his act. He would, he announced, make no effort to maintain himself in office if he should be forced out, though "still claiming that I am its Chief Executive. It is perhaps but meet that my career should close thus. I have seen the patriots and statesmen of my youth, one by one, gathered to their fathers, and the Government which they had created, rent in twain. . . . I stand the last almost of a race. . . . I am stricken down now, because I will not yield those principles, which I have fought for. . . . The severest pang is that the blow comes in the name of the State of Texas."[53] It would have been a blood-curdling speech—had he chosen to deliver it. No good would have come, however, from giving his enemies the satisfaction of hearing him roar in defeat. No minds would have been changed, no policy mended, and no more time gained. Faced with the moment, Houston returned in gloom to the Governor's Mansion and contented himself with having the paper published. The governor had told the legislature that he intended to continue in office until he was no longer able, and the next morning, March 17, he arrived at his office, toting his usual lunch basket, only to discover Ed Clark sitting at the gubernatorial desk. "Well, *Governor*," Houston said sarcastically, "you are an early riser."

Clark would not have any of it. "Yes, *General*, I am illustrating the old maxim, the early bird catches the worm."

"Well, *Governor* Clark, I hope you will find it an easier chair than I have found it."

"I'll endeavor to make it so, *General*, by conforming to the clearly expressed will of the people of Texas."

Houston made room in his lunch basket and began collecting personal effects from his office. At one point he caught his foot on the edge of the carpet and stumbled, remarking that the government should afford to replace it, but Clark huffed he could get on very well without a new carpet. "Having gathered up his duds," wrote a hostile newspaper, "Old Sam made a little farewell speech very much in the style of Cardinal Wolsey. . . . Halting at the door the General made a profound bow, and with an air of elaborate dignity said, 'Good-day, *Governor* C-l-a-r-k.'"[54] (Houston legend has it that soon after, when he chanced across Ed Clark on a street, the former governor affected not to know him.) Houston returned to the mansion, and he, Margaret, and the servants began packing. Houston's standing in the North as a lone Southern Unionist prompted letters imploring him, as his poet friend Lydia Sigourney wrote, to "save Texas for us if you can." Some appealed to his reputation as a wit and raconteur. "Flee out of the land of secession," pleaded Judge Thomas Shankland. If the Houstons would but come to New York, where he was enormously

popular, he "could be interminably amused with the antics of the abolitionists and
the strong minded women."[55] Other letters were far more serious and substantive. Colonel Waite, in San Antonio commanding what was left of U.S. forces in
Texas, offered Houston his aid in sustaining him in office. Houston had heard of
the Federals' plan to fortify themselves in Indianola until help should arrive and
refused any part. "Allow me most respectfully to decline any such assistance of the
United States Government, and to most earnestly protest against the concentration
of troops in fortifications in Texas, and request that you remove all such troops out
of the State at the very earliest day practicable." It then occurred to him that war
might begin regardless of what Waite did. "At any rate, by all means take no action
towards hostile movements till further ordered . . . by the Government." Waite forwarded Houston's letter to the army command, with the advisory that Houston could
not be counted on to take up arms against his own people; while a loyal Unionist,
he intended to use only "the press and the ballot-box . . . to effect a peaceable
change in the views of the inhabitants of the State."[56]

Lincoln was not ready to concede Houston's loss just yet. He had seen a published version of the governor's letter to Twiggs offering state troops to resist a mob
seizure of the federal arsenal and stores. In addition, the president had heard the
rumors that Houston was raising a pro-Union army. There was in Washington on
collateral business during the first week in March one Frederick W. Lander, a well-
known explorer and California Democrat as well as Unionist, preparing to return
home. Secretary of State William Seward ushered in Lander to see Lincoln. The
president entrusted to him a message to Houston offering federal support to hold
Texas in the Union. Almost simultaneously, a local Texas postmaster named George
Giddings was in Washington to lobby for the continuation of his contract, and
one of Lincoln's minions similarly summoned him to the White House to carry a
second letter to Houston.

It was now nearing the end of March, and while Houston had been deposed
from office and the family was packed to leave, no attempt had been made to evict
them from the mansion. The former governor, one day, was on his way to Belton to
speak when, according to Jeff, who was driving him, they were overtaken by a fagged
horse ridden hard by a courier waving a letter with a wax seal. Houston read it
seriously and had Jeff turn around to hurry back to Austin. This apparently was the
Lander letter, for Giddings recalled that he delivered his message to the mansion
himself at one o'clock in the morning, but it is no longer certain which of Lincoln's
pleas Houston received first. He answered Lander's letter straightaway in the same
manner in which he had answered Colonel Waite, that he would not accept U.S.
troops to maintain Texas in the Union. With Lander's failure, the army abandoned
its plan to fortify Indianola as a Federal foothold in Texas and allowed Colonel
Waite to proceed with his evacuation.

The letter brought by Giddings late at night contained, if the Lander letter did
not, some specifics: fifty thousand troops would be at Houston's disposal, and he
would hold the rank of major general, to keep Texas in the Union. At this Houston
wavered. He summoned to the mansion four of his closest friends, Ben Epperson,

David Culberson, James Throckmorton, and William Rogers, and read them the letter. A rarity for Sam Houston, he asked their advice. Only one, Epperson, a wealthy state legislator who had been a Houston delegate at the Baltimore convention, advocated accepting Lincoln's offer. In the late night in the mansion library, Houston stepped to the fireplace and burned the letter. "Gentlemen," he said, "I had resolved to act in this matter on your advice, but if I was ten years younger I would not." All were sworn to secrecy. At times later, the very existence of Lincoln's offer was disputed. However, both Giddings and Culberson left accounts of the meeting, and Jeff told Lenoir Hunt that he "saw with his own eyes" the letter Lincoln sent Houston and that the offer was fifty thousand troops, but he did not say, and probably could not have known, which letter it was.[57]

Judging from Houston's decision to quietly decamp, it might seem that Lincoln and his cabinet miscalculated the strength of his Unionism. They had not. They misapprehended not the strength of it but the nature of it. Houston's devotion to the Union was as complete as his understanding of the U.S. Constitution could admit of, but it stopped short of contravening the will of the people. To him, the supreme law of the land was not the constitution but the ballot box, and the choice of the whole people had to be upheld no matter how odious or calamitous the result. Colonel Waite understood Houston well and seemed to attach little blame to the governor's decision to canvass for loyalty to the Union through solely peaceful means. Houston was consistent in this philosophy. It was the only way he could have argued that the South accept Lincoln's election (at least until Lincoln might prove himself a tyrant, at which point a revolution might well be called for) but still cast his lot with the people if they spurned his counsel. As early as January 30, before the popular referendum that ratified secession, Houston had told the legislature: "Whatever the sovereign will may be when fairly expressed, it must be maintained. . . . While the Executive would not counsel foolish bravado, he deems it a duty we owe the people to declare that even though their action should bring upon us the consequences which now seem impending, we will all, be our views in the past or the present what they may, be united."[58]

And these words were spoken only one day before he wrote the memo to John Reagan's committee confirming to them that if the people overruled him and opted for secession, he would stand with them, whatever ruin might befall them all. Nor is this tone inconsistent with the bitter attack of his farewell on March 16; his quarrel with the delegates was not that they had met and ratified the referendum but that after doing so they had bounded far and then further beyond their powers in annexing Texas to the Confederacy and imposing an almost martial law compelling obedience. Sam Houston might argue to the limit of his wit and strength against breaking up the Union, and he did, but if Texans themselves in their voting on the issue turned him down, and they had, no choice was left him but to take his place in their ranks. Under Houston's code, there was no alternative.

Having packed to leave the Governor's Mansion, the evening of March 19 found the governor and Mrs. Houston sitting with a few final callers in the flicker of a single candle, including Ed Sharp, who had buggied Houston more than fifteen hundred miles in the 1857 campaign. Suddenly there came a heavy knock at the door. The sight of armed men outside made them think that the convention meant to put them out of the house that very night, but they soon learned that the party came to offer their service in maintaining Houston in the governor's chair. Noah Smithwick, whose ties to Texas were almost as Gordian as Houston's own—he was the black-smith who had repaired the Gonzales cannon that had opened the revolution—seems to have been among them. "My God," said Houston, "is it possible that all the people have gone mad?" He thanked them, but ordered them to disperse.[59]

Like Houston, Smithwick also opposed secession and found himself in the same predicament as all Unionists in Texas: how to hang on to his life and property in the face of the lawless local "Committees of Public Safety" that were already begin-ning to loot the holdings of those who refused to wave the Confederate firebrand. Smithwick wrote in his memoir a recollection of that evening: "'General,' said I, 'if you will again unfurl the Lone Star from the capitol, I will bring you 100 men to help maintain it there.'" "My friend," Houston told him, "I have seen Texas pass through one long, bloody war. I do not wish to involve her in civil strife. I have done all I could to keep her from seceding, and now if she won't go with me I'll have to turn and go with her." Already dispossessed of his sawmill, Smithwick sold Houston his remaining property, a slave, for half price, and moved to California.[60] If Lincoln could not persuade him with fifty thousand men, Smithwick had little chance with one hundred—but one suspects that the sad old campaigner was more tempted by the latter offer.

19

ALL IS WELL

When the Houstons vacated the mansion at the end of March, it is uncertain whether this was out of good manners toward Ed and Martha Clark or because the legislature ordered them out. They might even have left to avoid Lincoln's bombardment of letters offering to sustain him in office, since their departure coincided quite exactly with the Waite, Landers, and Giddings missions. Sam Houston had said repeatedly that whatever Texas chose for herself, he would stand by her. He meant it, and neither Lincoln nor anyone else did him any favors by making him a focus for Unionist intrigue.

Thus, the Houston caravan took to the road again; Margaret, the children, and the maids in the big yellow coach driven by Tom Blue and the other servants following in a wagon, rumbling out of Austin toward Independence to visit Nancy Lea. Jeff drove the former governor in his top buggy; usually they led the procession, far enough ahead that their dust would settle and not aggravate Margaret's asthma. On this occasion, however, Houston teased Jeff that, since they were "both out of office," time did not press. As the family headed east, Houston guided Jeff on a side-trip to see the Treaty Oak, a giant live oak near the banks of the Colorado River, several blocks west of the site of the old capitol of the Republic. Descending from the buggy, Houston paced off 130 feet across the diameter of its canopy, walked around it slowly, and then seated himself on a fallen branch and meditated for some moments. When they finally departed, the general reminisced that when he lived in Houston as president of Texas, he had sent the great naturalist John James Audubon inland to see the tree, and he returned effusing that it was as grand as Houston had promised. It was at least five hundred years old, Audubon said, and was still in a thriving maturity.[1]

Heading leisurely east with Jeff, Houston had some time to reflect. For once, he had not waited to be out of office before considering how to make ends meet, but where other men of his station might have thought how to build a fortune or peddle their influence, Houston's thoughts were of a different turn. Two weeks before he was deposed, he wrote to Margaret's nephew, Martin Lea: "Today I wrote to Mr. Armstrong about going to Houston for a Boar of the Woburn breed, & a Cashmire Goat. These I bought on my own account, but if you wish, you can have an interest in them. . . . I want the Woburn Boar should be there so as to mix with the new sows. We ought to be able to sell 1,000 lbs. of Pork and Bacon per year. . . . Do the best that you can. We are almost crazy to go down to the point, and Andrew and Willie are nearly crazy to 'see Cousin Mart Lea.' Do write to me. All are anxious to hear from you and send love." As Margaret had always made certain, when Houston was wounded in his public life, he found comfort in family—which now included virtually her entire clan.[2]

When they stopped in Brenham, several of Houston's old veterans who lived in the town asked him to give a speech and explain himself to the gathering crowd. This he declined to do numerous times until one insolent secessionist declared that he should not speak. His contrary nature finally aroused, Houston angrily agreed to speak his mind. "The excitement was intense," wrote one observer.

> The court house was densely packed, and as Governor Houston arose to speak, cries were heard: "Put him out; don't let him speak; kill him." At this moment, Mr. Hugh McIntyre, a wealthy planter of the community, and a leading secessionist, sprang upon the table and drew a large Colt revolver saying: "I and 100 other friends of Governor Houston have invited him to address us. . . . I myself think that Governor Houston ought to have accepted the situation, and ought to have taken the oath . . . but he thought otherwise. . . . There is no other man alive who has more right to be heard by the people of Texas. Now, fellow-citizens, give him your close attention; and you ruffians, keep quiet, or I will kill you."

There was a time when Sam Houston would have wondered what he had sunk to, requiring armed men to quiet a room with death threats just so he could be heard, but after the past year, he was almost used to it. Still, his speech was short and terse, as one more time he explained his reasons and purpose. He conceded that the clamor for secession had been loud. There was a popular political maxim of the day, "*Vox populi, vox dei*," which was used as a kind of natural-rights justification for secession. Houston cautioned them against such a platitude: "the Vox Populi is not always the voice of God, for when demagogues and selfish political leaders succeed in arousing public prejudice and stilling the voice of reason, then on every hand can be heard the popular cry of 'Crucify him, crucify him.' The Vox Populi then becomes the voice of the devil, and the hiss of mobs warns all patriots that peace and good government are in peril." He denied again that the South had yet suffered any injury that would justify breaking up the Union, declared that the structure of the new Confederate government was fatally flawed, and debunked the idea, as he had to John Reagan, that foreign nations would sail to their aid. The secessionists "also tell us if war comes that the superior courage of our people . . .

will enable us to triumph in battle over ten times our number of Northern forces. Never was a more false or absurd statement ever made. . . . The civil war which is now near at hand will be stubborn and of long duration. . . . The soil of our beloved South will drink deep the precious blood of our sons and brethren. . . . The die has been cast by your secession leaders, whom you have permitted to sow and broadcast the seeds . . . , and you must ere long reap the fearful harvest of conspiracy and revolution." Brenham was in a part of the state deeply divided over the issue, and Sam Houston knew that while he was cheered by his friends, he did not win many converts that day.[3]

The family stopped briefly in Independence for a visit with Mrs. Lea and clan before proceeding on to Cedar Point. On April 12, 1861, Confederate batteries opened up on Fort Sumter in Charleston Harbor, South Carolina, and three days later the Union effectively declared war on the seceded states. Houston again decided to speak his mind, this time in Galveston on April 19. Friends posted notices in the town, and Jeff watched as Houston paid the manager of the Tremont Hotel for permission to use his premises. As at Brenham, his life was threatened. A large and hostile crowd assembled and a deputation called on him, apparently including his good friend Hamilton Stuart. According to the *Houston Telegraph*, they "advised him not to speak, or if he did speak, to say nothing against the Convention, the State Government, or the Government of the Confederate States." Houston announced, to his friends' dismay, that he would, as he always had, speak his conscience. At 11 A.M. from the Tremont's balcony, Houston glowered down at the angriest mob he had yet faced. In Brenham it was Hugh McIntyre who brandished a pistol to quiet the crowd; here it was X. B. DeBray, a French-born military officer who was shortly to assume command of Galveston's defenses, backed up by a company of recruits. DeBray and Houston were friends, and moreover he owed Houston a favor, for it was he to whom the governor had let the contract to translate the laws of Texas into Spanish at a dollar and a quarter per page. When the grumbling died away, Houston intoned a defiant prophecy:

> Some of you laugh to scorn the idea of bloodshed as the result of secession. But let me tell you what is coming. Your fathers and husbands, your sons and brothers, will be herded at the point of the bayonet. You may, after the sacrifice of countless millions of treasure and hundreds of thousands of lives, as a bare possibility, win Southern independence, if God be not against you, but I doubt it. I tell you that, while I believe with you in the doctrine of state rights, the North is determined to preserve this Union. They are not a fiery, impulsive people as you are, for they live in colder climates. But when they begin to move in a given direction, they move with the steady momentum of a mighty avalanche. My fear is, they will overwhelm the South.[4]

This from the man who in slightly different circumstances and with slightly different timing, and with slightly greater willingness to political management might have been president of the United States and forestalled it all. The German philosopher G. W. F. Hegel once wrote that the mark of a great man is his ability to tell the people of his era what their will is and accomplish it. The tragedy of Sam Houston was that he told his era what its will should have been and it cost him everything. His Galveston remarks were recorded by a private hand, for by now Houston's stance was so unpopular that the *Galveston News* declined to publish the speech and risk the wrath of its readership. (Part of the speech did take place in a lighter vein; while Houston was speaking, a horse got spooked and tried to kick out of its harness. It became tangled in the bridle and reins and fell, and was whipped back into compliance by its owner. "Let Old Dobbin alone," Houston advised gravely, "he's just trying a little practical secession. See how it works?")[5]

Cast from the Governor's Mansion without employment or pension, Houston was anxious to get to Cedar Point and get the farm working again to provide for his family. Sam Junior was now freed from the Bastrop Military Institute, and the former governor left his son in charge at the Point while returning to Independence to tend to their stock there. The heir found this frustrating; he was pressing his parents to allow him to volunteer for the Confederate army, and Houston had to remind him: "We will be hard run to live, for the first year. . . . Do you, my son, not let anything disturb you; attend to business, and when it is proper, you shall go to war, if you really wish to do so. It is every man's duty to defend his Country; and I wish my offspring to do so at the proper time and in the proper way." Margaret was dead set against it and remonstrated to her uttermost. She found the son too much like the father, however, and Sam Senior placated her, easing his own mind by rationalizing to the son: "We are not wanted or needed out of Texas, and we may soon be wanted and needed in Texas. Until then, my son, be content." Houston was delayed by rain in Independence but sent detailed instructions to Sam Junior about the farm: "Keep the Hoes in the corn, if it is too wet to plow. . . . If it is too wet to do anything in the corn, put up a cow pen; also one for the goats—a brush pen will do for the goats. . . . You must think for yourself, as I cannot be there to see, while the rain continues. Do the best you can, and be industrious. . . . I intend to be satisfied with whatever you may do—We all send kindest love." Considering the tone of his speeches in Brenham and Galveston, it seems astonishing how quickly he was able to return to bucolic concerns. "The flock looks quite formidable, and the ewes are still lambing," he continued to Sam Junior and noted that six-year-old Andrew, with no state senators to imprison now, was trying to make himself useful in his own way. He "is quite busy, and feels much responsibility rests in his hands. He wishes to return with you from the Point & assist you down with the stock, but I am in hopes that the Goats will engross his attention when he gets home!"[6]

When he arrived in Independence, Houston was asked again to explain himself, this time to the students at Baylor University. He had had time to calm down by now, and as always, he took a softer tone with young people: "Whether the Convention was right or wrong is not now the question. Whether I was treated justly or unjustly is not now to be considered. I put all that under my feet and there it shall stay. . . . Burying in the grave of oblivion all our past differences, let us go forward determined not to yield until our independence is acknowledged; or, if not acknowledged, wrung from our enemies by force of valor. It is no time to turn back now."

Sam Houston then gave his final advice on military matters, which summarized all that he had learned in battle, hearkening straight back to Andrew Jackson and the ragtag Tennessee militia and reinforced by his grating experience in the Texas Revolution—including the Matamoros idiocy and the policy of voting for officers. Discipline, he told them, was paramount. For their own safety, he urged the students, many of whom were soon to meet their fate in the service of their state: "Organize your forces; yield obedience to orders from headquarters. Do not waste your energies in unauthorized expeditions; but in all things conform to law and order, and it will be ten times better than running hither and thither. . . . I give this advice as an old soldier. I know the value of subordination and discipline."[7]

The Houstons desired to settle finally in Huntsville, but when the general tried to buy back his beloved Woodland, which he had sold to pay debts from his 1857 gubernatorial campaign, the new owner would not sell. Several blocks north and a little east of Woodland, though, stood an odd-looking new house built by Rufus Bailey. Two stories high but only one room wide, it had a spacious front porch flanked by square turrets, and behind the turrets long, covered gallery porches stretched down both sides, upstairs and down. For obvious reasons, it became locally known as the Steamboat House. The Houstons rented this curious dwelling, dividing their time between it, Cedar Point, and trips to Independence. The Union blockade had cut off most of the commercial flow that people had come to take for granted, but the Houston household got by. For instance, no store-bought ink could be had, so they made their own from indigo roots and purple pokeberries. Jeff remembered roasting acorns for what he described as "pretty good coffee," but that may have been just for the slaves' consumption. Real coffee cost $3.75 a pound when it was in stock, but the family's connections in the North managed to keep them supplied.

For six months after his eviction from the Governor's Mansion, Houston was annoyed by but tried to ignore the conclusion on the part of most Texans that he had really been in favor of holding Texas in the Union by force. Hopeful rumor-mongering by the Northern press did not help him any, and the appearance of a piece in the *New York Herald* that implied that a pro-Union Texas force might still be led by Houston finally prompted him to protest. In a letter to the *Civilian* in Galveston, he pointed out that he had had that chance and chosen not to take it:

> Had I been disposed to involve Texas in civil war, I had it in my power, for I was tendered the aid of seventy thousand men and means to sustain myself in Texas by adhering to the Union; but this I rejected. . . . When my message was reported to Mr. Lincoln by his own messenger, it appeared . . . that he did not believe that his agent had been faithful to the discharge of his trust in reporting my opinion. To this conclusion he was led, no doubt, by editors . . . piling up and repeating the charges upon my reputation of abolition and treason to the South. So strong was his belief . . . in these slanders that he immediately resolved to send another messenger and troops. . . .
>
> The time has been when there was a powerful Union sentiment in Texas, and a willingness on the part of many true patriots to give Mr. Lincoln a fair

trial. . . . Those times have passed by. . . . Mr. Lincoln and his cabinet have usurped the powers of Congress, and have waged war against the sovereign States, and have thereby absolved . . . all the people from their allegiance to his government.[8]

Much of Houston's remaining time in Huntsville he spent cultivating the art of the old timer, sitting with his San Jacinto foot propped up in a chair on the front lawn of the Steamboat House amid its crepe myrtles and fig trees—there was also one large oak—eager to chat and swap yarns with passers by. In his final months he showed that he had not lost his taste for showy hats; his favorite now was a curious blue velvet smoking cap with gold embroidery, resembling rather a cross between a Russian monomakh and a night-stocking.[9] There were always a number of callers, for Rufus Bailey's house fronted on the principal thoroughfare of the city, across the street and just down from the Oakwood Cemetery.

Although he was now a political persona non grata, he was personally still vene-rated by his friends. On the days he felt up to it, he might stroll the neighborhood and call on one acquaintance or another, and he showed himself no less courtly than he had been in his prime. With the ladies, especially, his manners were still dictated by Robert Burns. The Houstons' near neighbors, Pleasant and Mary Frances Kittrell, had a son named Norman enrolled in Austin College, of which Houston sat on the board of directors. As Norman recalled,

> [Houston] used to come down the walk under the cedars from the front gate to our house, walking as erectly as if his age were one score, instead of . . . three score years. As he neared the front door, he would remove his broad-brimmed fur hat, and lay it on his left arm. He carried his buggy whip in his left hand, and as he ascended the steps my mother would greet him. Extending his right hand, on which were usually two or three seal rings, he would take my mother's hand, and bending with chivalric dignity and courtesy until his lips almost touched her finger tips, would say with his characteristic delibera-tion and distinctness, "My lady, I am charmed to meet you again. . . . Mrs. Houston bade me bring you assurance of her love."[10]

Not all visitors were welcome in the Steamboat House, however. Houston was sometimes visited by Alabama and Coushatta Indians, and Margaret was disap-proving and watchful of these echoes from his wilder past. Houston would instead receive them in some state at the spring near Woodland House a few blocks away, smoking a pipe with them and conversing in what Jeff remembered as "the Indian language," presumably Cherokee. One call had a particular purpose—the chief, Billie Blount, complained to Houston that the Confederate army had drafted many of his young men into service and taken them far away to fight in a war that they had no part in. He asked Houston's influence in getting his boys back. The general dispatched Jeff to the house, and when he returned with sheets of foolscap and a pot of their homemade ink, Houston wrote a letter to the Confederate War Department requesting the Indians' discharge. Several weeks later the effort proved successful, and a pair of young Indian men showed up in Huntsville to deliver a letter of thanks from Chief Blount.

He had more luck keeping his Indians out of the army than he did his own son. There was no longer any dissuading Sam Junior from joining the ranks, and in spite of Margaret's histrionics, he enlisted in the Second Texas Infantry. Perhaps instinctively, Sam Junior lifted a page out of his father's tactics, writing her letters swearing how much he would rather be with her had not duty kept him away, though knowing full well that he would go mad if he remained tied to her apron strings. "I would give anything to be at home," he wrote her from Galveston, where his regiment was forming: "I think, however, that the war will not last long and then I can (if it is the Lord's will) return home and live in peace. . . . I have forgotten none of the promises I made you. . . . I read my bible every night and say my prayers."[11] As the military legacy of Houston men settled in a new generation, other chapters from the old general's past quietly closed. Eliza Allen died on March 3, 1862, at the age of fifty-two, still residing in Gallatin, Tennessee. Once it became clear late in 1836 that Houston would neither return to her nor send for her, she had married Dr. Elmore Douglass, a widower with ten children, to whom she bore three—some say four—more. No image of her survives. Perhaps haunted by the might-have-beens of her life, she destroyed all the photographs and artists' likenesses ever made of her. When she entered her grave she entered oblivion, for she had instructed that no marker be erected.

On the first of March, Houston paid a visit to the city that bore his name to visit Col. John C. Moore's Second Texas Infantry, Sam Junior's unit. While in camp another visitor arrived: Frank Lubbock, now governor of Texas since defeating Ed Clark by 124 votes in the 1861 elections, had been in Galveston to attend a memorial service for Hugh McLeod, leader of Mirabeau Lamar's Santa Fe expedition of 1841. Lubbock had parted company with Houston over the latter's Know-Nothing dalliance, but the store of affection accumulated over a quarter-century ran too deep not to meet now as friends. Lubbock made a brief speech, after which, according the local newspaper: "General Houston was then called upon for an address. He indorsed everything the Governor had said. He observed that he had differed with many of them in the beginning of the difficulties, but we were now in for it, and all his feelings and interests were bound up in the success of our cause. . . . The general's speech was received with loud cheers, which fact must have shown him that, however much the people may have disliked his course at times, he has yet, personally, a warm place in their affections."[12]

This may have been the time (for there are not many other possibilities) when he was invited to drill the company, and Sam Houston on his sixty-ninth birthday still knew how to dress for an occasion: "He was the hero of San Jacinto sure enough," wrote one observer, "for there he stood in the same military suit he had worn in 1836 at the battle of San Jacinto . . . his pants tucked in the top of military boots; suspended at his side was the same old sword, and on his head was a weather-beaten, light-colored, broad-brimmed planter hat, the left side buttoned up to the crown." Jeff had helped his master get into the old uniform, recalling that the snuff-colored breeches were frayed and his high military boots "looked much the worse for wear." Nevertheless, "My master was as excited as a school-boy on circus day." Upon being asked whether he would care to drill the soldiers, the old general replied that he would do so with pleasure; his eye took on some of its wonted twinkle, and he decided it was time to have some fun at the expense of a couple of Confederate blowhards. "The day was sunny and beautiful; the hour ten in the forenoon; the regiment was in complete uniform and perfectly armed; their arms glistened in the sunbeams."

Colonel Moore gave Houston his sword, and Houston drew himself up and ordered, "Shoulder arms, about face!" and then inquired of the regiment, "Do you see anything of Judge Campbell or Williamson S. Oldham here?"

"No," was the emphatic reply.

"Well," said the General, "they are not found at the front, nor even at the rear. Right about, front face! Eyes right!"

The regiment whirled and snapped, faces turning to the right in unison. "Do you see anything of Judge Campbell's son here?"

"No, he has gone to Paris to school," responded the regiment.

"Eyes left! Do you see anything of young Sam Houston here?"

"Yes!"

"Eyes front. Do you see anything of old Sam Houston here?" The regiment and the crowd erupted, "united in a triple round of three times three and a tiger for the old hero." Houston returned Moore's sword with a remark that the regiment was well drilled, indeed.[13] Once the recruits were rested from parade, the general bade farewell to his son, handing over numerous mementoes from his siblings, a Bible that Margaret had inscribed to him—and what an eventful Bible it would prove to be—and finally Sam Houston did what all fathers do: he slipped his son some extra spending money.[14]

That night, with the Houston hotels being mostly full, Houston and Governor Lubbock shared a room at the Fannin House, where the old soldier showed himself no less fond of talking deep into the night than he was when he kept Ashbel Smith up all hours reading to him from the classics. And Houston used this occasion to attempt to close some business left unfinished at the abrupt end of his own gubernatorial term. Addressing Lubbock as "Governor Frank," he requested the pardon of a particular convict in the penitentiary. Lubbock refused, saying the man was the foreman of the shoe factory; the army's need for shoes was desperate and he could not be spared. Houston would not concede the point, and according to Lubbock, argued:

> "Why, Governor Frank, would you keep a poor fellow in the pen because you need his services?"
>
> To this I made answer: "General, he is there. We are needing shoes very much for our soldiers, and I would dislike very much to lose so valuable a man. . . . Why was it you failed to exercise the pardoning power?"
>
> "Governor Frank, . . . I will tell you the reason for the failure. I had the papers all prepared and they were upon my desk for action upon them. I got

up quite early the next morning, but upon arriving at my office I found *little Eddy Clark* in my chair claiming to be Governor. I presume he must have gotten up before daylight so as to precede me in possession. Governor Frank, that is the reason I failed to sign the papers; all of which facts I can prove by my Secretary of State, Major Cave."

Lubbock promised to look into the case, and a few months later he did indeed pardon the man.[15]

During his visit to Sam Junior's regiment, one fact came to the old soldier's attention that displeased him. His son had volunteered for the duration of the war but was away from town when the unit was organized. He returned to find all the officers' billets taken—not a proper situation for a Houston. When his own friends had criticized him for entering the army as a ranker, the elder Sam Houston had scolded them, "Go to, with your stuff," and then made much of the fact that he rose by his own merit with no exercise of family influence. That was one hardship, however, that he did not intend for his son to have to duplicate. From Nancy Lea's farm in Independence on April 5, 1862, after the Second Texas Infantry had marched off, he took up a pen and wrote a letter to Williamson Oldham, whom he had lampooned before the cadets the month before. The secessionist Democrat who had dogged his campaign trail speaking against him in 1857 now sat in the Confederate Senate, where he had come to play a leading role. Sam Junior, the general wrote:

> was offered a situation of Brevet Lieutenant, if he would consent to be transferred and be stationed in Galveston, but he preferred the glory of an active, and immediate campaign. . . .
>
> Sam is 18 years of age, 6 feet high, and rather a well-made and good looking boy. He was two sessions at Colonel Allen's Military School at Bastrop. . . . He is a very good scholar, his habits are good, and he is ardently devoted to the cause in which he is engaged, as well as to the life of a soldier. . . . If you can procure him a Lieutenancy, or any promotion that you may think proper, you will confer upon me an enduring obligation, and I trust and believe, he will never disgrace his *patron*.[16]

What happened to Sam Junior over the next three days bears one eerie echo after another from his father's life. Not waiting around for an officer's appointment, Sam Junior was marching as a private in Company C; his company commander was his father's best friend, Ashbel Smith. On the very day that Houston was writing Oldham about a promotion, the Second Texas was in Tennessee, forming up to attack a Union army near a place called Shiloh Church. In command was the Confederacy's western theater commander, Albert Sidney Johnston, who had been General of the Army of the Republic of Texas during his father's first term as president. With a reputation now as one of the South's most capable professionals, he suspected that the Union troops under U. S. Grant were not anticipating an attack and, therefore, decided to do exactly that. Sam Junior's company was part of the force that crushed the Union right flank, and Private Houston tasted a hot breakfast from the

Federal campsite they overran. Seeking to press the advantage the following day, the Confederates attacked again, unaware that Grant had been heavily reinforced. As the Second Texas advanced toward a fence, they were met by a volley fire from the Third Iowa. Sam Junior was struck by a Minié ball and fell wounded, like his father, in the groin. After the Union troops drove the Confederates back, Federal doctors scanned quickly over the wounded; the one who examined Sam Junior determined from the copious bleeding that the femoral artery had been severed and that the young man was a goner. Like his father, Sam Junior was abandoned to die on the battlefield. He lay there most of the day and, like his father, refused to die.

Eventually, a Union chaplain walking nearby thought he saw movement and tried to identify him; from the rebel private's knapsack he pulled a small Bible whose binding was shattered by a bullet. In the front he read, "Sam Houston, Jr., from his mother, March 6, 1862." The chaplain was one of those who had petitioned the U.S. Senate not to repeal the Missouri Compromise and had been deeply moved by Senator Houston's defense of them.

The chaplain knelt. "Are you related to General Houston of Texas, who served in the United States Senate?"

"My father."

Back in Texas, Margaret and Sam Houston knew nothing of these events. They read of the butchery at Shiloh and read that Sam Houston Junior was listed as dead or missing. His name was dropped from the company roll. Torn by grief but refusing to give up hope, Houston wrote to Governor Lubbock of the "unutterable anguish that I have witnessed in my domestic circle." But he was bearing up the best he could. "It would be unmanly in me were I to pine at my lot, when I witness all around me many others who have suffered greater bereavements." Margaret, however, was under no such compulsion to be brave; in fact, she had been beside herself since Sam Junior had left. The battle at Shiloh was still more than two weeks in the future when she poured out her heart in a letter to Nancy Lea. "My dear husband leaves nothing unsaid that can give me hope and consolation," she admitted, "but I cannot forget that my boy, my darling . . . is from me, probably never to return. . . . Oh, Mother, what shall I do? How shall I bear it?"[17]

Then hope grew stronger: Mary Jones, widow of Texas's last president, bridged her late husband's hatred of Houston and her own estrangement from Margaret with an act of enormous kindness. She had seen a letter from another soldier, which she enclosed to Margaret, saying that Sam was alive and a prisoner of war. Of details there were none, but it was something. The Houstons moved from Independence to summer at Cedar Point, and then in September 1862, Sam Junior like his father, came home to a family that did not at first recognize him. Eliza was tending a kettle of vegetable soup in the kitchen and Margaret was instructing Jeff in how she wanted some flowers planted when they each looked up and saw a gaunt, wounded young soldier supporting himself on the fence. Once they realized who it was, Margaret barely contained joyful hysteria as she and Jeff helped Sam Junior into the house and got him into bed. The general was away visiting a neighbor, but soon "my mistress and I looked out the window," recalled Jeff, "and coming down the road at full speed was the General, his crutch swinging from his saddle." Jeff helped him from the horse and he stumped into the house on his crutch. Something told him, he kept saying, something told him his son was coming home.[18]

This exertion and joyous outpouring depleted Houston's physical resources; he fell dreadfully ill, and in the isolation of Cedar Point a trusted doctor was not at hand. Down in Galveston, the general's warmly regarded newspaper editor Hamilton Stuart learned of his danger and journeyed up to the Point.

> The wind blew and the rain fell. The surroundings were about as desolate as could be. A young doctor, who had n't had much experience, was attending Mr. Houston. One night he came up and called me out. He said he thought the end was near, and asked me to tell Mr. Houston. I did n't much like the duty. After thinking it over I went into the room where Mr. Houston was lying, and told him what the doctor said. He did n't make any reply for a few minutes. Then he turned to me, and said, "Call the family." I went out and aroused Mrs. Houston and the children. After they came in Mr. Houston said, "Call the servants." All gathered about the bedside. Mr. Houston proceeded calmly and slowly to give detailed instructions about what he wanted done. He had some advice for each one present. When he had finished he called for the Bible and had a psalm read. Turning to two daughters he asked them to sing a hymn, which he designated. The girls began, but broke down sobbing. Mr. Houston took it up and finished it. After that he sent them all to bed again. He was very low.

Having orchestrated and performed the perfect farewell, Houston's reservoir of strength began to refill. Hamilton Stuart returned to Galveston, and when he looked in again on Houston some time later, he found vast improvement. Through Stuart, the general sent his warmest appreciation to his friends, and then with his old twinkle added, "Tell my enemies I am not dead yet."[19]

As his retirement lengthened, mentions of his projected Mexican protectorate faded, perhaps evidence that he intended the scheme primarily to head off the Civil War by unifying the country against a common enemy. With Texas now in the Confederacy but not ravaged by war as other regions throughout the South, Houston now expended what little political capital he had on the idea that Texas look to her own security—which involved resisting Confederate conscription of recruits within Texas. Jeff remembered that Margaret saw "what a foolish thing it was," not to say risky. The general mentioned the topic in letters to Ashbel Smith and Lubbock but received no encouragement, so he let the subject pass. Probably for this sentiment, Houston was suspected in some quarters of still being a Union sympathizer—a sin for which many other Texans had been burned out and even lynched. Confederate detectives so badgered him that by August of 1862, a month before Sam Junior's return, Houston groused to his friend, Austin businessman Swen Swenson, that the snoops had been "especial in their inquisitions about matters . . . at my house, or what my children may say in their prattlings. . . . I have started an inquiry into some things I have heard. You may hear more of it by and bye. It is not enough that we have given our son." The rest of the letter, though, reveals a sunny disposition and even includes an impromptu poem ("So . . . my muse was not asleep") in avowing that the Houstons regarded Swenson as one of the family. "We would be delighted if you would visit us . . . , we shall try to give you some of the best oysters and fish in the Bay. We live poorly, but we will try to dress our diet with a hearty welcome. Can't you come to see us?"[20]

The next day the promised inquiry took the form of a protest to the Harris County Provost Marshal, a man named Frazier: "communicate to me the . . . authors who have complained to you, or have made any charges against my loyalty to the government. . . . I claim no more than the humblest man in the community, and I am always ready to answer to the Laws of my Country."[21] Nor was it nosy provost marshals alone that made life at Cedar Point difficult. Houston still had a large family to support, and with neither employment nor pension, he was forced to turn to the trees of his beloved "fairy region," which he had once protected from poaching woodcutters. Houston in retirement made ends meet by shipping firewood to Galveston.

Early in October 1862, a Union fleet steamed into Galveston harbor and Federal forces occupied the city. With the firewood enterprise shut down, the Houstons prepared a return to Huntsville. Incessant rains rendered the road impassable, however, so instead they sojourned a time with Margaret's mother back in Independence. Still a hoop-skirted caryatid of the local Baptist church, Nancy Lea was now eighty-two years old, a stern woman made the more formidable by her growing eccentricity. In a burst of zeal, she had pledged her silver to add to the alloy in casting a bell for the Independence Baptist Church "to sweeten its tone." A note on the back of a family photo adds, "Grandma Lea sent a man to Ohio (I think) to see that the silver really went into the bell."[22] Of particular concern to her lately was the possibility, when her time came, that she would be buried in a wooden coffin. Such an end for a lady of her station was too horrible to contemplate, thus Nancy Lea used her means and connections to have a steel casket shipped from Alabama, which she stored, upright, in her bedroom closet. The Houstons stayed with her for a month, not entirely unleavened by the general's wonted sense of mischief. Better supplied with luxuries than most Southern families during the wartime scarcity, Houston noticed the larder of coffee and sugar disappearing faster than it should. Jeff Hamilton recalled in his memoir that Houston kept vigil until he discovered that two of the little slave girls, Hanna and Mary, were filching it for secretive "tea parties." Knowing the servants' terror of spirits, Houston opted for a little fun. "One night after supper," recalled Jeff, "he called us all together, and said that there must be some ghosts thieving about the place every night, and wanted us to help him find a safe place for his sugar and coffee." He then handed the staples to none other than Mary and Hanna and led them to Nancy Lea's stored steel casket. "They almost dropped dead," wrote Jeff. "And they did drop the packages, and ran from the house screaming. After that night, my master always had enough coffee and sugar for his usual two morning cups."[23]

Eliza, Jeff, and most of the servants may have been content with their situation in the Houston household, but back in Huntsville an incident occurred that reminded the family of the true nature of slavery. Tom Blue, a West Indian mulatto who had been in Houston's service ever since the early days of the republic, ran away. He escaped in company with a young boy named Walter, who was the son of a slave owned by a Huntsville smithy. Tom Blue was light complexioned enough to pass for white, spoke elegant English, and convinced young Walter that the best way for them to get to Mexico was for them to play master and slave. Walter agreed, addressing Tom Blue as "massa," until they reached Laredo—where Tom Blue sold the hapless boy and entered Mexico with eight hundred dollars in his pocket. Sam Houston told Alexis de Tocqueville thirty years earlier that he believed blacks to be as innately intelligent as anybody, but this was probably not the kind of evidence he would have wished to cite.[24]

Jeff Hamilton recalled with some amusement that Tom Blue should have been just a little more patient, for soon after he fled, the general called the servants to the front porch of the Steamboat House and instructed them to pay close attention. With Margaret beside him, he read them Lincoln's proclamation of September 22, 1862, declaring that slaves in the rebelling states would be free the following first of January. Putting the paper away, Houston announced that he had the right to emancipate his people whenever he chose. "You, and each of you, are now free." Eliza got the idea that they were going to be sent away and started wailing; Jeff recalled that she was known as a great shouter at revivals, and her protests against being separated from the family were punctuated with hallelujahs and glories to God. The general managed to hush her and assured the slaves that as long as they cared to stay and work for him, he would pay them as long as he could. Historians now debate whether this was a theatrical performance or whether, in his own mind, Houston did emancipate his slaves; generally in recent years concluding the former.[25] And, in fact, Texas at the time of secession outlawed the voluntary manumission of slaves by their owners—a law that Sam Houston would have taken defiant satisfaction in breaking. There may have been more to it than that, however. Houston had always believed the war was hopeless; Lincoln published his intention to free the Southern slaves on September 22; Galveston fell to a Federal invasion barely two weeks later, and Houston "freed" his slaves shortly thereafter. By emancipating his people before Union troops did it for him, perhaps he felt the boot of occupation would tread more lightly on his family. As far as not turning them out on their own, Lafayette had depicted for him nearly forty years earlier his vision of a South overrun by unemployed, indigent blacks and the disaster it would mean for the economy. Houston knew perfectly well that free blacks in the North were often treated just as hideously as slaves in the South, and he knew what his people would suffer if he dismissed them from the household; it is doubtful that he would have done that either to them or to Texas. In his own mind, he did free his slaves, as indeed he declared on his deathbed, but did not drive them from the family situation with which they were familiar.

On New Year's Day of 1863, there was wonderful news, although not the emancipation Lincoln had promised: the Union occupation of Galveston was broken. J. Bankhead "Prince John" Magruder attacked the Yankee positions on the wharf

with scaling ladders too short to reach the top, but just as it appeared that the
Rebels were doomed by fire support from Federal gunboats, a gallant little task force
of "cotton-clads" puffed into the harbor and saved the day. Two of them rammed and
captured the rakish new USS *Harriet Lane*, and the USS *Westfield* ran aground and
was blown up. About fifty Union troops onshore were killed and the remaining six
hundred, without fire support or a means of retreat, surrendered. Houston rose from
a sick bed to send a congratulatory message to Texas's newest hero. Perhaps uncon-
sciously drawing from his own history, he wrote: "all that Texans want is a General
who is capable of leading them to victory. . . . You have breathed new life into everything; you have illustrated to Texans what they can do, and most sincerely do I trust
that the past may be only the dawning of the future." Magruder delayed replying
until he had secured the city's defenses, but in a few weeks sent a courtly response:
"No hostile foot now treads the soil of Texas, and it gives me peculiar pleasure to
announce that fact to the Hero of San Jacinto. . . . Please accept my warmest thanks
for the Kind expressions conveyed in your letter."[26]

The Federal prisoners taken at Galveston were shipped to Huntsville and clapped
into the penitentiary. Houston had long been a good friend of the superintendent,
Maj. Thomas Carothers, and feeling renewed energy had Jeff drive him in his top
buggy over to have a look at the POWs. Houston still felt keenly obliged to the
alert Union soldiers who had safely repatriated Sam Junior, and when he "found
that both the officers and privates were being closely confined in convict cells like
common criminals," Jeff remembered, "the General was so angry that it looked
for a minute like he was going to start a riot. He protested so strongly and with such
unprintable words that the superintendent . . . apologized to my master and the
prisoners. He took some of them to his own home, and other Huntsville citizens
had the others live with them until arrangements could be made to exchange them."

Sam Houston's closing months afforded many chances to make peace and say
good-bye. Hearing that his health was failing, Chief Blount sent a delegation of
Alabama and Coushatta Indians, whose young men, thanks to Houston's intercession, had been exempted from Confederate conscription, to see him. Up to now,
Houston had customarily received them at the spring near Woodland, but at Bailey's
odd Steamboat House he was now too infirm to make the walk and chatted quietly
with them on the porch, seating the four men and eight young women in a circle
around him, utilizing the lilting native tongue for a last time. "Before they started
back," remembered Jeff, "my master asked them to sing his favorite Indian song. This
pleased the Indians very much. They sang two or three songs for him, and wound
up with the one he liked so well, which was sung in a low chant. It was a pretty song,
but sad."[27]

On one of their trips to Houston, the general had Jeff drive him out to San Jacinto. The usually garrulous Houston said nothing; arriving at the battleground, he
sought out the great oak tree where he had received Santa Anna's surrender. He sat
pensively beneath its boughs "for a long time. . . . He had a far-off look in his eyes,
which I couldn't help but notice were wet." Night had fallen, and Houston noticed
Jeff becoming restive at being, after dark, on a battlefield where so many men had

died. His communion completed, it was time for a little mirth. "Jeff," said Houston softly, "twenty-seven years ago I lay wounded for many days and nights under this very tree. There were hundreds of dead Mexicans all around me; and I always noticed that about midnight the ghosts of every one of those dead men jumped right out of the corpses and ran straight toward me, yelling at the top of their voices." The general, Jeff recalled, nearly frightened him to death as well.[28]

The day after his seventieth birthday, Houston dictated a letter to Maggie (Nannie was at her grandmother's in Independence while attending school) for Eber Cave, who had resigned as secretary of state shortly after Houston was deposed as governor. Cave had relocated to Houston city where he, like Houston, lived as a Unionist under compulsion to demonstrate some loyalty to the Confederacy. Cave invited the general to stay with his family if he could manage a visit to his namesake city. "I need not write to you about politics," Houston answered through Maggie, "as you wrote to me on a former occasion that you had eschewed them. For my own part I cannot for the life of me keep from thinking about them; though without any design of ever mingling in them again." But he accepted the offer. Jeff drove him down in the top buggy, but they were stopped by a short and delicately built Confederate sentry at White Oak Bayou on the edge of town. He informed them that the city was under martial law and demanded their passes. The general descended painfully from the buggy and, towering over the sentry, told him to "go to San Jacinto, and there learn my right to travel in Texas!" They passed unmolested, although Houston had Jeff stop at some railroad tracks so they could watch a train pass. "I was so terrified that I let the reins drop from my hands and would have jumped out of the buggy and run away had not the General caught me by the arm."

Once in Houston city, he was, inevitably, invited to give a speech. One last time, Robert Burns gave him an opening: "I have been buffeted by the waves, as I have been borne along time's ocean, until shattered and worn, I approach the narrow isthmus, which divides it from the sea of eternity beyond. Ere I step forward to journey through the pilgrimage of death, I would say, that all my thoughts and hopes are with my country."

His voice was hollow and did not carry. Sam Houston often took a melodramatic pose before an audience, and he had been talking for four years about how little time he had left. But now the audience could plainly see that he was failing. A photograph taken about this time, which he gave to Ashbel Smith, shows a dramatic change —wan, sunken, disappearing within himself.

"Once I dreamed of empire," he admitted, "vast and expansive for a united people.... The dream is over. The golden charm is broken.... From one nation we have become two ... to attest how vain were the dreams of those who believed that the Union was a thing of forever." Again he warned that the South ought not depend on foreign intervention to save them. "Wiser men than myself have thought that sympathy for our unequal condition and horror at the barbarism of our enemies, would bring interference in our behalf. History tells a different tale of national humanity.... Nations, like corporations, are soulless. England, to whom we may have looked for aid, has nothing in common with us, save what interest dictates."

Sam Houston in 1863. Houston's decline since 1859 is evident in this photograph, taken probably in Houston city and presented to his old friend, Ashbel Smith, who kept it in his papers until his own death twenty-three years later.

Courtesy Center for American History, University of Texas

France, he speculated, might be a different story now that Napoleon III had gilded a Mexican throne and set Maximilian von Hapsburg upon it. He could not resist a last defense of his protectorate idea. "Once, actuated by a desire for the glory of my country as it then was, I presented to the American Senate a scheme for the regeneration of Mexico under American auspices. . . . The Protectorate over Mexico was rejected by the American Senate," and now Napoleon had stepped "forward to grasp the prize" that America had been too timid to reach for. France might now be cultivated, and he spent some minutes talking up French virtues, but the result, he said, could not be certain.

The South, he advised, would do better to look to the strength of her own arms. "Let us go forward, nerved to nobler deeds than we have yet given to history. Let us bid defiance to all the hosts our enemies may bring against us. Can Lincoln expect to subjugate a people thus resolved? No! From every conflict they will arise stronger and more resolute." He praised Magruder's liberation of Galveston and naval victories off the mouth of the Sabine three weeks later. Northern currency was depressed, the conservative Northwest was disgusted with Lincoln, and, he pointed out hopefully, the Northern soldiers were mercenaries who had it better at home than they did in the field. They were more likely to give up than Confederate patriots, who were fighting for their homes and way of life and were accustomed to privations. All, he hoped, might yet come right. "I come to the conclusion. May the blessings of Heaven be upon us and our cause. May our glorious heroes living return to bless their kindred and friends, and over the fallen may monuments imperishable rise to show posterity where lie the men who fell for liberty. May the prayers of woman . . . win from Heaven, as they ever have done, its approving smiles, until upon us and the generations that shall come after us, shall fall the blessings of peace and prosperity."29

The general's pep talk was not sufficiently ardent for one drunk in the crowd, who interrupted him by shouting "Hurrah for Jeff Davis! Down with the damn Yanks!" Still not one to be heckled while holding a floor, Houston answered: "My friend, I do not approve of cussing your worst enemy, if you can find some sensible argument to use against him. I have personally known Mr. Davis for many years. I first met him when he was a member of Congress from Mississippi, later when he was Secretary of War under President Pierce, and when he was a United States Senator while I was in the Senate. He was a distinguished colonel in the United States army during the War with Mexico, and was badly wounded near Buena Vista. He is a gentleman imbued with all the instincts of Southern honor and chivalry, but I want to tell you something you may not know about him: Jeff Davis is as ambitious as Lucifer and cold as a lizard." (Unknown to Houston, Jeff Davis at about this same time was getting his own back on the Texan, characterizing him as, "a worthless man with some good points.")30

It was on this trip that Houston, one final time, ran into Alexander Terrell, his former political adversary who had become a good friend. Shortly before Terrell's wife died in 1860, the Houstons attended a church service beneath a live oak tree in the front yard of Terrell's house two miles south of Austin, and all took communion together. Recently an Austin newspaper had alleged that Terrell made an unfavorable allusion to Houston in a speech. Meeting Houston near the Fannin Hotel, Terrell disclaimed any ill intent. "I know, Judge," said Houston, "I know you did not refer to me, and if you had it would only have excited regret. I feel that my time is short and I have not a root of bitterness here," he tapped his chest, "towards any human being that breathes."31

Houston met him again that night at Eber Cave's house. According to Terrell, Houston sounded them out about his scheme to split Texas from the rest of the Confederacy and resume her status as an independent republic. "He asked my opinion," Terrell recalled, "as to how our people would feel in Texas about unfurling the Lone Star flag and calling the boys home, saying to the North and South, 'hands off.' I declared my belief that it would cause the sacrifice of any man who proposed it. The subject was then dropped." Houston may have believed he was in sympathetic company, for since his relocation to Houston city, Cave had limited his support for the war effort to organizing home guard units for Texas's defense, if it became necessary. Cave and Terrell, however, were too watchful of Houston's safety and reputation to let such sentiments go beyond Cave's front door. "It was agreed between Major Cave and myself that the conversation should be kept secret for obvious reasons. . . . The idea of a separate republic for Texas was naturally dear to General Houston, but he failed to realize that such a move as he proposed during the madness of the hour would be regarded as treachery."[32]

From this trip Houston returned to Huntsville, where his health spun into an alarming decline. Margaret, who had lost a brother and a brother-in-law to consumption, began to fear the worst. On April 2 the general made out his will, naming his wife his executor to be assisted by Gibbs, Carothers, Anthony Branch, and J. Carroll Smith. One of the few special bequests was "to my eldest son, Sam Houston, Jr., I bequeath my sword worn in the Battle of San Jacinto, it never to be drawn only in defence of the Constitution, the Laws, and the Liberties of his Country." All else he left to Margaret. Houston's great personal force once again began to dispel the deathwatch, however. By April 14 he recovered sufficiently to send a letter to Nannie in Independence, "with mine own hand," he was happy to inform her. She was now sixteen and a half, and her father remembered enough of his worldly ways to give her sound advice on extricating herself from the attentions of a young man. "I presume that you made no professions of Love," he wrote; since she had not been indiscreet, she should "make no fuss about it." As for discontinuing correspondence with her suitor, "give as reasons that it would cause me to withdraw a portion of my time from my studies. It is a rule of Mr. Clark's school that no scholar of his . . . shall correspond with any gentleman unless he is a relative." All in all, it was "not . . . a matter of so much importance as to give it the appearance of a 'Love Scrape.'" He also wrote family news, among other things that "Sam has leave to go with his Uncle Charles to Mexico," part of a geological expedition with Francis Moore, who had been his state geologist. The general knew he was declining and was loath to let his firstborn go. "I could not spare Sam, but as he wishes to be doing something for himself, I yield."

"April 15," reads a brief postscript, "Today I am afraid I have taken a relapse. Write *weekly* at least."[33]

It is possible that early in 1863, all the talk of him running again for governor and the earliest rumbles of antiwar dissent turned Houston's head, but if so, his April visit to death's door brought him back to his senses. To the editor of the *Huntsville Item*, he sent a letter at the end of May forswearing any further thought of office, but though his body was feeble, his mind had lost none of its sarcasm: "Having for some time past noticed the agonizing distress of some of the presses of Texas . . . relative to my permitting my name to go before the people as a candidate for

Governor of this State, I am disposed to relieve them from their painful apprehensions. For months past when spoken to on that subject, I have invariably replied that 'under no circumstances will I permit my name to be used as a candidate.' ... A man of three score years and ten, as I am, ought, at least, be exempt from the charge of ambition." Of course, he added in his inimitable way, if he did run, "I might be assured that I would receive a much larger vote than I have ever done in Texas."[34]

The general's health began to sink again, his old wounds causing him such pain that Margaret sent him to take the waters at Sour Lake. In the tangled fastness of a dark forest known as the Big Thicket northwest of Beaumont, an entrepreneur had raked out body-sized basins in tepid mineral springs, where the sore and the agued sought relief in the tarlike mud. "It is my daily prayer that you may be benefitted by the springs," she wrote him. "We have been very well since you left, but miss you very much. . . . If you find you are improving at Sour Lake I would not . . . change it for any other place." In his last speech in Houston, the general had pinned his remaining hope for the survival of the Confederacy on the fact that they still had access to the Mississippi River. News of the fall of Vicksburg on July 3, therefore, which placed the entirety of the waterway in Union hands and severed the Confederacy, was a crushing blow to his fragile and largely artificial optimism. He could still read a map, and the doom of the South, sooner or later, was now inevitable. Their genteel, antebellum way of life would, he knew, now meet a fate every bit as terrifying as he had repeatedly, and futilely, predicted. There is no record of it, but one suspects that Houston's legendary gift of forecast had already envisioned a Union occupation army seeking to impose him as a puppet governor over his own people. Whatever Texas's future, he probably did not want to live to see it. Margaret did not help his frame of mind when she wrote him that, when news of Vicksburg's loss reached Huntsville, a gang of hot-blooded patriot boys tried to pick a fight with the Union prisoners whose release from prison cells Houston had demanded. Still, she tried to cheer him with family and church news, penning an addition to her hope for his improvement at the springs: "Mr. Seat preaches tonight on the prophecies and the Confederate government. I hope he will have better luck in predicting than he has had heretofore."[35]

Four long weeks at Sour Lake gave him no relief. The midsummer heat closed about the Piney Woods like an Indian sweat lodge, and when Houston returned to Huntsville on July 8 in the grip of a cold and cough, it was apparent—even to himself, for he told Jeff he would not last fifteen days—that he was a dying man. He made one more solicitous visit to the Union prisoners of war in the penitentiary and then went home to await the end. The coolest place in Rufus Bailey's strange house was the lower front room, and a couch was hauled to the center of it for Houston to lie on, where he was visited almost daily by his friend and Huntsville's state representative Judge Joab H. Banton.

Margaret sent urgently for Ashbel Smith, who arrived in his captain's uniform of the Second Texas Infantry. He stayed four days, but there was nothing he could do.[36] The general began having trouble breathing, and in increasing desperation Margaret sent for Dr. Pleasant W. Kittrell, who had parted from Houston politically

Judge Joab Banton; Dr. Pleasant W. Kittrell. Jodge Joab Banton served as Huntsville's representative in the state legislature. He visited Sam Houston almost daily during the general's last illness and delivered the eulogy at his funeral. He reprised the address for the legislature during their next session and presented a transcript of it to Margaret. Dr. Pleasant W. Kittrell came to differ with Houston politically, but the two families remained friendly, owing in part to the fact that Kittrell's wife, Frances, had attended the same school in Alabama as Margaret Houston. They were close neighbors; Houston frequently called on them during his walks, and it was Dr. Kittrell who rendered the general's final diagnosis of pneumonia.

Both courtesy Sam Houston Memorial Museum

but remained a personal friend. He called, accompanied by Dr. J. W. Markham, and rendered the diagnosis of severe pneumonia. Markham recommended stimulation by brandy, a suggestion that the general himself roused long enough to rebuke. He had been a teetotaler this long; he did not intend to abandon the principle at the end.[37]

Jeff tended his master—or former master—continually, day and night alike, fanning away flies, administering medicine, and as always, changing the bandages on the wounds that never healed. The bullet hole in Houston's arm, rent in the spring of 1814, "run as fresh the day that he died as ever it did." During the nights, the rest of neither master nor servant was peaceful, for Jeff was awakened by Houston's groaning and muttering. "I could hear him turn over and hear him say, 'Oh, my country'—he would speak it three times."[38] The general's condition deteriorated. On July 25, as Jeff fanned him and Margaret sat by his side, the exhausted Jeff dozed off, and the general was awakened by the fan that fell on his face. "Margaret," he said, "you and that boy go and get some rest. There is no use in both of you breaking yourselves down." Later in the day Houston began slipping in and out of a coma. In a lucid moment, he sent one of the servants over to the penitentiary to fetch Major Carothers. "He soon arrived," remembered Jeff, "bringing with him a Presbyterian preacher, whose name I have forgotten, and two other friends, Judge A. B. Wiley and Colonel [Robert] Hays."

The minister whom Jeff Hamilton could not recall was the distinguished missionary Samuel McKinney, who had come to Huntsville in 1850, served three years as president of Austin College, gone home to Mississippi, and then returned to Huntsville in 1862. Despite Houston's scarred history with the Presbyterian denomination, he and McKinney had become quite friendly. When the group filed into the Steamboat House, they found Houston alert, and they talked quietly with him about slavery and the war. Carothers asked the general what he was going to do with Jeff. Houston replied that he had already freed all his people, but that he wanted Sam Junior to look after Jeff and was certain he would do so. The general soon tired and began to sink again, when Reverend McKinney asked him gently how things stood with him and the Lord. Houston stalled his oblivion just a second longer and gave him a penetrating look. "All is well," he whispered. "All is well."[39]

McKinney led the family in prayer, and Margaret spent the night at Houston's bedside. During the morning of July 26, the children except for the absent Sam Junior joined her by the bedside; all the children were weeping. Margaret, with astonishing composure, opened her Bible and read to him quietly from the fourteenth chapter of John: "Let not your heart be troubled: ye believe in God, believe also in me. In my Father's house are many mansions: if it were not so, I would have told you."

At that, Houston moved. Like Stephen Austin a quarter-century before, Houston roiled from his darkening sleep with a hallucination of his life's work. "We heard in his voice a tone of entreaty," remembered Maggie, "and . . . we caught the words, 'Texas! Texas!' Soon afterward my mother was sitting by his bedside with his hand in hers, and his lips moved again. 'Margaret.'"[40] He sank again, the thought unfinished, and passed over at a quarter after six that evening.[41] From the little finger of his left hand, she pulled the thin gold band that Elizabeth Paxton Houston had fitted on him a half-century earlier and passed it among the children to read the word engraved along the inner curve: *Honor*. She said a prayer, less for the safety of the soul she had so watchfully guarded for twenty-three years, but prayed that their children might one day be worthy of him.

Over the years, many people asked Houston's pastor in Washington, George Samson, whether such a notorious wildman could ever really become a Christian. "The world," he wrote after Houston's death, "and even the mass of Christians . . . see only occasional exhibitions of Christian principle, seldom called out in the routine of busy life. . . . The angels see more clearly; they know who truly repents, and they rejoice over him; they come when he dies to bear him to their home; and they will gather all such with unerring certainty into one band, in the day of the revelation of God's righteous judgment. It is more than a hope, it is the intelligent confidence of his long-attached pastor, that Sam Houston will be there found among that band."[42]

After the general's body was laid out, his lodge brethren arrived and dressed him in Masonic regalia. A coffin large enough to hold the giant, spent frame was fashioned by the ship's carpenter of the *Harriet Lane*, for the comfort of whose captive crew Houston had been so watchful. Bob Hayes and A. B. Wiley made the funeral arrangements and saw to it that the small black-bordered announcements were printed and distributed. Dr. Kittrell wrote out the announcement of the death to the newspapers. "To his numerous friends it will doubtless be a matter of great satisfaction that in his last hours he was sustained by the Christian hope that he died the death of the righteous." Margaret's choice to preach the service was the Presbyterian, John M. Cochran, a default appointment, the Baptist minister being out of town. With Oakwood Cemetery lying just across and a few blocks down the street, it was decided to hold the service in the upstairs parlor. With the coffin placed there, the room could accommodate little seating. Because of this, and perhaps because the heat wave finally broke in a deluge of rain, only a dozen or so family intimates attended the funeral, although other accounts describe a throng lining the lane to the cemetery. Margaret had spent her sleepless night composing a poem for Reverend Cochran to read, which concluded: "And now may peace, within thy breast, / From him descend, and there remain! / Each night mayst thou sweetly rest / And feel thou hast not liv'd in vain." Judge Banton delivered the eulogy:

> Profound, far-seeing, and comprehensive in statesmanship; bold, daring, glorious in war; a dear lover of peace, with wonderful capacity to enjoy private life and the family circle, he combined all the elements necessary to constitute him a truly great man.
>
> I was with General Houston in his last illness and in his last moments on earth. He who was Sam Houston in life was emphatically and characteristically Sam Houston in death. The same reverence-inspiring form, the same piercing eye, the same gigantic mind.... There is ... something majestic, magnificent, and yet instructive and beautiful, in such a life and such a death....
>
> And now that the war of faction and of party is over with him, and the tongue of envy is hushed, all can see and acknowledge his great worth, and honor his immortal memory.... We might say of Texas, that she was his handiwork. And I doubt not that as long as there are those who love Texas, and as long as her glorious history is read, the name of Houston will be honored and revered.[43]

At some time when she was alone, Margaret opened her family Bible and wrote: "Died on the 26th of July 1863, Genl Sam Houston, the beloved and affectionate Husband, father, devoted patriot, the fearless soldier—the meek and lowly Christian."[44] In the days following the death, Margaret's serenity collapsed. Daily she unloaded flowers at the grave and wept so bitterly over it that the children began to fear for her sanity. It was only an entreaty from Nancy Lea to come recover in Independence that pulled her together.

The following session of the Texas Legislature, in which sat many of the dandies and firebrands who had bounced him out of the Governor's Mansion, decided they could be generous, and they

> *Resolved,* That in his death the State has lost one of its most distinguished citizens and public servants, and one of its ablest and most zealous advocates, and defenders of its rights, liberties, and its honor; and
>
> *Resolved,* That so great a light can be illy spared in this dark hour of our country's existence, and its going out is alike a State and a national calamity; and
>
> *Resolved,* that the sympathies and condolence of the people of the State be tendered the afflicted family of the deceased. . . .

Of more practical comfort, having heard of Margaret's circumstances, the legislature later appropriated for her relief seventeen hundred dollars—the remaining salary of Houston's unfilled gubernatorial term. Judge Banton, who had delivered the eulogy, conveyed to Margaret nearly two years later the manuscript copy of the legislature's resolution, and his handwritten reprise of the eulogy that he delivered to the legislature. With them was Judge Banton's apology: the legislature had intended to honor Houston's memory by having the resolutions and Banton's speech published, but the depreciation of the currency was such that the printer refused to perform his contract. Times were indeed hard in Austin, and Banton's tender letter was itself written on scrap sheets of ledger paper.[45]

War and, not unimportantly, disgrace had also been hard on the Houstons' means. The general had named Margaret his executor, and her inventory of the estate valued it at $89,288, only somewhat more than half what it was at the time they were forced out of the Governor's Mansion. That might still seem a comfortable sum, but almost none of it was in cash, and Margaret had hardly ever even opened an account book. Two-thirds of the estate was in land and mortgages—seventeen tracts in eleven counties, not all of it of accurate survey or certain title. (The league at Cedar Point was appraised at $22,140.) Only $1,100 was in personal property: five horses, four cows, the wagon, the carriage, the top buggy, a Burnside rifle, and a brace of pocket pistols. The dozen slaves ranging in age from four to fifty-five (their ages mostly understated) were valued at $10,530—their presence in the accounting having ought to do with whether or not Sam Houston in his own mind had freed them. The largest remaining asset, totaling nearly $17,000, was in uncollected loans from six months to twelve years old. Only after the will was probated at the end of August was it apparent how generous Houston had been with friends in need, even during the recent couple of years when times for his own family were far from easy. He had lent Eber Cave $2,000 while he was governor, which was still owing, and since his retirement had lent Carothers over $700. Reverend G. W. Baines, whose counsel won Houston for the Baptist church, had borrowed $300 in January of 1858; Baines had never been able to scrape enough together to repay the loan, and Houston had renewed his note annually. Now Margaret had to face up to her husband's generosity: to manage herself, eight children, and twelve dependent servants, she had receipts for cash on account of only $250 and a draft on Austin College for $1,002.59, which might or might not be collectible or even negotiable.[46]

It was true that in his will Houston desired his debts to be paid out of his personal effects, without resort to "disposing of any of my family servants," and one could construct an argument that their emancipation had faded from his mind once its usefulness disappeared when the Union occupation was driven from Galveston. More likely, however, enumerating them as part of the estate may have been a way of protecting them from the kind of abuse that most freedmen were subjected to after real emancipation arrived. It is possible that the law in Confederate Texas would not have recognized their freedom anyway, and keeping them in the estate was a way to prevent their falling back into the hands of men like James McKell, from whom Houston bought Jeff. Margaret, in fact, kept the extended family together as best she could after the general died, and when the servants were finally left on their own, the times did not compare favorably to their former situation.[47]

Margaret's first decision as a widow was sensible. She left Joshua, perhaps free and perhaps in a kind of detached service, in Huntsville, where he could support himself amply as a wheelwright. By October she accepted her mother's offer and moved the family to Independence. With Eber Cave's help she bought a small, two-story, severely Greek revival house just south of her mother's farm, but her comfort was brief, for Nancy Lea passed on to her reward on February 7, 1864, a couple of months short of her eighty-fourth birthday. Sealed into her treasured steel vault, she was laid to rest in the stone crypt she had overseen so diligently across the road from the Baptist church. Her mother's death, following so closely after the general's, nearly unhinged Margaret. Cloaked in mourning, she sat alternately gazing into the fire and reading her Bible through small spectacles. In time she steeled herself; she still had small children to not only rear but also provide an example, and her widowhood was one of generosity extended despite personal privation. She could have rented out the farmhouse where she and the general had lived, southwest of the church, but chose instead to provide it, rent-free, as a parsonage to the Reverend William Carey Crane. Ashbel Smith had been detached from his regiment to be inspector general of the troops Texas was contributing to the Confederate cause. Margaret heard of this and wrote him that a large tent had been left at the summer house at Cedar Point, and he should acquire it to shelter those of his Second Texas Infantry most in need of it. It was soon well known throughout Texas that Sam Houston's widow was not well off, and one day Joshua, who had become a successful ferrier in Huntsville and had taken the last name of Houston, appeared in Independence. During his lifetime, the general had allowed his slaves to accept outside employment, and even though as master he could have claimed the money, he saw to it that they saved what they earned. Joshua got off his mule and offered Margaret an old leather pouch containing two thousand dollars in prewar gold and silver coin—his entire life's savings. Margaret, moved to tears by such kindness, declined, advising Joshua that the general would want him to use the money to get a Christian education for his children, which he did.[48] It is unknown whether she had by this time received her relief funds from the legislature, but it did not matter. The kindness she returned with kindness stands on its own merit.

Perhaps in defiance of their circumstances, the cheeky Nannie declared she would have no man who could not pay the preacher fifty dollars in gold and take her to Niagara Falls for their honeymoon—a laughable taunt in Texas during Reconstruction. But then she met Joseph Clay Stiles Morrow, a gifted and ambitious young merchant from Georgetown who traveled over to Independence to assay the parties at Baylor. He met her price, she adored him, and Margaret knew in a flash that it was a splendid match. It was their engagement that finally lifted her from her long, frightening depression. Whatever her privations, she intended Nannie to have a wedding befitting her father's daughter. Reverend Crane's wife bought lace for the wedding gown in New Orleans at twelve dollars per yard and labored over it for weeks at Margaret's sewing machine. For the wedding, on August 1, 1866, the shutters of Margaret's high grim house were thrown open, the Houston silver and china set out gleaming.

Margaret found something else to live for during these days. She had approached Reverend Crane about writing the general's biography. At first he demurred. He had only seen Houston twice in his life, and though he maintained a lively interest in history, he did not feel qualified for such an undertaking. Margaret would not be denied, however. Her attic was stuffed with chests of Houston's lifetime of manically saved papers, and she would help him as much as he needed. They labored mightily on the project, with Margaret taking an active role in editing the life to be presented, truthful as far as the public would be edified, but discreet. His drinking was left in, for instance, but Diana Rogers was cut out.

When the volume was complete, they drew up a list of the general's friends who could help find a publisher for the book and wrote each. Not one of them agreed to help. Reverend Crane quoted one without identifying him: "At the present time every mind that thinks is powerfully, often painfully preoccupied with the strange anomalous, grave condition of our affairs, with the uncertainty of our future. . . . It does not seem to me that there is any pressing urgency to present the Life and Labors of General Houston to the world. It is true that they will possess a paramount interest . . . yet there is an advantage in bringing out a book in an opportune time." Crane condoled with her over the lack of support, but after he was gone Margaret became enraged, lighting the parlor fireplace and exhausting herself in burning Sam Houston's papers.[49] Fortunately for history, her fury was soon spent, and thousands of letters, notes, and speeches were spared.

By the time Joe and Nannie returned from their honeymoon—at Niagara Falls—Nannie was expecting a baby. The Morrows were to settle in Georgetown, and the only way Margaret would consent to not herself looking after her pregnant daughter was to send her indispensable Eliza to help them. Joe, in turn, offered to take Andrew as well, for Margaret had found herself unable to control him. Again, kindness was returned for kindness. Maggie married suddenly soon afterward to a hardworking young rent farmer from Labadie's Prairie named Weston Williams. Sam Junior discovered that his war wounds, like his father's, placed some limitation on his ability to run a farm, and he decided to become a doctor. Margaret could ill afford paying for his education, but rather than disappoint him she sought

Margaret Houston, c. 1860. Shattered by widowhood at forty-four and then prostrated by the death of her mother six months later, it was Margaret's grim faith and her determination to raise her children that kept her going until her own death of yellow fever late in 1867.

Courtesy Sam Houston Memorial Museum

out Eber Cave's help again; they managed to rent out Cedar Point for three hundred dollars, one-third down, and it was probably Cave who lent her the balance to get Sam Junior on his way.

By September of 1867, Margaret's finances had deteriorated to the point that when wagons loaded with supplies for Joe Morrow's mercantile in Georgetown passed through Independence, Margaret hailed them. "I took the liberty of appropriating two of your bacon sides," Margaret wrote him. "I did not pay for them, for the simple reason that I had not the money." She did not ask Morrow for cash, but she did remind him that her longtime treasured friend Brother George Washington Baines now lived in Salado, just up the road from Georgetown. Since Houston's death he had managed to scrape together a hundred dollars to pay on his debt that the general had renewed every year, but now if Morrow were to "represent my situation to him . . . he would let you have something for me."[50]

Other relief soon came to hand in a macabre way. The yellow fever had come to Independence, claiming so many casualties that white sheets flew from the windows of afflicted households. Marquis James wrote in *The Raven* that Margaret was a volunteer nurse during the epidemic—one of his literary encapsulations based on the truth that she did in fact receive and return visits from afflicted households. She had always sat with the sick, and doubtless did so now, but she was not a volunteer in the modern understanding of the word.[51] Maggie and West Williams were doing well, beyond the reach of the sickness on their rented farm, but when Margaret received a message from Maggie that she was contemplating a visit to Independence, Margaret quickly trumped her, hustling the children into the great yellow coach and fleeing, shaken but safe, to high and healthy Labadie's Prairie. She spent the autumn of 1867 with West and Maggie, and then a letter came from Nannie inviting her to stay with her family in Georgetown. Nannie was by far the best off of all the family—even Eliza was seen sporting a yellow hat with an ostrich feather. Nannie invited the whole family for Christmas but intended for her mother to stay much longer, a welcome respite from the perennial struggle to make ends meet. Passing back through Independence, Margaret stopped to pack the things she would need and was delayed by a stream of callers who noticed her back in residence. The yellow fever had been merciless in Independence, where resort was even made to a medieval public dead-wagon to carry away casualties. Margaret, faultlessly courteous, returned calls to her friends' households, many of whom were in mourning, and she soon fell ill. On December 3, 1867, after two days of scripture-mumbling delirium, she died. The burial had to be deep and immediate; one of the remaining servants, Bingley, dug the grave next to Nancy Lea's tomb; Major Cave assisted Nettie and Mary Willie in the lonely, lantern-beamed task of laying her to rest. They sent over to the farm, where the preacher, William Carey Crane, had lived in grace and favor. Fearful of contamination, he refused to come out and conduct a service.

If James's characterization of Margaret as a nurse was a dash of his metaphorical license, it was not an unreasonable one. Stern, formidable, and caring, she was a woman of good works—above all of which, perhaps, was her husband.

AFTERWORD

Along with the Alamo and the monument at San Jacinto, Huntsville is one of the most important destinations for students of the Texas heritage. General Houston's Woodland, which sits on its original site, and Rufus Bailey's Steamboat House where the general died, which was relocated to the Woodland property, are both preserved as memorials. Visitors and researchers come in a steady stream to the Sam Houston Memorial Museum on the same tract, its low dome and Greek revival portico reminiscent of a kind of art deco Monticello. Houston's shaded resting place in the Oakwood Cemetery a few blocks away is dominated by a great stone monument with Andrew Jackson's prophetic epitaph, "The World Will Take Care of Houston's Fame." To Texas history pilgrims, Huntsville is a shrine of the first rank.

Work on this volume was almost complete before I had an opportunity to visit Margaret's grave in Independence. Reached by turning from a U.S. highway onto a state highway and then a final nine miles on a two-lane farm road with no shoulder, Independence is a village of fewer than 150 persons. Nancy Lea's establishment, just east of the Baptist church, no longer exists. The church building she knew burned down a few years after her death and was replaced by a sturdy stone edifice. The bell for whose casting she donated her silver no longer hangs in the belfry but is displayed in a small museum attached to the current structure.

The house that Margaret shared with the general, across the creek to the west and south, is no longer there, its site marked by a granite ebenezer. Of the original Baylor University for boys southeast of there, nothing remains. A reconstructed portico and a single imploding ruin of the kitchen and refectory is all that remains of the college for girls, which stood on a hill west of the church. The modest Greek revival home where Margaret lived out her brief widowhood was, at the time of my visit, for sale. (But not all things change—Margaret would be happy to know that the "Baptizing Hole" on Rocky Creek, about a mile and a half south and a little east of the town, still ripples with the occasional immersion of converts.)

More surprising, if I had not recognized from photographs the grim, squat outline of Nancy Lea's crypt as it blurred by, I would have missed the family burial plot altogether; some later hand added a cedar shake roof so that it resembles something more like a well house. The faux-ashlar exterior of the tomb has mostly crumbled away to the naked stone and mortar she so doggedly jabbed at with her cane. Some twenty years after her entombment, her prized metal vault cracked, and she now lies in a grave next to the crypt, with Margaret beside her. A few feet away stands a headstone that affectionately reads, "Aunt Eliza Faithful unto Death." She lived until 1898.

In 1936 the Texas Centennial Commission obtained an appropriation to exhume Margaret's remains and reinter them next to those of her husband, as she no doubt would have wished. The plan met with the approval of her only surviving child, Andrew Jackson Houston, and most of the grandchildren, but there was sufficient opposition from the rest of the family that the idea was dropped, and Margaret continued to lie in her obscure roadside grave. At some later time when the highway was widened, a cut was made into the hillside so that, from the narrow sidewalk, Margaret Lea Houston lies, not six feet deep but perhaps three. She who began life in gentility, in a social station far above that of her husband, now lies with her head a couple of yards—barely—from the blast and suction of semi-trailer trucks that scarcely slow through Independence on their run from Brenham to College Station.

One of my last tasks in writing this book, I once thought, would be to craft a way once the facts were written to give it a sense of literary closure, or perhaps symmetry. Only upon visiting Independence with a flower for Margaret's grave did I discover that Life, the great leveler, had done it for me.[1]

Notes

PREFACE

1. Many, indeed most, elements of the Houston story as traditionally related are now in conflict with the contemporary revisionist interpretation. Somehow one is not surprised to see a skirmish on only the second page of the book. Compare Roberts, *Star of Destiny*, 320, with Gregg Cantrell, "Whither Sam Houston?" *Southwestern Historical Quarterly* 96 (October 1993): 350. While this incident might not have occurred in the way it is traditionally related, its complete dismissal is probably not warranted either. In this volume, the possible emancipation of the Houston slaves will be dealt with at its proper place in the chronology.

2. Flanagan, *Sam Houston's Texas*, ix.

3. Heiskell, *Andrew Jackson and Early Tennessee History*, 1:1–2.

4. Cantrell, "Whither Sam Houston," 345, 350.

5. Houston to G. F. H. Prockett, 2 May 1855, in Barker and Williams, *Writings of Sam Houston*, 6:180.

6. Walter Prescott Webb, "An Honest Preface," *Southwest Review* 36 (autumn 1951): 312.

7. Haley, *Most Excellent Sir*, x.

CHAPTER 1

1. Williams, *Following General Sam Houston*, 9. Houston Castle has long since disappeared. "Padivan" is sometimes rendered "Padvinan." James, *The Raven*, 437n.

2. "Sam Houston Genealogy," Sam Houston Memorial Museum Website, <www.shsu.edu/~smm_www/geneology/>. James in *The Raven* gives the date as 1730.

3. Morton, *History of Rockbridge County*, 189–90; Boley, *Lexington in Old Virginia*, 38, 49–50. When the Liberty Hall Academy had earlier entered perilous financial straits, Washington endowed the school with James River Canal stock awarded him by the Virginia legislature for his war services. This became the nucleus of the Washington and Lee University endowment.

4. Boley, *Lexington in Old Virginia*, 119, 224–25. In later years, Thompson was one of the trustees who offered the presidency of Washington College to Robert E. Lee. After Lee's tenure, the school became Washington and Lee University.

5. Williams, *Following General Sam Houston*, 13; Boley, *Lexington in Old Virginia*, 150, 185. This particular vignette may be apocryphal, for it has the adolescent Sam replying, "Uncle, some day I will come back through here on my way to Congress." Interesting, if true. Matthew Houston was the sixth child of grandfather Robert Houston's younger brother, John.

6. Heiskell, *Andrew Jackson and Early Tennessee History*, 2:152.

7. Lester, *Life of Sam Houston*, 17ff.

8. One of the more colorful Anglo residents was a Bavarian vegetarian named Frederici, who was decades ahead of his time in his views on living with the land. The Cherokees had allotted him six acres to farm, on which he said he grew enough to feed ten families and intended to give four acres back. Williams, *Early Travels*, 480–85.

9. Wilkins, *Cherokee Tragedy*, 3–4.

10. Heiskell, *Andrew Jackson and Early Tennessee History*, 2:154. Late in his life, Houston spoke of clerking at Sheffy's to Alexander Terrell. Terrell, "Recollections of General Sam Houston," 114.

11. Williams, *Houston and the War of Independence*, 9. This reminiscence was made to Peter Burke, described by Williams as "an old comrade of the Indian wars." The Sam Houston School is now a state historic site, located off Highway 33 just south of Rockford, Tennessee.

12. James, *The Raven*, 438n.

13. Maj. Will A. McTeer to Samuel Heiskell, 17 July 1919, in Heiskell, *Andrew Jackson and Early Tennessee History*, 2:149.

14. Heiskell, *Andrew Jackson and Early Tennessee History*, 2:154 (quoting Willoughby Williams to Josephus Guild, 1 April 1878, first published in Guild, *Old Times in Tennessee*, 274–75). I am inclined to give Williams's recollection to Guild credence because the vigor of his memory, even though "written from memory fifty-two years after the event," stood proof against challenges elsewhere. Moreover, Williams's widowed mother lived three miles south of Kingston, and he would not have mistaken it for Maryville. Guild, 274–75, 285, 287–88.

15. Lester, *Life of Sam Houston*, 27. The reader will notice very few citations hereinafter to this source. It seems odd that a subject's autobiography should not be a principal source of any biography, and indeed many biographers have used it as such. However, Sam Houston's later fireside manufacture of this carefully designed image of his career, while its scenes have become irremovable from his story, also erodes the probative value of the memoir. I have treated it with caution. The gold band inscribed "Honor" is now displayed in the San Jacinto Museum of History, Houston.

16. Blount County Court Records, 29 September 1810, quoted in Maj. Will A. McTeer to Samuel G. Heiskell, 17 July 1919, reproduced in Heiskell, *Andrew Jackson and Early Tennessee History*, 2:150. Cusack was later fined twenty dollars for a repeat offense.

17. Remini, *Andrew Jackson and the Course of American Empire*, 187–205.

18. Lester, *Life of Sam Houston*, 303; *Historical Register and Dictionary of the United States Army*, quoted in Wisehart, *Sam Houston*, 651n.

19. Jackson to Blount, 31 March 1814, quoted in Heiskell, *Andrew Jackson and Early Tennessee History*, 1:498.

20. Mrs. Thomas J. Wallace to Samuel Heiskell, quoted in Heiskell, *Andrew Jackson and Early Tennessee History*, 1:151. Mary, known within the family as Polly, was the eighth of Capt. Samuel and Elizabeth Houston's nine children; the last was Eliza, whose later estrangement from Polly over the second Wallace marriage caused Sam Houston enormous grief.

21. Heiskell, *Andrew Jackson and Early Tennessee History*, 2:155. John McEwen was Robert's brother.

22. Houston to John Rhea, 1 March 1815, A. J. Houston Collection, Texas State Library and Archives, typescript. It is also contained in Barker and Williams, *Writings of Sam Houston*, 1:1–2. Rhea was not actually a representative at this time; between 1803 and 1823, he was out of office for only two years, 1815–17. Houston wrote a similar plea to Tennessee senator Joseph Anderson but admitted to Monroe, "I have not influential relatives to support me with their influence & if merit does not support me, I must sink." Houston to Monroe, 1 March 1815, in Barker and Williams, *Writings of Sam Houston*, 1:3–4.

23. Rhea to Secretary of War, 11 March 1815, A. J. Houston Collection, typescript. This document contains a penciled note in the margin that the original is in the War Department, the typescript being made from a photostat furnished by the historical collector and writer Col. M. L. Crimmins.

24. Houston to Capt. Alexander Campbell, 25 April 1815, in Barker and Williams, *Writings of Sam Houston*, 1:4–5. The citation of this letter from the *Texas Historical Association Quarterly*, 14:160 (quoted in James, *The Raven*, 36–37), has it addressed to Houston's cousin, Robert McEwen. However, it was McEwen who carried the letter to Campbell. Barker and Williams, *Writings of Sam Houston*, 1:5n. In the days before postal regulation, the person by whom a mail conveyance was made was commonly credited on the letter in such a way that often confuses latter-day readers. This letter is the oldest of the original Sam Houston documents in the collection of the Center for American History at the University of Texas. This large repository of Houston materials consists partly of

original documents, partly photostats, and partly transcripts stored in various areas. Each area is unique in some respects and duplicative in others; most, but not all, of the collection's documents were published in Barker and Williams, *Writings of Sam Houston*, including those transcripts bound as "Unpublished Correspondence." I have chosen to cite all papers used from this collection as the "Sam Houston Papers" at the Center for American History because I anticipate that one day, more near than far, these holdings must be integrated into a more accessible system that will supersede a directional citation.

25. Yoakum, *History of Texas*, 1:305.

26. Houston to Robert Brent, 26 July 1815, Sam Houston Papers, Center for American History.

CHAPTER 2

1. As an army commander of state militia, Jackson of course would have submitted separate reports of the action. Jackson to Pinckney, 28 March 1814; and Jackson to Blount, 31 March 1814, quoted in Heiskell, *Andrew Jackson and Early Tennessee History*, 1:497–502.

2. George C. Henry to *Dallas Morning News*, [February 1927], Correspondence about Sam Houston, Catholic Archives of Texas, Chancery of the Austin Diocese.

3. I had determined to quote from this letter as excerpted in James, *The Raven*, 40, before I chanced across the original, Jesse Beene to Houston, 31 May 1817, Penny Thornall Remick Collection, Sam Houston Regional Library and Research Center. It seems that in his anxiety to get Houston and the "Princess of E.T." married, Beene was engaging in what psychologists today would call "projection" of his own disappointments onto his friend; as he wrote Houston, "Old Mrs. E has kept me out of six years happines by preventing my union with her daughter, and do not let Mrs. H play the same trick on you."

4. Meigs to Jackson, 24 May 1817, in Bassett, *Correspondence of Andrew Jackson*, 2:296.

5. Houston to [Jackson], 21 October 1817, A. J. Houston Collection, Texas State Archives.

6. Meigs to Houston, 9 October 1817, A. J. Houston Collection.

7. Houston to Jackson, 18 December 1817, A. J. Houston Collection. The Hiwassee subagency was located on the west bank of the river near the spot where it was later bridged by the rail line between Knoxville and Chattanooga. Guild, *Old Times in Tennessee*, 275.

8. Houston to George Graham, 28 December 1817, A. J. Houston Collection.

9. John Jolly to John C. Calhoun, 28 January 1818, quoted in James, *The Raven*, 42.

10. Houston to Jackson, 18 December 1817. Houston's subagency was not the only one in the history of the frontier to have the problem of Indians seeking to improve their material situation by sending in, separately, different members of the same family for rations and supplies, each claiming to be a family head. The Hiwassee Cherokees, however, were more sinned against than sinning.

11. McMinn to Houston, 2, 16 January 1818, A. J. Houston Collection.

12. Remini, *Andrew Jackson and the Course of American Empire*, 474n. Remini refers to *The Raven*, 44, for the Calhoun episode, and James makes no mention of previous offenses.

13. Houston to Jackson, 6 December 1818, A. J. Houston Collection.

14. Houston to Parker, 1 March 1818, Old Files, War Department, quoted in James, *The Raven*, 45; General Orders, 1 March 1818, Penny Thornall Remick Collection.

15. Hamilton, *My Master*, 26.

16. James, *The Raven*, 28–29.

17. Ashbel Smith, "Life Sketch of Sam Houston," Ashbel Smith Papers, Center for American History, University of Texas.

18. Allen Johnson and Dumas Malone, eds., *Dictionary of American Biography*, 22 vols. (New York: Charles Scribner's Sons, 1958), 8:524–25.

19. Johnson and Malone, *Dictionary of American Biography*, 6:145–46.

20. McMinn to Houston, 24 January 1818, Sam Houston Papers, Catholic Archives of Texas.

21. McMinn to Houston, 22 April, 1 May 1818, Sam Houston Papers, Catholic Archives of Texas. Other Cherokee villages are enumerated in this fragment but are no longer legible.

22. See Gregory and Strickland, *Houston with the Cherokees*, 20–21.

23. McMinn to Houston, 13 June 1818, Sam Houston Papers, Catholic Archives of Texas.

CHAPTER 3

1. Houston, *Life*, 3; Ludlow, *Dramatic Life*, 166.

2. Houston to McMinn, 30 April 1819, Joseph McMinn Papers, Tennessee State Library and Archives. Curiously, this bucolic motif in the McMinn-Houston correspondence helps trace Houston's evolution from protégé to trusted friend. Three and a half years after this letter, McMinn confided to Houston: "I never have had the least inclination to make my religious opinions known except to my best friends. . . . I can say to you and you alone" that the Lord had laid His personal hand on McMinn's farming effort. "I have neither sowed nor planted a single article of vegitable matter which has not produced . . . beyond my most sanguine expectations." McMinn to Houston, 4 August 1822, Sam Houston Papers, Catholic Archives of Texas, Chancery of the Austin Diocese.

3. Hemphill et al., *Papers of John C. Calhoun*, 4:354–55, quoted in Remini, *Andrew Jackson and the Course of American Empire*, 476–77n. When Houston declined the Cherokee Agency it went, ironically, to McMinn.

4. I. V. Drake to William Carey Crane, 30 April 1867, quoted in Crane, *Life and Select Literary Remains*, 33; Heiskell, *Andrew Jackson and Early Tennessee History* 2:159. Houston biographies have modernized the title to attorney general, but in fact the office was still carried on in its archaic form of solicitor general. Joseph McMinn, "Proclamation of Election of Samuel Houston as Solicitor General of Nashville District," 11 October 1819, Penny Thornall Remick Collection, Sam Houston Regional Library and Research Center.

5. Quoted in Friend, *Sam Houston*, 9.

6. McMinn to Houston, 20 October 1821, Sam Houston Papers, Catholic Archives of Texas.

7. Richard Cutts to Stephen Pleasanton, 5 December 1821; Pleasanton to Henry Crabb, 10 December 1821; William Lee to Pleasanton, 8 April 1822; and Pleasanton to Crabb, 10 April 1822, Sam Houston Papers, Catholic Archives of Texas.

8. Houston to Calhoun, 4 June 1822, Sam Houston Papers, Center for American History, University of Texas.

9. Houston to Calhoun, 8 July 1822, in Barker and Williams, *Writings of Sam Houston*, 1:12; Houston, "Draft for Pay for $170.09," 15 June 1821, A. J. Houston Collection, Texas State Library and Archives.

10. Houston to McMinn, 15 February 1823, in Barker and Williams, *Writings of Sam Houston*, 1:17. This is one of about one hundred Houston papers that formed part of the Philpott Collection, which was canvassed for inclusion in *Writings of Sam Houston*. No record of the entire contents, however, was made before the collection was auctioned in 1986, so unique information was almost certainly lost into private albums at that time. Philpott Collection Auction Catalog, 16–17 October 1986; Tony Altermann to author, 4 June 1990.

11. Houston to McMinn, 30 March 1823, in Barker and Williams, *Writings of Sam Houston*, 1:19. McMinn had apparently served as a go-between for Graham and Houston before, the nature of which is mentioned but not clarified in a partly illegible letter (as are many of McMinn's letters), McMinn to Houston, 4 August 1822, Sam Houston Papers, Catholic Archives of Texas.

12. Wisehart, *Sam Houston*, 28.

13. Crane, *Life and Select Literary Remains*, 35 (quoting Jackson to Jefferson, 4 October 1823, reproduced in its entirety on p. 42). The original is on display at the Sam Houston Regional Library and Research Center in Liberty. Jefferson had almost three more years of "happy days" at Monticello,

playing with his grandchildren and experimenting with his vast garden. He went on to his reward the same day as John Adams, 4 July 1826, the fiftieth anniversary of American independence.

14. Remini, *Andrew Jackson and the Course of American Freedom*, 60; Boley, *Lexington in Old Virginia*, 54.

15. Lubbock, *Six Decades in Texas*, 73. Some daguerreotypes of Houston show glimpses of the size of his hands. Perhaps I should not admit this, but when I curated the annexation exhibit at the Texas State Capitol's visitor center, one of the items chosen for display was a topaz ring that Houston appears to be wearing in a daguerreotype by B. P. Paige. When no one was looking, I tried it on, and the ring fitted to his little finger slid loosely on and off my index finger. Printed exaggeration of Houston's height seems to have begun with Josephus Guild, who in his *Old Times in Tennessee* asserted the figure of six feet, six inches; six feet, four inches was a more common estimate. Despite the various heights later assigned to him, Houston himself once told Alexander Terrell that he stood six feet, two inches, the same figure shown on the passport he obtained to visit Texas in 1832 and on his Texas passport a few years later. Terrell, "Recollections of General Sam Houston," 114. The U.S. passport of 1832 is transcribed in Barker and Williams, *Writings of Sam Houston*, 4:11; the original is in the Franklin Williams Collection, Sam Houston Memorial Museum, Huntsville, Texas. As to the oft-related brilliant color of his eyes, I once met Sam Houston IV, grandson of Temple Houston. In his mature years by that time, he was a man in whom his great-grandfather's physical features surfaced to a degree that was unnerving. (Realizing this, he delighted in wearing a checkered vest similar to the one Gen. Sam Houston wore in the 1859 Brady series.) He had the bluest eyes that I have ever seen, and they could hold one's attention like magnets.

16. E. G. M. Butler to William Carey Crane, 9 April 1881, quoted in Crane, *Life and Select Literary Remains*, 249–50.

17. Houston to Calhoun, 15 April 1824, Records of the Governor, Texas State Library and Archives, photostat.

18. Sam Houston, "Audited Expense Account," 29 April 1824, Sam Houston Papers, Catholic Archives of Texas.

19. "Supporting Recognition of Greek Independence," *Annals of Congress*, 18th Cong., 1st sess., 1823–24, 1:1160–63, reprinted in Barker and Williams, *Writings of Sam Houston*, 1:21–24.

20. Crane, *Life and Select Literary Remains*, 178.

21. Houston to A. M. Hughes, 22 January 1825, in Barker and Williams, *Writings of Sam Houston*, 1:24–25. John Martin later served as the first Chief Justice of the Cherokee Supreme Court.

22. "Houston to the Freemen of the Ninth Congressional District," A. J. Houston Collection.

23. Houston to Hughes, 22 January 1825, 1:25.

24. Houston to John Houston, 20 April 1825, in Barker and Williams, *Writings of Sam Houston*, 8:1; De Bruhl, *Sword of San Jacinto*, 74.

25. Houston to William J. Worth, 24 January 1826, in Barker and Williams, *Writings of Sam Houston*, 1:28. Worth later became West Point commandant and distinguished himself in the Mexican War, perishing of cholera, which ravaged the American army during that campaign. The letter to Worth is also interesting as a restatement of Houston's dread, bordering on paranoia, of losing friends. "I have received [your letter] with great pleasure," he wrote Worth, "because it assures me that you are my Friend." The Worth letter is known only from an extract printed in a 1929 sale catalog of literary Americana; it was priced at $120. As with an unknown, but probably considerable, number of other early Houston papers, it disappeared into a private collection. Barker and Williams, *Writings of Sam Houston*, 28n.

26. Williams, *Following General Sam Houston*, 47; James, *The Raven*, 56.

27. Affidavit of A. R. Mathis, 10 May 1825; affidavit of T. Scruggs, 13 May 1825; affidavit of William D. Phillips, 14 May 1825; affidavit of J. F. Williams, 14 May 1825; and affidavit of Benjamin Williams, [May 1825], A. J. Houston Collection.

28. Friend, *Sam Houston*, 13; S. Hall to Houston, 4 October 1825, A. J. Houston Collection; Jonathan Bell to Houston, 5 October 1825, Sam Houston Papers, Catholic Archives of Texas; Houston to "My Next Friend, Shou'd I Perish," 27 May 1826, quoted in part in James, *The Raven*, 64. James obtained the letter from Houston Williams, son of Maggie; it later passed, as did many others, to Williams's sister, Madge Houston Williams Hearne, and ultimately to the University of Texas.

29. According to General White, he had known "Col." Smith in previous years and noted that he had killed seven men in single combat. Gen. William White to "My Dear Friend," 21 December 1826, quoted in Guild, *Old Times in Tennessee*, 286–87. Quotations from Dr. George Frederick Mellen, scrapbook, Tennessee State Library, quoted in James, *The Raven*, 65.

30. Jackson to Houston, 22 November 1826, quoted in Heiskell, *Andrew Jackson and Early Tennessee History*, 3:159; Houston to Jackson, 13 December 1826, Jackson Papers, Library of Congress, photostat in Sam Houston Papers, University of Texas Library, printed in Barker and Williams, *Writings of Sam Houston*, 1:65–66. See also Remini, *Andrew Jackson and the Course of American Freedom*, 120–21.

31. Jackson to Houston, 22 November 1826.

32. *National Banner*, 10 August 1827, quoted in Heiskell, *Andrew Jackson and Early Tennessee History*, 2:161–62. This piece also appears in Barker and Williams, *Writings of Sam Houston*, 1:113–14 (citing *Niles Register*, 32:412–14).

33. Crawford, *Tennessee*, 104–7, 123.

34. Guild, *Old Times in Tennessee*, 262; Williams, *Houston and the War of Independence*, 33; Heiskell, *Andrew Jackson and Early Tennessee History*, 3:346.

35. "Inaugural Address as Governor of Tennessee," *National Banner and Nashville Whig*, 6 October 1827, quoted in Barker and Williams, *Writings of Sam Houston*, 4:9–11.

CHAPTER 4

1. Friend, *Sam Houston*, 16.

2. Wisehart, *Sam Houston*, 35; Houston to the Governor of Ohio, 8 April 1827, in Barker and Williams, *Writings of Sam Houston*, 1:110–11.

3. "Houston to the Legislature of Tennessee," 15 October 1827, in Barker and Williams, *Writings of Sam Houston*, 1:120–21.

4. Carter Beverly to Houston, 21 January 1828; and Houston to Mrs. [Nathan] Morse, 30 January 1828, Sam Houston Papers, Center for American History, University of Texas. The original of the latter is in the San Jacinto Museum of History, LaPorte, and is reprinted in Barker and Williams, *Writings of Sam Houston*, 6:1. Mrs. Morse had ingratiated herself to Jackson and his party during the triumphal visit to New Orleans. Houston complied with Beverly's request and hand delivered his letter to Jackson, who declined to act on it, citing insufficient acquaintance with Beverly but not holding him responsible for what others may have written. Houston to Beverly, 18 February 1828, in Barker and Williams, *Writings of Sam Houston*, 1:122–23. More correspondence on the mountain-out-of-a-molehill Carter Beverly affair can be found in the Penny Thornall Remick Collection, Sam Houston Regional Library and Research Center.

5. William White, "To the People," *National Banner and Nashville Whig*, 25 August 1827.

6. Hamilton, *Reminiscences of James A. Hamilton*, 66–69. He is not to be confused with James Hamilton, the well-intentioned South Carolina governor during Texas's revolutionary and independent periods.

7. L. M. Price to Houston, 3 July 1827; and I. McClean to Houston, 7 July 1827, Sam Houston Papers, Catholic Archives of Texas.

8. Houston to John H. Houston, 10 November 1828, Records of the Governor, Texas State Library and Archives, photostat, also published in Barker and Williams, *Writings of Sam Houston*,

2:10–11. John H. Houston, known to the family as "Jack," was Sam Houston's first cousin, the son of Capt. Samuel Houston's older brother, John.

9. Robert Allen to Houston, 12 May 1828, A. J. Houston Collection, Texas State Library and Archives.

10. Houston to John Marable, 4 December 1828, quoted in James, *The Raven*, 72.

11. Frank Chambers, "Houston's First Wife," *Dallas News*, 4 April 1892. This is a source that I used with some caution, as the identical story appeared elsewhere under another name. See Crook, "Sam Houston and Eliza Allen," 8–9. However, his ultimate telling of Houston's side of the story matches so closely with Houston's own statements of many years later that I include it for its evidentiary value. See also note 28 below.

12. Will T. Hale and Dixon L. Merritt, *A History of Tennessee and Tennesseans*, 8 vols. (New York and Chicago: Lewis Publishing, 1913), 2:379.

13. Sam Houston's grandfather, Robert, had a brother, John, whose daughter Margaret married Alexander McEwen and begat Robert Houston McEwen, making him Sam Houston's second cousin. Roberts, *Personal Correspondence of Sam Houston*, 1:372–73.

14. Burleson, *Life and Writings of Rufus C. Burleson*, 554. A coincidence from the "Small World" file: Burleson was a student at Nashville University and boarded with the Allen cousin who imparted the story. Who knew that in after years Burleson, as president of Baylor College in Independence, Texas, would serve as Sam Houston's pastor and baptize him in November of 1854.

15. Crook, "Sam Houston and Eliza Allen," 13–14; Wisehart, *Sam Houston*, 39–40; James, *The Raven*, 139–40. The exact sequence of events is open to some quarrel, but the best guess is that Houston wrote John Allen the "What is to be done?" letter on the ninth in an attempt to convince Eliza to stay. I doubt that Houston would have gone on with the Cockrell's Springs debate on the eleventh if she had left before then, and at least one contemporary letter asserts that the split did occur on the eleventh. Houston's later divorce petitions give the date as the fifteenth, probably the date of their final interview.

16. "M.B.H.," *New Orleans Republican*, 14 September 1871; Samson, "Sam Houston's Exile: Explained after Many Years," *Nashville Banner and Whig*, 17 November 1880; Roberts, *Star of Destiny*, 30. (Both "M.B.H." and Samson are quoted in Crook, "Sam Houston and Eliza Allen," 6.)

17. In 1857 Alexander Terrell would not write to Houston to disavow the campaign smears against him until he was himself safely elected; a rapprochement could then be made without his motives being questioned. Terrell, "Recollections of General Sam Houston," 121.

18. Houston to John Allen, 9 April 1829, in Barker and Williams, *Writings of Sam Houston*, 1:130. The editors of this correspondence observe in a footnote that Marquis James's quote of this letter in *The Raven*, 143–44, "does not faithfully follow the original," which is found among the Andrew Jackson Papers in the Library of Congress, a photostat of which reposes in the Center for American History at the University of Texas. The presence of the original in Jackson's papers would seem to indicate an attempt by Houston's victorious rivals to discredit him by piling his dirty laundry in Old Hickory's hamper. Many of James's changes in the text seem to be for style or clarity and might even have been the work of an overzealous copyeditor. In defense of James, one ought to say that Sam Houston's frequent run-on sentences, dashes, and ampersands make it tempting to want to make his writing more comprehensible to a modern reader. Other changes, however, seem to add or subtract emphasis—and therefore meaning—a complication, as pointed out in the Preface, not overly dreaded during the era in which *The Raven* was written. Some particular attention is drawn to it here in lieu of repeating this caveat at every juncture where it might be appropriate.

19. "M.B.H.," *New Orleans Republican*, 14 September 1871.

20. Louise Davis, "New Light on the Mystery of Sam Houston," *Nashville Tennesseean Magazine*, 5, 12, 19 August 1962. For more on Balie Peyton, see Guild, *Old Times in Tennessee*, 89–91; and Crook, "Sam Houston and Eliza Allen," 11 (and other sources there cited).

21. Emily Peyton, untitled manuscript, Center for American History.

22. Hamilton, *My Master*, 93, 117.

23. Emily Drennen to Emily Austin Perry, [1829], James F. Perry Papers, Center for American History, quoted in Friend, *Sam Houston*, 22.

24. Peyton, untitled manuscript.

25. Davis, "New Light on the Mystery of Sam Houston," *Nashville Tennesseean*, 5, 12, 19 August 1962. When Marion Wisehart was researching his biography, *Sam Houston: American Giant*, he contacted Allen descendents who, a century and a third after the events in question, were not only still of the "running sore" school but also were still touchy on the point of Eliza's father and uncle pressuring her into the marriage. "No one forced her or over-persuaded her. It is absurd to suggest such a thing. I know the Allens. I am one. It's just one of the things they simply could not have thought of doing. In one of the Indian wars Houston had been struck by a poisoned arrow. It left a festering wound which never healed." Mrs. Eleanor Allen Sullivan, quoted in Wisehart, *Sam Houston*, 653n.

26. Crook, "Sam Houston and Eliza Allen," 5n.

27. Lester, *Life of Sam Houston*, 46–47. While this source often poses for effect, it is in substantial agreement, differing in details of the quotes, with the account left by Williams. Willoughby Williams to Josephus Guild, 1 April 1878, quoted in Guild, *Old Times in Tennessee*, 278.

28. Chambers, "Houston's First Wife." When I first read this article, I rather dismissed it as likely the product of one of Houston's after-the-fact groupies. Once I realized, however, that it was exactly the same story that Houston told Reverend Samson in the early 1850s and gave Ed Sharp in 1857, I decided to include it. All three could not have made up the same story independently, and it shows the consistency of Houston's seldom-cited position.

29. "Resignation as Governor of Tennessee," 16 April 1829, in Barker and Williams, *Writings of Sam Houston*, 1:131–32.

30. Crockett reported Houston's response in a letter to friends two days later. Davis, *Three Roads to the Alamo*, 170, 621n.

31. Wise, *Seven Decades of the Union*, 148.

32. Quoted in James, *The Raven*, 81.

CHAPTER 5

1. Burleson, *Life and Writings of Rufus C. Burleson*, 552. Burleson was thirty years younger than Houston and, at the time he entered Houston's life in the early 1850s, irritated the older man with his righteous insistence that belief in omens was unchristian. Houston's relation of such incidents to him was one method he employed to wrinkle the minister's shirt.

2. Roberts, *Star of Destiny*, 5–6. The Howser family kept the document in a safe-deposit box for three generations, unopened, until it was removed in 1933 to serve as source material for a Tennessee history. It burned in a fire, still unread.

3. That this was one of James's Sitwellian embellishments is indicated in Davis, *Three Roads to the Alamo*, 649n, 680n (citing Wooten, *Comprehensive History of Texas*, 1:152, who cites to Yoakum, *History of Texas*, 1:309). Yoakum, who prepared his history with access to Houston's papers, does not actually state that Houston and Bowie first met at San Felipe on Christmas 1832, but he mentions no previous meeting. Davis's overall interpretation of Houston is quite negative. Thus, his commentary on some of the more extreme revisionist work in recent years (for example, 649n) is particularly interesting.

4. James, *The Raven*, 90–91 (citing vertical files in the Tennessee State Library). Practical jokes on the frontier were frequently merciless, as Houston himself discovered to his cost more than once. (For example, see chap. 12.)

5. Charles F. M. Noland to William Noland, 11 May 1829, Sam Houston Papers, Center for American History, University of Texas. (Original in Berkeley Papers, University of Virginia.)

6. H. Haralson to John Eaton, 22, 24 June 1829, quoted in Gregory and Strickland, *Houston with the Cherokees*, 143, 161.

7. Lester, *Life of Sam Houston*, 51; Gregory and Strickland, *Houston with the Cherokees*, 9–12.

8. This was a phenomenon discovered separately by David Crockett at the time of his estrangement from the Jackson camp. See Davis, *Three Roads to the Alamo*, 168.

9. Friend, *Sam Houston*, 51. See also Stanley F. Horn, ed., "Holdings of the Tennessee Historical Society," *Tennessee Historical Quarterly* 3 (1944): 349–51. It has to be admitted, however, that William Wharton was a destabilizing influence almost from the time he entered Texas, which raises the possibility that it might have been Wharton who was trying to interject Houston into Texas' affairs to further erode the Austin regime. See Tyler et al., *New Handbook of Texas*, 6:907–9.

10. H. Haralson to Houston, 19 August 1829, Sheriff Williams Collection, Sam Houston Memorial Museum.

11. Green, in his newspaper, had earlier defended the reputation of Rachel Jackson, not with depositions of her good character but with scurrilous attacks on the wife of John Quincy Adams, the man who was Jackson's principal detractor. Green had the audacity to boast to Jackson of his bald lying, and the president had rebuked him, "*I never war against females* & it is only the base and cowardly that do." When Calhoun finally split from Jackson, Duff Green went with him. "Calhoun and Duff Green are both sunk into insignificance," Jackson wrote a couple of years later, "and will be both soon in oblivion." Jackson to Martin Van Buren, 17 December 1831, quoted in Heiskell, *Andrew Jackson and Early Tennessee History*, 3:491.

12. Houston to Jackson, 11 May 1829, in Barker and Williams, *Writings of Sam Houston*, 1:132–33. The editors' assertion (in note at 1:134) that Houston may have heard at this early date of Robert Mayo's story (see below in chap. 5) is improbable. Mayo did not make Houston's acquaintance, if it was much of an acquaintance, for another nine months. The Donelsons bore the tales Houston heard about, and more particularly Green's tale, as evidenced by Green's relation of the "emperor in two years" motif.

13. William Carroll to Jackson, 25 May 1829, Jackson Papers, Library of Congress, quoted in Crook, "Sam Houston and Eliza Allen," 22.

14. Daniel Graham to Houston, 20 May 1829; General Dunlap to Houston, 12 July 1829; J. P. Clarke to Houston, 6 July 1829; General Howard to Houston, 16 July 1829; and Richard S. Williams to Houston, 25 July 1829, Sheriff Williams Collection. There are perhaps half a dozen other letters in the same vein in this file; all bear notes and endorsements in the handwriting of Andrew Jackson Houston and undoubtedly at one time were part of his hoard of Sam Houston papers.

15. Haralson to Eaton, 23 June 1829, quoted in James, *The Raven*, 107.

16. Houston to Matthew Arbuckle, 8 July 1829, in Barker and Williams, *Writings of Sam Houston*, 1:136–39.

17. Houston to John H. Houston, 24 June 1829, Records of the Governor, Texas State Library and Archives, photostat (published in Barker and Williams, *Writings of Sam Houston*, 2:12).

18. H. Haralson to Houston, 29 July 1829, Sheriff Williams Collection.

19. Gregory and Strickland, *Houston with the Cherokees*, 117–25. The photograph of the house in the WPA Historic American Buildings survey identified as "Wigwam Neosho" was located on the Scott place, regarded as the Boling site's closest competitor. It was destroyed by a tornado in 1943.

20. Terrell, "Recollections of General Sam Houston," 118.

21. Jackson to Houston, 21 June 1829, quoted in Yoakum, *History of Texas*, 1:307.

22. James, *The Raven*, 176.

23. Andrew Jackson, notebook, Library of Congress, quoted in James, *The Raven*, 176.

24. James, *The Raven*, 176.

25. Houston to Overton, 28 December 1829, in Barker and Williams, *Writings of Sam Houston*, 1:145.

26. Quoted in Remini, *Andrew Jackson and the Course of American Freedom*, 202. Jackson's framing of the issue as the reacquisition of Texas stemmed from his interpretation that the region was included in the Louisiana Purchase.

27. Sam Houston Certificate of Citizenship in the Cherokee Nation, 21 October 1829, Catholic Archives of Texas, Chancery of the Austin Diocese, photostat. Because of a procedural defect, this certificate was later found to be invalid, and a new one was issued.

28. Houston to John Overton, 28 December 1829, 1:144–45.

29. Houston to Jackson, 19 September 1829, in Barker and Williams, *Writings of Sam Houston*, 1:140–43.

30. *Cherokee Phoenix*, 4 March 1830, quoted in Gregory and Strickland, *Houston with the Cherokees*, 159; Elijah Haywood to Hon. David Hinshaw, 27 February 1830; and Thomas Harrison to Joseph Loving, [February 1830], A. J. Houston Collection, Texas State Library and Archives. Haywood invited his recipient's civilities to "Gen. Samuel Houston, late Governor of Tenesee, who visits Boston for the first time. . . . Gen. Houston is a gentleman of great intelligence, extensively acquainted with mankind, and of the highest sense of honour."

31. James, *The Raven*, 134; Houston to John Van Fossen, 4 April 1830, in Barker and Williams, *Writings of Sam Houston*, 1:147–49. Jackson's enemies engaged in some artful disinformation on the ration scandal, leaving Houston to believe that Eaton had told the War Department that he (Houston) had imposed himself on the bidding process. This prompted Eaton to send Houston a letter that he was hurt that Houston could believe such a thing of him. "In high party times a man should be quite slow to believe even a portion of what he hears—certainly not the whole. In the present instance you have suffered your credibility to be imposed upon." Eaton to Houston, 28 July 1830, Sam Houston Papers, Center for American History.

32. Report of the Committee, Sam Houston Papers, Center for American History. The transcript in this collection was taken from the *Alabama State Intelligencer*, but their call for publication was also given to the *Gallatin Journal*, the *Nashville Republican*, and the *National Banner*.

33. Randolph to Arbuckle, 11 September 1830, Sam Houston Papers, Center for American History.

34. Houston to Jackson, 15 December 1830, in Barker and Williams, *Writings of Sam Houston*, 1:193–94, 195n. Nathaniel Pryor was also a descendent by marriage of Pocahontas. The town of Pryor, Oklahoma, located some thirty miles north of Cantonment (later Fort) Gibson, was named for him.

35. Jonathan Stump to Houston, 20 January 1831, Sam Houston Papers, Catholic Archives of Texas.

36. Nicholas Dean to Houston, 16 December 1830, A. J. Houston Collection.

37. Jackson to Fulton, 10 December 1830; and Fulton to John Forsyth, 6 March 1838, in Bassett, *Correspondence of Andrew Jackson*, 4:212–14, 5:540. The correspondence was the subject of a complex political and legal wrangle well summarized in Friend, *Sam Houston*, 52–53.

38. Robert Mayo, *Political Sketches of Eight Years in Washington* (Baltimore: Fielding Lucas Jr., 1839), 119.

39. James, *The Raven*, 180; Friend, *Sam Houston*, 51. The idea of a Jackson-Houston collaboration on the conquest of Texas forms an important thesis of *The Raven*. James's book was surely influenced at least in part by the earlier work of Richard R. Stenberg, who was so certain of the connection that he asserted that Jackson's letters to other officials to keep a watch on Houston, and even his personal memos, were deliberate plants to mislead future generations. Stenberg, "Texas Schemes of Jackson and Houston," 231. While Stenberg does cite some evidence of Jackson's ability to do this sort of thing, the propensity of some writers to interpret the lack of evidence of a conspiracy only as itself evidence of a cover-up is not unknown in our own time. What questions Stenberg does raise are fatally undercut by a complete lack of objectivity, as shown in his assessment of

the abortive rations contract (239), and his acceptance of Robert Coleman, Nicholas Labadie, David Burnet, and Anson Jones as unimpeachable sources of Houston's conduct before and during the battle at San Jacinto (250).

40. Benton to Houston, 15 August 1829, in Barker and Williams, *Writings of Sam Houston,* 1:140.

41. Z. N. Morrell, *Fruits and Flowers in the Wilderness,* 4th ed. (Dallas: W. G. Scarff, 1886), 20.

42. Yoakum, *History of Texas,* 1:281.

43. Wallis and Hill, *Sixty Years on the Brazos,* 267.

44. Isaac H. Howlett, William M. Hinton, Austin Gresham, James D. Parrish, James Cooper, and C. Lanier to Houston, 30 June 1831; and Houston to Howlett et al., 1 July 1831, quoted in Heiskell, *Andrew Jackson and Early Tennessee History,* 3:347–49.

45. "A Proclamation," in Barker and Williams, *Writings of Sam Houston,* 1:196. The editors of Houston's correspondence cite numerous newspapers that republished the piece over many years.

46. Gregory and Strickland, *Houston with the Cherokees,* 14–15. The modern trend to depict Houston as a racist is, like graffiti, prevalent, but the authors' lack of citation to direct statement and authorship quickly becomes nebulous. As pointed out by James Crisp in his article ("Sam Houston's Speechwriters," 203n), the issue is treated less as an accusation than an assumption, but it is an integral part of such recent works as De Bruhl, *Sword of San Jacinto*; Long, *Duel of Eagles*; and even forms a "dubious sub-theme" of Lack, *Texas Revolutionary Experience.* (Lack was misled at least in part by relying on Ehrenberg's "phlegm of the indolent Mexicans" hoax. See chap. 8, note 22, below.) With these sources to draw upon, the popular and trade presses now adopt these assumptions as fact. See Anne Dingus, "Sam the Man . . . ," *Texas Monthly,* 21 March 1993. The more circumspect Gregg Cantrell, in his article "Sam Houston and the Know-Nothings: A Reappraisal," offers an admirable summary of Houston's thinking, and limitations, on the status of the different races.

47. Quoted in Gregory and Strickland, *Houston with the Cherokees,* 91, 99. Houston had argued that the location of Union Mission created frictions between the Osages on the one hand and the Creeks and Cherokees on the other. Four years after Houston's departure, the argument carried in his favor, and Union Mission was removed from the Cherokee Nation.

48. Pierson, *Tocqueville and Beaumont,* 611–15. For a man who cared so much for the fate of the Indians, it seems remarkable that Tocqueville mistook the name of the tribe that took in Houston, although since Houston spent so much effort on behalf of the Creeks, Tocqueville might be forgiven. Terrell, "Recollections of General Sam Houston," 124, identifies the real source of the beaver-collared coat.

CHAPTER 6

1. Quoted in James, *The Raven,* 163.

2. Houston to William Stanbery, 3 April 1832, in Barker and Williams, *Writings of Sam Houston,* 1:199–200.

3. This is the traditional account typified by James, *The Raven,* 163–64.

4. Stanbery to Stevenson, 14 April 1832, in Barker and Williams, *Writings of Sam Houston,* 1:202.

5. Terrell, "Recollections of General Sam Houston," 126. Houston told Terrell that he was at home in the Indian Territory when he read of Stanbery's outrage and went to Washington specifically to avenge it. This was an embellishment, for Houston had been in Washington since February 5. Terrell, 124; Gregory and Strickland, *Houston with the Cherokees,* 162.

6. James Reily to Houston, 13 April 1842, Sam Houston Papers, Catholic Archives of Texas, Chancery of the Austin Diocese.

7. *Congressional Debates,* vol. 8, pt. 2 (1831–32), 1810–21 (reprinted in Barker and Williams, *Writings of Sam Houston,* 1:207–24). The speech was also published in the Knoxville Register, 30

June 1832 (reprinted in Heiskell, *Andrew Jackson and Early Tennessee History*, 3:350–64). The texts are in substantive concordance. I have added a couple of emphases in the final summation where Houston's meaning may not have been clear.

8. Houston's fourth daughter, Antoinette Power Houston, received a visit in 1888 from Edwin Booth (Junius's son) to request an autograph of Sam Houston, "who had been the hero of so many of his father's anecdotes." Nettie Houston Bringhurst to Marquis James, quoted in *The Raven*, 170.

9. Paschal, "Last Years of Sam Houston," 631.

10. Houston to James Prentiss, 28 June 1832, in Barker and Williams, *Writings of Sam Houston*, 1:248–49.

11. Houston, "To the Public," 9 July [publ. 10 July] 1832, *The Globe*, quoted in Barker and Williams, *Writings of Sam Houston*, 1:250–57.

12. Houston to James Prentiss, 10 July 1832, in Barker and Williams, *Writings of Sam Houston*, 1:253.

13. "Agreement between Houston and Prentiss," 1 June 1832, in Barker and Williams, *Writings of Sam Houston*, 1:229–30.

14. Wharton to Houston, 2 June 1832, in Barker and Williams, *Writings of Sam Houston*, 1:230–31. Whether or not Houston and Archer met at this time, the doctor served Texas well. He was a representative at the Convention of 1833; helped open the revolution at Gonzales in October of 1835; acted as chairman of the Consultation, where he joined forces with Austin and Houston to forestall a vote for independence, the following month; and then accompanied Austin and William Wharton on the first mission to the United States for loans. In later years he was more hawkish than Houston, serving a stint as Mirabeau Lamar's secretary of war. Dr. Archer retired into relative obscurity and died on his Oyster Creek plantation in 1856. See Tyler et al., *New Handbook of Texas*, 1:223.

15. Houston to Charles F. M. Noland, 10 June 1832, Sam Houston Papers, Center for American History, University of Texas. Houston seemed resigned to Noland's departure, and his own attitude toward Noland's participation seems to have paled. On 17 June Houston informed Prentiss that he was willing to pay Noland out of his (Houston's) share of the land proceeds, but in telling Prentiss of Noland's departure a few weeks later wrote, "nor do I know that he would be of any advantage; unless some accident taking place with me, which I do not anticipate." Houston to Prentiss, 17 June, 10 July, 1832, Sam Houston Papers, Center for American History. "Fent" Noland was a brilliant and funny consumptive who had washed out of West Point and whose father had sent him to Arkansas to get into business. Merry and adventurous, he was also a favorite of Gen. Albert Pike. Noland later became an author of at least regional celebrity for his Arkansas lore. It was just as well Houston parted company with him when he did, as Noland defected from Jackson and became a Whig in 1836. See Walter Lee Brown, *A Life of Albert Pike* (Fayetteville: University of Arkansas Press, 1997), 119.

16. Houston to Prentiss, 18 August 1832, in Barker and Williams, *Writings of Sam Houston*, 1:263–64. According to the editors, the Dr. Dillard mentioned was Dr. Thomas Dillard of Washington-on-the-Brazos. The possibility of recruiting Indian "auxilliaries" against Mexico became a recurring Houston motif over a number of years.

17. See Wisehart, *Sam Houston*, 655n. James cites Augustus Buells's *History of Andrew Jackson* (1904) in the affirmative but spins it to sound like the loan was financing for a filibuster. *The Raven*, 182.

18. Houston to Prentiss, 16, 17, 20, 27, 28 June, 10 July, 18 August, 11, 15 September 1832, in Barker and Williams, *Writings of Sam Houston*, 1:240–66. In the overlapping arrangement of Houston papers at the Center for American History at the University of Texas, the Prentiss correspondence is segregated into its own folder.

19. James, *The Raven*, 183–85. Houston still had his partisans, but his popular standing was so low that, as he himself later related, during one of his early returns to Tennessee he stayed at a tav-

ern near the Mississippi line and inquired incognito about the proprietor's opinion of former governor Houston. "Oh! He was all sorts of a fellow, was very much liked, made us an excellent Governor—*but he disgraced himself and the State and ran off amongst the Indians*." Guild, *Old Times in Tennessee*, 290–91.

20. Sam Houston, U.S. passport, Franklin Williams Collection, Sam Houston Memorial Museum.

21. The merits of the various possible resting sites are examined in Gregory and Strickland, *Houston with the Cherokees*, 50–54.

22. James, *The Raven*, 186 (citing Journal of Washington Irving, notebook no. 6, New York Public Library).

23. De Bruhl, *Sword of San Jacinto*, 139.

24. Houston to Henry L. Ellsworth, commissioner of Indian affairs, 1 December 1832, in Barker and Williams, *Writings of Sam Houston*, 1:267–71.

25. Wisehart, *Sam Houston*, 84. Many years later, when Rector was serving a stint as Indian superintendent, an expedition to the Wichita Mountains to locate a suitable site for an agency turned unpleasant owing to the heat, and "the supply of whisky was exhausted long before the party" reached their destination. Wilbur Nye, *Carbine and Lance: The Story of Old Fort Sill* (Norman: University of Oklahoma Press, 1937), 34.

26. Paschal, "Last Years of Sam Houston," 631; Creel, *Sam Houston*, 61–62. This story is related in some guise in virtually all Houston biographies.

27. James, *The Raven*, 186 (quoting a memoir by Pike in an issue of the *Nashville News* of 1905).

28. Houston to Ellsworth, 1 December 1832, in Barker and Williams, *Writings of Sam Houston*, 1:267–71.

29. Wallis and Hill, *Sixty Years on the Brazos*, 267.

30. Samuel May Williams to Houston, 26 December 1832, A. J. Houston Collection, Texas State Library and Archives. Williams not wanting his name revealed was understandable, for such an incendiary passage of information might well get Austin in trouble. Williams was shortly to form a business partnership with one Thomas F. McKinney. Engaged primarily in cotton brokering in New Orleans, the firm of McKinney and Williams also provided indispensable cash for the revolution, funds that were never fully repaid.

31. "Application for Headright in Austin's Colony," n.d., in Barker and Williams, *Writings of Sam Houston*, 1:271. In April of 1835, Houston applied for a second land grant, this one in Burnet's colony, a move of dubious legality.

32. Davis, *Three Roads to the Alamo*, 680n.

33. Caiaphas Ham, "Recollections," John Salmon Ford Papers, Center for American History.

34. Friend, *Sam Houston*, 58.

35. P. E. Bean to Houston, 4 February 1833, A. J. Houston Collection.

36. Houston to Jackson, 13 February 1833, in Barker and Williams, *Writings of Sam Houston*, 1:274–76. The expulsion of Mexican troops alluded to was a reference to the Anahuac disturbance of April 1832. At least in the first draft of this letter, according to the editors, Houston intended one more nudge, warning Jackson that his minister to Mexico, Anthony Butler, was no friend of annexation and had interests to the contrary. Raguet Family Papers, Center for American History.

37. See Morton, *Terán and Texas*, and the more recent, Manuel de Mier y Terán, *Texas by Terán* (Austin: University of Texas Press, 2000).

38. For both the traditional and revisionist assessments of the Anahuac disturbances, see respectively Rowe, "Disturbances at Anahuac," versus Margaret Swett Henson, *Juan Davis Bradburn: A Reappraisal of the Mexican Commander of Anahuac* (College Station: Texas A&M University Press, 1982).

39. "Notes of Speech of General Houston to Convention at San Felipe," April 1833, Washington Miller Papers, Texas State Library and Archives.

40. Campbell, *Sam Houston and the American Southwest*, 25.

41. Houston to John H. Houston, 31 July 1833, in Barker and Williams, *Writings of Sam Houston*, 5:5–6.

CHAPTER 7

1. Houston, "Petition for Divorce," 30 November 1833, in Barker and Williams, *Writings of Sam Houston*, 1:277–79. In Greek mythology, Hymen was the god of marriage; it was not a biological reference.

2. See *The Arlington (Texas) Post*, 10 January 1891. One must note, however, that old Jonas "The Hunter" Harrison was acknowledged to have out-orated Houston at Independence Day festivities in San Augustine on 4 July 1836, so the petition may possibly be his work after all. John Salmon Ford Papers, Center for American History, University of Texas. Curiously, Harrison's political leanings also paralleled Houston's own, having been conservative to moderate before converting to the independence movement at about the same time as Houston. Tyler et al., *New Handbook of Texas*, 3:485.

3. Kenney, "Questions and Answers," 228.

4. Friend, *Sam Houston*, 60.

5. A. C. Allen to Houston, 28 February 1834, A. J. Houston Collection, Texas State Library and Archives.

6. James Prentiss to Houston, 8 March, 1 April 1834; and Houston to Prentiss, 28 March 1834, in Barker and Williams, *Writings of Sam Houston*, 1:279–85. Houston to Lewis Cass, 6, 12 March 1834. The object of Cass's inquiry was Lt. George B. Abbay, who was captured by Indians on 2 June 1833 but was, as subsequently learned, killed soon after. The 12 March letter was the subject of a research note. Staff notes, "Sam Houston: Interpreter of Indian Strategy," *Chronicles of Oklahoma* 31 (summer 1953): 212–14.

7. Houston to Prentiss, 11 April 1834, in Barker and Williams, *Writings of Sam Houston*, 1:285–86; Friend, *Sam Houston*, 60.

8. Houston to Prentiss, 11, 20, 24 April 1834, in Barker and Williams, *Writings of Sam Houston*, 1:285–91; Davis, *Three Roads to the Alamo*, 389–90, 688n. Crockett left town the next day, and as I have found no Houston letters written from Washington after the twenty-fourth, they may have traveled together.

9. N. B. Hamilton to William Carey Crane, 19 May 1866, quoted in Crane, *Life and Select Literary Remains*, 22–23. Capt. Samuel Houston's youngest sister, Mary, wed John Letcher. Their daughter Sallie wed Robert Hamilton; Narcissa Bertonia Hamilton was their only child. Roberts, *Personal Correspondence of Sam Houston*, 1:372–73.

10. Flanagan, *Sam Houston's Texas*, 15; see also Friend, *Sam Houston*, 60. Friend and Flanagan were not the first to be intrigued by this disappearance. When the periodical that later evolved into the *Southwestern Historical Quarterly* began publication in 1897, so many frontier-era Texans still survived that the journal undertook to solicit, in the back of each number, their recollections on various unsolved questions of early Texas. The very first query, posed by Judge C. W. Raines, was, "Where was General Houston, and what was he doing, in the interval between the adjournment of the San Felipe convention, April, 1833, and the beginning of hostilities with Mexico . . . ?" *Quarterly of the Texas State Historical Associationtion* 1 (January 1898):129.

11. Friend, *Sam Houston*, 60 (quoting Davis, *Jefferson Davis*, 156–57).

12. Featherstonhaugh, *Excursion*, 2:161.

13. Williams, *Old Town Speaks*, 8–13. A later chapter of the same volume gives a detailed account of the life of James Black, his collaboration with Bowie on the knife, and his loss of recol-

lection on his twelve-step process of tempering the steel. Ibid., 154–63. One should observe, for the benefit of followers of the Bowie knife cult, that since Bowie gave Black a pattern for the knife he wanted, Black's Bowie knife may not have been the first. See also J. Frank Dobie, "Bowie and the Bowie Knife," *Southwest Review* 16 (1931).

14. One should note that by now Austin was in Santa Anna's dungeon; further news of treasonable scheming might cause him to be shot. If Houston was indeed at the center of this "deeper game than faro," perhaps he removed it beyond the boundary for the Austin's sake.

15. Friend, *Sam Houston*, 59.

16. Houston to John Wharton, 14 April 1835, in Barker and Williams, *Writings of Sam Houston*, 1:293–94. "I was provoked at [Austin's] first letter," Houston went on to say, "where he *broke into prison*, but when I read his letter of August, I must confess that it awakened no other emotion in my breast, than *pity* mingled with contempt."

17. The overall tone of this correspondence certainly adds nothing to attempts to color Houston an early conspirator with the Whartons in a design to overthrow Mexican authority in Texas. It is not clear from the record whether Houston was aware that William Austin and his brother, John, while warm friends with the empresario, were Connecticut Austins and only distantly related, if related at all, to Stephen F. Austin. Tyler et al., *New Handbook of Texas*, 1:291–92. This Wharton-Austin duel was a momentary flash of passion, since both John and William Austin participated in the Velasco troubles of 1832 and were the Whartons' natural partisans. The two families later reconciled. See Barker and Williams, *Writings of Sam Houston*, 1:294–95n.

18. Tyler et al., *New Handbook of Texas*, 6:94–95. Probably looking forward to a life with Anna Raguet, Houston later bought a town lot in Nacogdoches but sold it after his marriage to Margaret Lea.

19. C. S. Sterne to Fr. Joseph O'Donohoe, 8 February 1927, Correspondence about Sam Houston, Catholic Archives of Texas, Chancery of the Austin Diocese. The exact circumstances are unclear. Contrary to other information, the Sternes' daughter Rosine Ryan told William Zuber that the jewelry was given later on the occasion of the Declaration of Independence, a time when Houston would seem to have been preoccupied with other matters. Zuber, "Captain Adolphus Sterne," 215.

20. See Barker and Williams, *Writings of Sam Houston*, 1:297n.

21. "Character Certificate for Samuel Pablo Houston," 21 November 1835, Texas Land Office, Austin; James, *The Raven*, 211.

22. Houston to Anna Raguet, 12 January 1838, in Barker and Williams, *Writings of Sam Houston*, 2:184–85.

23. "Affidavit, District Court of Nacogdoches County," 14 June 1849, *Nacogdoches Transcripts*, 2:107, Center for American History, University of Texas, quoted in Barker and Williams, *Writings of Sam Houston*, 1:272n.

24. John M. Dor, "Invoice for Articles left in Care," 13 May 1835, Nancy Burch Collection, Sam Houston Regional Library and Research Center. Judge Dor was a figure of some importance in Nacogdoches before the revolution, and he and Houston were quite friendly. However, as indicated by papers in the A. J. Houston Collection, he seems to have been pummeled back into obscurity by relentless bad luck.

25. Friend, *Sam Houston*, 61–62 (quoting Mosely Baker to Houston, October [1844], University of Texas Library and Archives, typescript).

26. Houston et al. to Andrew Jackson, 11 September 1835, in Barker and Williams, *Writings of Sam Houston*, 1:299–301. The United States–Mexican Treaty of Amity, Navigation, and Commerce of 15 April 1831, provided in pertinent part that the two principals would prevent, by force if necessary, incursions of one's native inhabitants into the territory of the other.

27. Thomas J. Rusk to Houston, 30 January 1837, A. J. Houston Collection; Haley, *Most Excellent Sir*, 43. Complicating further the question of who had figured out what about Houston's

machinations, Santa Anna's right-hand man, Col. Juan Almonte, was also in Nacogdoches in the spring of 1834, reporting that Houston had returned from the United States with authority to negotiate afresh for the American purchase of Texas. Jack Jackson to author, 30 August 2000.

28. Friend, *Sam Houston*, 62. Friend also cites Grant Foreman (*Pioneer Days in the Early Southwest*, 206) in asserting that Houston considered another Creek settlement plan in 1837 but seemed unaware of its circumstances, remarking that no similarity existed between Houston's willingness to allow a Creek settlement in 1837 and his possible attempt to utilize them in 1835.

29. Barker and Williams, *Writings of Sam Houston*, 1:205n, 299.

30. Porter, "Hawkins Negroes," 57.

31. See, for instance, Wilkins, *Cherokee Tragedy*, 2.

32. Houston to Isaac Parker, 5 October 1835, in Barker and Williams, *Writings of Sam Houston*, 1:302.

33. *Red River Herald*, 7 October 1835. The story got the widest possible play and was soon reprinted in the *Arkansas Gazette*, the *Lexington Observer*, the *Kentucky Reporter*, and *The Commonwealth*. The rapidity with which the news spread, even for such an important story, reinforces earlier suspicion that Houston's "lost" months of 1834 were indeed spent clearing the pike for supplies and volunteers.

34. "To the Troops of the Department of Nacogdoches," 8 October 1835, in Barker and Williams, *Writings of Sam Houston*, 1:304–5.

CHAPTER 8

1. Angus McNeill to Houston, 2 November 1835; Ira Davis to Houston, 7 November 1835; and Felix Huston to Houston, 18 November 1835, Sam Houston Papers, Catholic Archives of Texas, Chancery of the Austin Diocese.

2. John Salmon Ford Papers, Center for American History, University of Texas.

3. Bowie himself seems to have been aware that he was becoming a problem. Upon finding the Indian situation a complicated one, he left for the United States to check on family and business without returning to Nacogdoches. Davis, *Three Roads to the Alamo*, 426–28.

4. Smithwick, *Evolution of a State*, 111.

5. Ibid., 110.

6. This particular episode is repeated as fact in, for instance, Davis, *Three Roads to the Alamo* (439). Baker's screed takes the form of an open letter to Houston, a typescript of which requires some fifty pages. He wrote it in vengeance for Houston's part in Baker's defeat in a run for the Texas Senate in 1844. Mosely Baker was a man to whom no calumny about Houston was too grotesque to place in circulation; the whoppers in this pamphlet were so silly that Baker could not find a publisher, and he discarded the manuscript. Ashbel Smith found it when he purchased Baker's home, Evergreen plantation, kept it, and in time gave it to Baker's daughter, Fannie Darden. It eventually was deposited in the Texas State Archives, where it has been chuckled over ever since. The typescript is in the Center for American History at the University of Texas, where it shares a box with some of Bowie's papers, which is likely where Davis saw it. Interestingly, Baker did not even claim firsthand witness of Houston's behavior, but stated that Bowie, who was conveniently dead, told him about it later.

Using similarly poisoned sources, some mostly amateur historians have in recent years created a cottage industry of allegations that Houston was not only a coward who was forced to fight at San Jacinto but was also a vicious cant who deliberately allowed the slaughter at the Alamo because he was jealous of Bowie's and Travis's growing influence. I do not find their conclusions to be consistent with the preponderance of known facts nor rhetorically persuasive.

7. See Cantrell, *Stephen F. Austin*, 321–23.

Using similarly poisoned sources, some mostly amateur historians have in recent years created a cottage industry of allegations that Houston was not only a coward who was forced to fight at San Jacinto but was also a vicious cant who deliberately allowed the slaughter at the Alamo because he was jealous of Bowie's and Travis's growing influence. I do not find their conclusions to be consistent with the preponderance of known facts nor rhetorically persuasive.

7. See Cantrell, *Stephen F. Austin*, 321–23.

8. Austin to Houston, 13 November 1835, Penny Thornall Remick Collection, Sam Houston Regional Library and Research Center. This letter is consistent with others that Austin wrote to the Consultation pressing for organization. Cantrell, *Stephen F. Austin*, 326; Hardin, *Texian Iliad*, 58.

9. Barrett was five years Houston's senior and a resident of Texas possibly as early as 1833. A lawyer and leading citizen of the town of Mina—later known as Bastrop—he represented that community at the Consultation. It is apparent from Houston's correspondence that he held him in high regard, but Barrett became a casualty of the Consultation squabbles and left Texas after falling out with Henry Smith. He returned after the republic was established but died in 1838. Tyler et al., *New Handbook of Texas*, 1:391–92. Beyond transmitting necessary information, Houston's letters to him are peppered with the chatter and puns he reserved for those he considered his friends. See, for example, Houston to Barrett, 2 January 1836, in Barker and Williams, *Writings of Sam Houston*, 1:330–31.

10. Houston, "Commission as Commander-in-Chief of the Texas Army," Sam Houston Memorial Museum. Long mislaid, the document was unveiled at a special ceremony at the Museum on 2 March 1996.

11. Thomas Jefferson Rusk to Houston, 14 November 1835, Remick Collection.

12. Mosely Baker had made restitution for the forgery and later served in a variety of posts, from which he struck at Houston until dying of yellow fever in Houston in 1848. Tyler et al., *New Handbook of Texas*, 349–50.

13. See generally Steen, "Analysis of the Work of the General Council."

14. Jones, *Memoranda and Official Correspondence*, 12–13. Austin's most recent biographer found little to support the story of Houston machinations against Austin. Cantrell, *Stephen F. Austin*, 326. Nevertheless, revisionists repeat Jones's story with approval. For one example, see Hardin, *Texian Iliad*, 57–58.

15. Yoakum, *History of Texas*, 2:446–47.

16. Fannin to Houston, 18 November 1835, Remick Collection. As an ally on the issue of organization, Houston gave Fannin his commission as a colonel on 7 December. Stephen Hardin found Fannin "ambitious" and his agreement with Houston's strategy "obsequious." Of course, it could just be that he agreed with him. *Texian Iliad*, 62.

17. See, for instance, the overarching tone of Hardin in his *Texian Iliad* even more stridently expressed in his *Alamo Parras* website essay. See Hardin, "San Jacinto Campaign."

18. Houston, "Review of the San Jacinto Campaign: A Speech at Houston in the Summer of 1845," in Barker and Williams, *Writings of Sam Houston*, 6:7.

19. Houston to United States volunteers, 27 December 1835, printed in *Arkansas Gazette*, 20 February 1836.

20. Houston to Powers, 28 December 1835, in Barker and Williams, *Writings of Sam Houston*, 1:326. Houston complained to Governor Smith of difficulty in getting these volunteers to enlist, presumably because of ambiguity in the terms of enlistment and the bounties they would receive. Most of the men died with Fannin at the Goliad mass murder, but their leader, Peyton Wylie, was spared by his having been on leave. He later served as a representative in the Texas Congress.

21. Houston to Don Carlos Barrett, 30 December 1835, 2 January 1836; and Houston to Henry Smith, 30 December 1835, in Barker and Williams, *Writings of Sam Houston*, 1:327–31.

22. The spurious speech is found in Barker and Williams, *Writings of Sam Houston*, 1:337–39. For its shrewd deconstruction, see James Crisp's article, which also contains interesting citations, with commentary, on Houston's revisionist makeover as a racist. "Sam Houston's Speechwriters," 203–37.

23. On 17 December, Houston had reluctantly and with wordy prevarication, "in obedience to the order" of the government, directed Bowie to Matamoros, but Houston had probably seen Bowie in Washington-on-the-Brazos on 27 December, when he undoubtedly clarified to Bowie that those orders left plenty of discretion not to attempt the expedition. "Army Orders," 17 December 1835, in Barker and Williams, *Writings of Sam Houston*, 1:322–23. "It is said that Bowie will be here tomorrow." Houston to Henry Smith, 26 December 1835, in Barker and Williams, *Writings of Sam Houston*, 1:325. William C. Davis places a typically modern, anti-Houston spin on events, speculating that he intended Bowie to have only temporary command of the Matamoros venture, and that "Houston apparently intended that *he* in the end would himself command the expedition" because he was jealous of Bowie's abilities. *Three Roads to the Alamo*, 489. In truth, Houston tried every way humanly possible to thwart the scheme and was grimly engaged in trying to impose some order on the military. There is no way in the world he would have even considered leading a pillaging excursion to the Rio Grande.

24. Henry Smith to Houston, 17 December 1835, Nancy Burch Collection, Sam Houston Regional Library.

25. Houston to Henry Smith, 17 December 1835, in Barker and Williams, *Writings of Sam Houston*, 1:321; Marshall Pease to Wyatt Hanks, 8 February 1836, Burch Collection.

26. Houston to Don Carlos Barrett, 2 January 1836, in Barker and Williams, *Writings of Sam Houston*, 1:330.

27. Houston to Henry Smith, 30 January 1836, in Barker and Williams, *Writings of Sam Houston*, 1:346.

28. Henry Smith to General Council, 17 December 1835, Burch Collection.

29. Henry Millard to Houston, 5, 7 February 1836, Sam Houston Papers, Catholic Archives of Texas. Millard later joined Houston along the Brazos, and for bravery at San Jacinto, the commanding general presented him with Santa Anna's confiscated dueling pistols.

30. William Wharton to Houston, 16 February 1836, Burch Collection.

31. Houston to Henry Smith, 30 January 1836, in Barker and Williams, *Writings of Sam Houston*, 1:354. Henry Smith was a Kentuckian, five years older than Houston. He had been on hand for virtually every step Texas took toward separation from Mexico: nearly killed at the battle of Velasco in 1832 and delegate to both the Convention of 1833 and the Consultation of 1835. The Mexican government recognized his ability, though, and appointed him political *jefe* of the Department of the Brazos in 1834; Houston also respected his abilities. Smith served one term in the Congress of the Republic of Texas and then left with two of his sons to seek gold in California in 1849. He died alone in their mining camp in 1851. His first two wives were sisters who widowed him in succession: Harriet (d. 1820) and Elizabeth (d. 1833) Gillet. He then wed Elizabeth's twin, Sarah, who survived him. See John Henry Brown, *Life and Times of Henry Smith: The First American Governor of Texas* (Dallas: A. D. Aldridge, 1887); and Smith, "Reminiscences," *Quarterly of the Texas State Historical Association* 12 (July 1910).

32. Travis to The People of Texas, 24 February 1836, Chalberg Photograph Collection, Austin History Center. Fearing the capture and loss of this dispatch, Travis wrote out multiple copies to send by different messengers, and their texts varied slightly. See, for instance, Yoakum, *History of Texas*, 2:76.

33. Travis to Houston, [17 February] 1836, quoted in Yoakum, *History of Texas*, 2:59. William C. Davis seems correct in his assessment of Yoakum's erroneous substitution of "January" for "February." *Three Roads to the Alamo*, 722n.

34. Ellis to Houston, 5 March 1836, Sam Houston Papers, Center for American History.

35. Fischer, *Robert Potter*, 24. After first entering politics, Potter stood for a seat in the North Carolina State Assembly, but election judges called off the contest on account of the violence of Potter's campaign.

36. Houston, "Proclamation Concerning the Enemy's Occupation of Bexar," 2 March 1836, in Barker and Williams, *Writings of Sam Houston*, 1:360–61; W. W. Thompson affidavit, 1 December 1840, Secretaries of the State, Domestic Records, Texas State Library and Archives; Thomas Ricks Lindley, "Drawing Truthful Conclusions," *Journal of the Alamo Battlefield Association* 1 (September 1995): 31–33. While, like everyone else's interpretation of documents and events, Lindley's view may be open to review, he performs a service to the craft of Texas history with his examination of seldom-visited files of documents.

37. Hardin, *Texian Iliad*, 162; Houston to Sterling C. Robertson, 5 March 1836, in Barker and Williams, *Writings of Sam Houston*, 1:362; Houston to Henry Raguet, 13 March 1836, in ibid., 4:17–18.

38. Houston to Collinsworth, 13 March 1836, in Barker and Williams, *Writings of Sam Houston*, 1:367–68.

39. In 1821 Potter had resigned from the U.S. Navy in a huff, reputedly over lack of promotion. He had also, while reading for the law, boarded at the home of the foster-father of John Paul Jones. For a synopsis of Potter's Texas career, see Tyler et al., *New Handbook of Texas*, 5:299.

40. Houston to Collinsworth, 15 March 1836, in Barker and Williams, *Writings of Sam Houston*, 1:374.

41. Taylor's leaving the army must have been a great loss to Houston, as by Taylor's own modest reckoning he was "known through all the settlements as one of the best trailers in the country. . . . As a scout I had no superior and at a very early age I knew every landmark, stream and valley from the Nueces to the San Jacinto." John Warren Hunter, "Literary Effort Concerning Creed Taylor and Others in the Mexican War," Texas State Library and Archives, 32B–32D. Taylor later rejoined the army at Harrisburg the day before San Jacinto—his sixteenth birthday. See Tyler et al., *New Handbook of Texas*, 6:215.

42. "Kuykendall's Account," quoted in Barker, "The San Jacinto Campaign," 295–96. Jonathan Hampton Kuykendall was in Chihuahua, Mexico, when he was alerted to Mexican plans to invade Texas. After a daring escape, his reports to Fannin on 16 February and to James W. Robinson four days later were the first warning Texans had of Santa Anna's march. In later years he was a newspaper editor and wrote a history of Texas, which would have been interesting, but when he could not interest a publisher in it, he burned the manuscript. He died in Rockport in 1880. Tyler et al., *New Handbook of Texas*, 3:1169.

43. Jenkins, *Recollections of Early Texas*, 40.

44. Houston to Collinsworth, 15 March 1836, in Barker and Williams, *Writings of Sam Houston*, 1:374.

45. "Kuykendall's Account," quoted in Barker, "The San Jacinto Campaign," 297. S. F. Sparks remembered this incident as occurring the night after the Brazos crossing was completed, which seems doubtful because that was the evening Houston dined at Groce's with Anson Jones and several other officers. It is possible, of course, that two separate but similar instances occurred. Sparks, "Recollections," *Quarterly of the Texas State Historical Association* 12 (July 1908): 67.

46. Houston to Fannin, 17 March 1836; and Houston to Collinsworth, 17 March 1836, in Barker and Williams, *Writings of Sam Houston*, 1:377, 378–79.

CHAPTER 9

1. Houston to Thomas J. Rusk, 23–24 March 1836, in Barker and Williams, *Writings of Sam Houston*, 1:380–82.

2. Flanagan, *Sam Houston's Texas*, 23.

3. Weyand and Wade, *History of Early Fayette County*, 134–35.

4. Houston to Rusk, 23 March 1836, in Barker and Williams, *Writings of Sam Houston*, 1:381.

5. "W. B. Dewees Letters," *The Colorado Citizen*, May 1922.

6. Weyand and Wade, *History of Early Fayette County*, 137.

7. Houston wrote Baker on 5 April criticizing "the destruction . . . at San Felipe, under your command," which he would not have done if he had ordered the town burned. "Every means in your power should have been used to preserve and protect the stores, until such were ordered to be destroyed." Houston advised that other units had been ordered to cooperate with Baker and, fearing that the captain was getting beyond his control, emphasized, "the utmost harmony of action, subordination, and discipline, must be observed. The safety of the country requires it, and the commanding general orders a rigid adherence to it." Houston to Mosely Baker, 5 April 1836, in Barker and Williams, *Writings of Sam Houston*, 1:396. During January, Stephen F. Austin, while in the United States, trying to raise loans for Texas, became alarmed at a rumor that Baker intended to burn San Felipe to disrupt the government, to protect his interest in Monclova land speculations. Cantrell, *Stephen F. Austin*, 336.

8. Zuber, *My Eighty Years in Texas*, 71; Terrell, "Recollections of General Sam Houston," 115.

9. Houston to Rusk, 31 March 1836, in Barker and Williams, *Writings of Sam Houston*, 1:388–89.

10. "Message to the People East of the Brazos," 31 March 1836, in Barker and Williams, *Writings of Sam Houston*, 1:390.

11. Houston to John E. Ross, 2 April 1836; and Ross to Houston, 11 April 1836, in Barker and Williams, *Writings of Sam Houston*, 1:391, 408. Built in 1831, the *Yellow Stone* was designed for the rigors of the Upper Missouri and Yellowstone Rivers and was a formidable asset to have. After ferrying Houston's army across the Brazos, she steamed down the flooding river and was ambushed by Santa Anna's 6-pounder and some massed musketry—without effect. Not surprisingly, the Republic of Texas was remiss in validating Houston's pledge, although years later, when the state legislature granted land to Ross's widow, the *Yellow Stone*'s engineer memorialized the legislators that bounties were promised to the entire crew. Undated Petition to Legislature, Dorothy Loe Collection, Sam Houston Regional Library and Research Center. He did have some basis for this, as Houston at the time promised him a league of his own land if he would stay and help. Houston to Louis C. Ferguson, 3 April 1836, in Jenkins, *Papers of the Texas Revolution*, 5:308.

12. Edward Harcourt to Houston, 3 April 1836, Sam Houston Collection, Catholic Archives of Texas, Chancery of the Austin Diocese.

13. Houston to Rusk, 3, 4 April 1836, in Barker and Williams, *Writings of Sam Houston*, 1:393–96.

14. Houston to Burnet, 6 April 1836, in Barker and Williams, *Writings of Sam Houston*, 1:398. Burnet's famous "laughing to scorn" letter is quoted in nearly all the histories, but I have yet to locate the original. The editors of Houston's correspondence cite it at Barker and Williams, *Writings of Sam Houston*, 1:412, but only in a footnote; its earliest appearance seems to have been in the *Telegraph and Texas Register* of 9 June 1841. Another early April letter, this one from Burnet to Rusk, may well have been carried in the same packet as the one he delivered to Houston. It implored Rusk to make Houston understand that he must fight. It is nearly obliterated by rot and water damage, suggesting that the "laughing to scorn" letter possibly did not survive similar damage. Burnet to Rusk, [2 April 1836], Thomas Jefferson Rusk Papers, Center for American History, University of Texas.

15. Jesse Benton to Rusk, 3 April 1836, Rusk Papers.

16. Houston to Henry Raguet, 7 April 1836; and Houston to Colonel Bowl, 13 April 1836, in Barker and Williams, *Writings of Sam Houston*, 1:400, 409–10.

17. Houston to Mosely Baker, 5 April 1836; Houston to "Major," 6 April 1836; Houston to David Thomas, 6, 9, 11 April 1836; and Houston to John Forbes, 7 April 1836, in Barker and Williams, *Writings of Sam Houston*, 1:396, 398, 399, 404, 406–7, 401. The editors of Houston's correspondence believed "Major" to be Henry Karnes. 398n. They were probably correct; Karnes was only twenty-three and had been in the service a couple of weeks at most, having attained his rank by virtue of

the fact that it was he who had organized his company of volunteers. Houston did, however, use him to spy out the Mexican positions at San Jacinto shortly thereafter, and that summer, as a Texas commissioner in Matamoros, Karnes smuggled information on Mexican troop movements back to Texas in the incident of the "Whip-handle Dispatches." He died, untimely, of yellow fever in 1840. Tyler et al., *New Handbook of Texas*, 3:1034, 6:922, and articles there cited. Acting Secretary of War Thomas was accidentally killed during the flight of the government from Harrisburg to Galveston, struck by a ball from a gun inadvertently fired on President Burnet's ship.

18. Proceedings of the Court-Martial, 2 April 1836, Rusk Papers. Scales's clemency recommendation became separated from the other papers and eventually came to reside in the formidable Texana collection of W. A. Philpott of Dallas. That collection has since been auctioned into private hands, but many of its Houston documents were published in the canon of Writings. Scales's desertion three days after his release was cited in a letter by Philpott. Philpott to Editors, undated, in Barker and Williams, *Writings of Sam Houston*, 2:23–24. Houston's inclination to mercy was natural, but he would also have remembered that when Jackson executed a mutinous militiaman during the Creek War, the incident returned to haunt him politically in 1828. Remini, *Andrew Jackson and the Course of American Freedom*, 122.

19. Houston to John M. Allen, 8 April 1836, in Barker and Williams, *Writings of Sam Houston*, 1:403.

20. Houston to David Thomas, 13 April 1836, in Barker and Williams, *Writings of Sam Houston*, 1:410–11. With Rusk having come to the army, Thomas was the acting secretary of war.

21. "Santa Anna's Report," quoted in Barker, "The San Jacinto Campaign," 268.

22. Jones, *Memoranda and Official Correspondence*, 16; James, *The Raven*, 380; Tyler et al., *New Handbook of Texas*, 5:161. James Hazard Perry should not be confused with James Franklin Perry, brother-in-law of the great empresario. Barker and Williams, *Writings of Sam Houston*, 1:415n. The entirety of the offending letter is reproduced in Barker and Williams, *Writings of Sam Houston*, 4:274–76.

23. "Kuykendall's Account," quoted in Barker, "The San Jacinto Campaign," 298; Tolbert, *Day of San Jacinto*, 49; Clarke, *Chief Bowles and the Texas Cherokees*, 68. Houston mentioned his "hartshorn Phial," which he wanted replenished, in a letter to Ashbel Smith. Houston to Smith, 10 July 1838, in Barker and Williams, *Writings of Sam Houston*, 2:263.

24. Houston to the Citizens of Texas, 13 April 1836, in Barker and Williams, *Writings of Sam Houston*, 1:408–9.

25. Steele, *Biography*, 9.

26. Tolbert, *Day of San Jacinto*, 92.

27. Sparks, "Recollections," *Quarterly of the Texas State Historical Association* 12 (July 1908): 66–67.

28. Labadie, "San Jacinto Campaign," 40–64. Considered scurrilous in respectable quarters, Labadie's account was hotly disputed, and the author was even sued for libel by John Forbes, who was commissary general of the Texas army at the time of San Jacinto.

29. Quoted in Tolbert, *Day of San Jacinto*, 93–94; Turner, *Houston and His Twelve Women*, 51.

30. See, for instance, Hardin, "San Jacinto Campaign." However, the resurrection of century-old calumny as newfound gospel is one aspect of revisionism that future historians will likely look back on with little charity.

31. Winters, "Account of the Battle of San Jacinto," 140. The Winters family came from Tennessee in 1834 and settled in the Big Thicket on the Upper San Jacinto River. When Cós occupied San Antonio in the fall of 1835, Winters, his father, and brothers all volunteered but apparently arrived after the fight. "We met Sam Houston, who told us to go back home and make all the corn we could, for in the spring would come the clash," which reiterates the same message Houston was broadcasting at that time. Ibid., 139; Tyler et al., *New Handbook of Texas*, 6:1026.

32. "R. J. Calder's Account," quoted in Barker, "The San Jacinto Campaign," 336. Calder later was one of the men who carried news of the victory to Ad Interim President Burnet in his sanctuary on Galveston Island. In later years he served as Brazoria County sheriff and mayor of Brazoria and Richmond, where he ultimately settled. When a monument to the San Jacinto dead was finally dedicated in 1881, it was Calder who unveiled it. He died in 1885. Tyler et al., *New Handbook of Texas*, 1:893.

33. Williams, *Following General Sam Houston*, 161; Betty Nibbs Roberts Tucker, "Application for Membership in the Daughters of the Republic of Texas," 20 January 1951, Applications, Republic of Texas Museum. Ann Nibbs was widowed soon thereafter, but in 1852 she married another Houston compatriot, Judge Constantine W. Buckley. Tyler et al., *New Handbook of Texas*, 1:803. Willis Nibbs could be fussy about the care of his horses. See Jenkins, *Papers of the Texas Revolution*, 5:7.

CHAPTER 10

1. James, *The Raven*, 243.

2. Sparks, "Recollections," *Quarterly of the Texas State Historical Association* 12 (July 1908): 68–69.

3. Labadie, "San Jacinto Campaign," 154–55.

4. Houston and Rusk to the People of Texas, 19 April 1836, in Barker and Williams, *Writings of Sam Houston*, 1:415–16.

5. Houston to Henry Raguet, 19 April 1836, in Barker and Williams, *Writings of Sam Houston*, 1:413–14.

6. "Zuber's Account," quoted in Barker, "The San Jacinto Campaign," 338. Zuber was a member of this camp guard. For his estimation of General Houston, see Barker, 279–80. Zuber later fought in Somervell's expedition and in the Civil War. In his dotage, as the last survivor of the battle of San Jacinto, he was given an honorary life membership in the Texas Historical Society and lived until 1913.

7. "Y. P. Alsbury's Account," quoted in Barker, "The San Jacinto Campaign," 339–40. Alsbury was one of the volunteers who undertook to torch Vince's Bridge, and in his article he mentions the others who took part. Alsbury's account disagrees in no important aspects with a rendering that Houston gave to minister and historian Chester Newell in 1838 and repeated to William S. Taylor, who apparently happened across the Newell inquiry twenty years later. Houston to Chester Newell, 18 April 1838, in Barker and Williams, *Writings of Sam Houston*, 2:202–3; William S. Taylor to Houston, 20 April 1859, A. J. Houston Collection, Texas State Library and Archives.

8. Lyman F. Rounds, audited pension application, Republic Claim Files, Texas State Library and Archives. Rusk promoted Rounds to second lieutenant the day after the battle.

9. Some sources describe a quartet of fifers but that this was the only tune they all knew. Another records that at Houston's order they switched to "Yankee Doodle" a hundred yards from the breastworks. Tolbert's *Day of San Jacinto* is the overall best account of the battle; Hardin's *Texian Iliad*, even with its interpretive shortcomings, is an excellent chronological condensation.

10. McCulloch, "Recollections of the Battle of San Jacinto," reprinted in Barker and Williams, *Writings of Sam Houston*, 7:325–26. Young McCulloch's family had been neighbors of Crockett in Tennessee, and Ben had planned to rendezvous with Crockett in Nacogdoches on Christmas Day of 1835. He missed the date, and only a subsequent bout of measles prevented him from joining his mentor in the Alamo. Tyler et al., *New Handbook of Texas*, 4:384–85.

11. "Santa Anna's Report," and "Delgado's Account," quoted in Barker, "The San Jacinto Campaign," 270–86.

12. Hunter, *Narrative*, 16. These accounts are further confused by the fact that Houston apparently gave another order to halt when he was informed that some of the army were looting the

Mexican camp, and he angrily insisted the pillaging stop. This order to halt had nothing to do with the actual fighting, a fact that the anti-Houston partisans ploughed over undeterred. "Amasa Turner's Account," quoted in Barker, "The San Jacinto Campaign," 342.

13. Winters, "Account of the Battle of San Jacinto," 142–43.

14. "Amasa Turner's Account," quoted in Barker, "The San Jacinto Campaign," 341–42. A Massachusetts yankee, Turner was thirty-five, an old timer by Texas army standards. After a succession of military commands during the early years of the republic, Turner failed at planting and town building but served several terms in the state legislature. He ended his days in 1877 in Gonzales, where Houston's retreat had begun. Tyler et al., *New Handbook of Texas*, 6:592.

15. Winters, "Account of the Battle of San Jacinto," 143.

16. Moses Austin Bryan Papers, University of Texas, quoted in Hardin, *Texian Iliad*, 215.

17. Wallis and Hill, *Sixty Years on the Brazos*, 46.

18. John Forbes, audited pension application, Republic Claim Files. Writing in 1870, Forbes believed the young man who brought Santa Anna in was named Robertson. He was close; it was Joel Robison, a twenty-one-year-old Georgian. Another account of waking General Houston has him uttering a stunning profanity when roused from his painful sleep.

19. Houston, *Life*, 11. This account, recalled for readers during the 1855 presidential campaign, is really no less posturing in tone than most of the others.

20. De Leon, *They Called Them Greasers*, 67.

21. "Guard Report," G. Kuykendall to Houston, 2 May 1836, Sam Houston Papers, Catholic Archives of Texas, Chancery of the Austin Diocese. Gibson Kuykendall, the company commander, was the brother of Hamp.

22. Rusk to Houston, 23 April 1836, Penny Thornall Remick Collection, Sam Houston Regional Library and Research Center; Dilue Rose Harris, "Reminiscences," 171. In his memoir Noah Smithwick added (in his outrageous fashion) that after the battle the coyotes fed only upon the dead horses, refusing to touch the Mexicans, "presumably because of the peppery condition of the flesh." Smithwick, *Evolution of a State*, 131. Smithwick's reminiscences may not be politically correct today, but the Mexican dead certainly lay unburied until they decomposed, for John James Audubon collected several skulls from the battleground a year later. The circumstances of the eventual burial are seconded in Zuber, *My Eighty Years in Texas*, 97.

23. Houston, "A Review of the San Jacinto Campaign: A Speech at Houston in the Summer of 1845," in Barker and Williams, *Writings of Sam Houston*, 6:5–13.

24. Ibid., 13n.

25. Hardin, "San Jacinto Campaign." The author of the less stridently anti-Houston *Texian Iliad*, Hardin here also cites Labadie's account of Pamela Mann as "proof" of Houston's cowardice.

26. Carson to Houston, 14 April 1836, quoted in Friend, *Sam Houston*, 70. A useful summary biography of Carson is found in Kemp, *Signers of the Texas Declaration of Independence*, 45–56.

27. These are cited in Hardin, *Texan Iliad*, 177. Hardin's further "speculation" (283n) that there was at least an understanding between Gaines and Houston is probably right on the money.

28. Carson to Burnet, 14 April 1836; and Carson to Houston, 28 November 1836, in Garrison, *Diplomatic Correspondence*, pt. 1, 84–85, 145; Burnet to Carson, 25 May 1836, Secretaries of State, Domestic Records, Texas State Library and Archives. It is apparent from the wording of Carson's letter that the Indian threat was perceived to be more than a pretext, but the expressed fear that the Indians were supported by a thousand Mexican cavalry seems far-fetched. Carson reported that on his arrival in Natchitoches, "I met with Genl Gains and have had with him a full and *satisfactory* conversation." Carson surely would not have told his president ad interim that Gaines would take an active role west of the Sabine without some token of that fact from Gaines himself. Once Burnet was made aware that Houston was following a plan to lure Santa Anna into a trap (at least until Santa Anna separated himself from his army), it did not alter his opinion of the commanding general. He later

wrote a vicious letter to Mary Austin Holley: "Sam Houston has been generally proclaimed the hero of San Jacinto. No fiction of the novelist is farther from the truth. Houston was the only man on the battlefield that deserved censure. Was absolutely compelled into the fight." Quoted in Stenberg, "Texas Schemes of Jackson and Houston," 250.

29. Carson to Burnet, 4 April 1836; and Carson to Houston, 14 April 1836, in Jenkins, *Papers of the Texas Revolution*, 5:316–17, 470. The editors of this correspondence note that the original of the letter to Houston has been lost and cite to Yoakum, *History of Texas*, 2:169. Since Yoakum prepared his history largely from Houston's papers, the original may have been among Margaret Houston's fireplace casualties in later years.

30. Gen. Richard G. Dunlap to Samuel Carson, 1 June 1836, in Jenkins, *Papers of the Texas Revolution*, 6:471.

31. J. W. Gaines to Burnet, 28 March 1836, Secretaries of State, Domestic Records. Gaines had opposed the Fredonian Rebellion in 1826 but later became an independence radical. See Kemp, *Signers of the Texas Declaration of Independence*, 127–34. The editors of Houston's correspondence erred in their description of James Gaines as E. P. Gaines's brother, but they were amply correct in their assessment that he "had had scant opportunities for a formal education, a fact he seems to have felt keenly . . . but he had learned economic independence in the hardships of life, had a somewhat mean and spiteful disposition, and was always ready to make trouble in public matters in which he had even a slight personal interest." Barker and Williams, *Writings of Sam Houston*, 2:102n.

32. J. W. Gaines to Burnet, 28 March 1836; J. W. Gaines to Houston, 5 May 1836, Thomas Jefferson Rusk Papers, Center for American History, University of Texas. He wrote an almost identical letter to Rusk on the same day. A third letter of similar text, to President Burnet, now reposes in Secretaries of State, Domestic Records, Texas State Library and Archives. Fifty-nine at the time of San Jacinto, James Gaines was far from through with his adventures. He served three terms in the Senate of the Republic of Texas, led the campaign for annexation in Nacogdoches, and opened a hotel in Bastrop, all before leaving for California during the gold rush. Contrary to the impoverished obscurity in which most prospectors ended their days, Gaines and his sons struck it rich in the Mount Gaines Mine. He became prominent in Mariposa County politics and died two days short of his eightieth birthday. Tyler et al., *New Handbook of Texas*, 3:42–43.

33. Jones, *Memoranda and Official Correspondence*, 83–84. Jones did not pen this until 1850. It is unclear when the light first dawned for him, but this elliptical rant may come closer to uncovering Houston's actual thinking than anything else ever written on the topic.

34. Yoakum, *History of Texas*, 2:170.

35. For instance, see Hardin, *Texian Iliad*, 163. Hardin faults Houston for not hastening to reinforce the Alamo because "he could not have been aware" that it had already fallen.

36. E. P. Gaines to Houston, 25 April 1836, Rusk Papers. In fairness, it must also be said that later in the year Gaines actually did post troops in Nacogdoches at the invitation of the Texas government to cow truculent Indians. Even then, however, the move seemed calculated as much for Mexican notice as for the Cherokees. James, *The Raven*, 260–61.

37. See, for a general example, Margaret Swett Henson, *Juan Davis Bradburn: A Reappraisal* (College Station: Texas A&M University Press, 1982). For a particularly vociferous summary of the personalities and events leading up to the revolution, see Long, *Duel of Eagles*, chap. 2.

38. As an example of this earlier mentality, when I first began research in Texas history, there were still a few surviving museum docents of the first generation of the Daughters of the Republic of Texas and the United Daughters of the Confederacy. When I inquired of one after photographs relating to the 1865 battle of Palmito Ranch, the final land action of the Civil War, she could not place it in her mind and so asked me, "Who was the hero?"

39. George William Boyd to Houston, 6 June 1836; and William Johnston to Houston, 29 May 1836, Sam Houston Papers, Catholic Archives of Texas. Johnston surfaced again, if it was the same

man, during the Mexican invasion crisis of 1842, offering to bring a company of volunteers, to which Houston responded heartily. Houston to Johnston, 10 May 1842, in Barker and Williams, *Writings of Sam Houston*, 4:99.

40. H. K. Grimker to Houston, 4 June 1836; Francis Mahan to Houston, 9 June 1836; John G. Stewart to Houston, 10 June 1836; Samuel Mabson to Houston, 19 June 1836; and Joseph and Sarah Shepard to Houston, 23 June 1836, Sam Houston Papers, Catholic Archives of Texas.

41. John D. Bowen to Houston, 30 May 1836, Sam Houston Papers, Catholic Archives of Texas; Houston to Robert McEwen, 7 September 1836, in Barker and Williams, *Writings of Sam Houston*, 2:25.

42. John Salmon Ford Papers, Center for American History.

43. Felix Huston to Houston, 2 August 1836, Sam Houston Papers, Catholic Archives of Texas. This document exists partly in Huston's handwriting and partly as a file copy in the hand of James Izod, his aide-de-camp.

44. Thomas Jefferson Green to Houston, 10 August 1836, Sam Houston Papers, Catholic Archives of Texas.

45. I. M. Glassell to Houston, 19 October 1836; and P. P. Harney to Houston, 10 October 1836, Sam Houston Collection, Catholic Archives of Texas. W. J. Kyle went on to settle in Brazoria County, where in partnership with Benjamin Franklin Terry (of later Civil War fame) he accumulated vast wealth as a planter and slaveowner. See Tyler et al., *New Handbook of Texas*, 3:1172.

46. Gard, *Rawhide Texas*, 30.

47. James, *The Raven*, 277–78. James obtained the letter from Madge Hearne; it is now in the Sam Houston Hearne Collection, University of Texas.

48. J. P. Clark to Houston, 5 October 1836, Sam Houston Papers, Catholic Archives of Texas.

CHAPTER 11

Oath of Office, 22 October 1836, in Barker and Williams, *Writings of Sam Houston*, 1:448.

1. Inaugural Address, 22 October 1836, in Barker and Williams, *Writings of Sam Houston*, 1:448–52. In 1996 I curated an exhibition of memorabilia for the sesquicentennial of statehood at the Texas State Capitol's visitor center, and we borrowed the original of this document from the Texas State Library and Archives. Like many of Houston's papers, it bore signs of passage through private hands—a price of $1,000 was penciled in the margin.

2. Samuel Swartwout to Houston, 4 December 1836, A. J. Houston Collection, Texas State Library and Archives.

3. Houston to Major Moody, [undated], Sam Houston Papers, Thomason Room (Special Collections), Newton Gresham Library, Sam Houston State University; Houston to the Texas Senate, 26, 27 October 1836, in Barker and Williams, *Writings of Sam Houston*, 1:457, 459. In the first submissions for confirmation, Houston pointed out to the Senate that in such a frontier republic as Texas, it was virtually impossible to find highly qualified professionals for each post, and "should any one of them be rejected, I should feel myself at a loss where, or by whom to supply his place."

4. Potter was, apparently, not a success as navy secretary. Within days of taking office, Fisher sent Houston a meticulous and scathing report on the disorganization of the department. Fisher to Houston, 12 November 1836, A. J. Houston Collection. Houston's willingness to utilize Pease's considerable abilities may have been curried by John Wharton, who had become Pease's law partner. He did not keep the job long, though, quitting in December of 1837. His letter of resignation was respectful, citing the presence of a business opportunity that a young man like himself could not afford to pass up. Pease, of course, later went on to serve Texas as an able governor. Marshall Pease to Houston, 9 December 1837, Penny Thornall Remick Collection, Sam Houston Regional Library and Research Center.

5. Felix Huston to Army, 29 October 1836; Huston to Houston, 5 November 1836, Sam Houston Papers, Catholic Archives of Texas, Chancery of the Austin Diocese.

6. Almanzon Houston to Houston, 16 November 1836; and Felix Huston to Houston, 10 November 1836, Sam Houston Papers, Catholic Archives of Texas.

7. Houston to Thomas Toby, 25 October, 1 November 1836, in Barker and Williams, *Writings of Sam Houston*, 1:454–55, 465.

8. "Appointment of Commissioners to Make Indian Treaties," 12 November 1836, in Barker and Williams, *Writings of Sam Houston*, 1:480.

9. James Collinsworth to Houston, 13 November, 1836; and Samuel P. Carson to Houston, 28 November 1836, in Garrison, *Diplomatic Correspondence*, pt. 1, 125–26, 145–47.

10. Houston to Toby, 17 November 1836, in Barker and Williams, *Writings of Sam Houston*, 1:485.

11. Lubbock, *Six Decades in Texas*, 36. As was not the case with many of the family inquiries addressed to Houston, Tom Lubbock was safe and sound. After participating in the siege of Béxar, he took a job on a Brazos riverboat, working the river's upper reaches. Texas independence was won before he ever learned there had been a revolution. He lived to help recruit Terry's Texas Rangers into the Civil War.

12. Houston, "To the Mexican Minister at Washington," 25 October 1836; "Revocation of Blockade," 1 November 1836; and "Proclamation Recalling Letters of Marque," 16 December 1836, in Barker and Williams, *Writings of Sam Houston*, 1:453–54, 466–67, 508–9.

13. Houston to the Texas Senate, 16 November 1836, in Barker and Williams, *Writings of Sam Houston*, 1:469–74. An apparent misprint in the Writings misdates this message as 6 November.

14. Houston, "Safe Conduct Pass for Santa Anna and Almonte," 20 November 1836, A. J. Houston Collection, photocopy; Henson, "Politics and the Treatment of the Mexican Prisoners," 204–5; Hockley to Houston, 13 December 1836 (two letters); and Bee to Houston, 14 December 1836, in Garrison, *Diplomatic Correspondence*, pt. 2, 425–27.

15. Huston to Houston, 10, 14, 24, 26 November, 3, 16 December 1836, Sam Houston Papers, Catholic Archives of Texas. In these letters Huston thanks the president for his replies, but I have not located these documents.

16. Houston to Andrew Jackson, 20 November 1836 (two letters), in Barker and Williams, *Writings of Sam Houston*, 1:487–88. Collinsworth's pessimistic letter was written from Brazoria, only eight miles from Columbia, on 13 November. It provides a more urgent motivation for Houston's private message to Jackson than has been previously connected.

17. See chap. 5, note 39.

18. Barker and Williams, *Writings of Sam Houston*, 2:42. The editors' summary of Morfit's population estimate as including 45,000 Anglos does not square with the 30,000 in Yoakum, *History of Texas*, 2:197 (quoting Morfit to Forsyth, 27 August 1836). Morfit estimated that Texas also held about 3,500 resident Mexicans, 5,000 Negroes, and some 14,000 Indians.

19. Richardson, *Messages and Papers of the Presidents*, 3:1456.

20. Houston to John H. Houston, 20 November 1836, in Barker and Williams, *Writings of Sam Houston*, 2:27–28. It is worth mentioning that the mail in this era was quite uncertain; Houston in this letter acknowledges receiving one from Jack, but others from Gertrude "have never met my eye. For all I truly thank you, tho' not received."

21. Gammel, *Laws of Texas*, 1:132.

22. Houston, "Veto of the Post Office Bill," 17 December 1836, in Barker and Williams, *Writings of Sam Houston*, 1:509.

23. Lubbock, *Six Decades in Texas*, 91–92.

24. Jackson, "Message on Texas and Mexico," 21 December 1836, quoted in Heiskell, *Andrew Jackson and Early Tennessee History*, 3:314–17.

25. "General Orders," 27 December 1836, in Barker and Williams, *Writings of Sam Houston,* 2:28–29.

26. "Appointment of Commissions to the United States," 31 December 1836, in Barker and Williams, *Writings of Sam Houston,* 1:524. Hunt was a North Carolinian who arrived in Texas too late to fight for independence, but he was appointed a brigadier by Ad Interim President Burnet to resist the anticipated reinvasion from Mexico. Tyler et al., *New Handbook of Texas,* 3:783–84. His early work on behalf of Texas was creditable, but he later passed into the Lamar camp and became a burr under Houston's saddle.

27. Commission of Memucan Hunt, 31 December 1836, Remick Collection.

28. Madge Thornall Roberts cites the dissimilarity of the "I" and "S" in the general's hand to dispute this element of the Houston legend. It is not part of the family tradition. However, the similarity of Houston's "S" to the "I" of many other hands of the day, along with the sometimes imperial dimensions of his signature and the recurring apparent distance between the "S" and "am," does tempt one to accept the story. Roberts, interview with the author, 4 May 2000.

29. Houston to Toby, 27 January 1837, in Barker and Williams, *Writings of Sam Houston,* 2:41. Houston's confusing blur of present, past, future, and subjunctive case caused his editors to comment, "This sentence is as in the original." His phrase "get over" regarding U.S. recognition of Texas independence in that time would be read "get around" or "ignore" today as opposed to its modern vernacular.

30. William Wharton to Houston, 2 February 1837, in Garrison, *Diplomatic Correspondence,* pt. 1, 179–81. The perspicacity of Wharton's observations is that of an intelligent and diligent observer. He resigned his mission soon after; on his way home, he was captured at sea by a Mexican warship, taken to Matamoros, and imprisoned—telling evidence of Santa Anna's peaceable intentions. He escaped and might have done further good service for his country, but William Wharton was killed by an accidental pistol discharge in 1839. See Tyler et al., *New Handbook of Texas,* 6:908–9.

31. Felix Huston to Houston, 27 December 1836, 8 January 1837, Sam Houston Papers, Catholic Archives of Texas. These two missives are in Huston's hand. An additional account that Major Morse heard Felix Huston characterize the president's homily as "damned lies" exists in a transcript, but I have not located the original.

32. Styles to Houston, 10 November 1836, A. J. Houston Collection. The president already had received a similar letter from William R. C. Hays, sent from New Orleans. Hays to Houston, 20 December 1836, Sam Houston Papers, Catholic Archives of Texas. Styles later made it back to Columbia, where he was shot through the leg and mortally wounded by a resident on account "of some *night* prank of his." Gail Borden to Houston, 18 January 1837, A. J. Houston Collection. During the spring Houston received an anguished letter from the young man's mother in Baltimore, seeking news of his fate, which is one of the most poignant documents in the A. J. Houston Collection. S. E. Styles to Houston, 13 April 1837, A. J. Houston Collection; Haley, *Most Excellent Sir,* 21n.

33. William Patterson to Houston, 20 January 1837; and John H. Wallace to Houston, 22 December 1836, Sam Houston Papers, Catholic Archives of Texas.

34. William N. Hill to Houston, 6 February 1837, A. J. Houston Collection. The other letters of introduction mentioned in the text and not individually cited—and others besides—are located in the same repository and in the Sam Houston Papers, Catholic Archives of Texas.

35. Henry Karnes to Houston, 29 April 1837, A. J. Houston Collection. Houston's confidence in Ricord seems not to have been misplaced, at least based on previous experience with him. Most of Houston's tediously duplicated file copies of his official business during this period are in Ricord's precise, angular, and somewhat difficult hand. Additionally, Ricord sometimes served as Houston's eyes and ears in New Orleans, sending back detailed and, all things considered, reliable dispatches.

See, for instance, Ricord to Houston, 26 January 1837, A. J. Houston Collection. Ricord's personal story is less happy. He seems to have lived his whole life as a man in search of a place. He left Texas later in 1837 and traveled widely, serving for a time as attorney general to King Kamehameha III of Hawaii. He also turned up in Siam, the Malay States, and the Philippines. Back in Texas in 1861, Ricord successfully lobbied the legislature into granting him compensation for his services to Houston and soon afterward died in France while *en route* to Liberia. Tyler et al., *New Handbook of Texas*, 5:577.

36. David Gallaher to Houston, 15 October 1837, Sam Houston Papers, Catholic Archives of Texas.

37. Houston to Anna Raguet, 1 January 1837, in Barker and Williams, *Writings of Sam Houston*, 2:29. Sue Flanagan believed the reference to "armour" was connected to the story that Raguet had made Houston the sash from which he drew his sword at San Jacinto. "Thus, as did maidens of old, Anna Raguet sent forth her knight." Flanagan, *Sam Houston's Texas*, 45; Barker and Williams, *Writings of Sam Houston*, 2:30n.

38. Houston, "March, Chieftain," in Barker and Williams, *Writings of Sam Houston*, 2:31–32. Handed down for many years in Anna Raguet's family, it was published in the *Dallas Morning News*, 12 October 1930.

39. Among the secondary sources, this letter, like the John Campbell letter of 6 October, is unique to James's work, and subsequent citations stem from there. James, *The Raven*, 278–79. James obtained it from Houston descendent Marian Williams, and it is now housed, along with the Campbell letter, in the Sam Houston Hearne Collection, Center for American History, University of Texas.

40. James, *The Raven*, 278. Elizabeth Crook makes the point that despite these letters, Eliza Allen remained silent on the subject of reuniting with Houston. That is not surprising, as it would have been almost impossible for her to commit such a humiliating act as to correspond with Houston directly to take her back. Moreover, McEwen, if not Campbell, had been Houston's partisan in the separation scandal and knew how shamelessly the Allens had dragged him through the mud to vindicate Eliza. It's hard to imagine that McEwen would have urged Houston to reconcile without prompting. Crook, "Sam Houston and Eliza Allen," 34.

41. Daniel Elam to Houston, 2 January 1837, A. J. Houston Collection. The reader should not be confused by this apparently inexplicable geography. The "China Grove" where Elam lived was not the present town just southeast of San Antonio but refers to a place name now defunct, the neighborhood of Gen. Albert Sidney Johnston's China Grove plantation on the W. D. C. Hall grant in Brazoria County. This is made quite certain by two other references in the Elam letter. One was to "R. R. Royal," who was Richardson Royster Royall of Matagorda. The other was to "Hardimans Crossing on Caney Creek," apparently a reference to William P. Hardeman, who settled on Caney Creek in Matagorda County. The "public cattle" mentioned here were part of a large wild, or feral, herd that had been driven up the previous year from south of the Nueces River. Coincidentally, it was R. R. Royall who had been placed in charge of rounding them up and driving them to the Matagorda area, where they could be used to feed the army. See Barker and Williams, *Writings of Sam Houston*, 1:384n.

42. Houston to Neill, undated, in Barker and Williams, *Writings of Sam Houston*, 2:61. Camp Independence was on the east bank of the Lavaca River about four miles southwest of the present town of Edna. Tyler et al., *New Handbook of Texas*, 1:939–40.

43. Houston to Capt. B. J. White, 12 February 1837, in Barker and Williams, *Writings of Sam Houston*, 2:51–52.

44. Gail Borden to Houston, 18 January 1837, A. J. Houston Collection; *Telegraph and Daily Register* [January 1837].

45. Houston to Catherine Duane Morgan, 31 January 1837, in Barker and Williams, *Writings of Sam Houston*, 2:45–46. Houston's eye was keen regarding the possibilities of George Washington Morgan; he left Texas two years later, attended West Point, fought in the Mexican War, entered the

foreign service as American consul in Marseilles and Lisbon, fought as a Union general in the Civil War, and then served three terms in Congress from Ohio. Tyler et al., *New Handbook of Texas*, 4:835.

46. Houston to Anna Raguet, 29 January 1837, in Barker and Williams, *Writings of Sam Houston*, 2:43–44. The Mrs. Long referred to was probably the indomitable Jane Herbert Wilkinson Long, niece of the General Wilkinson who signed the Neutral Ground Agreement, widow of the filibuster James Long, and mother of the first Anglo baby—as popularly believed—born in Texas, for which feat she is sometimes awarded the sobriquet "Mother of Texas." (This latter claim, however, is hotly disputed by the descendents of Helena Dill Berryman of Nacogdoches. Corinne Moore to author, undated [1986]. The Berryman claim has received some academic acknowledgment in recent years. See Tyler et al., *New Handbook of Texas*, 1:504.) Jane Long reentered Texas with Austin's colonists, opened a hotel, and had her name romantically linked to various leading men of the day, including Ben Milam and Mirabeau Lamar. Despite Houston's hopeful assessment of her age, Jane Long was five years his junior. Tyler et al., *New Handbook of Texas*, 4:274–75.

47. Houston to John Marable, 4 December 1828, quoted in James, *The Raven*, 72.

48. James Allan to Houston, 25 January 1837, Sam Houston Papers, Catholic Archives of Texas; Yoakum, *History of Texas*, 2:207.

49. Henry Teal to Houston, 5 March 1837, A. J. Houston Collection.

50. Marshall de Bruhl places the letter and Teal's murder on the same day, 5 May, but the letter is clearly dated 5 March. De Bruhl, *Sword of San Jacinto*, 240.

51. Houston to soldiers, [May 1837], A. J. Houston Collection. Teal's murderer was later discovered to be not one of his men but a Mississippi ne'er-do-well named Schultz.

52. Houston to Thomas Toby, 17 March 1837, in Barker and Williams, *Writings of Sam Houston*, 2:72.

53. John Ricord to Houston, 26 January 1837, A. J. Houston Collection.

54. Houston to Col. Juan N. Seguín, 16 January 1837, in Barker and Williams, *Writings of Sam Houston*, 2:34. Houston later provided Seguín a letter of introduction to Judge E. D. White of New Orleans, in which he characterized Seguín as "an officer in our service. The Colonel commanded the only Mexican company in the Battle of San Jacinto. His chivalrous and estimable conduct in the battle earn him my warmest regard and esteem." Houston to E. D. White, 31 October 1837, ibid., 2:147.

55. Houston to Capt. Randall Jones, 7 February 1837, Sam Houston Papers, Thomason Room (Special Collections), Newton Gresham Library, Sam Houston State University.

56. Ricord to Houston, 26 January 1837, A. J. Houston Collection.

57. R. H. Smith to Houston, 24 February 1837, Sam Houston Papers, Catholic Archives of Texas. The handwriting of this letter is about on a par with its grammar; his name may have been B. H. Smith.

58. William M. Price to Houston, 24 February 1837, A. J. Houston Collection. Houston had been receiving desultory reports of ominous troops movements within Mexico for months. See, for instance, William H. Howell to Houston, 7 June 1836, A. J. Houston Collection.

59. Houston to Toby, 27 January, 1 February 1837, in Barker and Williams, *Writings of Sam Houston*, 2:41, 47. Ricord's aspersions on the conduct of Toby and Brothers' Texas agency were later considered, if not actually found to be, unsubstantiated, although sufficient irregularities were discovered in their handling of land scrip to discontinue its issuance. The government acknowledged the validity of its debt to them, to the amount of over $76,000, but the Republic of Texas never had enough money to pay in full. Thomas Toby's heirs finally collected a settlement of $45,000 in 1881, thirty-two years after his death. See Tyler et al., *New Handbook of Texas*, 6:513, and sources there cited.

60. Rusk to Houston, 30 January 1837, A. J. Houston Collection; Houston to Lt. Peter Harper, 9 February 1837, in Barker and Williams, *Writings of Sam Houston*, 2:49–51; Armstrong to C. A. Harris, 10 May 1837, quoted in ibid., 50n.

61. Houston to A. S. Thruston, 17 March 1837, in Barker and Williams, *Writings of Sam Houston*, 2:71–72.

62. Houston to "Any Captain of a Steam Boat," 11 February 1837, in Barker and Williams, *Writings of Sam Houston*, 2:51; Gail Borden to Houston, 3 March 1837, Sam Houston Papers, Catholic Archives of Texas.

63. Houston to Samuel Swartwout, 22 March 1837, in Barker and Williams, *Writings of Sam Houston*, 6:3. This was not the first time Houston rendered his literary impression of Lafayette; he had been doing it at least as early as a letter to his cousin Jack on 10 November 1828: "Your former letters never reached me, and for that, I will no 'die appie.'" Houston to John H. Houston, in Barker and Williams, *Writings of Sam Houston*, 2:10. Houston had been acquainted with the Allen brothers for some time. It was A. C. Allen who had written him of Austin's imprisonment in 1834, and a letter the following year from Houston's New York friend James Auchincloss had offered to settle some of J. K. Allen's business affairs there if he could have a commission payable in Allen lands in the Red River country. A. C. Allen to Houston, 28 February 1834; and James Auchincloss to Houston, 25 March 1835, A. J. Houston Collection.

CHAPTER 12

1. Sam Hewes to Houston, 7 March 1837, A. J. Houston Collection, Texas State Library and Archives. See also Friend, *Sam Houston*, 88. This hat may have been the large plumed one of which LeRay de Chaumont wrote incredulously to Mirabeau Lamar in July. Houston wore it then to complement a black velvet suit lined with white satin while in the company of J. K. Allen and the English consul, J. T. Crawford.

Captain Hewes had been sent to New Orleans on duties attached to Col. A. S. Thruston, commissary general of the republic. Houston's letters of introduction for them both, addressed to Toby, are dated 20 January, although he waited until 10 May to present his nominations to fill army positions to Congress, which confirmed the list on 22 May. Houston to Thomas Toby, 20 January 1837, in Barker and Williams, *Writings of Sam Houston*, 2:34–35 (and notes).

2. William D. Redd to Lamar, 23 May 1837, in Gulick et al., *Papers of Mirabeau Buonaparte Lamar*, 1:552. The reference to "the wounded Achilise" was tactless but appropriate, both heroes having been wounded in the foot. It was the kind of witticism Lamar would have appreciated—and Houston too, if it had been made to his face. Redd had accompanied Lamar out from Georgia and served off and on in the army. It is interesting from his spelling of the word "longer" that his regional accent claimed equal place with the classical allusion in his writing. He died, like a good Southerner, in a duel with his commanding officer shortly after the Council House fight in 1840. Redd did manage to mortally wound his opponent, Lysander Wells.

3. John Roberts to Houston, 8 March 1837, A. J. Houston Collection.

4. Houston to Anna Raguet, 20 May 1837, quoted in *Dallas Morning News*, 21 March 1915, and in James, *The Raven*, 293.

5. Houston to F. H. Rankin, 8 May 1837, Sam Houston Papers, Thomason Room (Special Collections), Newton Gresham Library, Sam Houston State University. This document is a draft for sixty dollars to pay for rations fed to the Indians during their visit, an interpreter's fee, and includes fifteen dollars for the cost of sending an express to the Trinity River, perhaps to summon the natives to Houston.

6. Hogan, *Texas Republic*, 50.

7. Lubbock, *Six Decades in Texas*, 57–60.

8. Ibid., 49–50.

9. Barker, "The African Slave Trade in Texas," 145 ff.

10. "Speech to the Texas Congress on Annexation (Following Recognition by the United States)," 5 May 1837, in Barker and Williams, *Writings of Sam Houston*, 2:82–90.

11. John H. Houston to Houston, 2 March 1837, Penny Thornall Remick Collection, Sam Houston Regional Library and Research Center.

12. "Speech to the Texas Congress," 21 November 1837, in Barker and Williams, *Writings of Sam Houston*, 1:152–61.

13. J. P. Henderson to Houston, 20 July 1837, in Garrison, *Diplomatic Correspondence*, pt. 1, 243–44.

14. Houston to Chief The Bowl, 3 July 1837, in Barker and Williams, *Writings of Sam Houston*, 2:131.

15. Quoted in Lubbock, *Six Decades in Texas*, 53–54.

16. Robert Irion to J. P. Henderson, 25 June 1837, in Garrison, *Diplomatic Correspondence*, pt. 3, 809. Houston had already been teasing Anna Raguet on the eligibility of Irion as a rival and now threw Henderson into the balance: "Bye the bye, Genl Henderson . . . is a bachelor, *young*, *noble*, and *rich*—a man of genius. Note this will you and look out!!" Safe enough to say when he was sending Henderson across the Atlantic. Houston to Anna Raguet, 7 March 1837, in Barker and Williams, *Writings of Sam Houston*, 2:63–64.

17. Friend, *Sam Houston*, 87.

18. According to Marquis James, President Houston's fear that the military might seize the government was justified, as Huston's second in command, a Colonel Rodgers, had been whipping up the soldiers into an ardor to march on the capital if General Huston came away unsuccessful. *The Raven*, 284–85; see also Creel, *Sam Houston*, 220. The episode received a final ironic twist nearly four years later, when Fisher, after various personal reverses, tried to make common enterprise with Huston in a private conquest of Mexico. James, *The Raven*, 317.

19. Lubbock, *Six Decades in Texas*, 74–75. Houston City was still being platted out by the Allen brothers when Lubbock arrived with his first boatload of goods. He missed the "landing," which was the merest thread of a path down to Buffalo Bayou, and continued upstream until he lost steerage. Lubbock, of course, after much legislative duty, served a term as governor of Texas during the Civil War.

20. Huston to Houston, 16 March 1837; Huston and Johnston to Houston, [24 May] 1837, Sam Houston Papers, Catholic Archives of Texas.

21. Houston to Fisher, 18, 19 May 1837; and Fisher to Houston, 24 May 1837, A. J. Houston Collection.

22. Houston to Anna Raguet, in Barker and Williams, *Writings of Sam Houston*, 3:8.

23. Huston to Houston, 3, 8 June 1837; and Houston to Huston, 3 June 1837, Catholic Archives of Texas.

24. Ashbel Smith, "Life Sketch of Sam Houston," Ashbel Smith Papers, University of Texas, quoted in Crane, *Life and Select Literary Remains*, 246–47; Yoakum, *History of Texas*, 2:183. Either Smith was confused as to the date of this incident or it repeated itself, for A. C. Allen carried a message from Houston to Western, requiring the latter's presence, during his weeks as president-elect before Houston's second term. Houston to Western, 2 November 1841, Nancy Burch Collection, Sam Houston Regional Library and Research Center.

25. Peter W. Grayson to Houston, 21 October 1837, in Garrison, *Diplomatic Correspondence*, pt. 1, 264–65.

26. Parma, the ducal seat of the ancient Farnese family, had been annexed to France by Napoleon, and after the emperor's exile, the Congress of Vienna gave Parma as a kind of charitable domicile to his Austrian wife, Marie Louise, who still ruled it in 1837. The count's warm references to the emperor in his proposal would indicate that he was a Napoleonic Farnese, not an Italian Farnese. John C. Williams to Houston, 11 July 1837; and Charles, Comte de Farnese to Houston, 28 July 1837, [typescripts in French and English] Sam Houston Papers, Catholic Archives of Texas. The original of Houston's reply to Farnese, dated 5 August 1837 and reprinted in Barker and Williams, *Writings of Sam*

Houston (2:135–37), is in the Ashbel Smith Papers at the University of Texas, which may hint at who translated the letter into French. Henderson Yoakum reprints salient points of Farnese's plan with some editorializing on the impropriety of the land grant angle. *History of Texas,* 2:224–27. President Houston would probably have agreed with Yoakum, but saw no need to discourage a well-connected nobleman willing to befriend the country. See also Francis Richard Bayard, *Lone-Star Vanguard: The Catholic Re-Occupation of Texas, 1838–1848* (St. Louis: Vincentian Press, 1945.)

27. T. W. Ashton to Houston, 8 May 1838, Sam Houston Papers, Catholic Archives of Texas. There were three Captains English in Texas at the time who could have been his intended business partner.

28. George C. Henry to *Dallas Morning News* [February 1927], Correspondence about Sam Houston, Catholic Archives of Texas; *Texas Telegraph and Register,* 17 March 1838, quoted in Flanagan, *Sam Houston's Texas,* 46.

29. Gard, *Rawhide Texas,* 8.

30. Mann was sentenced to death the following year for forgery, but she was ultimately pardoned and died a woman of property in 1840. See Hogan, "Pamela Mann."

31. Lubbock, *Six Decades in Texas,* 66.

32. Smith, "Life Sketch of Sam Houston"; Hogan, *Texas Republic,* 187.

33. Silverthorne, *Ashbel Smith of Texas,* 16. This is the only book-length biography of Smith, an excellent chronicle of an excellent life.

34. "Nominating Ashbel Smith Surgeon General of the Texas Army," 7 June 1837, in Barker and Williams, *Writings of Sam Houston,* 2:115. Marion Wisehart inexplicably has Smith in Houston in time to hear the president open Congress on the fifth. Sam Houston, 301. Smith's journal fixes his arrival on the ninth. See Silverthorne, *Ashbel Smith of Texas,* 38.

35. Smith, "Sketch Life of Sam Houston"; Houston to Anna Raguet, 2 December 1837, in Barker and Williams, *Writings of Sam Houston,* 3:8.

36. "A Prohibition Wager," 7 January 1838, in Barker and Williams, *Writings of Sam Houston,* 2:180.

37. Stuart, "Hamilton Stuart," 382–83. Stuart, incidentally, became one of the most influential newspaper editors in Texas, and the friendship between the two lasted until Houston's death.

38. "The Amount Due Houston for Military Services, 1835–36," 23 February 1838, in Barker and Williams, *Writings of Sam Houston,* 2:198–99.

39. Houston to Anna Raguet, 12 January, 1 February 1838, in Barker and Williams, *Writings of Sam Houston,* 2:184–85, 189–90. Houston bought the land from the common-law wife of the original settler to whom it was patented and to whom the settler bequeathed it. Her claim was contested, however, by his son from a first (legal) marriage, and he sold the parcel to someone else. In this case it was merely a coincidence, however unsurprising, that Houston's sympathies lay with a common-law arrangement; she did have the superior claim. Houston to William Duncan, 6 December 1847, in Barker and Williams, *Writings of Sam Houston,* 6:17–18n. See also *Texas State Gazette,* 16 March 1850. The entire legal proceeding is in the William Hale Papers, Center for American History, University of Texas.

40. Roberts, *Star of Destiny,* 13. After Houston's marriage, the house was expanded to serve as the summer home for his large family.

41. Quoted in Flanagan, *Sam Houston's Texas,* 49.

42. Harris, "Reminiscences," 36.

43. Hogan, *Texas Republic,* 109, 118–19. Trask was in Houston to collect the headright of her late brother, Olwyn, who was killed in a firefight shortly before the battle at San Jacinto. She had been since 1835 the proprietress of a girls' boarding school at Cole's Settlement, which later became the town of Independence, and late in 1838 she was awarded an additional section of land in recognition of her contribution to society as a frontier schoolmarm. She did not marry until 1851 and then

was widowed six months later; after teaching at various locations in Texas, she returned to Massachusetts, where she died in 1892. See "Thompson, Frances Judith Somes Trask," in Tyler et al., *New Handbook of Texas*, 6:471.

44. Arthur, "Jottings," 82; Lubbock, *Six Decades in Texas*, 84. In San Augustine some months earlier, Fowler procured a letter of introduction to President Houston from Almanzon Huston, a shrewd choice of intermediary. Huston, who had dispatched the Twin Sisters to the army from Brazoria, stood high in the president's esteem, and Fowler managed to overlook Huston's Catholicism. Fowler was a man of "high exalted talents as a Preacher," Huston wrote the president, "I have seen none in Texas equal to him." Almanzon Huston to Houston, 7 November 1837, Sam Houston Papers, Catholic Archives of Texas; Tyler et al., *New Handbook of Texas*, 3:801–2. Not one to leave anything to chance, Fowler, before ever coming to Texas, procured a separate letter of introduction to Sam Houston, this one from a higher authority than Almanzon. Andrew Jackson to Houston, 19 September 1837, General Collections, Sam Houston Memorial Museum.

45. Randolph Ross to Houston, 8 January 1837, Sam Houston Collection, Catholic Archives of Texas.

46. "I set Mr. Johnson on *Sam Patch* for the sake of dispatch." Houston to Smith, 10 July 1838, Ashbel Smith Papers, quoted and annotated in Barker and Williams, *Writings of Sam Houston*, 2:262–63. The letter restates the urgency of the situation several times.

47. Houston to Robert Irion, 7 July 1838, in Barker and Williams, *Writings of Sam Houston*, 2:261–62.

48. "Election Proclamation," 11 July 1838, in Barker and Williams, *Writings of Sam Houston*, 2:264–65.

49. Francis W. Johnson to Houston, 24 April 1838, Burch Collection; Houston to Colonel Bowl, 12, 14, 15 August 1838, in Barker and Williams, *Writings of Sam Houston*, 2:274–75, 277.

50. Houston to Rusk, 12, 13 August 1838; "General Orders," 18 August 1838, in Barker and Williams, *Writings of Sam Houston*, 2:275–76, 278.

51. Houston to Anna Raguet, 3 August 1838, in Barker and Williams, *Writings of Sam Houston*, 2:265–66.

52. Houston to Jackson, 11 August 1838, in Barker and Williams, *Writings of Sam Houston*, 2:270–72.

53. Tyler et al., *New Handbook of Texas*, 2:220, 3:297.

54. Tom Rusk Jennings, "General Houston and the Ticks," *Nacogdoches Daily Sentinel*, 15 May 1909, quoted in *Yesterdays* [the journal of the Nacogdoches Genealogical Society] 11, no. 2. The playing of practical jokes on men who were too drunk to defend themselves was something of a frontier art form, and this was by no means the only time such mirth was made at Houston's expense. The term "cap box" in this usage almost certainly refers to a container for percussion caps, not—mercifully—a hatbox.

55. Houston to Mrs. Ross, 28 August 1838, in Barker and Williams, *Writings of Sam Houston*, 2:280–82.

56. Lubbock, *Six Decades in Texas*, 69.

57. Houston to Robert Irion, 7 July 1838, in Barker and Williams, *Writings of Sam Houston*, 2:261–62.

58. Harris, "Reminiscences," 218–19. While Houston did not view the play until autumn, the playbill shows that it opened on 11 June in tandem with another comedy, "The Hunchback." Tyler et al., *New Handbook of Texas*, 6:455.

59. Hogan, "Theater in the Republic of Texas," 394–400; Turner, *Houston and His Twelve Women*, 54–56. A "gill" is an archaic term for a half-pint measure.

60. McKinney to Samuel May Williams, quoted in James, *The Raven*, 302. Allen, if he was victorious, probably took little notice, having suffered the death of his brother John in August, and

entered a long decline of illness and poverty. See note appended to the "Prohibition Wager," in Barker and Williams, *Writings of Sam Houston*, 2:181–83. Houston's drinking during this time became so storied that a document signed by his shaking hand commanded a premium when it passed onto the market because it was signed "while intoxicated, $250.00" Houston to F. H. Rankin, 4 December 1838, Sam Houston Papers, Thomason Room (Special Collections), Newton Gresham Library, Sam Houston State University.

61. "To the Texas Congress," 19 November 1838, in Barker and Williams, *Writings of Sam Houston*, 2:299–304.

62. Houston to Martin, 5 December 1838, in Barker and Williams, *Writings of Sam Houston*, 2:306.

63. Statement of Stephen Z. Hoyle, [October 1838], Sam Houston Papers, Catholic Archives of Texas.

64. Extract from the *Telegraph*, 24 November 1838, Sam Houston Papers, Catholic Archives of Texas.

65. Guild, *Old Times in Tennessee*, 289; Red, "Allen's Reminiscences of Texas," 295. Judge Guild's informant erred in ascribing this circumstance to Houston's first inaugural.

CHAPTER 13

1. *Houston Morning Star*, 27 April 1839; *Houston Telegraph and Texas Register*, 20 February, 10 April 1839; Red, "Allen's Reminiscences of Texas," 287–88.

2. Houston to Anna Raguet, 8 February 1839, in Barker and Williams, *Writings of Sam Houston*, 2:310.

3. "Terms of Partnership," 8 January 1839, in Barker and Williams, *Writings of Sam Houston*, 2:308; Houston to John Birdsall, 4 August 1838, Sam Houston Papers, Thomason Room (Special Collections), Newton Gresham Library, Sam Houston State University. In between his appointment and the end of the administration, Birdsall had served as acting chief justice. His partnership with Houston was short lived, as Birdsall died of yellow fever seven months later.

4. "Proprietor's Notice Concerning the City of Sabine," 1 May 1839, in Barker and Williams, *Writings of Sam Houston*, 2:312–14. The best job of placing the scheme in perspective is De Bruhl, *Sword of San Jacinto*, 258ff. It was Sublett who had nominated Houston for president in 1836 and, indeed, had signed the resolution nominating him to command the Nacogdoches militia in 1835. He remained a Houston intimate until his death in 1850. Many other papers of the City of Sabine venture, including the company's constitution, the conveyances of Houston's lots, and announcements of shareholder meetings, which continued for many years, are in the Franklin Williams Collection, Sam Houston Regional Library and Research Center.

5. Terrell, "Recollections of General Sam Houston," 117. Sublett related the story to his older brother, Henry, who took Alexander Terrell's place in a law partnership in 1857.

6. Sam Houston, passport, Secretaries of the State, Domestic Records, Texas State Library and Archives.

7. Hunt to Lamar, 31 May 1839, in Gulick et al., *Papers of Mirabeau Buonaparte Lamar*, 3:7.

8. Hunt to Lamar, 13 July 1839, in Gulick et al., *Papers of Mirabeau Buonaparte Lamar*, 3:42. Hunt had spent six months as Lamar's secretary of the navy until, just previous to his departure, the new president appointed him to the Boundary Commission.

9. William Christy to Houston, 20 July 1839, Penny Thornall Remick Collection, Sam Houston Regional Library and Research Center.

10. Seale, *Sam Houston's Wife*, 11; Roberts, *Star of Destiny*, 18–19.

11. "Contract with Hickman Lewis for Blooded Stock," 30 August 1839, in Barker and Williams, *Writings of Sam Houston*, 2:313–14. Houston may have done very well by the stock purchased with his land scrip. After the horses were safely landed in Texas, Houston received a letter

from one breeder very anxious to see and buy them. John W. Floyd to Houston, 30 December 1841, Sam Houston Papers, Catholic Archives of Texas, Chancery of the Austin Diocese.

12. Scrapbook of clippings, Tennessee State Library and Archives, quoted in James, *The Raven*, 309. James identified the "Judge Wallace" who recalled the scene as Houston's cousin. I suspect it may have been Judge William Wallace, husband of Houston's younger sister, Mary.

13. Margaret Moffette Lea, "Lines to a Withered Pink," June 1839, General Collections, Sam Houston Memorial Museum.

14. Lubbock, *Six Decades in Texas*, 43.

15. Ibid., 93.

16. Tyler et al., *New Handbook of Texas*, 5:1109, 6:847.

17. Ashbel Smith, "Sketch Life of Sam Houston," Ashbel Smith Papers, University of Texas.

18. Anson Jones et al., to Houston, 11 November 1839, Sam Houston Papers, Thomason Room (Special Collections), Newton Gresham Library, Sam Houston State University.

19. Houston to Anna Raguet, 10 December 1839, in Barker and Williams, *Writings of Sam Houston*, 2:322–23.

20. "In Behalf of the Cherokee Land Bill," 22 December 1839, in Barker and Williams, *Writings of Sam Houston*, 2:342.

21. "On the Removal of the Capital from Austin," 2–3 December 1839, in Barker and Williams, *Writings of Sam Houston*, 2:315–21.

22. "In Behalf of the Cherokee Land Bill," 22 December 1839, 2:323–48.

23. John M. Hansford to Houston, 4 January 1840, Sam Houston Papers, Catholic Archives of Texas.

24. Marquis James (*The Raven*, 310) refers to the following tale as traditional.

25. For a more general history of this proposed legislation, see Denton, "Count Alphonso de Saligny."

26. J. P. Henderson to Houston, 8 July 1839; and I. Maria McManus to Houston, 20 April 1840, Sam Houston Papers, Catholic Archives of Texas. Followers of Houston's sobriety will be reassured to know that McManus meant the word "saloon" in its European, not its American, usage.

27. Houston to Robert Irion, 27 January 1840, Texas Collections, University of Texas, photocopy, quoted in Flanagan, *Sam Houston's Texas*, 55.

28. Houston to Anna Raguet, 19 June 1838, Sam Houston Papers, Center for American History, University of Texas.

29. Houston to Anna Raguet, 29 January 1840, Margaret B. Rost Collection, Sam Houston Memorial Museum.

30. Quoted in Crook, "Sam Houston and Eliza Allen," 2.

31. Lubbock, *Six Decades in Texas*, 98.

32. "The Reply to a Dinner Invitation," 28 August 1840, in Barker and Williams, *Writings of Sam Houston*, 2:351. If the meeting was ultimately held, no extract seems to have survived, but as the editors of the correspondence point out, this was not unusual even for Houston's appearances.

33. Bernard Bee to Ashbel Smith, 5 June 1840, Ashbel Smith Papers; Crane, *Life and Select Literary Remains*, 253. Reverend Crane was well acquainted with the Leas before the time of Margaret's marriage.

34. Houston to Margaret, 28 September 1840, in Barker and Williams, *Writings of Sam Houston*, 2:352.

35. "Speech Concerning the Cherokee Bill," 4 December 1840, in Barker and Williams, *Writings of Sam Houston*, 2:354–62.

36. Houston to Anthony Butler, 2 February 1841, in Barker and Williams, *Writings of Sam Houston*, 2:365–66. Butler was by now a citizen of Texas and lately congressman from Washington County.

37. Williams, *Houston and the War of Independence*, 256–57.

38. Washington Miller to Houston, 27 February 1841, Washington Miller Papers, Texas State Library and Archives.

39. Citizens of San Augustine to Houston, 8 April 1841, Sam Houston Papers, Thomason Room, Sam Houston State University.

40. G. W. Terrell to Houston, 25 July 1841, Sam Houston Papers, Catholic Archives of Texas.

41. Ford, *Rip Ford's Texas*, 17.

42. Houston to William G. Harding, 17 July 1841, in Barker and Williams, *Writings of Sam Houston*, 3:10–11.

43. Lamar, "To the People of Santa Fé," April 14, 1840, Texas Army Papers, Texas State Library and Archives. The subsequent history of this outfit so disposed itself that memoirs stemming from it are virulently anti-Houston. See George Wilkins Kendall, *Narrative of the Texan Santa Fe Expedition* (Chicago, R. R. Donnelly and Sons, 1929); and Thomas Falconer, *Letters and Notes on the Texan Santa Fe Expedition, 1841–1842* (New York: Dauber and Pine, 1930). For a more scholarly treatment, see H. Bailey Carroll, *Texan Santa Fe Trail* (Canyon, Tex.: Panhandle-Plains Historical Society, 1951).

44. Houston to [*Austin City Gazette*], 10 August 1841, in Barker and Williams, *Writings of Sam Houston*, 2:372–73.

45. Miller to Houston, 10 July 1841, Washington Miller Papers.

46. Barker and Williams, *Writings of Sam Houston*, 2:389n.

47. Wallis and Hill, *Sixty Years on the Brazos*, 292.

48. "Replies to Publius," 16, 18 August 1841, in Barker and Williams, *Writings of Sam Houston*, 2:376–86.

49. Houston to Ashbel Smith, 4 August 1841, in Barker and Williams, *Writings of Sam Houston*, 2:371. The Frank mentioned was Houston's slave.

50. Houston to Samuel May Williams, 28 July 1841, in Barker and Williams, *Writings of Sam Houston*, 2:369–70; Linn, Reminiscences, quoted in Williams, *Houston and the War of Independence*, 31.

51. The entirety of the "Publius" diatribe was carried in the *Telegraph and Texas Register*, August–September 1841.

52. B. J. White to Houston, 19 March 1842; and George W. Terrell to Houston, 25 July 1841, Sam Houston Papers, Catholic Archives of Texas.

53. Bateman, "Waterloo Scrapbook," *Austin American-Statesman, 12 December 1986. The* green velvet cap, minus its feathers but otherwise in pristine condition, was recently acquired by the Sam Houston Memorial Museum in Huntsville, Texas. Du Bois de Saligny did not overstate its appearance.

54. Edward Winfield to Ashbel Smith, 22 September 1841, Ashbel Smith Papers.

55. "To a Committee of Supporters at Crockett," 30 October 1841, in Barker and Williams, *Writings of Sam Houston*, 2:389–90.

56. Houston to Ashbel Smith, 11 November 1841, in Barker and Williams, *Writings of Sam Houston*, 2:390.

57. "Address of General Sam Houston, President Elect, at Houston, November 25, 1841," Barker and Williams, *Writings of Sam Houston*, 2:391–97.

58. Margaret to Houston, 10 November 1840, in Roberts, *Personal Correspondence of Sam Houston*, 1:38. Pamela Mann had since become Mrs. T. K. Brown.

59. Margaret to Houston, 6 December 1841, in Roberts, *Personal Correspondence of Sam Houston*, 1:120–23.

60. Houston to Margaret, 30 November 1841, in Roberts, *Personal Correspondence of Sam Houston*, 1:112–14.

61. Margaret to Houston, 6 December 1841, in Roberts, *Personal Correspondence of Sam Houston*, 1:120–23. Margaret's ability to anticipate her husband's thoughts extended once during this

period to whether or not to hire out her slave, Joshua. Houston to Margaret, 30 November 1841; and Margaret to Houston, 5 December 1841, in ibid., 1:114, 118.

62. Crane, *Life and Select Literary Remains*, 248–49. James W. Scott is one of Houston's less remembered protégés but apparently enjoyed a high degree of favor. He arrived in Texas, at the age of about twenty, the day San Jacinto was fought and by the end of the year was a lieutenant, later accompanying Houston to Stephen F. Austin's funeral at Peach Point. By 1841 he had married and gone into business with Frank Lubbock in Houston; he later represented Harris County in the Third and Fourth Legislatures. Tyler et al., *New Handbook of Texas*, 5:937.

63. "Address of Austin Committee to Sam Houston upon Inauguration as Third President of the Republic of Texas," 20 November 1841, Washington Miller Papers.

64. Houston to Margaret, 9 December 1841, in Roberts, *Personal Correspondence of Sam Houston*, 1:125.

65. As Angelina Peyton, she married her cousin, Jonathan Peyton, and came to Texas in 1822. They operated a tavern in San Felipe from 1825; she was widowed in 1834, and then after her business was destroyed in the Runaway Scrape in 1836, she removed to Columbia. Peyton married Jacob Eberly and moved to Bastrop and then to Austin when it became the capital of the country. Never a shrinking violet where business matters were concerned, Mrs. Eberly later operated establishments in Galveston and Indianola, leaving behind a fortune of fifty thousand dollars when she died in 1860. See Kemp, "Mrs. Angelina B. Eberly," 196.

66. Houston to Margaret, 12 December 1841, in Roberts, *Personal Correspondence of Sam Houston*, 1:130. Judge G. W. Terrell is not to be confused with Judge A. W. Terrell, for whom Terrell County was named.

67. Lubbock, *Six Decades in Texas*, 141–42.

68. Gregg, *Diary and Letters of Josiah Gregg*, 109.

69. Lubbock, *Six Decades in Texas*, 142.

70. *Austin Daily Bulletin*, 14 December 1841; Houston to Margaret, 13 December 1841, in Roberts, *Personal Correspondence of Sam Houston*, 1:134.

CHAPTER 14

1. Houston to Hockley, 13 December 1841; Houston to Jones, 13 December 1841; Houston to Miller; 13 December 1841; and Houston to Brigham, 16 December 1841, in Barker and Williams, *Writings of Sam Houston*, 2:397–99.

2. I. F. Winfred to Houston, 24 August 1841; and "A. L. Kern and 63 Others" to Houston, 12 October 1841, Sam Houston Papers, Catholic Archives of Texas.

3. Houston to Margaret, 13 December 1841, in Roberts, *Personal Correspondence of Sam Houston*, 1:135–36; "Report to the Congress Concerning the Condition of the President's Residence," 23 December 1841, in Barker and Williams, *Writings of Sam Houston*, 2:409–14.

4. "Washington Miller, Appointment as Private Secretary to the President," Washington Miller Papers, Texas State Library and Archives.

5. Jones, *Memoranda and Official Correspondence*, 34–36.

6. "First Message to Congress, Second Administration," 20 December 1841, in Barker and Williams, *Writings of Sam Houston*, 2:399–408.

7. "Recommendation that March 2, Be Made a National Thanksgiving Day," 17 January 1842, in Barker and Williams, *Writings of Sam Houston*, 2:431.

8. G. W. Terrell to Houston, 25 July 1841, Sam Houston Papers, Catholic Archives of Texas.

9. "Proclamation against the Regulators," 31 January 1842, in Barker and Williams, *Writings of Sam Houston*, 2:459–61. For a general history of the feud itself, see Oran M. Roberts, "The Shelby War, or, the Regulators and the Moderators," *Texas Magazine* 3 (August 1897). Roberts, later a governor of Texas, was a lawyer in San Augustine and Shelbyville throughout much of the dispute.

10. "Houston to the House of Representatives," 1 February 1842, in Barker and Williams, *Writings of Sam Houston*, 2:462–65.

11. Houston to Robert A. Irion, 6 January 1842, Margaret B. Rost Collection, Sam Houston Memorial Museum.

12. "Houston to the Texas Congress," 2 February 1842, in Barker and Williams, *Writings of Sam Houston*, 2:471–72. It would be interesting to learn whether King Leopold's interest in Texas might have owed in some part to his father-in-law and player in the Texas game, Louis Philippe.

13. Gard, *Frontier Justice*, 200n (citing *Houston Morning Star*, 7 October 1842).

14. Houston, "A Proclamation Concerning Free Negroes in Texas," 5 February 1842, in Barker and Williams, *Writings of Sam Houston*, 2:476–77. See also Tyler et al., *New Handbook of Texas*, 2:1165.

15. Houston to Miller, 15 February 1842, in Barker and Williams, *Writings of Sam Houston*, 2:484–85. "Wynnes" was Houston lawyer Archibald Wynns, who represented Harris County in the Sixth Congress.

16. Silverthorne, *Ashbel Smith of Texas*, 72–73. The site of the Texan mission in London, located a short distance from St. James's Palace, is now the headquarters of Cutty Sark distillers.

17. James Hamilton to Houston, 24 February 1842, enclosing Du Bois de Saligny to Hamilton, 28 January 1842; and Sir Charles Elliot to Houston, 10 January 1842, Sam Houston Papers, Catholic Archives of Texas; Silverthorne, *Ashbel Smith of Texas*, 74.

18. Houston to George W. Brown, 3 March 1842, in Barker and Williams, *Writings of Sam Houston*, 4:73–76. Brown later came on anyway after Houston did call for volunteers shortly afterward. He rose to distinction as a district attorney and representative to the Convention of 1845.

19. G. W. Hockley to Houston, 28 February 1842, Sam Houston Papers, Catholic Archives of Texas.

20. Miller to Houston, 16, 23 February 1842, Washington Miller Papers.

21. Miller to Houston, 6 March 1842, Washington Miller Papers.

22. Hockley to Houston, 7 March 1842, Sam Houston Papers, Center for American History, University of Texas.

23. "Houston to the House of Representatives," 1 February 1842, in Barker and Williams, *Writings of Sam Houston*, 2:462–65.

24. Houston to Alexander Somervell, 10 March 1842, in Barker and Williams, *Writings of Sam Houston*, 2:492–93.

25. Houston to Edwin Morehouse, 18 March 1842, in Barker and Williams, *Writings of Sam Houston*, 2:511.

26. Houston to Robert Irion, 14 April 1842, Rost Collection; G. W. Terrell to Houston, 18 March 1842; and W. Richardson to Houston, 7 May 1842, enclosing Thomas O'Connor et al. to Houston, Sam Houston Papers, Catholic Archives of Texas. The president's letter to Irion conveyed "our love to your Lady, young Sam, and yourself." Sam Houston Irion was followed by four more children; with a growing family to feed, Irion could not afford to work for a government with not a dollar in the treasury, and returned to his medical practice. He died in 1861; Anna Raguet Irion survived until 1883. Tyler et al., *New Handbook of Texas*, 3:868–69.

27. Houston to Washington Miller, 17 March 1842, in Barker and Williams, *Writings of Sam Houston*, 2:507–8.

28. G. W. Terrell to Houston, 8 February 1842, Sam Houston Papers, Catholic Archives of Texas; Miller to Houston, 9 February 1842, Washington Miller Papers.

29. Houston to A. D. Coombs and N. H. Watrous, 24 March 1842, in Barker and Williams, *Writings of Sam Houston*, 2:533–34.

30. Houston to Santa Anna, 21 March 1842, in Barker and Williams, *Writings of Sam Houston*, 2:513–27; Guy M. Bryan et al. to Houston, 28 March 1842, Sam Houston Papers, Thomason Room (Special Collections), Newton Gresham Library, Sam Houston State University.

31. Houston to W. H. Daingerfield, 1 April 1842, in Barker and Williams, *Writings of Sam Houston*, 3:14–16.

32. Houston, "A Proclamation to All Texans," 14 April 1842, in Barker and Williams, *Writings of Sam Houston*, 3:26–32.

33. Houston to Barry Gillespie, 14 June 1842, Sam Houston Papers, Center for American History.

34. P. Edmunds to Houston, 3 February 1842, Sam Houston Papers, Catholic Archives of Texas; Houston to Daingerfield, 16, 17 May 1842; and Houston to Captain Rollins, or Captain Wright, 23 May 1842, in Barker and Williams, *Writings of Sam Houston*, 3:53–54, 57. The bearer was Frank Lubbock's brother, Thomas, then in the employ of Texas' New Orleans bankers, McKinney and Williams.

35. Joseph Waples to Houston, 31 July 1842, enclosing draft of Waples to Eve, 30 July 1842, in Garrison, *Diplomatic Correspondence*, pt. 1, 574–75 (with supporting documents cited or reproduced at 580–89); Houston to Eve, 30 July 1842, in Barker and Williams, *Writings of Sam Houston*, 3:135. Waples was appointed acting secretary of state when Anson Jones took an approved leave of absence. Houston to Waples, 5 February 1842, in Barker and Williams, *Writings of Sam Houston*, 2:478. Not surprisingly, Means was, like most Texas creditors, still trying to collect at the end of the year. Joseph Eve to Anson Jones, 30 December 1842, in Garrison, *Diplomatic Correspondence*, pt. 1, 644–45.

36. James Reily to Houston, 9 February 1842, Sam Houston Papers, Catholic Archives of Texas.

37. Houston to Terrell, 16 May 1842; and Houston to L. B. Franks, 21 May 1842, in Barker and Williams, *Writings of Sam Houston*, 3:52, 55–56; Tyler et al., *New Handbook of Texas*, 2:1156.

38. Houston to "Mr. Lumsden," 18 May 1842, in Barker and Williams, *Writings of Sam Houston*, 3:55. The president sent a similar and even lengthier injunction to Col. Lewis M. H. Washington four days later. Ibid., 56–57.

39. P. Edmunds to Houston, 18 March 1842; and B. J. White to Houston, 19 March 1842, Sam Houston Papers, Catholic Archives of Texas.

40. P. Edmunds to Houston, 23 March 1842; and James Reily to Houston, 13 April, 9 May 1842, Sam Houston Papers, Catholic Archives of Texas.

41. Reily to Houston, 13 April 1842, Sam Houston Papers, Catholic Archives of Texas.

42. Houston, "An Election Proclamation," 24 May 1842, in Barker and Williams, *Writings of Sam Houston*, 3:59. Potter had returned to his home on Caddo Lake, where he tried to arrest a neighbor to claim the five hundred dollar reward on his head. The neighbor escaped by hiding in a brush pile, and several days later a mob surrounded the Potter house and demanded his surrender. Potter sought escape by diving into the lake but was shot through the head when he came up for air. See, generally, Fischer, *Robert Potter*.

43. "Houston to the Texas Congress," 22 July 1842, in Barker and Williams, *Writings of Sam Houston*, 3:116–24.

44. Houston to Jones, 2 August 1842, with endorsements, in Barker and Williams, *Writings of Sam Houston*, 3:137–39. The Mr. Johnson mentioned in Houston's letter was R. D. Johnson, the postmaster in Galveston. Jones's second amendment to this letter must have been a symptom of his later growing derangement, for he accurately assessed Houston's policy to Isaac Van Zandt early the following year: "The late Campaign under Gen. Somervell was not projected or recommended by the President. It was merely sanctioned to satisfy popular clamor, and . . . to clothe the expedition with legal authority that in case it was unfortunate . . . they could not be regarded or treated by [Mexico] otherwise than lawful belligerents." Jones to Van Zandt, 16 February 1843, in Garrison, *Diplomatic Correspondence*, pt. 2, 125–27.

45. Houston to Richard Roman, 10 August 1842, in Barker and Williams, *Writings of Sam Houston*, 3:142–45. Roman was a hero of San Jacinto who had since seen action inside Mexico as a soldier of fortune in the service of the Federalist army in 1839. It is not surprising that he was eager to go.

46. William Christy to Houston, 22 July 1842, Nancy Burch Collection, Sam Houston Regional Library and Research Center; Tyler et al., *New Handbook of Texas*, 6:824–25. These sources list his birth year as 1799, although Christy's intimate knowledge of Warfield at age twenty-six would place his birth year about 1816. His early history has largely fallen from Texas' memory, although he served in the Eighth Legislature.

47. "Memorandum of Conference between Houston and Eve and Elliot," 10 September 1842; and Joseph Waples to Joseph Eve, 14 September 1842, in Garrison, *Diplomatic Correspondence*, pt. 1, 606–8.

48. Hockley to Houston, 1 September 1842, Burch Collection; Houston to Hockley, 1, 2 September 1842; and Houston to Terrell, 1 September 1842, in Barker and Williams, *Writings of Sam Houston*, 4:135–41.

49. Flanagan, *Sam Houston's Texas*, 63; undated manuscript, Ashbel Smith Papers.

50. Houston to Daingerfield, 2 April 1842, in Barker and Williams, *Writings of Sam Houston*, 3:37–40.

51. "Orders to the Country," 15 September 1842, in Barker and Williams, *Writings of Sam Houston*, 7:6–7.

52. Houston to William Y. McFarland, 10 September 1842, in Barker and Williams, *Writings of Sam Houston*, 3:155. This individual is not to be confused, as the editors of Houston's correspondence did, with the William McFarland whom Houston appointed chief justice of San Augustine County in 1836 (who died in 1840). See Barker and Williams, *Writings of Sam Houston*, 2:66; and Tyler et al., *New Handbook of Texas*, 4:399–400.

53. Lubbock, *Six Decades in Texas*, 148; "Houston to the Texas Senate," 13 January 1843, in Barker and Williams, *Writings of Sam Houston*, 3:291–92. This text is cited as from the *Congressional Record Book*, no. 40, 207. The duplicate text in the papers of the Sixth Congress appears in Barker and Williams, *Writings of Sam Houston*, 2:430, as a result of the file copy being misdated as the previous year—a common January error.

54. T. W. Ward to Houston, 30 October 1842, Sam Houston Papers, Center for American History; Wallis and Hill, *Sixty Years on the Brazos*, 161–64. Pettus, who had been one of the camp guards at San Jacinto, died two years later at Washington-on-the-Brazos. Hall was a longtime resident of the town, and it was he who rented the building in which the Texas Declaration of Independence was written. Hall died a few months after Pettus. Tyler et al., *New Handbook of Texas*, 3:414, 5:173.

55. Ward sent two letters on the same day, the official one advising that he had closed the Land Office, and this private one (quoted in the text) pleading for money. Thomas William Ward to Houston, 28 September 1842 (two letters), Burch Collection.

56. Roberts, *Star of Destiny*, 94–95.

57. Wallis and Hill, *Sixty Years on the Brazos*, 156–57.

58. Houston to Anson Jones, 19 September 1842, in Jones, *Memoranda and Official Correspondence*, 196–97. The editors of Houston's correspondence curiously omitted the "Truly your friend" from the signature, a substantive omission in a letter from one who only closed letters in such manner to those he believed loyal. Barker and Williams, *Writings of Sam Houston*, 3:160–61.

59. Wallis and Hill, *Sixty Years on the Brazos*, 41; Holland, "Reminiscences of Austin and Old Washington," 94–95. The other saloon was the enterprise of John Rumsey, who because he did extend credit was sometimes reduced to collecting bills with statements like, "Dad blame you, pay me what you owe me!"

60. Wallis and Hill, *Sixty Years on the Brazos*, 264–65. A later letter from Houston to Margaret confirms Lockhart's unusual observation, for he signed it, "Thy devoted Husband, Sam Houston—with a steel pen!!!" Houston to Margaret, 9 November 1848, in Roberts, *Personal Correspondence of Sam Houston*, 3:3.

61. Houston to Franks, 26 September 1842, in Barker and Williams, *Writings of Sam Houston*, 3:168.

62. Wallis and Hill, *Sixty Years on the Brazos*, 158.

63. For these services Chisholm received a $150 payment the following spring. Houston to Asa Brigham, 12 April 1843, in Barker and Williams, *Writings of Sam Houston*, 3:354–55 (and documents following). Similar payments were made to Thomas M. Hawkins, a brother of Ben Hawkins of the previous Creek Indian business, to Luis Sanchez and to several Delaware Indians.

64. Houston to Chenoweth, 8 October 1842, in Barker and Williams, *Writings of Sam Houston*, 3:174–75. Chenoweth, like so many others whom Houston considered reliable, was a San Jacinto veteran. He was furloughed from the army long enough to represent Goliad in the First Congress of the republic. Houston's closing reference to fair compensation may have hearkened back to the army privations of summer and fall of 1836, when Chenoweth had been forced to provide for his men out of his own pocket. Tyler et al., *New Handbook of Texas*, 2:58.

65. Houston to Indian Commissioners, 9, 17 October 1842, in Barker and Williams, *Writings of Sam Houston*, 3:175–77, 184–85. The addendum may have been a late-night afterthought, for it is entirely in Houston's handwriting. Ibid., 185n.

66. Chandler, in fact, took seventeen with him, and they were gone twenty-five days. A note penned on his bill for services by G. W. Terrell indicates that the rangers were depended on "to preserve order at the treaty—as we apprehend danger of disturbance from our own people as well as from the Indians." Houston to Chandler, 18 October 1842, in Barker and Williams, *Writings of Sam Houston*, 3:185.

67. Houston to G. W. Terrell, 21 October 1842, in Barker and Williams, *Writings of Sam Houston*, 3:189.

68. Houston to Terrell et al., 13 November 1842; and Houston to Col. L. B. Franks, 13 November 1842, in Barker and Williams, *Writings of Sam Houston*, 3:195–96.

69. Wallis and Hill, *Sixty Years on the Brazos*, 96.

70. Houston to Bagby, 18 December 1842, in Barker and Williams, *Writings of Sam Houston*, 3:236. The originals of this and other letters to Bagby are in the Houston Public Library, of which Bagby was a founder, and which now occupies the site of his house. Tyler et al., *New Handbook of Texas*, 1:333.

71. "Annual Message to the Texas Congress," 1 December 1842, in Barker and Williams, *Writings of Sam Houston*, 7:203–16.

72. Houston to Charles Elliot, 5 November 1842, in Barker and Williams, *Writings of Sam Houston*, 3:191–92.

73. Wisehart, *Sam Houston*, 379; Wallis and Hill, *Sixty Years on the Brazos*, 59.

74. Orders and separate letter to Smith and Chander; "Proclamation Ordering the Removal of the Archives from Austin"; and Houston to Ward, all 10 December 1842, in Barker and Williams, *Writings of Sam Houston*, 3:226–30.

75. Kemp, "Mrs. Angelina Eberley," 196ff.

76. Ward to Houston, 8 January 1843, in Barker and Williams, *Writings of Sam Houston*, 3:230–31.

77. Houston to A. B. Roman, 12 September, 29 October 1842, in Garrison, *Diplomatic Correspondence*, pt. 2, 101–2.

78. "Houston to the Texas Congress," 22 December 1842, in Barker and Williams, *Writings of Sam Houston*, 3:241–48. Houston made a point of labeling this communication SECRET, "so the world will not know the deplorable condition" to which the navy had degraded.

79. Anson Jones to Isaac Van Zandt, 25 December 1842, enclosing James Hamilton to Houston, 6 November, 27 December 1842, in Garrison, *Diplomatic Correspondence*, pt. 1, 636–40; Jones to Hamilton, 26 December 1842, in *Diplomatic Correspondence*, pt. 2, 784–85. This was not the first time that Almonte had been mentioned as a possible alternative Mexican authority; Houston had received a letter on the identical subject the day after the revolutionary cannon boomed at Gonza-

les. Samuel Sawyer to Houston, 3 October 1835, A. J. Houston Collection, Texas State Library and Archives.

CHAPTER 15

1. "Houston to the Texas Congress," 4 January 1843, in Barker and Williams, *Writings of Sam Houston*, 3:262–67.

2. Houston to Washington Miller, 31 August 1855, Sam Houston Papers, Catholic Archives of Texas, Chancery of the Austin Diocese.

3. Roberts, *Star of Destiny*, 100.

4. James, *The Raven*, 212 (quoting Samuel Swartwout to Houston, 10 May 1835, "in the possession of a Houston descendent"). In the spring before the revolution, Swartwout sought to engage Houston to track down a land investment that had gone awry, expressing the hope that Houston would stay sober "till you get my land, I hope." Afterward, "I long to have a bottle of old Madeira with you." Swartwout further said that Houston's description of his lands on the Red River "made me too *appy* as poor old Genl. La fayette used to say."

5. Wallis and Hill, *Sixty Years on the Brazos*, 119; Roberts, *Star of Destiny*, 99. These two sources are the most authentic, the first being the only eyewitness account, and the second being the tradition that has endured in the Houston family. The incident is, of course, replayed in nearly all the biographies, with various ornaments and elaborations.

6. Houston to William Bryan, 24 January 1843, in Barker and Williams, *Writings of Sam Houston*, 3:304–5. Bryan was called upon to shop for everything from guitar strings (two sets) to a barrel of herrings to a four-seat Barouche. Houston arranged for payment on goods and freight to be made by his old friend Gail Borden in Galveston so that there was no raid on the national funds—which did not prevent Houston enemy Thomas Jefferson Green from penning a snide note on a certified copy now in the Rosenberg Library. The original of Green's note is in the Burnley Papers, Texas State Library and Archives. Houston's eager young protégé at Washington-on-the-Brazos, John Lockhart, overheard Houston dictating this letter, and the imagery of wild boars and stud horses painted such a picture in his mind that, half a century later, he was able to recall the phrase almost exactly. Wallis and Hill, *Sixty Years on the Brazos*, 120.

7. Houston to Elliot, 24 January 1843, in Barker and Williams, *Writings of Sam Houston*, 3:299–302.

8. Houston to Bagby, 20 February 1843, in Barker and Williams, *Writings of Sam Houston*, 3:323–34. All of Houston's letters to young Tom Bagby evince great and genuine affection, and it is plain that the president enjoyed both the relationship and the correspondence. "You write with so much ease and eloquence that you ought to write often. And furthermore, I am always happy to hear from you. . . . Bagby, do write, I pray you?"

9. J. A. Eaton, "Instructions to Agents," 16 February 1830, A. J. Houston Collection, Texas State Library and Archives. "Agents will inform the Indians, that the Government in future will not pay their expenses to the seat of Government, unless specifically authorized to come." Houston to Bryant, 24 February 1843, in Barker and Williams, *Writings of Sam Houston*, 3:324–25.

10. Houston to James Ross, 24 February 1843, in Barker and Williams, *Writings of Sam Houston*, 3:325. Ross was a Washington-on-the-Brazos merchant from whom Houston requisitioned the goods, and he then had to endorse the order, "Judge Toler, Be so good if you please to call on Maj. Brigham for the amount necessary, and I will give him an order on the Indian fund for the current year."

11. "A Testimony of John Castro's Friendship for the People of Texas," 28 March 1843; Houston to Asa Brigham, 29 March 1843; and Houston to Stephen Z. Hoyle, 1 April 1843, in Barker and Williams, *Writings of Sam Houston*, 3:343–50. David Torrey, head of the firm, was ironically killed by Brazos Indians a couple of years later. His brother James fell victim to the "Black Bean" incident

at Hacienda Salado. Houston to Hoyle. Little is known of Hoyle, although he had been secretary of the Senate and became Anson Jones's private secretary in 1845. Tyler et al., *New Handbook of Texas*, 3:754.

12. "Notes of Indian Talks &c at Council Held at Washington, April 1843," Washington Miller Papers, Texas State Library and Archives.

13. Wallis and Hill, *Sixty Years on the Brazos*, 104–5; "Treaty with Various Indian Tribes," 24 August 1842, Penny Thornall Remick Collection, Sam Houston Regional Library and Research Center.

14. Wallis and Hill, *Sixty Years on the Brazos*, 105–6.

15. Houston to Asa Brigham, 25 April 1843, in Barker and Williams, *Writings of Sam Houston*, 3:365–66.

16. Houston to Pah-Hah-You-Co, Comanche Chief, 4 May 1843; and Houston to Asa Brigham, 6 May 1843, in Barker and Williams, *Writings of Sam Houston*, 3:372–75.

17. Houston to A-Cah-Quash, Waco Chief, 19 April 1843, in Barker and Williams, *Writings of Sam Houston*, 3:363–64. The chief's words, in which Houston took confidence, were recorded by Miller at the council: "Foolish young men may come in to steal horses, not knowing" that peace had been concluded. "Notes of Indian Talks," Miller Papers.

18. Wallis and Hill, *Sixty Years on the Brazos*, 107–8.

19. "Notes on Indian Talks," Miller Papers.

20. Houston to J. F. Torrey and Company, 14 April 1843 (four different warrants), in Barker and Williams, *Writings of Sam Houston*, 3:356–58.

21. Houston to Joseph Eve, 17 February 1843, in Garrison, *Diplomatic Correspondence*, pt. 2, 128.

22. Wallis and Hill, *Sixty Years on the Brazos*, 187.

23. Houston to Santa Anna, 10 April 1843, in Barker and Williams, *Writings of Sam Houston*, 3:351–53.

24. Lubbock, *Six Decades in Texas*, 154.

25. Houston to Joseph Eve, 6 May 1843; Houston to Charles Elliot, 6 May 1843; and Houston to Cramayel, 6 May 1843, in Garrison, *Diplomatic Correspondence*, pt. 2, 174–75, 1089, 1445.

26. Houston to Elliot, 15 June 1843, in Barker and Williams, *Writings of Sam Houston*, 4:211.

27. Houston to Dr. Cornelius McAnelly, 24 April 1843, in Barker and Williams, *Writings of Sam Houston*, 4:193.

28. Roberts, *Star of Destiny*, 99; treasury warrant, 6 January 1843, Sam Houston Papers, Thomason Room (Special Collections), Newton Gresham Library, Sam Houston State University.

29. The biographer who provided this excerpt also noted with considerable perceptiveness that this was a key element of Houston's gaining and keeping popular favor. "It was [his] custom to acquaint himself with the antecedents of new-comers to Texas as far as he could, and attach them to himself by friendly interest and hospitality. If, however, they showed signs of rivalry or opposition to him, he was apt to . . . be as harsh and sarcastic as he had before been friendly." Williams, *Houston and the War of Independence*, 292–93.

30. Guild, *Old Times in Tennessee*, 289–90. Guild erroneously remembered the man in question as named Hall, but it would have had to be a brother of John C. Hale, a lieutenant in Sherman's regiment, who was killed; both Halls at San Jacinto survived. There is no record, of course, of anyone dying in Houston's arms at San Jacinto. Guild himself was no exception to Houston's incessant link-forging; Guild's wife was a cousin of William and Richardson Scurry.

31. Houston to Anson Jones, 10 June 1843, in Garrison, *Diplomatic Correspondence*, pt. 2, 785–86.

32. Joseph Eve to Houston, 10 June 1843, in Garrison, *Diplomatic Correspondence*, pt. 2, 190–91; biographical note on Eve, in Barker and Williams, *Writings of Sam Houston*, 3:135–36n. See also Tyler et al., *New Handbook of Texas*, 2:908; 4:894–95.

33. Isaac Van Zandt to Houston, 16 October 1843, Remick Collection.

34. *National Vindicator*, 2 December 1843.

35. See Davis, *Three Roads to the Alamo*, 167.

36. "To the Texas Congress—Annual Message," 12 December 1843, in Barker and Williams, *Writings of Sam Houston*, 3:459, 464. For more on the ineffective but, all things considered, lucky expedition, see Carroll, "Steward A. Miller and the Snively Expedition."

37. Jackson to Houston, 18 January 1844, Nancy Burch Collection, Sam Houston Regional Library and Research Center; William Rozier, 1874, Audited Pension Application, Republic Claim Files, Texas State Library and Archives.

38. "Houston's Opinion of the Reverend James Hazard Perry," in Barker and Williams, *Writings of Sam Houston*, 4:272–74.

39. Washington Miller to Jackson, 7 April 1844, in Bassett, *Correspondence of Andrew Jackson*, 6:276–77; Jackson to Houston, 15 March 1844, quoted in Remini, *Andrew Jackson and the Course of American Democracy*, 492–95.

40. Houston to Isaac Van Zandt and J. Pinckney Henderson, 29 April 1844, in Garrison, *Diplomatic Correspondence*, pt. 2, 274–76.

41. Houston to Isaac Van Zandt and J. Pinckney Henderson, 17 May 1844, in Garrison, *Diplomatic Correspondence*, pt. 2, 281–83.

42. Ashbel Smith to Houston, Burch Collection.

43. W. S. Murphy to Houston, 3 July 1844, Sam Houston Papers, Catholic Archives of Texas.

44. Houston to Santa Anna, 29 July 1844, in Barker and Williams, *Writings of Sam Houston*, 4:346–47.

45. "An Open Letter to My Countrymen," 16 August 1844, in Barker and Williams, *Writings of Sam Houston*, 4:361–62.

46. Gard, *Frontier Justice*, 39.

47. Travis Broocks to Houston, 23 August 1844, Sam Houston Papers, Catholic Archives of Texas. In another letter three days previous, Brooks apparently suggested asking supplies from the American army at Fort Jessup, which Houston advised him would be against U.S. Army regulations. Houston to Travis Broocks, 23 August 1844; Houston to Gen. James Smith, 23 August 1844; and Houston to Smith, 26 August 1844, in Barker and Williams, *Writings of Sam Houston*, 4:365–67. Smith had won Houston's respect when, during the terrible army privations of 1837, Smith spent large sums of his own money to care for the volunteer company he had raised and brought to Texas. He and Houston parted company over the 1839 Cherokee War, for which Smith also raised a company of volunteers, but it is clear from their 1844 correspondence that the general still held Houston's regard. Ibid., 363n. Smith later donated acreage from his family farm for the town site of Henderson.

48. See generally C. L. Sonnichsen, *I'll Die before I'll Run: The Story of the Great Feuds of Texas* (New York: Harper, 1951).

49. "An Open Letter to My Countrymen," 4:361–62.

50. Houston *Telegraph and Texas Register*, 21 August 1844.

51. Tyler et al., *New Handbook of Texas*, 3:962. J. W. Lockhart remembered Johnson as the editor of the *Register*, the name to which he changed the paper the following December. Wallis and Hill, *Sixty Years on the Brazos*, 157.

52. Houston to J. C. Neill, 10 September 1844, in Barker and Williams, *Writings of Sam Houston*, 4:368.

53. Gard, *Rawhide Texas*, 35.

54. "Treaty of Tehuacana Creek," 9 October 1844, Texas State Library and Archives, quoted in Wallace and Vigness, *Documents of Texas History*, 144–46.

55. Several weeks before the treaty actually failed, Jackson wrote one of his lieutenants to instruct Mississippi senator Robert J. Walker that should this happen to reconsider it in the form

of a bill, which would be as legal and constitutional as a treaty. Walker was a key Texas backer in the Senate. Jackson to William B. Lewis, 8 April, 3 May 1844, quoted in Remini, *Andrew Jackson and the Course of American Democracy*, 495.

56. Rachel Jackson's brother, Samuel Donelson, was Andrew Jackson's law partner. When Donelson died, Jackson took in his namesake nephew and, while not legally adopting him, bestowed on him the full share of affection and advantages that Jackson habitually showed all of Rachel's family. See, generally, Heiskell, *Andrew Jackson and Early Tennessee History*, vol. 1, chap. 9.

57. Andrew Jackson to Houston, 12 March 1845, General Collections, Sam Houston Memorial Museum. This letter is published only in Yoakum's book, the result of Houston giving his historian-friend access to his trunks of papers that subsequently disappeared from critical assay. *History of Texas*, 2:441.

58. Calhoun to Donelson, 9 January 1845, quoted in Heiskell, *Andrew Jackson and Early Tennessee History*, 1:170.

59. Undated manuscript, Ashbel Smith Papers, Center for American History, University of Texas, quoted in Crane, *Life and Select Literary Remains*, 247.

60. E. G. M. Butler to William Carey Crane, 9 April 1881, quoted in Crane, *Life and Select Literary Remains*, 250.

61. Ibid., 249.

62. Donelson to Thomas Ritchie, 28 May 1845, quoted in Heiskell, *Andrew Jackson and Early Tennessee History*, 1:171–72.

63. Donelson to Jackson, 28 May 1845, quoted in Heiskell, *Andrew Jackson and Early Tennessee History*, 1:171.

64. Butler to Crane, 9 April 1881, quoted in Crane, *Life and Select Literary Remains*, 251. The chronology of Houston's speaking in these weeks is complicated and leads me to believe that he gave not one but two speeches during his brief stay in New Orleans. The temperance speech mentioned by Donelson is not included in the canon of his writings. The speech explaining his coquetry with Europe (quoted in the text) is published (Barker and Williams, *Writings of Sam Houston*, 6:5–13), and Butler's satisfaction that it was in response to his letter seems to place it in New Orleans. The editors of Houston's correspondence, however, can affix no certain date or place but speculate that it was given in the city of Houston in the summer of 1845. That is not possible because the Houstons did not return to Texas until October. Immediately before his departure for the United States, Houston did plan to speak in Houston city on 16 May, having accepted an invitation from Lubbock, Gray, and others to do so. Barker and Williams, *Writings of Sam Houston*, 4:422. There are elements of the speech that seem to indicate both a Houston and New Orleans delivery. Throughout his career, Houston often repeated himself in successive speeches on the same topic, and if this actual text, which was recorded by the stenographer William Weeks, was given in Houston city, the same sentiments and surely many of the same phrases would have been repeated in New Orleans. Placement of the speech in Texas stems apparently not from Weeks but from William Lewis, cobbler, judge, and author of *Biographical Sketch of the Life of Sam Houston, with a Condensed History of Texas from Its Discover to 1861* (Dallas: Herald Printing House, 1882). Willard Richardson of the Galveston News is not to be confused with David Richardson, who came to work for him at the same newspaper and later published issues of the *Texas Almanac* that also aroused Houston's ire. Houston and Francis Moore later seemed to have made up, for Houston appointed him state geologist in the summer of 1860. See Tyler et al., *New Handbook of Texas*, 4:817–18, 5:567, 572.

Chapter 16

1. Boney, "*The Raven* Tamed," 90–91. The Aunt Gillespy referred to was the offspring of the marriage of Houston's grandfather Robert's sister, Isabelle, to William Gillespy (sometimes Gillespie). Letcher was Houston's first cousin, the first born of Capt. Samuel Houston's youngest sister, Mary. Roberts, *Personal Correspondence of Sam Houston*, 1:372–73.

2. Crane, *Life and Literary Remains*, 255–56; Roberts, *Star of Destiny*, 107–8.

3. Polk to Donelson, 6 May 1845, quoted in Heiskell, *Andrew Jackson and Early Tennessee History*, 1:172–73.

4. Houston to A. B. Allen, 1 December 1845, in Barker and Williams, *Writings of Sam Houston*, 4:430–32.

5. Houston to Anthony Butler, 25 December 1845, in Barker and Williams, *Writings of Sam Houston*, 4:444–48. For a summary of Butler's own fall from standing with Jackson, see Remini, *Andrew Jackson and the Course of American Democracy*, 352–56.

6. Quoted in Roberts, *Star of Destiny*, 110, 112.

7. Quoted in Friend, *Sam Houston*, 164.

8. Flanagan, *Sam Houston's Texas*, 10; Houston to Joseph Ellis, 12 June 1847, in Barker and Williams, *Writings of Sam Houston*, 5:13–14.

9. Temple Houston Morrow notes, 15 January 1957, Sam Houston Papers, Center for American History, University of Texas, quoted in Flanagan, *Sam Houston's Texas*, 198n.

10. James Patton to author, 2 March 1996. Patton is Walker County clerk as well as chairman of the Walker County Historical Commission.

11. Gard, *Rawhide Texas*, 64. I have found no corroboration on this point. However, Houston is said to have once spent the night at John Coffee's similar house in Georgetown, where, according to tradition, a messenger arrived with Lincoln's offer of aid to keep Texas in the Union in 1861. This house was built in 1847. Flanagan, *Sam Houston's Texas*, 182.

12. See, generally, Terry G. Jordan, *Texas Log Buildings: A Folk Architecture* (Austin: University of Texas Press, 1978), 119ff.

13. Margaret to Houston, 8 May 1848; and Houston to Margaret, 20 June 1848, in Roberts, *Personal Correspondence of Sam Houston*, 2:323, 340–42.

14. Houston, "Remarks on the Bill to Establish Territorial Government in Oregon," 2 June, 12, 14 August 1848, in Barker and Williams, *Writings of Sam Houston*, 5:53–56, 58–61.

15. Houston to Margaret, 7 February 1849; and Margaret to Houston, 13 February 1849, in Roberts, *Personal Correspondence of Sam Houston*, 3:69, 74.

16. Mrs. John L. Norton to Houston, 12 February 1849, Sam Houston Papers, Catholic Archives of Texas.

17. Houston to James Gadsden, 20 September 1849, in Barker and Williams, *Writings of Sam Houston*, 5:95–107. Ironically, four years later as U.S. minister to Mexico, Gadsden accomplished something that Houston had never done. In successfully purchasing a strip of territory for a southern rail route, Gadsden made Santa Anna so unpopular that he was toppled from power.

18. Ever since his days as a besieged infantry lieutenant, Houston had kept a death-grip on his papers, and when Yoakum approached him with the idea to write a compendious Texas history, the senator gave him unfettered access to his trunks of letters. As a result, Yoakum's history as published in 1855 contained documentation of items that either disappeared when the Houston papers vanished into descendents' attics and private collections or were destroyed in Margaret's Independence fireplace. See Tyler et al., *New Handbook of Texas*, 6:1121–22.

19. Ashbel Smith to Houston, 7 June 1850, Sam Houston Papers, Center for American History.

20. Houston to Ashbel Smith, 2 August 1848, in Barker and Williams, *Writings of Sam Houston*, 5:57; Mrs. Thomas J. Wallace quoted in Heiskell, *Andrew Jackson and Early Tennessee History*, 2:151; James, *The Raven*, 423. At the time of his death, Mrs. Wallace's father, the son of Houston's brother-in-law, still had in his possession "a letter which Governor Houston wrote . . . thanking [Judge Wallace], in terms of tenderest affection, for the great devotion that had been given his sister." Mrs. Wallace's father knew Mary Houston Wallace as "Aunt Polly," but Madge Roberts identifies her second husband not as Matthew's brother but his nephew. Roberts, *Personal Correspondence of Sam Houston*, 3:71, 73.

21. Houston to Margaret, 13 April 1850, in Roberts, *Personal Correspondence of Sam Houston*, 3:176–77. Phoebe Jane and Mary Moore were Eliza's daughters.

22. Guild, *Old Times in Tennessee*, 273.

23. Houston to Margaret, 30 April 1850, in Barker and Williams, *Writings of Sam Houston*, 5:145–46.

24. Ibid.

25. G. Barrett to Houston, 29 May 1850, Sam Houston Papers, Catholic Archives of Texas.

26. Narcissa Hamilton to Houston, 14 February 1850, Penny Thornall Remick Collection, Sam Houston Regional Library and Research Center; Houston to John Letcher, 24 January 1851, published in *The Northern Standard*, 12 April 1851, and quoted in Barker and Williams, *Writings of Sam Houston*, 5:261–67. Letcher was the eldest grandson of Capt. Samuel Houston's youngest sister, Mary Houston Letcher, making him Sam Houston's first cousin once removed. Curiously, Letcher was, like Houston, a Unionist who remained loyal to his state once the war began. After eight years in Congress, he served as governor of Virginia from 1860 to 1864.

27. Houston, "Lecture on Trials and Dangers of Frontier Life," 28 January 1851, in Barker and Williams, *Writings of Sam Houston*, 5:267–81.

28. Houston to Margaret, 20, 28 February 1851, in Roberts, *Personal Correspondence of Sam Houston*, 3:306–8. He had been invited to the Harrisburg event by Mrs. James R. Jones on 11 February. He replied to her from his Senate desk; perhaps he was distracted by a speaker, for he addressed the letter to her at Harrisburg, Tennessee (there is no Harrisburg, Tennessee). Houston to Mrs. James R. Jones, 11 February 1851, in Barker and Williams, *Wriings of Sam Houston*, 5:283.

29. Houston to Robert Wilson, 8 February 1851; and Houston to Henderson Yoakum, 10 February 1851, in Barker and Williams, *Writings of Sam Houston*, 5:281–83.

30. Houston to Margaret, 28 February, 5, 6 March 1851, in Roberts, *Personal Correspondence of Sam Houston*, 3:309–10. Writers have long quoted another Houston to Margaret letter of 5 March regarding his intention to take communion at the E Street Baptist Church the following day, which has led to considerable confusion on the state of Houston's standing in grace. James, *The Raven*, 381, citing Raines, *A Year-Book for Texas*, 2 vols. (Austin: Gammel-Statesman Publishing, 1902–3), 452. This even confused the usually meticulous Llerena Friend (*Sam Houston*, 215) and prompted Donald Braider in his *Solitary Star* to conclude that the 1854 baptism was a repeat performance. The red-herring letter is actually dated 5 March 1856, not 1851. Domestic Correspondence, Sam Houston Papers, Texas State Library and Archives, published in Barker and Williams, *Writings of Sam Houston*, 6:244–45. William Seale (*Sam Houston's Wife*, 179) got it right.

31. Carrol Williams to author, 4 May 1996. Mr. Williams is the current minister of education of the First Baptist Church.

32. Ibid.; James Patton to author, May 1996; Walker County Minutes, Book A, 30 September 1851, 368; "The State vs. Margaret Houston," Henderson Yoakum Papers, Center for American History. As Madge Roberts notes (*Star of Destiny*, 222), Yoakum miswrote the year 1851 as 1850, to the confusion of later writers. See Seale, *Sam Houston's Wife*, 152–53.

33. Margaret to Houston, 8 February 1851, in Roberts, *Personal Correspondence of Sam Houston*, 3:298.

34. Houston to Nicholas Dean, 8 May 1851, in Barker and Williams, *Writings of Sam Houston*, 5:297–99. "Tar barrel" was common vernacular for a keg of molasses.

35. Lester to Houston, 18 October 1851, quoted in Barker and Williams, *Writings of Sam Houston*, 5:283n.

36. Houston to John H. Houston, 8 May 1851, in Roberts, *Personal Correspondence of Sam Houston*, 3:315.

37. Houston to John H. Houston, 11 October 1851, in Barker and Williams, *Writings of Sam Houston*, 5:316.

38. Quoted in Flanagan, *Sam Houston's Texas*, 112.

39. Quoted in Friend, *Sam Houston*, 284–87.

40. Houston to Washington Miller, n.d., Margaret Bell Houston Collection, Sam Houston Memorial Museum.

41. George W. Samson, "Sam Houston's Exile, Explained after Many Years," *New York Tribune*, 13 November 1880, quoted in James, *The Raven*, 138; Braider, *Solitary Star*, 74–75.

42. See, for instance, "Records of an Early Texas Baptist Church," *Quarterly of the Texas State Historical Association* 11, 12 (October 1907, July 1908).

43. Col. John B. Brownlow quoted in Heiskell, *Andrew Jackson and Early Tennessee History*, 2:183–84. The Mr. Swan referred to was William G. Swan, later a representative in the Confederate Congress.

44. Guild, *Old Times in Tennessee*, 291–92.

45. Houston, "Opposing Legislation Concerning Religion and Prohibition," [1853], in Barker and Williams, *Writings of Sam Houston*, 6:21–25.

46. Margaret to Houston, 28 November 1848, in Roberts, *Personal Correspondence of Sam Houston*, 3:15.

47. Houston to Miller, 10, 30 June 1853, Washington Miller Papers, Texas State Library and Archives. Houston's handwriting here is a bit above the usual degree of difficulty, and my reading of them differs in small particulars (for example, "auxiliary forces" rather than "auxiliary for us") from the interpretation in Barker and Williams, *Writings of Sam Houston*, 5:447–52. Houston had appointed Peter W. Gray attorney general in Houston City during his second presidential term; Gray later became a founder of the Houston Public Library along with Houston's great friend there, Tom Bagby. See Tyler et al., *New Handbook of Texas*, 3:294–95.

48. Houston to Miller, 13 September 1853, in Barker and Williams, *Writings of Sam Houston*, 5:457.

49. Frederick Golladay in Williams, *Houston and the War of Independence*, quoted in Heiskell, *Andrew Jackson and Early Tennessee History*, 2:158–59. The infant with whom Margaret was confined would have been Nettie, who was a year old at that time.

50. Houston to Miller, 13 September, 7 October 1853, in Barker and Williams, *Writings of Sam Houston*, 5:457–58. Miller was not singled out for Houston's matchmaking. Ashbel Smith was still enduring the same thing: "I wish you luck in marrying. If you can marry a fine woman, and she should have a *large fortune*, do not let it be a reason for breaking off the match!!! Write to me." Houston to Ashbel Smith, 2 August 1848, in Barker and Williams, *Writings of Sam Houston*, 5:58.

51. Hamilton, *My Master*, 7–9.

52. Hamilton's lack of bitterness over his slavery, indeed his stout defense of Houston as a kind master, is undoubtedly one reason why the latest "politically correct" generation of scholars has taken to treating his memoir somewhat curtly. Of course, the occasionally ham-handed editing of Lenoir Hunt sometimes gives the impression of her putting words in Hamilton's mouth, which excuse is now given for dismissing the memoir. But there are places in the narrative that are resoundingly Hamilton's own memory, and these are the passages cited in this volume.

53. Hamilton, *My Master*, 21–22. Exactly how long after Jeff's purchase Houston tried to acquire the rest of his family is difficult to determine, but it must have been reasonably soon, for Hamilton recalled that at the time of the trip to Independence, Sam Junior was ten years old, and the latter was already ten and a half when Jeff entered the family's service six months later. Long after the demise of slavery, Hamilton did celebrate a joyous reunion with his mother, "Aunt Big Kittie," in her old age. Martin Roysten was the youngest of Robertus and Varilla's six children. Roberts, *Personal Correspondence of Sam Houston*, 1:374.

54. A. Meggett and John Willard to Houston, 26 November 1853, Sam Houston Papers, Catholic Archives of Texas.

55. James Auchindort to Houston, 10 February 1854, Sam Houston Papers, Catholic Archives of Texas. Due to a clerical misread, this letter was filed chronologically as 10 February 1837.

56. James H. Stuart to Houston, 12 December 1853; and N. Rudder to Houston, 14 December 1853, Sam Houston Papers, Catholic Archives of Texas. Rudder, a resident of Velasco, did not mention what office he was grateful to have received, but he hailed Houston as the savior of his "poor wife and helpless children."

57. Houston, "A Motion to Admit Ladies to the Floor of the Senate," 8 February 1854, *Congressional Globe* 24:376, quoted in Barker and Williams, *Writings of Sam Houston*, 5:468–69.

58. Sam Houston, "Opposing the Kansas-Nebraska Bill," 14–15 February 1854, in Barker and Williams, *Writings of Sam Houston*, 5:469–502, 504–22.

59. Wilson, *Rise and Fall of Slave Power*, 2:393.

60. Pierce, *Memoir and Letters of Charles Sumner*, 3:366–67.

61. Houston, "Defending the Right of Petition," 14 March 1854, in Barker and Williams, *Writings of Sam Houston*, 5:523–30.

62. Elijah B. Stackpole to Houston, 10 March 1854, Sam Houston Papers, Catholic Archives of Texas. Stackpole asked for a copy of Houston's speech on the Kansas-Nebraska bill; his place of residence appears to be, in his handwriting, Kenduskeag, Maine, which I have been unable to locate. A copy of this speech, printed as a pamphlet, resides in the Remick Collection.

63. Heiskell, *Andrew Jackson and Early Tennessee History*, 1:14–15. Charles Sprague on the disappearance of the Indian was an Independence Day oration delivered in Boston in 1825.

64. Crane, *Life and Select Literary Remains*, 240. Lemuel Dale Evans of Fannin County was a political force in East Texas for years, was later Houston's ally in opposing secession, and after Houston's death served as chief justice of the Texas Supreme Court. Friend, *Sam Houston*, 250; Tyler et al., *New Handbook of Texas*, 2:906.

65. Houston "as firmly believed in the divine instincts of the eagle as Romulus or any of the Grecian or Roman philosophers and kings." Burleson, *Life and Writings of Rufus C. Burleson*, 552.

66. Burleson continued to serve the Baptist denomination as an educational administrator until 1897. See Haynes, "Dr. Rufus C. Burleson."

67. Burleson, *Life and Writings of Rufus C. Burleson*, 579.

68. Margaret to Houston, 24 May 1854; Houston to Margaret, 13 May 1854; and Margaret to Houston, 31 May 1854, quoted in Roberts, *Star of Destiny*, 240–41; Nannie to Houston, Dorothy Loe Collection, Sam Houston Regional Library and Research Center.

69. Margaret to Houston, 14 June 1854, Sam Houston Hearne Collection, Sam Houston Regional Library and Research Center, quoted in Seale, Sam Houston's Wife, 166.

70. Seale, *Sam Houston's Wife*, 168. Baylor's "Jesus Wept" must have been quite a production. The faithful in Waco once coerced Baylor to deliver it by coating the town with advertisements for it, and the first that the crestfallen Judge Baylor learned of it was when he arrived in town after an exhausting ride. Unable to disappoint the throng that had gathered, he delivered the oration. Wallis and Hill, *Sixty Years on the Brazos*, 184. Any thought that Sam Houston would have considered the political advantages of being baptized in such a public setting are negated by Jackson's example, which bears a curious parallel to Houston's case. "My dear," Old Hickory once answered a plea from Rachel to join the church, "if I were to do that now, it would be said, all over the country, that I had done it for the sake of political effect. My enemies would all say so. I can not do it *now*, but I promise you that once I am clear of politics I will join the church." Unlike Margaret, Rachel Jackson never lived to triumph. Remini, *Andrew Jackson and the Course of American Freedom*, 108.

71. Born at the end of 1809 in Georgia and raised in Alabama, Baines reached adulthood an illiterate but goodhearted bumpkin. Ignorance ill suited him, however; after educating himself in the basics, he worked his way through the University of Alabama. He was licensed to preach in 1834 and ordained two years later. Baines located to Huntsville, Texas, in 1850 after wide religious and

public service in Arkansas and Louisiana. His modesty and humility were best summed up in a family observation: "He so loved a back seat." Johnson, *A Family Album*, 96. Texas Baptists knew a good thing when they saw it, and although Baines was never in robust health, they never allowed him to stay in retirement. The great-grandfather of Pres. Lyndon Baines Johnson, he passed on the day before his seventy-third birthday. See also Tyler et al., *New Handbook of Texas*, 1:340.

72. M. V. Smith quoted in Johnson, *A Family Album*, 91.

73. See Ernest C. Shearer, "Sam Houston and Religion," *Tennessee Historical Quarterly* 20 (March 1961).

74. George Washington Baines to William Carey Crane, n.d., quoted in Crane, *Life and Select Literary Remains*, 244–45.

75. Houston to Margaret, 18 January 1842, in Roberts, *Personal Correspondence of Sam Houston*, 1:175.

76. Burleson, *Life and Writings of Rufus C. Burleson*, 166–67. This was not the only time that Rufus Burleson managed to insinuate himself, perhaps beyond propriety, into the Houston history. At one time he told Mrs. Thomas J. Wallace (great-niece by marriage of Houston's youngest sister) that he had accompanied Houston to New Orleans for treatment of his San Jacinto wound and witnessed Margaret Lea's dockside swoon. If her memory was accurate, for a twelve-year-old boy living in Decatur, Alabama, this would have been an astral projection worthy of higher sainthood than Baptists generally recognize. Heiskell, *Andrew Jackson and Early Tennessee History*, 2:153. "General Houston and I were exceedingly intimate. He was converted under my preaching, and I buried him in holy baptism." Ibid., 2:551.

77. Goree Papers, Thomason Room (Special Collections), Newton Gresham Library, Sam Houston State University. In the mid-nineteenth century, unlike today, Methodists were considered more evangelical and demonstrative than Baptists. More than a dozen others were immersed on the same occasion, but their conversions were far overshadowed by Houston's. Madge Thornall Roberts, interview by author, 4 May 2000.

78. James, *The Raven*, 385. James cites a statement of Houston's grandson, Franklin Williams. Of all the anecdotes in *The Raven* that lack corroboration, this is the one that I most hope is true, and there is independent confirmation in the family tradition to support it. Madge Roberts interview, 4 May 2000.

CHAPTER 17

1. Houston to J. W. Stone, 25 January, 7 February 1855, in Barker and Williams, *Writings of Sam Houston*, 6:108–9, 156–57. In the following session, Banks was elected Speaker of the House, and as a Union general during the Civil War was given the assignment, over his own objection, of invading Texas via the Red River. He and Adm. David Dixon Porter were roundly defeated in Louisiana.

2. Wisehart, Sam Houston, 565; Houston to "Dear General," 20 February 1855, in Barker and Williams, *Writings of Sam Houston*, 6:166–67. The editors of Houston's correspondence note that Houston and Rusk had two mutual friends named Burke, both of them businessmen in Houston City, but the orator Edmund Burke is a far likelier candidate. Houston's appeal to the principles of Jackson was not unique. A few years before, he had written Gideon Welles (coincidentally also a resident of Connecticut and who later served Lincoln as secretary of the navy) that, in a given situation, "it is a good rule to recur to first principles and by way of doing so, it seems to me a wise plan would be to ask what would General Jackson decide to be proper." Houston to Welles, 15 August 1852, in Barker and Williams, *Writings of Sam Houston*, 5:354.

3. Houston to Mrs. Sigourney, 6 March 1855, in Barker and Williams, *Writings of Sam Houston*, 6:179.

4. "Extracts from a Speech on Slavery, Tremont Temple, Boston," 22 February 1855, in Barker and Williams, *Writings of Sam Houston*, 6:167–77. Houston's view of the probable condition of

emancipated slaves was not far different from the actual condition of most freedmen after the Civil War.

5. *Texas State Gazette*, 31 March 1855.

6. See, for example, De Bruhl, *Sword of San Jacinto*, 363.

7. Pierson, *Tocqueville and Beaumont*, 613.

8. "Uncle Joshua told me later that the General fed his slaves much better than most other owners did." Hamilton, *My Master*, 16–19. Houston's mother-in-law apparently was less progressive in her policy toward hiring out slaves. During her early residence in Galveston, a man whom Houston had trusted to keep an eye out for her interest confessed: "Upon inquiring of Mrs. Lea I find that she has been most shamefully imposed upon by those to whom she has been hiring her negroes to. I shall endeavor, however, in the future to make those who hire pay promptly." James H. Cocke to Houston, 9 December 1841, Sam Houston Papers, Catholic Archives of Texas, Chancery of the Austin Diocese. James H. Cocke is not to be confused with James Decatur Cocke, a loud Lamar partisan and Houston hater who later "died with grace" in the "Black Bean" episode.

9. Houston to William J. Worth, 24 January 1826, in Barker and Williams, *Writings of Sam Houston*, 1:23; Houston to Anna Raguet, 15 May 1838, in Barker and Williams, *Writings of Sam Houston*, 2:228; Williams, *Houston and the War of Independence*, 256–57.

10. See also Olmsted, *A Journey through Texas*. While relentless in his condemnation of slavery, Olmsted freely refers to African American children as "pickininnies." Houston met Harriet Beecher Stowe once and wrote Margaret about her. "Last night I went to a party at Speaker Banks, and saw 'Uncle Tom's Cabin,' alias Madam Beecher Stowe. She is certainly a hard subject to look on. I was at the party an hour, ate an ice cream, and left." Houston to Margaret, 18 April 1856, in Barker and Williams, *Writings of Sam Houston*, 6:305.

11. Hamilton, *My Master*, 26, 38–39.

12. Terrell, "Recollections of General Sam Houston," 122; Flanagan, *Sam Houston's Texas*, 123.

13. George W. Samson to William Carey Crane, 28 March 1866, quoted in Crane, *Life and Select Literary Remains*, 243.

14. Houston, "On an Increase of the Army, and the Indian Policy of the Government," 29, 31 January 1855, in Barker and Williams, *Writings of Sam Houston*, 6:151–52.

15. Houston, "Opinion Concerning the 'American Order,'" 24 July 1855, in Barker and Williams, *Writings of Sam Houston*, 6:192–99.

16. Cantrell, "Sam Houston and the Know-Nothings," 337–38.

17. A. M. Hunt to Houston, 15 May 1855, Sam Houston Papers, Catholic Archives of Texas.

18. Houston to Ashbel Smith, 20 November 1855, in Barker and Williams, *Writings of Sam Houston*, 6:207–8.

19. *New York Herald*, 28 April 1856, clipping in A. J. Houston Collection, Texas State Library and Archives; A. L. Meredith to Houston, 3 May 1856, Sam Houston Papers, Catholic Archives of Texas; Narcissa Hamilton to Houston, 20 June 1852, Baldwin Collection, Sam Houston Memorial Museum.

20. Houston to Mrs. Ana S. Stephens, 22 March 1856, in Barker and Williams, *Writings of Sam Houston*, 6:299–300.

21. Houston to Margaret, 16 December 1856, Dorothy Loe Collection, Sam Houston Regional Library and Research Center. In 1824, citizens of Lancaster County, Pennsylvania, had placed Houston's name on a ballot in opposition to Buchanan. Houston wrote Buchanan that he would have withdrawn from "opposition to my worthy friend" if he could have done so without insulting the parties; Buchanan considered Houston's note "a new mark" of their friendship and joked that he was sure Houston would mount a very respectable showing. Houston to Buchanan; and Buchanan to Houston, 21 September 1824, Records of the Governor, Texas State Library and Archives.

22. Margaret to Houston, 19 January 1856, Loe Collection.

23. Ed Sharp, "Reminiscences," *Dallas News*, 4, 5 April 1892.

24. *Huntsville Recorder* quoted in *Texas State Gazette*, 6 June 1857; *The Texas Sentinel*, 20 June 1857. In his haste to publish the first half of the itinerary, a couple of miscalculations were made— 29 June, for instance, was a Monday, not a Tuesday—and a couple of small adjustments were made in the second half. See Flanagan, *Sam Houston's Texas*, 134.

25. Sharp, "Reminiscences"; Houston to Rusk, 28 May 1857, in Barker and Williams, *Writings of Sam Houston*, 6:445.

26. Sharp, "Reminiscences."

27. Terrell, "Recollections of General Sam Houston," 118–19.

28. Ibid., 130.

29. Austin State Gazette, 25 July 1857. There was a well-known grove of oak trees favored for such gatherings, but it was later decimated to make room for the University of Texas' Graduate School of Business.

30. Terrell, "Recollections of General Sam Houston," 119–20. John Marshall was another Austin newspaper editor; Terrell pointed out later that Steiner was acquitted in Arnold's murder, having pled self-defense.

31. Flanagan, *Sam Houston's Texas*, 152–53.

32. Rose, *History of Victoria County*, 36–37. The day before speaking in Victoria, Houston gave a speech in Clinton, the seat of DeWitt County. The town of Cuero, established across the Guadalupe River at the same time (1846) three miles to the north, eventually won most of the business, the railroad, and afterward became the county seat. All that remains of Clinton is an overgrown cemetery and a well in a pasture. Tyler et al., *New Handbook of Texas*, 2:155–56; Flanagan, *Sam Houston's Texas*, 154.

33. Houston to Smith, 22 August 1857, in Barker and Williams, *Writings of Sam Houston*, 6:447–48.

34. Terrell, "Recollections of General Sam Houston," 121.

35. Houston to Washington Miller, 1 September 1857, A. J. Houston Collection. Henderson Yoakum had died at the end of 1856, so Houston's remark on the unpaid debt must have been occasioned by disappointment with the progress of probating the estate.

36. "Remarks on the Admission of Kansas," 19 March 1858, in Barker and Williams, *Writings of Sam Houston*, 7:41.

37. "Remarks on the Death of Thomas J. Rusk," 19 January 1858, in Barker and Williams, *Writings of Sam Houston*, 6:463–66.

38. Houston to Hon. H. Cobb, Secretary of the Treasury, 12 January 1858, in Barker and Williams, *Writings of Sam Houston*, 6:466.

39. "Against Increase of the Regular Army," 11 February 1858, in Barker and Williams, *Writings of Sam Houston*, 6:505.

40. Speeches to the Senate, 1, 25 February 1858, *Congressional Globe*, (1857–58), 1:492–97, 873–75, quoted in Gard, Frontier Justice, 222.

41. "Remarks Concerning His Resolution Authorizing a Protectorate over Certain Latin-American States," 16 February 1858, in Barker and Williams, *Writings of Sam Houston*, 6:508–12.

42. Houston, "Favoring a Protectorate over Mexico," 20 April 1858, in Barker and Williams, *Writings of Sam Houston*, 7:84–99.

43. Flanagan, *Sam Houston's Texas*, 160.

44. Houston, "Concerning a Mexican Protectorate," 2 June 1858, in Barker and Williams, *Writings of Sam Houston*, 7:131.

45. "Remarks on the Pacific Railroad Bill," 17 April 1858, in Barker and Williams, *Writings of Sam Houston*, 7:79–83.

46. "Remarks on the Admission of Kansas," 19 March 1858, in Barker and Williams, *Writings of Sam Houston*, 7:37–41. Regarding Houston's alleged inability to perceive the moral dimension of slavery, see De Bruhl, *Sword of San Jacinto*, 363.

47. Houston, "Concerning the Appropriation for the Distribution of Seeds and Cuttings," 28 May 1858, in Barker and Williams, *Writings of Sam Houston*, 7:122.

48. Houston to Mrs. Houston, 17, 19 May 1858, in Barker and Williams, *Writings of Sam Houston*, 7:108. Georgia native, doctor, and lawyer William Peleg Rogers, with his wife and six children, were neighbors of the Houstons in Independence, where Rogers donated time as a law professor at Baylor University. He was a man of deeply held principles and had distinguished himself in the Mexican War. See Tyler et al., *New Handbook of Texas*, 5:665.

49. Houston, "A Synopsis of a Speech at Danville," 11 September 1858, in Barker and Williams, *Writings of Sam Houston*, 7:183–86.

50. Hamilton, *My Master*, 40.

51. Houston to Ashbel Smith, 29 October 1858, in Barker and Williams, *Writings of Sam Houston*, 7:189.

52. Houston, "On the Death of James Pinckney Henderson," 5 June 1858, in Barker and Williams, *Writings of Sam Houston*, 7:140–43.

53. "Concerning the Pacific Railroad and Other Matters," 12, 13 January 1859, in Barker and Williams, *Writings of Sam Houston*, 7:194–216. The reference to Aesop was recalled by Henry Watterson of the *Louisville Courier-Journal*, quoted in Heiskell, *Andrew Jackson and Early Tennessee History*, 2:189.

54. Houston to Mrs. Houston, 20, 21, 29 January 1859, in Barker and Williams, *Writings of Sam Houston*, 7:218–20, 224–25.

55. Unknown to Houston, 24 February 1859, in Barker and Williams, *Writings of Sam Houston*, 7:327–28.

56. Houston, "A Refutation of Calumnies Produced and Circulated against His Character as Commander-in-Chief of the Army of Texas," 28 February 1859, in Barker and Williams, *Writings of Sam Houston*, 7:306–35.

57. Houston, "Remarks on the Post Office Appropriation Bill," 1 March 1859, in Barker and Williams, *Writings of Sam Houston*, 7:336–39.

58. *Washington Evening Star*, 11 March 1859, subsequently reprinted in *Southern Intelligencer*, 6 April 1859.

59. Houston to Washington Miller, 14 February 1859, A. J. Houston Collection; Houston to Margaret, 29 January 1859, in Barker and Williams, *Writings of Sam Houston*, 7:224–25.

Chapter 18

1. "Authorization to Draft on Riggs & Co.," 10 March 1859, A. J. Houston Collection, Texas State Library and Archives.

2. Swante Palm to Houston, 21 May 1859, A. J. Houston Collection. Palm later won a consular appointment to Sweden. Friend, *Sam Houston*, 182.

3. Hamilton Stuart to Houston, 24 May 1859; C. B. Way et al. to Houston, 27 May 1859; and A. J. McGown to Houston, 28 May 1859, A. J. Houston Collection. Bearing a commission as "Missionary to the United States," McGown was probably responsible for recruiting more Presbyterian ministers into Texas service than any other man in the mid-1840s. He published a Presbyterian newspaper in Huntsville from 1847 to 1856. See Tyler et al., *New Handbook of Texas*, 4:406.

4. Houston to George W. Paschal, 3 June 1859, in Barker and Williams, *Writings of Sam Houston*, 7:339–40.

5. Terrell, "Recollections of General Sam Houston," 117–18.

6. Houston, "Speech at Nacogdoches," 9 July 1859, in Barker and Williams, *Writings of Sam Houston*, 7:343–67. Nacogdoches University was the earliest nonsectarian college in Texas, and it remained doctrinally unaffiliated for most of its existence, which ended in 1904. The 1858 Greek revival building is now listed on the National Register of Historic Places. See Tyler et al., *New Handbook of Texas*, 4:930. The first point of Houston's exposition on the economics of the slave traffic

reflects the facts of the day, as revealed in any of the newspapers, that slaves born in Texas or else-where in the South sold at premiums over "wild negroes" freshly imported, who were angry, frightened, and spoke only native tongues.

7. Houston, "Synopsis of a Speech Made at Huntsville," September 1859; and "Extracts from a Speech at a Barbecue in Montgomery," 15 September 1859, in Barker and Williams, *Writings of Sam Houston*, 7:374–78.

8. Houston to Washington Miller, 30 August 1859, in Barker and Williams, *Writings of Sam Houston*, 7:373; [Miller] to Houston, 20 September 1859; and Houston to Miller, 8 October 1859, A. J. Houston Collection. The letter of 20 September is missing a signature, but the handwriting is unquestionably Miller's.

9. Houston, "Proclamation Ordering Armed Bands within the State to Disperse," 28 December 1859; and Houston to Xavier Blanchard DeBray, 5 May 1860, in Barker and Williams, *Writings of Sam Houston*, 7:389–90, 8:45.

10. Robert E. Lee to A. M. Lea, 1 March 1860; and A. M. Lea to Houston, 24 February, 3 April 1860, Records of the Governor, Texas State Library and Archives. These letters are frequently cited; see, for example, Friend, *Sam Houston*, 303; Seale, *Sam Houston's Wife*, 199; and Webb, *The Texas Rangers*, 208–11.

11. Terrell, "Recollections of General Sam Houston," 131–32; Houston to Francis Moore Jr., 25 August 1860, in Barker and Williams, *Writings of Sam Houston*, 8:125–26. As a state senator in 1862, A. J. Hamilton fled Austin before being caught by a mob bent on punishing his continuing Unionist opinions. Reaching the North via Mexico, he accepted an appointment in the Union army and later served a stormy term as provisional governor during Reconstruction. "Dirtyshirt" Bill Scurry was the younger brother, by ten years, of Richardson Scurry, who had provided Houston with able service during his tenure in the Seventh and Eighth Congresses of the Republic. Tyler et al., *New Handbook of Texas*, 3:427–28, 5:945–46.

12. Houston to the Directors of the Penitentiary, 24 January 1860; and Houston to Sheriff of Walker County, 30 January 1860, in Barker and Williams, *Writings of Sam Houston*, 7:447–49, 460–61.

13. Terrell, "Recollections of General Sam Houston," 133; Roberts, *Star of Destiny*, 293.

14. Houston to Lewis Cass, 23 January 1860, in Barker and Williams, *Writings of Sam Houston*, 7:411–12.

15. "A Pardon for a Negro Slave, Bill," 8 February 1861, in Barker and Williams, *Writings of Sam Houston*, 8:258–59.

16. Houston to S. F. Jones, 6 August 1860; and Houston to Joseph M. Cox, 7 August 1860, in Barker and Williams, *Writings of Sam Houston*, 8:116–17. The subject of Anglo outlaws covering their crimes by disguising themselves as Indians was not rare in the newspapers of the day. See, for instance, a representative clipping in the appendix of Olmsted, *A Journey through Texas*.

17. Friends of the Governor's Mansion, *Governor's Mansion of Texas*, 36–39. Nearly eighty years later, another Texas first lady, Jo Betsy Allred, gave birth in this bed to a son named, inevitably, Sam Houston Allred.

18. Jean Houston Daniel, Price Daniel, and Dorothy Blodgett, *The Texas Governor's Mansion* (Austin: Texas State Library and Archives Commission; and Liberty, Tex.: Sam Houston Regional Library and Research Center, 1984), 324. This was the first physical alteration done to the house since its completion in 1856.

19. Col. R. T. P. Allen was the founder and superintendent of Bastrop Military Institute. He was apparently unrelated to the Allen brothers who had founded Houston city as a namesake and memorial for the general. The school was closed during the Civil War, reopened in 1867, and for want of patronage moved to Austin in 1870. Tyler et al., *New Handbook of Texas*, 1:113.

20. Terrell, "Recollections of General Sam Houston," 123–30. The captain of cadets on this visit was Joseph Draper Sayers, governor of Texas from 1899 to 1903.

21. Burnet to Smith, 30 April 1860, Ashbel Smith Papers, Center for American History, University of Texas, quoted in Friend, *Sam Houston*, 314.

22. Quoted in Friend, *Sam Houston*, 316.

23. Houston to John H. Manly, 17 May 1860, in Barker and Williams, *Writings of Sam Houston*, 8:58–61.

24. Quoted in Friend, *Sam Houston*, 319.

25. Houston, "To Friends in the United States," 18 August 1860, in Barker and Williams, *Writings of Sam Houston*, 8:121–22.

26. Houston to A. Daly, 14 August 1860, in Barker and Williams, *Writings of Sam Houston*, 8:118–20.

27. Houston to Ashbel Smith, 25 July 1860, in Barker and Williams, *Writings of Sam Houston*, 8:109.

28. Houston to Sam Jr., 4, 14, 23, 30 April 1860, in Barker and Williams, *Writings of Sam Houston*, 7:7–9, 12–13, 27, 33–34. The father's advice on the hat would doubtless have been well taken, for in his own day General Houston was accounted something of an expert in the field of showy headgear.

29. See Houston to Sam Jr., 27 January 1860, Sam Houston Hearne Collection, Sam Houston Regional Library and Research Center, quoted in Seale, *Sam Houston's Wife*, 196; and Houston to Sam Jr., 30 January 1860, in Barker and Williams, *Writings of Sam Houston*, 7:457–58.

30. The "Andrew dear" to whom the work was addressed was Andrew Hunter Aiken of Ayr, who later established a business career in Liverpool before being named British consul to Riga. He died in 1831, doubtless unaware of the part he had played in shaping Sam Houston's consciousness. William Ernest Henley and Thomas F. Henderson, eds., *The Complete Poetical Works of Burns*, Cambridge Edition (Boston: Houghton-Mifflin, 1897), 39–40.

31. Houston to Joseph Ellis, n.d., Correspondence on Sam Houston, Catholic Archives of Texas, Chancery of the Austin Diocese. The editors of Houston's correspondence note that they copied this document from the original in the collection of Temple Houston Morrow. Barker and Williams, *Writings of Sam Houston*, 7:462. When I found what appeared to be the original in the Catholic Archives of Texas, it was not in the Sam Houston papers but in an unrelated file of twentieth-century letters arguing the true nature of Houston's religious sentiments, which seems inexplicable. Its text, quoted here, varies somewhat from the published version.

32. Roberts, *Star of Destiny*, 288.

33. Seale, *Sam Houston's Wife*, 197–98. Austin's climate is still famous as torture to those suffering from allergies and asthma. In defense of Margaret's reputation as a nonhostess, Lucadia Pease, who had selected the mansion's location, found the Austin summers as intolerable as Margaret did and usually managed to visit her family in New England during the hottest months. Friends of the Governor's Mansion, *Governors Mansion of Texas*, 98–102.

34. Hamilton, *My Master*, 43–55; Roberts, *Star of Destiny*, 287–88, 291.

35. Roberts, *Star of Destiny*, 288.

36. "Address at the Union Mass Meeting, Austin, Texas," 22 September 1860, in Barker and Williams, *Writings of Sam Houston*, 8:145–60.

37. Fletcher Stockdale to Guy Bryan, 16 October 1860, Bryan Papers, Center for American History, quoted in Friend, *Sam Houston*, 329–30. Stockdale served as acting governor of Texas for a brief period after the fall of the Confederacy.

38. Houston to Ed Burleson, 9 November 1860, Edward Burleson Papers, Center for American History, quoted in Friend, *Sam Houston*, 330.

39. Houston to H. M. Watkins and others, 20 November 1860, in Barker and Williams, *Writings of Sam Houston*, 8:192–97.

40. Burleson, *Life and Writings of Rufus C. Burleson*, 581.

41. Friend, *Sam Houston*, 331; Maher, "Sam Houston and Secession," 453. Bell was a Harvard graduate, quite an accomplishment for one of the rare native Anglo Texans, born at Bell's Landing in 1825.

42. Maher, "Sam Houston and Secession," 454. It cannot be doubted, however, as Maher points out in his article, that a majority of Texans did support secession.

43. Kittrell, *Governors Who Have Been and Other Public Men* (Houston: Dealey-Adey-Elgin, 1921), quoted in Welch, *The Texas Governor*, 36. Texas' fourth governor, James Wilson Henderson, known as "Smoky," a lieutenant governor who became chief executive for a month after the resignation of P. H. Bell in November 1853, should not be confused with Texas' first governor, James Pinckney Henderson.

44. Pardon of Mary Monroe, 11 February 1860, Sam Houston Executive Record Book, Texas State Library and Archives. It seems clear from Henderson's account that he had not mistaken the case, but the Monroe pardon was dated a year before the secession convention met—probably an error in the date the document was recorded in Houston's record book or possibly a gaffe on Houston's part in applying the old year to the paper, an unusual mistake six weeks into the new year but not unheard of.

45. Hamilton, *My Master*, 72–73; Houston to a Committee of the Secession Convention, 31 January 1861, in Barker and Williams, *Writings of Sam Houston*, 8:253–54. W. P. Rogers later made good on his vow, killed by multiple rifle shots in the battle of Corinth, Mississippi, on 3 October 1862.

46. Reagan, "A Conversation with Governor Houston," 279–81.

47. Houston to D. E. Twiggs, 20 January 1861, in Barker and Williams, *Writings of Sam Houston*, 8:234–35. Other passages in Houston's letter further this conclusion; he authorized Twiggs to call upon San Antonio authorities to defend the army supplies from such an unauthorized attack and promised to keep him informed of the activities of the legislature, which was called to meet the next day.

48. Maj. Gen. Winfield Scott to Waite, 12, 19 March 1861, quoted in Westwood, "President Lincoln's Overture," 133.

49. First daughter Nannie passed this story on to her son, Temple Houston Morrow, who recounted it to the Texas Legislature the day before the commencement of Texas's Statehood Centennial Celebration. "Address by Temple Houston Morrow," Senate Journal, Forty-ninth Texas Legislature, reg. sess. (27 February 1945), 282. This incident, of course, became part of the Houston legend and was paraphrased and retold so often that details became unclear. Either the children followed Margaret upstairs and retired to their rooms (Seale, *Sam Houston's Wife*, 206) or Margaret, unable to sleep, remained downstairs (Roberts, *Star of Destiny*, 298). Nannie's account is not specific as to where Margaret spent the night, but it has her downstairs when Houston came down in the morning. I have opted to leave her downstairs, as Roberts cites a similar version that descended through second daughter Maggie, who was thirteen at the time.

50. Raglin, H. W. "Inventory of Articles and Furniture in the Governor's House," 8 November 1861, State of Texas, Comptroller's Office, Texas State Library and Archives.

51. "Address by Temple Houston Morrow," 282–83. This tradition, if accurate, may provide insight into the debate that has occurred over the years as to whether the actual "Sam Houston Bedroom" was the southwest (left rear) bedroom, where his great mahogany bedstead reposed for many years, or the southeast (left front), where it is now. If Margaret passed the night downstairs, she would most likely have spent it in the family parlor, now the library, which was the most comfortably furnished room in the mansion. The library is beneath the southeast bedroom, and if she heard the floor creaking above her, that would be the chamber indicated as the proper "Sam Houston Bedroom."

52. Baker, "A Pivotal Point," 566.

53. "To the People of Texas," 16 March 1861, in Barker and Williams, *Writings of Sam Houston*, 8:271–78.

54. Quoted in Williams, *Houston and the War of Independence,* 358–59.

55. Governors' Letters, Texas State Library and Archives, quoted in Friend, Sam Houston, 340.

56. Houston to Charles A. Waite, 29 March 1861, in Barker and Williams, *Writings of Sam Houston,* 8:294; Waite to Assistant Adjutant General, 1 April 1861, quoted in Westwood, "President Lincoln's Overture," 135.

57. Hamilton, *My Master,* 75; Culberson, "General Sam Houston and Secession," 586. It was probably Culberson, father of Texas senator Charles Culberson, who gave an account of the meeting that Alexander Terrell relates. "Recollections of General Sam Houston," 135. Terrell wrote that he had heard others say the letter was from F. W. Lander, but Culberson told him it was from Giddings. Like Jeff, he was unaware there were two letters. Giddings's own accounts were elicited by Lincoln's biographer Ida M. Tarbell in sources cited in Westwood, "President Lincoln's Overture," 138–39. Epperson, like Houston, espoused the Confederacy after secession was effected, and though he was too disabled to serve, he contributed to the cause from his sizeable fortune. Tyler et al., *New Handbook of Texas,* 2:878–79.

58. "Message to the Texas Legislature," 30 January 1861, in Barker and Williams, *Writings of Sam Houston,* 8:253.

59. *Galveston Daily News,* 3 April 1892, quoted in Barker and Williams, *Writings of Sam Houston,* 8:293. The editors of Houston's correspondence did not identify the source of this quote, but the following day's issue of the *Dallas News,* 4 April 1892, makes it clear that it was Ed Sharp.

60. Smithwick, *Evolution of a State,* 334. Smithwick remained in California, eventually settling in the town of—nice irony—Santa Ana. He died in 1899. His memoir, dictated to his daughter owing to his near blindness, remains one of the most vivid extant portraits of Texas during its frontier heyday.

CHAPTER 19

1. Hamilton, *My Master,* 78–80. Houston may have been just spinning an enjoyable tale for Jeff, for there is no record that Audubon ever actually visited the Austin area. Ron Tyler to Susan Garrett, 3 April 2000, in manuscript evaluation. Tyler is the author of *Audubon's Great National Work: The Royal Octavo Edition of "The Birds of America* (Austin: University of Texas Press, 1993). The Treaty Oak remained a popular Austin landmark and gathering place until it was vandalized by lead poisoning in the 1990s. About a third of the tree survived.

2. Houston to Martin Lea, 2 March 1861, in Barker and Williams, *Writings of Sam Houston,* 8:264. Martin Lea was the third child of Margaret's older brother Henry, not to be confused with Varilla's son, Martin Royston. The editors of Houston's correspondence, who were not stock raisers, misread "Woburn" as "Wohurn" in the general's handwriting. A suitable valedictory of Houston's lifelong fiduciary character is given in Wisehart, *Sam Houston,* 564.

3. Houston, "Speech at Brenham," 31 March 1861, in Barker and Williams, *Writings of Sam Houston,* 8:295–300.

4. North, *Five Years in Texas,* 89–90. The Telegraph did publish an emasculated extract, characterizing the speech as reasonably mild—Houston declared that he had never intrigued with Lincoln nor sought federal aid, ridiculed Ed Clark, and attacked secessionist demagogues. But "he advised the people now, no matter what were the causes that had brought on this state of affairs, to counsel wisely and to be united . . . and to repel the enemy." *Houston Telegraph,* 23 April 1861. The editors of Houston's correspondence were apparently unacquainted with the North book when they wrote that no verbatim extract exists of this speech. Barker and Williams, *Writings of Sam Houston,* 8:301n.

5. Hamilton, *My Master,* 77.

6. Houston to Sam Houston Jr., 15, 22 May 1861, in Barker and Williams, *Writings of Sam Houston,* 8:305–7.

7. Houston, "Speech at Independence," 10 May 1861, in Barker and Williams, *Writings of Sam Houston*, 8:301–5; also quoted in Williams, *Houston and the War of Independence*, 366–67. Not confident that Confederate organization would be much better than under the republic, Houston tried to make his serious point with a stripe of humor that strikes one as somewhat lame today: "Do not be making companies to-day and unmaking them tomorrow. If you are dissatisfied with your captain, wait until the battle day comes, and he gets killed off, then you can get another."

8. Houston to the editors of the *Civilian*, 12 September 1861, published in the *Civilian*, 16 September 1861, and reprinted in Barker and Williams, *Writings of Sam Houston*, 8:310–14. Lincoln's offer of troops is here increased to seventy thousand, for Houston was always flexible with figures when recounting his story. The number of Mexicans who attacked the Alamo, for instance, increases regularly through the canon of his later writings.

9. Hamilton, *My Master*, 85. The blue felt cap remains on display at the Sam Houston Memorial Museum in Huntsville.

10. Quoted in Heiskell, *Andrew Jackson and Early Tennessee History*, 2:186.

11. Sam Houston Jr. to Margaret, 26 August [1861], typescript in A. J. Houston Collection, Texas State Library and Archives.

12. Lubbock, *Six Decades in Texas*, 381. Lubbock remembered McLeod's memorial service as having taken place on the first, but according to the *Telegraph* of 6 March, his and Houston's speeches took place the preceding Saturday, which was the first. Texas Almanac 1992–93 (Dallas: *Dallas Morning News*, 1991), 111.

13. Quoted in Williams, *Houston and the War of Independence*, 368–69. A very similar incident, probably the same occasion, is described by William Carey Crane, though with the victims of Houston's humor discreetly omitted. *Life and Select Literary Remains*, 236. Jeff recalled decking out the general in his old uniform. *My Master*, 103.

14. Hamilton, *My Master*, 106.

15. Lubbock, *Six Decades in Texas*, 672–73.

16. Houston to Williamson Oldham, 5 April 1862, in Barker and Williams, *Writings of Sam Houston*, 8:315–16. During his years in the Confederate Senate, Oldham developed a curiously Houston-like independence, occasionally colliding with Jefferson Davis's administration on matters touching, ironically, states' rights. "So far as I understand your senatorial action," Houston wrote him, "I entirely approve it."

17. Houston to Francis Lubbock, 9 August 1862, in Barker and Williams, *Writings of Sam Houston*, 8:316–20; Margaret to Mother [Nancy Lea], 17 March 1862, typescript in A. J. Houston Collection.

18. Sam Houston Jr., "Shiloh Shadows," 329–33. The battle of Shiloh also cost the life of General Johnston, whose femoral artery, unlike Sam Junior's, was severed by a bullet. Ashbel Smith was also wounded.

19. Williams, *Houston and the War of Independence*, 370–71.

20. Houston to S. M. Swenson, 14 August 1862, in Barker and Williams, *Writings of Sam Houston*, 8:320–22. Swen Swenson was the first Swedish settler in Texas, made a great success of himself, and through his informal immigration office was responsible for landing hundreds of Swedes in Texas. His pro-Union sentiments forced him to flee to Mexico the following year, however, and after the war he relocated his business empire to New York City. He did, however, bequeath to the University of Texas a coin collection worth $100,000 at the time he died in 1896. Tyler et al., *New Handbook of Texas*, 6:176.

21. Houston to Frazier, 15 August 1862, in Barker and Williams, *Writings of Sam Houston*, 8:322.

22. Independence Baptist Church photo, Sam Houston Hearne Collection, Sam Houston Regional Library and Research Center.

23. Hamilton, *My Master,* 116–17. The names of these two girls do not appear on the inventory of Houston's estate, but Hannah was Eliza's eldest daughter and Mary a daughter of old Aunt Mary. Hamilton, 16–17. The latter may have been entered as "Mariah" on the roster. There are other inaccuracies on the slave inventory.

24. Hamilton, *My Master,* 97–99. Tom Blue came to a poor end in Houston, offering to tell people his recollections of Sam Houston for spare change.

25. See, for instance, De Bruhl, *Sword of San Jacinto,* 401. For an excellent examination of slavery in Texas, see Randolph B. Campbell, *An Empire for Slavery: The Peculiar Institution in Texas, 1821–1865* (Baton Rouge and London: Louisiana State University Press, 1989).

26. Houston to John B. Magruder, 7 January 1863, in Barker and Williams, *Writings of Sam Houston,* 8:321; Magruder to Houston, 11 February 1863, A. J. Houston Collection. Houston's laud to Magruder overlooked the fact that Magruder had been assigned the Texas command to get him out of the real war, where he was blamed for bungling the Seven Days' Battles.

27. Hamilton, *My Master,* 114–15.

28. Ibid., 93.

29. Houston, "Speech at Houston," 18 March 1863, in Barker and Williams, *Writings of Sam Houston,* 8:327–39.

30. Bruce, *Life of General Houston,* 215; Davis, *Three Roads to the Alamo,* 352, 679n.

31. Terrell, "Recollections of General Sam Houston," 122.

32. Ibid., 122–23. Initially, I read this account with some doubt, for Houston by this time should have been past such thoughts. However, Terrell quotes Houston as saying, "We will soon have no one in Texas but old men and boys to defend our homes," which is very similar to what Houston had said in public, and given the limited scope of Cave's involvement in the war effort, I give Terrell some credence here. This is also recounted by Jeff Hamilton, although this is one of those passages where one suspects that Hamilton's editor, Lenoir Hunt, used the availability of previously published sources to flesh out Jeff's own words. *My Master,* 90.

33. Houston to Nannie, 14 April 1863, in Barker and Williams, *Writings of Sam Houston,* 8:344–45.

34. Houston to G. Robinson, 27 May 1863, in Barker and Williams, *Writings of Sam Houston,* 8:346–47.

35. Margaret to Houston, 8 June 1863, Sam Houston Papers, Center for American History, University of Texas.

36. Ashbel Smith, "Sketch Life of Sam Houston," Ashbel Smith Papers, Center for American History.

37. Roberts, *Star of Destiny,* 323. Other sources spell the doctor's name as T. H. Markam. However, his own assertion of his presence at the deathbed is subscribed J. W. Markham. Sam Houston Hearne Collection.

38. "Uncle" Jeff Hamilton, interview, 16 March 1938, Louis Lenz Collection, University of Houston, quoted in Flanagan, *Sam Houston's Texas,* 191; Hamilton, *My Master,* 117.

39. Roberts, *Star of Destiny,* 323; Hamilton, *My Master,* 119. Samuel McKinney continued to lead Austin College until 1871. The school moved to Sherman, Texas, in 1876.

40. Williams, *Houston and the War of Independence,* 366; Bruce, *Life of General Houston,* 217; Hamilton, *My Master,* 119.

41. *Houston Tri-Weekly Telegraph,* 29 July 1863.

42. George W. Samson to William Carey Crane, 28 March 1866, quoted in Crane, *Life and Select Literary Remains,* 244.

43. *Houston Tri-Weekly Telegraph,* 29 July 1863, reprinted in Barker and Williams, *Writings of Sam Houston,* 8:348–49; Margaret Lea Houston, "To My Husband," Franklin Williams Collection, Sam Houston Memorial Museum and Research Center; J. H. Banton, quoted in Crane, *Life and*

Select Literary Remains, 238–39. There was no stenographer at the funeral, but Banton reprised the oration for the legislature when it met the following November, from which this excerpt is taken. Undoubtedly, many of the sentiments expressed on the first occasion were repeated at the second.

44. Margaret Houston, Bible, Sam Houston Memorial Museum and Research Center.

45. Resolutions on the Death of Sam Houston, 3 November 1863; Remarks of Joab H. Banton, 3 November 1863; and Banton to Margaret, 10 April 1865, A. J. Houston Collection.

46. "Inventory and Appraisement of the Estate of Sam Houston," 2 December 1863, in Barker and Williams, *Writings of Sam Houston,* 8:341–44.

47. "The first two men I worked for were the biggest hypocrites and the meanest men I ever knew. They were even worse than Mr. McKell. . . . The first man . . . was named Ross, a Baptist preacher, who was always praying and shouting and claimed to be so holy . . . but if his flock could have seen how stingy and mean he was at home . . . they wouldn't have listened to him much. . . . The next man, a Mr. Taylor, was just as bad. He was a deacon in some other church." Hamilton, *My Master,* 128.

48. Silverthorne, *Ashbel Smith of Texas,* 161; James, *The Raven,* 456–57. William Seale substantiated James. *Sam Houston's Wife,* 244. Joshua Houston went on to become one of the most prominent leaders of Huntsville's black community.

49. Crane, *Life and Select Literary Remains,* 3; Seale, *Sam Houston's Wife,* 247. Madge Roberts traces the origin of the story to second daughter Maggie. *Star of Destiny,* 345. Many of the Sam Houston papers in the Catholic Archives of Texas show fire damage, but this is from a 1960 blaze in the LaPorte home of Andrew Jackson Houston, the papers then being in the custody of two of his daughters, Ariadne and Marguerite Houston. Reverend Crane's book finally appeared in 1884.

50. Margaret to Joe Morrow, 3 September 1867, Margaret Houston Papers, Center for American History.

51. James, *The Raven,* 457.

Afterword

1. On a return visit to Independence in 2004, I found it undergoing a renaissance of historical consciousness. Projects have included excavation at the original Baylor Male Campus and restorative work on the Margaret Houston house and the nearby dwelling of General Jerome B. Robertson. The virtually intact ante-bellum Seward Plantation east of town has long been the object of private conservation.

Bibliography

MANUSCRIPTS

Catholic Archives of Texas, Chancery of the Austin Diocese, Austin.
    Correspondence about Sam Houston.
    Sam Houston Papers.
Center for American History, University of Texas, Austin.
    Louise Davis, typescript.
    John Salmon Ford Papers.
    Margaret Houston Papers.
    Sam Houston Papers.
    Raguet Family Papers.
    Thomas Jefferson Rusk Papers.
    Ashbel Smith Papers.
    Henderson Yoakum Papers.
Republic of Texas Museum, Austin.
    Applications.
Sam Houston Memorial Museum, Huntsville, Texas.
    Artifacts.
    Baldwin Collection.
    General Collections.
    Margaret Bell Houston Collection.
    Margaret B. Rost Collection.
    Website <www.shsu.edu/>.
    Franklin Williams Collection.
    Sheriff Williams Collection.
Sam Houston Regional Library and Research Center, Liberty, Texas.
    Artifacts.
    Nancy Burch Collection.
    Sam Houston Hearne Collection.
    Dorothy Loe Collection.
    "Private Executive Records of the Second Term of Sam Houston's Administration of the Government of the Republic of Texas, December 13, 1841, to December 9, 1844." Microfilm.
    Penny Thornall Remick Collection.
Tennessee State Library and Archives, Nashville.
    Joseph McMinn Papers.
    Rhea Family Papers.
Texas State Library and Archives, Austin.
    Audited Pension Applications, Republic Claim Files.
    Houston Family Correspondence.
    A. J. Houston Collection.
    Sam Houston, Executive Record Book.
    Hunter, John Warren. "Literary Effort Concerning Creed Taylor and Others in the Mexican War."
    Washington Miller Papers.

Records of the Governor.
Secretaries of State, Domestic Records.
Texas Army Papers.
Thomason Room (Special Collections), Newton Gresham Library, Sam Houston State University, Huntsville, Texas.
Goree Papers.
Sam Houston Papers.

NEWSPAPERS

Alabama State Intelligencer
Arkansas Gazette
Arlington (Texas) Post
Austin Centinel
Cherokee Phoenix
Colorado (Texas) Citizen
Congressional Globe
Dallas News
Huntsville Item
Knoxville Register
Lexington Observer
Nashville News
Nashville Tennesseean
National Banner and Nashville Whig
National Vindicator
New Orleans Republican
Red River Herald
Telegraph and Texas Register

PUBLISHED DOCUMENTS

Barker, Eugene C., and Amelia W. Williams, eds. *The Writings of Sam Houston, 1813–1863.* 8 vols. Austin: University of Texas Press, 1938–43.

Bass, Feris A., Jr.; and B. R. Brunson, eds. *Fragile Empire: The Texas Correspondence of Samuel Swartout and James Morgan.* Austin: Shoal Creek Publishers, 1978.

Bassett, John Spencer, ed. *Correspondence of Andrew Jackson.* 7 vols. Washington, D.C.: Carnegie Institution of Washington, 1926–35.

Gammel, H. P. N., ed. *The Laws of Texas, 1822–1897.* 10 vols. Austin: Gammel, 1898.

Garrison, George P., ed. *Diplomatic Correspondence of the Republic of Texas.* Annual Reports of the American Historical Association for the Years 1907 and 1908. 3 vols. Washington, D.C.: Government Printing Office, 1907–11.

Gulick, C. A., Jr., et al., eds. *The Papers of Mirabeau Buonaparte Lamar.* 6 vols. Austin: Von Boeckmann-Jones, 1921–27.

Hemphill, W. Edwin, et al., eds. *The Papers of John C. Calhoun.* 25 vols. Columbia: University of South Carolina Press for the South Caroliniana Society, 1959–91.

Jenkins, John H., III, ed. *The Papers of the Texas Revolution, 1835–1836.* 10 vols. Austin: Presidial Press, 1973.

Jones, Anson. *Memoranda and Official Correspondence Relating to the Republic of Texas, its History, and Annexation.* New York: D. Appleton, 1859.

Nevins, Allan, ed. *Polk: The Diary of a President, 1845–1849.* New York: Longmans, Green, 1929.

Pierce, Edward Lillie, ed. *Memoir and Letters of Charles Sumner.* 4 vols. Boston: Roberts Brothers, 1877.

Roberts, Madge Thornall, ed. *The Personal Correspondence of Sam Houston.* 4 vols. Denton: University of North Texas Press, 1996–99.

Wallace, Ernest, and David M. Vigress, eds. *Documents of Texas History.* Austin: Steck, 1963.

Books

Baker, DeWitt Clinton. *A Texas Scrap-Book, Made up of the History, Biography, and Miscellany of Texas and Its People.* New York: A. S. Barnes, 1875.

Barker, Eugene C. *The Life of Stephen F. Austin, Founder of Texas, 1793–1836.* Nashville and Dallas: Cokesbury Press, 1925.

———. *Mexico and Texas, 1821–1835: University of Texas Research Lectures on the Causes of the Texas Revolution.* Dallas: P. L. Turner, 1928.

Barr, Alwyn. *Texans in Revolt: The Battle for San Antonio, 1835.* Austin: University of Texas Press, 1990.

Binkley, William C. *The Expansionist Movement in Texas, 1836–1850.* Berkeley: University of California Press, 1925.

———. *The Texas Revolution.* Baton Rouge: Louisiana State University Press, 1952.

Boley, Henry. *Lexington in Old Virginia.* Reprint, Richmond: Garrett and Massie, 1974.

Bollaert, William. *William Bollaert's Texas.* Edited by W. Eugene Hollon and Ruth Lapham Butler. Norman: University of Oklahoma Press, 1956.

Braider, Donald. *Solitary Star: A Biography of Sam Houston.* New York: G. P. Putnam's Sons, 1974.

Branda, Eldon Stephen, ed. *The Handbook of Texas: Volume III, A Supplement.* Austin: Texas State Historical Association, 1976.

Bruce, Henry. *The Life of General Houston.* New York: Dodd, Mead, 1891.

Buenger, Walter L. *Secession and the Union in Texas.* Austin: University of Texas Press, 1984.

Burleson, Georgia J. *The Life and Writings of Rufus C. Burleson, D.D., LL.D.* N.p., 1901.

Calcott, Wilfred Hardy. *Santa Anna: The Story of an Enigma Who Once Was Mexico.* Norman: University of Oklahoma Press, 1936.

Campbell, Randolph B. *Sam Houston and the American Southwest.* New York: HarperCollins College Publishers, 1993.

Castañeda, Carlos E., trans. *The Mexican Side of the Texas Revolution.* Dallas: P. L. Turner, 1928.

Clarke, Mary Whatley. *Chief Bowles and the Texas Cherokees.* Norman: University of Oklahoma Press, 1971.

———. *David G. Burnet.* Austin: Pemberton Press, 1969.

———. *Thomas J. Rusk: Soldier, Statesman, Jurist.* Austin: Jenkins Publishing, 1971.

[Coleman, Robert M.] *Houston Displayed: Or, Who Won the Battle of San Jacinto? By a Farmer in the Army.* Velasco, Tex.: [priv. pr.], 1837.

Crane, William Carey. *Life and Select Literary Remains of Sam Houston of Texas.* Philadelphia: J. B. Lippincott, 1884.

Crawford, Charles H. *Tennessee: Land, Government and History.* Austin: Steck-Vaughn, 1984.

Creel, George. *Sam Houston: Colossus in Buckskin.* New York: Cosmopolitan, 1928.

Davis, Varina Howell. *Jefferson Davis, Ex-President of the Confederate States of America: A Memoir by his Wife.* 2 vols. New York: Bedford, 1890.

Davis, William C. *Three Roads to the Alamo: The Lives and Fortunes of David Crockett, James Bowie, and William Barret Travis.* New York: Harper Collins, 1998.

Day, Donald, and Harry Herbert Ullom, eds. *The Autobiography of Sam Houston.* Norman: University of Oklahoma Press, 1954.

Day, James M. Day, comp. and ed. *The Texas Almanac, 1857–1873: A Compendium of Texas History.* Waco: Texian Press, 1967.

De Bruhl, Marshall. *Sword of San Jacinto: A Life of Sam Houston.* New York: Random House, 1993.

De Leon, Arnoldo. *They Called Them Greasers: Anglo Attitudes toward Mexicans in Texas, 1821–1900.* Austin: University of Texas Press, 1983.

Dixon, S. H., and L. W. Kemp. *Heroes of San Jacinto.* Houston: Anson Jones Press, 1932.

Everett, Dianna. *The Texas Cherokees: A People between Two Fires.* Norman: University of Oklahoma Press, 1990.

Featherstonhaugh, G. W. *Excursion through the Slave States, from Washington on the Potomac to the Frontier of Mexico.* 2 vols. London: John Murray, 1844.

Fischer, Ernest G. *Robert Potter: Founder of the Texas Navy.* Gretna, La.: Pelican, 1976.

Flanagan, Sue. *Sam Houston's Texas.* Austin: University of Texas Press, 1964.

Ford, John Salmon. *Rip Ford's Texas.* Edited by Stephen B. Oates. Austin: University of Texas Press, 1967.

Fornell, Earl W. *The Galveston Era: The Texas Crescent on the Eve of Secession.* Austin: University of Texas Press, 1961.

Friend, Llerena B. *Sam Houston: The Great Designer.* Austin: University of Texas Press, 1954.

Friends of the Governor's Mansion. *The Governor's Mansion of Texas.* 2d ed. Austin: Friends of the Governor's Mansion, 1997.

Gambrell, Herbert P. *Anson Jones: The Last President of Texas.* Garden City, N.J.: Doubleday, 1948.

———. *Mirabeau Buonaparte Lamar: Troubador and Crusader.* Dallas: Southwest Press, 1934.

Gard, Wayne. *Frontier Justice.* Norman: University of Oklahoma Press, 1949.

———. *Rawhide Texas.* Norman: University of Oklahoma Press, 1965.

Gray, William Fairfax. *From Virginia to Texas, 1835: Diary of Col. Wm. F. Gray, Giving Details of his Journey to Texas and return in 1835–1836 and Second Journey to Texas in 1837.* Houston: Gray, Dillaye, 1909.

Green, Thomas Jefferson. *Journal of the Texian Expedition against Mier.* New York: Harper and Brothers, 1845.

Gregory, Jack, and Rennard Strickland. *Sam Houston with the Cherokees, 1829–1833.* Austin: University of Texas Press, 1967.

Guild, Josephus Conn. *Old Times in Tennessee, with Historical, Personal, and Political Scraps and Sketches.* Nashville: Travel, Eastman, and Howell, 1878.

Haley, James L. *Most Excellent Sir: Letters Received by Sam Houston, President of the Republic of Texas, at Columbia, 1836–1837.* Austin: Duncan and Gladstone, 1987.

Hamilton, James A. *Reminiscences of James A. Hamilton, or, Men and Events, at Home and Abroad, during Three Quarters of a Century.* New York: Charles Scribner, 1869.

Hamilton, Jeff. *My Master: The Inside Story of Sam Houston and His Times.* Edited by Lenoir Hunt. Dallas: Manfred, Van Nort, 1940. Reprint, Austin: State House Press, 1992.

Hardin, Stephen L. *Texian Iliad: A Military History of the Texas Revolution, 1835–1836.* Austin: University of Texas Press, 1994.

Haynes, Sam W. *Soldiers of Misfortune: The Somervell and Mier Expeditions.* Austin: University of Texas Press, 1990.

Heiskell, Samuel G. *Andrew Jackson and Early Tennessee History.* 2d ed. 3 vols. Nashville: Ambrose Publishing, 1920.

Hogan, William R. *The Texas Republic: A Social and Economic History.* Norman: University of Oklahoma Press, 1946

Hopewell, Clifford. *Sam Houston: Man of Destiny.* Austin: Eakin Press, 1987.

Houston, Sam. *Life of General Sam Houston: A Short Autobiography.* Washington: J. T. Towers, 1852. Reprint, Austin: Pemberton Press, 1964.

Hunter, Robert Hancock. *Narrative of Robert Hancock Hunter.* Reprint, Austin: Encino Press, 1966.

James, Marquis. *The Raven: A Biography of Sam Houston.* New York and Indianapolis: Bobbs-Merrill, 1929.

Jenkins, John H., and Kenneth Kesselus. *Edward Burleson: Texas Frontier Leader.* Austin: Jenkins Publishing, 1990.

Jenkins, John Holland. *Recollections of Early Texas: The Memoirs of John Holland Jenkins.* Edited by John Holmes Jenkins III. Austin: University of Texas Press, 1958.

Johnson, Rebekah Baines. *A Family Album.* New York and London: McGraw-Hill, 1965.

King, Alvy L. *Louis T. Wigfall: Southern Fire-Eater.* Baton Rouge: Louisiana State University Press, 1970.

Lack, Paul D. *The Texas Revolutionary Experience: A Political and Social History, 1835–1836.* College Station: Texas A&M University Press, 1992.

Lester, Charles Edwards. *The Life of Sam Houston, The Only Authentic Memoir of Him Ever Published.* Rev. ed. New York: J. C. Derby, 1855. Originally published as *Sam Houston and His Republic,* New York: Burgess, Stringer, 1846.

Linn, John Joseph. *Reminiscences of Fifty Years in Texas.* New York: D. & J. Sadlier, 1883.

Long, Jeff. *Duel of Eagles: The Mexican and U.S. Fight for the Alamo.* New York: William Morrow, 1990.

Lubbock, Francis R. *Six Decades in Texas, or Memoirs of Francis Richard Lubbock.* Austin: Ben C. Jones, 1900.

Ludlow, Noah M. *Dramatic Life as I Found It: A Record of Personal Experience, with an Account of the Rise and Progress of the Drama in the West and South.* St. Louis: G. I. Jones, 1880.

McGrath, Sister Paul of the Cross. *Political Nativism in Texas, 1825–1860.* Washington, D.C.: Catholic University of America, 1930.

Merk, Frederick. *Slavery and the Annexation of Texas.* New York: Knopf, 1972.

Miller, Edmund T. *A Financial History of Texas.* Bulletin of the University of Texas, No. 37. Austin, 1916.

Miller, Thomas Lloyd. *The Public Lands of Texas, 1519–1970.* Norman: University of Oklahoma Press, 1972.

Morton, Ohland. *Terán and Texas: A Chapter in Texas-Mexican Relations.* Austin: Texas State Historical Association, 1948.

Morton, Oren F. *A History of Rockbridge County, Virginia.* Staunton: McClure, 1920.

Nance, Joseph Milton. *After San Jacinto: The Texas-Mexican Frontier, 1836–1841.* Austin: University of Texas Press, 1963.

———. *Attack and Counter-Attack: The Texas-Mexican Frontier, 1842.* Austin: University of Texas Press, 1964.

North, Thomas. *Five Years in Texas, from 1861 to 1866.* Cincinnati: [priv. pr.], 1871.

Olmsted, Frederick Law. *A Journey through Texas; Or, A Saddle-Trip on the Southwestern Frontier.* New York: Dix, Edwards, 1857.

Pierson, George Wilson. *Tocqueville and Beaumont in America.* New York: Oxford University Press, 1938.

Pletcher, David M. *The Diplomacy of Annexation: Texas, Oregon, and the Mexican War.* Columbia: University of Missouri Press, 1973.

Pohl, James W. *The Battle of San Jacinto.* Austin: Texas State Historical Association, 1989.

Potter, David M. *The Impending Crisis, 1848–1861.* New York: Harper and Row, 1976.

Prather, Patricia Smith, and Jane Clements Monday. *From Slave to Statesman: The Legacy of Joshua Houston, Servant to Sam Houston.* Denton: University of North Texas, 1993.

Proctor, Ben H. *Not without Honor: The Life of John H. Reagan.* Austin: University of Texas Press, 1962.

Remini, Robert. V. *Andrew Jackson and the Course of American Empire, 1767–1821.* New York: Harper and Row, 1977.

———. *Andrew Jackson and the Course of American Freedom, 1822–1832.* New York: Harper and Row, 1981.

———. *Andrew Jackson and the Course of American Democracy, 1833–1845.* New York: Harper and Row, 1984.

Richardson, James D., ed. *Messages and Papers of the Presidents.* 18 vols. New York: Bureau of National Literature, 1897–1928.

Roberts, Madge Thornall. *Star of Destiny: The Private Life of Sam and Margaret Houston.* Denton: University of North Texas Press, 1993.

Roland, Charles P. *Albert Sidney Johnston: Soldier of Three Republics.* Austin: University of Texas Press, 1964.

Rose, Victor M. *History of Victoria County.* Laredo, Tex.: Daily Times Printers, 1883.

Schmitz, Joseph W. *Texas Statecraft, 1836–1845.* San Antonio: Naylor, 1941.

Seale, William. *Sam Houston's Wife: A Biography of Margaret Lea Houston.* Norman: University of Oklahoma Press, 1970.

Siegal, Stanley. *A Political History of the Texas Republic.* Austin: University of Texas Press, 1956.

Silverthorne, Elizabeth. *Ashbel Smith of Texas: Pioneer, Patriot, Statesman, 1805–1886.* College Station: Texas A&M University Press, 1982.

Smith, Ashbel. *Reminiscences of the Texas Republic.* Galveston, Tex.: Historical Society of Galveston, 1876.

Smith, Justin H. *The Annexation of Texas.* New York: Baker and Taylor, 1911.

Smithwick, Noah. *The Evolution of a State: Or, Recollections of Old Texas Days.* Compiled by Nanna Smithwick Donaldson, Austin: Gamel Books, 1900.

Steele, Alfonso. *Biography of Alfonso Steele, Last Survivor of the Battle of San Jacinto.* Mexia, Tex.: [priv. pr.], 1906.

Sterne, Adolphus. *Hurrah for Texas! The Diary of Adolphus Sterne, 1838–1851.* Edited by Archie P. McDonald. Waco: Texian Press, 1969.

Sumner, Charles. *Memoir and Letters of Charles Sumner.* Edited by Edward L. Pierce. 4 vols. Boston: Roberts Brothers, 1877–93.

Tarbell, Ida M. *The Life of Abraham Lincoln.* 2 vols. New York: Macmillan, 1928.

Tolbert, Frank X. *The Day of San Jacinto.* New York: McGraw-Hill, 1959.

Turner, Martha Anne. *Sam Houston and His Twelve Women: The Ladies Who Influenced the Life of Texas' Greatest Statesman.* Austin: Pemberton Press, 1966.

Tyler, Ron, et al., eds. *The New Handbook of Texas.* 6 vols. Austin: Texas State Historical Association, 1996.

Wallace, Ernest. *Texas in Turmoil: 1849–1875.* Austin: Steck-Vaughn, 1965.

Wallis, Jonnie Lockhart, with Laurance L. Hill. *Sixty Years on the Brazos: The Life and Letters of Dr. John Washington Lockhart.* Priv. pr., 1930. Reprint, New York: Argonaut Press for University Microfilms, 1966.

Webb, Walter Prescott. *The Texas Rangers: A Century of Frontier Defense.* Boston: Houghton Mifflin, 1935.

Webb, Walter Prescott, et al., eds., *The Handbook of Texas.* 2 vols. Austin: Texas State Historical Association, 1952.

Weber, David J. *The Mexican Frontier, 1821–1846: The American Southwest under Mexico.* Albuquerque: University of New Mexico Press, 1982.

Weems, John Edward. *Dream of Empire: A Human History of the Republic of Texas, 1836–1846.* New York: Simon and Schuster, 1971.

Welch, June Rayfield. *The Texas Governors.* Dallas: G. L. A. Press, 1977.

Weyand, Leonie Rummel, and Houston Wade. *An Early History of Fayette County.* La Grange, Tex.: *La Grange Journal,* [1936].

Wilkins, Thurman. *Cherokee Tragedy: The Story of the Ridge Family and the Decimation of a People.* New York: Macmillan, 1970.

Williams, Alfred M. *Sam Houston and the War of Independence in Texas.* Boston: Houghton Mifflin, 1893.

Williams, Amelia W. *Following General Sam Houston from 1793 to 1863.* Austin, Steck, 1935.

Williams, Charlean Moss. *The Old Town Speaks: Reflections of Washington, Hempstead County Arkansas, Gateway to Texas, 1835, Confederate Capital, 1863.* Houston: Anson Jones Press, 1951.

Williams, John Hoyt. *Sam Houston: A Biography of the Father of Texas.* New York: Simon and Schuster, 1993.

Williams, Samuel Cole, ed. *Early Travels in the Tennessee Country.* Johnson City, Tenn.: Watauga Press, 1928.

Wilson, Henry. *Rise and Fall of Slave Power in America.* 3 vols. Boston: Houghton Mifflin, 1872.

Winchester, Robert G. *James Pinckney Henderson: Texas's First Governor.* San Antonio: Naylor, 1971.

Wise, Henry Alexander. *Seven Decades of the Union: The Humanities and Materialism.* Philadelphia: J. B. Lippincott, 1881.

Wisehart, Marion K. *Sam Houston: American Giant.* Washington, D.C.: Robert B. Luce, 1962.

Wooten, Dudley G. *A Comprehensive History of Texas, 1685–1897.* Dallas: William G. Scarff, 1898.

Yoakum, Henderson. *The History of Texas, from Its First Settlement in 1685 to Its Annexation to the United States in 1846.* New York: Redfield, 1855.

Zuber, William Physick. *My Eighty Years in Texas.* Edited by Janis Boyle Mayfield. Austin: University of Texas Press, 1971.

Articles

Arthur, Dora Fowler. "Jottings from the Old Journal of Littleton Fowler." *Quarterly of the Texas State Historical Association* 2 (July 1898).

Baker, William Mumford. "A Pivotal Point." *Lippincott's Magazine* 26 (November 1880).

Barker, Eugene C. "The African Slave Trade in Texas." *Quarterly of the Texas State Historical Association* 6 (October 1902).

———. "The San Jacinto Campaign." *Quarterly of the Texas State Historical Association* 4 (April 1901).

Boney, F. N., ed. "The Raven Tamed: An 1845 Sam Houston Letter." *Southwestern Historical Quarterly* 68 (July 1964).

Bragg. J. D. "Baylor University, 1851–1861." *Southwestern Historical Quarterly* 49 (July 1945).

Campbell, Randolph B. "Texas and the Nashville Convention of 1850." *Southwestern Historical Quarterly* 76 (July 1972).

Cantrell, Gregg. "Sam Houston and the Know-Nothings: A Reappraisal." *Southwestern Historical Quarterly* 96 (spring 1993).

Carroll, H. Bailey. "Steward A. Miller and the Snively Expedition of 1843." *Southwestern Historical Quarterly* 54 (January 1951).

Crisp, James R. "Sam Houston's Speechwriters: The Grad Student, the Teenager, the Editors, and the Historians. *Southwestern Historical Quarterly* 97 (spring 1994).

Crook, Elizabeth. "Sam Houston and Eliza Allen: The Marriage and the Mystery." *Southwestern Historical Quarterly* 94 (July 1990).

Culberson, Charles A. "General Sam Houston and Secession." *Scribner's Magazine* 39 (May, 1906).

Denton, Bernice Barnett. "Count Alphonso de Saligny and the Franco-Texienne Bill." *Southwestern Historical Quarterly* 45 (October 1941).

Frantz, Joe B. "Texas Giant of Contradictions: Sam Houston." *American West* 17 (July–August 1980).

Hardin, Stephen L. "The San Jacinto Campaign: The Generalship of Sam Houston." *Alamo Parras* Website. <http://www.flash.net/~alamo3/archives/feature/hardin.htm>.

Harris, Dilue Rose. "Reminiscences of Mrs. Dilue Harris." *Southwestern Historical Quarterly* 4 (October 1900, January 1901).

Haynes, Harry. "Dr. Rufus C. Burleson." *Quarterly of the Texas State Historical Association* 5 (1901–2).

Henson, Margaret Swett. "Politics and the Treatment of the Mexican Prisoners after the Battle of San Jacinto." *Southwestern Historical Quarterly* 94 (October 1990).

Hogan, William Ransom. "Pamela Mann: Texas Frontierswoman." *Southwest Review* 20 (July 1935).

———. "The Theater in the Republic of Texas." *Southwest Review* 19 (1933–34).

Holland, J. K. "Reminiscences of Austin and Old Washington." *Quarterly of the Texas State Historical Association* 1 (October 1897).

Houston, Sam, Jr. "Shiloh Shadows." *Southwest Historical Quarterly* 34 (April 1931).

Jennings, Tom Rusk. "Sam Houston and the Ticks." *Yesterdays* 11:2 (1990).

Kemp, L. W. "Mrs. Angelina B. Eberley." *Southwest Historical Quarterly* 36 (1932–33).

Kenney, M. M. "[Note:] Questions and Answers." *Quarterly of the Texas State Historical Association* 1 (January 1898).

Labadie, N. D. "The San Jacinto Campaign." *Texas Almanac* (1859).

Maher, Edward R., Jr. "Sam Houston and Secession." *Southwestern Historical Quarterly* 55 (April 1952).

Muir, Andrew F. "Sam Houston and the Civil War." *Texana* 6 (fall 1968).

Nance, John M. "Letter Book of Joseph Eve." *Southwestern Historical Quarterly* 43 (October 1939).

Narrett, David E. "A Choice of Destiny: Immigration Policy, Slavery, and the Annexation of Texas." *Southwestern Historical Quarterly* 100 (January 1997).

Paschal, George W. "Last Years of Sam Houston." *Harper's New Monthly Magazine* 32 (1865–66).

Pohl, James W., and Stephen L. Hardin. "The Military History of the Texas Revolution: An Overview." *Southwestern Historical Quarterly* 89 (October 1985).

Porter, Kenneth Wiggins. "The Hawkins Negroes Go to Mexico," *Chronicles of Oklahoma* 24 (spring 1946).

Rains, C. W. "The Alamo Monument." *Quarterly of the Texas State Historical Association* 6 (1902–3).

Reagan, John H. "A Conversation with Governor Houston." *Quarterly of the Texas State Historical Association* 3 (April 1900).

Red, William S. "Allen's Reminiscences of Texas, 1838–1842." *Southwestern Historical Quarterly* 17 (January 1914); 18 (January 1915).

Roberts, Oran M. "The Shelby War, Or, The Regulators and the Moderators." *Texas Magazine* 3 (August 1897).

Rowe, Edna. "The Disturbances at Anahuac in 1832." *Quarterly of the Texas State Historical Association* 6 (April 1903).

Shearer, Ernest C. "Sam Houston and Religion." *Tennessee Historical Quarterly* 20 (March 1961).

Sparks, S. F. "Recollections of S. F. Sparks." *Quarterly of the Texas State Historical Association* 12 (July 1908).

———. "Recollections of S. F. Sparks." *Yesterdays* 10:2 (September 1989).

Steen, Ralph W. "Analysis of the Work of the General Council, 1835–1836." *Southwestern Historical Quarterly* 41 (January 1938).

Stenberg, Richard R. "The Texas Schemes of Jackson and Houston, 1829–1836." *Southwestern Social Science Quarterly* 15 (December 1924).

Stuart, Ben C. "Hamilton Stuart: Pioneer Editor." *Southwestern Historical Quarterly* 21 (April 1918).

Terrell, A. W. "Recollections of General Sam Houston." *Southwestern Historical Quarterly* 16 (October 1912).

Webb, Walter Prescott. "The Last Treaty of the Republic of Texas." *Southwestern Historical Quarterly* 25 (January 1922).

Westwood, Howard C. "President Lincoln's Overture to Sam Houston." *Southwestern Historical Quarterly* 88 (October 1984).

Winters, James Washington. "An Account of the Battle of San Jacinto." *Quarterly of the Texas State Historical Association* 6 (October 1902).

Zuber, William P. "Captain Adolphus Sterne." *Quarterly of the Texas State Historical Association* 2 (January 1899).

Index

*Subentries are in chronological order. References to illustrations are in **boldface** type.*

S

Sabine, Tex., 210–13

Salado, Tex., 420

Saligny, Alphonse Du Bois, Comte de, 216, 226–27, 241, 281

Samson, Rev. George, 52, 314, 329, 336, 340, 348, 415

San Antonio (Texas warship), 262

San Antonio de Béxar, Tex., 91, 93, 109, 112–13, 117, 242, 251

San Augustine, Tex., 99, 103, 109, 162, 220, 222, 283, 364, 385

San Felipe de Austin, 91–92, 99, 112, 130–31

San Jacinto, battle of, 148–52, 279, 309, 358

San Marcos, Tex., 350

San Patricio, Tex., 121, 124

Santa Anna, Antonio López de, 96, 99–100, 113, 116, 122–25, 129–30, 135–36, 138–39, 141, 144–48, 150, 153–60, 171–72; 176–77, 241, 262, 266, 272–73; 274, 277–78, 280–82, 290, 293, 297

Santa Fe Expedition, 221, 223, 237–39, 259, 460n.43

Scales, Pvt. A., 135, 445n.18

Scott, Maj. James W., 229, 461n.62

Scruggs, T., 42

Scurry, Richardson, 260

Scurry, William Read, 364, 367

Seguín, Col. Juan, 148, 172, 182–83, 238, 453n.54

Sequoyah (Cherokee syllabist), 78

Sesma, Gen. Joaquín Ramirez y, 129

Sevier, John, 46

Seward, William, 392

Shankland, Judge Thomas, 391

Sharp, Ed, 344–45, 347–50, 393

Shaw, Jim, 270

Sheffy's Store, 10, 425n.10

Shelby, Dr. John, 52, 58, 61, 307

Sherman, Col. Sidney, 121, 128, 145–47

Shumard, Benjamin Franklin, 367

Sigourney, Lydia H. H., 335, 391

Simmons, Cleveland Kinlock, 161

Smallwood, Miss; 84, 248

Smith, Ashbel: on Houston's memory, 90; relationship with Houston, 198–200; on Houston's drinking, 209; edits "Truth" letters, 225; appointed chargé d'affaires, 240; proposes international mediation, 262–63; conversation with King Louis Philippe, 281; returns from Europe, 287; operates on Margaret, 298; reports politics favorable to Houston, 305; treats Houston's sister for lunacy, 306; political rift from Houston 342; personal letter from Houston, 348–49; cheered by Houston, 352; Houston offers to buy sheep from, 356; assured of Houston's contentment, 375; as member of secessionist deputation, 383–**84**; as captain in 2nd Texas Infantry, 403; treats Houston, 413; heckled by Houston to marry, 472n.50

Smith, Benjamin Fort, 189

Smith, Erastus "Deaf," 124, 200

Smith, George A., 163

Smith, Henry, 117, 120, 167, 442n.31

Smith, Gen. James, 238, 282–83, 468n.47

Smith, J. Carrol, 374, 412

Smith, John T., 43, 430n.29

Smith, R. H., 183

Smith, Capt. Robert, 215

Smith, Thomas I., 260–61

Smithwick, Noah, 394, 481n.60

Snively, Jacob, 266

Snively Expedition, 266, 278

Somervell, Gen. Alexander, 243, 258

Southard, Samuel, 44

"Southern Conspiracy," 111

Sparks, S. F., 138–39, 143–44

Stanbery, William, 81–86, 435n.5

Steiner, J. M., 350

Sterne, Adolphus, 91, 104–5; 178, 215, 364

Sterne, Eva Catherine Rosine, 104–5; 439n.19

Stevens, Ana, 343

Stevenson, Andrew, 81, 85

Steward, John G., 161